Trade Secrets and Employee Mobility

In the increasingly knowledge- and innovation-based economy in which the mobility of the workforce is vital, employees and ex-employees are considered to be the biggest threats to the existence of trade secrets. The interests of the former parties to the employment relationship are contradictory: employers want to safeguard their competitive position by limiting use of information and employees want to use that information to pursue their professional career. Magdalena Kolasa analyses existing guidelines that determine the extent to which former employees may use information learned during service. She proposes criteria for a balanced enforcement of trade secrets, discussing the statutory and implicit confidentiality duties, contractual protection and remedies. Drawing from the laws of Germany, the United Kingdom and the United States, and considering the EU Trade Secrets Directive, this book advocates an approach that recognises the value and functions of trade secrecy both within companies and in the context of public policy.

MAGDALENA KOLASA specialises in the law of intellectual property. Having worked for several years in private practice, she conducted her doctoral research in the area of trade secrets at the Max Planck Institute for Innovation and Competition, and obtained her Ph.D. at the Ludwig-Maximilians University in Munich, Germany. She currently works as a lawyer in the European Patent Office.

Cambridge Intellectual Property and Information Law

As its economic potential has rapidly expanded, intellectual property has become a subject of front-rank legal importance. Cambridge Intellectual Property and Information Law is a series of monograph studies of major current issues in intellectual property. Each volume contains a mix of international, European, comparative and national law, making this a highly significant series for practitioners, judges and academic researchers in many countries.

A list of books in the series can be found at the end of this volume.

Trade Secrets and Employee Mobility

In Search of an Equilibrium

Magdalena Kolasa

CAMBRIDGE
UNIVERSITY PRESS

CAMBRIDGE
UNIVERSITY PRESS

University Printing House, Cambridge CB2 8BS, United Kingdom

One Liberty Plaza, 20th Floor, New York, NY 10006, USA

477 Williamstown Road, Port Melbourne, VIC 3207, Australia

314–321, 3rd Floor, Plot 3, Splendor Forum, Jasola District Centre, New Delhi – 110025, India

79 Anson Road, #06–04/06, Singapore 079906

Cambridge University Press is part of the University of Cambridge.

It furthers the University's mission by disseminating knowledge in the pursuit of education, learning, and research at the highest international levels of excellence.

www.cambridge.org
Information on this title: www.cambridge.org/9781108424226
DOI: 10.1017/9781108545921

First published 2018

Printed in the United Kingdom by Clays, St Ives plc

A catalogue record for this publication is available from the British Library.

Library of Congress Cataloging-in-Publication Data
Names: Kolasa, Magdalena, author.
Title: Trade secrets and employee mobility : in search of an equilibrium / Magdalena Kolasa.
Description: New York : Cambridge University Press, 2018. | Series: Cambridge intellectual property and information law ; 44 | Includes bibliographical references and index.
Identifiers: LCCN 2017038385| ISBN 9781108424226 (hardback) | ISBN 9781108439565 (paperback)
Subjects: LCSH: Trade secrets–Law and legislation. | Confidential business information–Law and legislation. | Conflict of interests. | Labor contract. | BISAC: LAW / Intellectual Property / General.
Classification: LCC K1577 .K65 2018 | DDC 346.04/8–dc23 LC record available at https://lccn.loc.gov/2017038385

ISBN 978-1-108-42422-6 Hardback

Contents

Preface

Former employees are widely considered as the biggest threat to the maintenance of trade secrets, which are one of the central mechanisms for protecting a company's intangible assets. This is an issue of growing importance due to the rising value of information in our increasingly knowledge- and innovation-based economy. In this environment, interests of the former parties to the employment relationship are contradictory: employers want to safeguard their competitive position by limiting use of information and their former employees want to use that information to pursue their professional careers. This conflict of interests is a major issue in the enforcement of trade secrets. This book critically analyses the law relating to the extent to which former employees may use information learned during service. It proposes criteria for a balanced approach to enforcement of trade secrets discussing the statutory and implicit confidentiality duties, contractual protection of trade secrets, as well as application of remedies. Drawing from the laws and experience of Germany, the United Kingdom and the United States and considering the EU Trade Secrets Directive, this book proposes an approach to trade secrets enforcement which recognises the value and functions of trade secrecy on a private level and in the context of public policy relating to innovation, economic growth and welfare.

Acknowledgements

I would like to thank Professor Ansgar Ohly for his valuable and kind support in the process of writing this book and Professor Annette Kur for her comments on the first draft.

The research presented here owes much to the Max Planck Institute for Innovation and Competition which provided me with financial support in the form of a scholarship and an optimal academic work environment.

Finally, I am grateful to a number of people who helped me along the way to work on this book, including Stephen, Nicole and Seyhan, and to those who simply kept me going, Asia, Kasia and Maciej, to name only a few. Most importantly, special thanks goes to my Parents.

Abbreviations

Am Bus L J	*American Business Law Journal*
Ann/Loschelder/Grosch	Ann C, Loschelder M and Grosch M, *Praxishandbuch Know-how-Schutz* (1st edn, Carl Heymanns Verlag 2010)
ArbnErfG	Gesetz über Arbeitnehmererfindungen [ArbnErfG] [Act on Employee Inventions], 25 July 1957, BGBl I 2521 as amended
B2B	business to business
BAG	Bundesarbeitsgericht (Federal Labour Court of Germany)
Baker&McKenzie Study	Study on Trade Secrets and Confidential Business Information in the Internal Market, Baker & McKenzie – Milan MARKT/2011/128/D http://ec.europa.eu/internal_market/iprenforcement/docs/trade-secrets/130711_final-study_en.pdf accessed 1 June 2017
Bauer/Diller	Bauer J-H and Diller M, *Wettbewerbsverbote* (7th edn CH Beck 2015)
BGB	Bürgerliches Gesetzbuch [BGB] [Civil Code], 18 August 1896, RGBl at 195 as amended
Busche/Stoll/Wiebe	Busche J, Stoll P-T and Wiebe A, *TRIPs: Internationales und europäisches Recht des geistigen Eigentums. Kommentar* (2nd edn, Carl Heymanns Verlag 2013)
BVerfG	Bundesverfassungsericht (Federal Constitutional Court of Germany)
CA 1998	Competition Act 1998
Cal Bus & Prof Code	California Business and Professions Code
CDPA	Copyright, Designs and Patents Act 1988
CJEU	Court of Justice of the European Union. Until 2009: European Court of Justice

CJQ	*Civil Justice Quarterly*
Comm	High Court of Justice Queen's Bench Division Commercial Court
Cov L J	*Coventry Law Journal*
CSOH	Outer House Scottish Court of Session
CTLR	*Computer and Telecommunications Law Review*
Database Directive	Directive 96/9/EC of the European Parliament and of the Council of 11 March 1996 on the legal protection of databases [1996] OJ L77/20
DB	*Der Betrieb*
Del Ch	Court of Chancery of Delaware
DTSA	Defend Trade Secrets Act
ECHR	European Convention on Human Rights of 4 November 1950
Enforcement Directive	Directive 2004/48/EC of the European Parliament and of the Council of 29 April 2004 on the enforcement of intellectual property rights [2004] OJ L 157
GC	General Court
DesignG	Gesetz über den rechtlichen Schutz von Design [DesignG] [Design Act] 12 March 2004, BGBl I 122 as amended
GewO	Gewerbeordnung [GewO] [Act on Trade], 21 June 1896, BGBl I 202 as amended
GG	Grundgesetz für die Bundesrepublik Deutschland [GG] [Basic Law for the Federal Republic of Germany], 23 May 1949, BGBl III 100–1 as amended
Goulding	Goulding P, *Employee Competition. Covenants, Confidentiality and Garden Leave* (3rd edn, Oxford University Press 2016)
GRUR	*Gewerblicher Rechtsschutz und Urheberrecht*
GRUR-Int	*Gewerblicher Rechtsschutz und Urheberrecht – Internationaler Teil*
GRUR-RR	*Gewerblicher Rechtsschutz und Urheberrecht – Rechtsprechungs-Report*
Gurry on Breach of Confidence	Aplin T and others, *Gurry on Breach of Confidence: The Protection of Confidential Information* (2nd edn, Oxford University Press 2012)
GWB	Gesetz gegen Wettbewerbsbeschränkungen [GWB] [Act against Restraints of Competition], 26 August 1998, BGBl I 1750, 3245 as amended

Harte/Henning	Harte-Bavendamm H, Henning-Bodewig F, *Gesetz gegen den unlauteren Wettbewerb (UWG)* (4th edn, CH Beck 2016)
Harv J L Techn	*Harvard Journal of Law & Technology*
HGB	Handelsgesetzbuch [HGB] [Commercial Code], 5 May 1897, BGBl III at 4100–1 as amended
Hogan Lovells Report	Report on Trade Secrets for the European Commission, Hogan Lovells International LLP, Study on Trade Secrets and Parasitic Copying (Look-alikes) MARKT/2010/20/D http://ec.europa.eu/internal_market/iprenforcement/docs/parasitic/Study_Parasitic_copying_en.pdf accessed 1 June 2017
HRA	Human Rights Act
HTLJ	*High Technology Law Journal*
IBLJ	*International Business Law Journal*
IDS Emp L Brief	*IDS Employment Law Brief*
ILJ	*Industrial Law Journal*
IP	intellectual property
IPR/IPRs	intellectual property right/rights
IT	information technology
JA	*Juristische Arbeitsblätter*
JBL	*Journal of Business Law*
JuS	*Juristische Schulung*
Kalbfus	Björn H Kalbfus, *Know-how-Schutz in Deutschland zwischen Strafrecht und Zivilrecht – welcher Reformbedarf besteht?* (Carl Heymanns Verlag 2011)
LQR	*Law Quarterly Review*
Milgrim on Trade Secrets	Milgrim RM and Bensen EE, *Milgrim on Trade Secrets* (102nd edn, Lexis Nexis 2013)
MMR	*MultiMedia und Recht*
MPI Position Paper	Stellungnahme des Max-Planck-Instituts für Innovation und Wettbewerb vom 3 Juni 2014 zum Vorschlag der Europäischen Kommission für eine Richtlinie über den Schutz vertraulichen Know-hows und vertraulicher Geschäftsinformationen (Geschäftsgeheimnisse) vor rechtswidrigem Erwerb sowie rechtswidriger Nutzung und Offenlegung vom 28.11.2013, COM (2013) 813 final www.ip.mpg.de/fileadmin/ipmpg/

	content/stellungnahmen/stellungnahme-geschaeftsgeheimnisse_2014-05-12_final_7.pdf accessed 1 June 2017
MünchKommBGB	*Münchner Kommentar zum Bürgerlichen Gesetzbuch* (6th edn, CH Beck 2012)
NCA	agreement not to compete
NDA	agreement not to disclose
NSA	agreement not to solicit (clients or employees)
NJ Super	Superior Court of New Jersey, Chancery Division
NStZ	*Neue Zeitschrift für Strafrecht*
NVwZ	*Neue Zeitung für Verwaltungsrecht*
NZA	*Neue Zeiteschrift für Arbeitsrecht*
NZA-RR	*NZA-Rechtsperchungs-Report Arbeitsrecht*
NZG	*Neue Zeitschrift für Gesellschaftsrecht*
Ohly/Sosnitza	Ohly A and Sosnitza O, *UWG: Gesetz gegen den unlauteren Wettbewerb* (7th edn, CH Beck 2016)
PatG	Patentgesetz [PatG] [Patent Act], 5 May 1936, BGBl 1981 I 1 as amended
PC	Paris Convention for the Protection of Industrial Property of 20 March 1883, as revised and amended
Peterson	Peterson GR, *Trade Secret Protection in an Information Age* (Glasser Legal Works 1997)
PI	preliminary injunction
Pooley	Pooley J, *Trade Secrets* (6th edn, Law Journal Press 2002)
Quinto/Singer	Quinto DW, Singer SH and McCauley CA, *Trade Secrets: Law and Practice* (Lexis Nexis 2016)
R&D	research and development
RDBER	Commission Regulation (EC) No 1217/2010 of 14 December 2010 on the application of Article 101(3) TFEU to certain categories of research and development agreements [2010] OJ L355/36
Schlötter	Schlötter R, *Der Schutz von Betriebs- und Geschäftsgeheimnissen und die Abwerbung von Arbeitnehmern* (Carl Heymanns Verlag 1997)
Sherman Act	Sherman Act, US Code Title 15
SMEs	small and medium-sized enterprises

Stanley	Stanley P, *The Law of Confidentiality: A Restatement* (Hart Publishing 2008)
StGB	Strafgesetzbuch [StGB] [Criminal Act] 15 May 1871, BGBl I 3322 as amended
SVP	Senior Vice President
TFEU	Treaty on the Functioning of the European Union, consolidated version [2012] OJ C 326
Toulson/Phipps	Roger G Toulson and Charles M Phipps, *Confidentiality* (3rd edn, Sweet&Maxwell 2012)
Trade Secrets Directive	Directive (EU) 2016/943 of the European Parliament and of the Council of 8 June 2016 on the protection of undisclosed know-how and business information (trade secrets) against their unlawful acquisition, use and disclosure [2016] OJ L 157
TRIPS	Agreement on Trade-related Aspects of Intellectual Property Rights
TSD	Trade Secrets Directive
TTBER	Commission Regulation (EU) No 316/2014 of 21 March 2014 on the application of Article 101(3) of the Treaty on the Functioning of the European Union to categories of technology transfer agreements [2014] OJ L 93/17
UNCTAD	United Nations Conference on Trade and Development
UrhG	Gesetz über Urheberrecht und verwandte Schutzrechte [UrhG] [Copyright Act], 9 September 1965, BGBl I 1273, as amended
US Patent Act	US Patent Act, US Code Title 35
USCA	US Copyright Act, US Code Title 17
USDC	United States District Court
UTSA	Uniform Trade Secrets Act 1985
UWG	Gesetz gegen den unlauteren Wettbewerb [UWG] [Act against Unfair Competition], 3 March 2010, BGBl I at 254, as amended
WL	Westlaw
WLR	*Wisconsin Law Review*
ZPO	Zivilprozessordnung [ZPO] [Civil Procedure Statute], 12 September 1950, BGBl at 455 as amended

Introduction

Trade secrets, i.e. undisclosed information valuable for its holder's competitive position, have been described as 'the key appropriability mechanism in most industries'.[1] Indeed, up to 74 per cent of companies declare that they rely on trade secrets.[2] At the same time, former employees are reported to be one of the major sources of leakage of valuable undisclosed information[3] and the law surrounding the post-employment phase is described as 'perhaps the most significant part of the law on trade secrets'.[4]

In the increasingly service- and innovation-oriented markets, employees may be one of the most valuable assets of a company. With their knowledge, skills and ingenuity, they add to their employer's value by creating new technical solutions and products, building the company's relations with clients, creating marketing strategies and maintaining image. In doing so, they not only create, but also learn their employer's

[1] Wesley M Cohen, Richard R Nelson and John P Walsh, 'Protecting their Intellectual Assets: Appropriability Conditions and Why US Manufacturing Firms Patent (or Not)' (2000) NBER Working Paper Series Working Paper No 7552, 24 www.nber.org/papers/w7552.pdf accessed 1 June 2017.

[2] According to a survey prepared in 2013 for the European Commission, 74 per cent of EU companies ranked trade secrets as of medium or high importance for their competitiveness and/or innovative growth, see Baker&McKenzie Study 12, 122. By way of example, 70 per cent of Alstom's value depends on trade secrets, according to Alain Berger, SVP European Affairs – Alstom, 'Why Europe Must Reform its Trade Secrets Rules' (Managing Intellectual Property, 10 February 2015) www.managingip.com/Blog/3426227/Guest-blog-Why-Europe-must-reform-its-trade-secrets-rules.html accessed 1 June 2017. The problem with most of the statistical data concerning trade secrets is that it is based on anecdotal evidence, precisely due to the confidential character of the subject-matter.

[3] In 2013 in the EU, former employees were declared to be responsible for 45 per cent of all attempts or acts of trade secrets misappropriation, see Baker&McKenzie Study 13. Employees or former employees were defendants in 59 per cent of trade secrets misappropriation cases litigated in the US federal courts in 2008, according to David S Almeling, Darin W Snyder, Michael Sapoznikow, Whitney E McCollum and Jill Weader, 'A Statistical Analysis of Trade Secret Litigation in Federal Courts' (2010) 45:2 *Gonz L Rev* 291, 302–303.

[4] William van Caenegem, *Trade Secrets and Intellectual Property. Breach of Confidence, Misappropriation and Unfair Competition* (1st edn, Kluwer Law International 2014) 223.

trade secrets, such as information about products and processes; production plans; pricing structures; or preferences of clients. Much of that information is carried in the heads of those employees and thus, when they leave service, consciously or not they take that knowledge with them.

If an ex-employee starts his own competitive activity or enters employment for another company, using the information learned in previous employment, this may have a negative impact on the competitive position of the former employer, who until then might have been the only market participant to profit from use of this data. Moreover, once the secret information leaves its holder's enterprise and control, the risk of its disclosure increases.

The threats connected with the departure of employees who know the intricacies of their employer's business grow with the changing economic landscape. Automation and the advance of information technology result in a shift from labour markets based on manufacturing of goods to a knowledge-based service economy which relies essentially on human knowledge.[5] At the same time, the pace of social development and economic change is increasing, and with it the mobility of employees. Life-time employment with one company is no longer a reality in most industries,[6] and the booming IT and Internet-based services require quick change and adaptation; promote entrepreneurship; and increase the number of start-ups.[7] Decreasing job security is accompanied by reduced workforce loyalty.[8] This setting has been described as a 'new psychological contract' under which the employees accept lower job security in return for training provided by the employers.[9]

The rising value of information in the economy and reliance on its use by both employers and employees, combined with increasing work mobility, cause tensions. On the one hand, the employers wish to protect their competitive advantage stemming from the use of valuable information,

[5] Darin W Snyder and David S Almeling, *Keeping Secrets: A Practical Introduction to Trade Secret Law and Strategy* (1st edn, Oxford University Press 2012) 29.

[6] Norman D Bishara, 'Covenants Not to Compete in a Knowledge Economy: Balancing Innovation from Employee Mobility against Legal Protection for Human Capital Investment' (2006) 27 *Berk J Emp & Lab L* 287, 292; Snyder and Almeling, *Keeping Secrets: A Practical Introduction to Trade Secret Law and Strategy* 27.

[7] On these developments in the United States, see Bishara, 'Covenants Not to Compete in a Knowledge Economy: Balancing Innovation from Employee Mobility against Legal Protection for Human Capital Investment' 287, 291–292. In the context of computer industries, see Miles J Feldman, 'Towards a Clearer Standard of Protectable Information: Trade Secrets and the Employment Relationship' (1994) 9 *HTLJ* 151, 157.

[8] Snyder and Almeling, Keeping Secrets: A Practical Introduction to Trade Secret Law and Strategy 28.

[9] Katherine VW Stone, 'Human Capital and Employee Mobility: A Rejoinder' (2002) 34 *CTLR* 1233, 1243.

and to protect their investments in developing and securing this data. On the other hand, use of this information by a departing employee may be essential for him to continue his professional activity, and thus decisive for the exercise of his freedom of self-determination in choosing a place of work. At the same time, trade secrets are used as means to protect innovation. Thus, their enforcement is an important element of public policy relating to incentivising innovation, entrepreneurship and dissemination of knowledge.[10]

When compared to patents, copyright or trademarks, trade secrets are often referred to as the 'Cinderella of IP law'[11] due to a lack of comprehensive regulation and research.

Secrecy may, like IPRs, protect intellectual creations. At the same time, there exist considerable discrepancies with respect to treatment of trade secrets in various jurisdictions, both as regards secrecy alone and as regards its relationship with the classical IPRs. It seems that one of the reasons for such a situation is that, while trade secrets may cover the same subject-matter as patents, utility models, designs or copyright, they are not uniformly recognised as a right of intellectual property and their regulation is fragmented.[12] While in some countries they are seen as a right of intellectual property or administered by a dedicated statute,[13]

[10] The conflicting interests as well as policy considerations pertaining to protection of secrecy in the post-employment context are the subject of the analysis presented in Chapter 1.

[11] Report on Trade Secrets for the European Commission, Hogan Lovells International LLP, Study on Trade Secrets and Parasitic Copying (Look-alikes) MARKT/2010/20/D para 34 http://ec.europa.eu/internal_market/iprenforcement/docs/parasitic/Study_Parasitic_copying_en.pdf accessed 1 June 2017 (Hogan Lovells Report); 'The Cinderella of IP (or not)' (*The IP Kat*, 18 December 2012) http://ipkitten.blogspot.de/2012/12/the-cinderella-of-ip-or-not.html accessed 1 June 2017; Ansgar Ohly, 'Der Geheimnisschutz im deutschen Recht: heutiger Stand und Perspektiven' [2014] GRUR 1, 1.

[12] The general framework is laid down in Art 39 TRIPS. For an account of the situation within the EU, see Hogan Lovells Report. For a discussion of the legal nature of trade secrets, see Chapter 2, part III.

[13] Trade secrets are considered an IPR in Italy. For details, see Hogan Lovells Report paras 130–136. Sweden on the other hand seems to be the only EU country which has a statute dedicated to the regulation of the use of trade secrets, see Hogan Lovells Report para 217. This seems also to be the case in the United States, under the framework of protection of trade secrets is laid down in the UTSA, see Milgrim on Trade Secrets vol 1A 2-2; Richard A Epstein, 'Trade Secrets as Private Property: Their Constitutional Protection' (2003) John M Olin Law & Economics Working Paper No 190 (2d Series) 1 http://papers.ssrn.com/sol3/papers.cfm?abstract_id=421340 accessed 1 June 2017; Mark A Lemley, 'The Surprising Virtues of Treating Trade Secrets as IP Rights' (2008) 61 *Stanf L R* 311, 325; Robert G Bone, 'Trade Secrecy, Innovation and the Requirement of Reasonable Secrecy Precautions' in Rochelle C Dreyfuss and Katherine J Strandburg (eds), *The Law and Theory of Trade Secrecy: A Handbook of Contemporary Research* (Edward Elgar 2011) 48.

other countries address infringement of a trade secret within the framework of unfair competition,[14] general tort or contract law.[15]

The lack of uniform treatment and developed doctrinal approaches increases legal uncertainty, also where disputes between employers and their former staff are concerned.

The discrepancies between national approaches to protection of trade secrets within the European Union have been recognised as an obstacle to the smooth functioning of the Internal Market. To address this problem, in 2013 the European Commission issued a Proposal for the Directive on the protection of undisclosed know-how and business information (trade secrets) against their unlawful acquisition, use and disclosure.[16] The Trade Secrets Directive was enacted on 8 June 2016 and entered into force on 5 July 2016.[17] The Member States are to implement it by 9 June 2018.[18] The Directive lays down a definition of trade secrets; regulates their acquisition, use and disclosure; and provides for measures and procedures of enforcement as well as remedies in cases of misappropriation.

As a result of the United Kingdom European Union membership referendum (broadly referred to as the Brexit referendum) which took place on 23 June 2016 and in which the majority voted to leave the EU, the implementation of the Directive in the United Kingdom is uncertain. The Article 50 TEU process of withdrawing from the EU has been triggered on 29 March 2017 and the terms of withdrawal have not yet been negotiated. In the meantime, the United Kingdom remains a full member of the EU, and in this book, references to implementation of the Trade Secrets Directive in the United Kingdom are made under this assumption.

[14] For example, Germany, Austria and Poland, Hogan Lovells Report paras 251–252.

[15] Hogan Lovells Report para 253. In the United Kingdom, protection of trade secrets is ensured by way of action for breach of confidence, Hogan Lovells Report para 257, but the nature of the ex-employee's obligations remains unclear, Gurry on Breach of Confidence paras 12.152–12.153. Most EU Member States provide for contractual protection of trade secrets, Hogan Lovells Report para 258.

[16] Proposal COM(2013) 813 of 28 November 2013 for a Directive of the European Parliament and of the Council on the protection of undisclosed know-how and business information (trade secrets) against their unlawful acquisition, use and disclosure http://ec.europa.eu/internal_market/iprenforcement/docs/trade-secrets/131128_proposal_en.pdf accessed 1 June 2017.

[17] Directive (EU) 2016/943 of the European Parliament and of the Council of 8 June 2016 on the protection of undisclosed know-how and business information (trade secrets) against their unlawful acquisition, use and disclosure [2016] OJ L 157 (hereinafter Trade Secrets Directive or TSD). References in this book are made to the final text of the Directive. Legal literature referring to the previous drafts of the Directive is cited only in so far as it pertains to the final text.

[18] Art 19(1) TSD.

The conflict of interests between employers and their former employees is at the centre of the discussion presented in this book. It examines the approaches towards enforcement of trade secrets against ex-employees in Germany, United Kingdom, United States and under the Trade Secrets Directive. The analysis focuses on the balancing of the private and public interest and its role in the determination of the scope of post-employment duties and in the framing of remedies.

Recognising the necessity of a case-by-case assessment, the existing guidelines for determination of the extent to which former employees may use information learned during service are identified and critically assessed. They are systematised and the guidelines which might help to reconcile the conflicting interests are put forward. The overreaching considerations in this respect are the need to allow for sufficient flexibility in order to accommodate the varying circumstances and interests, and the necessity to ensure legal certainty in the enforcement of rights to valuable information.

The concept of 'employee' used in this analysis relates to people who are in an employment relationship; perform their duties in furtherance of the employer's interests; are bound by instructions given by the employer; and work under the employer's control and at his risk, not as part of an independent business. Therefore, unless otherwise indicated, members of organs of companies, contractors, fiduciaries and staff whose duties are otherwise regulated by special legislation are not within the realm of the discussion.

The discussion presented in this book starts with an introduction of the role which protection of trade secrets plays in the economy as well as in the market for innovation and employment (Chapter 1). The interests which come into conflict, where trade secrets are enforced against former employees, are presented on the private and on the policy level.

This background discussion is continued in Chapter 2 with a comparative analysis of the definitions of trade secrets adopted in the legal orders; the types of information which may be protected as trade secrets; and the relationship between secrecy and IPRs. The discussion of the legal nature of trade secrets completes the introductory part. Furthermore, this part of the book contains a discussion on the terminology used to designate trade secrets.

The following two chapters present an analysis of the scope of post-employment duties which employees have with regard to information they learned during service. The statutory and implied (default) duties are discussed in Chapter 3, and the framework within which those duties may be regulated by way of contract is presented in Chapter 4.

Chapter 5 contains a discussion of the basic remedies available for aggrieved employers in case of a found or threatening infringement of a right to a trade secret.

The discussion is followed by a summary in which the findings are recapitulated.

The analysis presented in this book is based on the state of law and research as it stands on 1 June 2017.

The terms 'employer' and 'employee' used in this book refer equally to both men and women.

1 Conflict of Interests

Confidentiality, Mobility of Employees and Innovation Policy

'When a secret is revealed, it is the fault of the man who confided it'.[1] As true as this statement by Jean de la Bruyère may be in philosophical terms, it does not provide for a solution of legal and economic problems arising in the context of information-sharing between employers and employees. After all, information kept absolutely secret is not useful. Trade secrets need to be shared within the company in order to allow the employees to carry out a secret process, develop a product using the secret information on previous failures, or to enable them to manage customer relations on behalf of the employer. That information, learned or developed by the employee during service, is what the employer treats as his asset. However, that same information, embodied in the employee as part of his experience, may at the same time be decisive for his position in the job market. As long as the employee remains active for his principal, his and his employer's interests in the use of the information are synergetic and based on the general duty of good faith that any employee owes to his principal.[2] The problems may start when the employee leaves the service and, consciously or not, takes the information with him. That is when the conflict between the interest of the former employer in maintaining the secrecy of the information and the interest of the ex-employee in using the information to continue his professional activity becomes most apparent.[3]

This chapter presents an overview of interests which may become relevant in the context of employee mobility. The discussion starts with an introduction of the interests of employers and those of the employees. It is followed by

[1] Orig. 'Toute révélation d'un secret est la faute de celui qui l'a confié', Jean de la Bruyère (1645–1696) https://sites.google.com/site/texteschoisis/home/jean-de-la-bruyere accessed 1 June 2017. Unless indicated otherwise the translations are made by the author.

[2] For more information in Germany, see Schlötter 171–172; in the United Kingdom, Gurry on Breach of Confidence para 11.08; in the United States, Peterson 7-3–7-4.

[3] According to a survey prepared in 2013 for the European Commission, in the EU former employees were declared to be responsible for 45 per cent of all attempts or acts of trade secrets misappropriation, see Baker&McKenzie Study 13.

an analysis of policy considerations presented in the legal and economic literature, which derive from the incompatible interests of those parties.

I Interests of the Employers

Information that is useful for a business and which is not known to others is valuable.[4] The higher the number of competitors who make use of the information, the lower is its value. And it disappears entirely once the information loses secret status. Therefore, preserving confidentiality allows the employer to maintain his market position and competitive advantage over others who do not have access to that particular information.[5]

The resources generated from secret information are derived not only from its use in an employer's own business, but also from 'licensing'[6] it to others. However, despite such sharing, as long as the information is not accessible to the general public[7] and thus remains under the control

[4] Under TRIPS and US law, information may only be a trade secret if it derives value from being secret: 'has commercial value because it is secret' (Art 39(2)(b) TRIPS), 'derives independent economic value (. . .) from not being generally known to (. . .) other persons' (S 1(4)(i) UTSA), similarly Restatement (Third) of Unfair Competition S 39 comment e. German and UK laws do not explicitly require that the information has an economic value derived from the fact that it is secret. Still, 75 per cent of companies in EU rank trade secrets as strategically important for their growth, competitiveness and innovative performance, Baker&McKenzie Study 12. The requirement of value is contained also in the definition of trade secrets contained in Art 2(1) TSD.

[5] Kalbfus para 508.

[6] Under German law 'licensing' of a trade secret is, strictly speaking, not an appropriate way to describe revealing the information to others ia under the condition that the information be kept secret. The term 'licensing' relates to allowing others to use the exclusive right of the licensor. Trade secrets are not regarded as exclusive rights under German law and therefore the 'licensing' of a trade secret relates to transfer of the information rather than to agreeing to the use of an exclusive right. See Kalbfus para 94 with further references. Still, the German authors use the term 'licence', see e.g. Ohly in Ohly/Sosnitza Vor §§17–19 para 5, Huber in Ann/Loschelder/Grosch 74. The same applies for the United Kingdom, see Gurry on Breach of Confidence para 9.17. The term 'trade secrets licence' is accepted under US law, due to recognition of trade secrets as an IPR.

[7] None of the analysed legal systems requires absolute secrecy of the information in order to protect it as a trade secret. According to Art 39(2)(a) TRIPS, the information must be 'not (. . .) generally known among or readily accessible to persons within the circles that normally deal with the kind of information in question'. This concept is also contained in Art 2(1)(a) TSD. Under German law, the information must be 'not publicly accessible but known only to a limited group of persons' (Ohly in Ohly/Sosnitza Vor §§17–19 para 1, with further references). Under UK law, the lack of requirement of absolute secrecy arises from the nature of the action for breach of confidence, see *Prince Albert v Strange* [1849] EWHC Ch J20 (EWHC), Gurry on Breach of Confidence para 5.21. For the lack of requirement of absolute secrecy in the United States, see e.g. Restatement of Unfair Competition S 39 comment f, Ruth E Leistensnider, 'Trade Secret Misappropriation: What is the Proper Length of an Injunction after Public Disclosure?' (1987) 51 *Alb L Rev* 271, 275, note 24.

of the business that generated it, it allows it to reap profits from both its own and others' use of that information.

A further consideration in respect of the interests of employers in protecting their trade secrets is that undisclosed know-how is one of many assets of a business, especially of an innovative company.[8] Very often, trade secrets accompany classical IPRs, for example as improvements to a patented process, information about a product for which patent or design protection has not been applied yet, or as information on source code complementing the protection granted by copyright. Disclosure of such trade secrets necessarily lowers the value of the IPR they accompany and in some circumstances may even destroy it completely, especially in case of disclosure of information about an invention before a patent application is filed.[9]

One of the main arguments put forward as a justification for granting legal protection for trade secrets is that it saves costs that businesses would otherwise spend on factual measures to protect secrecy.[10] Preserving the information's secrecy allows the employer to accumulate resources and possibly invest them in research and development or in human capital by training his employees.[11]

The protection of economic interests of the employer also involves the consideration that, at least with regard to some types of trade secrets, such as information relating to the company's clients, this protection allows the employers to safeguard the business relations developed by the employees on behalf of the employer.[12] The departure of an employee who generated those relations might be detrimental to the employer's business as a whole.

The considerations of the interests of the employers may be well summarised by the statement that since people as carriers of skill and

[8] As explained by Feldman, ideas and methodologies developed in computer firms are viewed by their management as the company's primary asset, see Miles J Feldman, 'Towards a Clearer Standard of Protectable Information: Trade Secrets and the Employment Relationship' (1994) 9 *HTLJ* 151, 157.

[9] Trade secrets have been recognised by companies in the EU as both complementary and supplementary to other means of protecting their intangible assets, see Baker&McKenzie Study 2.

[10] See ia Kalbfus para 508. For a more detailed analysis, see Chapter 1, part III, point B.1.

[11] Orly Lobel, 'Intellectual Property and Restrictive Covenants' (2008) Legal Studies Research Paper Series, Research Paper 08-059, 12 with further references http://ssrn.com/abstract=1226463 accessed 1 June 2017; Norman D Bishara, 'Covenants Not to Compete in a Knowledge Economy: Balancing Innovation from Employee Mobility against Legal Protection for Human Capital Investment' (2006) 27 *Berk J Emp & Lab L* 287, 300.

[12] This is achieved most effectively by use of covenants not to compete, see Sampsa Samila and Olav Sorenson, 'Non-Compete Covenants: Incentives to Innovate or Impediments to Growth' (2010) 9 http://papers.ssrn.com/sol3/papers.cfm?abstract_id=1411172 accessed 1 June 2017.

knowledge 'are the most valuable asset of any organisation',[13] their leaving poses a real threat to the employer's business. Therefore employers have a strong interest in keeping employees and their knowledge of the company's secrets under control. Restricting the use of expertise and information acquired during employment after it has terminated may be a key factor in that respect.

II Interests of the Employees

Just as data is of value to an enterprise, it is of importance to an individual. Any information learned by employees as part of their professional experience may form part of their knowledge and skills. Those in turn are decisive for both the person's position in the company where he is employed as well as on the job market. In times of growing specialisation of labour, a shift from a market driven by manufacturing of goods to a service-oriented economy[14] and increased movement of employees between companies, it is knowledge above all that may decide on employment opportunities and economic success.

Any restraint on the person's use of the skill, knowledge and information accumulated during his work experience effectively limits his freedom to choose employment[15] and consequently his freedom of self-determination.[16] This aspect becomes particularly clear in the case of specialised and highly qualified employees. The knowledge they have obtained during employment is decisive for their attractiveness on the market. Were they not to rely on their work experience, any change of employment would result in a deterioration of their professional position, with a direct knock-on effect for their financial situation.

The interest of employees in an unrestricted choice of their employment or business activity is supported by the general freedom to compete with the former employer, even by imitation.[17] From this perspective, the former employee should not be restrained in the use of information acquired during employment.

[13] Keith Hodkinson and Martin Wasik, *Industrial Espionage Protection and Remedies* (Longman Intelligence Reports, Longman Group UK Ltd 1986) 5.

[14] Bishara, 'Covenants Not to Compete in a Knowledge Economy: Balancing Innovation from Employee Mobility against Legal Protection for Human Capital Investment' 287, 291.

[15] In Germany, the employee's interest in occupational freedom is protected as basic constitutional right under Art 12 GG. For a more detailed analysis, see ia Kalbfus para 508; Ohly in Ohly/Sosnitza § 17 para 40a with further references. See also Stanley 80.

[16] Which includes the right to choose best career opportunity, Stanley 79–80; *Herbert Morris Ltd v Saxelby* [1916] 1 AC 688 (HL) 699 (Lord Atkinson).

[17] Kalbfus para 508; Peterson 1–66, 2–33.

Access to information and the possibility of its unrestricted use, some argue, provides creative employees with incentives to invent. The comparison is drawn with the incentives that drive the development of open-source software. According to Hyde,[18] some creative employees are encouraged not so much by the remuneration that they get directly from their employer, but rather by the possibility to freely use the information they have obtained and the recognition they achieve for creations made with the use of such information. This appreciation as such is of value in the job market, giving creative employees better opportunities for their professional future. For many scientists and engineers their success is a function of the progress and development to which they contribute, and measured not solely in economic terms. Keeping the information secret undermines this because it limits the possibility to present and share their achievements, e.g. in scientific publications.[19]

The argument that protection of trade secrets allows employers to accumulate resources and spend them, e.g. on investment in human capital, may be used also in support of the interests of employees, albeit in the reverse way. Since employees acquire skills and knowledge not only through the training obtained from their employers, but also through their own investment in their training and broadening of expertise, strong protection of trade secrets might discourage them from making that investment.[20] Should employees be restricted in their choice of activity after employment, they might not be interested in developing themselves outside the employment relationship. This would possibly harm the employers too, since they could not profit from such skills either.

The ability of employees to use skills, knowledge and information obtained during employment may have an essential bearing on their livelihood by influencing their choice of best employment and the possibility to change jobs. Overly strong legal protection against trade secrets misappropriation might limit their mobility.

[18] Alan Hyde, 'Intellectual Property Justifications for Restricting Employee Mobility: A Critical Appraisal in Light of Economic Evidence' in Cynthia L Estlund and Michael L Wachter (eds), *Research Handbook on the Economics of Labor and Employment Law* (Cheltenham: Edward Elgar 2012) 369.

[19] Feldman, 'Towards a Clearer Standard of Protectable Information: Trade Secrets and the Employment Relationship' 151, 157.

[20] Matt Marx, Jasjit Singh and Lee Fleming, 'Regional Disadvantage? Non-Compete Agreements and Brain Drain' (2010) 22 http://papers.ssrn.com/sol3/papers.cfm?abstract_id=1654719 accessed 1 June 2017.

III Policy Considerations

A Introduction

The considerations of interests of employers and employees presented above indicate that information has value for the former just as it has for the latter. The resolution of the conflict between those interests in legal terms is decisive for the extent to which information may be used after termination of employment. Thus, it may influence the development of the market for employment and innovation and therefore the economy in general. For that reason it is crucial to see the conflict of interests in a broader context of policy and economics. The analysis presented below, although based on policy considerations, may be transferred to an analysis of an inter partes conflict on a private-law level, since the public interest in fact reflects the interests of the employer and the employee.[21]

That is also the reason why the interests as well as the argumentation presented in this chapter will serve as reference throughout the further analysis presented in this book. Since the courts' decisions in trade secrets cases are strongly fact-related, the balancing exercise between the interests of the employers, employees and the public may play an essential role in both defining the scope of a right to use a trade secret in a post-employment scenario, as well as granted remedy once misappropriation has been found. The extent to which such considerations are part of decisions on enforcement of trade secrets is looked at in the course of the analysis.

The policy considerations underlying employee mobility include the will to incentivise innovation[22] and investment in research and development as well as training,[23] while at the same time encouraging dissemination of knowledge by enabling unrestricted change of employment.[24]

For the purpose of the present analysis, the arguments put forward in the discussion on policy issues are grouped into economic arguments, including reduction of costs, incentives to innovate and economic growth, followed by considerations relating to competition policy. After

[21] Stanley 79–80.

[22] Which includes competing notions of innovation: by breakthrough moments and by collective effort in incremental stages, see Lobel, 'Intellectual Property and Restrictive Covenants' 3–4.

[23] Bishara, 'Covenants Not to Compete in a Knowledge Economy: Balancing Innovation from Employee Mobility against Legal Protection for Human Capital Investment' 287, 301.

[24] Lobel, 'Intellectual Property and Restrictive Covenants' 18.

that the discussion on social policy is presented. The analysis is concluded by presentation of arguments based on fairness.

B Economic Arguments

In the economic analysis, trade secrets are often juxtaposed against the IPRs, in particular, patents and copyright. The main areas of discussion include the role of trade secrecy in encouraging innovation, reducing costs and facilitating economic growth and the impact that enforcement of trade secrets may have on competition.

1 Reduction of Costs through Protection of Investments

One of the main economic arguments for granting protection to trade secrets is that the existence of a legal framework to which an aggrieved party has recourse in a situation of unauthorised use of its trade secrets allows it to reduce the expenses which it would otherwise spend on gaining a level of de facto protection it deems sufficient (e.g. by introducing security measures, limiting access to premises, employment policy based on informal relations of trust rather than on skills).[25] This argumentation is looked at more closely below and followed by a critique to the effect that stronger protection of trade secrets does not necessarily guarantee reduction of businesses' expenditure.

1) Legal Protection of Trade Secrets as a Cost-Reducing Factor

The theory according to which legal protection of trade secrets allows cost-cutting, focuses on the reduction of indirect and transaction costs, i.e. costs generated by efforts to misappropriate the secrets on the one hand and endeavours to guard the secret information against theft and to securely transfer it on the other.[26] The existence of legal protection deters potential perpetrators from investing in theft of the information and encourages licensing instead. On the part of those holding valuable and secret know-how, the existence of legal protection allows reduction of expenditure on factual protection, by implementing secure access and

[25] Mark A Lemley, 'The Surprising Virtues of Treating Trade Secrets as IP Rights' (2008) 61 *Stanf L R* 311, 335; Robert G Bone, 'A New Look at Trade Secret Law: Doctrine in Search of Justification' (1998) 86 *Cal L Rev* 241, 272–273; Robert G Bone, 'The (Still) Shaky Foundations of Trade Secret Law' (2014) 92 *Tex L R* 1803, 1808–1809.

[26] Bone, 'A New Look at Trade Secret Law: Doctrine in Search of Justification' 241, 272–273; Bone, 'The (Still) Shaky Foundations of Trade Secret Law' 1803, 1808–1809; Michael Risch, 'Why Do We Have Trade Secrets?' (2007) 11 *Marq IP L Rev* 1, 41, 43, 67; Michael Risch, 'Trade Secret Law and Information Development Incentives' in Rochelle C Dreyfuss and Katherine J Strandburg (eds), *The Law and Theory of Trade Secrecy: A Handbook of Contemporary Research* (Edward Elgar 2011) 160.

an elaborate confidentiality policy, or employing loyal but possibly less-skilled employees with a view to averting misappropriation.[27] Should the party who possesses the information wish to profit from licensing it, in the absence of legal protection they would need to ensure an elaborate contractual framework in order to preserve the secrecy of the information and prevent its misuse. The same considerations may be raised in the context of an employment relationship.[28]

The legal protection of trade secrets aims at reducing the costs of self-help. However, granting such protection without any de facto measures would be costly as well, albeit not for the employer. The requirement that those who want to profit from the secret information must protect it by taking reasonable efforts to maintain that secrecy allows 'filtering' of information which is deemed more valuable (and therefore more strongly protected using factual measures) and easier sharing of information which is considered less crucial by a business.[29] Not requiring reasonable measures to maintain secrecy would result in protection of any information, irrespective of its subjective value for the employer.[30] That, in turn, would increase costs for other market participants for whom such information might be of use, and would furthermore severely limit the mobility of the employees, not allowing them to use any information they had learned from their former employer, irrespective of whether he had taken any steps to alert them to the secret nature of the know-how.

The existence of legal protection of trade secrets is furthermore argued to lead to a reduction of wasteful expenditures on an 'arms race' between those who have trade secrets and those who want to obtain them.[31] The

[27] Bone, 'A New Look at Trade Secret Law: Doctrine in Search of Justification' 241, 272–273; Douglas Lichtman, 'How the Law Responds to Self-Help' (2004) John M Olin Law & Economics Working Paper No 232, 24 http://papers.ssrn.com/sol3/papers.cfm?abstract_id=629287 accessed 1 June 2017.

[28] Risch, 'Why Do We Have Trade Secrets?' 1, 41, 67; Risch, 'Trade Secret Law and Information Development Incentives' 161–162.

[29] Risch, 'Why Do We Have Trade Secrets?' 1, 45–46. The level of de facto protection may furthermore serve as an indicator of the information's value, ibid; Michael V Risch, 'Comments on Trade Secrets Sharing in High Velocity Labor Markets' (2008) 339, 345 http://ssrn.com/abstract=1269039 accessed 1 June 2017; Lichtman, 'How the Law Responds to Self-Help' 19.

[30] That proposition seems to be supported by Chally who advocates lowering the hurdle needed to profit from protection, in particular by eliminating the requirement that reasonable steps be taken to preserve secrecy. This, he argues, will allow the holders of information to save the costs spent on de facto protection and, instead, spend more on research and development, Jonathan R Chally, 'The Law of Trade Secrets: Toward a More Efficient Approach' (2004) 57 *Vand L Rev* 1269, 1310–1311.

[31] Risch, 'Why Do We Have Trade Secrets?' 1, 62–63; Lichtman, 'How the Law Responds to Self-Help' 26–27, although, as the author admits (at 32), the law may only reduce the arms race, but not eliminate it completely.

threat of expensive litigation serves as a deterrent against misappropriation. Thus, potential infringers are encouraged to obtain trade secrets in a legal way, e.g. by reverse engineering or independent research instead of employee poaching. Those who 'own' trade secrets are in turn discouraged from overinvesting in protecting the information by recourse to self-help.

Another aspect of the cost-reducing effect of the legal protection of trade secrets is that it allows the safeguarding of expenses spent on developing valuable information[32] and human capital. As regards the latter, Samila and Sorenson differentiate between firm-specific skills, which are not of use for competitors, and more general skills from which also others may profit. The employee's move to another company does not pose a threat to investment in the firm-specific skills, and therefore legal protection of trade secrets does not influence investment in those skills and knowledge, even if they are trade secrets. However, in the case of training which can be valuable also for competitors, the legal protection of trade secrets allows the employer to protect his expenditure[33] by limiting the probability of his competitors reaping the fruit of the investment he has made in his (former) employees' training.

2) Legal Protection of Trade Secrets as a Factor Increasing Overall Costs

According to the view presented partially in the older literature, there is no need for extensive trade secrets protection since information is in fact self-protecting (it is difficult to steal as it is rarely contained in a single document).[34] Consequently, legal protection of such information would not reduce costs, due to the fact that there is no need for any active protection in the first place. It is submitted here that this argument may apply only to some types of information that may be protected as a trade secret. A secret formula is not self-protecting if it is contained in a single document. Of course, ensuring that none of the employees knows the entire formula lowers the possibility of the secret being disclosed or misappropriated. However, that does not result from the self-protecting nature of that information, but rather from how it is being actively protected by its holder. Therefore, the argument that information is self-protecting may be more valid in relation to information on, e.g.,

32 For a more detailed analysis, see Chapter 1, part III point B.1-2.

33 Samila and Sorenson, 'Non-Compete Covenants: Incentives to Innovate or Impediments to Growth' 8.

34 Edmund W Kitch, 'The Law and Economics of Rights in Valuable Information' (1980) 9 (4) *JLS, The Law and Economics of Privacy* 683, 711–715.

the organisation of a company, which quickly loses its value if applied by more enterprises, rather than to secret formulas or processes.

Another argument, which remains an important criticism of the theory that legal protection of trade secrets results in reduction of costs, is that, while that protection allows for reduction of the indirect and transaction costs of guarding against theft, it increases the enforcement costs and transaction costs of licensing.[35] The possibility to protect secret information through courts may reduce investment in factual measures to protect secrets, but it invites litigation, which is also costly.[36] The costs of detecting misappropriation, litigation costs deriving from the complexity of the factual issues and difficulties in providing evidence of misappropriation are emphasised by the commentators as factors that may make the overall costs of trade secrets protection higher than the profits gained from it.[37] Another critical argument raised by Bone is that while the transaction costs of licensing of secret know-how exist irrespective of legal protection of trade secrets, the existence of such legal protection does not decrease those costs. This is because the licensing negotiations are complicated by the fact that the licensor does not want to disclose the information, while the licensee is not interested in entering the discussions if uncertain as to the object of the prospective contract. For similar reasons transaction costs are further increased by the fact that the valuation of the secret information poses problems,[38] making it difficult to agree on remuneration. Trade secrets law, as opposed to the patent system, is also seen as a cause of wasteful duplication of efforts in developing information which already exists, even if kept secret.[39]

[35] Bone, 'A New Look at Trade Secret Law: Doctrine in Search of Justification' 241, 273; Bone, 'The (Still) Shaky Foundations of Trade Secret Law' 1803, 1809.

[36] Litigation costs are especially high in the United States, to which Bone refers, due to discovery proceedings and the fact that each party is required to bear its own legal expenses. However, the costs of litigation in Germany and the United Kingdom should not be disregarded. Even in those jurisdictions, the costs of gathering evidence and of litigation are often decisive for enforcement of trade secrets. According to a market survey among companies in the EU conducted in 2013, 43% of respondents cited difficulties in collecting evidence, and 30% of respondents litigation costs, as reasons not to seek a remedy in case of actual or threatened misappropriation, see Baker&McKenzie Study 13.

[37] Bone, 'A New Look at Trade Secret Law: Doctrine in Search of Justification' 241, 275, 278–279.

[38] Ibid 241, 280.

[39] Bone, 'A New Look at Trade Secret Law: Doctrine in Search of Justification' 241, 266–267; Bone, 'The (Still) Shaky Foundations of Trade Secret Law' 1803, 1813. Lemley is not convinced by this argument. He suggests that, on the one hand, parallel research may bring valuable effects and, on the other, patent law does not serve the function of informing society, because patent applications and patents are not read by

Bone suggests however that the cost reduction argument, although generally misguided, might be applicable in the employee mobility scenario. According to him, in such cases the theft is relatively easy to detect, since the competing firm (new employer) will start producing an identical product in a relatively short period of time after the employee's departure. This also supports the argument of improper acquisition and use of the information, which significantly increases the probability of successful litigation and consequently lowers its costs. At the same time, the indirect costs of safeguarding the information used by an employer's own employees are particularly high and therefore the existence of legal protection of trade secrets proves efficient. However, according to Bone, the statutory protection of trade secrets is most efficient in cases in which the former employee is hired by a competitor. He suggests that post-employment contracts provide a better deterrent against misappropriation by former employees starting their own business.[40]

In view of the efficiency of contractual protection of trade secrets, it has been suggested that the law should step in only in cases where the costs of negotiations between the parties are too high or where such negotiations are not possible.[41] As regards licensing, Landes and Posner suggest therefore that informal sharing of information achieved by weaker protection granted to trade secrets (in the example given by them: by the unenforceability of covenants not to compete) may be more efficient than licensing of the valuable information, taking into account the transaction costs involved.[42]

From the perspective of the employees, it has been stressed that, since any protection of trade secrets limits mobility, it entails higher opportunity costs for creative employees. Research based on a comparison of enforcement of non-compete agreements in various US states has shown that the inventive employees moved from the states which enforced NCAs to those which did not.[43] As limited job mobility reduces the

competitors, see Lemley, 'The Surprising Virtues of Treating Trade Secrets as IP Rights' 311, 336 note 103, with further references.

40 Bone, 'A New Look at Trade Secret Law: Doctrine in Search of Justification' 241, 281–282.

41 As summarised in Bishara, 'Covenants Not to Compete in a Knowledge Economy: Balancing Innovation from Employee Mobility against Legal Protection for Human Capital Investment' 287, 304–307, with further references. Also in support of contractual regulation, see Bone, 'A New Look at Trade Secret Law: Doctrine in Search of Justification' 241, 297, 303; Bone, 'The (Still) Shaky Foundations of Trade Secret Law' 1803, 1836.

42 William A Landes and Richard A Posner, *The Economic Structure of Intellectual Property Law* (The Belknap Press of Harvard University Press 2003) 366.

43 This phenomenon has been described as 'brain drain', see Marx, Singh and Fleming, 'Regional Disadvantage? Non-Compete Agreements and Brain Drain' 5.

possibilities for those employees to use their skills in a new company, it increases their costs by not allowing them a free choice of the best professional opportunity.

Another argument presented with regard to post-employment covenants not to compete is that their aggressive enforcement discourages employees from investing in their own education and broadening their skills.[44] It is argued here that strong legal protection of trade secrets outside contract law may have a similar effect: if employment mobility is limited due to strong protection of trade secrets, employees will be discouraged from incurring the costs of investing in their human capital.

2 Encouraging Innovation: Incentives to Create

Since protection of trade secrets allows reduction of companies' costs, it provides them with resources which they can invest in research and development. That stimulates innovation, which is further encouraged by legal protection of the secret know-how which is thereby developed. This argument is typically used to justify the exclusive rights of intellectual property,[45] although it is also put forward to support the protection granted to trade secrets. The line of argumentation based on the incentive theory of trade secrets is presented below, together with a critical appraisal stemming primarily from the fact that trade secrets may not be seen as typical IPRs.[46]

1) Legal Protection of Trade Secrets as Incentive to Create

The traditional role of trade secrecy is to allow entrepreneurs to 'recoup their investments in small-scale innovation without creating barriers to entry and without impeding qualified second comers from making follow-on applications of others' routine innovations'.[47] However, trade secrets protection is not limited to small-scale improvements and is often

44 Ibid 22.

45 William Cornish, David Llewelyn and Tanya Aplin, *Intellectual Property: Patents, Copyright, Trade Marks and Allied Rights* (8th edn, Sweet&Maxwell 2013) paras 3–36–3–37.

46 Trade secrets are not generally recognised as another type of intellectual property. Even in the United States, where they are referred to as a right of intellectual property, the differences from other IPRs, in particular patents, are stressed, see e.g. Landes and Posner, The Economic Structure of Intellectual Property Law 355.

47 Jerome H Reichman, 'How Trade Secrecy Law Generates a Natural Semicommons of Innovative Know-How' in Rochelle C Dreyfuss and Katherine J Strandburg (eds), *The Law and Theory of Trade Secrecy: A Handbook of Contemporary Research* (Edward Elgar 2011) 193.

seen as an alternative or an addition to the traditional IPRs.[48] Thus, it may be regarded as a tool for protection of innovation as such.[49]

Innovation stems not only from patentable inventions or creations protected by other types of intellectual property. An innovative process or product may not be novel and inventive in patent-law terms or susceptible of protection by copyright. Even if eligible for IP protection, the costs of obtaining such protection may not be covered by the prospective income from marketing the innovation. This as such does not render the information worthless. The value of the secret know-how lies in the lead time (competitive advantage) that it provides over other companies.[50] Therefore, the protection granted by the law of trade secrets particularly benefits innovation in non-patentable inventions. It has even been proposed by Bone that secrecy should not be relied on in case of inventions eligible for patent protection, due to the fact that it might undermine the existence of the patent system. According to him, the only instance when such protection could be accepted would be during the development phase,[51] since applying for a patent for each stage of research might prove too costly and might furthermore render the next steps of the innovative process obvious and thus not patentable.

The fact that the law protecting trade secrets provides a remedy in cases of misappropriation of information results in companies spending less on factual protection of that information.[52] As in the case of revenues derived from monetisation of IPRs, the originators of valuable information are expected to invest those resources in research and development of further innovative products and services. The information considered particularly valuable will be enforced more aggressively, therefore providing a natural 'filter' by which the more valuable information will be preserved and the less valuable made available for everyone to use.[53] Of course, the fact that a company has additional revenues derived from the protection that the law grants to the trade secrets at its disposal does not ensure that all of that income will be invested in innovation. It may be

[48] Ibid 190; Baker&McKenzie Study 2.

[49] Reichman, 'How Trade Secrecy Law Generates a Natural Semicommons of Innovative Know-How' 187–190.

[50] Ibid 189.

[51] Bone, 'A New Look at Trade Secret Law: Doctrine in Search of Justification' 241, 267–269, 271.

[52] Risch, 'Comments on Trade Secrets Sharing in High Velocity Labor Markets' 339, 345; Lichtman, 'How the Law Responds to Self-Help' 24.

[53] Risch, 'Comments on Trade Secrets Sharing in High Velocity Labor Markets' 339, 345; David D Friedman, William M Landes and Richard A Posner, 'Some Economics of Trade Secret Law' (1991) 5(1) *J Econ Pers* 61, 68; Landes and Posner, *The Economic Structure of Intellectual Property Law* 366.

spent on monetisation, promotion and marketing or divided between the company's shareholders. A reasonable company would however be expected to invest at least part of that income in development of its products and services.

Another argument in support of trade secrets as an incentive to innovate is that, despite the limiting effect on employee mobility, the protection granted to secret know-how encourages innovation based on tacit knowledge, such as routines and practices, which cannot be codified and which is inseparable from the employee who possesses it. Any departure of such an employee would invariably deprive the employer of the possibility to innovate based on that knowledge. Due to those characteristics of tacit knowledge, there is no other way of appropriating it than by limiting employee mobility.[54]

Consequently, reliance on trade secrecy is usually a complementary way used by creative entrepreneurs to protect innovation.[55] Others include the classical IPRs (patents, utility models, copyright, design rights, trademarks), lead time, use of limited distribution channels, factual monopolies and development of customer loyalty.[56] Secrecy is considered to be especially suitable for protection of processes. In case of alleged unauthorised use of a method or procedure, it is oftentimes difficult to prove infringement of an IPR due to difficulties in collecting evidence. If the process can be kept secret, those problems may be avoided.[57]

According to Risch, trade secret law encourages innovation in cases in which neither self-help nor legal remedies would suffice. He mentions situations in which it is impossible or too costly to achieve absolute secrecy by recourse to de facto measures.[58] Further areas of positive correlation between trade secrecy and innovation are multi-stage manufacturing (in which the transaction costs of negotiating non-disclosure contracts with all the participants of the manufacturing process are saved due to the existence of legal protection) and information typically owned by the employer

[54] Samila and Sorenson, 'Non-Compete Covenants: Incentives to Innovate or Impediments to Growth' 7; Marcus Oehlrich, 'Know-how und Tacit Knowledge als vernachlässigte Vertragsbestandteile bei Lizenzverträgen' (2010) GRUR 33, 34.

[55] For example, protection of innovation by patents is often complemented by NCAs, see Samila and Sorenson, 'Non-Compete Covenants: Incentives to Innovate or Impediments to Growth' 7.

[56] Oliver Gassmann and Martin A Bader, *Patentmanagement. Innovationen erfolgreich nützen und schützen* (3rd edn, Springer 2011) 5.

[57] Gassmann and Bader, *Patentmanagement. Innovationen erfolgreich nützen und schützen* 61, giving the Coca-Cola composition and manufacturing process and the operating algorithms used by Schindler as examples of successful recourse to secrecy for protection of innovative products.

[58] Risch, 'Trade Secret Law and Information Development Incentives' 160.

(usually data related to sales and contacts).[59] Bone suggests that secrecy might be a good way to protect non-technical information such as market studies, long-term business plans and customer information; although he admits that it is not clear whether trade secrets law encourages the production of such information in the first place.[60]

In this regard it is submitted here that legal protection of trade secrets might be an efficient way to incentivise innovation characterised by a relatively short life-cycle. Even in the cases of eligibility of protection of such know-how under the patent system, the costs[61] and duration[62] of obtaining an exclusive right might be too high, in view of the fact that in some fields of technology[63] the life-span of a product does not exceed a few years or even months. In those cases an exclusive right lasting for up to 20 years might simply be inefficient. Keeping such an invention secret allows lead time to be gained,[64] which is an important factor in creating and maintaining a competitive advantage.[65]

2) *Legal Protection of Trade Secrets as an Obstacle to Incentivising Innovation*

Economic research based on the analysis of migration of inventor-employees who obtained patents in the United States shows that inventors changing employment are more likely to leave states which enforce NCAs and move to states which do not. The increase in migration proved strongest for more productive and collaborative employees.[66] A similar conclusion was reached in another piece of research, in which empirical evidence showed that stronger trade secrets protection lowers the mobility of highly specialised and educated employees.[67]

[59] Ibid 161.

[60] Arguably such information is created as a result of conducting business as such, Bone, 'A New Look at Trade Secret Law: Doctrine in Search of Justification' 241, 272.

[61] Baker&McKenzie Study 91.

[62] Lemley, 'The Surprising Virtues of Treating Trade Secrets as IP Rights' 311, 331.

[63] Notably IT and software, cf Peterson 1–70 – 1–71.

[64] Even if the secret is disclosed upon marketing of the product, Pooley 4–47.

[65] Wesley M Cohen, Richard R Nelson and John P Walsh, 'Protecting their Intellectual Assets: Appropriability Conditions and Why US Manufacturing Firms Patent (or Not)' (2000) NBER Working Paper Series Working Paper No 7552, 1, 6 www.nber.org/papers/w7552.pdf accessed 1 June 2017; in the survey reported on by Arundel, 54.4% of companies relied on lead time as an appropriation mechanism for product innovation and 46.7% for process innovation, see Anthony Arundel, 'The Relative Effectiveness of Patents and Secrecy for Appropriation' (2001) 30 *Research Policy* 611, 616.

[66] Marx, Singh and Fleming, 'Regional Disadvantage? Non-Compete Agreements and Brain Drain' 5–6, 19.

[67] Ivan PL Png and Sampsa Samila, 'Trade Secrets Law and Mobility: Evidence from "Inevitable Disclosure"' (2015) 23 http://papers.ssrn.com/sol3/papers.cfm?abstract_id=1986775 accessed 1 June 2017.

Dissemination of knowledge, apart from investment in research and development, is one of the ways of encouraging innovation. Since knowledge spill-overs are correlated with the mobility of employees,[68] strong protection of trade secrets, while fostering investment in research and development by employers, might still have a negative impact on innovation. This may be caused by hampering diffusion of knowledge and result in limiting the number of new spin-offs and start-ups.[69]

In contrast to patent law, trade secrecy prevents disclosure of innovative information. In this way, for a possibly unlimited time, it denies access to information which could lead to further developments and therefore, as argued by Bone, increases duplication of efforts to find innovative solutions which might already exist in the market.[70]

Bone and Risch draw attention to the fact that for certain types of information, namely that which would have been created anyway as part of a company' daily activity (e.g. marketing plans or customer lists)[71] or where information sharing between firms is a better way to maximise profits,[72] trade secrets protection does not encourage innovation.

A nuanced approach is presented by Bessen and Nuvolari. Based on historical analysis they argue that knowledge-sharing between innovators is more likely to occur in the early phases of development of a technology, while proprietary incentives, such as patent law, seem to encourage improvements of developed technologies. Therefore, as a policy consideration, they propose that for most efficient promotion of innovation, a combination of various models should be chosen.[73]

Finally, it is observed that in the analysis of the influence of trade secrecy on incentivising innovation, any one type of legal protection may not be seen as the only means of promoting it.[74] In certain industries, lead time and

[68] Hyde, 'Intellectual Property Justifications for Restricting Employee Mobility: A Critical Appraisal in Light of Economic Evidence' 366–368. Among companies in the EU, employee mobility was recognised as a source of information spill-overs by 17% of the respondents (after clients and customers: 34% and suppliers: 22%), see Baker&McKenzie Study 125.

[69] Samila and Sorenson, 'Non-Compete Covenants: Incentives to Innovate or Impediments to Growth' 10; Png and Samila, 'Trade Secrets Law and Mobility: Evidence from "Inevitable Disclosure"' 24.

[70] Bone, 'A New Look at Trade Secret Law: Doctrine in Search of Justification' 241, 266–267; Bone, 'The (Still) Shaky Foundations of Trade Secret Law' 1803, 1813.

[71] Bone, 'A New Look at Trade Secret Law: Doctrine in Search of Justification' 241, 272; Bone, 'The (Still) Shaky Foundations of Trade Secret Law' 1803, 1812.

[72] Risch, 'Trade Secret Law and Information Development Incentives' 163.

[73] James Bessen and Alessandro Nuvolari, 'Knowledge-Sharing Among Inventors: Some Historical Perspectives' (2011) Boston University School of Law Working Paper No 11–51 11–12 http://ssrn.com/abstract=1944201 accessed 1 June 2017.

[74] As argued in the case of patents by Bessen and Nuvolari, see 'Knowledge-Sharing among Inventors: Some Historical Perspectives' 3, 12.

learning curve may play a more effective role in securing competitive advantage for innovative companies than legal protection. Other factors that may play a similar role include taxation; public support for research and development; the degree of connectedness between academic, business and financial communities;[75] and general change in the economic or social situation, in particular economic decline.[76] Therefore, while supporters of the incentive theory of trade secrets law put forward many valid arguments, to date it has not been shown that there is a clear correlation between protection of trade secrets and innovation as such on the policy level.

3 Facilitation of Economic Growth

Apart from being a cost factor and an element of the incentive system of innovation, trade secrets protection may encourage market participants to introduce new products, thus strengthening their competitive position and market wealth in general. On the other hand, it may limit creation of start-ups and have a negative impact on the level of investment and employment.[77] The various considerations regarding the influence of the protection of trade secrets on economic growth are presented below.

1) Legal Protection of Trade Secrets as Incentive to Experiment in the Market

Enabling entrepreneurs to reap profits from secret information they possess may lead to a reduction in prices and an increase in the quality of products and services.[78]

The introduction of a new and better product on the market is referred to by Abramowicz and Duffy as a justification for the protection of trade secrets.[79] They argue that, unlike classical IP law, which encourages technical experimentation, the law protecting trade secrets encourages market experimentation,[80] i.e. the introduction of new products, which

[75] Samila and Sorenson, 'Non-Compete Covenants: Incentives to Innovate or Impediments to Growth' 28.

[76] Marx, Singh and Fleming, 'Regional Disadvantage? Non-Compete Agreements and Brain Drain' 17–18.

[77] The varying regimes of protection granted to trade secrets by various Member States of the EU may also conflict with the fundamental principle of free movement of workers and provision of services, see Ansgar Ohly, 'Harmonising the Protection of Trade Secrets: Challenges and Perspectives' in Jacques de Werra (ed), *La protection des secrets d'affaires. The Protection of Trade Secrets* (Schulthess 2013) 39.

[78] Stanley 79.

[79] Michael Abramowicz and John F Duffy, 'Intellectual Property for Market Experimentation' (2008) 83 *NYULRev* 337.

[80] Market experimentation being a commercial test of a new product on the market, as opposed to technical experimentation in which products are tested in laboratories. In market experimentation the product is being launched in a situation in which it has

are not necessarily novel and inventive in patent-law terms.[81] According to them, market experimentation explains why the law protects not only innovative information, but also information that is naturally produced as a result of any entrepreneurial activity, such as business plans and customer lists. The goal of the protection granted to trade secrets is not the protection of such information, but rather of the business that produced the information. By protecting the information, the law allows a company to secure a first-comer position on the market and thereby creates incentives for further market experiments. The authors admit that trade secrets law protects innovative companies in the same way as it does possible misappropriators, but they argue that on the whole these are innovative companies that are more prone to conduct market experimentation.[82]

2) *Legal Protection of Trade Secrets as Factor Limiting Creation of New Firms and Employment*

The argument that trade secrets protection may lead to reduced prices and higher quality of products and services may lose its force in a situation in which, as explained below,[83] the protection of information leads to creation of a monopoly. A company which has a dominant position in a certain market, for example due to a successfully safeguarded trade secret, may dictate the prices of products and services at levels higher than those which would apply if the information was accessible to all competitors.

Additionally, under general economic considerations, information is seen as non-rivalrous (i.e. consuming it does not exclude others from consuming it)[84] and as a crucial factor in economic growth.[85] According to Hyde, who refers to the example of Silicon Valley, where companies base their activities on outsourcing and networking rather than vertical integration,[86] weaker protection for employers' intellectual property[87] is positive for start-ups, venture capital and economic growth in general.[88]

uncertain prospects of commercial success, Abramowicz and Duffy, 'Intellectual Property for Market Experimentation' 337, 339 note 4.

81 Ibid 337, 342.

82 Ibid 391.

83 Chapter 1, part III point C.

84 Jan G Tönnies, 'Erfindungen – ein Kollektivgut oder die Gedanken sind frei' (2013) GRUR 796, 796.

85 Hyde, 'Intellectual Property Justifications for Restricting Employee Mobility: A Critical Appraisal in Light of Economic Evidence' 358.

86 Ibid 363.

87 In his article, Hyde refers to the US legal system, which recognises trade secrets as a type of IPRs.

88 Hyde, 'Intellectual Property Justifications for Restricting Employee Mobility: A Critical Appraisal in Light of Economic Evidence' 359, with further references to empirical studies.

Employee-friendly legal regimes not enforcing NCAs were found to profit from greater employment than those with stronger protection of trade secrets. Samila and Sorenson found that enforcement of NCAs limits entrepreneurship. According to the authors, the effect that strict labour law, e.g. rigid enforcement of covenants protecting trade secrets, has on the economy may not be offset even by promotion of venture capital investment.[89] A further argument points out that broad post-employment fiduciary duties of employees have a similar effect as NCAs by impeding the development of spin-offs and new firms.[90]

It can be concluded that the question of whether legal protection of trade secrets facilitates economic growth, in particular the creation of start-ups and promotion of employment, has not been conclusively answered in the economic literature. Like other arguments presented in this part of the book, it is to be approached with due account of various interests that collide in the context of employee mobility.

C Considerations Rooted in Competition Law

The overlap between trade secrecy and competition is an area of controversy, as exemplified ia by the battle between Microsoft and the European Commission, concerning abuse of a dominant position safeguarded by the company's secret information on inter-operability of software.[91]

Although trade secrets may be relevant for both anti-competitive agreements[92] and abuse of dominant position,[93] the focus of this book is the effect that the protection granted to trade secrets may have in the context of employee mobility. This area is dominated by private-law enforcement between the former employer and the employee or his new employer.

[89] Samila and Sorenson, 'Non-Compete Covenants: Incentives to Innovate or Impediments to Growth' 26–27; similarly Hyde, 'Intellectual Property Justifications for Restricting Employee Mobility: A Critical Appraisal in Light of Economic Evidence' 366.

[90] Samila and Sorenson, 'Non-Compete Covenants: Incentives to Innovate or Impediments to Growth' 28.

[91] Case T-201/004 *Microsoft v Commission* (2007) ECR II-03601.

[92] Agreements between undertakings, decisions by associations of undertakings and concerted practices which may affect trade between Member States and which have as their object or effect the prevention, restriction or distortion of competition within the internal market, Art 101 TFEU. To that effect in the United States, see S 1 Sherman Act.

[93] Art 102 TFEU, defined as 'a position of economic strength enjoyed by an undertaking which enables it to prevent effective competition being maintained on the relevant market by giving it the power to behave to an appreciable extent independently of its competitors, customers and ultimately of its consumers', Case 27/76 *United Brands Company and United Brands Continentaal BV v Commission of the European Communities* [1978] ECR 1978 00207 [65]. To that effect in the United States, see S 2 Sherman Act.

Competition law on the other hand belongs to the domain of public law.[94] Thus, the arguments presented below serve as an indication of policy issues that are rooted in competition law and may be taken into consideration in the context of employee mobility.[95] Those considerations are of particular relevance with regard to obtaining and keeping a dominant position[96] by an employer as well as in the assessment of post-employment covenants under the common-law doctrine of restraint of trade.[97]

1 Legal Protection of Trade Secrets as a Factor Encouraging Competition by Innovation

Legal protection granted to trade secrets, by limiting access to information and thereby the possibility of imitation of products and services developed by others, may encourage competition by innovation, in a similar way as the IPRs do.[98] If companies are not allowed to rely on what others have developed, they will be forced to come up with their own ideas and compete by introducing better innovative products or

[94] Cf Jürgen Basedow (ed), *Private Enforcement of EC Competition Law* (Kluwer Law International 2007) 1–2. However, defences based on competition law have been recognised also in inter partes civil enforcement, see ia Case C-126/97 *Eco Swiss China Time Ltd and Benetton International NV* [1999] I-3079, in which the ECJ ruled that a national court deciding on an arbitration award must take into account the possible anticompetitive effect of the arbitration award, and the German case BGH GRUR 2009, 694, 696 *Orange Book Standard*, in which the BGH recognised a patent-infringement defence based on the abuse of dominant position by the patentee. See also Case C-170/13 *Huawei Technologies Co. Ltd v ZTE* [2015] not published in ECR.

[95] Competition law, strictly speaking, does not apply in this context, e.g. Art 101 TFEU will not apply to post-employment agreements since employees may not be seen as 'undertakings' within the meaning of that provision, Alexandra Kamerling and Christopher Goodwill, *Restrictive Covenants under Common and Competition Law* (Sweet&Maxwell 2010) 204. See also Chapter 4, part III.

[96] Mary-Rose McGuire, Björn Joachim, Jens Künzel and Nils Weber, 'Der Schutz von Geschäftsgeheimnissen durch Rechte des Geistigen Eigentums und durch das Recht des unlauteren Wettbewerbs (Q215)' (2010) 829, 835.

[97] The purpose of many post-employment contracts is to limit competition, e.g. with regard to the use of information obtained by the employee during employment, Alexandra Kamerling and Christopher Goodwill, *Restrictive Covenants under Common and Competition Law* (Sweet&Maxwell 2010) 2. In German law, no explicit limitation of the possibility to conclude post-employment contracts based on competition law considerations has been identified. However, post-employment agreements limiting competition are regulated by statute (Ss 74–75f HGB). In UK law the doctrine of restraint of trade may limit the scope of post-employment covenants, see Kamerling and Goodwill, Restrictive Covenants under Common and Competition Law 1. In the United States the doctrine of restraint of trade also exists, see e.g. Katherine VW Stone, 'The New Psychological Contract: Implications of the Changing Workplace for Labor and Employment Law' (2001) 48 *UCLA L Rev* 519, 583. For a more detailed analysis of this doctrine, see Chapter 4, part II, points B and C.

[98] Trade secrets have been recognised ia by Schumpeter, together with IPRs, as one of the factors that may help innovators to destroy existing monopolies and thereby increase innovation and dynamic competition, Joseph A Schumpeter *Capitalism, Socialism and Democracy* (5th edn, Routledge reprinted 1996) 88.

services. At the same time they will be encouraged to do so by a prospect of exclusivity in the use of the information developed by them, which may be achieved by a successful trade secret strategy.[99]

An example, although not directly related to the employee mobility scenario, is the acceptance of exemptions from scrutiny under competition law for certain kinds of agreements, with the argumentation that their efficiency-enhancing effect and facilitation of innovation outweigh the anti-competitive effect they might have.[100] In the EU such block exemption covers transfers of technology containing secret know-how[101] and agreements relating to research and development.[102]

2 Legal Protection of Trade Secrets as an Aid to Secure Market Dominance

Unlike patent and copyright laws, which presuppose disclosure and only a time-limited exclusion of others, secrecy may allow a company to reap benefits from information for an unlimited period of time, not conditional on disclosure that would benefit society. Even though exclusivity granted to the proprietors of IPRs limits competition by imitation, at the same time it encourages competition by innovation: with access to disclosed patent specifications, competitors can work around the exclusive right and deliver innovative products.[103] The differences in the nature and effects of trade secrets call for a particularly careful analysis under that doctrine. Precisely the lack of disclosure of the information which is at the core of the protection of trade secrets makes the argumentation less convincing in the case of confidential information. Therefore, while it should not be assumed that the possession of secret information has an anticompetitive effect through creation of a monopolistic position,[104] the mere fact that the object of enforcement is a trade secret should not create a presumption of lack of such effect either. Regardless of any such presumptions, the courts in assessing claims for misappropriation of

99 See Chapter 1, part III point B.2.

100 Recitals 4 and 5 Commission Regulation (EU) No 316/2014 of 21 March 2014 on the application of Article 101(3) of the Treaty on the Functioning of the European Union to categories of technology transfer agreements [2014] OJ L 93/17 (TTBER); Recital 4 Commission Regulation (EC) No 1217/2010 of 14 December 2010 on the application of Article 101(3) TFEU to certain categories of research and development agreements [2010] OJ L355/36 (RDBER).

101 Art 2 TTBER.

102 Art 2 RDBER.

103 Josef Drexl, 'Intellectual Property and Antitrust Law. IMS Health and Trinko – Antitrust Placebo for Consumers Instead of Sound Economics in Refusal-to-Deal Cases' (2004) IIC 788, 792–793.

104 Cf Recital 13 TTBER; Antitrust Guidelines for the Licensing of Intellectual Property, US Department of Justice and the Federal Trade Commission, 6 April 1995 para 2.2.

confidential information should take due account of effects that such enforcement might have on competition and consumer welfare.[105]

Imitation allows for lowering of prices and as such is not a reprehensible practice. Rather, together with competition by innovation, competition by imitation is an inherent feature of a well-functioning market.[106] Therefore, in the case of strong legal protection granted to trade secrets, the benefits achieved by encouraging innovation may be counterbalanced by the strengthening of the market position of the company which asserts its rights to secret information. This in turn may safeguard that company's dominant position[107] and allow it to dictate prices at monopolistic levels. As a consequence, protection granted to trade secrets may result in creation of barriers to entry for competitors and in reduced consumer welfare.[108]

One of the ways in which abuse of a dominant position may limit competition is abusive litigation.[109] The problem arises most commonly when patents are enforced.[110] With regard to trade secrets it is most evident in a situation of enforcement of an alleged trade secret against the former employee or his new employer, where misappropriation has in fact not occurred.[111] Other examples of abusive litigation recognised as having anticompetitive effect include asserting trade secret protection for a manufacturing process after the expiry of patent protection for that process.[112] Initiation of enforcement in such cases may result in prohibitive litigation costs on the part of the former employee or his new employer and as a consequence eliminate them from the market and chill competition.[113] In the years 2003–2013, between 8.9% and 11.2%

105 Harry First, 'Trade Secrets and Antitrust Law' in Rochelle C Dreyfuss and Katherine J Strandburg (eds), *The Law and Theory of Trade Secrecy: A Handbook of Contemporary Research* (Edward Elgar 2011) 333, 380.

106 Kalbfus para 59.

107 Kalbfus para 59; Gintare Surblytė, *The Refusal to Disclose Trade Secrets and Abuse of Market Dominance - Microsoft and Beyond* (Stämpfli Publishers Ltd Berne 2011) 203–205. It is observed that while in Europe only abuse of an existing dominant position is seen as anti-competitive under Art 102 TFEU, in the United States already an attempt at monopolisation is considered illegal under S 2 Sherman Act.

108 Stanley 79.

109 In Europe also referred to as vexatious litigation, see e.g. Case T-111/96 *ITT Promedia v Commission (1998) ECR II-02937* (with regard to copyright); in the USA sham litigation, see *Professional Real Estate Investors Inc v Columbia Pictures Industries Inc* 508 US 49, 60 (US Supr Ct 1993).

110 First, 'Trade Secrets and Antitrust Law' 363.

111 For example, due to earlier disclosure by the former employer and 'failure to follow its own established procedures for the protection of trade secrets', *CVD Inc v Raytheon Co* 769 F2d 842 paras 32, 36 (1st Cir 1985).

112 As explained in First, 'Trade Secrets and Antitrust Law' 365.

113 Lobel, 'Intellectual Property and Restrictive Covenants' 13; Bone, 'A New Look at Trade Secret Law: Doctrine in Search of Justification' 241, 279; Bone, 'The (Still) Shaky Foundations of Trade Secret Law' 1803, 1815.

of companies in the EU experienced abusive litigation relating to alleged trade secrets.[114]

Where strong protection is granted to trade secrets, the same effect is suggested not only with regard to direct competitors. If post-employment confidentiality obligations are strictly enforced, former employees may be effectively prevented from pursuing remote lines of business on their own or in employment with an existing company.[115]

The argumentation presented above shows that while the discussion on whether legal protection of trade secrets benefits innovation seems to provide equally valid arguments for and against that proposition, the discussion approached from the perspective of competition law, on the policy level, seems to present more arguments in favour of trade secrecy as a factor impacting competition in a negative way. This consideration is reflected ia in the Trade Secrets Directive, which confirms the primacy of Articles 101 and 102 TFEU[116] and sanctions abusive litigation.[117]

D *Arguments Relating to Social Policy and Human Welfare*

The level of protection granted to trade secrets may have an impact on employee welfare and the creation of certain structures in the employment market.

1 **Arguments for Granting Legal Protection to Trade Secrets**

Intuitively, any restriction of employee mobility, e.g. through putting boundaries on the information they may use after termination of their employment, should have a negative impact on their welfare. Nevertheless, the limitation of the use of information acquired from the employer might be a necessary consideration for the employment in the first place. Were the employers not able to rely on trade secrets protection, including post-employment non-disclosure, non-compete and invention-assignment[118] contracts, they might limit the hiring of new workers,[119] with a negative impact on employee welfare at a general level.

[114] Baker&McKenzie Study 132. This report refers to abusive litigation in general and is not limited to litigation by dominant undertakings.

[115] Samila and Sorenson, 'Non-Compete Covenants: Incentives to Innovate or Impediments to Growth' 10.

[116] Recital 38 TSD.

[117] Art 7(2), Recital 22 TSD.

[118] For example, for assignment of any post-employment improvements made to the invention created while working for the former employer.

[119] *Hulse v Bonsack Machine Co*, 65 F 864, 866 (4th Cir 1895), as reported in Catherine L Fisk, '"An Ingenious Man Enabled by Contract": Entrepreneurship and the Rise of

Additionally to the negative influence on the level of employment, limitation of protection granted to trade secrets might affect employees by lowering the level of their remuneration.[120] As with patentable inventions, it is not possible to assess in advance which trade secret is going to prove valuable enough to allow the recoupment of the investment in developing the information. Lack of ex ante regulation on who – the employer or the employee – will be able to use that information after the end of the employment relationship would create a situation of uncertainty. The use of the secret information would need to be negotiated individually in each case. Allowing such a situation would discourage employers from taking the risk of investing in research into areas in which the uncertainty of success is considerable.[121] On the other hand, it would allow employees to benefit from the use of the information in a situation in which they did not bear any risk of its creation. As argued by Risch, only the possibility to appropriate all the results of the research may be the way to induce the employer to take that risk.[122] Therefore, if employees were allowed to use after employment the trade secrets which are valuable to their ex-employer, employers would not be ready to agree on a high remuneration in the employment contract, since they would not be able to expect compensation for their expenses on that remuneration by reaping profits from information developed during employment.[123]

2 Legal Protection of Trade Secrets as Impediment to Productivity, Entrepreneurship and Mobility

Strong protection granted to trade secrets may lower competitiveness in the labour market. If employees are prevented from using any information they might have obtained during previous employment, they may in practice be precluded from finding any occupation in the same or related field. Such an effect of the legal protection of trade secrets contradicts the public interest in free exercise of skill and experience[124] and reduces employee welfare.

This approach is supported by empirical research which has shown that an employee-friendly legal environment results in greater overall

Contract' (2007) Duke Law School Legal Studies Research Paper Series, Research Paper No 157 43–44 http://ssrn.com/abstract=983739 accessed 1 June 2017.

120 Risch, 'Comments on Trade Secrets Sharing in High Velocity Labor Markets' 343.

121 Requiring bargaining over use of any information would also significantly raise the employer's transaction costs.

122 Risch, 'Comments on Trade Secrets Sharing in High Velocity Labor Markets' 343 note 53.

123 Risch, 'Comments on Trade Secrets Sharing in High Velocity Labor Markets' 343.

124 Stanley 79–80; *Herbert Morris Ltd v Saxelby* [1916] 1 AC 688 (HL) 699 (Lord Atkinson).

employment. This is caused by the fact that strong legal protection of trade secrets (in particular by enforcement of NCAs) lowers the mobility of labour, which makes it generally more difficult for companies to find an appropriate employee[125] in terms of skill, knowledge and experience.

The classic example of a market in which the lack of strong trade secrets protection generated positive social effects is the Silicon Valley in California. Due to the fact that Californian law ia does not allow enforcement of post-employment non-competition agreements, employees are free to change jobs or start their own commercial activity, possibly competing with their former employer. This is put forward as one of the reasons for the development of the successful high-technology market in that area.[126]

Markets characterised by high mobility of labour profit from a social environment in which employees are able to decide on their professional development and are encouraged to take full advantage of their individual skills and experience. Such an environment has been recognised as promoting productivity,[127] entrepreneurship, innovation and development, especially in areas where investments in R&D and technology are highest.[128]

E Arguments Based on Fairness[129]

The legal protection of trade secrets stems not only from economic considerations in the broad sense, as presented above. It is also rooted in the desire to safeguard commercial morality, as evidenced by the important role that equity and law of unfair competition play in the protection of undisclosed information.[130] The desire to preserve

[125] Samila and Sorenson, 'Non-Compete Covenants: Incentives to Innovate or Impediments to Growth' 11, 26.

[126] Lobel, 'Intellectual Property and Restrictive Covenants' 17.

[127] Hyde, 'Intellectual Property Justifications for Restricting Employee Mobility: A Critical Appraisal in Light of Economic Evidence' 370.

[128] Hyde, 'Intellectual Property Justifications for Restricting Employee Mobility: A Critical Appraisal in Light of Economic Evidence' 365–372; Lobel, 'Intellectual Property and Restrictive Covenants' 17.

[129] Justifications for legal protection based on fairness are also referred to as deontological, see Ohly, 'Harmonising the Protection of Trade Secrets: Challenges and Perspectives' 36.

[130] At international level the protection of undisclosed information is safeguarded with reference to Art 10bis PC which assures protection against unfair competition (Art 39 (1) TRIPS). In Germany the main provisions safeguarding protection of trade secrets are codified in the statute regulating fairness of competition, Ss 17–18 UWG. In the United Kingdom the main ground of protection is provided under breach of confidence and not unfair competition. However, this concept is based on equity, which in turn is originally rooted in the consideration of fairness (Penny Darbyshire, *Darbyshire on the English Legal System* (10th edn, Sweet&Maxwell 2011) para 8-009, John Wheeler, *Essentials of the English Legal System* (2nd edn, Pearson Longman 2006) 366). In the

commercial fairness was expressed ia by the US Court of Appeals in *EI DuPont v Christopher*, where the court defined one of the commandments of a 'catalogue of commercial improprieties' as '"thou shall not appropriate a trade secret through deviousness under circumstances in which countervailing defences are not reasonably available"'.[131]

1 Legal Protection of Trade Secrets as Means of Maintaining Standards of Commercial Ethics

Allowing employees to use any information they might have acquired during employment would be unfair to the employer who invested in developing that information, bearing the risk of failure to profit from it. Regardless of whether the information as such is seen as property, it is used to produce both tangible and intangible assets. Therefore, it is argued that it is fair that the law should grant protection to trade secrets, as it reflects the protection granted to property and to investments.[132] This argument may be seen as a reflection of the labour theory of John Locke, which concentrates on the investment made in development of a good (here: information) and the natural right to control the fruit of one's own labour (investment).[133]

The existence of legal protection of trade secrets may furthermore be justified by a contract-based argument. As explained by Bone, even if any given protection of confidential information was lacking but the market participants were allowed to bargain with each other, they would agree on some rules for protecting trade secrets either for reasons of efficiency or because of the will of the negotiating parties to maintain commercial morality from which they could all profit.[134]

Generally, the underlying argument based on fairness in support of legal protection of trade secrets is that it serves as a tool for maintaining

United States the main act regulating protection of trade secrets is the UTSA, which has been developed on the basis of the common law of the states. Despite the adoption of the UTSA by most of the states, the law of unfair competition still plays a role in protection of trade secrets (S 40 Restatement (Third) of Unfair Competition). Introduction of a civil cause of action under federal law by way of the DTSA did not change this situation.

131 *EI DuPont de Nemours & Co v Christopher* 431 F 2d 1012, 1017 (5th Cir 1970).

132 Stanley 80.

133 John Locke, 'The Second Treatise of Government. An Essay Concerning The True Original, Extent, and End of Civil Government' in Paul E Sigmund (ed), *The Selected Political Writings of John Locke* (W W Norton & Company 2005) 28–29.

134 Bone acknowledges the existence of the contract-based arguments for the existence of legal protection of trade secrets (at 290–294), but goes further and proposes contracts as a way to regulate protection of trade secrets, instead of independent legal norms, Bone, 'A New Look at Trade Secret Law: Doctrine in Search of Justification' 241, 297. See also Bone, 'The (Still) Shaky Foundations of Trade Secret Law' 1803, 1836–1838.

the standards of commercial ethics.[135] Since ethical behaviour excludes any misappropriation, and not only blatant cases of industrial espionage or theft,[136] it is fair to protect market participants' rights in confidential business-related information.

2 Legal Protection of Trade Secrets as Unfair Limitation of Former Employee's Activities

The critics of strong legal protection granted to trade secrets in favour of employers argue that the function of maintaining commercial ethics should be corrected taking into account the special relationship between the employees and their employers and in particular the lack of balance of bargaining powers between those parties. Consequently, the ethical standards in an employment relationship should be designed in a way that would even out this difference.

According to one argument, since free competition benefits society, it is fair to allow former employees to use in the course of trade all the skill and knowledge that they have obtained during employment, as long as this does not constitute a violation of a fiduciary obligation towards the ex-employer.[137] That consideration should be present when deciding on the enforcement of confidential information, since it allows delineation of the border between the interests of employers and employees, as a fiduciary relationship creates an elevated duty of care on the part of the latter.

A strong protection granted to secret information may furthermore be unfair to society as a whole, since it constitutes a restriction of trade and keeps information from the public. In that way the legal protection deprives society of valuable services, which could be developed, if the information were accessible to the former employee. Moreover, since employees usually have weak bargaining power when contracting with their employer, they may be forced to agree to post-employment

[135] Mathias M Siems, 'Die Logik des Schutzes von Betriebsgeheimnissen' (2007) WRP 1146, 1152; William G Porter II and Michael Griffaton, 'Identifying and Protecting Employers' Interests in Trade Secrets and Proprietary Information' (2001) 68 *Def Couns J* 439, 442; Chally, 'The Law of Trade Secrets: Toward a More Efficient Approach' 1269, 1271.

[136] There is little doubt that employers should be protected against industrial espionage or theft. Such protection is granted in all of the jurisdictions analysed, often by criminal law. However, this book concentrates on the cases where the information was learned by the employee in the course of employment and where for that reason the decision on liability may be difficult to make.

[137] P Guthrie, 'Employee's duty, in absence of express contract, not to disclose or use in the new employment special skills or techniques acquired in earlier employment' 30 ALR 3d 631, 12.

obligations which might result in excessive limitation of their rights. If all such contracts were enforceable, the law would limit employees in pursuit of their chosen livelihood.[138]

Others argue that there is no need to create legal norms to protect trade secrets at all. According to Hyde, markets in which information is not protected by law develop informal norms that achieve a balance between employee mobility and protection of information. The market of open-source software developers is given as an example. They are rewarded for their creative contribution through community recognition, which makes them more valuable on the employment market, rather than by direct compensation and IPRs.[139] It is observed that this argument is convincing only in situations in which all the market participants have similar bargaining power. The open-source software community is generally composed of individuals who act with their own resources and at their own risk. It is difficult to imagine the development of informal norms in industries in which the employers dictate the conditions of contracts, such as those which require major investments in research and development.

An argument based on fairness which relates to the interest of employers is that secondary liability for trade secrets misappropriation creates legal uncertainly among those who hire employees who have previously worked for a competitor. The candidate might be interested in presenting confidential information as part of his knowledge and skills to raise his value in the eyes of the prospective employer[140] who is not able to judge whether the employee is using his own skills or the trade secrets of the former employer. This situation of uncertainty might result in the new employer becoming liable together with the former employee towards his competitor for misappropriation of trade secrets. Furthermore, even if no secondary liability arises, the new employer might need to start the recruitment process again, or be limited in profiting from the input that he thought the newly hired employee would provide for his business. Such a situation raises the costs of the recruitment process and thus of business.

Finally, Bone, who is a proponent of protecting trade secrets solely on the basis of already existing legal norms such as trespass, fraud or

138 Bishara, 'Covenants Not to Compete in a Knowledge Economy: Balancing Innovation from Employee Mobility against Legal Protection for Human Capital Investment' 287, 311.

139 Hyde, 'Intellectual Property Justifications for Restricting Employee Mobility: A Critical Appraisal in Light of Economic Evidence' 369, 372.

140 Kitch, 'The Law and Economics of Rights in Valuable Information' 683, 691.

contractual regulation,[141] states that 'commercial relationships have economic value, not intrinsic moral value'.[142] Therefore, any type of protection granted to trade secrets should not be based on ethical arguments but rather should be the result of bargaining. It is observed here that similarly as in the case of protection under informal norms, the bargaining position of most employees does not allow them to freely negotiate their employment conditions and post-employment obligations.

IV Summary

Many commentators[143] present Silicon Valley in California as an example of an environment in which the right balance between protection of secret know-how and employee mobility has been struck. Risch explains that Californian law protects trade secrets only where valuable and directly competitive information has been taken, and as a result the departing employees rarely compete directly with their former employers. The analysis of that market shows furthermore that the allegedly misappropriated information is rarely as important as initially argued and that it is generally difficult for a plaintiff to win a trade secrets case. This discourages employers' aggressive enforcement against ex-employees since it might constitute a waste of their resources. Such a result is welcome, since most of the litigation referred to by Risch proved to be punitive or abusive in nature.[144]

It is suggested here that although the success of Silicon Valley is remarkable, it may not be simply reproduced in any given country and in any industry.[145] As discussed above, particularly in industries which require high investment in research and development, a certain limitation of employee mobility may prove more efficient in terms of encouraging innovation than unrestricted sharing of knowledge.[146]

141 Bone, 'The (Still) Shaky Foundations of Trade Secret Law' 1803, 1836.

142 Bone, 'A New Look at Trade Secret Law: Doctrine in Search of Justification' 241, 288.

143 See ia Risch, 'Comments on Trade Secrets Sharing in High Velocity Labor Markets'; Lobel, 'Intellectual Property and Restrictive Covenants' 12; Samila and Sorenson, 'Non-Compete Covenants: Incentives to Innovate or Impediments to Growth' 27; Marx, Singh and Fleming, 'Regional Disadvantage? Non-Compete Agreements and Brain Drain' 23.

144 Risch, 'Comments on Trade Secrets Sharing in High Velocity Labor Markets' 341–342.

145 The largest industries represented in the Silicon Valley in 2001 and 2008, judged by employment, related to information products and services (computer systems design, semiconductor manufacturing, Internet, telecommunication and data processing), United States Department of Labor, Bureau of Labor Statistics www.bls.gov/opub/regional_reports/200908_silicon_valley_high_tech.htm accessed 1 June 2017.

146 A similar question is posed in Hyde, 'Intellectual Property Justifications for Restricting Employee Mobility: A Critical Appraisal in Light of Economic Evidence' 377–378.

The correlation between the protection of secret and valuable information and the movement of employees is undisputed. There also seems to be little doubt as to whether trade secrets should be protected at all. The ongoing discussion concentrates rather on the extent to which that information should be protected and how that protection should be designed, taking into account the conflicting interests presented in this chapter.

The protection of trade secrets attempts to strike a balance between exclusivity on the one hand and access to information on the other.[147] The need to find that balance is of particular importance and difficulty in the context of movement of employees, since this is where, as explained above, lack of equilibrium might have negative consequences for individuals and society as a whole.

Thus, it is suggested that the considerations presented in this chapter, such as incentivising innovation, economic growth, employment, commercial morality and fair competition should be taken into consideration in the discussion of enforcement of trade secrets in the context of employee mobility.[148] Even though enforcement is rooted in private law, it constitutes a reflection of public policy towards innovation, investment and personal freedom. Therefore, considerations stemming from public policy, such as possible anticompetitive effects or impact on the market,[149] may be reflected in the enforcement of trade secrets together with considerations of the interests of the parties to a particular dispute.

Giving due consideration to the conflicting interests when determining the scope of the right to information and upon enforcement may help to reach the desired equilibrium between the protection of trade secrets and employee mobility.

[147] Landes and Posner, *The Economic Structure of Intellectual Property Law* 364.

[148] Similar proposals are also made in the context of patent prosecution and enforcement, see Tönnies, 'Erfindungen – ein Kollektivgut oder die Gedanken sind frei' 796, 797–798.

[149] Madison suggests taking into account collective interests, stemming e.g. from the positive effects of spill-overs, see Michael J Madison, 'Open Secrets' in Rochelle C Dreyfuss and Katherine J Strandburg (eds), *The Law and Theory of Trade Secrecy: A Handbook of Contemporary Research* (Edward Elgar 2011) 244.

2 Concept of Trade Secrets

Chapter 1 analysed the role that the protection of trade secrets plays in the economy and society, as well as the influence of the level of such protection on innovation, economic growth and employment. This chapter takes a closer look at what trade secrets are, in both legal and practical terms.

Confidential information has been aptly compared to an ice cube:

> Give it to the party who undertakes to keep it in his refrigerator and you still have an ice cube by the time the matter comes to trial. (. . .) Give it to the party who has no refrigerator or will not agree to keep it in one, and by the time of the trial you just have a pool of water which neither party wants. It is the inherently perishable nature of confidential information which gives rise to unique problems.[1]

The difficulties in defining trade secrecy are addressed in this part of the book. The following analysis presents the international legal framework and national definitions of the concept, as well as the definition of trade secrets harmonised for the European Union (EU). The various types of information that may be protected as trade secrets are described, and after that the discussion of the legal nature of trade secrets is outlined. This is followed by a comparison of trade secrets with patents and copyrights which are commonly used as a point of reference in the analysis of the protection granted to secret information.

I Definitions of Trade Secrets

A Definition of Trade Secrets under the TRIPS Agreement: Undisclosed Information

TRIPS is said to contain 'the first multilateral acknowledgement of the essential role that trade secrets play in industry'.[2] It generally provides a

[1] *Attorney General v Newspaper Publishing Plc* [1989] 2 FSR 27 (Ch) 48 (Donaldson MR).

[2] François Dessemontet, 'Protection of Trade Secrets and Confidential Information' in Carlos M Correa and Abdulqawi A Yusuf (eds), *Intellectual Property and International Trade: The TRIPS Agreement* (3rd edn, Wolters Kluwer 2016) 339.

minimum standard of protection[3] for its Member States and in Article 39 (1) obliges them to safeguard undisclosed information in the course of ensuring effective protection against unfair competition pursuant to Article 10*bis* PC.

Article 39(2) TRIPS contains a definition of undisclosed information.[4] Since TRIPS is the result of negotiations between countries which already had developed concepts of trade secrecy in their own jurisdictions, it was difficult to find a common understanding of the notion referred to in Article 39 TRIPS. Therefore, instead of referring to the concepts of 'trade secrets' or 'know how', which already had a meaning in national laws, it was decided to apply the more neutral term of 'undisclosed information'.[5] It is defined as information which is lawfully within the control of its holder; is secret; has a commercial value because it is secret; and has been subject to reasonable steps to keep it secret.[6]

1 Information

The notion of undisclosed information is understood broadly, to mean any information developed, or learned by accident, composed of isolated facts or complex sets of data; also negative knowledge is covered by the definition.[7] Moreover, unlike IP law, ideas may be protected as undisclosed information. Since TRIPS is a trade-related agreement, the protection safeguarded therein concerns in the first place information related to trade activity, whether of a technical, commercial, administrative or financial nature. Nevertheless, it is not restricted to a purely business context. The information may also relate to the activities of non-profit or charity organisations. It is protected as long as it is related to economic competition of any sort.[8]

Although not strictly limited to business information, the definition under TRIPS does not go as far as to cover information relating to the intimate or private sphere.[9] Moreover, it does not cover tacit knowledge, since it is not transferable to others and may not be separated from its

[3] Art 1(1) TRIPS; Daniel Gervais, *The TRIPS Agreement: Drafting History and Analysis* (4th edn, Sweet&Maxwell 2012) para 2.24.

[4] The protection of test data under Art 39(3) TRIPS relates to different subject-matter from Art 39(2) TRIPS, see Nuno Pires de Carvalho, *The TRIPS Regime of Antitrust and Undisclosed Information* (Kluwer Law International 2008) paras 39.1.56–39.1.60.

[5] UNCTAD, *Resource Book on TRIPS and Development* (Cambridge University Press 2005) 521; Peter/Wiebe in Busche/Stoll/Wiebe Art 39 para 7.

[6] As argued by Dessemontet, 'Article 39 TRIPS unifies the American definitions of trade secrets and the European concepts of unfair competition and honest commercial practices', see Dessemontet, 'Protection of Trade Secrets and Confidential Information' 358.

[7] Pires de Carvalho, *The TRIPS Regime of Antitrust and Undisclosed Information* para 39.2.36.

[8] Ibid para 39.2.37.

[9] Dessemontet, 'Protection of Trade Secrets and Confidential Information' 347; Peter/Wiebe in Busche/Stoll/Wiebe Art 39 para 7.

holder. Thus, this type of know-how must indeed be qualified as 'knowledge' rather than 'information'.[10]

2 Lawfully within the Control of Its Holder

The information must be lawfully within 'control' of the holder.[11] It follows that the quality of the information as undisclosed information protected under TRIPS is not determined with regard to the type of the title that the holder has in respect of the information. In particular, it leaves open the question of whether the holder is supposed to have a property right in the information.[12]

However, only those persons may claim rights in undisclosed information who obtained it lawfully, i.e. have a legal title which supports their control over the information. It is not required that the information has been developed by the holder himself. The 'lawfulness' of the control is judged under national law and may encompass acquiring the information by way of sale or licensing. Accordingly, 'control' and 'lawfulness' need to be seen as two separate elements of the definition.[13]

As long as the information is under de facto control of the person who obtained it in a lawful way, it may qualify as undisclosed information.

Finally, the requirement of lawfulness of the control over the information says nothing about the content of the information itself. Thus, it appears that under TRIPS information about illegal behaviour may be qualified as protectable undisclosed information, as long as it is lawfully within control of its holder; is secret; has commercial value stemming from secrecy; and is subject to reasonable steps to maintain secrecy.

3 Secret

The information must be objectively secret,[14] i.e. it must not be generally known or readily accessible to persons who normally deal with the kind of information in question.[15] The individual elements may be or become generally known, but as long as the conglomerate remains a secret, it is protected.[16] In this sense secrecy may protect the idea to put the information

[10] Peter/Wiebe in Busche/Stoll/Wiebe Art 39 para 7.

[11] Pires de Carvalho, *The TRIPS Regime of Antitrust and Undisclosed Information* para 39.2.38.

[12] Ibid.

[13] Peter/Wiebe in Busche/Stoll/Wiebe Art 39 para 17.

[14] Dessemontet, 'Protection of Trade Secrets and Confidential Information' 349.

[15] Art 39(2)(a) TRIPS.

[16] Dessemontet, 'Protection of Trade Secrets and Confidential Information' 351; Jacques de Werra, 'How to Protect Trade Secrets in High Tech Sports? An Intellectual Property Analysis Based on the Experiences in the America's Cup and in the Formula One Championship' (2010) 32(4) *EIPR* 155, 157; Peter/Wiebe in Busche/Stoll/Wiebe Art

together or the link between the known elements. No absolute secrecy or novelty, in the sense in which it is understood in patent law, is required.[17]

The information remains undisclosed if it is neither known nor readily accessible to interested persons. In the first place these are the holder's competitors for whom the information might be valuable for competitive reasons, but they may also be other persons who have a commercial interest in knowing the information.[18]

Rather than absolute secrecy, the concept of undisclosed information under TRIPS relates more to the fact that the information remains under control of the person who asserts it.[19] As expressed by Pires de Carvalho, the information must not be absolutely secret, but it must not be accessible by honest means.[20] Ann argues that as a result of an illegal act of reverse engineering, the information becomes neither generally known nor readily accessible.[21] It is suggested that Article 39 TRIPS aims at safeguarding protection only against disclosure which is 'contrary to honest commercial practices',[22] and at the same time it requires that the information is objectively secret in order to profit from protection. Therefore, a disclosure which destroys that objective secrecy results in the termination of the information's status as undisclosed. The way in which the disclosure occurred, e.g. whether it was reverse-engineered and whether it was in breach of copyright,[23] is irrelevant. It is the result of the disclosure which is decisive. Thus, reverse-engineering alone does not terminate secrecy. The information must become generally known to lose its trade secret status.[24]

39 para 18; Justin Malbon, Charles Lawson and Mark Davison, *The WTO Agreement on Trade–Related Aspects of Intellectual Property Rights* (Edward Elgar 2014) para 39.23.

17 UNCTAD, *Resource Book on TRIPS and Development* 529; Dessemontet, 'Protection of Trade Secrets and Confidential Information' 349–350.

18 Peter/Wiebe in Busche/Stoll/Wiebe Art 39 para 19.

19 Pires de Carvalho, *The TRIPS Regime of Antitrust and Undisclosed Information* paras 39.2.50, 39.2.52; Peter/Wiebe in Busche/Stoll/Wiebe Art 39 para 18.

20 Pires de Carvalho, *The TRIPS Regime of Antitrust and Undisclosed Information* para 39.2.51.

21 Ann in Ann/Loschelder/Grosch 8, which corresponds to the prevailing view in Germany; TRIPS is not conclusive on the question of reverse engineering, see Gurry on Breach of Confidence para 15.24 note 48.

22 Reverse engineering is not uniformly recognised as contrary to honest commercial practices. In Germany the majority opinion seems not to accept it (RGZ 149, 329, 334 *Stiefeleisenpresse*; Ohly in Ohly/Sosnitza §17 paras 10, 26a, pleading for acceptance of reverse engineering as a fair commercial practice), while in the United Kingdom and in the United States it is generally seen as legitimate (Gurry on Breach of Confidence para 15.30). In particular, information which may be easily reverse engineered is arguably 'readily accessible' and therefore not 'undisclosed' within the meaning of Art 39 (2) TRIPS.

23 Peter/Wiebe in Busche/Stoll/Wiebe Art 39 para 21.

24 Ibid.

4 Commercial Value Derived from Secrecy

Undisclosed information protected under Article 39 TRIPS furthermore needs to have commercial value derived from the fact that it is secret. Thus, there must exist a causal link between secrecy and the information's value.[25] Nevertheless, secrecy need not be the only source of this value. It may be complemented by other factors such as a useful technical solution which the information carries.[26]

Like the information itself, the commercial character of its value is understood broadly. The information must give its holder some competitive advantage[27] and therefore its value usually stems from the lead time that it secures.[28]

Whether the information's value must be actual or potential is a matter of discussion in the literature. Pires de Carvalho argues that it is sufficient if the information has potential value, i.e. the value of the information does not need to be precisely established for the protection to be granted.[29] Correa, as well as Malbon, Lawson and Davison argue that the wording 'has commercial value because it is secret' indicates that the value must be actual.[30] It is submitted here that for the purpose of qualifying information as undisclosed within the meaning of Article 39 TRIPS it is sufficient that the information has any value, even potentially. It must be remembered that the value stems mainly from the competitive advantage which the information provides to its holder and thus might change depending on the circumstances. Nevertheless, for the purpose of enforcement of rights in undisclosed information, its value might need to be determined, especially if the holder wishes to obtain damages for infringement of his rights.

5 Subject to Reasonable Steps to Maintain Secrecy

The final element of the definition of undisclosed information under TRIPS is that it must be subject to some reasonable steps to keep it secret,[31] undertaken by the person who is lawfully in control of the

25 Ann in Ann/Loschelder/Grosch 7.

26 Peter/Wiebe in Busche/Stoll/Wiebe Art 39 para 22.

27 Pires de Carvalho, *The TRIPS Regime of Antitrust and Undisclosed Information* para 39.2.58.

28 Dessemontet, 'Protection of Trade Secrets and Confidential Information' 347; Ann in Ann/Loschelder/Grosch 8.

29 Pires de Carvalho, *The TRIPS Regime of Antitrust and Undisclosed Information para* 39.2.56.

30 Carlos M Correa, *Trade Related Aspects of Intellectual Property Rights. A Commentary on the TRIPS Agreement* (Oxford University Press 2007) 373; Malbon, Lawson and Davison, The WTO Agreement on Trade-Related Aspects of Intellectual Property Rights para 39.24.

31 Art 39(2)(c) TRIPS.

information (the holder of the information). Reasonable steps are those which 'make it clear that the information in question has a confidential nature' and which do not go beyond what is proportional to the value of the information.[32] By maintaining secrecy, the purpose of those measures is to keep the information under the control of its holder.[33]

Therefore, whether and to what extent the holder took any measures to maintain the information's secrecy indicates the information's value as perceived by its holder.[34] Accordingly, the type and extent of steps which are considered reasonable will vary depending on the circumstances.[35] Nevertheless, the holder of the information must take some active steps to prevent disclosure. They may include encryption and other technical solutions, marking the information as confidential, and the conclusion of confidentiality agreements.[36]

Even though TRIPS foresees minimum harmonisation with respect to protection of undisclosed information, it has been convincingly argued by Peter and Wiebe that a national definition of secret information which would require keeping the data completely secret, or taking measures to maintain secrecy going beyond what may be reasonably expected from a person active in trade, might be incompatible with TRIPS.[37]

Making the protection by trade secrets law conditional on active steps taken by the holder of the information to maintain secrecy ensures that the holders 'filter' the information they control. They will invest in de facto protection of information they deem particularly valuable, thus allowing the less valuable information to become public and available for others to use. The investment in protection is likely to be proportional to the information's competitive value, which minimises the risk of overprotection. Removing this requirement might introduce uncertainty for competitors as well as employees. They might be faced with a claim for misappropriation of trade secrets even though they were not alerted to their existence. Furthermore, the requirement that reasonable measures are taken to maintain secrecy forms the basis for finding infringement in the current framework of unfair competition. If the holder of the information did not

[32] Pires de Carvalho, *The TRIPS Regime of Antitrust and Undisclosed Information* para 39.2.62.
[33] Peter/Wiebe in Busche/Stoll/Wiebe Art 39 para 23.
[34] Michael Risch, 'Why Do We Have Trade Secrets?' (2007) 11 *Marq IP L Rev* 1, 45.
[35] de Werra, 'How to Protect Trade Secrets in High Tech Sports? An Intellectual Property Analysis Based on the Experiences in the America's Cup and in the Formula One Championship' 155, 159.
[36] Peter/Wiebe in Busche/Stoll/Wiebe Art 39 para 23.
[37] Peter/Wiebe in Busche/Stoll/Wiebe Art 39 para 24.

even attempt to keep it secret, it would be possible neither to find unauthorised use or disclosure of information, nor its unfairness.

6 Summary

The definition of undisclosed information codified in Article 39(2) TRIPS provides for a minimum standard of protection for trade secrets and confidential information which is recognised by all Member States of the WTO.[38] Application of this standard requires balancing the interests of the holders of the information with those of the public which might profit from the diffusion of information. In particular, too stringent interpretation of the TRIPS minimum standard may hinder employee mobility.[39]

Even though Germany, United Kingdom and United States are members of the WTO,[40] the definitions of industrial/commercial secrets (Germany), confidential information (United Kingdom) and trade secrets (United States) are not the same, as explained below.

B Definition of Trade Secrets in German Law: Industrial and Commercial Secrets

German law does not contain a legal definition of a trade secret[41] and this concept is not uniformly regulated.[42] Instead of referring to 'trade secrets', the law speaks of 'industrial and commercial secrets'. Commercial secrets (*Geschäftsgeheimnisse*) relate to business aspects of a commercial activity, and industrial secrets (*Betriebsgeheimnisse*) to technical information. In spite of this dual terminology, it is often difficult to draw a clear line between the one and the other category. Such a distinction is also superfluous, since both industrial and commercial secrets are legally equal.[43] This leads to suggestions in the literature to use a single term such as business secrets (*Unternehmensgeheimnisse*) or trade secrets

[38] Ann in in Ann/Loschelder/Grosch 5.

[39] Correa, *Trade Related Aspects of Intellectual Property Rights. A Commentary on the TRIPS Agreement* 373.

[40] All of those countries have been members of WTO since its creation on 1 January 1995, i.e. they have been taking part in TRIPS since the same date.

[41] Christoph Ann, 'Know-how – Stiefkind des Geistigen Eigentums?' (2007) GRUR 39, 41.

[42] For the various legal acts regulating protection of trade secrets, see Ohly in Ohly/Sosnitza Vor § 17–19 paras 9–10 and Swantje Richters and Carolina Wodtke, 'Schutz von Betriebsgeheimnissen aus Unternehmenssicht "Verhinderung von Know-how Abfluss durch eigene Mitarbeiter"' (2003) NZA-RR 281, 282.

[43] Mary-Rose McGuire, Björn Joachim, Jens Künzel and Nils Weber, 'Der Schutz von Geschäftsgeheimnissen durch Rechte des Geistigen Eigentums und durch das Recht des unlauteren Wettbewerbs (Q215)' (2010) GRUR Int 829, 829; Ann, 'Know-how – Stiefkind des Geistigen Eigentums?' 39, 41.

(*Wirtschaftsgeheimnisse*) instead of the present notions.[44] Due to lack of legal differences between the two concepts, both commercial secrets and industrial secrets are commonly referred to as trade secrets in the course of the analysis presented in this book.

The basic rules on trade-secrets misappropriation are contained in the criminal provisions of Sections 17–19 UWG.[45] The case-law defines commercial and industrial secrets as any information relating to a commercial activity which is not public but known only to a limited number of persons and which is to be kept secret according to the will of the owner of that commercial activity and in his interest.[46]

It follows that the definition of a trade secret under German law contains four elements:

1) the information relates to a commercial activity,
2) the information is not public,
3) there is a will on the part of the holder of the information to keep the information secret,
4) there exists an interest on the part of the holder of the information in keeping it secret.

1 Relation to Commercial Activity

The protected information must relate to activities of a specific business. This requirement is derived from the aim of granting protection to trade secrets, which is to allow businesses to maintain their competitive advantage over others.[47]

The notion of commercial activity is understood broadly and covers not only privately owned companies, but also independent professionals and publicly owned entities, as long as they are active in commerce.[48] Moreover, the information must relate to a specific business and not to business in general. Therefore, the information that a company is using a process widespread in the industry has been accorded protection as a trade secret, since the unpublicised fact of use was related to the activities of that particular business, even though the application of the process

[44] Ohly in Ohly/Sosnitza §17 para 5 with further references.
[45] Gesetz gegen den unlauteren Wettbewerb (UWG).
[46] NJW 1983, 134 (BAG) *Thrombosol*; BGH GRUR 1955, 424, 425 *Möbelpaste* with further references; BGH GRUR 2003, 356, 358 *Präzisionsmessgeräte*; BGH GRUR 2006, 1044, 1046 *Kundendatenprogramm;* Harte-Bavendamm in Harte/Henning §17 para 1; Ohly in Ohly/Sosnitza §17 para 5; Josef Molkenbur, 'Pflicht zur Geheimniswahrung nach Ende des Arbeitsverhältnisses?' (1990) BB 1196, 1197.
[47] Harte-Bavendamm in Harte/Henning §17 para 2.
[48] Markus A Mayer, 'Geschäfts- und Betriebsgeheimnis oder Geheimniskrämerei?' (2011) GRUR 884, 885.

could be associated with many enterprises and even though the process as such could not be protected as secret.[49]

The relationship to the commercial activity of a specific undertaking does not cease to exist upon sale of a product containing the secret information.[50]

As under TRIPS, personal information is not covered by the definition, since it does not relate to commercial activity. However, unlike TRIPS, the definition under German law does not seem to encompass information which is produced by research institutions which do not perform commercial activities.[51]

2 Information Which Is Not Public

Industrial or commercial information may be treated as a trade secret only if it is in fact secret. Like TRIPS, German law does not contain a requirement of absolute secrecy. The information is considered to be a trade secret as long as it is neither public nor readily ascertainable by the interested public.[52]

The information is considered public if it is accessible to anyone from among those who normally deal with information of the particular type.[53] It is the objective assessment which is decisive in that respect. How the information lost its secret status, whether as a result of a decision of its holder, a breach of confidence or a criminal act, is irrelevant.[54]

As absolute secrecy is not required, information does not become public if it is known only to a limited circle of persons. This is to be decided under circumstances of each case. In any event, the number of persons who know the information is not decisive. Rather, it can be said that information is not public as long as it remains under the control of the person who asserts rights to it.[55] Therefore, disclosing the information to

[49] BGH GRUR 1955, 424, 425 *Möbelpaste*; Mayer, 'Geschäfts- und Betriebsgeheimnis oder Geheimniskrämerei?' 884, 885.

[50] McGuire, Joachim, Künzel and Weber, 'Der Schutz von Geschäftsgeheimnissen durch Rechte des Geistigen Eigentums und durch das Recht des unlauteren Wettbewerbs (Q215)' 829, 830.

[51] Ohly in Ohly/Sosnitza §17 para 6.

[52] Harte-Bavendamm in Harte/Henning §17 para 3; Ohly in Ohly/Sosnitza §17 para 7 with further references.

[53] Ohly in Ohly/Sosnitza §17 para 7.

[54] Harte-Bavendamm in Harte/Henning §17 para 4; Mayer, 'Geschäfts- und Betriebsgeheimnis oder Geheimniskrämerei?' 884, 885; McGuire, Joachim, Künzel and Weber, 'Der Schutz von Geschäftsgeheimnissen durch Rechte des Geistigen Eigentums und durch das Recht des unlauteren Wettbewerbs (Q215)' 829, 829.

[55] BGH GRUR 2012, 1048, 1049 (para 31) *MOVICOL-Zulassungsantrag;* Harte-Bavendamm in Harte/Henning §17 para 4; Ralph Grunewald, 'Fern der Quelle – Geheimnisschutz und Outsourcing' (2007) WRP 1307, 1309.

employees or even to competitors does not make it publicly available, as long as the recipients are bound by a duty not to disclose the information[56] and, naturally, as long as they observe that duty. Of course, the wider the circle of persons to whom the holder discloses the secret information, the stronger the measures he needs to take in order to maintain its secrecy.[57]

The lack of the requirement of absolute secrecy differentiates this element of the definition from the concept of novelty in patent law. Even information which is not new in patent-law terms may still be a trade secret.[58] This is because the question of whether the information was made available to the public is, unlike in patent law,[59] assessed by answering the question of whether the information is accessible for those active in the relevant commercial area in the territory of Germany without extensive time expense and cost[60] and without recourse to unfair methods.[61] It follows that if the information is available on the Internet, in the media, in publicly accessible databases, in professional journals[62] or if it was publicly presented e.g. at a trade fair, the secrecy no longer exists. If, however, only the elements of the information are available in such a manner, the complete information as such may still be considered secret, as long as the reconstruction of the entire information from the publicly accessible sources is burdensome.[63] According to Westermann, secrecy ceases to exist when information becomes part of the routine

[56] The duty with regard to employees in service stems from S 242 BGB (as any obligor in a contract of service pursuant to S 611 BGB is obliged to perform his duties in good faith, see e.g. NJW 1967, 125, 126 (BAG)). For the analysis of the post-employment duty of secrecy, see infra Chapter 3, part II point A. The duty with regard to competitors arises usually from contract, and may arise even during pre-contractual negotiations under the concept of culpa in contrahendo (S 311 BGB). See also Harte-Bavendamm in Harte/Henning §17 para 4; Westermann 14–17; Richters and Wodtke, 'Schutz von Betriebsgeheimnissen aus Unternehmenssicht "Verhinderung von Know-how Abfluss durch eigene Mitarbeiter"' 281, 283.

[57] Grunewald, 'Fern der Quelle – Geheimnisschutz und Outsourcing' 1307, 1310.

[58] For a detailed comparison of novelty under patent law and secrecy under UWG, see Thomas Reimann, 'Einige Überlegungen zur Offenkundigkeit im Rahmen von §§ 17 ff UWG und von §3 PatG' (1998) GRUR 298.

[59] Art 54(2) EPC, S 3 PatG.

[60] BGH GRUR 2003, 356, 358 *Präzisionsmessgeräte*. Therefore, while published patent applications and published patents destroy novelty of an invention, they terminate the secrecy of information only if they are accessible for the interested commercial circles from Germany without undue burden, Ohly in Ohly/Sosnitza §17 para 9; Harte-Bavendamm in Harte/Henning §17 para 4.

[61] Mayer, 'Geschäfts- und Betriebsgeheimnis oder Geheimniskrämerei?' 884, 886. Of course, once the secret is revealed, even as an effect of application of unfair methods, the information loses its secret status.

[62] BGH GRUR 2012, 1048, 1049 (para 20) *MOVICOL-Zulassungsantrag.*

[63] Ohly in Ohly/Sosnitza §17 para 9; Westermann 19. It is irrelevant whether the information as a whole ('als Paket') can be obtained from the public sources. Rather it is decisive whether the elements of the information can be obtained from public sources

knowledge of an undefined circle of persons.[64] Harte-Bavendamm sets a higher threshold for the loss of secrecy. In his opinion, even if the information becomes known to some outsiders, this does not generally destroy the secrecy. The information rather needs to become generally known.[65] It is proposed here that the decisive factor should be whether the information is still under the control of its holder. If he ceases to be able to decide on its use or disclosure, the information may not be regarded as his secret any more. At the same time, the information does not need to be used by its holder in order to be protected. Thus, a list of potential clients has been recognised as a trade secret.[66]

The issue of whether the information is accessible for those active in the relevant area without significant cost in time and money and without recourse to unfair methods relates in particular to whether reverse engineering[67] leads to termination of secrecy. Under the definition of secrecy presented above, the possibility of reverse engineering of a product or process means that it was not secret only where an interested person would have been able to discover the underlying information without undue burden and upon application of not more than average skills and knowledge.[68] For example, if the information is accessible only through disassembling a product which is not intended to be disassembled and through precise measurements of its component parts, the fact that the product is available on the market does not in itself make the information contained therein public.[69] It follows that if reverse engineering is possible only under exceptionally high cost in time and money, it does not render

without undue burden, see BGH GRUR 2012, 1048, 1049 (para 21) *MOVICOL-Zulassungsantrag*.

64 Westermann 16.

65 Harte-Bavendamm in Harte/Henning §17 para 4.

66 OLG Köln GRUR-RR 2010, 480 *Werbeadressen als Geschäftsgeheimnis*.

67 Understood as 'starting with the known product and working backward to divine the process which aided in its development or manufacture', *Kewanee Oil Co v Bicron Corp* 416 US 470, 476 (US Supr Ct 1974). The Trade Secrets Directive in Art 3(1)(b) describes reverse engineering as acquisition of trade secrets by observation, study, disassembly or test of a product or object that has been made available to the public or that is lawfully in the possession of the acquirer of the information who is free from any legally valid duty to limit the acquisition of the trade secret. For a comprehensive comparative study of reverse engineering in Germany and in the United States, see Florian Schweyer, *Die rechtliche Bewertung des Reverse Engineering in Deutschland und den USA* (Mohr Siebeck 2012).

68 Harte-Bavendamm in Harte/Henning §17 para 3; Ohly in Ohly/Sosnitza §17 para 10; Westermann 12; Mayer, 'Geschäfts- und Betriebsgeheimnis oder Geheimniskrämerei?' 884, 886.

69 RGZ 149, 329, 334 *Stiefeleisenpresse*; Harte-Bavendamm in Harte/Henning §17 para 3; Ohly in Ohly/Sosnitza §17 para 10; Mayer, 'Geschäfts- und Betriebsgeheimnis oder Geheimniskrämerei?' 884, 886.

the obtained information public. Thus, such an act of reverse engineering may potentially be seen as misappropriation of a trade secret.[70]

This approach has been criticised by Ohly.[71] Arguably, to the extent that reverse engineering is considered as not destroying secrecy regardless of whether it occurred without application of unfair means, it seems at odds with the underlying principles of trade secret protection and protection against unfair competition. If the object of reverse engineering is a product obtained in the open market, the level of effort spent on its analysis should not be regarded as an indication of whether the information contained therein is secret. If it can be reverse engineered with recourse to legal methods only, even if expensive and time-consuming, it is not a secret.[72] Although acknowledging such an argumentation, Ohly suggests that secrecy is a factual matter and that a better solution may be achieved by recourse to a more flexible interpretation of the requirement of 'due cause' under Section 17 UWG. He proposes an interpretation compliant with Article 39 TRIPS, according to which even if the information obtained by reverse engineering is considered secret, its disclosure, obtaining or use must be 'contrary to honest commercial practices' in order to be prohibited.[73] As a result, he proposes that 'reverse engineering should be permissible in general, whereas the use of the information that is so obtained may be restricted'.[74]

3 Will to Keep the Information Secret

Information which is secret must be distinguished from information which is not known. Therefore, the holder of the information must be aware of its existence and must be willing to keep it secret. However the 'will to keep the information secret' is construed broadly: it does not need to be expressed and may be inferred from the circumstances or from the nature of the information in question.[75] In the case of employee inventions it is furthermore assumed that there exists a will to keep the

70 As explained by Ohly in Ohly/Sosnitza §17 paras 10, 26a.

71 Ansgar Ohly, 'Reverse Engineering: Unfair Competition or Catalyst for Innovation?' in Wolrad Prinz zu Waldeck und Pyrmont, Martin J Adelman, Robert Brauneis, Josef Drexl and Ralph Nack (eds), *Patents and Technological Progress in a Globalized World. Liber Amicorum Joseph Straus* (Springer 2009) 535; Ohly in Ohly/Sosnitza §17 para 26a.

72 Ohly, 'Reverse Engineering: Unfair Competition or Catalyst for Innovation?' 551.

73 Art 39(2) TRIPS.

74 Ohly, 'Reverse Engineering: Unfair Competition or Catalyst for Innovation?' 551.

75 BGH GRUR 2006, 1044, 1046 *Kundendatenprogramm*; Mayer, 'Geschäfts- und Betriebsgeheimnis oder Geheimniskrämerei?' 884, 886. Grunewald is of the opinion that the will to keep the information secret should not be assumed and that it should be assessed taking into consideration the measures that the holder of the information took in order to maintain its secrecy and his control over it, Grunewald, 'Fern der Quelle – Geheimnisschutz und Outsourcing' 1307, 1311.

invention secret (at least until the day of the filing of the patent application), even though the employer might not (yet) be aware of his employee's achievement.[76]

The will to keep the information secret will normally be derived either from an express statement by the holder of the information, or from the measures that he undertakes to maintain the secrecy of the information. Application of such 'reasonable measures to keep the information secret' as required under Article 39(2)(c) TRIPS is not mentioned as an element of the definition of trade secrets under German law. Nevertheless, it may often be regarded as an indication of the will to keep the information secret and thus be incorporated into the national definition of a trade secret.

Furthermore, by contrast to Article 39(2)(b) TRIPS, there is no requirement that the secret information has any particular value.[77]

According to Harte-Bavendamm, in an employment relationship it is to be assumed by the employees that any internal procedures and data which are not known to the outside world and which influence the competitive position of the company are to be kept secret according to the will of the employer, which needs not be expressed in any particular form, but derived from the circumstances.[78] It is submitted here that while this may be so during employment, due to the general duty of the employee to act in good faith,[79] for a departing employee the employer's will to keep the information secret might be difficult to assess, if he does not express it. Since the contractual relationship is over, the duty of good faith derived therefrom is reduced.[80]

The requirement that there must exist a will to keep the information secret is criticised.[81] According to Ohly, the fact that the will to keep the

[76] BGH GRUR 1977, 539, 540 *Prozessrechner*; Mayer, 'Geschäfts- und Betriebsgeheimnis oder Geheimniskrämerei?' 884, 886.

[77] BGH GRUR 2006, 1044, 1046 *Kundendatenprogramm*; Ohly in Ohly/Sosnitza §17 para 11; McGuire, Joachim, Künzel and Weber are of a different opinion and argue that compliance with the requirement of Art 39(2)(b) TRIPS is achieved through the requirements of connection to a specific undertaking and commercial interest in maintaining the secrecy of the information, see McGuire, Joachim, Künzel and Weber, 'Der Schutz von Geschäftsgeheimnissen durch Rechte des Geistigen Eigentums und durch das Recht des unlauteren Wettbewerbs (Q215)' 829, 830.

[78] Harte-Bavendamm in Harte/Henning §17 para 5.

[79] S 242 BGB, see note 56.

[80] A post-employment duty of good faith has been recognised by the BAG, see e.g. NZA 1994, 502, 505 (BAG) *Titanoxid.* See also Molkenbur, 'Pflicht zur Geheimniswahrung nach Ende des Arbeitsverhältnisses?' 1196, 1198; Ohly in Ohly/Sosnitza §17 para 40.

[81] It has not been included in the definition of trade secrets applied by the Federal Constitutional Court, who referred to trade secrets as information relating to commercial activity, which is not public and with regard to which its holder has an interest in maintaining its secrecy, see NVwZ 2006, 1041, 1042 (BVerfG).

information secret is in fact assumed makes this requirement superfluous and does not fit the objective approach otherwise taken in the UWG.[82] Mayer suggests that the requirement of will to keep the information secret is redundant in view of the last requirement of the trade secrets definition, namely an interest in keeping the information secret. He argues that wherever there exists an interest in keeping the information secret, there is also a will to do that.[83] Maume proposes to abandon this requirement and to base the definition of trade secrets on objective indicia.[84] In a similar vein, Redeker, Pres and Gittinger argue that as a result of the implementation of the Trade Secrets Directive in the proposed wording, the 'will to keep the information secret' will need to be replaced by the requirement of reasonable steps to keep the information secret.[85] It is submitted here that the taking of 'reasonable measures to maintain secrecy'[86] by the holder of the information is a more suitable requirement. While it in fact reflects the will of the holder of the information to keep it undisclosed, it is at the same time based on objective considerations.

4 Interest in Keeping the Information Secret

Interest in keeping the information secret is present if disclosure of the information would have a negative impact on the competitiveness of the holder's business. The interest must be legitimate and have a commercial character, which has a corrective function towards the requirement of will to keep the information secret, i.e. the holder of the information may not rely on the protection granted to trade secrets by simply stating that specific undisclosed information relating to his company is a trade secret.[87]

The existence of a legitimate interest in keeping the information secret, like the will to do that, is judged taking into account the circumstances of each case. Here too the decisive consideration is whether the disclosure

[82] Ohly in Ohly/Sosnitza §17 para 11; see also Ansgar Ohly, 'Der Geheimnisschutz im deutschen Recht: heutiger Stand und Perspektiven' (2014) GRUR 1, 5.

[83] Mayer, 'Geschäfts- und Betriebsgeheimnis oder Geheimniskrämerei?' 884, 886.

[84] Philipp Maume, 'Know-how-Schutz – Abschied vom Geheimhaltungswillen?' (2008) WRP 1275, 1280.

[85] Sandra S Redeker, Sascha Pres and Corin Gittinger, 'Die Entwürfe zur Know-how-Richtlinie, deren Konsequenzen für das innerbetriebliche Vertragsmanagement (Teil 1)' (2015) WRP 681, 683.

[86] A required by Art 39(2)(c) TRIPS, S 1(4)(ii) UTSA, 18 US Code §1839(3)(A), as amended by the DTSA, and Art 2(1)(c) TSD.

[87] Mayer, 'Geschäfts- und Betriebsgeheimnis oder Geheimniskrämerei?' 884, 887; Ohly in Ohly/Sosnitza §17 para 12.

of the information would influence the position of the holder of the information towards his competitors.[88]

In view of the requirement that there must exist a legitimate interest in keeping the information secret, a question can be posed, whether any considerations of public interest could play a role in this assessment and whether the existence of the employer's interest could be balanced against the interest of the (former) employee. It seems that under German law such considerations are not present. It is generally recognised that the employer has an interest in maintaining secrecy even if the information relates to his unlawful acts and that an exception may be made only in special cases in which an obviously higher interest prevails.[89] According to the minority opinion, there can be no trade secrets in case of 'illegal' secrets, since any interest in keeping such information secret would not be legitimate.[90] Still, under this more lenient approach it is not considered necessary to go so far as to balance the interests of the parties involved. The requirement of an interest in keeping the information secret has been described as confusing, as it suggests a need to include a balancing of interests in the definition of trade secrets.[91] However since secrecy is a matter of fact[92] and its definition is rooted in the provisions of criminal law, it would be advisable to interpret the provision strictly and not invite judgement in the definition. Thus, it would be desirable to include in the definition of trade secrets more objective elements such as measures taken in order to maintain the secrecy of the information, rather than the will and the interest in keeping the information secret. Reliance on subjective factors is problematic in the context of criminal provisions. On the other

[88] Harte-Bavendamm in Harte/Henning §17 para 6.

[89] For example, in case of emergency, which is explicitly provided in S 34 StGB, see Harte-Bavendamm in Harte/Henning §17 para 6; Ohly in Ohly/Sosnitza §17 para 12; McGuire, Joachim, Künzel, and Weber, 'Der Schutz von Geschäftsgeheimnissen durch Rechte des Geistigen Eigentums und durch das Recht des unlauteren Wettbewerbs (Q215)' 829, 830; Mayer, 'Geschäfts- und Betriebsgeheimnis oder Geheimniskrämerei?' 884, 887. Generally on so-called whistleblowing, see Eileen Gaugenrieder and Dagmar Unger-Hellmich, 'Know-How Schutz – gehen mit dem Mitarbeiter auch die Unternehmensgeheimnisse?' (2011) WRP 1364, 1378–1379 and Ansgar Ohly, 'Harmonising the Protection of Trade Secrets: Challenges and Perspectives' in Jacques de Werra (ed), *La protection des secrets d'affaires. The Protection of Trade Secrets* (Schulthess 2013) 44.

[90] Mayer, 'Geschäfts- und Betriebsgeheimnis oder Geheimniskrämerei?' 884, 887; Richters and Wodtke, 'Schutz von Betriebsgeheimnissen aus Unternehmenssicht "Verhinderung von Know-how Abfluss durch eigene Mitarbeiter"' 281, 282; Stefan Rützel, 'Illegale Unternehmensgeheimnisse?' (1995) GRUR 557, 557.

[91] Ohly, 'Der Geheimnisschutz im deutschen Recht: heutiger Stand und Perspektiven' 1, 5.

[92] Ohly, 'Reverse Engineering: Unfair Competition or Catalyst for Innovation?' 551; Harte-Bavendamm in Harte/Henning §17 para 4.

hand, the definition is based on the law against unfair competition, which is characterised by its flexibility and relied on in civil enforcement, where general clauses are often applied by courts and legislators. Thus, even though the civil law has the tools allowing for application of general concepts, it is desirable to base the definition on objective elements also for the purposes of civil enforcement, as it increases the legal certainty of the application of the law.

5 Summary

Given that the German definition of trade secrecy is rooted in criminal provisions, it is interesting to see that it contains a considerable number of imprecise concepts (such as 'secrecy', 'will to keep the information secret' and 'interest in keeping the information secret'). After all, the provisions of criminal law should be as clear as possible in order to prevent their broad interpretation which reduces legal certainty.[93] This inconsistency may however be explained by the fact that the notion of trade secrecy is frequently, if not mostly, assessed in civil litigation, and most of the case-law defining it stems from the BAG and the BGH. These courts are more accustomed to applying general clauses and unclear concepts than criminal courts.

Although satisfying the requirement of Article 39(1) TRIPS by linking the protection of secret information to protection against acts of unfair competition, the elements of the concept under German law are not the same as those contained in TRIPS. In particular, German law does not contain a requirement that the information has value derived from secrecy. Nevertheless, it contains the requirements of will and interest in keeping the information secret, which in practice may indicate the information's value.

C *Definition of Trade Secrets in the United Kingdom: Confidential Information*

A different approach to the concept of trade secrecy is presented in the law of the United Kingdom, where it forms part of a broad notion of confidential information. This concept encompasses not only information relating to commercial activity (technical secrets[94] and business secrets[95]) but also

[93] Grunewald, 'Fern der Quelle – Geheimnisschutz und Outsourcing' 1307, 1311. The application of unclear concepts in this context has been criticised, see e.g. Maume, 'Know-how-Schutz – Abschied vom Geheimhaltungswillen?' 1275, 1278.
[94] Gurry on Breach of Confidence paras 6.09–6.13.
[95] Gurry on Breach of Confidence paras 6.14–6.34.

artistic and literary information (such as the plot of an unpublished book), government secrets (information which ensures proper functioning of government agencies) and personal information (related to the private and intimate sphere of a person).[96] Despite the fact that trade secrets form only a part of the broad notion of confidential information in the United Kingdom, the 'primary economic importance of the action [for breach of confidence] lies in protection it affords to trade secrets'.[97]

Even as part of the concept of 'confidential information', the term 'trade secrets' is not uniformly applied: particularly in the context of post-employment agreements 'trade secrets' are meant as the type of confidential information which the employee is not allowed to use after termination of employment.[98] However, the preferred approach is to understand trade secrets in a more general way, as a synonym for commercial or industrial confidential information.[99] This is how the term is used in this book.

The courts struggle with clarifying the notion of trade secrets within the broader concept of confidential information.[100] According to a 'tentative' definition applied by Meggary VC, an information which possesses the following qualities will be protected as trade secret:[101]

1) the owner[102] of the information believes that its release would be injurious to him or of advantage to his competitors,
2) the owner of the information believes that the information is confidential or secret,
3) the owner's belief regarding potential injury and secrecy is reasonable,
4) the information is to be judged in the light of usage and practices of the industry or trade concerned.

This definition has been criticised, since it introduces a subjective element into the assessment of the quality of confidence, while generally the

96 Gurry on Breach of Confidence para 6.02; Gintare Surblytė, *The Refusal to Disclose Trade Secrets and Abuse of Market Dominance - Microsoft and Beyond* (Stämpfli Publishers Ltd Berne 2011) 75; for justification of the approach, see Stanley 161–162.
97 Gurry on Breach of Confidence para 1.07.
98 *Faccenda Chicken v Fowler* [1987] 1 Ch 117 (CA) 137.
99 Cf the notions of commercial and industrial secrets in German law. Such an application of the term is applied ia in Gurry on Breach of Confidence, see ibid para 6.06.
100 John Hull, 'Trade Secret Licensing: The Art of the Possible' (2009) 4(3) *JIPLP* 203, 205–206.
101 *Thomas Marshall v Guinle* [1979] 1 Ch 227 (Ch) 248 (Meggary VC). Meggary VC did not exclude that other information could be protected as trade secrets too.
102 Even though the question of whether trade secrets are property has not been finally resolved in the United Kingdom, the courts generally refer to the person asserting his rights in a trade secret as 'owner' of the information. For a discussion of the approach regarding the legal nature of trade secrets, see infra Chapter 2, part III point C.

courts tend to propose an objective analysis.[103] Although the critique is justified, it is considered here that the subjective elements of potential injury and secrecy may be to some extent corrected by the third requirement, i.e. that the subjective expectation must be reasonable.

1 Confidentiality

Despite various attempts at defining trade secrets[104] or confidential information, the general principle that the courts and the commentators agree on is that the information must not be something which is in public knowledge. Under this test, the information will be considered confidential even if it can be reproduced from publicly accessible sources, but only by application of considerable amount of skill, effort, time and labour.[105]

As under German law and under TRIPS, this requirement is not absolute.[106] This differentiates the quality of confidence from the patent-law notion of novelty. If the information is accessible to anyone, it is not confidential. However, a niche publication of the information, even if prejudicial to novelty in patent-law terms, does not terminate secrecy. The test question in that respect is 'whether such a degree of secrecy remains that, except by improper means, a member of the public would have difficulty in acquiring the information'.[107]

The public is defined as anyone interested in accessing the information. However, even if the information is not easily accessible to any such person, it may already be considered not confidential if it is known in a narrow field or industry.[108] On the other hand, as under German law, secrecy does not terminate where information is disclosed to persons who need to know the information because they are employed by the holder of the information to execute the secret process.[109]

Information is not deemed disclosed if its release occurred outside of the territory of the United Kingdom. This is rightly criticised by Hull, who contends that in view of modern means of communication, the geographical place of publication may no longer play a decisive role when determining accessibility of the information.[110]

[103] John Hull, *Commercial Secrecy: Law and Practice* (Sweet&Maxwell 1998) para 3.09.
[104] Hull, *Commercial Secrecy: Law and Practice* paras 3.03–3.10.
[105] Gurry on Breach of Confidence para 5.15.
[106] *Prince Albert v Strange* [1849] EWHC Ch J20 (EWHC); Gurry on Breach of Confidence para 5.21.
[107] Hull, *Commercial Secrecy: Law and Practice* para 3.11.
[108] Ibid para 3.15.
[109] Hull, *Commercial Secrecy: Law and Practice* para 3.18; Gurry on Breach of Confidence para 5.22.
[110] Hull, *Commercial Secrecy: Law and Practice* para 3.18.

Whether the information is in the public domain is determined, again as in Germany, by assessing the amount of effort, time and cost needed to discover the information. Therefore, even if a product containing the confidential information is available on the market and could, at least theoretically, be reverse engineered, this does not of itself mean that the information is in the public domain.[111] However, in one decision, Jacob J observed by way of an *obiter dicta* that in a situation in which encrypted information contained in a product available on the market was reverse engineered by a person spending a considerable amount of time and effort, it lost the quality of confidence.[112] It was presumed that this conclusion refers only to the person who decrypted the information, although it is not clear at which point such information becomes public.[113] In view of this comment by Jacob J, it seems that the necessary quality of confidence may be judged under inclusion of a subjective element: the information contained in a product available on the market may not be confidential towards a person who has the skills to reverse engineer it, and it may remain confidential as regards persons who do not possess the necessary skills to understand the underlying information.[114]

Even though there is some controversy as to whether unauthorised disclosure puts a limit to the confidentiality of the information towards the party who has disclosed it,[115] it is to be stated that any disclosure of the information, whether by its holder[116] or a third person and whether authorised or not, if it makes the information available to those interested in obtaining it, terminates the confidential status of the information.[117]

It follows that the determination of whether certain information is (still) confidential is of an objective character and requires detailed consideration of the facts of the case. Even publication on the Internet, which is often given as a 'classical' example of publication leading to automatic loss of secrecy, does not make the information public, if it was disseminated there on a limited scale and subsequently removed.[118]

[111] Ibid para 3.19.

[112] *Mars v Teknowledge* [1999] EWHC 226 (Pat) [31]–[33] (Jacob J).

[113] Gurry on Breach of Confidence para 5.34.

[114] Similarly Toulson/Phipps para 3-130.

[115] There are arguments stating that if an unauthorised party discloses the information, the secrecy terminates with regard to everyone but that party. It has been suggested by Hull that the question should not be answered by defining confidentiality, but rather by application of the springboard doctrine upon grant of the remedy, see Hull, *Commercial Secrecy: Law and Practice* para 3.22.

[116] For example, by filing of a patent application which is published, as in *Mustad v Allock and Dosen* (1928) [1964] 1 WLR 109 (HL) 111 (Lord Buckmaster).

[117] Hull, *Commercial Secrecy: Law and Practice* para 3.22.

[118] Gurry on Breach of Confidence para 5.30.

Like the definitions analysed above, the concept of confidential information under UK law does not require that the elements of a trade secret are confidential. If publicly available elements are combined, the information as a whole is still considered confidential as long as the combination as such is not in the public domain.[119] This allows for protection of e.g. customer lists or incremental improvements to known processes or products. The concept however does not go so far as to protect any combination of known elements. There must be some skill in making or selecting the information. Mere labour and expense in collection is insufficient to render a combination of known elements confidential.[120]

2 Value

UK law does not contain an express condition that the information which is claimed to be a trade secret must possess an objective or commercial value.[121] However, the first requirement under the definition applied by Megarry VC,[122] i.e. the belief of the holder of the information that its release would be injurious to him or of advantage to his competitors, may be seen as an indication that the information is expected to have some, albeit subjective, value. Value of the information, or at least its attractiveness from a commercial perspective, may also be seen as an indication of confidentiality: if competitors are ready to pay to acquire the information, it can be inferred that the information is not publicly available.[123] It is considered here that, due to the broad notion of confidential information applied in UK law, which encompasses also personal and intimate information, value may not be a condition of granting protection.

119 *Coco v Clark Ltd* [1968] FSR 415 (Ch) 420 (Meggary J); Stanley 12.

120 *Ocular Sciences Ltd v Aspect Vision Care Ltd* [1997] RPC 289 (Pat) 375 (Laddie J); Gurry on Breach of Confidence para 5.20. The requirement that the selection of known elements requires some 'skill of human brain' to be considered confidential resembles the condition of copyright protection for a database contained in Art 3(1) Database Directive. A database must be the 'author's own intellectual creation' in order to be protected by copyright, regardless of any rights residing in its contents (Art 3(2) Database Directive). This standard has been applied by the CJEU also for grant of copyright protection in the unharmonised area, see e.g. Case C-5/08 *Infopaq* [2009] ECR I-06569 [37], Case C-393/09 *BSA* [2010] ECR *I-13971* [45]–[46], Combined cases C-403/08 and C-429/08 *Murphy* [2011] *I-09083* [97], [155]. The application of a threshold of protection characteristic of copyright law may be seen as an indication of the closeness of trade secrecy to the 'classical' IPRs. This aspect is analysed more closely infra in Chapter 2, part IV.

121 Gurry on Breach of Confidence para 5.51. For a different position, see Toulson/Phipps para 3-081.

122 *Thomas Marshall v Guinle* [1979] 1 Ch 227 (Ch) 248.

123 Gurry on Breach of Confidence para 5.54.

However, as regards the sub-category of confidential information, namely trade secrets, the consideration of value may be a helpful tool in determining whether the information is confidential.

3 Identification

The information must also be sufficiently identified. On the one hand this requirement ensures a delimitation of the asserted secret from the public domain – so that the person acquiring the information in confidence is aware of the breadth of his duty – and on the other hand plays an important role upon grant of remedy where breach of confidence is found – so that the losing party can determine which acts are to be desisted from. The proper identification of the information has been recognised as particularly important in the employment context. Due to the existence of an often thin borderline between the employer's trade secrets and the employee's general skill and knowledge, precise identification of the confidential information makes it possible to avoid intrusion in the employee's freedom of self-determination.[124]

The law protecting confidential information in the United Kingdom does not contain an express requirement that reasonable steps must be taken in order to preserve the secrecy of the information, as laid down in Article 39(2)(c) TRIPS. Nevertheless, such measures, and in particular the marking of the information as confidential, are considered useful to draw the recipient's attention to the quality of confidence attached to the data.[125] Furthermore, since the assessment of the nature of information, as well as the duty of confidentiality, is objective,[126] the application of some measures to maintain the secrecy of the information indicates that a reasonable person would regard it as confidential. Even though certain information may be regarded as confidential by nature, this usually relates to personal data. In the business context, and in particular in an employment relationship, such measures may be decisive for the determination of the quality of confidence.[127]

124 *Herbert Morris Ltd v Saxelby* [1916] 1 AC 688 (HL) 699, 703 (Lord Atkinson); Gurry on Breach of Confidence para 5.74.

125 Gurry on Breach of Confidence para 5.79. Such measures are also routinely applied by the holders of valuable information, see Keith Hodkinson and Martin Wasik, *Industrial Espionage Protection and Remedies* (Longman Intelligence Reports, Longman Group UK Ltd, 1986) 73–79.

126 Toulson/Phipps para 3-081.

127 The existence of confidentiality clauses is put forward as an indication of the secret character of the information covered by that clause, William van Caenegem, *Trade Secrets and Intellectual Property. Breach of Confidence, Misappropriation and Unfair Competition* (1st edn, Kluwer Law International 2014) 202.

4 Consideration of Public Interest

The consideration of public interest is not routinely present in the definition of confidential information. Public interest used to be a defence against a claim for breach of confidence, if the information disclosed related to crimes or civil wrongs.[128] According to Aplin, this changed upon the introduction of the Human Rights Act 1998, with regard to both personal and commercial confidential information in a situation in which the defendant asserts the right to exercise his freedom of expression (Article 10 ECHR). Since the nature of the relationship between the parties is taken into consideration in any assessment under Article 10 ECHR, the obligation of confidence which usually exists between the employers and their (former) employees may be a factor when assessing the weight of the claim to freedom of expression under Article 10 ECHR. Even though the appraisal has changed, Aplin suggests that the considerations which gave weight to the public interest in disclosing crimes and civil wrongs remain valid.[129] Thus, it seems doubtful whether the public interest in supporting innovation by dissemination of knowledge or entrepreneurship could be given weight upon application of Article 10 ECHR.

5 Summary

The above analysis shows that even though the definition of trade secrets in the United Kingdom is founded on a conceptually different basis from the definition in German law, they share some notions, such as lack of requirement of absolute secrecy. Although the UK concept of confidential information is broad, its scope includes information related to commercial activity, while the will to keep the information confidential and the interest in keeping it confidential are not expressly contained in the definition. As in the German definition, the decision whether certain information may be protected as trade secret (confidential information) is made on a case-by-case basis, under consideration of all circumstances of the case. In that respect the relationship between an employer and his former employee has been generally recognised as a special case, in which the employee's 'know-how' (skill and knowledge) defines a limit of confidential information.[130] The concept of trade secrets in the

[128] Lionel Bently and Brad Sherman, *Intellectual Property Law* (4th edn, Oxford 2014) 1180–1184.

[129] Tanya Aplin, 'Commercial Confidences after the Human Rights Act' (2007) 29(10) *EIPR* 411, 418.

[130] Hull, *Commercial Secrecy: Law and Practice* paras 3.45–3.52.

relationship between the employer and his former employee is looked at more closely in Chapter 3.

D Definition of Trade Secrets in the United States: Trade Secrets

The protection accorded to trade secrets is not uniformly codified in the law(s) of the United States. The civil protection of trade secrets has until recently been regulated almost exclusively by state laws, which apply the definition based on the Uniform Trade Secrets Act (UTSA), or on common-law principles summarised in either the Restatement (First) of Torts or the Restatement (Third) of Unfair Competition.[131] As of May 2016, Defend Trade Secrets Act (DTSA) introduced a federal cause of action for misappropriation of trade secrets.[132] The DTSA takes over the definition of trade secrets as applied in the federal law (Economic Espionage Act).[133]

The definition contained in Section 1(4) UTSA closely resembles the definition of undisclosed information from Article 39(2) TRIPS,[134] in that a trade secret is considered to be a piece of information which is not generally known; which derives economic value from not being generally known and not being readily ascertainable by proper means; and which is subject to reasonable measures to maintain its secrecy.

The definition contained in Section 39 of the Restatement (Third) of Unfair Competition is deemed consistent with that prescribed in the UTSA[135] and encompasses information which can be used in the operation of a business and which is secret so that it can afford its holder an economic advantage over others.

The definition contained in comment b to Section 757 of the Restatement (First) of Torts defines a trade secret as a formula, pattern, device or compilation of information which is used in a business and which allows its holder to obtain an advantage over competitors who do not know or use it.

The definition of trade secrets applied in the federal law encompasses all forms and types of information, if the owner thereof has taken

131 Quinto/Singer 1. New York and Massachusetts are the only states which have not adopted the UTSA yet, see Randy Bruchmiller, 'Texas Adopts the Uniform Trade Secrets Act' (*Trading Secrets*, 3 May 2013) www.tradesecretslaw.com/2013/05/articles/trade-secrets/texas-adopts-the-uniform-trade-secrets-act/ accessed 1 June 2017.

132 Defend Trade Secrets Act of 2016, Public Law 114–153, 11 May 2016.

133 18 US Code §1839.

134 de Werra, 'How to Protect Trade Secrets in High Tech Sports? An Intellectual Property Analysis Based on the Experiences in the America's Cup and in the Formula One Championship' 155, 157.

135 Quinto/Singer 32.

reasonable measures to keep such information secret and this information derives independent economic value, actual or potential, from not being generally known to, and not being readily ascertainable through proper means by, another person who can obtain economic value from the disclosure or use of the information. In this way it appears to be consistent with the definition laid down in the UTSA.

Despite the fact that the definitions outlined above differ, their application is based on similar fundamental ideas.[136] Due to the adoption of the DTSA on the federal level and the UTSA in the vast majority of states, it seems that the notion of a trade secret which should be seen as representative of the law of the United States is the concept contained in the UTSA interpreted in the light of the Restatements,[137] and which defines trade secret as:

1) information,
2) which is not generally known or readily ascertainable,
3) which derives value from not being generally known or readily ascertainable and
4) which is the subject of reasonable measures to maintain its secrecy.

These cumulative elements are analysed more closely below.

1 Information

The information which may be protected as a trade secret is understood broadly under all four definitions presented above. Even despite the requirement of 'continuous use' contained in the definition from the Restatement (First) of Torts, which is not included in the UTSA and the Restatement (Third) of Unfair Competition, it has been recognised that the information does not need to be used in order to be protected.[138] This allows to include in the scope of protected subject-matter also negative information ('negative know-how'[139]), e.g. information about experiments which failed or products which are not marketable.

Under the US law, the content of the information is not decisive regarding whether it may be protected as a trade secret. Therefore, theoretically, even information relating to illegal acts may be granted such protection. However, in some instances the constitutional protection of freedom of speech has been granted priority over the right of the owner of secret information. Consequently, it seems that, while considerations of freedom

[136] Peterson 1–79.
[137] William G Porter II and Michael Griffaton, 'Identifying and Protecting Employers' Interests in Trade Secrets and Proprietary Information' (2001) 68 *Def Couns J* 439, 440.
[138] Peterson 2–9, 2–29; Quinto/Singer 16.
[139] Quinto/Singer 18.

of speech are not taken into account in order to define the right to a trade secret, they may be decisive in its enforcement.[140]

2 Not Generally Known or Readily Ascertainable

A trade secret must be neither generally known, nor readily ascertainable by proper means by others who can obtain economic value from its disclosure or use.[141]

As in the other jurisdictions analysed, no requirement of absolute secrecy exists under US law.[142] The information does not need to be completely unknown[143] to the outside world, it is sufficient that it is not known to those who could profit from its use or disclosure (i.e. 'persons outside plaintiff's enterprise but within the same trade'[144]). The required level of awareness among competitors varies in the case-law from recognition that secrecy is lost when the majority of competitors know the information, to the consideration that secrecy is preserved as long as there remains at least one competitor who does not have the information.[145]

On the other hand, the information is not considered secret if it is known in the relevant industry[146] or if it is readily ascertainable by proper means, i.e. accessible to those interested in obtaining it (e.g. through searching of a publicly available database or patent register, or the Internet).[147] If the information is 'not economically feasible to obtain'[148] it is not considered readily ascertainable. Therefore, as in Germany and the United Kingdom, if the information may be obtained only through investment of a considerable amount of time, effort, skills and money, it will be deemed not readily ascertainable and therefore secret.[149] If, on the other hand, the information can be reverse engineered without effort, it will not be a trade secret.[150]

[140] Victoria A Cundiff, 'Reasonable Measures to Protect Trade Secrets in a Digital Environment' (2009) 49(3) *IDEA* 359, 397.

[141] S 1(4)(i) UTSA; 18 US Code §1839(3)(B).

[142] Peterson 2–37.

[143] *Kewanee Oil Co v Bicron Corp*, 416 US 470, 475 (US Supr Ct 1974).

[144] Milgrim on Trade Secrets vol 1 1–468.58.

[145] Robert Unikel, 'Bridging the "Trade Secret" Gap: Protecting "Confidential Information" Not Rising to the Level of Trade Secrets' (1998) 29 *Loy U Chi LJ* 841, 869–870.

[146] Comment to S 1 UTSA; *Silicon Image Inc v Analogix Semiconductor Inc* No C-07-00635 JCS (not reported in F Sup 2d) 2008 WL 166950 (ND Cal 2008) 16.

[147] *Paramanandam v Herrmann* 827 NE 2d 1173, 1177 (Ind CA 2005); Mark A Glick, Lara A Reymann and Richard Hoffman, *Intellectual Property Damages: Guidelines and Analysis* (John Wiley & Sons, Inc 2003) 284.

[148] Quinto/Singer 22.

[149] Quinto/Singer 22; Peterson 2–38.

[150] As rightly pointed out by Quinto and Singer, the fact that the information is readily ascertainable and therefore not secret does not exonerate from liability a person who obtained by improper means information which 'could easily have been reverse engineered

Therefore, if a competitor reverse engineers a product but does not disseminate the obtained information, the information contained in that product will remain secret. In fact, it can be a trade secret of both the original holder and the competitor. But it will remain 'not generally known'.[151]

The inclusion in the definition of a trade secret of the requirement that the information is 'not readily ascertainable by proper means' has been criticised by various authors.

As argued by Risch, this consideration should not form part of the definition, but rather be treated as an exception to misappropriation of a secret. He considers such an approach more efficient ia because it is easier for the defendant to prove that he obtained the information by proper means (e.g. by reverse engineering a product he purchased) than for the plaintiff to prove the negative, i.e. that the defendant took a 'short cut' and accessed the information in an improper way even if he could have reverse engineered it.[152] As attractive as this argument may be in terms of procedural economy, it is submitted here that the removal of this requirement would lower the already low threshold for obtaining trade secret status for some information. Consequently, it might lead to attempts at appropriation of general knowledge and invite abusive litigation.

Pursuant to the argumentation developed by Unikel, the 'not readily ascertainable by proper means' requirement should be eliminated so that only information which is not generally known (i.e. which is known only to a minority[153]) could be protected as a trade secret. In exchange for that narrowing of the definition, he proposes the creation of an additional category of protectable information: 'confidential information', which would lie between the category of public domain and trade secrets. He defines it as 'data, technology or know-how that is known by a substantial number of persons in a particular industry (. . .) but that, nonetheless, retains some economic and/or competitive value by virtue of the fact that it is unknown to certain industry participants'.[154] Therefore it could be said that it is information which is less known in an industry than information in the public domain (generally known), but which nevertheless does not reach the level of inaccessibility required for a trade secret. This 'confidential information' would be protected if it was subjectively novel to a company or an individual that could obtain economic value from it,

but was not'. The legal ground for enforcement will however not be misappropriation of trade secrets, but rather unfair competition, see Quinto/Singer 22 note 95.

151 Quinto/Singer 22.

152 Risch, 'Why Do We Have Trade Secrets?' 1, 54–55.

153 Unikel, 'Bridging the "Trade Secret" Gap: Protecting "Confidential Information" Not Rising to the Level of Trade Secrets' 841, 875.

154 Ibid 841, 844.

if it was treated by that company or individual as confidential and as long as it was not necessary for entry into or participation in the relevant industry.[155] Unikel suggests that introducing the requirement that the information is not necessary for entry into or participation in the industry would make it possible to balance the interests of employers and employees, by excluding from protection information which is necessary for the latter to allow them to continue to work in the field in which they specialise.[156] It is considered here that the proposal to allow unrestricted use of information which is not generally known but which is necessary for participation in the industry is attractive, although the criteria proposed by the author seem imprecise[157] and might be difficult to interpret in a uniform way. Instead of introducing a new category of information, a flexible interpretation of the 'generally known' requirement, bearing in mind the employee's interest in remaining active in the field in which he specialises, might ensure a proper balance between the interests of employees and their former employers. As regards information which under the current definition does not reach the level of trade secrecy, it is submitted here that a more appropriate legal ground for liability in such cases might be not the broadening of the law protecting trade secrets, but rather the application of laws against unfair competition or theft, which the author also accepts.[158]

Moreover, a limited disclosure does not make information 'generally known' if it is taken under precautions such as an explicit or implied obligation on the part of the recipient not to disseminate the information.[159]

Furthermore, the information does not need to be new in patent-law terms. This enables protection of improvements that do not reach the level of novelty or inventive step, as long as other requirements of the definition of a trade secret are met.[160]

Trade secret protection may also subsist in a combination of known facts or procedures,[161] as long as the combination as such remains

155 Ibid 841, 876–879.

156 Ibid 841, 881.

157 For example, the requirement proposed by Unikel that information is considered 'not generally known', and therefore susceptible of being a trade secret, if it is known by less than half of persons who could obtain economic value from it (Unikel, 'Bridging the "Trade Secret" Gap: Protecting "Confidential Information" Not Rising to the Level of Trade Secrets' 841, 875). It seems that the difficulties in determining that threshold would make this standard no more workable than the current requirement.

158 Unikel, 'Bridging the "Trade Secret" Gap: Protecting "Confidential Information" Not Rising to the Level of Trade Secrets' 841, 882–888.

159 Peterson 2-40, 2-42.

160 Quinto/Singer 11.

161 Also referred to as 'combination trade secrets', David S Almeling, Darin W Snyder, Michael Sapoznikow, Whitney E McCollum and Jill Weader, 'A Statistical Analysis of Trade Secret Litigation in Federal Courts' (2010) 45(2) *Gonz L Rev* 291, 305.

inaccessible.[162] Therefore 'a trade secret can exist in a combination of characteristics and components, each of which, by itself, is in the public domain, but the unified process, design and operation of which, in unique combination, affords a competitive advantage.'[163] This statement aptly expresses the approach which the US trade secrets doctrine shares with those taken in the other jurisdictions discussed here.

If a piece of information is generally known, it is not a trade secret. Under this consideration, the general knowledge and skill of departing employees is not considered to be a trade secret of their former employers.[164] Disclosure of the information in such a way that it becomes generally known terminates its secret status.[165] It is irrelevant whether or not the disclosure is authorised by the owner of the information. What is decisive is the objective assessment of the level of accessibility of the information.[166] And, as the US Supreme Court stated in *Bonito Boats v Thunder Craft Boats*, the use of what has entered the public domain may not be restricted.[167] Of course, in view of the above, the determination of whether certain information has entered the public domain is not an easy task and must take account of all of the circumstances of the case. The 'not generally known' requirement in the context of employee mobility is assessed in Chapter 3.

3 Value Derived from Not Being Generally Known or Readily Ascertainable

A trade secret derives independent economic value, actual or potential, from not being generally known or readily ascertainable.[168]

The value of the information must be independent, i.e. it must stem from secrecy and not e.g. from other characteristics of the good or service which encompasses the undisclosed information or from external factors such as the marketing techniques applied.[169] This relationship also

[162] Porter II and Griffaton, 'Identifying and Protecting Employers' Interests in Trade Secrets and Proprietary Information' 439, 442.
[163] *Imperial Chemical Industries Ltd v National Distillers and Chemical Corp* 342 F 2d 737, 742 (CA 2nd Circuit 1965).
[164] Quinto/Singer 14; Porter II and Griffaton, 'Identifying and Protecting Employers' Interests in Trade Secrets and Proprietary Information' 439, 443. The boundary between trade secrets and general skill and knowledge in the employee movement context is explored more closely infra in Chapter 3, part II, point C.2.
[165] Deliberate disclosures to destroy the novelty of another's invention, publication in a patent or patent application, as well as registration of software as copyrighted work, lead to loss of secrecy, see Quinto/Singer 26.
[166] Quinto/Singer 11.
[167] *Bonito Boats v Thunder Craft Boats* 489 US 141, 156 (US Supr Ct 1989).
[168] S 1(4)(i) UTSA; 18 USC §1839(3)(B).
[169] *Dynamics Research Corp v Analytic Sciences Corp* 400 NE 2d 1274, 1285 (Mass CA 1980); Pooley 4–45.

implies the existence of a causal link between the quality of secrecy of the information and the value that it possesses.

The economic value of a trade secret must be actual or potential. Therefore it is not necessary to show what exact value the information has. It suffices that the information has some value. Various courts apply different tests for establishing the existence of the economic value of a trade secret. Some acknowledge the existence of value where the information provides its owner with some competitive advantage over his competitors.[170] Other courts use multi-factor tests which include considerations such as the measures taken to protect the secrecy of the information,[171] the level of difficulty in duplicating the information, the level to which the information is accessible from public sources and the effort and cost of developing the information.[172]

Quinto and Singer criticise using the cost of developing the information as a factor in determining its value. Not all valuable data is a result of costly research or development, and not every costly research activity results in the creation of valuable information.[173] The determination of the value of secret information is generally a difficult task. Therefore, it is considered here that, while the amount of effort in its development should not be decisive in determining the value of information, it may be helpful in some cases, when combined with other factors such as the factual measures taken to maintain the secrecy of the information or the level of difficulty in reverse engineering or independent discovery.

4 Reasonable Measures to Maintain Secrecy

Even though no absolute inaccessibility is required, the party asserting a right to a trade secret must show that it has taken all the precautions reasonable under the circumstances to preserve the secrecy of the information.[174] The economic justification of this requirement is said to lie in its role in alerting others to the existence of the trade secret and also in the positive effect that it has on litigation by limiting frivolous enforcement of claims to information which was not subject to reasonable secrecy precautions.[175]

170 *Ruckelshaus v Monsanto* 467 US 986, 1011 note 15 (US Supr Ct 1984).

171 Measures taken in order to protect secrecy of the information are put forward as a factor indicative of value also on a policy level e.g. by Lichtman in Douglas Lichtman, 'How the Law Responds to Self-Help' (2004) John M Olin Law & Economics Working Paper No 232, 19 http://papers.ssrn.com/sol3/papers.cfm?abstract_id=629287 accessed 1 June 2017.

172 Quinto/Singer 19–20; Peterson 2–30.

173 Quinto/Singer 20.

174 *EI DuPont de Nemours & Co v Christopher* 431 F 2d 1012, 1015 (5th Cir 1970).

175 Robert G Bone, 'Trade Secrecy, Innovation and the Requirement of Reasonable Secrecy Precautions' in Rochelle C Dreyfuss and Katherine J Strandburg (eds), *The*

Which measures are sufficient to be regarded as reasonable, and therefore as satisfying the final requirement of the definition of a trade secret under US law, needs to be determined taking into account the circumstances of each case. No exhaustive catalogue may be provided and no single measure or set of measures may be considered as always sufficient.

The precautions taken in order to keep the information secret must not go below, but do not have to go above, what can be expected from a reasonably diligent person. In *EI DuPont v Christopher*, the court recognised that requiring the holder of a trade secret 'to put a roof over the unfinished plant to guard its secrets would impose an enormous expense to prevent nothing more than a school boy's trick'[176] (in this case aerial photography of the plant in order to discover the details of a secret process which was to be conducted there). Although the general rule remains good law,[177] since the reasonableness of the measures must be judged in the light of all circumstances of the case, what the courts recognised as unreasonable in 1970 might not be so now, because of the availability of aerial documentation e.g. via Google Earth.[178] The determination of the type of measure which is reasonable under the circumstances depends furthermore on the size of the company, the expense that it would need to incur in order to safeguard secrecy as well as the level of security that those measures could be expected to ensure.[179]

In the employment context, the catalogue of measures that have been recognised as reasonable in order to preserve secrecy include informing the employees about the confidential nature of certain documents and educating them in their handling, signing non-disclosure agreements, marking the documents containing the information as confidential, restricting access to documents on a need-to-know basis, use of passwords and security systems, dividing a secret process into steps and assigning the execution of the steps to different employees so that no single employee knows the entire process, as well as auditing the files of the employees.[180] The measures to be applied upon the employee's departure include: interviews drawing the employee's attention to the confidential data;

Law and Theory of Trade Secrecy: A Handbook of Contemporary Research (Edward Elgar 2011) 67–75; Mark A Lemley, 'The Surprising Virtues of Treating Trade Secrets as IP Rights' (2008) 61 *Stanf L R* 311, 317.

176 *EI DuPont de Nemours & Co v Christopher* 431 F 2d 1012, 1016 (5th Cir 1970).

177 Quinto/Singer 27.

178 Quinto/Singer 27.

179 *In re Innovative Construction Systems Inc* 793 F2d 875, 884 (7th Cir 1986).

180 Quinto/Singer 28–29; Glick, Reymann and Hoffman, *Intellectual Property Damages: Guidelines and Analysis* 285; Gary E Weiss, 'Biting the Hand that Stops Feeding: How to Protect Trade Secrets from Misappropriation by Laid Off Employees' (2001) 661 *PLI/Lit* 469, 489.

instructing him not to use it; and the signing of non-disclosure and non-compete covenants.[181] While marking the information as secret is a measure to maintain secrecy, simply designating information as secret does not make it secret if it was not such in the first place.[182]

In view of the role that the *de facto* measures taken in order to maintain secrecy play in determining the existence of a trade secret, but above all in keeping the information under the control of its holder, it is not surprising that companies like Coca-Cola or KFC spend a considerable amount of time, money, effort and ingenuity[183] in creating and maintaining effective methods ensuring exclusive control over their legendary formulas.

5 Summary

US law contains various definitions of trade secrets, prescribed in the state and federal laws. The definition which has been predominantly applied is based on the UTSA and mirrors the concept contained in Article 39(2) TRIPS. The US concept of trade secrecy differs from the definitions used in Germany and in the United Kingdom in particular in that it contains an express requirement of value and reasonable steps to maintain secrecy. The lack of absolute secrecy is outlined in a similar way as in the United Kingdom and Germany.

E Definition of Trade Secrets under the Trade Secrets Directive: Uniform Concept of Trade Secrecy for the European Union

In Article 2(1) the Trade Secrets Directive introduces a homogenous definition of trade secrets with the view to ensuring a sufficient and consistent level of civil redress.[184] The proposed definition describes trade secrets as information which is not, as a body or in the precise

[181] Darin W Snyder and David S Almeling, *Keeping Secrets: A Practical Introduction to Trade Secret Law and Strategy* (1st edn, Oxford University Press 2012) 42, 49–53.

[182] *Dynamics Research Corp v Analytic Sciences Corp* 400 NE 2d 1274, 1288 (Mass CA); Glick, Reymann and Hoffman, *Intellectual Property Damages: Guidelines and Analysis* 286.

[183] In the case of the Coca-Cola Company this includes ia disclosing the ingredients to two people in the company who are not allowed to travel together and keeping the complete formula in a bank vault, see Glick, Reymann and Hoffman, *Intellectual Property Damages: Guidelines and Analysis* 285; KFC stores its secret recipe in a secure room, in a safe with a dual-opening system that requires both a smart key and a personal identification number, with a silent alarm and time lock allowing access to the safe only during pre-set periods of time, Press release, 'To Launch The Ultimate Value Menu KFC Offers First-Ever Look Into New High-Tech Home Of One Of America's Most Valued Secrets' (10 February 2009) www.kfc.com/about/news/2009/021009.asp accessed 9 February 2015. Of course these are the measures which the companies have decided to publicise.

[184] Recital 10 TSD.

configuration and assembly of its components, generally known among or readily accessible to persons within the circles that normally deal with the kind of information in question, which has commercial value because it is secret and which has been subject to reasonable steps, under the circumstances, by the person lawfully in control of the information, to keep it secret.

This corresponds to the definition of undisclosed information contained in Article 39(2) TRIPS[185] and to the definition laid down in the UTSA and DTSA. Therefore, the discussion presented supra with regard to TRIPS and the UTSA seems to apply also to the concept of trade secrecy presented in the Directive.

It is clarified in the Directive that trade secrets extend neither to the employee's skill and experience gained in the normal course of employment, nor to information which is generally known or accessible to circles that normally deal with the kind of information in question.[186]

Rauer argues that, due to the fact that the Directive does not require that the information is connected to a business, the harmonised definition includes also 'private' secrets.[187] Aplin considers that private commercial information should be excluded from the notion of trade secrets under the Directive, but admits that the wording is not entirely clear in this respect, since private commercial information may be relevant for a person's business or financial interests, without being held by a business.[188] It is considered that, like the definitions laid down in TRIPS and in the UTSA, the definition under the Directive does not cover private data in the sense of personal or intimate information. Rather, it covers information held by both business and, unlike German law, non-commercial institutions,[189] which is relevant for their 'scientific and technical potential, business or financial interests, strategic positions or ability to compete'.[190] Even though this could admittedly be made clearer in the Directive,[191] it appears that it was not the legislative

185 Which is acknowledged and stressed in Recital 5 in view of the fact that both the Member States and the EU itself are bound by TRIPS. See also Anette Gärtner, 'Zum Richtlinienentwurf über den Schutz von Geschäftsgeheimnissen' (2014) NZG 650, 651; Gill Grassie, 'Trade Secrets: The New EU Enforcement Regime' (2014) 9(8) *JIPLP* 677, 679.

186 Recital 14 TSD.

187 Nils Rauer, 'Richtlinienentwurf: Europaweit einheitlicher Schutz von Geschäftsgeheimnissen' (2014) GRUR-Prax 2, 2.

188 Tanya Aplin, 'A Critical Evaluation of the Proposed EU Trade Secrets Directive' (2014) 4 *IPQ* 257, 263.

189 Recital 1 TSD. See also Nuno Sousa e Silva, 'What Exactly is a Trade Secret under the Proposed Directive?' (2014) 9(11) *JIPLP* 923, 927.

190 Cf Recital 14 TSD.

191 Aplin, 'A Critical Evaluation of the Proposed EU Trade Secrets Directive' 257, 263.

intention to include private commercial information in the definition of a trade secret, just as it is not included in the definitions under TRIPS and the US law on which the Directive was modelled, and as it was not the subject of the discussion preceding the publication of the Proposal for the Trade Secrets Directive.[192]

With regard to the requirement of reasonable measures to maintain secrecy, clarification has been called for in the form of a clear statement that these may be de facto measures as well as confidentiality agreements.[193] This would admittedly serve the goal of harmonisation. However, as far as the jurisdictions analysed are concerned, such a flexible concept of 'reasonable measures' has already been accepted.[194]

The adoption of the definition as laid down in TRIPS and the US law allows inspiration to be drawn from the rich US jurisprudence and literature on the concept of trade secrets. Nevertheless, in view of the fact that the definition has a character of minimum harmonisation,[195] the Member States will be free to include or maintain further elements in their national definitions, even after implementation of the Directive.

Despite the fact that the Directive recognises the existence of a conflict of interests,[196] the balancing of rights is not part of the definition of secrecy. Rather, it is to be taken into account when determining whether a right to a trade secret has been infringed[197] and when granting a remedy where infringement is found.[198]

F *Definitional Conundrum: Undisclosed Information, Industrial and Commercial Secrets, Confidential Information, Trade Secrets, Know-How*

The terminology applied by national laws in defining the notion of trade secrets varies considerably, as can be seen from the analysis presented

[192] Proposal COM(2013) 813 of 28 November 2013 for a Directive of the European Parliament and of the Council on the protection of undisclosed know-how and business information (trade secrets) against their unlawful acquisition, use and disclosure http://ec.europa.eu/internal_market/iprenforcement/docs/trade-secrets/131128_proposal_en.pdf accessed 1 June 2017.

[193] MPI Position Paper paras 19–20.

[194] For a discussion of 'reasonable measures to maintain secrecy' under German law in view of the definition contained in the Directive, see Björn Kalbfus and Henning Harte-Bavendamm, 'Protokoll der Sitzung des Fachausschusses für Wettbewerbs- und Markenrecht zum Richtlinienvorschlag über den Schutz von Geschäftsgeheimnissen' (2014) GRUR 453, 454.

[195] Art 1(1), Recital 10 TSD.

[196] Recitals 21, 22, 26, 28, 29, 34 TSD.

[197] Cf Art 3(1)(c), 4(2)(b), Art 5(d) TSD.

[198] Cf Art 6(2), 7 TSD.

above. The discussion is additionally complicated by the fact that some legal acts, commentators and courts use further terms when referring to trade secrets.

The term 'undisclosed information' used in TRIPS is an 'umbrella term' and the result of a compromise reached during the international negotiations.[199] Taking into account that the jurisdictions analysed are all party to TRIPS, it can be said that the term 'undisclosed information' encompasses (or at least should encompass[200]) the national concepts presented above.

The term 'trade secrets' may also be used to designate the concept in all of the legal orders analysed. Even though neither German nor UK law contains a legal definition, the literature in Germany[201] uses the common term '*Unternehmensgeheimnisse*', which can be translated as 'trade secrets' and in the United Kingdom the term 'trade secrets' is used by the courts and commentators[202] to designate that part of confidential information which relates to commercial activities.

Another term much used in the discussion relating to trade secrets is 'know-how'. Even though the definition of this term contained in the TTBER and in the RDBER[203] resembles the concept of trade secrets, in that it is not generally known or easily accessible and useful (which may signify value), it may not be equated with any of the definitions analysed above, since it relates only to non-patented information resulting from experience and testing, which is furthermore identified. Therefore, the term know-how in this meaning may be used only in the context of the application of the TTBER or the RDBER. They relate to agreements between undertakings and therefore their scope does not cover relations between employees and employers. In the United Kingdom, know-how has been referred to as general skills and knowledge, which the employee may freely use after termination of the employment relationship, as opposed to 'trade secrets' which must remain with the employer.[204]

199 UNCTAD, *Resource Book on TRIPS and Development* 521; de Werra, 'How to Protect Trade Secrets in High Tech Sports? An Intellectual Property Analysis Based on the Experiences in the America's Cup and in the Formula One Championship' 155, 156.

200 As noted at various occasions supra, the national definitions seem to differ from the provision of Art 39(2) TRIPS, e.g. neither the German nor the UK definitions contain requirements of value and reasonable measures to maintain secrecy.

201 Ohly in Ohly/Sosnitza §17 para 5 with further references.

202 Gurry on Breach of Confidence para 6.02.

203 Pursuant to Art 1(1)(i) TTBER and Art 1(1)(i) RDBER, know-how means a package of practical information, resulting from experience and testing, which is secret, substantial and identified.

204 Hull, 'Trade Secret Licensing: The Art of the Possible' 203, 206.

A more widespread although not purely legal use of the term 'know-how' relates to its general meaning derived from economics, to designate knowledge or skills about how to solve problems, and which can be applied commercially. Such application of the term does not limit the notion to technical or business contexts, it also says nothing about secrecy. In that meaning 'know-how' may be secret, but does not need to be. Also, not every trade secret relates to know-how, it may relate to pure facts. Nevertheless, because the notion of know-how is relatively broad, it is handy to describe some trade secrets which are often referred to as 'secret know-how'.

'Confidential information' is the legal term referring to any information that is protected under the tort of breach of confidence in the United Kingdom and encompasses, but is not limited to, confidential trade information. In the United States, it is referred to as information which is not generally known, but not so inaccessible as to be qualified as a trade secret and which, before the introduction of the UTSA, was protected under Section 759 of the Restatement (First) of Torts.[205] Therefore, under the law of the United States, information 'may be considered confidential in the context of a business relationship without rising to the level of a trade secret'.[206] Moreover, such information is identified by the existence of a confidential relationship usually rooted in an agreement, not by examination of the factors described above.[207] German law does not use a separate notion of confidential information, but sometimes refers to a confidentiality obligation (*Verpflichtung zur Vertraulichkeit*) between the holder and a recipient of the secret information.[208]

In view of the lacking harmonisation of the terminology used in respect of trade secrets, in this book the notions of trade secrets or undisclosed information are applied as general concepts, and the national terminology is used in situations in which national particularities are being referred to.

205 Edmund W Kitch, 'The Expansion of Trade Secrecy Protection and the Mobility of Management Employees: a New Problem for the Law' (1996) 47 *SCLRev* 659, 661–662; Unikel proposes re-introduction of this category of protectable information in Unikel, 'Bridging the "Trade Secret" Gap: Protecting "Confidential Information" Not Rising to the Level of Trade Secrets' 841.

206 *Roboserve Ltd v Tom's Foods Inc* 940 F 2d 1441, 1456 (11th Cir 1991). Trade secrets and confidential information are often used as synonyms, see e.g. *Ed Nowogroski Insurance Inc v Michael Rucker et al.* 137 Wash 2d 427 (Washington Supr Ct 1999) and the case-law cited therein.

207 Glick, Reymann and Hoffman, *Intellectual Property Damages: Guidelines and Analysis* 287.

208 Ohly in Ohly/Sosnitza §17 para 45.

G Summary: A Uniform Understanding of What Trade Secrets Are?

The concepts of trade secrecy differ under the definitions discussed above. While all of the legal systems analysed protect information which is related to commercial activity, including negative information, the notion of confidential information in the United Kingdom seems to be broadest and covers any type of data, including private information. On the other hand, German law seems to include in the concept of industrial and commercial secrets only information held by businesses while all of the other definitions analysed include in the scope of protected information the data which is held by non-commercial institutions.

All of the definitions discussed contain a requirement that the information is secret. This condition is not absolute. Therefore, the information may be known to some people, as long as it remains under the control of its holder. Furthermore, the concept differs from the requirement of novelty under patent law in that the information may still be considered a secret if it remains generally unknown to competitors, even if some of them know it, e.g. if they discovered the information independently but decided to keep it secret as well. Individual elements of the information may be publicly accessible or even form part of common general knowledge, but as long as the entire composition of the information remains unknown and is not readily accessible to anyone interested in obtaining it, the requirement of secrecy is met.

The information may be a trade secret if it is not generally known or readily accessible by honest means. The information is considered not readily accessible if it can be obtained only by employing costly and complicated measures, e.g. by expensive, burdensome and time-consuming analysis of a product available on the market or by collecting information which, although its elements are available to the public, may be accumulated only at considerable expense and with a lot of effort. All of the systems analysed acknowledge that secrecy is lost when the information is disclosed in such a way that it is available to the interested circles. However, they differ in the assessment of the influence which reverse engineering may have on the secrecy of the information. While German law generally maintains the quality of secrecy with regard to information which has been reverse engineered using honest means, and treats such reverse engineering as misappropriation of trade secrets, under the laws of the United Kingdom and the United States such information is no longer considered secret, at least with regard to the person who reverse engineered it.[209] As discussed above, even though

[209] This seems also to be the approach taken in Art 3(1)(b) TSD.

this approach presented in German law is criticised, it remains the majority opinion. Therefore, while the German assessment of secrecy remains strict, the other systems accept a 'narrowing down' of secrecy with regard to persons who reverse engineered the information without recourse to dishonest means and did not disseminate it in such a way that it would become available to anyone interested.

The further elements of the definition are not uniformly present in the legal systems analysed. While TRIPS, the US law and the Trade Secrets Directive require that the information has value which is derived from secrecy in order for it to be protected, neither German nor UK laws contain such an explicit requirement. Nevertheless, under German law it is considered that the information must give its holder some competitive advantage in order to be protected. This requirement may be seen as akin to the understanding of value in the jurisdictions which contain such an explicit requirement, since also under TRIPS and the US law the value does not need to be precisely estimated and its existence is confirmed if the information improves the competitive position of its holder. Confidential information does not need to have value in order to be protected by the courts in the United Kingdom. This is due to the broad concept applied there. Even though it is not an element of the definition, in the context of trade secrets, which are only a part of the notion of confidential information, it is considered that in practice only such information will be enforced which gives its holder some competitive advantage. Otherwise its enforcement would not be economically viable.

Reasonable steps taken in order to maintain secrecy of the information are an element explicitly contained in the definition of trade secrets only under TRIPS, US law and the Trade Secrets Directive. Nevertheless, the considerations relating to whether such self-help measures have been taken will usually be present in all the legal systems analysed. Although in Germany the implementation of such measures is not an explicit element of the definition, they are taken into account upon assessment of the existence of the will of the holder to keep the information secret. Moreover, both in Germany and in the United Kingdom, the circumstance that the holder of the information took measures to maintain its secrecy will be an indication of the secret status of this information.

The existence of a will to keep the information secret and an interest in keeping it secret are elements of the definition which exist only in German law. While the will to keep the information secret may effectively be compared to the requirement of value contained in US law, TRIPS and the Trade Secrets Directive, the requirement of interest in keeping the information secret seems to be unique. This condition might open the door for inclusion of a balance of interests in the definition of the notion of trade secrecy. However, as discussed above, such a balancing exercise is not supported by the majority opinion. Furthermore, even those who advocate the inclusion of some considerations of public interest when defining a trade secret, support it only in cases of 'illegal' secrets.

On the other hand, UK law seems to be the only legal system analysed here, in which the definition contains a requirement that the information is identified. Even though no such condition is foreseen in the other jurisdictions, in practical terms the information needs to be identified in order to be enforced. This requirement may also be compared to the condition of a will to keep the information secret, contained in German law. This would indicate that by requiring identification of the information, UK law makes the protection dependent on an expressed will to keep the information secret.[210] German law, on the other hand, grants protection to the information even if the will to keep it secret can be implied from the circumstances.

It is concluded that, while generally the main requirement that the information must be secret in order to be protected is shared by all of the legal systems analysed and is construed in a similar way, further conditions differ, at least with regard to their formulation as part of the definition of a trade secret.[211] The balancing of rights is not generally present in the definitions analysed, even though they contain broad terms such as 'readily accessible by honest means' or 'reasonable measures to maintain secrecy'. This is to be accepted, since legal definitions should aim at achieving unambiguous results. Nevertheless, the determination of whether a particular information is a trade secret often poses considerable problems and requires a case-by-case assessment. These challenges are addressed in more detail infra.[212]

In view of the broadness of the definitions discussed here, the notion of trade secrecy may encompass various kinds of information. The types of data that are susceptible of being protected as trade secrets are presented below and the elements of the definition are looked at more closely again infra.[213]

[210] Schlötter 228.

[211] Still, it is argued that the definitions are compliant with the minimum requirements of TRIPS. With regard to Germany and United States, see Charlotte Sander, 'Schutz nicht offenbarter betrieblicher Informationen nach der Beendigung des Arbeitsverhältnisses im deutschen und amerikanischen Recht' (2013) GRUR-Int 217, 227; Ohly, 'Der Geheimnisschutz im deutschen Recht: heutiger Stand und Perspektiven' 1, 4.

[212] Chapters 3–4.

[213] Ibid.

II Types of Information Which Can Be Protected as Trade Secrets

The legal definitions of trade secrets discussed above are broad and flexible. Thus, the 'identification of trade secrets is a dynamic process',[214] which requires a case-by-case consideration not only of the attitude of the holder but also of the type and characteristics of the information itself.

Even though no strict categorisation may be provided, usually the information susceptible of protection as a trade secret of an employer is divided into technical and non-technical.[215] This dualism may bring to mind the German definition of trade secrets comprising industrial and commercial secrets. However it is referred to also in other jurisdictions.[216] Generally, technical trade secrets encompass information on research and development as well as information on products and means of production, while non-technical trade secrets cover information relating to conducting a business activity and to the company's clients. Those two categories are to some extent overlapping and, as a rule, qualifying certain information as technical or not does not influence the level of protection it may be accorded. However, in the particular scenario in which an employee moves to another company or starts his own business, the balance of interests between the employers and the ex-employees may result in different treatment of the various kinds of information.[217] This is discussed in more detail infra in Chapter 3.

The examples of technical information which can be protected as trade secrets include manufacturing processes; software (in particular source code and object code); algorithms of search engines;[218] designs, drawings and models; specifications; formulas;[219] testing procedures and test

[214] Glick, Reymann and Hoffman, *Intellectual Property Damages: Guidelines and Analysis* 281.

[215] Huber in Ann/Loschelder/Grosch 64–65.

[216] See e.g. Gurry on Breach of Confidence para 6.08; Almeling, Snyder, Sapoznikow, McCollum and Weader, 'A Statistical Analysis of Trade Secret Litigation in Federal Courts' 291, 304. This dualism may also be found in the Trade Secrets Directive which already in its title refers to undisclosed 'know-how' on the one hand and 'business information' on the other.

[217] A similar suggestion is made in Almeling, Snyder, Sapoznikow, McCollum and Weader, 'A Statistical Analysis of Trade Secret Litigation in Federal Courts' 291, 305.

[218] Michael J Madison, 'Open Secrets' in Rochelle C Dreyfuss and Katherine J Strandburg (eds), *The Law and Theory of Trade Secrecy: A Handbook of Contemporary Research* (Edward Elgar 2011) 241.

[219] For example, the Coca-Cola formula, Big Mac Special Sauce, Chartreuse liqueurs, as explained in Gurry on Breach of Confidence para 6.13; see also Quinto/Singer 12–13.

results; inventions (up to publication of the patent application, which is generally recognised as terminating secrecy); and negative technical information.[220] Within the category of technical information, both patentable inventions and information not reaching that level due to lack of novelty or inventive step (obviousness) may be protected.

Non-technical information which may be the subject of protection as a trade secret includes strategic and marketing plans; research and development plans; customer lists;[221] client information; information on suppliers and other business partners; information about prices and costs; organisational methods;[222] information about a particular transaction; or terms of an offer.[223]

A special category of information which has been recognised by the courts in the United Kingdom as susceptible of protection as a trade secret is commercialised private information, and in the particular case, the photographs of a celebrities' wedding.[224] The information was granted protection as a trade secret, which is criticised in the literature as lacking justification and as resulting in overprotection of such information.[225]

A category which becomes particularly relevant in the context of employee mobility is the so-called tacit knowledge, defined by Oehlrich as non-transferable knowledge, strictly connected with a person, which cannot be transmitted otherwise than with the transfer of the person

[220] The lack of requirement that the information be used to be protected allows protection of negative knowledge which derives its value from the savings that a competitor would make by not pursuing research or a line of business which the holder of the secret has already proved inefficient. Similarly, the lack of a use requirement allows protection of 'second best' information, i.e. information about e.g. a process which is not known to competitors, but which is not used by the company, since it has created a better process. Such information may also be valuable for competitors and therefore can be protected as a trade secret, see Risch, 'Why Do We Have Trade Secrets?' 1, 48–49.

[221] According to Stone, customer lists are the most litigated type of trade secrets, although not every customer list is a trade secret, see Katherine VW Stone, 'The New Psychological Contract: Implications of the Changing Workplace for Labor and Employment Law' (2001) 48 *UCLA L Rev* 519, 586–587. A current threat to the secrecy of customer lists lies in the use of social media by employees, e.g. a customer list may be disclosed by including the customers as contacts in LinkedIn. For the discussion of this problem, see e.g. Marisa Warren and Arnie Pedowitz, 'Social Media, Trade Secrets, and Yes, the Sky is Falling' (2011) www.americanbar.org/content/dam/aba/administrative/labor_law/meetings/2011/tech/a_03.authcheckdam.pdf accessed 1 June 2017.

[222] Even though they may be difficult to distinguish from general information about how to conduct business, see Gurry on Breach of Confidence para 6.17.

[223] Glick, Reymann and Hoffman, *Intellectual Property Damages: Guidelines and Analysis* 286; Richters and Wodtke, 'Schutz von Betriebsgeheimnissen aus Unternehmenssicht "Verhinderung von Know-how Abfluss durch eigene Mitarbeiter"' 281, 282.

[224] *Douglas v Hello! Ltd (No3)* [2006] 1 QB 125 (CA) [111], [113], [118].

[225] Gurry on Breach of Confidence paras 6.23–6.31.

carrying it.[226] It is argued here that such tacit knowledge may not be considered as a trade secret of the employer due to its inseparability from the person of the employee. This results in the lack of the employer's control of such information and, if the employer is not able to identify the information in question (as required by UK law), it would be difficult for him to undertake any measures to keep this information secret (as required in the United States) as well as to identify the will and interest in keeping it secret (under German law). Furthermore, due to the inseparability of that type of information from the person of the employee, it may not be considered to relate to a specific business enterprise (as required by German law).[227] It seems that the limitation of use of such information after termination of employment might be possible only through limitation of the employee's competitive activity altogether, e.g. by a non-compete agreement, and not with recourse to the protection of trade secrets per se.

Thus, in view of the broadness of the definitions of trade secrets applied in the jurisdictions analysed, any information that the employee may learn during his employment can potentially be a trade secret.

III Discussion on the Legal Nature of Trade Secrets

Whether trade secrets are a property right similar to IPRs or merely a relative right is a contentious issue in the literature.[228]

A proposal for a conclusive resolution of this dispute goes beyond the scope of this book. For the sake of completeness of the introduction to the analysis of the enforcement of rights to trade secrets in a post-employment setting, the positions taken in the analysed jurisdictions as regards the legal nature of trade secrets and the main arguments put forward for and against recognising a property right in trade secrets are presented below.

A Protection against Unfair Conduct under TRIPS

At the international level, even though pursuant to Article 1(2) TRIPS undisclosed information is considered to be a category of intellectual

[226] Marcus Oehlrich, 'Know-how und Tacit Knowledge als vernachlässigte Vertragsbestandteile bei Lizenzverträgen' (2010) GRUR 33, 34.

[227] Kalbfus para 514.

[228] For an overview, see e.g. van Caenegem, *Trade Secrets and Intellectual Property. Breach of Confidence, Misappropriation and Unfair Competition* 15–51. For a discussion from the perspective of fundamental rights, see Tanya Aplin, 'Right to Property and Trade Secrets' in Christophe Geiger (ed), *Research Handbook on Human Rights and Intellectual Property* (Edward Elgar 2015) 421.

property,[229] its legal nature has not been conclusively determined in that agreement. Due to the fact that Article 39 TRIPS uses the term 'control' rather than 'property', it requires only that there is a de facto dominion over the information.[230] This is in clear contrast to the concept of ownership used with regard to classical IPRs.[231] Moreover, Article 39 TRIPS, unlike provisions relating to the classical IPRs,[232] obliges the contracting states to grant protection to trade secrets by reference to Article 10bis Paris Convention, which regulates protection against acts of unfair competition.[233] By taking such an approach, TRIPS does not protect undisclosed information as such, but rather prohibits certain means of obtaining, disclosing or using it.[234] In this way trade secrets are protected against particular unfair conduct, which makes this form of protection considerably weaker than the one prescribed for IPRs.[235] It follows that under TRIPS trade secrets could only be seen as an IPR if the concept of intellectual property is construed broadly.[236]

B 'Imperfect Intellectual Property Right' in German Law

Neither are trade secrets to be seen as property under German law. This is not a straightforward conclusion, since they are sometimes included in

[229] Ohly, 'Harmonising the Protection of Trade Secrets: Challenges and Perspectives' 33.

[230] Pires de Carvalho, *The TRIPS Regime of Antitrust and Undisclosed Information* para 39.2.38.

[231] UNCTAD, *Resource Book on TRIPS and Development* 527.

[232] In particular, Art 9 TRIPS with regard to copyright, Art 16 TRIPS with regard to trade marks, Art 26 TRIPS with regard to industrial designs, Art 28 TRIPS with regard to patents, which create an obligation for the Member States of TRIPS to protect those rights as exclusive rights. Art 22(2) TRIPS in regulating the protection to be granted to geographical indications refers to protection against confusion and acts of unfair competition.

[233] de Werra, 'How to Protect Trade Secrets in High Tech Sports? An Intellectual Property Analysis Based on the Experiences in the America's Cup and in the Formula One Championship' 155, 156; Ohly, 'Harmonising the Protection of Trade Secrets: Challenges and Perspectives' 33–34.

[234] Pires de Carvalho, *The TRIPS Regime of Antitrust and Undisclosed Information* para 39.1.49.

[235] Surblytė, *The Refusal to Disclose Trade Secrets and Abuse of Market Dominance - Microsoft and Beyond* 28.

[236] Jerome H Reichman, 'How Trade Secrecy Law Generates a Natural Semicommons of Innovative Know-How' in Rochelle C Dreyfuss and Katherine J Strandburg (eds), *The Law and Theory of Trade Secrecy: A Handbook of Contemporary Research* (Edward Elgar 2011) 186. A proposition that trade secrets are intellectual property under TRIPS is put forward ia in Marco Bronckers and Natalie McNelis, 'Is the EU Obliged to Improve the Protection of Trade Secrets? An Inquiry into TRIPS, the European Convention on Human Rights and the EU Charter of Fundamental Rights' (2012) 34(10) *EIPR* 673. For a contrary view, see e.g. Peter/Wiebe in Busche/Stoll/Wiebe Art 39 para 9; Malbon, Lawson and Davison, *The WTO Agreement on Trade-Related Aspects of Intellectual Property Rights* para 39.11.

the catalogue of rights encompassed by Article 14(1) GG, which grants constitutional protection to property.[237] Some authors recognise secret information as a property right,[238] others argue that it is protected indirectly, as part of a company, which in turn profits from the property guarantee of Article 14(1) GG.[239] Similarly divided are the arguments based on civil law.[240] The majority opinion seems not to ascribe proprietary character to trade secrets. This argumentation is based on the interpretation of Section 832(1) BGB, which contains a general provision of the law of torts which prescribes compensation for wilful or negligent wrongful interference with another's ia property or a special right. Unlike 'property' under constitutional law, the notion of property under the BGB relates strictly to rights in rem of an absolute and exclusive character and does not encompass trade secrets, which are seen merely as assets.[241] Nor are trade secrets as such considered a 'special right' under Section 823(1) BGB, which distinguishes them from 'classical' IPRs, such as copyright and patent.[242] However, due to the fact that the notion of 'special right' covers a right to established and exercised business, they may be protected indirectly as part of a business.[243]

[237] Ohly in Ohly/Sosnitza Vor §§17–19 para 8. Enders considers that trade secrets are included in the scope of Art 14(1) GG, Theodor Enders, 'Know How Schutz als Teil des geistigen Eigentums' (2012) GRUR 25, 28. On the other hand Wolff does not see trade secrets as covered by Art 14(1) GG, Heinrich Amadeus Wolff, 'Der verfassungsrechtliche Schutz der Betriebs- und Geschäftsgeheimnisse' (1997) NJW 98, 100–101.

[238] For example, Erhard Denninger, 'Die Zweitanmelderproblematik im Arzneimittelrecht' (1984) GRUR 627, 633. See also Mary-Rose McGuire, 'Der Schutz von Know-how im System des Immaterialgüterrechts. Perspektiven für die Umsetzung der Richtlinie über Geschäftsgeheimnisse' (2016) GRUR 1000.

[239] Ohly in Ohly/Sosnitza Vor §§17–19 para 8 with further references. Trade secrets are also protected as part of a business under Art 12 GG which safeguards the freedom of commercial activity, see Ohly in Ohly/Sosnitza Vor §§17–19 para 8; Wolff, 'Der verfassungsrechtliche Schutz der Betriebs- und Geschäftsgeheimnisse' 98, 101 (considering it a more appropriate legal ground than Art 14(1) GG). It is interesting to note that Art 12 GG at the same time safeguards the employees' right of occupational freedom, see BVerfG NVwZ 2006, 1041 at [79]–[85].

[240] For treatment of trade secrets as an absolute right, see ia BGH GRUR 1955, 388, 389 *Dücko;* Peter Mes, 'Arbeitsplatzwechsel und Geheimnisschutz' (1979) GRUR 584, 590–593. For protection of trade secrets as part of the right to establishment and exercise of a business, see ia BGH GRUR 1963, 367, 369 *Industrieböden*; Ohly in Ohly/Sosnitza §17 para 49.

[241] Cf Wagner in MünchKommBGB §823 paras 165, 228.

[242] Wagner in MünchKommBGB §823 para 228; Mes, 'Arbeitsplatzwechsel und Geheimnisschutz' 584, 591. Mes acknowledges this distinction but argues for the inclusion of trade secrets in the notion of 'special right' under S 823(1) BGB, ibid. Similarly Nastelski in Karl Nastelski, 'Der Schutz des Betriebsgeheimnisses' (1957) GRUR 1, 6.

[243] Surblytė, *The Refusal to Disclose Trade Secrets and Abuse of Market Dominance - Microsoft and Beyond* 55–56; Kalbfus para 411; Ann, 'Know-how – Stiefkind des Geistigen

Other tort,[244] unfair competition[245] and criminal provisions[246] protecting trade secrets do not make their protection conditional on the existence of a proprietary right, but rather on the type of behaviour which is deemed unfair.[247] It may therefore be useful to refer to trade secrets as an 'imperfect intellectual property right': from an economical point of view they form part of the assets of a company, just like patents or works protected by copyright, but they do not have the exclusive character required for a property right.[248] Ohly refers to the imperfect character of trade secrets as a right of intellectual property in the sense that it is ascribed to its holder but only conditionally: the rights to secret information terminate with disclosure and their protection is limited to unfair attacks.[249]

C *Property as a Shorthand to Describe Complex Relations in the United Kingdom*

In the United Kingdom some confusion is caused by the fact that the courts, when referring to trade secrets as a sub-category of confidential information, routinely use the terminology characterising property. The existence of a right to prevent publication of etchings was based on the recognition of proprietary nature of ideas in *Prince Albert v Strange*.[250] The majority of the House of Lords in *Boardman v Phipps*[251] was also of the opinion that know-how is to be considered property.[252] This recognition seems to stem at least partially from the fact that information may be a valuable asset. Those considerations are also present in the German literature, although the recognition of the existence of the value of information did not result in its treatment as another category of intellectual property.

Eigentums?' 39, 43; Enders, 'Know How Schutz als Teil des geistigen Eigentums' 25, 28.

244 S 823(2) BGB in combination with Ss 17–19 UWG, S 826 BGB.

245 S 3 UWG. UWG was last amended by the Act dated 2 December 2015 (BGBl at 2158). Unless otherwise indicated, in this book reference is made to the UWG as amended.

246 ia Ss 17–19 UWG.

247 Kalbfus para 408.

248 Mathias M Siems, 'Die Logik des Schutzes von Betriebsgeheimnissen' (2007) WRP 1146, 1149, with further references.

249 Ohly, 'Der Geheimnisschutz im deutschen Recht: heutiger Stand und Perspektiven' 1, 4.

250 *Prince Albert v Strange* [1849] EWHC Ch J20 (EWHC).

251 *Boardman v Phipps* [1967] 2 AC 46 (HL) 107 (Lord Hodson).

252 For examples of case-law recognising and denying the proprietary nature of information, see John Hull and Sarah Abbott, 'Property Rights in Secrets – Douglas v Hello! In the Court of Appeal' (2005) 27(10) *EIPR* 379, 381–382.

While the majority in *Boardman v Phipps* considered that know-how was property, it was in fact the minority opinion of Lord Upjohn which prevailed in the modern approach to the legal nature of secret information. He expressed the view that information 'is not property in any normal sense but equity will restrain its transmission to another if in breach of some confidential relationship'.[253] Thus, the prevailing view in the United Kingdom seems to be that information is not considered property (a right in rem enforceable erga omnes), but part of relationships in personam.[254]

Still, in some circumstances information is treated as property, especially where it is a convenient 'shorthand' to describe a complex relationship, such as the one between the person holding confidential information and the confidant. In such a situation the confider is often referred to as the 'owner' of the information.[255]

Some authors argue that due to the fact that action for breach of confidence is rooted in contract and property law at the same time, and additionally in tort law, the nature of the protected right cannot be ascribed to a single category and therefore confidential information should be regarded as a sui generis right combining characteristics of a right in rem and a right in personam.[256]

D Intellectual Property Right in the United States

The position taken in the United States towards the legal nature of trade secrets seems to be dominated by the view that trade secrets are rights of intellectual property, together with patents, copyright, trademarks, trade dress and industrial designs.[257]

This is based on the analysis of the catalogue of rights that the holder of secret information has. Since the possessor of the information has the right

[253] *Boardman v Phipps* [1967] 2 AC 46 (HL) 127–128 (Lord Upjohn).

[254] Stanley 149. Lack of proprietary nature of confidential information was confirmed ia in *Douglas v Hello! Ltd (No 3)* [2006] 1 QB 125 (CA) [119] and *Fairstar v Adkins* [2012] EWHC 2952 (TCC) [58], [69]. This opinion is shared by the commentators. For example, Hull stresses the differences in the legal treatment of confidential information as a right in personam and IPRs which are rights in rem, Hull, 'Trade Secret Licensing: The Art of the Possible' 203, 206–207.

[255] Stanley 150; Gurry on Breach of Confidence paras 4.74–4.76.

[256] Gurry on Breach of Confidence paras 4.09–4.11.

[257] Milgrim on Trade Secrets vol 1A 2-2; Richard A Epstein, 'Trade Secrets as Private Property: Their Constitutional Protection' (2003) John M Olin Law & Economics Working Paper No 190 (2d Series) 1 http://papers.ssrn.com/sol3/papers.cfm?abstract_id=421340 accessed 1 June 2017; Lemley, 'The Surprising Virtues of Treating Trade Secrets as IP Rights' 311, 325; Bone, 'Trade Secrecy, Innovation and the Requirement of Reasonable Secrecy Precautions' 48.

to use it and to disclose it, he is also authorised to petition the courts for a remedy against the use or disclosure of that information by others. The rights to possess, use and dispose of are inherent in the relationship to a physical object and therefore the rights of the holder of the secret information must be seen as having a proprietary character.[258] This was the opinion expressed by the US Supreme Court in *Ruckelshaus v Monsanto*[259] and confirmed in numerous decisions by both federal and state courts.[260]

Despite this prevalent view, the legal nature of trade secrets remains a topic of discussion in the literature.[261] The proprietary nature of secret information is reflected in the possibility of its sale and assignment; eligibility for securitisation, licensing and use as an object of trust; or as a testamentary device and property in bankruptcy.[262] Risch acknowledges the existence of those rights in respect of trade secrets which are associated with real property, personal property or intellectual property, but proposes that they reflect the 'bundle' rather than 'property' nature of a right to a trade secret and suggests that secret information should be treated accordingly.[263]

E *Discussion on the Legal Nature of Trade Secrets and Its Impact on the Balance of Interests between Employers and Departing Employees*

Despite the continuing debate on the nature of the right to a trade secret, the question of whether trade secrets are property in general and an IPR in particular has not been given a conclusive answer. Even in jurisdictions which do not recognise trade secrets as property, it is difficult to describe them without recourse to the notion of 'ownership'. Due to the fact that the information has value, for practical reasons it is often treated in a similar way to intellectual property: even in jurisdictions in which they are considered a relative right they can be assets in bankruptcy proceedings[264] and can be

[258] Milgrim on Trade Secrets vol 1A 2-12–2-14.

[259] *Ruckelshaus v Monsanto* 467 US 986, 1002–1004 (US Supr Ct 1984).

[260] Milgrim on Trade Secrets vol 1A 2-12 note 7 with further references.

[261] Ia Risch as well as Quinto and Singer deny property character of trade secrets under Restatements, see Risch, 'Why Do We Have Trade Secrets?' 1, 15; Quinto/Singer, 32. For criticism of ascribing proprietary nature to trade secrets, see also David D Friedman, William M Landes and Richard A Posner, 'Some Economics of Trade Secret Law' (1991) 5(1) *J Econ Pers* 61, 71; Robert G Bone, 'A New Look at Trade Secret Law: Doctrine in Search of Justification' (1998) 86 *Cal L Rev* 241, 304; van Caenegem, *Trade Secrets and Intellectual Property. Breach of Confidence, Misappropriation and Unfair Competition* 70–71.

[262] Milgrim on Trade Secrets vol 1A 2-2.

[263] Risch, 'Why Do We Have Trade Secrets?' 1, 24–26.

[264] In Germany, see e.g. BGH GRUR 1955, 388, 389 *Dücko*; Mes, 'Arbeitsplatzwechsel und Geheimnisschutz' 584, 592. In the United Kingdom, see Gurry on Breach of Confidence paras 8.99–8.101.

licensed.[265] Furthermore, the value of the information is sometimes taken into consideration when assessing a remedy for trade secrets misappropriation.[266] The application of these practical solutions may indicate a temptation to treat secret information as property. However this alone does not confer property status to data.[267]

On the other hand, even in the United States, despite the prevailing opinion as to the proprietary nature of the right to trade secrets, the differences to 'classical' property are stressed[268] and arguments against proprietary character of protection are raised.[269]

There are also voices in the literature speaking in favour of compromise solutions. Reichman argues that the nature of trade secrets is semi-commons, i.e. an area between the public domain (commons) and exclusive rights.[270]

Under the law of the EU, albeit in the context of competition law, the General Court stated that 'trade secrets must be treated as equivalent to intellectual property rights'.[271] Currently, Italy is the only EU country which explicitly recognises trade secrets as an IPR.[272] This strengthening of the protection granted to trade secrets has been criticised[273] and seems not to have gained support in the industry. The survey which was one of the elements of the Study on Trade Secrets and Confidential Business Information in the Internal Market, prepared for the European

265 In Germany, see e.g. BGH GRUR 1955, 468, 472 *Schwermetall-Kokillenguß*; Mes, 'Arbeitsplatzwechsel und Geheimnisschutz' 584, 592. For United Kingdom, see Gurry on Breach of Confidence para 9.17.

266 (indirectly) Ingo Westermann, *Handbuch Know-How Schutz* (CH Beck 2007) 121; Gurry on Breach of Confidence para 19.26; Friedman, Landes and Posner, 'Some Economics of Trade Secret Law' 61, 62.

267 Risch, 'Why Do We Have Trade Secrets?' 1, 21; Stanisław J Sołtysiński, 'Are Trade Secrets Property?' (1986) IIC 331, 354–355.

268 For example, that the right of the 'owner' of a trade secret to exclude others is not absolute, and does not extend to those who developed the information independently or by reverse engineering a product, see Lemley, 'The Surprising Virtues of Treating Trade Secrets as IP Rights' 311, 330, although stressing that the same holds true of copyright.

269 Friedman, Landes and Posner warn against strengthening the protection, and argue that treating trade secrets as property would 'be tantamount to a perpetual patent law without public disclosure', Friedman, Landes and Posner, 'Some Economics of Trade Secret Law' 61, 71.

270 Reichman, 'How Trade Secrecy Law Generates a Natural Semicommons of Innovative Know-How' 192–193.

271 Case T-201/04 *Microsoft v Commission* [2007] ECR II-03601 [289].

272 Trade secrets are also to some extent protected as an IPR in France, see Ohly, 'Harmonising the Protection of Trade Secrets: Challenges and Perspectives' 27.

273 Gustavo Ghidini and Valeria Falce, 'Trade Secrets as Intellectual Property Rights: a Disgraceful Upgrading – Notes on an Italian "Reform"' in Rochelle C Dreyfuss and Katherine J Strandburg (eds), *The Law and Theory of Trade Secrecy: A Handbook of Contemporary Research* (Edward Elgar 2011) 140.

Commission in 2013, suggests that European business circles would find it beneficial to harmonise the definition of trade secrets. However, no proposal as to the treatment of secret information as intellectual property has been put forward.[274] The findings of the Study are reflected in the Trade Secrets Directive. While it contains a harmonised definition of the concept of trade secrets,[275] it explicitly states that it does not aim at creating any exclusive right to the information, stressing the lawfulness of independent discovery and reverse engineering.[276]

Admittedly, trade secrets share many features of property rights. Nevertheless, it is argued here that they are better placed in the category of relative rights. Secrecy does not protect information. Rather, it protects access to information. Only unfair taking of the trade secret is restricted by law. Independent discovery is accepted. In this sense, trade secrets appear to be inherently relative: a secret exists because it is not known to the general public, not because it is completely unknown to anyone. The right to a trade secret is infringed where the information has been taken in an unfair manner, but not where it was created independently.

Thus, every act of infringement must be seen in a broader context of the rights of others: was the information taken from its holder, developed independently or learned from a third party? Was it misappropriated from the employer, or is it part of the employee's skill and knowledge? Is the information still a secret, or has it been disclosed and available to the public, even if its holder is not yet aware of that fact? The balancing of rights is an indispensable feature of trade secrets protection.

Therefore, the acts of infringement are defined differently in the case of trade secrets and absolute rights. In the case of trade secrets the balancing of rights may to some extent be relevant already when determining whether an infringing act has occurred. In the case of absolute rights, if at all, the balancing may step in when determining a remedy.

Moreover, the argument that secret information has value is not conclusive as to its character as a property right. Goodwill or personality rights have value as well, which does not confer proprietary character on them.

The recognition of trade secrets as property might have an impact on the balance of rights between employers and departing employees who have extensive knowledge of the functioning of the business of their former employer.[277] When rights are balanced against one another, property as an absolute right usually outweighs a relative right, which is

[274] Baker&McKenzie Study 154.
[275] Art 2(1) TSD.
[276] Art 3(1), Recital 16 TSD.
[277] It would also have a bearing on constitutional law, conflict of laws and remedies, see Ohly, 'Harmonising the Protection of Trade Secrets: Challenges and Perspectives' 34–35.

assessed under the circumstances and in view of the relationship between the parties to a dispute. Therefore, ascribing proprietary character to trade secrets as such might overly favour the interests of employers at the cost of the positive effects that enhanced mobility of employees might have on innovation, knowledge-sharing and entrepreneurship.

Due to the multifaceted nature of trade secrets, the pragmatic approach is to see rights in trade secrets as relative, belonging to the domain of protection against acts of unfair competition. At the same time, wherever similarities to property rights are identified, it is advisable to consider analogical application of solutions which proved appropriate in the property context. In particular, rights of intellectual property may serve as point of reference for handling trade secrecy.[278]

IV Similarities and Differences between Trade Secrets, Copyright and Patents

The difficulties in describing undisclosed information as property stem ia from its intangible nature. The immateriality of the subject-matter of protection as well as the broad range of information thus protected indicate the conceptual closeness of trade secrets to the rights of intellectual property,[279] namely copyright and patents.[280] This calls for a comparison of the characteristics of trade secrets with those of patents and copyright.

Unlike patents or copyright, the object of a trade secret may be any kind of information. In particular it is irrelevant whether it is new, inventive or has a technical character.[281] Copyright requires originality,[282] which is not

[278] It has been suggested that stronger regulation of trade secrets along the lines of the rules governing IPRs would increase legal certainty, Mary-Rose McGuire, 'Know-how: Stiefkind, Störenfried oder Sorgenkind? Lücken und Regelungsalternativen vor dem Hintergrund des RL-Vorschlags' (2015) GRUR 424, 426–427.

[279] William Cornish and others, *Intellectual Property: Patents, Copyright, Trade Marks and Allied Rights* (8th edn, Sweet&Maxwell 2013) paras 8-02–8-05.

[280] The object of trade mark protection cannot overlap with that of a trade secret, due to the fact that the value of a trade mark stems from its function as a communicator, Michael Risch, 'Trade Secret Law and Information Development Incentives' in Rochelle C Dreyfuss and Katherine J Strandburg (eds), *The Law and Theory of Trade Secrecy: A Handbook of Contemporary Research* (Edward Elgar 2011) 178.

[281] Even though trade secrets and confidential information are often grouped into technical and non-technical, this categorisation does not influence the protectability of the information. See Lemley, 'The Surprising Virtues of Treating Trade Secrets as IP Rights' 311, 331; Risch, 'Trade Secret Law and Information Development Incentives' 169–172; McGuire, Joachim, Künzel, and Weber, 'Der Schutz von Geschäftsgeheimnissen durch Rechte des Geistigen Eigentums und durch das Recht des unlauteren Wettbewerbs (Q215)' 829, 829; Ann, 'Know-how – Stiefkind des Geistigen Eigentums?' 39, 41.

[282] 'Author's own intellectual creation' pursuant to Art 2(2) UrhG; 'original' pursuant to S 1(1)(a) CDPA; 'original' pursuant to S 102(a) USCA. It should be recalled however

a condition of protection by secrecy. In that sense, trade secrecy is very 'democratic': any information, no matter how trivial, may be protected as long as it is in fact secret.[283] If the information may be derived from e.g. examination of a product available on the market and without recourse to unfair means and without extensive efforts, it is to be seen as readily accessible and therefore not secret. A design of a product will cease being secret the moment it is put on the market or presented at a trade fair. Therefore, particularly information which is not self-disclosing may profit from the legal protection granted to trade secrets. This is the case for process innovations. On the one hand, such information usually may not easily be reverse engineered from the end product. On the other, obtaining a patent for such a process might not simplify its protection, since enforcement of a process patent is usually burdensome due to problems in gathering evidence, i.e. for the same reasons which make the reverse engineering of a secret process difficult.[284] Furthermore, independent discovery of the information does not terminate secrecy, even though it limits the scope of the right to a trade secret.[285] In comparison to copyright, which requires originality, facts and ideas may be protected as trade secrets, e.g. in the form of customer lists and business plans.[286]

Lack of protection against independent creation is a common feature of copyright and trade secrecy. In both cases, for infringement to be found there must be an act of copying, i.e. the infringer must derive the information from the data controlled by the holder of a trade secret or the owner of the copyright.[287] Patent law is stricter in this sense and provides a remedy even against independent inventors.[288] Moreover, again similarly to copyright, but differently from the rules of patent protection, trade

that under UK law 'skill of human brain' is required for treatment of collection of known facts as confidential information, see supra note 120 in Chapter 2.

283 According to Recital 14 TSD the definition of trade secrets should not be construed so as to encompass trivial information and the skills and knowledge acquired by employees in the normal course of employment.

284 Huber in Ann/Loschelder/Grosch 90.

285 Due to the concept of relative secrecy, the secrecy is lost only when the information becomes generally known or readily accessible. Even if the information is known to some competitors, it may still be secret in the legal sense.

286 This is of particular importance in the United States where protection by copyright was denied to collections of facts under *Feist Publications Inc v Rural Telephone Service Co*, 499 US 340, 349 (Supr Ct 1991). In Germany and the United Kingdom the implementation of the Database Directive provides for a sui generis protection of collections of facts even if they do not reach the level of originality required for copyright protection.

287 Cornish and others, *Intellectual Property: Patents, Copyright, Trade Marks and Allied Rights* para 8-04.

288 Ibid para 8-02; Louis Altman and Malla Pollack, *Callmann on Unfair Competition, Trademarks and Monopolies* (4th edn, Clark Boardman Callaghan 2012) para 14:15. In

secret law allows for protection of identical information in favour of different holders, as long as it was independently discovered by those claiming rights to it.[289] Despite those similarities, what differentiates the protection of trade secrets from that provided by copyright is the fact that secret information is protected only where it is copied using some improper means.[290]

Trade secrecy allows for appropriation of information for as long as it is secret, and not subject to formalities such as examination and registration.[291] Patent law grants exclusivity after registration and only in exchange for disclosure of the invention. Copyright demands expression or fixation.[292] Due to the lack of the requirement of disclosure, in comparison to patent law, the protection offered by secrecy may be attractive for inventions that can be kept secret.[293] Compared to copyright, even though not necessary for grant of protection as such, some kind of fixation or expression of the information might be useful to show the existence of a trade secret in order to licence or enforce it.

Furthermore, both patents and copyright have limited duration.[294] By contrast, a successfully managed trade secret can potentially be protected for ever.[295] However the duration of trade secrecy is very fragile: public disclosure terminates the existence of the secret altogether, even if it occurred in a reprehensible manner or was a criminal act.[296] The time-limited exclusivity granted by the IPRs allows the owners of patents or copyright to rely on this foreseeable duration when making business decisions.

Nevertheless, not every information, even if it concerns an invention or copyrightable subject-matter, needs to be protected for the fixed periods

Germany and in the United Kingdom, prior user rights are an exception, see, in Germany, S 12 PatG, in the United Kingom, S 64 Patents Act 1977.

289 Risch, 'Trade Secret Law and Information Development Incentives' 166.

290 Ibid.

291 Ibid 167.

292 For Germany, see Gunda Dreyer in Gunda Dreyer, Jost Kotthoff, Astrid Meckel and Hans-Joachim Zeisberg, *Urheberrecht* (3rd edn, C F Müller 2013) §2 para 34 with further references; for United Kingdom, see *Donoghue v Allied Newspapers Ltd* [1938] Ch 106 (Ch) 109–110 (Farwell J); for United States, see S 102(a) USCA.

293 Mark A Lemley, 'The Myth of the Sole Inventor' (2012) 110 *MILR* 709, 747–748.

294 20 years in case of patents, Art 33 TRIPS, 70 years after the author's death in case of copyright, S 64 UrhG, S 12(2) CDPA, S 302(a) USCA.

295 For example, the recipe for Angostura Bitters has remained secret since 1824, see http://en.wikipedia.org/wiki/Angostura_bitters accessed 1 June 2017; the Coca-Cola formula has been kept secret since 1886, http://en.wikipedia.org/wiki/Coca-Cola_formula#Physical_security_of_the_secret_recipe accessed 1 June 2017.

296 Average life-time of a trade secret is 3–5 years, according to Jon Cavicchi, 'Jorda on: Trade Secrets are not Trade Secrets' (*Jorda on Trade Secrets* 18 October 2007) http://blogs.law.unh.edu/tradesecrets/2007/10/jorda-on-trade-secrets-are-not.html accessed 1 June 2017.

of time that can be secured by an IPR. In some industries, an exclusive right might not be relevant for an innovator after a short period, due to the fast pace in which the relevant technology changes. Furthermore, grant proceedings may take longer than the life-span of some inventions. Therefore, even though reliance on trade secret protection might not secure long-lasting exclusivity, it might provide a valuable head start.[297]

Another aspect which is often put forward as a factor distinguishing the protection granted to trade secrets from IPRs is cost. Obtaining a patent is thought to be expensive.[298] Trade secrets, on the other hand, do not require registration or maintenance through payment of fees. The protection of trade secrets is primarily based on the factual measures taken by their holders to maintain their secrecy, such as encryption or access control. These efforts naturally incur costs, which however depend on the industry and the type of information to be protected. Therefore, it is difficult to estimate them and compare them with the costs of patent protection.[299] Friedman, Landes and Posner suggest that trade secrets protection is often cheaper than patent protection, since the holder of a secret will likely invest in this protection only as much as is reflected by its value, while the costs of obtaining a patent are not relative to its value. Therefore, less valuable trade secrets will incur lower costs of de facto protection.[300] Copyright protection does not require registration and maintenance costs. However, as explained above, not every kind of information can be protected as work under copyright.

Due to the fact that copyright does not require disclosure, the subject-matter which is kept secret may at the same time be protected under copyright. The example may be a computer source code, which is often subject to secrecy in the proprietary software and at the same time protected by copyright. Patent law on the other hand, with its requirement that the invention be sufficiently disclosed, compels the holder of the information to make a choice between applying for a patent and keeping the information secret. Still, the prevalent view in the literature is that secrecy is not simply an alternative to patent protection. The relationship between patents and trade secrets is considered to be

297 Lemley, 'The Surprising Virtues of Treating Trade Secrets as IP Rights' 311, 331.

298 The costs during prosecution comprise not only the various fees payable to the granting authority, but also the fees of a professional representative, whose involvement may be compulsory (see e.g. Art 133(2) EPC). After grant, the costs of maintaining the exclusive right include the need to pay renewal fees, which increase with time.

299 Ann in Ann/Loschelder/Grosch 20.

300 William A Landes and Richard A Posner, *The Economic Structure of Intellectual Property Law* (The Belknap Press of Harvard University Press 2003) 357; Friedman, Landes and Posner, 'Some Economics of Trade Secret Law' 61, 63.

complementary.[301] It is suggested by Landes and Posner that trade secret protection is more attractive than the protection offered by patent law in three groups of cases: where disclosure would deprive the information of value (in cases of compilations of known data, such as incremental improvements), where the inventor believes that no one would come up with the invention during the term of a patent, and where an invention is not patentable but the inventor believes that his competitors would take long enough to realise this invention for him to gain a head start and thereby secure a market position.[302] Lemley suggests that reliance on secrecy is the best solution in situations in which the invention can actually be kept secret. He argues that in such a case the inventor has no incentive to apply for a patent.[303] Another observation presented in the literature is that trade secrets often complement the technical information covered by a patent. They may be improvements to a patented solution which are not considered inventive enough to obtain a separate patent, or know-how relating to operating the invention covered by the exclusive right. The fact that a patent is accompanied by secret know-how may make licensing the invention more attractive.[304] Yet another approach is presented by Hussinger, who explains that firms may rely on secrecy to protect inventions in the early phases of the innovative process, while the research outcome is still uncertain, rather than when the inventions have already entered the market.[305] Taking into account Lemley's argumentation, this effect is likely to be stronger for inventions which are self-disclosing.

The costs of obtaining and enforcing patents and the requirement to disclose the invention are given as the main reasons for relying on trade secrets instead of patents for protecting innovation. As suggested by numerous studies, this consideration is particularly important for smaller firms.[306] Due to the fact that reliance on trade secrecy may not grant

[301] Landes and Posner, *The Economic Structure of Intellectual Property Law* 371; Lichtman, 'How the Law Responds to Self-Help' 24; Baker&Mckenzie Study 2, 91–93 (with further references). Dessemontet is of the opinion that functional competition is stronger between utility models and trade secrets than between patents and trade secrets, since utility models do not protect against technical equivalents and the term of their protection is shorter than that of patents, see Dessemontet, 'Protection of Trade Secrets and Confidential Information' 342.

[302] Landes and Posner, The Economic Structure of Intellectual Property Law 356–357.

[303] Lemley, 'The Myth of the Sole Inventor' 709, 747.

[304] Risch, 'Trade Secret Law and Information Development Incentives' 170.

[305] The research was based on an analysis of the market success of inventions protected by patents and by trade secrecy by product-innovating firms in German manufacturing in 2000, Katrin Hussinger, 'Is Silence Golden? Patents Versus Secrecy at the Firm Level' (2006) 15(8) *Econ Innov New Techn* 735, 749.

[306] See e.g. Nicola Searle and Gavin C Reid, 'Firm Size and Trade Secret Intensity: Evidence from the Economic Espionage Act' (2012) Scottish Institute for Research in

exclusivity, its value is seen mostly in the fact that it makes it possible to gain lead time over competitors. As discussed above, in fast-moving industries this type of protection may be sufficient to encourage innovation.

This brief description of the similarities and the differences between the protection offered by secrecy and that provided by IPRs shows that, depending on the type of industry,[307] trade secrets may be an attractive solution for protecting various types of information. Lemley even argues that, apart from incentive theory and prospect theory justifications, trade secrecy may satisfy the disclosure theory of patents: their legal protection avoids overinvestment in secrecy and enables limited disclosure for purposes of contractual negotiations and licensing, which in effect allows for commercialisation of the secret information, thereby disseminating its content.[308] Ultimately, the choice between relying on protection offered by patent law and by trade secrecy involves legal, strategic and economic considerations, such as the ability to keep the information secret, costs, type of subject-matter to be protected, effect on competitors and employee mobility. Due to the fact that a high employee turnover is one of the biggest threats to secrecy, in those circumstances businesses are advised to apply for patent protection rather than rely on secrecy.[309]

In view of the numerous similarities, keeping in mind the differences between the two types of protection and the fact that trade secrets are not generally seen as property, it seems justified, when analysing trade secrets, to make references and rely on some of the arguments put forward in the discussion about IPRs.

Economics Discussion Paper 23 http://repo.sire.ac.uk/bitstream/10943/372/1/SIRE-DP-2012_60.pdf accessed 1 June 2017; Wesley M Cohen, Richard R Nelson and John P Walsh, 'Protecting their Intellectual Assets: Appropriability Conditions and Why US Manufacturing Firms Patent (or Not)' (2000) NBER Working Paper Series Working Paper No 7552 25 www.nber.org/papers/w7552.pdf accessed 1 June 2017 (stressing the reliance on patents by large companies); Josh Lerner, 'Using Litigation to Understand Trade Secrets: A Preliminary Exploration' (2006) Harvard Business School Working Papers 4–5 http://papers.ssrn.com/sol3/papers.cfm?abstract_id=922520 accessed 1 June 2017; Hussinger, 'Is Silence Golden? Patents Versus Secrecy at the Firm Level' 735, 749. The tendency among SMEs to rely on protection by secrecy is confirmed in the Baker&McKenzie Study at 149.

307 The attractiveness of secrecy as an appropriability mechanism was found to exceed that of patent protection in chemicals, metal, textiles, petroleum, machine tool and semi-conductor industries, as explained in the Baker&McKenzie Study at 99–100.

308 Lemley, 'The Surprising Virtues of Treating Trade Secrets as IP Rights' 311, 333–337.

309 Andrew Beckerman-Rodau, 'The Choice Between Patent Protection and Trade Secret Protection: A Legal and Business Decision' (2002) 13 http://papers.ssrn.com/sol3/papers.cfm?abstract_id=704644&download=yes accessed 3 March 2016, on file with the author, presenting a list of legal and business factors relevant for choice between patent and secrecy.

V Summary: The Concept of Trade Secrecy

This chapter presented the overview of the concept of trade secrecy at international level, in Germany, the United Kingdom and United States, and under the Trade Secrets Directive. Initially, the definitions of trade secrecy were analysed. After that, the types of information that can be protected as trade secrets were looked at. This assessment was followed by a discussion of the legal nature of trade secrets and their comparison with IPRs.

This analysis shows that the concept of trade secrecy in all of the jurisdictions scrutinised is broad and flexible. Despite there being an overarching regulation in Article 39(2) TRIPS, the legal orders analysed apply varying terminology and present differing approaches to the legal concept of trade secrecy. In Germany, trade secrets are regulated as part of unfair competition and criminal law, in the United Kingdom they are considered a sub-category of the broad notion of confidential information protected ia under rules of equity, whilst in the United States they profit from a special regulation under state and federal laws.

All of those jurisdictions refer to the notion of information when defining trade secrets. Nevertheless, their common feature is that the protection is granted not to information as such. Rather it is a protection of access to the information, which safeguards the undisclosed data only indirectly.

The breadth of the concept allows to encompass practically any type of information as a trade secret, whether technical or not, as long as it relates to a business (with the exception of the United Kingdom, where confidential information covers also e.g. private information). The fact that they protect information, i.e. intangible subject-matter, and the functions they serve are common characteristics of both trade secrets and IPRs, in particular copyright and patents. This conceptual similarity stimulates the discussion as to whether trade secrets are property rights, just like the IPRs. This is an unresolved dispute. While in the United States undisclosed information is generally counted as an IPR, in Germany, in the United Kingdom and under the Trade Secrets Directive it is considered to be a relative right. Despite this, on both sides of the Atlantic Ocean, the proponents and critics of treating trade secrets as property are ready to acknowledge the arguments of the other side.

It is submitted here that trade secrets do not fit well within the framework of property rights. They are to be seen as relative rights, akin to IPRs, which complement the types of protection offered by copyright and patent law. This balance should be safeguarded, as providing enhanced protection to trade secrets might not only have a negative impact on employee mobility, but might even undermine the patent system, were they an attractive alternative for patent protection.

This analysis of the concept of trade secrecy on a general level paves the way for a more focused discussion of how far the right to a trade secret extends into the relationship between an employer and his former employee. This debate is continued in the subsequent chapters of this book.

3 Trade Secret, Employee's Skill and Knowledge or Public Domain Information

Where to Draw the Line?

I Introduction

The discussion of what trade secrets are, in both legal and practical terms, presented in Chapter 2 shows that in all of the jurisdictions analysed no absolute secrecy is necessary. The information is considered a trade secret as long as it remains under the control of the person asserting rights to it. Therefore, a limited disclosure, in particular to employees executing the secret process or managing relations with the company's customers, does not necessarily terminate secrecy.

The sharing of information with employees – whether to enable them to do their job or for training purposes – is an essential part of running a business. It enhances performance and efficiency and enables the employees to improve the employer's processes, goods and services. However, after termination of the employment relationship, the employee necessarily departs with his head full of those ideas, data and projects. In many cases the former employer considers the information provided to the employee and developed by him during employment as his trade secrets. The employee, on the other hand, is often not able to distinguish such information from the knowledge he obtained over time, as part of his work experience. What is more, a specialist in a narrow field might not be able to pursue any activity in the same line of commerce, if he were unable to draw on his previous experience. If ex-employees were prevented from using any information they learned during previous service, they might in theory have to perform a 'pre-frontal lobotomy' on themselves.[1]

This part of the book presents a discussion of the solutions applied to determine what information learned or developed during employment can be used by the former employee, where the parties did not expressly regulate this in a contract.

[1] *Fleming Sales Company Inc v Joseph W Bailey* 611 F Supp 507, 514 (Ill Distr Ct 1985).

II Comparative Analysis

A Post-Employment Duty of Confidentiality in Germany

In Germany the conflicts which may arise against the background of the relationship between the employer and his (former) employee may be brought before both general civil[2] and specialised labour[3] courts. These courts have developed diverging approaches with regard to the extent to which the former employee may rely on knowledge and information obtained during employment after its termination.[4] The BGH generally allows the use of any information honestly obtained before the termination of employment. The BAG follows a stricter approach and, as a rule, recognises the existence of a duty of confidentiality with regard to trade secrets even after termination of employment.

1 BGH: Theory of Inseparability

The BGH takes the view that trade secrets cannot be distinguished from general skill and knowledge and therefore, as a rule, considers the use by a former employee of all of the knowledge and information he obtained in an honest way during his employment as allowable, without making an exception for trade secrets of the former employer (theory of inseparability).[5]

The line of argumentation followed by the BGH is based on the considerations rooted in the law against unfair competition and in particular the provisions of Section 17 and Section 3 UWG.[6] Section 17 UWG prohibits unauthorised disclosure of a trade secret during employment (Section 17 (1) UWG) and any unauthorised obtaining of a trade secret by use of technical means, by creating an embodied communication of the secret or by removing an item in which the secret is embodied, as well as the use and disclosure of information so obtained or otherwise secured without

[2] With the BGH as the highest instance.

[3] With the BAG as the highest instance. Reuter pleads for exclusive competence of labour courts in cases concerning alleged acts of unfair competition by former employees, see Wolf J Reuter, 'Wettbewerbsrechtliche Ansprüche bei Konflikten zwischen Arbeitgebern und Arbeitnehmern – Terra Incognita?' (2008) NJW 3538, 3542.

[4] For an analysis of the historical developments, see e.g. Karl-Heinz Fezer, 'Der Zivilrechtliche Geheimnisschutz im Wettbewerbsrecht' in Ulrich Loewenheim and Thomas Raiser (eds), *Festschrift für Fritz Traub zum 65. Geburtstag* (Deutscher Fachverlag 1994) 81.

[5] Untrennbarkeitsthese, as explained in Kalbfus para 513.

[6] Which replaced the former S 1 UWG, Sosnitza in Ohly/Sosnitza §3 para 1. The amendment of this statutory provision in 2008 and 2015 had mainly a terminological and not a substantive character (Sosnitza in Ohly/Sosnitza §3 para 11; BGBl at 2158) Therefore, in the course of this book, unless otherwise indicated, reference is made to the present version of the statute.

authorisation (Section 17(2) UWG).[7] This catalogue may not be interpreted broadly due to the criminal character of the provision.[8] Thus, uses of information going beyond those penalised in Section 17 UWG are to be seen as allowable under criminal law. However, this limitation of criminal character is not transferable to the regulations provided in civil law, in particular the general clause of Section 3(1) UWG prohibiting unfair commercial practices. Consequently, commercial behaviour may be found to be unfair independently of Section 17 UWG and regardless of the existence of any IPRs.[9] The assessment under Section 3(1) UWG is made taking into account all the circumstances of the case.

As explained in the decision *Spritzgießwerkzeuge*,[10] a clear distinction between a trade secret and the employee's skill and knowledge obtained through experience is not possible. The Court stressed that Section17 UWG penalises only behaviour relating to use of trade secrets of the employer committed during employment.[11] The court further observed that, according to the established case-law of both the Reichsgericht and the BGH, any information obtained honestly during employment can be used afterwards and its use may be restricted only if the requirements of Section 3(1) UWG are met.[12] Therefore, any limitation of such use is not to be made by reference to the type of information (employer's trade secret as opposed to employee's skill and knowledge), but rather by reference to the circumstances in which the information was obtained and the circumstances in which it is to be used.

Thus, the approach presented by the BGH may be described as containing two thresholds: if the employee obtained (any) information, skill or knowledge during employment in an honest way, he may use it after termination of the employment, unless such use would be unfair.

1) Information Obtained in an Honest Way

Whether information was obtained in an honest way is to be judged, as with any general clause, taking into account all the circumstances of the case at hand.

[7] For an analysis of the notion of unauthorised obtaining of information under criminal law, see e.g. Björn Kalbfus, 'Die neuere Rechtsprechung des BGH zum Schutz von Betriebs- und Geschäftsgeheimnissen' (2013) WRP 584, 587–589.

[8] BGH GRUR 1983, 179, 180 *Stapel-Automat*.

[9] Settled case-law, as confirmed in BGH GRUR 1983, 179, 181 *Stapel-Automat*, with further references; Harte-Bavendamm in Harte/Henning §17 para 45; Ansgar Ohly, 'Der Geheimnisschutz im deutschen Recht: heutiger Stand und Perspektiven' (2014) GRUR 1, 4, 10.

[10] BGH GRUR 2002, 91, 92 *Spritzgießwerkzeuge* with further references.

[11] As explained ia in BGH GRUR 1983, 179, 180 *Stapel-Automat*.

[12] BGH GRUR 1983, 179, 181 *Stapel-Automat*; Schlötter 182.

The means of obtaining information enumerated in Section 17(2) UWG are certainly indicative of what is regarded as dishonest. Espionage and theft are also dishonest.[13] However, since the protection granted by civil law may be broader than that regulated by the criminal provisions,[14] further situations may be identified in which information is to be considered as obtained in a dishonest way.

It is considered that the trade secret was obtained in a dishonest way in particular if the employee, while employed, but not as part of his duties, came into contact with technical drawings or other documents which he copied by technical means, or by preparing or memorising drawings, in such a way that he could use the information contained therein after termination of the employment.[15] Also information which the employee had access to as part of his duties but which is contained in documents or other records which he prepared while still employed may not be used for a competitive activity after termination of the employment.[16] Similarly, sending an electronic document containing confidential information to a private e-mail account, or copying it onto an external storage device, point to dishonesty.[17] Further examples of dishonest obtaining of information by employees include deliberately analysing the functioning of the company to an extent going beyond performance of their normal duties, or interviewing other employees, who e.g. deal with a secret process. Extracting large volumes of information from the employer may also be an indication of dishonesty. This will be particularly the case where the ex-employee's behaviour infringes the employer's rights to a database.[18] On the other hand, data regarding clients whom the ex-employee looked after and remembers is not excluded from use after termination of the employment relationship because such information was obtained in an honest way.[19]

[13] Falk Freiherr von Maltzahn, 'Wettbewerbsrechtliche Probleme beim Arbeitsplatzwechsel' (1981) GRUR 788, 793.

[14] Cf Fezer, 'Der Zivilrechtliche Geheimnisschutz im Wettbewerbsrecht' 97; Ohly, 'Der Geheimnisschutz im deutschen Recht: heutiger Stand und Perspektiven' 1, 4, 10; Harte-Bavendamm in Harte/Henning §17 para 53.

[15] BGH GRUR 1963, 367, 369 *Industrieböden*; BGH GRUR 1983, 179, 180–181 *Stapel-Automat*; Eileen Gaugenrieder and Dagmar Unger-Hellmich, 'Know-How Schutz – gehen mit dem Mitarbeiter auch die Unternehmensgeheimnisse?' (2011) WRP 1364, 1370.

[16] BGH GRUR 2006, 1044, 1045 *Kundendatenprogramm*; Harte-Bavendamm in Harte/Henning §17 para 45; BGH GRUR 2012, 1048, 1049 (para 17) *MOVICOL-Zulassungsantrag*.

[17] Kalbfus, 'Die neuere Rechtsprechung des BGH zum Schutz von Betriebs- und Geschäftsgeheimnissen' 584, 587.

[18] Both copyright and the sui generis right, S 87b UrhG.

[19] BGH GRUR 1999, 934, 935 *Weinberater*; BGH GRUR 2006, 1044, 1045 *Kundendatenprogramm*. Generally, see also Rudolf Kraßer, 'Grundlagen des Zivilrechtlichen Schutzes von Geschäfts- und Betriebsgeheimnissen sowie von Know-How' (1977) GRUR 177, 193.

In any case it is submitted here that the fact that the information in question did not form part of the data used by the employee when performing his duties during employment may be a strong indication of dishonesty. However, even in such a case a detailed consideration of the circumstances is recommended due to the fact that the information may have been obtained accidentally.[20] According to Kraßer, information obtained honestly may not be limited to data which was necessary for the employee to perform his duties. He proposes a flexible interpretation of this concept, bearing in mind that the use by proactive employees of certain information not directly connected to the performance of their duties may benefit the employer.[21]

2) *Unfair Use of Information Obtained Honestly*

The BGH has developed a further limitation to the use of information after termination of employment: even the use of data obtained in an honest way may be prohibited if such utilisation would be unfair.[22]

Unfairness of behaviour is one of the constitutive elements of Section 3 UWG, which prohibits commercial practices which are unfair. This includes behaviours which go against fair practices in trade.[23]

The determination of fairness of a competitive activity requires balancing the interests of the parties involved,[24] taking into account the goal of the UWG which is to ensure undistorted competition in the market.[25] In the scenario analysed, the interests in question are on the one hand the constitutionally protected interest of the employee in his professional advancement,[26] including the right to compete with the former employer, and on the other the interest of the employer in safeguarding his market

[20] Accidental obtaining of information may hardly be described as dishonest. However, it is to be remembered that even the use of information which was acquired in good faith may be limited if such use would be unfair.

[21] Kraßer, 'Grundlagen des Zivilrechtlichen Schutzes von Geschäfts- und Betriebsgeheimnissen sowie von Know-How' 177, 193.

[22] BGH GRUR 1963, 367, 368 *Industrieböden*. This decision is based on S 1 UWG then in force, which was based on the notion of 'contra bonos mores' (*Sittenwidrigkeit*). While S 3 UWG refers to the notion of 'unfair commercial practices', these concepts remain equal, see Sosnitza in Ohly/Sosnitza §1 para 12. Podszun considers that this change deprived the analysis under S3 UWG from any considerations of moral or subjective nature, see Podszun in Harte/Henning §3 para 123. It is to be stressed that the concept of unfairness of the behaviour is to be distinguished from the requirement of 'unauthorised' (*unbefugt*) as referred to in Ss 17, 18 UWG. In the context of criminal enforcement, 'authorised' use or obtaining is limited strictly to justifications provided in the criminal law (see Ohly, 'Der Geheimnisschutz im deutschen Recht: heutiger Stand und Perspektiven' 1, 6) and may not be equated with the general clause foreseen in S3 UWG.

[23] Sosnitza in Ohly/Sosnitza §3 para 17.

[24] Ibid para 33.

[25] S 1 UWG, Podszun in Harte/Henning §3 para 140.

[26] Art 12(1) GG; Karl Nastelski, 'Der Schutz des Betriebsgeheimnisses' (1957) GRUR 1, 6.

position through the use of the secret information.[27] The collective interest of the former colleagues of the departed employee in maintaining the competitive position of their employer and thus their own jobs was also suggested as a factor to be weighed up in the balancing exercise.[28]

As the general clause of Section 3 UWG is necessarily broad, it is for the courts to develop the guidelines[29] for distinguishing fair uses of information obtained during employment from those which are contrary to honest commercial practices. Taking into consideration the character of the provision as a general clause, the assessment of a behaviour must be made objectively and taking into account all the circumstances of the particular case.[30] The emphasis is put on the influence that the behaviour may have on the position of the market participants and not so much on the subjective attitude of the persons involved. Thus, elements such as moral judgement and awareness on the part of the employee that his behaviour could harm the former employer are generally not to be considered.[31] Self-interest and intention to harm expressly mentioned in Section 17 UWG should not be considered as factors in the assessment of fairness of the employee's behaviour, since they do not have an influence on the competitive interests of the employer.[32] Furthermore, it is sufficient to establish that a certain behaviour could have a negative impact on the interests in question. The actual effect, if any, is irrelevant.[33] This approach is to be welcomed. The subjective attitude of the parties involved should not be included in the analysis of whether a certain behaviour is fair. It might be taken into consideration upon determination of remedies once unfairness is found.[34] From the point of view of the right to use information and the goal of the statute to

[27] Art 2(1), 14 GG; BGH GRUR 2002, 91, 93 *Spritzgießwerkzeuge*; Nastelski, 'Der Schutz des Betriebsgeheimnisses' 1, 6; Ohly, 'Der Geheimnisschutz im deutschen Recht: heutiger Stand und Perspektiven' 1, 9.

[28] BGH GRUR 1963, 367, 370 *Industrieböden*; Harte-Bavendamm in Harte/Henning §17 paras 48, 54.

[29] Podszun in Harte/Henning §3 para 122.

[30] The 'objectivisation' of the protection against unfair commercial practices is a result of changes in law. Before 2004 subjective elements (knowledge) played a more important role in this assessment, even though their inclusion was criticised, see Sosnitza in Ohly/Sosnitza §3 paras 39–40. Still, in some cases subjective elements may play a role in the assessment of the fairness of a behaviour, see Sosnitza in Ohly/Sosnitza §3 para 42. It seems, however, that in the present context of use of undisclosed information by a former employee, the consideration of subjective elements, such as intent to harm the ex-employer, may become relevant only in the analysis of S 4(1) UWG, i.e. deliberate hindering of competitors.

[31] Podszun in Harte/Henning §3 paras 123, 153–157.

[32] Ibid paras 153–157.

[33] Ibid para 93.

[34] See infra Chapter 5, part IV, point A (grant of damages requires finding of fault).

protect undistorted competition, these are the actions that count and not the motivations. Even from the perspective that considers the protection of trade secrets as a tool to encourage ethical behaviours, these are still behaviours rather than motivations which are to be encouraged or deterred.

In *Industrieböden*[35] the BGH presented a list of factors to be taken into account when deciding on the unfairness of post-employment competitive activity.

It has not been recognised that the employment relationship as such gives ground for an obligation of confidentiality after termination of that relationship.[36] It is necessary that there exists a special confidentiality relationship, supported by consideration in the employee's remuneration. Entrustment of an employee with a general power of attorney (Prokura) typically creates such a special relationship.[37] In such a case there implicitly exists a special agreement supported by consideration under which the employee commits himself to post-employment confidentiality. The higher the remuneration underlying this special relationship, the longer the duration of post-employment confidentiality.[38] It is submitted here that, while linkage of a post-employment duty of confidentiality to the nature of the employment relationship is justified, the scope and duration of such duty should take into account the obligatory rule of Section 74 HGB. Accordingly, any such implicit duty may not have the effect of restricting competition, since for that a written agreement accompanied by remuneration is necessary.

Another factor that may be taken into consideration is the duration of the employment relationship. The longer the employment and the 'exposure' to the information lasted, the more that information becomes connected with the employee, and may become so strongly embedded in him that his further professional activity may not be possible without reliance on that information.[39] Shorter duration may indicate that the goal of the employee was merely to understand the details of the employer's business and later profit from that knowledge for competitive purposes.[40]

[35] BGH GRUR 1963, 367 *Industrieböden*.

[36] S 17 UWG is clearly limited to the duration of the employment relationship, Schlötter 187.

[37] BGH GRUR 1963, 367, 370 *Industrieböden*, BGH GRUR 1983, 179, 180 *Stapel-Automat*.

[38] Josef Molkenbur, 'Pflicht zur Geheimniswahrung nach Ende des Arbeitsverhältnisses?' (1990) BB 1196, 1199.

[39] BGH GRUR 1963, 367, 370 *Industrieböden*; Schlötter 188.

[40] BGH GRUR 1983, 179, 180 *Stapel-Automat*.

In the opinion of the BGH, that the employee's duty to safeguard his employer's secrets ends with the termination of his employment, as stipulated in Section 17 UWG, is justified by the need to safeguard professional freedom of former employees.[41] Even though the obligations under civil law may go beyond those prescribed by criminal provisions, the Court applied the same justification in favour of ex-employees when applying Section 1 UWG (currently Section 3 UWG). Accordingly, it ruled that any obligation to safeguard the ex-employer's secrets may survive the duration of the employment contract only in exceptional circumstances, for example if the employee 'provoked' an early termination of employment in order to sooner be able to use the legally obtained trade secrets.[42] This 'transfer' of considerations from criminal law to the civil understanding of the duration of the employee's duties has been criticised. As argued by Nastelski, under civil law there is no reason to refrain from imposing limitations on the use of the information by former employees going beyond the framework of Section 17 UWG.[43] This is accepted. Nevertheless, it needs to be stressed that also under civil law competition with the former employer is as such not considered unfair. Besides, the interest of the ex-employee in choosing his livelihood is protected by the German constitution. Thus, the interest of the former employee in being able to profit from his experience and use the information learned during employment which is necessary for remaining active in a certain area remains a valid factor in the assessment of the ex-employee's duties, often weighing more than the employer's interest in keeping the information for himself.[44]

It is furthermore suggested in the literature that even the use of information which is not essential for the continuation of professional activity by the ex-employee is not automatically to be seen as unfair in view of the balance of interests. However, disclosure of secrets to others will usually be prohibited, unless it was in fact essential for the furtherance of the employee's occupation.[45] Thus, it seems that the scope of accepted use of information is broader if the data is used by the ex-employee without disclosing it to other persons. This proposition is similar to the approach taken by the BAG in the *Kundenlisten* decision, where the court allowed the use of secret information acquired during employment by the ex-employee but not its sale to others.[46] It may also be supported by the

41 BGH GRUR 1955, 402, 404 *Anreißgerät*.
42 BGH GRUR 1955, 402, 404–405 *Anreißgerät*.
43 Nastelski, 'Der Schutz des Betriebsgeheimnisses' 1, 5; Kalbfus para 336.
44 Ohly, 'Der Geheimnisschutz im deutschen Recht: heutiger Stand und Perspektiven' 1, 10.
45 Harte-Bavendamm in Harte/Henning §17 para 48.
46 NJW 1988, 1686–1687 (BAG) *Kundenlisten*. This decision is discussed infra in Chapter 3, part II, point A.2.

consideration that disclosing the information to others increases the risk of loss of the secret character of the information.

The duration of employment as well as the position of the employee in the company as factors have been criticised by Mes, since this favours employees with fewer responsibilities and does not take into consideration the ever-faster pace of economic reality.[47] Also, Ohly does not accept this as a straightforward indication, arguing that a high position of an employee may be a sign of his particular qualifications and expertise. Thus, limiting his post-employment activities might result in depriving him of the possibility to be active in the same industry.[48] It is submitted here that the duration of the employment as a factor should be used only on an ancillary basis and depending on the industry: in IT and similar industries in which the mobility of employees is higher, the duration of employment is less likely to influence the employee's exposure to a trade secret. It is more his position in the company that would determine the amount of secret data that he might have learned. In more traditional industries, duration of employment may be an indication that the information has become connected to the (former) employee. With regard to the position of the former employee in the company it is submitted that indeed employees on lower positions, having fewer responsibilities, may not be aware of many secrets and may therefore be less limited in their mobility if a post-employment duty of confidentiality is found to apply. However, precisely in view of their position, the use of secret information of the former employer will usually not be a condition for the continuation of their professional activity elsewhere, i.e. they will not need to rely on such information to be able to work for a competitor. Thus, the duration of employment should help to determine whether certain information was obtained honestly and whether reliance on the use of such information is decisive for the employee's future activity. Nevertheless, it should not be assessed in isolation from other factors presented here.

The *Industrieböden* decision furthermore points to the importance of the information for the competitive position of the former employer as a factor indicating unfairness of the use of such information by an ex-employee.[49] The more essential the information is in order to safeguard the competitive position of the former employer, the more unfair it would be if the ex-employee was allowed to use it, as it might improve the

[47] Peter Mes, 'Arbeitsplatzwechsel und Geheimnisschutz' (1979) GRUR 584, 587.
[48] Ohly, 'Der Geheimnisschutz im deutschen Recht: heutiger Stand und Perspektiven' 1, 10.
[49] BGH GRUR 1963, 367, 370 *Industrieböden*.

competitive position of the former employee by way of 'reaping without sowing'. The value of the trade secret, or the particular importance of the information for the former employer as a factor has been criticised, since it makes the fairness of a behaviour conditional on the value of the underlying object and obliges the court to make a decision via an *ex post* analysis of the value or importance of the information.[50] It is argued here that while establishing the secret information's value may be particularly problematic, the importance of the information for the competitive position of the employer may be possible to assess, e.g. if the information relates to a core product of the company. Ohly admits that certain information may be of great importance for a particular business, even decisive for its survival, but he convincingly suggests that the importance of the information for the ex-employer generally should not weigh more than the interest of the employee in undertaking a competitive activity after termination of employment.[51]

With regard to information relating to the ex-employer's clients, even though generally competition with the former employer is allowed, it has been decided that a situation in which the employee immediately after termination of his employment takes over practically all the ex-employer's clients is unfair if it leads to annihilation of the basis of the former employer's commercial activity.[52] This may be compared with the consideration of the importance of a technical secret for the competitive position of the former employer. Accordingly, the taking of particularly important information or a particularly large volume of information might amount to the annihilation of the basis of the former employer's commercial activity and thus be unfair.

The circumstance that it was the former employee himself who developed the technical information while in service was given as a further factor in determination of fairness of the use by a former employee of information learned during employment.[53]

The case of inventions created by an employee is explicitly regulated in the ArbErfG, which protects both inventions and trade secrets.[54] It prescribes a general obligation for the employee to inform his employer

[50] Kalbfus para 525.
[51] Ohly, 'Der Geheimnisschutz im deutschen Recht: heutiger Stand und Perspektiven' 1, 10.
[52] BGH GRUR 1964, 215 *Milchfahrer.*
[53] BGH GRUR 1963, 367, 370 *Industrieböden.*
[54] Ss 17, 24 ArbnErfG; Mes, 'Arbeitsplatzwechsel und Geheimnisschutz' 584, 587. An employee invention is an invention conceived during employment. Gaul suggests that there should be a presumption that also inventions conceived within three months after termination of employment were conceived during service, Dieter Gaul, 'Erfindungen eines gekündigten Arbeitnehmers' (1979) GRUR 750, 750–751.

of any inventions[55] conceived during employment (Sections 4–5, 18, 19 ArbErfG) and a duty to keep the information relating to that invention confidential until the employer declares that it is free to be used (Sections 24(2), 8 ArbErfG).[56] The duty to keep confidential the information relating to an invention does not expire with the termination of employment (Section 26 ArbErfG) and extends not only to the employee-inventor but also to other employees who became aware of the invention as provided by the ArbErfG (Section 24(3) ArbErfG). Despite the clear obligation on the part of employee-inventors to keep the information confidential, the statute does not extend it to other employees who are not explicitly covered by its wording. This caused Kalbfus to doubt whether employees who became aware of the undisclosed information while employed, but not as provided in the ArbErfG (i.e. employees other than those who are inventors or act on behalf of the employer in executing the statutory obligations), are also bound by the duty of confidentiality that would survive the employment relationship.[57] It is considered here that in view of the lack of explicit regulation, the situation of those employees is to be assessed under general rules.[58] It seems however that, taking into account the duty of confidentiality borne by those aware of the invention, it is not likely that other employees would obtain such information honestly. And even if they found out about the invention accidentally and in good faith, the use of such information is likely to be seen as unfair, especially in case of disclosures leading to destruction of the novelty of a patentable invention.

With regard to technical improvements, which do not rise to the level of a patentable invention or utility model (Section 3 ArbErfG) and are not covered by the explicit duty of confidentiality as provided in Section 24 ArbErfG,[59] the BGH considered that their use by an ex-employee might be allowed if the employee developed the information himself. If he did not develop it himself, even if he obtained it honestly, its use after

[55] Which can be subject of an application for a patent or utility model, S2 ArbErfG.

[56] Kraßer, 'Grundlagen des Zivilrechtlichen Schutzes von Geschäfts- und Betriebsgeheimnissen sowie von Know-How' 177, 189.

[57] Kalbfus para 528.

[58] Kraβer argues that former employees who did not develop the information in question, and thus did not obtain special remuneration for the inventions under ArbErfG, should be generally free to use the information they might have learned while in service, unless they knew or had reason to know that the information related to an employee invention, see Kraßer, 'Grundlagen des Zivilrechtlichen Schutzes von Geschäfts- und Betriebsgeheimnissen sowie von Know-How' 177, 190. Similarly Schlötter 192–193.

[59] Mes, 'Arbeitsplatzwechsel und Geheimnisschutz' 584, 587. Such technical improvements are deemed worthy of protection because they improve the company's competitive position in a similar way to IPRs, often giving it a de facto monopolistic position, see Schlötter 191.

termination of employment would be unfair towards his former employer and co-employees because, by influencing the competitive position of the entire company, it might have a negative impact on the situation of his former colleagues.[60] This position has been criticised by Kalbfus, who is of the opinion that technical improvements should not be treated in the same way as inventions, since their use and disclosure by others does not threaten novelty.[61] A strict interpretation of the ArbErfG may support this argument. This statute has been recognised as applicable only to inventions which can be the subject of a patent or a utility model (Section 2 ArbErfG) or to those technical improvements which give the employer a competitive position comparable to a patent or a utility model (Section 20(1) ArbErfG).[62] Thus, other solutions developed by the employees may not profit from the rules provided for employee inventions.[63] It follows that, beyond the rules explicitly laid down by the ArbErfG, the fact that the employee developed the technical information himself may weigh in favour of a conclusion that his use of such information would be fair towards the former principal.

The *Industrieböden* decision, when explaining that the fact that the information was developed by the employee should weigh in favour of allowing him the continuous use of that information after termination of employment, considers only information of technical character developed by a technically active employee. The situation is different if an employee who was active in sales and marketing wants to rely on technical information after the employment.[64] If he was not supposed to know that information as part of his duties as employee, it could be considered to have been dishonestly obtained and for that reason excluded from use. If that is not the case, the use of such data might still be considered unfair under the balancing of interests prescribed in Section 3 UWG.

In the newer case-law of the BGH the consideration which seems to have gained strongest recognition regarding the fairness of the use of

[60] BGH GRUR 1963, 367, 370 *Industrieböden;* similarly BGH GRUR 2002, 91, 93 *Spritzgießwerkzeuge.*

[61] Kalbfus para 529.

[62] Kraßer, 'Grundlagen des Zivilrechtlichen Schutzes von Geschäfts- und Betriebsgeheimnissen sowie von Know-How' 177, 190.

[63] Bernd Fabry and Michael Trimborn, *Arbeitnehmererfindungsrecht im internationalen Vergleich* (1st edn, Carl Heymanns Verlag 2007) 19; Schlötter 191–192. This has been explicitly recognised in case of works protected by copyright in MMR 2001, 310, 312 (BGH) *Wetterführungspläne I* and MMR 2002, 99, 100 (BGH) *Wetterführungspläne II.* In view of this strict interpretation, the same argumentation may be applied to technical improvements not rising to the level of an invention.

[64] Mes, 'Arbeitsplatzwechsel und Geheimnisschutz' 584, 587.

information by an ex-employee is that the former employee should be allowed to use only the information which he retained in his memory in a natural way.[65] The use of data memorised on purpose or contained in documents is not considered necessary for the ex-employee.[66] Thus, according to some authors, the BGH, similarly to the BAG, does differentiate between skills and knowledge which the employee should be allowed to use after termination of the employment and data which he has not learned through the work itself, but which is bound to the organisation of a particular business, and which should remain with the ex-employer.[67]

Termination of employment by the employer due to the employee's fault, in particular because of misappropriation of trade secrets, has been given as a further example indicating that the use of the particular information by an ex-employee would be unfair.[68] This opinion was not shared by Kalbfus.[69] It is submitted here that such termination of employment by the employer may be relevant only if the basis for such justified termination was a dishonest obtaining or unfair use of the particular information in question and not a reason unrelated to the trade secret.

The fact that the duty of confidentiality generally does not survive the termination of employment allows the employee to use any information obtained during that time. However, some authors propose that in a situation in which the employee pretends to give the employer a reason for dismissal, in order to be released from the obligation of confidence, the use of the information would be unfair and therefore should not be allowed.[70]

The use of information in breach of a contractual provision explicitly requiring post-employment confidentiality from the employee was also taken into account for determining unfairness.[71] As explained supra,[72] for the existence of a trade secret under German law it is not required

[65] Harte-Bavendamm in Harte/Henning §17 para 49 citing BGH GRUR 2006, 1044, 1045 *Kundendatenprogramm*, BGH GRUR 1999, 934, 935 *Weinberater* (although concerning a former commercial agent and not an ex-employee), BGH GRUR 2003, 356, 358 *Präzisionsmessgeräte*.

[66] Cf S 18 UWG.

[67] Gaugenrieder and Unger-Hellmich, 'Know-How Schutz – gehen mit dem Mitarbeiter auch die Unternehmensgeheimnisse?' 1364, 1375.

[68] BGH GRUR 1963, 367, 370 *Industrieböden*.

[69] Kalbfus para 525.

[70] Carsten Salger and Anja Breitfeld, 'Regelungen zum Schutz von betrieblichen Know-how – die Sicherung von Geschäfts- und Betriebsgeheimnissen' (2005) BB 154, 156.

[71] BGH GRUR 2002, 91, 93 *Spritzgießwerkzeuge*. The limits of contractual regulation of the post-employment duty of confidentiality are analysed infra in Chapter 4, part II, point A.

[72] Chapter 2, part I, point B.3–4.

that the employer expresses his will and interest in confidential treatment of the information, as those elements of the definition may be derived from the circumstances. However, the existence of a contractual obligation of confidentiality or of a non-compete agreement are circumstances indicating the particular interest of the employer in keeping the information secret. Conversely, the lack of such agreement or clause might indicate a lack of the employer's interest in safeguarding the secret information[73] and tip the balance in the employee's favour.

On the other hand, in view of the general consideration that it is fair for the former employee to compete with his previous employer, the steps taken by the employee while in service, in preparation of his competitive activity, do not point to unfairness as long as they do not go beyond what is necessary for starting a competing activity after employment.[74] In particular, the commencement of production of competing products was not recognised as having a merely preparatory character.[75]

The change of employment as such, even if induced by the new employer, may also generally not be seen as unfair.[76]

Due to the fact that the protection of trade secrets is rooted in the law against unfair competition, the goal of this regulation, i.e. the safeguarding of free competition, must be kept in mind when determining the fairness of a certain behaviour.[77] This includes the interests of competitors, consumers and other market participants (Section 1 UWG). Thus, the public interest may be taken into consideration only to the extent that it relates also to the interests of those persons.[78] Already the acceptance of consideration of the interests of the former colleagues goes beyond the strict analysis of the interests of the parties involved in a particular dispute.[79] Thus, it seems that under the case-law of the BGH there is space for the inclusion of considerations relating to public interest, such as consumer welfare, economic growth or innovation, when determining the extent to which a former employee may use information obtained during employment.

While the anticompetitive character of a certain behaviour[80] may affect the interests of consumers, competitors and other market participants, it is unclear to what extent antitrust considerations may be taken into

[73] BGH GRUR 2002, 91, 94 *Spritzgießwerkzeuge.*
[74] BGH GRUR 1955, 402, 405 *Anreißgerät.*
[75] BGH GRUR 1983, 179, 181 *Stapel-Automat*, with further references.
[76] Freiherr von Maltzahn, 'Wettbewerbsrechtliche Probleme beim Arbeitsplatzwechsel' 788, 789.
[77] Sosnitza in Ohly/Sosnitza §3 para 21.
[78] Ibid.
[79] BGH GRUR 1963, 367, 370 *Industrieböden.*
[80] As understood under the antitrust regulations, Art 102 TFEU, S 18 GWB.

account when balancing rights under Section 3 UWG. In any case, as stressed by Sosnitza, the protection of smaller market participants[81] is a goal of neither antitrust regulation nor the UWG.[82] Podszun advocates the position that, while not every anticompetitive behaviour is automatically unfair,[83] considerations of the possible effect that a certain behaviour might have on free competition may be used to establish the fairness of behaviour of individual market participants as part of a 'more economic approach' to the law of unfair competition.[84] It is argued here that an anticompetitive effect of a particular behaviour may fall within the ambit of §4(4) UWG,[85] which defines the deliberate targeting of a competitor as unfair. Thus, under certain circumstances, abuse of a dominant position by an ex-employer by initiating abusive litigation against a former employee could tip the balance in favour of the use of the information by that employee for competitive purposes.

The analysis of the abovementioned factors shows that in order to find that the use of particular information by the ex-employee was unfair, certain circumstances must be found which go beyond the mere use of the information.[86] It seems that the *Industrieböden* decision is rather isolated and for the finding of the unfairness of a post-employment use of information some additional, more 'classical' circumstances need to be found, such as commencement of the employment with the purpose of preparation of a competitive activity or breach of a contractual confidentiality obligation.[87] It is argued that the factors presented in the *Industrieböden* decision present a maximum threshold beyond which any use of information may not be considered unfair[88] and that generally it is the interest of the ex-employee in continuation of competitive activities that prevails over the interests of the employer.

The BGH in *Spritzgießwerkzeuge* acknowledges the theory of separability applied by the BAG with regard to the use of trade secrets by the employee after termination of service, according to which a departed employee may rely only on his general skills and knowledge obtained during previous employment and may not use or disclose trade secrets that he became aware of during that time.[89]

[81] E.g. start-ups.
[82] Sosnitza in Ohly/Sosnitza §3 para 32.
[83] Podszun in Harte/Henning §3 para 140.
[84] Ibid para 143.
[85] Which entered into force on 10 December 2015 (BGBl at 2158).
[86] Schlötter 186; Freiherr von Maltzahn, 'Wettbewerbsrechtliche Probleme beim Arbeitsplatzwechsel' 788, 789; Fezer, 'Der Zivilrechtliche Geheimnisschutz im Wettbewerbsrecht' 97.
[87] Schlötter 188; Fezer, 'Der Zivilrechtliche Geheimnisschutz im Wettbewerbsrecht' 104.
[88] Fezer, 'Der Zivilrechtliche Geheimnisschutz im Wettbewerbsrecht' 99.
[89] BGH GRUR 2002, 91, 92 *Spritzgießwerkzeuge*.

2 BAG: Theory of Separability

While the considerations of the BGH are based on Section 17 UWG according to which the protection of trade secrets finishes with the termination of the employment relationship, the case-law of the BAG is rooted in the analysis of the duties under the service contract (Section 611 BGB). With this background, it is considered that even though the mutual relationship finishes with the termination of employment, certain duties may remain binding on the former parties.[90] This outcome is possible because the interests protected by criminal law (Sections 17ff UWG) differ from those safeguarded by civil law.[91] Thus, in the opinion of the BAG, an employment relationship may create duties which survive its duration.[92] These obligations encompass in particular a limited duty of fidelity towards the former employer and the duty to safeguard the former employer's trade secrets (duty of confidentiality), as opposed to the general skill and knowledge gathered during that employment, which the former employee is free to use, even in competition with the ex-employer.[93]

The post-employment duty of confidentiality relates only to the use of the former employer's trade secrets. In the *Thrombosol*[94] decision, the BAG shared the considerations of the BGH to the extent that the former employee is free to use the information which has become part of his knowledge and experience gathered during employment. However, according to the BAG, this freedom does not go so far as to allow trade secrets learned during employment to be used in competition with the former employer.[95] Unlike the BGH, the BAG held that the existence of a post-employment duty of confidentiality with regard to trade secrets does not depend on the conclusion of an agreement. Since trade secrets are given special legal protection, the limitation of the former employee in the use of such information does not exclude his competition with the former employer and merely puts him in the same position as other employees who were not exposed to the secret information.[96] However, the implied duty of confidentiality may not put the former employee in a

[90] Schlötter 184.

[91] Criminal law protects public interest in the first place, while civil law safeguards the interests of private parties, Gaugenrieder and Unger-Hellmich, 'Know-How Schutz – gehen mit dem Mitarbeiter auch die Unternehmensgeheimnisse?' 1364, 1373.

[92] Molkenbur, 'Pflicht zur Geheimniswahrung nach Ende des Arbeitsverhältnisses?' 1196, 1198. Described as duty of good faith (*Treuepflicht*) by Ohly in Ohly/Sosnitza §17 para 40.

[93] Theory of separability (*Trennbarkeitsthese*), as explained in Kalbfus para 513; NZA 1994, 502, 504–506 (BAG) *Titanoxid.*

[94] NJW 1983, 134 (BAG) *Thrombosol.*

[95] NJW 1983, 134, 135 (BAG) *Thrombosol.*

[96] Ibid.

worse competitive position than his former colleagues.[97] Any limitation of the employee's freedom to compete with the former employer going beyond that threshold must be safeguarded by way of contract.

This position has been somewhat qualified by the BAG in its *Kundenlisten* decision. According to the Court, a former employee is obliged to maintain the secrecy of the former employer's client lists. While it was considered not allowed for the former employee to use the information about clients by disclosing it to a third party, this duty did not prohibit him from soliciting clients of the former employer. The Court considered that this was necessary in order to enable competition between the former employee and his ex-employer.[98] This has been confirmed in the *Titanoxid* decision, in which the Court added that the former employee, regardless of the length of his service for the employer (in this case: 40 years) and regardless of the breadth of his duties and his awareness of the details of his former employer's business, can use his experience and knowledge of the former employer's clients (in particular names, preferences and tastes) gathered during employment, so long as he relies solely on what he remembers[99] and not on any written records. It was recognised as allowable for an ex-employee to poach his former employer's clients both as part of his own business activity, as well as to the benefit of another competitor.[100]

The duty of fidelity which survives the termination of a contract is more general and is based on considerations of fairness. The BAG accepts the position of the BGH to the extent that in the absence of a contract limiting post-employment competition by an employee, he is free to rely on skills and knowledge obtained honestly during employment in independent activities or in employment by others. However, such activity must be fair within the meaning of Section 3 UWG. Any limitation of such competitive activity not based on a contract but on a post-employment implicit duty of fidelity may relate only to specific behaviours and may not lead to limitation of the former employee's freedom to compete. Relying on the case-law of the BGH (*Stapel-Automat* and *Industrieböden*), the BAG concluded that since any limitation of the use of trade secrets after employment must be narrow, limitation of use of skills and knowledge must undergo even stricter scrutiny. The Court considered in particular that soliciting the former employer's clients may not be seen as unfair.[101]

[97] NZA 1994, 502, 506 (BAG) *Titanoxid.*
[98] NJW 1988, 1686–1687 (BAG) *Kundenlisten.*
[99] NZA 1994, 502, 505–506 (BAG) *Titanoxid.*
[100] NZA 1994, 502 (BAG) *Titanoxid.*
[101] NZA 1994, 502, 505–506 (BAG) *Titanoxid.*

The BAG, like the BGH, considered the conflict between the interests of the employer in safeguarding his competitive position in the market by protecting trade secrets and the interests of the employee in his occupational freedom. This was done in the context of post-employment agreements limiting competition (Section 74 HGB).[102] The BAG ascribed higher rank to the interest of the ex-employee enshrined in Article 12(1) GG and stressed his freedom to compete with his employer as a limitation of the constitutional protection of property.[103] Therefore, it can be said that despite the recognition of the post-employment duty of confidentiality, its limits are defined by the need to ensure fair competition between the former employer and employee.[104]

It seems that the approach taken by the BAG differentiates between post-employment duties depending on the type of information which is the object of a trade secret. While technical secrets were considered to be reserved for the former employer without exceptions,[105] the information relating to the clients of a company may be used by the former employee to support his professional activity but not as an object which is to be traded to third parties. Thus, in *Kundenlisten*[106] it was not considered a breach of the post-employment duties for the former employee to approach the clients of his ex-employer.

In summary, it can be stated that the BAG limits the duty of confidentiality of a departed employee to specific behaviours that could be considered unfair towards the former employer and does not attach it to an undefined class of any activities which could negatively influence the competitive position of the ex-employer.[107] Any limitation of the use of information obtained honestly during employment going beyond this threshold may be based only on a contract which requires additional compensation in accordance with Section 74 HGB. Otherwise, the freedom to compete with a former employer would be overly limited.[108]

Deriving a duty of confidentiality from a contractual relationship which had expired has been criticised. Molkenbur argues that an

[102] For the analysis of those agreements, see infra Chapter 4, part II, point A.
[103] NZA 1994, 502, 505 (BAG) *Titanoxid;* Swantje Richters and Carolina Wodtke, 'Schutz von Betriebsgeheimnissen aus Unternehmenssicht "Verhinderung von Know-how Abfluss durch eigene Mitarbeiter"' (2003) NZA-RR 281, 284.
[104] Salger and Breitfeld, 'Regelungen zum Schutz von betrieblichen Know-how – die Sicherung von Geschäfts- und Betriebsgeheimnissen' 154, 156.
[105] Cf NJW 1983, 134 (BAG) *Thrombosol.*
[106] NJW 1988, 1686 (BAG) *Kundenlisten.*
[107] Richters and Wodtke, 'Schutz von Betriebsgeheimnissen aus Unternehmenssicht "Verhinderung von Know-how Abfluss durch eigene Mitarbeiter"' 281, 284.
[108] NZA 1994, 502, 505 (BAG) *Titanoxid*; Gaugenrieder and Unger-Hellmich, 'Know-How Schutz – gehen mit dem Mitarbeiter auch die Unternehmensgeheimnisse?' 1364, 1374.

employment relationship is a special relationship of a reciprocal character and as such should not be interpreted beyond its explicit terms. Therefore no particular post-employment duty of fidelity should be construed on the basis of an employment contract. Instead, he proposes analogical application of Section 90 HGB which provides for an explicit duty to safeguard trade secrets on the part of a former commercial agent. This would ensure protection for trade secrets of the employer after the departure of his employee, as long as the ex-employer identified the information to be protected.[109]

On the whole, despite differentiating between trade secrets and general skill and knowledge, the BAG does not provide precise guidance that would make it possible to draw a clear line between those two categories of information that may be learned during employment. The Court rather relies on a general statement that knowledge which became part of the employee's experience may not be considered a trade secret of the employer.[110]

3 Common Position of the German Courts

Despite the differences in the approaches advocated by the BGH and the BAG, the outcomes of the analysis do not differ in most cases.[111] Both courts recognise that only information obtained in an honest way may be applied after termination of employment. In particular, reliance on records copied from the ex-employer disqualifies their use. Although the BAG acknowledges the existence of a post-employment duty of confidentiality,[112] the employee is restricted from the use of his former employer's trade secrets only to the extent that this post-employment duty does not limit him in competing against his ex-employer altogether and as long as it does not lead to unfair results.[113] Both courts recognise

[109] Molkenbur, 'Pflicht zur Geheimniswahrung nach Ende des Arbeitsverhältnisses?' 1196, 1198.

[110] NZA 1994, 502, 506 (BAG) *Titanoxid*; Gaugenrieder and Unger-Hellmich, 'Know-How Schutz – gehen mit dem Mitarbeiter auch die Unternehmensgeheimnisse?' 1364, 1374.

[111] Gaugenrieder and Unger-Hellmich, 'Know-How Schutz – gehen mit dem Mitarbeiter auch die Unternehmensgeheimnisse?' 1364, 1373, 1376; Ohly, 'Der Geheimnisschutz im deutschen Recht: heutiger Stand und Perspektiven' 1, 10; Harte-Bavendamm in Harte/Henning §17 para 55; Fezer, 'Der Zivilrechtliche Geheimnisschutz im Wettbewerbsrecht' 100.

[112] Some authors postulate introduction of an explicit post-employment time-limited duty of confidentiality, see Mary-Rose McGuire, Björn Joachim, Jens Künzel and Nils Weber, 'Der Schutz von Geschäftsgeheimnissen durch Rechte des Geistigen Eigentums und durch das Recht des unlauteren Wettbewerbs (Q215)' (2010) GRUR Int 829, 838. Under the current legal framework such an effect can be achieved by way of contract.

[113] Gaugenrieder and Unger-Hellmich, 'Know-How Schutz – gehen mit dem Mitarbeiter auch die Unternehmensgeheimnisse?' 1364, 1376.

the need to balance the interests of the former employer and the departed employee. While the BGH considers it part of the assessment of fairness of the behaviour, the BAG construes it as a limitation of the post-employment duty of confidentiality, beyond which a contractual restraint of competitive activity by the former employee is necessary.[114]

Both courts differentiate between technical data and information relating to clients. They consider client data to be more essential for the former employee to be able to compete with the former employer and generally allow for the use of such information after termination of employment as long as the ex-employee does not use materials taken from the employer. The BAG furthermore does not allow such information to be forwarded to third parties.

With regard to technical information, the courts present a stricter approach. They consider technical undisclosed information less essential to enable competition on the part of the former employee and thus they generally give more weight to the interest of the former employer in keeping the information for himself. The BAG argues that the limitation in the use of such information merely puts the former employee in the same position as his former colleagues who did not find out about it. The BGH makes a reservation with regard to information developed by the employee, allowing him exceptionally to use it after employment. In any case, technical information which may be the subject of a patent or utility model application may not be used without the ex-employer's explicit consent, as the ArbErfG with regard to such information clearly imposes a duty of confidentiality after termination of employment.

The fairness of the former employee's competitive activity is a factor assessed by both courts. This is done by balancing the interests of the former employer in safeguarding his competitive position by keeping secret information for himself and the employee's interest in his professional advancement, which includes activity competitive towards his ex-employer, undertaken independently or in employment for a third person.

Factors which are taken into consideration when making this assessment include the need to use the information by the ex-employee in order to remain active in a certain field, the importance of the information for the competitive position of the employer, the duration of employment, the position in the former employer's company, the reason

[114] Harte-Bavendamm stresses the fact that post-employment duties under civil law may not be limited by the strict interpretation of the criminal provision of S 17 UWG and thus finds the approach presented by the BAG more convincing; see Harte-Bavendamm in Harte/Henning §17 para 53.

for or the circumstances of the termination of the employment relationship as well as any breach of contractual provisions relating to handling the information in question. These factors are judged individually under consideration of the particular facts of the case and may be given different weight depending on the circumstances.

4 Attempts to Define the Borderline in the Literature

Taking into account the approach to the use of undisclosed information after termination of employment discussed here, it seems that the distinction between trade secrets which are reserved for the ex-employer and information which became part of the employee's skill and knowledge may be applied to the case-law of the German courts on a conceptual level.[115] Employee's skill and knowledge include information learned by the employee in an honest way while executing his duties and which is retained in his memory[116] as well as tacit knowledge which cannot be separated from the person of the employee.[117] This information may either not count as a trade secret at all or there exists a consensus that its use after employment is not unfair (e.g. information relating to clients the employee attended to during service). On the other hand there exists a consensus that technical trade secrets may not be used after termination of the employment relationship. They encompass information which may be the subject of an application for a patent or utility model.[118] However, apart from those two categories, no clear line may be drawn between data which the employee is free to use and that which must remain with his former employer.[119] Thus, in the case of information such as technical improvements which do not rise to the level of patentable inventions, large volumes of information relating to clients, marketing strategies or research plans, it remains important to determine

[115] According to Kraßer, such a distinction, even though attractive in theory, in practice is often not workable and is moreover irrelevant, since the decision whether certain information may be used by an ex-employee is made taking into account all the circumstances of a particular case, see Kraßer, 'Grundlagen des Zivilrechtlichen Schutzes von Geschäfts- und Betriebsgeheimnissen sowie von Know-How' 177, 186, 188.

[116] Kalbfus paras 511, 514.

[117] Kalbfus para 514; Marcus Oehlrich, 'Know-how und Tacit Knowledge als vernachlässigte Vertragsbestandteile bei Lizenzverträgen' (2010) GRUR 33, 33. As discussed supra in Chapter 2 part II, tacit knowledge may not be a trade secret.

[118] Ohly, 'Der Geheimnisschutz im deutschen Recht: heutiger Stand und Perspektiven' 1, 10; Mes, 'Arbeitsplatzwechsel und Geheimnisschutz' 584, 588.

[119] Ohly in Ohly/Sosnitza §17 paras 40–40a; Kalbus para 515; Schlötter 181; Kraßer, 'Grundlagen des Zivilrechtlichen Schutzes von Geschäfts- und Betriebsgeheimnissen sowie von Know-How' 177, 186.

the fairness of use of this information taking into account the conflicting interests of employers and employees.

Various attempts have been made in the literature at answering the question of what information obtained during employment may be used by the departed employee.

Kalbfus proposes that disclosure or use of such information is not to be considered unfair if it forms part of the employee's knowledge (learned honestly while executing his duties as an employee and retained in his memory) and is used or disclosed for the purpose of exercising professional activity. He proposes two exceptions to this rule: in the case of employee inventions and explicit contractual confidentiality agreements, the use of information learned during employment is to be considered unfair.[120]

In his seminal article Nastelski, basing his argumentation on Section 823(1) BGB, presents the view that generally the former employee has no claim to the use of the employer's secrets.[121] Only if reliance on certain information is necessary for the employee to remain professionally active in the same area, his interests may prevail over those of his former employer. He admits that such an approach strengthens the position of the employers. In order to reconcile this with the interests of the former employee, he proposes, in cases in which the information cannot be separated from the skill and knowledge of the ex-employee, to allow a limited use of the information: only in his own or his new employer's business, without a right to disclose the information to third parties, thus safeguarding the (relative) secrecy of that information.[122]

Mes considers the approach taken by the BGH based on the balancing of interests to be difficult to exercise in practice.[123] He stresses that employee inventions and information obtained in a dishonest way may never be used after termination of employment, and considers other information generally free to be used by the ex-employee.[124] In order to minimise the difficulties connected with the balancing of interests Mes proposes to treat the former employee as a guarantor of the employer's trade secrets and to generally prohibit the use of that information after termination of employment. That presumption should be stronger for technical and weaker for non-technical information since it is more likely to form part of the general skill and knowledge which the employee must use in order to find new occupation.[125]

120 Kalbfus paras 519–530.
121 Nastelski, 'Der Schutz des Betriebsgeheimnisses' 1, 6.
122 Ibid 1, 7.
123 Mes, 'Arbeitsplatzwechsel und Geheimnisschutz' 584, 587.
124 Ibid 584, 588.
125 Ibid 584, 593.

The proposals of Mes and Nastelski seem to go against the presumption represented in the case-law of the BGH. The courts start from the assumption that the ex-employee is free to use the information, unless such use would be unfair. The authors on the other hand propose an assumption that the former employee is not allowed to use the ex-employer's trade secrets, unless he needs to rely on that knowledge in order to continue his professional activity in a particular field.[126] A similar approach is proposed by Kalbfus, albeit based on procedural law. He explains that one of the main practical difficulties in enforcement of trade secrets lies in the fact that it is the former employer who needs to provide evidence as to dishonest acquisition of the information. That is often problematic, since they are neither able nor allowed to fully control the actions of their employees.[127] Accordingly, he proposes that as long as the ex-employer proves the existence of a trade secret and its use by the ex-employee, it should be presumed that the information was obtained in a dishonest way. The burden of proof would shift onto the employee to show that the information forms part of his skill and knowledge (learned honestly and retained in memory in a natural way). If he is able to do that, then the use of the information would not be considered unfair. Kalbfus argues that this application of a reversed burden of proof would solve the problems of the employer in showing circumstances which he did not have access to, while not overly prejudicing the position of employees, who are best equipped to show how they learned a particular piece of information and who can rely on testimony by their former colleagues.[128] This proposition recalls the suggestion by Risch who puts forward that it should be up to the alleged infringer to show that information was readily ascertainable and thus was not misappropriated.[129] Both proposals of reversed burden of proof raise concerns particularly in the employee scenario and particularly with regard to knowledge which was gained through experience. It might be difficult even for the employee to show how and when he found out about a particular piece of information, if it is part of extensive experience gained over time. Reliance on former colleagues is also problematic, taking into account their likely reluctance to testify against their employer.

[126] According to Harte-Bavendamm this approach too requires a balancing of interests, which will follow similar considerations to the balancing pursuant to S 3 UWG, see Harte-Bavendamm in Harte/Henning §17 para 50.

[127] Close monitoring of employees is both expensive and not reconcilable with the employee's right to privacy and data protection.

[128] Kalbfus paras 531–536.

[129] Michael Risch, 'Why Do We Have Trade Secrets?' (2007) 11 *Marq IP L Rev* 1, 54–55.

5 Duration of the Post-Employment Duties

The post-employment duty of confidentiality seems not to be limited in time and lasts as long as the information remains secret. This is the only way to maintain the quality of the information as a trade secret. Moreover, in view of the concept of relative secrecy, under which the use of the information by the employee may be accepted as long as he does not disclose it, the duty not to disclose does not overly limit the employee's freedom to undertake a competitive activity.

Also the duty not to use the information is generally of unlimited duration, even if it would amount to limitation of competition.[130] This is because the scope as well as duration of this duty may only be determined on a case-by-case basis. This is usually done upon grant of a remedy.[131]

Molkenbur proposes a time limitation on the prohibition of the use of particular information. He argues that post-employment duty of confidentiality should be based in the first place on contract, or on a special relationship supported by remuneration obtained during employment.[132] When no such contractual ground is present, the interest of the ex-employee in the continuation of his professional activity should prevail. Consequently, he proposes that any duty to safeguard the former employer's trade secrets based on balancing of interests should not outlive the duration of such limitation in a situation in which a contract has been concluded. Since pursuant to Section 74a(1) HGB, the maximum duration of a contractual limitation of competition supported by compensation amounts to two years after termination of employment, an implied duty should not last longer than that.[133]

McGuire, Joachim, Künzel and Weber seem to propose an introduction of a time-limited erga omnes prohibition of use of the information in case of disclosure of a trade secret, in order to remedy the loss of the information's competitive value, by reference to Section 6 DesignG, which allows for a restoration of novelty of a design in case of a disclosure in breach of confidence.[134] This solution is provided also in patent law (e.g. Article 55 EPC, Section 3(5) PatG), but does not seem to fit into

130 Frank Wertheimer, 'Bezahlte Karenz oder entschädigungslose Wettbewerbsenthaltung des ausgeschiedenen Arbeitnehmers?' (1999) BB 1600, 1600.

131 For a discussion of the duration of injunctions against use or disclosure of trade secrets, see infra Chapter 5 part II point A.3 and part III, point A.3.

132 As proposed by the BGH in BGH GRUR 1963, 367 *Industrieböden*.

133 Molkenbur, 'Pflicht zur Geheimniswahrung nach Ende des Arbeitsverhältnisses?' 1196, 1199–1200.

134 McGuire, Joachim, Künzel and Weber, 'Der Schutz von Geschäftsgeheimnissen durch Rechte des Geistigen Eigentums und durch das Recht des unlauteren Wettbewerbs (Q215)' 829, 838.

the context of trade secrets. Disclosure is an inherent risk which the holder of a trade secret takes when deciding to rely on secrecy. The extension of a remedy for disclosure beyond the person of the infringer would contradict this basic rule of trade secrecy. On the other hand, an erga omnes restoration of novelty in case of IPRs is acceptable, since those rights have an erga omnes effect, granted in return for ia publication and registration.

The duration of the post-employment duties of the employee with regard to his employer's confidential information determines the duration of an injunction which the court may impose in case of infringement of a right to a trade secret. Thus, it is discussed in more detail as part of the analysis of the remedy of injunctive relief.[135]

6 Summary: Balance between the Interests of Ex-Employers and Their Former Employees with Regard to Use of Information Learned During Service

Taking into consideration the current legal framework in Germany, it seems inevitable to determine the borderline cases of use of information after termination of employment on a case-by-case basis by way of balancing interests.

The starting point of the analysis of fairness of the use of information is the unquestioned principle that information obtained in a dishonest way may not be used by the former employee. This includes data copied or memorised on purpose.

As regards other data, which the employee retained in his memory in a natural way, there is an agreement, rooted in the provisions of the ArbErfG, as to the prevalence of the ex-employer's interest in case of employee inventions.

In other instances the fairness of the use of information is to be established under consideration of all circumstances of the case.

Where the information is essential for the former employee to continue an activity in the same area of technology or trade, the employee's interest in his professional advancement should be given particular weight.[136] This is usually the case when the information relates to clients and in particular clients with which the departed employee developed a long relationship based on trust. Similarly, when the employee is a specialist in a narrow field, in which he has been active for a long time,

[135] See infra Chapter 5 part II, point A.3.

[136] Thus, a post-employment duty of confidentiality will usually be justified in cases in which the former employee is not active in the same sector as his ex-employer, cf Harte-Bavendamm in Harte/Henning §17 para 54.

his interest in continuing activity in that area should be appreciated, as his occupational opportunities might be severely limited if the use of the information learned during employment is denied to him.

The importance of the information for the competitive position of the former employer is another relevant factor in the balancing exercise, but it should be considered in a nuanced way. There exists an interest on the part of the employer to limit the use of such information. However, competition with the ex-employer is as such not reprehensible behaviour. Technical information which is important for the employer, but which he chose not to make the subject of a patent or utility model application, should not be treated in the same way as employee inventions. Limiting the use of such information by a former employee might undermine the goals of the patent system, by rewarding suppression of information which could have benefited society through a disclosure in a patent application. Technical information not rising to the level of subject-matter of a patent or utility model application may also be the source of the employer's competitive advantage. It is suggested to treat such information as well as information for which no IP protection was obtained in a similar way and include this factor to support the employer's interest, particularly for cases in which the employee's ability to be professionally active is not dependent on the use of such data. This applies also to non-technical information. It may have great competitive value, in particular if it relates to the launch of a new product or marketing strategy or if it encompasses a large volume of data. It is submitted here that the former employee's possession of a large volume of information may be an indication that the information was obtained in a dishonest way. If so, the value of the information would be irrelevant, since dishonestly obtained information may not be used in any case.

The fact that it was the employee who developed the information in question weighs in favour of regarding it as having been learned in an honest way and naturally retained in his memory. Thus, unless it is explicitly covered by the ArbErfG, the use of such information must be subject to balancing of interests. As part of that assessment, the fact that the employee developed the information himself while in service for his employer should not be conclusive in favour of the employee's interests. This is because, as a rule, the fruits of employees' actions in execution of their duties are to be ascribed to the employer.[137] Thus, it is proposed to include this factor in the balancing exercise in favour of the employee in situations in which the information resembles tacit knowledge, i.e. if it

[137] NJW 2006, 3803 (BAG) paras 20–27 *Herausgabeanspruch*.

was obtained thanks to personal qualities of the employee. That is the case with regard to e.g. client information developed through relations based on trust. Where, on the other hand, the information relates rather to output of the employee's service, which can be directly incorporated in documents or products, the fact that it was the employee who developed the information should remain neutral in the assessment of the balance of interests.

The position of the employee in the ex-employer's company is not to be seen as a relevant factor in determination of the correct balance of interests. Even in the case of employees who, because of their position in the company, had access to valuable confidential information, if such information becomes imprinted in their memory in a natural way, the prohibition of its use might deprive them of the possibility to be professionally active. On the other hand, the fact that an ex-employee uses information which he did not have access to while in service is a strong indication that the information was obtained in a dishonest way. Thus, the position of the employee may in fact be a helpful argument in support of a finding of unauthorised access to the information in question rather than a factor in the balancing of interests.

The case-law of the German courts and the majority of commentators concentrate on the necessity to strike a balance between the interest of the former employer in protection of his business and the interest of the ex-employee in his professional advancement. The interest of the former colleagues in maintaining their employer's competitive position and thus their own jobs is also mentioned.[138] Other interests seem not to be in the focus of the discussion. However, it should be kept in mind that the assessment of the fairness of a particular behaviour under Section 3 UWG is to be made taking into account the goal of the statute, which is to safeguard free competition and thus it may include the consideration of the interests of competitors, consumers and other market participants (§1 UWG). Moreover, as explained supra[139] the interests of the employee and of the employer are in fact a reflection of policy considerations on a more general level, relating ia to reduction of costs and incentivising innovation. Thus, it seems that within the legal framework of trade-secrets enforcement in Germany, it is possible to assess the fairness of use of a particular information by a departed employee against a broader background which includes some of the policy considerations analysed in the initial part of this book.

[138] BGH GRUR 1963, 367, 370 *Industrieböden.*
[139] Chapter 1.

Although not explicitly mentioned, the considerations regarding maintaining standards of commercial ethics appear to be present as an element of both the assessment whether a particular information was obtained in an honest way and whether subsequent use of such information would be fair. Limiting the use of data to that which was learned in an ethical way and the use of which would not overly prejudice the interests of the parties involved supports the argument that protection of trade secrets as part of the law of unfair competition aims at safeguarding ethical behaviours in commerce.

Furthermore, it appears possible to include antitrust considerations in the assessment of fairness. Should limitation of use of particular information by a former employee be a result of abuse of dominant position by the ex-employer, e.g. by initiating abusive litigation,[140] this factor could be an argument for assessing the use of such information as fair (or, rather, the prohibition of the use of such information as unfair vis-à-vis the former employee). This would not only reflect the interest of the employee in pursuing a professional activity in competition with his former employer but at the same time would take into account the interests of consumers and other market participants in general, who would profit from enhanced competition.

Similarly, considerations of whether a particular behaviour encourages competition by innovation by introducing knowledge spill-overs may be taken into account. Even though it is not the goal of the UWG to protect small market players, a situation in which a former employee starting a competitive firm was not allowed to use particular information might reduce the number of competitors in an innovative market and thus harm the interests of consumers. Thus considering the effect of a certain behaviour on competition as such might be helpful in resolving the problem of the conflict of interests in some borderline scenarios. In this context the assessment must be nuanced as well. If the information relates to technology in an R&D-intensive industry, the argument that protection of trade secrets allows the accumulation of resources that could be invested in further R&D might weigh in favour of the employer. The argument relating to the positive effects of knowledge spill-overs might be more relevant in the fast-moving software area, in which accumulation of resources does not play an essential role in order to recoup investments.

Finally, the consideration of whether the employee was aware that particular information is the employer's trade secret may be helpful in the consideration of the balance of interests. Under the current definition of commercial and industrial secrets, the measures taken by the holder of

[140] For example, knowingly asserting rights in information which, in fact, is partially not a trade secret.

the information to maintain its secrecy are not a constitutive element. The assessment of whether particular data is a trade secret is based on ex post facto analysis of subjective factors such as will and interest in keeping the information secret, which may be implied. Introducing measures to maintain secrecy as part of the definition[141] would allow for a more objective assessment of whether particular information constitutes a trade secret. This would increase legal certainty for the recipients of information, in particular employees. However, apart from the objectification of the definition of a trade secret by including in it the assessment of measures taken to maintain secrecy, it is submitted that the ex-employee's awareness of the secret status of particular information and of the importance of this information for the employer's business, based on objective criteria, may be a factor in the assessment of fairness as well. The clear attitude of the employer supports his position in the balancing of interests. It will usually be expressed by way of a confidentiality agreement.[142]

Taking into account the convoluted legal argumentation surrounding the existence and scope of the post-employment use of information obtained during employment, there are arguments for resolving likely disputes by way of a contract and for denying any further-reaching duties of confidence.[143] However, even the general freedom of contract finds its limits where interests of employees come into play. The contractual duty of confidentiality as well as its boundaries are discussed in the subsequent chapter of this book.

B Post-Employment Implied Duty of Confidentiality in the United Kingdom

At first glance, the approach taken by the UK courts appears to combine the positions presented by the BGH and the BAG.

The employee's duties vis-à-vis the employer generally expire with the termination of the employment relationship. From that moment on, the ex-employee is free to undertake any competitive activity, including solicitation of the former employer's customers.[144] This general rule is

[141] As prescribed in Art 2(1)(c) TSD.

[142] Contractual tools for safeguarding secrecy of information as well as the conflict of interest in that context are analysed infra in Chapter 4, part II, point A.

[143] Fezer, 'Der Zivilrechtliche Geheimnisschutz im Wettbewerbsrecht' 104.

[144] *Helmet Integrated Systems Ltd v Tunnard* [2007] FSR (16) 437 (CA) 445–446; Gurry on Breach of Confidence para 12.150; Andrew Stewart, 'Confidential Information and Departing Employees: The Employer's Options' (1989) 11(3) *EIPR* 88, 89; John Hull, 'Making Preparations to Compete – A Note on Helmet Systems v Tunnard' (2009) 31 (12) *EIPR* 623.

limited in circumstances in which an implied duty of confidentiality may be found[145] because 'whilst the employment may terminate, the secrecy of the information does not terminate'.[146] The nature of this duty has so far not been clarified: there is case-law basing it on equity and on contract.[147] Currently the majority opinion seems to ascribe the post-employment obligation of confidence to an implied contract surviving the termination of the employment relationship.[148] However, in a more recent decision the UK Supreme Court acknowledged an equitable character of the post-employment duty of confidentiality.[149] Whatever the legal justification for its existence, the scope of the post-employment obligation of confidence under contract of employment does not differ from the one which would exist under equity.[150]

1 Existence of an Implied Duty

The existence of an implied duty is conditional on the ex-employee's knowledge of the confidential character of the information.[151] This may be a result of an explicit statement, or where the information is 'obviously confidential' judging by the way it was treated by the ex-employer, who e.g. restricted access to it or marked it as confidential. In particular, the employee's behaviour or his duties during employment (e.g. participation in meetings where strategic decisions were being discussed) may be an indication

[145] According to Kalbfus, the UK courts apply a similar approach to the theory of separability presented by BAG, see Kalbfus para 513.

[146] John Hull, *Commercial Secrecy: Law and Practice* (Sweet&Maxwell 1998) para 7.07.

[147] For a discussion of those developments, see Gurry on Breach of Confidence paras 12.152–12.153.

[148] *Faccenda Chicken v Fowler* [1987] 1 Ch 117 (CA) 135–136; Gurry on Breach of Confidence para 12.154. Hull explains that the post-employment implied duty of confidentiality stems from the implied contractual duty of fidelity and good faith, see Hull, *Commercial Secrecy: Law and Practice* para 7.07. See also AN Khan, 'Former Employee's Duty of Secrecy' (1988) 9(6) *Company Lawyer* 130, 130; Kenneth Miller, 'Implied Duties of Confidentiality in the Contract of Employment' (1986) 102 *LQR* 359, 361. For a theoretical analysis of contract as a source of post-employment duties, see Simon Honeyball and David Pearce, 'Contract, Employment and the Contract of Employment' (2006) 35(1) *ILJ* 30, 43–55.

[149] *Vestergaard Frandsen A/S & Ors v Bestnet Europe Ltd & Ors* [2013] UKSC 31 (UKSC) [23], [25]. Even though in the end the Court found no liability for breach of confidence on a different ground, namely that the recipient did not know that the information was confidential, ibid [45].

[150] Gurry on Breach of Confidence paras 12.157–12.158; Stewart, 'Confidential Information and Departing Employees: The Employer's Options' 88, 89 (arguing that the implied post-employment duty of confidentiality is in fact both contractual and equitable).

[151] Gurry on Breach of Confidence para 12.160. For an analysis of the notice of confidentiality test established on the basis of *Coco v Clark Ltd* [1968] FSR 415 (Ch), see Gurry on Breach of Confidence paras 7.36–7.45.

that he knew that the information was secret.[152] Thus, it is possible that even where the information was learned by the employee accidentally, he will be subject to an implied post-employment duty of confidentiality, if judging by the totality of circumstances the information has been obtained in circumstances imposing an obligation of confidence.[153] The nature of employment and the marking of the information as confidential by the employer were given by the Court of Appeal in *Faccenda Chicken* as factors for consideration in order to establish the scope of the post-employment duty of confidentiality.[154] It is suggested that these circumstances may be helpful to establish the existence of this duty as well.[155]

Generally, for the duty of confidentiality to apply, the knowledge of the secret status of the information must have existed both when the employee received the information and when he left the employment.[156] However, the UK Supreme Court expressed the opinion that even if at the time of receipt of the information the employee was not aware that it was confidential, the duty of confidentiality steps in when the recipient later finds out about the secrecy.[157] Even though the Court did not explicitly state this, it seems that the situation would be the same even if the notification took place after termination of the employment.

2 Scope of the Implied Duty

The leading case[158] on post-employment duty of confidentiality is *Faccenda Chicken.*[159] It concerned nine former employees of the plaintiff, who ia delivered fresh chickens in refrigerated vans and employed salesmen operating those vans in various geographical regions. The first defendant, who was the plaintiff's sales manager, established a competing business and left the company. Eight of the plaintiff's employees started working for him. The plaintiff alleged that the defendants used sales information, which covered names and addresses of the customers, routes of supply, customer's requirements, delivery times and prices

152 The assessment is made under consideration of both objective and subjective elements, see Gurry on Breach of Confidence paras 7.38–7.40.
153 *Coco v Clark Ltd* [1968] FSR 415 (Ch) 420–421. This is assessed from the perspective of a 'reasonable man standing in the shoes of the recipient of the information' (ibid 420–421). For the analysis of accidental acquisition of the information in general terms, see Gurry on Breach of Confidence paras 7.46–7.50.
154 *Faccenda Chicken v Fowler* [1987] 1 Ch 117 (CA) 137–138.
155 Gurry on Breach of Confidence para 12.165.
156 Gurry on Breach of Confidence para 12.164.
157 *Vestergaard Frandsen A/S & Ors v Bestnet Europe Ltd & Ors* [2013] UKSC 31 (UKSC) [25].
158 Gurry on Breach of Confidence para 12.166; Stewart, 'Confidential Information and Departing Employees: The Employer's Options' 88.
159 *Faccenda Chicken v Fowler* [1987] 1 Ch 117 (CA).

and that this use was in breach of an implied term of the contract of employment restricting the use of confidential information and trade secrets obtained during employment. In a first instance decision[160] Goulding J identified three classes of information which an employee may learn during employment: information which is public knowledge and may always be used, information which is confidential and which may not be used or disclosed during employment without breaching the duty of fidelity, but which may be used after termination of employment, unless there is an explicit contract prohibiting such use, and trade secrets which the employee may use or disclose neither during nor after employment. He considered that the sales information fell into second category and that in the absence of explicit regulation, the former employees were allowed to use it in competition with their ex-employer.

In its decision the Court of Appeal took a different view. It identified a special category of confidential information, which may not be used after termination of the employment by a departed employee. It described this type of information as 'trade secret' or 'highly confidential', equivalent to a trade secret.[161]

The Court differentiated between the implied duties owed to the employer during service and after its termination. It considered that obtaining the information fraudulently,[162] copying or memorising information (customer lists) during employment with the view to using it after termination of service, amounts to breach of the employee's implied duty of fidelity (good faith) towards the employer, even though solicitation of the ex-employer's customers is generally not restricted[163] and preparatory actions taken with the view to undertaking a competitive activity after termination of employment are generally considered legitimate.[164]

The post-employment duty of confidentiality was considered to be more restricted. Trade secrets and 'other information which is of a sufficiently high degree of confidentiality as to amount to a trade secret'

[160] *Faccenda Chicken v Fowler* [1984] ICR 589 (Ch) (Goulding J).

[161] *Faccenda Chicken v Fowler* [1987] 1 Ch 117 (CA) 137. Thus, the Court departed from referring to 'trade secrets' to designate the type of confidential information relating to business and trade, and, rather, used this term to describe a special category of information to which a particular duty of confidentiality is attached. This was criticised as 'altering the law', see Gurry on Breach of Confidence para 12.174.

[162] Hull, *Commercial Secrecy: Law and Practice* paras 7.56–7.57.

[163] *Faccenda Chicken v Fowler* [1987] 1 Ch 117 (CA) 136; *Roger Bullivant Ltd v Ellis* [1987] ICR 464 (CA) 474–475; Toulson/Phipps paras 14-018–14-019.

[164] *Crowson Fabrics Ltd v Rider* [2008] FSR 17 (Ch) 447–448, where it was held that copying the employer's documents containing pricing and discount information on suppliers and customers, in preparation of competitive activity after termination of service, was in breach of duties of fidelity and the fiduciary duty of a director.

may not be used after termination of the employment.[165] Secret processes of manufacture, chemical formulae, designs or methods of construction were given as examples. The Court considered further that certain kinds of information, which would have been considered as restricted from use by the employee during service, could be used after its termination.[166] As regards other information, the Court considered that the employee should be free to use it for himself or in service for a new employer.

Thus, information obtained during service may be classified into three categories:

a) Non-confidential information which the ex-employee is free to use.
b) Confidential information which the employee learned as part of his work experience and which became part of his skill and knowledge. The employee is not allowed to use it outside of service during employment, but may rely on such information after termination, also in competition with the former employer.
c) Trade secrets and highly confidential information, which the departed employee is not allowed to use, even if he remembers it.[167]

The decision whether particular information is to be considered a trade secret or highly confidential is made under consideration of all circumstances of the case. It is an objective assessment based on what a man of 'ordinary honesty and intelligence' would believe.[168] It includes, but is not limited to, the nature of the employment and whether the employee handled highly confidential information which would allow him to realise its sensitive nature, the nature of the information (as trade secret or 'of such a highly confidential nature as to require the same protection as a trade secret eo nomine'), whether the employer indicated to the employee the confidentiality of the information and whether the information can be easily isolated from the employee's general skill and knowledge.[169]

165 *Faccenda Chicken v Fowler* [1987] 1 Ch 117 (CA) 136.

166 *Faccenda Chicken v Fowler* [1987] 1 Ch 117 (CA) 136. In its argumentation the Court relied on *Printers & Finishers v Holloway* [1965] 1 WLR 1 (CA) 5–6, where a distinction was drawn between information which was disclosed by the employer in confidence and which was memorised by the employee on purpose, on the one hand, and information which the employee has learned as part of his employment duties and which may not be separated from his acquired skill and knowledge, on the other.

167 *Faccenda Chicken v Fowler* [1987] 1 Ch 117 (CA) 135–136; Gurry on Breach of Confidence paras 12.168–12.171.

168 *Printers & Finishers v Holloway* [1965] 1 WLR 1 (CA) 5; David Cran and Paul Joseph, 'Breach of Confidence Claim against Ex-employees and Consultants' (2011) 6 (10) *JIPLP* 688, 689.

169 *Faccenda Chicken v Fowler* [1987] 1 Ch 117 (CA) 137–138.

3 Trade Secrets and Highly Confidential Information under the Post-Employment Duty of Confidentiality – the Borderline Defined?

The classification presented in *Faccenda Chicken* has been criticised for not providing satisfactory guidance as to which information is to be regarded as a trade secret or highly confidential.[170] That is true, although taking into consideration the breadth of the concept of confidential information as well as the unlimited number of potential scenarios of its use, it may not be possible to provide a clear-cut differentiation between what the ex-employee may and may not use that would be applicable in any situation, regardless of the accompanying facts. Thus, like under German law, an overall assessment seems inevitable.[171]

The nature of the information in question appears to be the primary factor to consider: the information needs to be confidential (secret). Restricted circulation of the information within the company,[172] the fact that it is not known to outsiders, and is not readily available or easily reverse-engineered are factors speaking for confidentiality.[173] Furthermore, identification of the information as secret is to be considered, particularly since it is an element of the definition of confidential information under the law of the United Kingdom.[174] This requirement seems to have been developed in *Faccenda Chicken* as an aid to identify highly confidential information. The Court considered that it is relevant whether the employer 'impressed on the employee the confidentiality of the information'.[175] Even though merely informing an employee that an information is a trade secret does not make this information a trade secret, absent other factors, it points to the confidential nature of the particular data and may be helpful in the overall assessment.[176] Other practical steps taken by the employer to maintain the secrecy of the information, as well as the attitude of the employee (e.g. whether he resorted to surreptitious means to learn the information), may also

170 Gurry on Breach of Confidence para 12.175; Howe, Gupta, Wilkinson, Pritchard and Taylor in Goulding paras 4.31, 4.37.

171 'A multi-factored and contextual inquiry' as referred to by Howe, Gupta, Wilkinson, Pritchard and Taylor in Goulding para 4.46.

172 *Faccenda Chicken v Fowler* [1987] 1 Ch 117 (CA) 138; Hull, *Commercial Secrecy: Law and Practice* paras 7.71, 7.73.

173 Gurry on Breach of Confidence para 12.180. For a detailed analysis of the notion of secrecy under UK law, see supra Chapter 2, part I point C.

174 See supra Chapter 2, part I point C.3. Thus 'it will be unusual, though not impossible to envisage that business policy etc. will be protectable', Alexandra Kamerling and Christopher Goodwill, *Restrictive Covenants under Common and Competition Law* (Sweet&Maxwell 2010) 161.

175 *Faccenda Chicken v Fowler* [1987] 1 Ch 117 (CA) 138.

176 Gurry on Breach of Confidence para 12.197.

be helpful in determining the nature of the information and level of confidentiality.[177] Surreptitious acquisition of information (e.g. through theft, secret photography or hacking a computer) does not necessarily involve interference with property and therefore might not constitute a tort.[178] However, resorting to obtaining information in such a way may constitute an indication that the employee knew of the confidential character of the information and did not remember it in a natural way.[179]

Value of the information may be another factor. For certain information to be acknowledged as confidential under UK law it is not necessary that it is objectively valuable.[180] However, for the determination of information which is a trade secret or equivalent under the *Faccenda Chicken* definition it is proposed to include an objective assessment of value, i.e. to refer to the value of the information for competitors.[181] It is an interesting proposition, allowing for a more impartial assessment. Since the value of the information stems from the advantage that it gives its holder over his competitors, it seems more appropriate to assess it from their perspective, rather than from the standpoint of the business asserting rights to that information. The value of the information may stem e.g. from the 'proximity of the information to any core of secret process or know-how'.[182] However, the proposition that the older the information is, the less likely it is to retain the quality of being a valuable trade secret,[183] does not seem entirely convincing. Certain data, such as marketing plans, preparations for launch of a new product or technical data in IT may be short-lived, its value deteriorating rapidly with the passing of time. Nevertheless, often the value stems precisely from successful safeguarding of secrecy over a long period of time.[184]

[177] Gurry on Breach of Confidence paras 12.199–12.200.
[178] Gurry on Breach of Confidence para 7.53.
[179] Gurry on Breach of Confidence paras 7.70–7.71; Kamerling and Goodwill, *Restrictive Covenants under Common and Competition Law* 159.
[180] It seems however that some subjective value is taken into consideration. For an analysis of value as an element of the definition of trade secrets under UK law, see supra Chapter 2, part I point C.2.
[181] Gurry on Breach of Confidence para 12.181.
[182] Given as a separate factor for consideration by Howe, Gupta, Wilkinson, Pritchard and Taylor in Goulding para 4.46.
[183] Gurry on Breach of Confidence para 12.181.
[184] As the 'classic' example of the Coca-Cola formula shows. The recipe for Coca-Cola is still given as an example of a successfully guarded trade secret, even though some question secrecy of the composition and argue that in this case the value stems rather from a successful marketing strategy and branding, see Mark Pendergrast, *For God, Country & Coca-Cola: The Definitive History of the Great American Soft Drink and the Company That Makes It* (3rd edn, Basis Books 2013) 493.

Another way to consider the value of information may be to limit highly confidential information (trade secrets) to 'information which, if disclosed to a competitor, would be liable to cause real (or significant) harm to the owner of the secret'.[185] This is certainly true, however this test has rightly been criticised as over-inclusive as there are kinds of information which the employee might have learned during employment and the disclosure of which would cause harm to the employer, but which may not be sufficiently 'highly confidential' to be equated with trade secrets.[186] Thus, reliance solely on such a test might overly prejudice the interests of employees. However, it is suggested that the consideration of possible harm may be included as one of the factors in the assessment.[187]

The proposal to include the impact that disclosure of the information could have on the reputation of the former employer[188] as a factor for determination of highly confidential information seems to be a result of the broad understanding of the notion of confidential information under UK law, which includes also private information, not necessarily having commercial value. The examples given include the taking of personal data of patients.[189] The disclosure of such information is likely to damage the reputation of its holder, which may well have a commercial dimension in terms of loss of clients or contractors and thus influence the position of the ex-employer in the market.

The effort and cost of developing particular information, such as time and costs of research and development, costs of licensing of the confidential information from third parties or costs and effort in assembling commercial information, indicate a high level of confidentiality. On the other hand, information which is not generally known, but which is a 'by-product of doing business', such as information relating to sources of supply, may be confidential but not necessarily highly confidential or a trade secret.[190] The cost of developing the information is sometimes given as a factor in considering whether particular information was confidential in the first place. While the cost spent on the production of the information should not be decisive for protecting it at all,[191] it may be helpful as one of the considerations in an overall assessment of the narrow category of highly confidential data. Nevertheless, this factor should be applied

[185] *Lansing Linde v Kerr* [1991] 1 WLR 251, (CA) 260.

[186] Howe, Gupta, Wilkinson, Pritchard and Taylor in Goulding para 4.43.

[187] Stanley 81–82. It is nevertheless submitted that this factor should be applied with caution. 'Harm', like value, should be assessed objectively, i.e. from the perspective of damage to the ex-employer's competitive position in the case of use of the highly confidential information by a departed employee.

[188] Gurry on Breach of Confidence para 12.182.

[189] Ibid.

[190] Ibid para 12. 183.

[191] As explained in Quinto/Singer 16.

carefully in order to avoid overprotection of employers and thus it is proposed to generally limit this consideration to R&D costs in technical fields.

Difficulty of duplication of the information is another factor pointing to a high level of secrecy.[192] Even if information is confidential, if obtaining it through independent research is relatively easy, it should not be elevated to the category of trade secrets which the ex-employee is not allowed to use even if he learned it as part of his work experience. Such information must be defined narrowly. Recognition of easily duplicable data as highly confidential might lead to appropriation of facts and routine information which the employee has learned during service.

The above factors help to establish the 'level' of secrecy of the information and may generally be seen as an application of a higher threshold of the definition of confidential information under UK law. According to *Faccenda Chicken* it is also important to assess whether the information in question can easily be isolated from the general skill and knowledge[193] which the employee is free to use.[194] While the decision did not consider this factor as conclusive,[195] both courts and commentators seem to ascribe a central role to it.[196]

The reason for the centrality of the distinction between confidential information sensu stricto and the employee's skill and knowledge is public policy and in particular the need to ensure the employee's freedom to choose his occupation and to compete with the ex-employer.[197] The core question in the assessment is therefore whether preventing the ex-employee from the use of particular information which he learned during employment would impose an unreasonable restriction on his ability to find and carry out work in the area of industry or trade in which he is skilled.[198] And '[w]here the employer's right to restrain misuse of

[192] Gurry on Breach of Confidence para 12.184.

[193] Also referred to as the employee's 'subjective knowledge', 'know-how' or 'stock of knowledge', see Stewart, 'Confidential Information and Departing Employees: The Employer's Options' 88, 91.

[194] *Faccenda Chicken v Fowler* [1987] 1 Ch 117 (CA) 138.

[195] Ibid.

[196] *Lancashire Fires Ltd v SA Lyons & Comp Ltd and Others* [1996] FSR 629 (CA) 699; *Ocular Sciences Ltd v Aspect Vision Care Ltd* [1997] RPC 289 (EWHC) 370–371; Toulson/Phipps para 14-016; Stanley 81–82; Hull, *Commercial Secrecy: Law and Practice* para 7.03. For a critical appraisal of the increasing role of the 'separability' criterion, see Gurry on Breach of Confidence paras 12.193–12.194.

[197] Recognised e.g. in *Herbert Morris Ltd v Saxelby* [1916] 1 AC 688 (HL) 698–699 (Lord Atkinson).

[198] Toulson/Phipps para 14-016. The employee's skill and knowledge may in this context be defined as 'confidential information which (...) an employee acquires in order to be able to pursue a particular trade, calling or profession and which is so inseparable from (his) general stock of knowledge that to restrain its use would necessarily be to prevent the employee from carrying on that trade at all', see Stewart, 'Confidential Information and Departing Employees: The Employer's Options' 88, 91.

his confidential information collides with the public policy, it is the latter which prevails'.[199]

There have been various attempts at identifying the borderline between a trade secret which should remain with the employer and the skill and knowledge which the employee acquired through experience and which he should be free to rely on in his future professional activities. Some courts use a 'metaphor of property',[200] arguing that an employer's trade secret is something which 'a man of ordinary honesty and intelligence would recognise to be the property of his old employer and not his own'.[201] Another proposal is to make a distinction between what is 'objective' knowledge belonging to the ex-employer and what is 'subjective' and therefore necessary for the former employee to use.[202] These standards have been criticised.[203] In particular it is suggested that their application might suppress the mobility of employees in innovative industries. Instead, it is proposed to determine the borderline in some cases by an assessment of whether the information in question was obtained through employment for a particular employer, or whether it would have been learned through working for any employer in the particular area of trade.[204] It may also be helpful to consider whether the ex-employee may realistically be expected to refrain from using the information (whether consciously or unconsciously).[205]

Whether the information is embodied in a document is also given as a factor aiding the distinction, since in such a case it is more likely to be 'separable' from the skill and knowledge retained in the employee's memory.[206] On the other hand, the fact that the ex-employee did not take any documents with him does not enable him to use all the information he might remember, such as a chemical formula.[207] Even if information can

199 *Ocular Sciences Ltd v Aspect Vision Care Ltd* [1997] RPC 289 (EWHC) 370–371. See also Toulson/Phipps para 14-017.

200 Gurry on Breach of Confidence para 12.187.

201 *Printers & Finishers v Holloway* [1965] 1 WLR 1 (CA) 5. This standard has been referred to as 'the "honesty" test' by Howe, Gupta, Wilkinson, Pritchard and Taylor in Goulding para 4.40.

202 *Herbert Morris Ltd v Saxelby* [1916] 1 AC 688 (HL) 714 (Lord Shaw of Dunfermline); Hull, *Commercial Secrecy: Law and Practice* paras 7.39–7.42; Gurry on Breach of Confidence paras 12.63–12.64.

203 Howe, Gupta, Wilkinson, Pritchard and Taylor in Goulding paras 4.39–4.41; Hull, *Commercial Secrecy: Law and Practice* para 7.43.

204 Gurry on Breach of Confidence para 12.187, calling for a cautious application of such an assessment.

205 Howe, Gupta, Wilkinson, Pritchard and Taylor in Goulding para 4.46; Stanley 82; Stewart, 'Confidential Information and Departing Employees: The Employer's Options' 88, 91.

206 Gurry on Breach of Confidence para 12.188.

207 *Printers & Finishers v Holloway* [1965] 1 WLR 1 (CA) 5.

be memorised it does not automatically mean that it turns into the employee's skill and knowledge or stops being confidential.[208]

The way the information was learned by the employee may also be considered when distinguishing skill and knowledge from trade secrets. The notion of skill and experience relates to what has been inevitably learned in the course of service for the former employer. Thus, data which has been acquired outside the exercising of those duties, e.g. by interviewing other employees or memorising documents, may not be regarded as the employee's skill and knowledge. On the other hand, this does not automatically qualify it as a trade secret of the employer either, because separability of trade secrets from skill and knowledge is just one of the factors in the overall assessment of the post-employment duty of confidentiality.[209]

How and by whom the information was obtained or derived is a further factor put forward for consideration. It is proposed that the fact that it was the employee himself who developed the information, rather than the employer who communicated it to the employee, indicates that the information may belong to the employee's stock of knowledge.[210] Employee inventions are an exception. Even though, unlike under German law, no explicit duty of confidentiality is provided for the former employees, the implied duty of confidentiality applies. Pursuant to Section 39(1) Patents Act 1977, employee inventions[211] belong to the employer. Thus, it seems that for employee inventions a strict implied duty of confidentiality will apply after termination of service. Based on the definition provided in Patents Act 1977, such inventions may be separated from the employee's skill and knowledge. This is supported by the rule of prevalence of the duty of confidentiality when interpreting agreements relating to employee

[208] *Force India Formula One Team Ltd v Aerolab Srl & Another* [2013] EWCA Civ 780 (EWCA) [67] (Lewison J). This case is not, strictly speaking, a post-employment case. The plaintiff and the defendant were companies bound by a contract relating to development of Formula 1 racing cars. One of the issues to be decided was whether the details of the plaintiff's confidential CAD drawings of the car parts provided to the defendant as part of their co-operation could have become part of the skill and knowledge of the defendant's employees who had access to them as part of their work duties. Lewison J stressed the fact that even if some pieces of information could have been memorised, they were identifiable and traceable to the plaintiff. This made them independent of the employee's skill and knowledge.

[209] Gurry on Breach of Confidence para 12.192.

[210] Hull, *Commercial Secrecy: Law and Practice* para 7.79; Howe, Gupta, Wilkinson, Pritchard and Taylor in Goulding para 4.46.

[211] Inventions made by employees in the course of their normal duties or in the course of other duties specifically assigned to them, if the invention resulted from the carrying out of these duties, as well as inventions made in the course of the employees' duties when they had an obligation to further the interests of the employer's undertaking.

inventions (Section 42(3) Patents Act 1977). Moreover, it has been recognised that up to the filing of the patent application there exists an implied obligation of confidentiality with regard to the subject-matter of that application.[212]

In *Faccenda Chicken* the first factor on the non-exhaustive list to be considered for determining information which is trade secret or highly confidential was the nature of the employment.[213] Accordingly, employees who routinely handled confidential material are expected to appreciate its character and refrain from its use after termination of service. Thus, a court can assume that a regular employee would not learn any highly confidential information in the course of his employment.[214] On the other hand, employees occupying positions of trust, such as company directors,[215] are more likely to learn highly confidential information decisive for their employer's competitive position. Therefore the courts would be more willing to restrain them from using that information after termination of their service if it would be detrimental to their ex-employer's interests.[216] The post-employment implied duty of confidentiality was analysed also with regard to solicitors and patent attorneys who were employed. Their position while in service exposes them to highly confidential information.[217]

It is generally recognised that a departed employee may rely on his knowledge of the former employer's clients (their identity, preferences etc.) in competition with the ex-employer after termination of service. It is suggested that this is even more so in situations in which the ex-employee was responsible for contacts with those clients on behalf of the employer or where he attracted them.[218]

212 *Threeway Pressings Ltd* [2012] BL O/124/12 (UKIPO).
213 *Faccenda Chicken v Fowler* [1987] 1 Ch 117 (CA) 137.
214 Gurry on Breach of Confidence para 12.196.
215 The relationship between the company directors and the company is of a fiduciary character. Thus, the directors owe an obligation of loyalty towards their employer. While a fiduciary duty is independent of a duty of confidentiality (Linda Clarke, 'Breach of Confidence and the Employment Relationship' (2002) 31(4) *ILJ* 353, 356–358), the fiduciary relationship might be a factor pointing to the scope of data that the employee learned during service and to the particular importance of that data.
216 For example, in a situation where a former employee relied on the knowledge, obtained during performance of his duties as director, that a prior patent application is potentially prejudicial to the employer's patent application, in order to acquire the prior application after termination of the employment. This has been recognised in *Cranleigh Precision Engineering Ltd v Bryant and Another* [1965] 1 WLR 1293 (QB) 1310–1311, 1319. See also Hull, *Commercial Secrecy: Law and Practice* paras 7.63–7.65.
217 *Generics (UK) Ltd v Yeda Research and Development Co Ltd* [2012] EWCA Civ 726 (EWCA) [29] (Jacob J).
218 Hull, *Commercial Secrecy: Law and Practice* para 7.49.

Further factors have been considered to be helpful to determine the highly confidential information and trade secrets which may not be used by the employee after termination of service. In a situation in which the information related to a technical process and where the former employer neither covered the relevant information by a non-competition agreement nor applied for a patent, the Court of Appeal held that the courts should not be eager to qualify such information as subject to the implied duty, since this would prejudice the interests of the employee by exposing him to expensive and time-consuming litigation.[219]

In *Faccenda Chicken* the Court explicitly left open the question of 'whether additional protection should be afforded to an employer where the former employee is not seeking to earn his living by making use of the body of skill, knowledge and experience which he has acquired in the course of his career, but is merely selling to a third party information which he acquired in confidence in the course of his former employment'.[220] The balance of interests might be different in a situation in which the former employee needs to rely on the information in subsequent professional activity, whether independent or for the ex-employer's competitor, or where the disclosure would occur for other purposes.[221] Kamerling and Goodwill argue that there should be no difference as to whether the ex-employee uses the information in his own or his new employer's competitive activity or whether he sells the information to a third party. If the information has become part of the ex-employee's skill and knowledge, its use in any of these ways is arguably for the purpose of 'earning his living in the area in which he has the greatest experience'.[222] It is submitted that considering the justification for the distinction between the information which may be used and that which may not, which is to ensure the freedom of the former employee to remain active in the area of his expertise, the decisive factor should be whether the use of the particular information would further such an activity. This seems doubtful where the information would be used as a mere commodity. In a situation in which the former employee simply sells the information to a third party, he can hardly be considered to be competing with his former employer (it will be the

[219] This is because claims to confidential information 'are easily made but expensive and time-consuming to refute', *AT Poeton (Gloucester Plating) Ltd and Another v Horton and Another* [2000] ICR 1208 (CA) 1218–1219. How the information has been protected by the employer is also given as a factor by Howe, Gupta, Wilkinson, Pritchard and Taylor in Goulding para 4.46.

[220] *Faccenda Chicken v Fowler* [1987] 1 Ch 117 (CA) 138–139.

[221] As suggested in Toulson/Phipps para 14-024. Toulson and Phipps do not offer a conclusive opinion on that matter.

[222] Kamerling and Goodwill, *Restrictive Covenants under Common and Competition Law* 153.

purchaser who would possibly compete). On the other hand, use of the information in the former employee's activity independently or for a third party is to be seen as satisfying the policy consideration.

Taking into account that the implied duty of confidentiality with regard to information considered a trade secret or equivalent may have as an effect a limitation of the competitive activity of an employee without a contractual agreement and for an unlimited period of time, it is suggested to give it a narrow construction.[223] Where the employee did not breach his duty of fidelity while employed by obtaining the information in a reprehensible manner, the acquisition of the information will usually be regarded as inevitable and thus it will be fairly easy to convince the court that the information is inseparable from the ex-employee's skill and knowledge, resulting in him being allowed to use it in competition with his ex-employer.[224] Further-reaching limitations of the use of confidential information by employees after termination of their service may be imposed on a contractual basis.[225]

4 Duration of the Post-Employment Duty

As a result of the inherent perishability of trade secrets, the post-employment implied duty of confidentiality generally lasts only as long as the information remains secret.[226]

Thus, once the information is in the public domain so that it ceases to be confidential, the former employee may use it like anyone else.[227] Some authors argue that even in such circumstances the obligation of confidentiality may remain on the part of the former employee in order to mitigate the competitive head start which he has obtained by use of the information before other competitors had access to it,[228] but the majority opinion seems to be that even in such circumstances, a head start (springboard) injunction should terminate when the information enters the public domain.[229]

[223] Howe, Gupta, Wilkinson, Pritchard and Taylor in Goulding para 4.50; Brian Turner and Ian Purvis, 'More Chicken Pieces' (1989) 11(1) *EIPR* 3, 6.

[224] Stewart, 'Confidential Information and Departing Employees: The Employer's Options' 88, 92. See also Kamerling and Goodwill, *Restrictive Covenants under Common and Competition Law* 159.

[225] Discussed infra in Chapter 4 part II point B.

[226] In *Balston Ltd v Headline Filters Ltd* [1987] FSR 330 (Ch) 348 the Court expressed the opinion that the implied obligation of confidentiality is unlimited in time. However, apart from circumstances giving rise to springboard doctrine, it is hard to conceive of a duty of confidentiality covering information which is not confidential (any more).

[227] Gurry on Breach of Confidence para 14.38; Alex Batteson, 'Gaining Confidence in the Law of Confidence' (2006) 1(11) *JIPLP* 714, 715.

[228] Stewart, 'Confidential Information and Departing Employees: The Employer's Options' 88, 92.

[229] Gurry on Breach of Confidence para 14.38; Stanley 41 (inconclusive); Batteson, 'Gaining Confidence in the Law of Confidence' 714, 715.

Thus, the exact duration of the duty of confidentiality is determined on a case-by-case basis, usually when the court decides to grant a final injunction. The considerations made at this point are discussed infra.[230]

5 Summary: Balance between the Interests of the Ex-Employers and Their Former Employees with Regard to Use of Information Learned During Service

The factors allowing for the determination of highly confidential information and trade secrets which the ex-employee is under an implied duty not to use and disclose may be divided into those which relate to the determination of the confidentiality of the information; those which allow for the distinction between the employer's trade secrets and the employee's skill and knowledge; and other factors.

Any information covered by the duty of confidentiality must have the quality of confidence. However the implied post-employment duty relates only to information which is highly confidential. This is judged under consideration of the factors analysed supra.[231] In particular, the high level of confidentiality of the information is indicated by how it was treated by the ex-employer and by the importance of that information for his competitive position (value assessed objectively). The use or disclosure of highly confidential information would furthermore be more likely to negatively impact the ex-employer's commercial position or reputation. The more time and effort was spent on developing the information and the more difficult it is to duplicate the information without recourse to surreptitious means, the higher the level of its confidentiality. Despite the fact that these factors are helpful in determining the confidentiality of any information, particularly in a business setting, it is submitted that they need to be subject to a strict evaluation. This is because the implied duty attaches not to all confidential information but only to information which is highly confidential. Additional aspects such as the nature of the employment which requires handling of confidential information and whether the information was covered by an application for a patent or by a restrictive covenant[232] (thus stressing the value that the employer ascribes to that information) may be included in the assessment as well.

[230] Chapter 5 part II point B.3 and part III point B.3.

[231] Chapter 2 part I, point C.

[232] When a restrictive covenant cannot be enforced (e.g. as a result of repudiatory breach of contract by the employer, see Clarke, 'Breach of Confidence and the Employment Relationship' 353, 355), the implied duties remain applicable. Thus in such circumstances a restrictive covenant, rather than stipulating the extent of the duty of confidentiality, will be considered as an indication of the level of confidentiality ascribed to that information by the former employer.

The increasingly important group of considerations helping to determine the scope of the post-employment implied duty of confidentiality relates to the distinction between the information which became part of the former employee's skill and knowledge and information which may be separated and thus should remain with the employer. The various methods used in order to distinguish the information include the assessment from a standpoint of an 'honest man' and parallels to property. Information, which is particular to the ex-employer's business rather than to the entire trade or industry, is more likely to be considered separable from the employee's skill and knowledge. On the other hand, where the former employee may not realistically be expected to refrain from the use of the information, because it is not possible to dissect it in his mind from other information which he is free to use, the separability argument weighs in favour of considering the data as part of skill and knowledge. The fact that it was the employee who developed the information may indicate that he will not be able to distinguish it from his general skill and knowledge. Employee inventions are an exception in that respect since they may be defined. Data learned outside of the exercise of the employment duties may hardly be considered as general skill and knowledge acquired in the course of service for a particular employer. Incorporation of the data in a document also generally points to separability. Whether the information in question is to be used in furtherance of the ex-employee's professional career in the same field of trade or industry or sold as a commodity is another issue for consideration. Nevertheless it is proposed that only where such information is used in furtherance of the professional activity of the ex-employee should this weigh in his favour.

This list of factors is not conclusive and the assessment of the existence of the implied duty must be made under consideration of all the circumstances of a particular case. For this reason it is also neither possible nor desirable to establish a hierarchical relationship between those factors. In particular, despite the growing importance of the test on separability between the employee's skill and knowledge and the employer's trade secrets,[233] there is no ground for limiting the considerations only to this test. Trade secrets and highly confidential information to which the implied duty of confidentiality relates are a subcategory of confidential information which employees learn during employment. Thus, the first group of factors is not to be seen as used only for determining whether

[233] van Caenegem refers to a 'rule of thumb' applied by some courts, under which if the employer is not able to show that the information was learned by the employee deliberately and surreptitiously, the continued use of such information is likely to be accepted, William van Caenegem, *Trade Secrets and Intellectual Property. Breach of Confidence, Misappropriation and Unfair Competition* (1st edn, Kluwer Law International 2014) 200.

the information is confidential or not. The information in question must be confidential. The assessment made when determining the implied duty boils down to a consideration of whether the information has such a high level of confidentiality as to deny its use to the former employee. The separability of the information from the ex-employee's general stock of knowledge is important, albeit one of many factors to be considered. Thus, it may be possible that an employee will be denied the use of particular information even if it is so imprinted in his memory as to become an element of his general professional experience (e.g. highly confidential information relating to a particular chemical process used by the employer). Conversely, it is possible that a particular information is not covered by the implied duty even though it may be separated from the former employee's skill and knowledge (e.g. information relating to a technical process used by the ex-employer, which he did not treat as confidential).

As explained above, the reason for the creation of a subcategory of confidential information (highly confidential information and trade secrets) covered by the implied post-employment duty of confidentiality is the consideration that under certain circumstances the employer's interest in the preservation of his competitive position must prevail over the interest of the ex-employee in relying on the use, in his further professional activity, of the information he had learned during his career.

Thus, finding an equilibrium between those conflicting interests plays an important role in the assessment of the scope of post-employment duties under the law of the United Kingdom.

The primary interests under consideration are the private interests of the employer and the former employee. It is deemed unfair to deny former employees the right to use information which they need to rely on in order to continue their professional career. It is also considered unfair and often impossible to expect employees to be able to separate certain confidential information from their skill and knowledge. On the other hand, allowing the use of information of a highly confidential nature outside the ex-employer's business might threaten his competitive position. The *Faccenda Chicken* factors offer important guidelines for determining the balance between conflicting interests. The inclusion of those considerations as well as a general denial of use of information which has been obtained surreptitiously indicate the presence of considerations relating to the role that the protection of trade secrets plays in safeguarding ethical behaviours in trade.

Despite the centrality of the balancing of private interests, the courts seem to acknowledge that the interests of the ex-employer and of the ex-employee are in fact a reflection of the public interest. In particular it has been ruled that when enforcing implied confidentiality obligations against former employees the courts should recognise the need to ensure fulfilment of contractual obligations on the one hand, and on the other hand the need to respect the right and interests of employees to choose their trade and profession. This would at the same time 'promote the public interest by better use of servants' personal aptitudes, experience and skill'.[234] The Court went on to state that generally the mobility of employees and their changing of employment is a result of 'a healthy bargaining process' between employees and those wanting to use their services, which operates to the 'benefit of the employees and of the public, but in the short term, naturally to the disadvantage of the employer who loses in the competitive bargaining process'.[235] This disadvantage seems to be accepted in view of the benefits to the employees and the public in general.

The importance that the courts ascribe to the ability of former employees to advance their careers has been recognised also in the case of employees often exposed to highly confidential information during service. In *Generics (UK) Ltd v Yeda Research and Development Co Ltd*, Ward LJ was of the opinion that applying strict rules regarding the duty to avoid conflict of interests[236] to patent attorneys and solicitors in employment is not justified. Thus, the public interest in the administration of justice was not seen as prevailing over the ex-employee's interest in choosing his profession.[237] Consequently, the general rule specified in *Faccenda Chicken* remains applicable also to this category of employees.

The importance of placing the assessment of the duty of confidentiality in a broader context of policy considerations has been made clear by the UK Supreme Court, which explained that '(p)articularly in a modern economy, the law has to maintain a realistic and fair balance between (i) effectively protecting trade secrets (...) and (ii) not unreasonably inhibiting competition in the market place. The importance to the economic prosperity of the country of research and development in the commercial world is self-evident, and the protection of intellectual property, including trade secrets, is one of the vital contributions of the law to that end. On the other hand, the

[234] *GD Searle & Co Ltd v Celltech Ltd and Others* [1982] FSR 92 (CA) 99 (Cumming-Bruce LJ).

[235] *GD Searle & Co Ltd v Celltech Ltd and Others* [1982] FSR 92 (CA) 101 (Cumming-Bruce LJ).

[236] As developed in *Prince Jefri Bolkiah v KPMG* [1999] 2 AC 222 (HL) 235–236.

[237] *Generics (UK) Ltd v Yeda Research and Development Co Ltd* [2012] EWCA Civ 726 (EWCA) [105–106] (Ward LJ). Consequently, despite the proposition of Jacob J (ibid [19]–[39]) the obligation to avoid any risk of disclosure of confidential information of the former client, remains applicable only to external counsel under *Prince Jefri Bolkiah v KPMG* [1999] 2 AC 222 (HL).

law should not discourage former employees from benefitting society and advancing themselves by imposing unfair potential difficulties on their honest attempts to compete with their former employers'.[238]

In the same vein, it is proposed to approach the guidance provided in *Faccenda Chicken* from the perspective of 'information policy', i.e. to consider whether the employer would have been ready to share the information with the employee in the absence of its protection as a trade secret or highly confidential. With this consideration in mind, a higher level of protection should be granted to information which would not have been generated or disclosed in the absence of the implied duty of confidentiality, as it increases efficiency in the working environment. On the other hand, information which would have been shared or disclosed anyway should not be overprotected by qualifying it as a trade secret or highly confidential, as its use by the departed employees increases spill-over innovation.[239] It is suggested here that this argumentation may also be applied with regard to information which is a 'by-product' of any business activity, such as customer lists or some marketing plans. It seems that from the perspective of 'information policy' this data is less likely to qualify as highly confidential.

The analysis presented in this part of this book shows that the approach of UK law to the use by departed employees of confidential information obtained during employment is flexible. In particular, it includes considerations relating to balancing the interests of the ex-employer and the ex-employee. The role which the protection of trade secrets plays in incentivising innovation, spill-overs and entrepreneurship as well as commercial ethics has been recognised in both the case-law and the legal literature, although it does not seem to be routinely considered in practice.

The assessment of the use of particular information from the perspective of competition law does not seem to take place. The core of the analysis under the law of the United Kingdom lies in the determination of whether information is highly confidential. Unlike German law, which approaches the issue from the perspective of fairness of the use of trade secrets after termination of employment, UK law concentrates on the nature of the information. Thus, it seems that the effect on competition that the enforcement of particular information might have cannot be included when assessing the implied duty. Whether it can be included when assessing the enforceability of contractual obligations is considered below.[240]

[238] *Vestergaard Frandsen A/S & Ors v Bestnet Europe Ltd & Ors* [2013] UKSC 31 (UKSC) [44] (Lord Neuberger).
[239] Gurry on Breach of Confidence para 12.178.
[240] See Chapter 4 part II, point B.2–3.

Some authors argue that the public interest on a more general level may also be included in the balancing of interests. According to Khan, the fact that it is in the public interest to publish a particular piece of information may be a defence against an action for breach of confidence.[241] It seems however that such a defence would apply only in situations where the public interest at stake lies in the preservation of public order, i.e. where health, safety[242] or national security is at stake. It seems therefore that the considerations of public interest in this sense would be more pertinent in situations of whistle-blowers or confidential information of a private nature, and not in the context of employee mobility discussed here.

C Post-Employment Implied Duty of Confidentiality in the United States

In the United States, the protection of trade secrets is governed by state laws, which are to a large extent harmonised under the UTSA and by federal law which recently introduced an action for misappropriation of trade secrets.[243]

Similarly as in Germany and in the United Kingdom, US law recognises the general freedom of copying and the general freedom of the former employees to compete with their employer.[244] However, US law seems to be taking a different methodological approach in the determination of the extent to which that freedom may be limited by a duty of the former employee to preserve the confidentiality of information obtained during service. In the other jurisdictions analysed the distinction between the employer's secrets and the former employee's general skill and knowledge constitutes one of the considerations in the determination of the scope of information which the departed employee may use. In the United States it is this distinction itself which is decisive.[245] The assessment of whether a particular piece of information qualifies as a trade secret or belongs to the employee's general experience is made under consideration of all the circumstances of the case. As part of that assessment, the impact that defining a particular information as trade secret might have on the interests of the

[241] Khan, 'Former Employee's Duty of Secrecy' 130,132.

[242] *Schering Chemicals Ltd v Falkman Ltd and Others* [1982] QB 1 (CA) 27.

[243] Thus, the case-law presented here stems mostly from state courts. However, in cases between citizens of various states and where the claim value exceeds $75000, the federal district courts have had jurisdiction even before introduction of the DTSA, see 28 US Code S 1332.

[244] *Ed Nowogroski Insurance Inc v Michael Rucker et al* 137 Wash 2d 427 (Washington Supr Ct 1999); Milgrim on Trade Secrets vol 1A 5-21 – 5-33; Peterson 1–66.

[245] In this sense, the US approach recalls the theory of separability represented by the BAG in Germany, as well as the separability criterion used by the UK courts to determine highly confidential information and trade secrets, see Kalbfus para 513.

employer, of the employee, as well as on the public interest is taken into consideration. Thus, it appears that the balancing of private and public interests plays an important role in the determination of what a trade secret is in the context of employee mobility in the United States.

Under the UTSA, misappropriation of a trade secret includes its disclosure or use without express or implied consent of its holder by a person who at the time of disclosure or use knew or had reason to know that this knowledge of the trade secret was acquired under circumstances giving rise to a duty to maintain its secrecy or by a person who, before a material change of his position, knew or had reason to know that it was a trade secret and that knowledge of it had been acquired by accident or mistake.[246] This applies also under the DTSA.[247]

1 Existence of the Duty Not to Use or Disclose Trade Secrets

Employment generally gives rise to a duty to maintain secrecy of the information obtained in the course of that relationship, both during it and after its termination.[248] This duty encompasses trade secrets as well as confidential information, acquired in the course of service but which does not rise to the level of a trade secret and does not have a competitive value.[249] While such confidential information is often valuable also in an economic sense (e.g. information about personal preferences may be useful for marketing purposes), it seems that the notion of confidential information relates rather to personal and sensitive data which is not necessary for the employee to use for competitive purposes.[250]

The existence of a duty of confidentiality with regard to particular information may be inferred from the measures that the former employer took in order to maintain the secrecy of that information,[251] such as marking

[246] S 1(2)(ii)(B)(II) and (C) UTSA. The UTSA broadened the understanding of what a trade secret is, see Miles J Feldman, 'Towards a Clearer Standard of Protectable Information: Trade Secrets and the Employment Relationship' (1994) 9 *HTLJ* 151, 154 and Chapter 2, part I, point D.

[247] 18 US Code §1839(5) as amended by the DTSA.

[248] *Ed Nowogroski Insurance Inc v Michael Rucker et al* 137 Wash 2d 427 (Washington Supr Ct 1999); S 8.05 comment c Restatement (Third) of Agency; Milgrim on Trade Secrets vol 1A 5-17; Peterson 7-6.

[249] Such as information about the principal's health, life history or personal preferences, S 8.05 comment c Restatement (Third) of Agency.

[250] The distinction, if any, between trade secrets and confidential information in the context of the relationship between the employer and his former employee is furthermore complicated by the fact that the term 'confidential information' is often used as a synonym for trade secrets, see e.g. *Ed Nowogroski Insurance Inc v Michael Rucker et al* 137 Wash 2d 427 (Washington Supr Ct 1999) and the case-law cited therein.

[251] Feldman, 'Towards a Clearer Standard of Protectable Information: Trade Secrets and the Employment Relationship' 151, 155. The importance of delineating trade secrets from other information is also stressed, see Letty S Friesen, 'Distinguishing between an Employee's General Knowledge and Trade Secrets' (1994) 23 *Colo Law* 2123.

documents as confidential or limiting access to a research area. The existence of that duty may also be derived from the employee's experience and scope of employment duties which enabled him to appreciate the confidentiality attached to certain information[252] and from the context in which the information was disclosed to the employee.[253] Thus, the scope of the duty of confidentiality may depend on the position of the employee in his former employer's company. Consequently, a broader duty attaches to employees who held higher positions.[254] The consideration contained in the employment agreement, in particular the remuneration and other benefits that the employee is entitled to during employment (e.g. social security or medical insurance) plays an important role in the assessment of the scope of duties of a particular employee.[255] The higher the level of consideration, the broader the scope of the duty to maintain secrecy, as it can be said that the employee has been rewarded for restricting the use of the data learned during employment.

The circumstances giving rise to the duty to maintain secrecy may include not only acquisition of the information in the course of performance of the employment duties, but also accidental acquisition if the employee knew or had reasons to know that the information was a trade secret.[256]

No duty of confidentiality may arise with regard to information which is not a trade secret. Accordingly, the implied duty does not attach to the former employee's skill and knowledge, even if it was acquired during service for a particular employer.[257]

2 Scope of the Duty to Maintain Secrecy: The Employer's Trade Secret

The employee is free to use the general knowledge he has learned during service, but must refrain from using the employer's trade secrets and confidential information.[258]

252 Milgrim on Trade Secrets vol 1A 5-19.
253 Peterson 7-15.
254 This includes fiduciary duties of key personnel and officers, such as company directors or accountants, see Milgrim on Trade Secrets vol 1A 5-13.
255 Milgrim on Trade Secrets vol 1A 5-13 – 5-14.1.
256 S 1(2)(ii)(C) UTSA.
257 *SI Handling Systems v Heisley* 753 F 2d 1244, 1267 (3rd Cir 1985); Edmund W Kitch, 'The Expansion of Trade Secrecy Protection and the Mobility of Management Employees: a New Problem for the Law' (1996) 47 *S C L Rev* 659, 671.
258 Milgrim on Trade Secrets vol 1A 5-21; Peterson 7-4, 7-6 – 7-9; William G Porter II and Michael Griffaton, 'Identifying and Protecting Employers' Interests in Trade Secrets and Proprietary Information' (2001) 68 *Def Couns J* 439, 443; Feldman, 'Towards a Clearer Standard of Protectable Information: Trade Secrets and the Employment Relationship' 151, 154.

Neither the Restatement of Torts nor the UTSA or DTSA explain the difference between these two categories of information.[259] Thus the distinction needs to be made on a case-by-case basis, taking into consideration all the circumstances of a particular case.

The primary requirement is that the information satisfies the definition of a trade secret.[260] The measures taken in order to maintain secrecy play an important role in this respect. In particular, they alert the employee to the secret status of the information. Although a contract protecting trade secrets after termination of the employment relationship may be a ground for a separate cause of action,[261] it also points to the existence of a trade secret. At the same time, simply designating information as confidential or classified does not make it a trade secret if it was not confidential in the first place.[262] Information which was not kept secret by the employer may be freely used after employment.[263]

The courts consider further elements, including the value of the information to the ex-employer and to his competitors and the difficulty with which the information may be replicated or acquired independently, when determining whether information is to be considered a trade secret of the employer.[264] However, even valuable information which is part of the general experience of the former employee may not be regarded as the employer's trade secret.[265]

A long duration of employment might be an indication that information obtained during that employment has become part of the employee's general stock of knowledge.[266] However, it needs to be kept in mind that the mere fact that the former employee remembers particular information does not make it free for him to use after termination of service.

259 Feldman, 'Towards a Clearer Standard of Protectable Information: Trade Secrets and the Employment Relationship' 151, 166. Some guidance is provided in S 42 Restatement (Third) of Unfair Competition.

260 Information which derives independent economic value from not being generally known or readily ascertainable by proper means and which is subject to reasonable efforts to maintain its secrecy, S 1(4) UTSA, 18 US Code §1839(3), as amended by the DTSA. For a detailed analysis, see Chapter 2 part I, point D.

261 For a detailed analysis, see infra Chapter 4, part II, point C.

262 *Dynamics Research Corp v Analytic Sciences Corp* 400 NE 2d 1274, 1288 (Mass CA 1980).

263 *Jostens Inc v National Computer* Systems Inc 318 NW 2d 691, 702 (Supr Ct Minn 1982).

264 *SI Handling Systems v Heisley* 753 F 2d 1244, 1267 (3rd Cir 1985).

265 *Fleming Sales Company Inc v Joseph W Bailey* 611 F Supp 507, 516 (Ill Distr Ct 1985).

266 Feldman, 'Towards a Clearer Standard of Protectable Information: Trade Secrets and the Employment Relationship' 151, 165.

It may be easier for the ex-employer to show that particular information is a trade secret if it was incorporated into a document. Nevertheless, the circumstance of incorporation in material form is not conclusive and information which was not written down but which the former employee remembers might also be considered a trade secret of his former employer.[267]

Even though the law protects information based on its status as a trade secret, the manner in which it was taken may also be a factor for consideration. The circumstance that the employee has taken documents or data carriers incorporating the information or memorised the information on purpose may be an indication that the information is a trade secret of the employer rather than part of the former employee's general experience.[268] If it was part of his general knowledge, there would have been no need to copy documents. Similarly, even if the elements of the conglomerate information (e.g. a customer list) were publicly accessible, but the former employee resorted to taking or copying documents containing that information, this might weigh in favour of recognising the customer list as constituting the employer's trade secret.[269] On the other hand, trade secrets do not extend to 'memories casually retained from the ordinary course of employment'.[270]

Information which is unique to the employer's business as opposed to information widely known in the industry is more likely to be considered the employer's trade secret.[271]

The contribution of the employee to the development of that information may also be taken into consideration in the assessment.[272] For cases in which the information was developed by the employee himself, a method used to distinguish between the information which may be used by him after termination of the service and that which must remain with the former employer is an analogical[273] application of the guidelines

[267] *Al Minor & Assocs v Martin* 881 NE 2d 850, 855 (Supr Ct Ohio 2008); Darin W Snyder and David S Almeling, *Keeping Secrets: A Practical Introduction to Trade Secret Law and Strategy* (1st edn, Oxford University Press 2012) 56.

[268] *Ed Nowogroski Insurance Inc v Michael Rucker et al* 137 Wash 2d 427 (Washington Supr Ct), pointing out that there is no difference between deliberate copying of documents and deliberate memorisation; S 42 comment d Restatement (Third) of Unfair Competition.

[269] Porter II and Griffaton, 'Identifying and Protecting Employers' Interests in Trade Secrets and Proprietary Information' 439, 446.

[270] *Al Minor & Assocs v Martin* 881 NE 2d 850, 855 (Supr Ct Ohio 2008).

[271] S 42 comment d Restatement (Third) of Unfair Competition.

[272] Ibid.

[273] Taking into consideration the differences between trade secrets, patents and copyright, as analysed more closely in Chapter 2 part IV.

developed with regard to the 'classical' IPRs: copyright[274] and patents[275] and in particular employee inventions.[276]

If no explicit agreement assigning any inventions or ideas conceived during employment[277] has been entered into by the parties, where an employee was hired to develop or during employment instructed to create a specific solution in a specific field or as part of a specific project, this indicates an implied agreement that the result of his activities belongs to the employer.[278] Furthermore, where the ex-employer routinely required conclusion of assignment agreements and the ex-employee was aware of that practice, assignment of the developed solution may be implicit.[279] If the service has not been entered into for the purpose of solving a particular problem, the advances made during employment should be ascribed to the employee.[280] Some authors even suggest that information developed by the employee should be considered his skill and knowledge in every situation in which he has not signed an explicit assignment agreement.[281] It is argued here that this proposition would increase the legal certainty surrounding employer–employee relations, but it would be difficult to align with the general principle of law that, absent explicit regulation as to form, contractual obligations may accrue implicity.

The equitable doctrine of shop right is also put forward as an aid to determine whether the information is to be considered a trade secret

[274] Under S 101 USCA, a work of authorship belongs to the employer ab initio if it was created by the employee within the scope of his employment (work made for hire doctrine).

[275] The issue of ownership of employee inventions is governed by state laws, see Barton Beebe and others, *Trademarks, Unfair Competition, and Business Torts* (2nd edn Wolters Kluwer 2016) 791; Robert P Merges, 'The Law and Economics of Employee Inventions' (1999) 13(1) *Harv J L Techn* 1, 4. Even though the right to a patent originally rests with the inventor (S 111(a)(1) US Patent Act), under S 118 US Patent Act a person to whom the inventor assigned or is under an obligation to assign the invention may make an application for a patent.

[276] Milgrim on Trade Secrets vol 1A 5–84; for a more critical assessment of application of the common law rules to the obligation to assign inventions, see Beebe and others, *Trademarks, Unfair Competition, and Business Torts* 792.

[277] For more information on assignment of an employee's developments, see Milgrim on Trade Secrets vol 1A 6-5 – 6-6.1.

[278] Merges, 'The Law and Economics of Employee Inventions' 1, 5; Milgrim on Trade Secrets vol 1A 5–84 – 5–90, 5-102. This includes patentable inventions arrived at by the employee, S 42 comment e Restatement (Third) of Unfair Competition, referring to Restatement of Agency. Even though not compulsory, explicit assignment agreements are increasingly used to protect patentable inventions and other forms of intellectual property, Pooley 8-23.

[279] Milgrim on Trade Secrets vol 1A 5-103.

[280] S 42 comment e Restatement (Third) of Unfair Competition; *Structural Dynamics Research Corp v Engineering Mechanics Research Corp* 401 F Supp 1102, 1111 (ED Mich 1975); Milgrim on Trade Secrets vol 1A 5–97; Peterson 7–9.

[281] Feldman, 'Towards a Clearer Standard of Protectable Information: Trade Secrets and the Employment Relationship' 151, 167, 176.

reserved for the employer. Accordingly, even though the information might have been developed outside the performance of the employee's duties, if it was done within working hours; or using the employer's equipment, materials or premises; or with the help of other employees, it should be ascribed to the employer.[282]

These guidelines may help to establish the existence of an employer's trade secret in jurisdictions which do not provide explicit regulation. Some state laws contain provisions granting to the employer the right to 'everything which an employee acquires by virtue of his employment',[283] i.e. also trade secrets.[284]

Thus, as a general rule, it can be stated that whether the information was developed by the employee may be relevant in the distinction between the employer's trade secrets and the ex-employee's general skill and knowledge. Where the information was produced as a result of performance of the employment duties, or with the use of the employer's materials and equipment, it will be reserved for the employer. In other cases the employee will be allowed to use the information after termination of his service. The UTSA does not distinguish between information which was developed by the employee and other information. Therefore, according to Peterson, in the jurisdictions which have adopted the UTSA, the fact that it was the employee who developed the information may not be used in favour of allowing him the use of that data after termination of employment.[285] The same considerations apply to the DTSA.

Another factor which is given as an aid in differentiating between trade secrets and the general experience of the employee is whether the employee had any pre-employment experience in the field to which the information in question pertains. If the previous employment was his first job, it is more likely that the information the employee has learned was obtained from that particular employer, which speaks for considering it as the ex-employer's trade secret. In the case of highly experienced employees, who were active

[282] Milgrim on Trade Secrets vol 1A 5-104 – 5-108. Admittedly the shop right as applied to inventions does not give the employer a property right over the invention but merely a non-exclusive licence to practice the invention, see Milgrim on Trade Secrets vol 1A 5-104. Under S 42 comment e Restatement (Third) of Unfair Competition, the shop right is considered not to speak for ascribing the trade secret (or invention) to the employer, and the ex-employee is considered free 'to use the information or to disclose it to others even if the former employer retains a "shop right" in the trade secret' in the form of a non-exclusive licence. However, an analogical application of the doctrine, combined with other factors, might tip the balance of the right to the trade secret in favour of the employer. See also Feldman, 'Towards a Clearer Standard of Protectable Information: Trade Secrets and the Employment Relationship' 151, 168–169.

[283] See e.g. S 2860 California Labor Code.

[284] Milgrim on Trade Secrets vol 1A 5-114 – 5-115.

[285] Peterson 7-13, see also 8-5 – 8-17.

for many years in an industry and working for various companies or independently, it may be that they had learned the particular information on other occasions than during service for their last employer.[286]

The type of information is not a factor in the determination of trade secrecy. However it can generally be said that information relating to customers, such as their identity or preferences, is more often exchanged and transferred between market participants, and that therefore it is more likely to be readily ascertainable and thus not a trade secret.[287] Where the departing employee did not take with him any documents containing the information relating to clients, the awareness of contracts with particular customers of the employer which the employee was in charge of, products and personnel of those clients, or the knowledge of the products which are most attractive to particular customers may generally not be seen as a trade secret.[288] Technical information is less likely to be readily ascertainable if reasonable measures to maintain secrecy have been taken by the employer.

A particularly difficult situation occurs where the secret information of the former employer is 'inextricably tied up'[289] with the ex-employee's skills and knowledge. It is in those circumstances that the US courts have developed a highly controversial[290] doctrine of inevitable disclosure. The doctrine may be applied in a situation in which the ex-employee has learned a trade secret of the former employer in the course of service and where the parties did not explicitly agree, by way of a restrictive covenant, on the scope of the information which the employee is allowed to use after departure. If the position of the ex-employee with his new employer is such that there is a high probability that that secret will be used, the use of that information may be denied. It is done by way of an injunction prohibiting the employee from undertaking certain activities with the new

286 *Heyden Chemical Corp v Burrell & Neidig* 64 A 2d 465, 466 (NJ Super 1949); Friesen, 'Distinguishing between an Employee's General Knowledge and Trade Secrets' 2123, 2123.

287 *Fleming Sales Company Inc v Joseph W Bailey* 611 F Supp 507, 513 (Ill Distr Ct 1985).

288 *Fleming Sales Company Inc v Joseph W Bailey* 611 F Supp 507, 515 (Ill Distr Ct 1985).

289 Milgrim on Trade Secrets vol 1A 5-43.

290 As argued by Beebe et al., taking into consideration that S 2(a) UTSA allows for enjoining both actual and threatened misappropriation and the fact that the doctrine imposes a non-compete agreement where parties did not bargain to conclude such an agreement, the inevitable disclosure doctrine might not be efficient, see Beebe and others, *Trademarks, Unfair Competition, and Business Torts* 820–821. Many courts, particularly in California, reject the doctrine of inevitable disclosure, see Beebe and others, *Trademarks, Unfair Competition, and Business Torts* 819. For a critical appraisal of this doctrine, see also Katherine VW Stone, 'The New Psychological Contract: Implications of the Changing Workplace for Labor and Employment Law' (2001) 48 *UCLA L Rev* 519.

employer.[291] Due to the intertwining of the secrets with the employee's experience, the injunction necessarily stretches into the former employee's general skill and knowledge. Therefore, the application of this doctrine blurs the basic distinction between trade secrets and general skill and knowledge even more.

Various multifactor tests have been proposed for distinguishing the employee's skill and knowledge from the employer's trade secrets.[292] Feldman proposes to consider whether the employee developed the disputed information (suggesting that only an explicit assignment would transfer such information to the former employer), whether the information is unique to the employer's business, whether there were any unsuccessful attempts on the part of the competitors to develop the information independently,[293] whether the former employee had taken with him any materials in which the information was incorporated (such as documents, blueprints or drawings) or whether he has memorised the information on purpose. As a final factor he suggests considering whether the information has become so closely integrated into the ex-employee's general experience that denying him its use would effectively prevent him from working in his field of expertise.[294]

3 Duration of the Post-Employment Duty

Under the US law, as in the other jurisdictions analysed, the duration of the duty not to use or disclose trade secrets takes into account their perishable nature. Thus, as a rule, the secrecy of the information should be guarded by the departed employee for as long as the information remains secret.

However, in some circumstances, the duty may be extended beyond the point in time when the secret is disclosed. This is because under the UTSA an injunction granted with the aim to eliminate the competitive advantage (head start) which the ex-employee obtained over his competitors as a result of misappropriation may continue for a set period of time, even despite disclosure of the information.[295]

The determination of the duration of the duty is made on a case-by-case basis, upon enforcement. Since the length of the duty corresponds

[291] Milgrim on Trade Secrets vol 1A 5–50. For a discussion of this doctrine, see Chapter 5 part II, point C.2.

[292] See e.g. *Al Minor & Assocs v Martin* 881 NE 2d 850, 853 (Supr Ct Ohio 2008); *IBM v Papermaster* 2008 WL 4974508 7 (SDNY 2008).

[293] Cf S 42 comment d Restatement (Third) of Unfair Competition.

[294] Feldman, 'Towards a Clearer Standard of Protectable Information: Trade Secrets and the Employment Relationship' 151, 175–176.

[295] S 2(a) UTSA.

to the duration of an injunction imposed by a court in the given circumstances, it is discussed infra.[296]

4 Summary: Balance between the Interests of Ex-Employers and Their Former Employees with Regard to Use of Information Learned During Service

Even under consideration of the above-mentioned factors, the precise determination of the borderline between trade secrets and the skills and knowledge of the former employee may be a difficult task. To address this problem, the courts additionally consider the effect that allowing or prohibiting the use of particular information might have on the interests of the parties involved in the dispute, taking into account the public interest.[297] Thus, also under the law of the United States, the balancing of interests is the ultimate aid in determining the scope of the information which the departed employee may use for competitive purposes.[298]

The ex-employer's right to a trade secret is a property right.[299] Thus, the protection granted to that information should safeguard this property as well as the investment made in its production.[300] This would allow and invite the development of new methods and products to the benefit of the entire society, encourage the creation of new jobs and ensure stability of employment in general.[301] Nevertheless, protection of this property collides with the recognised freedom of employees to use their skill, knowledge and experience in competition with the former employer in order to earn a livelihood.[302]

These private interests should be seen in a broader framework of the public policy which they reflect. What needs to be taken into consideration on the policy level is in particular the recognition of the increasing mobility of the workforce, the public interest in competition and dissemination of ideas resulting from that mobility, which benefit

296 Chapter 5 part II point C.3 and part III point C.3.

297 See e.g. *Fleming Sales Company Inc v Joseph W Bailey* 611 F Supp 507, 514 (Ill Distr Ct 1985).

298 See e.g. *EI DuPont de Nemours and Co v American Potash & Chemical Corp* 220 A 2d 428, 437 (Del Ch 1964); *SI Handling Systems v Heisley* 753 F 2d 1244, 1267–1268 (3rd Cir 1985).

299 For a more detailed analysis of the legal nature of trade secrets under US law, see Chapter 2 part III point D.

300 *EI DuPont de Nemours and Co v American Potash & Chemical Corp* 220 A 2d 428, 437 (Del Ch 1964); Milgrim on Trade Secrets vol 1A 5–16.

301 Milgrim on Trade Secrets vol 1A 5-20; Feldman, 'Towards a Clearer Standard of Protectable Information: Trade Secrets and the Employment Relationship' 151, 155–156.

302 *Fleming Sales Company Inc v Joseph W Bailey* 611 F Supp 507, 514 (Ill Distr Ct 1985); Feldman, 'Towards a Clearer Standard of Protectable Information: Trade Secrets and the Employment Relationship' 151, 155.

society and consumers,[303] as well as the purpose of the trade secrets law which is to maintain standards of commercial ethics and to encourage innovation.[304]

Generally, employers may bind employees by contracts limiting their competitive activity after termination of employment, which would encompass the use of any competitive information and not only trade secrets. Absent such a contract, the law should not step in with the effect of restraining competition, since that would go against the public interest.[305] Accordingly, information which may well be covered by a restrictive covenant, such as the identity of the employer's customers with whom the employee was in contact, their needs and preferences or the identity of their representatives, product and service requirements or buying procedures, will not be recognised as the employer's property if it does not satisfy the definition of a trade secret.[306] Thus, while the protection of trade secrets as a property right is strong, considering the conflicting interests, the courts are reluctant to stretch the boundaries of the concept so that it encompasses information which may not clearly be qualified as a trade secret. Consequently, while valuable secret formulas which were subject to reasonable measures to maintain secrecy are likely to be seen as the employer's secrets, incremental developments or information about customers obtained in daily work, even if valuable, is more likely to be seen as part of the employee's general knowledge, absent taking of documentation or deliberate memorisation.

The consideration of other interests, such as those of employers other than the one claiming protection, is also present in the discussion in the United States. The public interest in the existence of an innovative and competitive economy is reflected in the consideration that limitation of employee mobility due to enforcement of trade secrets might impede the possibility to hire new workforce,[307] in particular experienced and highly specialised staff. This would adversely affect economic growth and social wellbeing in general.

303 S 42 comment b Restatement (Third) of Unfair Competition; *SI Handling Systems v Heisley* 753 F 2d 1244, 1267–1268 (3rd Cir 1985); Feldman, 'Towards a Clearer Standard of Protectable Information: Trade Secrets and the Employment Relationship' 151, 155–156.

304 *Fleming Sales Company Inc v Joseph W Bailey* 611 F Supp 507, 511 (Ill Distr Ct 1985).

305 *Fleming Sales Company Inc v Joseph W Bailey* 611 F Supp 507, 511 (Ill Distr Ct 1985). However some courts effectively impose such an effect by applying the doctrine of inevitable disclosure. For a discussion of this doctrine, see infra Chapter 5 part II, point C.2.

306 *Fleming Sales Company Inc v Joseph W Bailey* 611 F Supp 507, 511, 514 (Ill Distr Ct 1985).

307 Feldman, 'Towards a Clearer Standard of Protectable Information: Trade Secrets and the Employment Relationship' 151, 170.

Although not routinely present in the case-law on misappropriation of trade secrets, there exists, at least theoretically,[308] the possibility to include in the balancing exercise the general public interest in preserving undistorted competition in the market. As has been recognised in *CVD Inc v Raytheon Co*, assertion of claims to trade secrets in bad faith, i.e. with the knowledge that no trade secret exists, can be an antitrust violation,[309] if it is done with the purpose of restraining competition by monopolisation or attempted monopolisation.[310] Even a threat of litigation in such circumstances has been recognised as an anti-trust violation since the costs of such litigation would be ruinous for the start-up company founded by the ex-employees and in effect would foreclose competition in the relevant market.[311]

Taking into account the analysis presented in the initial part of this book,[312] it can be observed that the considerations of public interest, including promotion of innovation and entrepreneurship, dissemination of information and promotion of commercial morality, are present and vigorously discussed both in the case-law and in the literature in the United States.

The discussion is not limited to the analysis of the impact of the protection of trade secrets on private and public interests. Considering the need to strike a balance between the various interests and policies relating to innovation and competition,[313] Unikel proposes to create an additional category of information: confidential information. According to his proposal, the current level of protection should be awarded only to the most valuable information which is a result of extensive investment in R&D and which is not likely to be easily created through independent research. Granting protection to such information would reduce the

308 It seems that application of antitrust considerations, which are part of federal law, is not likely to occur in state courts, as illustrated by *CVD Inc v Raytheon Co* 769 F2d 842 (1st Cir 1985). In this case a separate action under S 2 Sherman Act was brought before the federal court by former employees, alleging that they were forced by their ex-employer to enter into a licensing agreement as a result of his attempt at monopolisation and that therefore that agreement was null and void.

309 As long as other conditions of finding such a violation are met. Under S 1 Sherman Act it needs to be shown by clear and convincing evidence that the ex-employer had market power in the relevant market and that he acted with specific intent to restrain competition. Under S 2 Sherman Act specific intent to monopolise (e.g. bad faith) and dangerous probability of success must be shown. See *CVD Inc v Raytheon Co* 769 F2d 842 [26] (1st Cir 1985).

310 *CVD Inc v Raytheon Co* 769 F2d 842 [25]–[26] (1st Cir 1985).

311 *CVD Inc v Raytheon Co* 769 F2d 842 [27], [67]–[70] (1st Cir 1985).

312 In Chapter 1.

313 Robert Unikel, 'Bridging the "Trade Secret" Gap: Protecting "Confidential Information" Not Rising to the Level of Trade Secrets' (1998) 29 *Loy U Chi LJ* 841, 850.

costs that its holders would spend on de facto protection.[314] As regards confidential information, i.e. information known to a considerable number of persons in the industry, but which still has some value stemming from the fact that it is not generally known, which is not necessary for participation in the field of industry or trade and which is treated as confidential by its holder,[315] he proposes to grant it a lower level of protection. He suggests that introduction of this category of protectable information would allow a balance to be achieved between the interests of employers in protecting their data and the interests of employees in being able to change jobs within an industry, because the employees would be allowed to use the information which is 'universally known, freely disseminated by their former employers or necessary for the participation in the field'.[316] It is suggested here that the current level of protection of trade secrets in the United States seems in line with the arguments presented by Unikel.[317] Nevertheless, whether the particular information asserted as a trade secret of the employer is necessary for the ex-employee's participation in the field might be helpful in determining the borderline between trade secrets and the employee's knowledge, as a factor supporting the interest of the former employee.

As regards confidential information not rising to the level of a trade secret because it does not have a competitive or other economic value and which may be described as personal,[318] it seems that there exists no interest of the employee that would speak in favour of allowing him to use it. Thus, the conflict of interests with regard to information such as health or life history does not seem to arise.

In the context of reverse-engineering, Risch proposes the introduction of a reversed burden of proof, so that it is up to the alleged misappropriator to show that he obtained the information by honest means.[319] In the context of employee mobility, considering that the taking of documents or deliberate memorisation indicates the existence of a trade secret of the ex-employer, this could transfer into a proposal to place the burden on the former employee to show that he has learned the information in a natural way. While attractive from the point of view of employers, such a reversed burden of proof might result in an obligation for the employee to prove the negative, i.e. that he did not take any documents, or to show that he has not memorised the information on purpose, which is an

[314] Ibid 841, 851.
[315] Ibid 841, 844, 877–879.
[316] Ibid 841, 881.
[317] As explained in Chapter 2 part I point D.
[318] Cf S 8.05 comment c Restatement (Third) of Agency.
[319] Risch, 'Why Do We Have Trade Secrets?' 1, 54–55.

equally difficult standard to meet. Such a result would not be welcome, in particular considering that departed employees are often the weaker party in litigation, having limited resources at their disposal. Increasing their burden of proof might invite litigation on the part of the former employers. Taking into account that the high costs of litigation in the United States are borne by the parties themselves, this might have an anticompetitive effect.

As the analysis presented here shows, in the United States the determination of the scope of information which a departed employee may use depends on the nature of that information and in particular on its recognition as a trade secret which is protected as the property of the employer. Thus, unlike in Germany and the United Kingdom, it seems that once particular information is considered a trade secret, its use by a departed employee is excluded. This strong protection is balanced by the fact that the assessment of the nature of the information is made under a comprehensive consideration of the circumstances of a case, including the impact of ascribing a secret status to the information on both the private and public interest. Furthermore, that assessment is placed in the broader context of public policy.

D Post-Employment Duties under the Trade Secrets Directive

The Trade Secrets Directive does not harmonise post-employment duties with respect to trade secrets. Skill and experience of employees gathered in the normal course of their employment is excluded from the definition of a trade secret laid down in the Directive.[320] Furthermore, Article 1(3) prescribes that the Directive does not offer any ground for restricting mobility of employees and in particular for restricting use of information not constituting a trade secret (Article 1(3)(a) Trade Secrets Directive) and use of employees' experience and skills honestly obtained in the normal course of employment (Article 1(3)(b) Trade Secrets Directive).[321]

Thus, Article 1(3) and Recital 14 limit the substantive scope of the Directive. Since employees' skill and experience are not trade secrets (Recital 14), they do not come under the ambit of the Directive. Use of information which is not a trade secret, i.e. also an employee's skill and experience, is not restricted by the Directive (Article 1(3)(a)). Also, as a separate point, in Article 1(3)(b), use of skill and experience honestly acquired in the normal course of employment is not restricted by the Directive. This may be seen as a repetition. After all, skills and experience

[320] Art 2(1), Recital 14 TSD.
[321] See also Recital 14 TSD.

are already encompassed by section (a) of Article 1(3). However, such a wording could also leave room for the interpretation that even information which could be qualified as a trade secret, if it has become part of the employee's experience and skill acquired honestly during employment, is beyond the scope of the Directive. This would weaken the dichotomy between trade secrets and skills and experience, which seems to be expressed in Recital 14. This would also be closer to the approach taken in the European legal orders analysed, which do not base the lawfulness of use of information by former employees solely on whether it counts as trade secrets or as skill and experience of the employee.

The statement that the employee's skill and experience is not a trade secret is rather confusing. Whether particular information has become part of his skill and experience seems more appropriately addressed within the framework of lawfulness of use (Articles 3–4 Trade Secrets Directive) rather than as part of a definition of trade secrets.[322]

The approach to the employee's skill and experience taken in the Directive seems closer to the one presented in US doctrine, which concentrates on the assessment of whether the information is the employer's trade secret or the employee's skill and knowledge, rather than on the assessment of the behaviour. Recognising the use of skill and experience by former employees in the framework of lawfulness of use of trade secrets would be more in line with the unfair competition approach presented in the Directive. Accordingly, the decision whether the ex-employee is to be allowed to use the information should depend on the assessment of the behaviour: if the trade secret has become part of the employee's skill and experience, is it fair for him to use it? Such an approach seems logical since information which is part of skill and knowledge may still fulfil the requirements of secrecy, value and reasonable steps to maintain secrecy in accordance with Article 2(1) of the Directive. Thus, the fact that information has become part of skill and experience should be considered as a factor in the assessment of fairness, rather than as an element of definition. This would allow for a more systematic approach to the determination of the scope of information which can be used by departed employees.

The lawfulness and unlawfulness of acquisition, use and disclosure of trade secrets are laid down in Articles 3 and 4 of the Directive.

Article 3, which has a character of full harmonisation,[323] regulates lawfulness of acquisition, use and disclosure. Some types of acquisition

[322] Tanya Aplin, 'A Critical Evaluation of the Proposed EU Trade Secrets Directive' (2014) 4 *IPQ* 257, 270.
[323] Art 1(1) TSD.

of information in conformity with honest commercial practices (such as reverse engineering) have been explicitly recognised as lawful under Article 3(1) of the Directive. Acquisition, use and disclosure are also lawful to the extent that they are required or allowed by Union or national law (Article 3(2) of the Directive). This weakens the maximum character of harmonisation of this provision.

Pursuant to Article 4(3) of the Directive, use or disclosure of a trade secret is deemed unlawful when the information has been acquired unlawfully[324] or where its use is in breach of a duty not to disclose or a duty not to use a trade secret, whether contractual or other. Article 4 has a character of minimum harmonisation[325] leaving it open for the Member States to provide for more far-reaching protection.

Furthermore, acquisition, use or disclosure of a trade secret ia for the purpose of protecting a legitimate interest has been recognised as a reason for denying a remedy against such acquisition, use or disclosure in Article 5(d) of the Trade Secrets Directive. It seems that the notion of legitimate interests under Article 5(d) may encompass the interest of the former employee in choosing an occupation or to conduct business,[326] i.e. private interests. Considerations of public interest seem not to be present for the purpose of determination of the infringing acts. The interest of both parties as well as the public interest are taken into account when applying remedies.[327]

The consideration that information acquired unlawfully may not be used by the departed employee is accepted in all the jurisdictions analysed. Since the unlawful use or disclosure of the information is defined by reference to breach of a contractual or implied duty,[328] it seems that the rules governing the scope of post-employment duties developed in those jurisdictions may remain in force once the Directive is implemented.[329]

Nevertheless, any doubts as to the meaning of Article 1(3) of the Directive will ultimately need to be resolved by the CJEU. Aplin suggests

324 That is, by unauthorised access to, copying or appropriation of any documents, objects, materials, substances or electronic files, lawfully under the control of the trade secret holder, containing the trade secret or from which the trade secret can be deduced (Art 4 (2)(a) TSD) or acquired by any other conduct which, under the circumstances, is considered contrary to honest commercial practices (Art 4(2)(b) TSD).

325 Art 1(1) TSD.

326 Recital 34 TSD; MPI Position Paper para 38.

327 Art 6 (measures are to be fair and equitable), Art 7 (proportionality, avoidance of creation of barriers to trade in the internal market) TSD.

328 Art 4(3)(b)–(c) TSD.

329 This conclusion refers to the use of information by former employees. It seems that implementation of the Directive in the proposed wording would require amendments of the national laws, e.g. as regards lawfulness of reverse engineering (Art 3(1)(b) TSD), which e.g. in Germany is not uniformly recognised as lawful.

that it is unclear whether the matters relating to employers and ex-employees altogether are to be governed by national laws or EU law (with ultimate jurisdiction lying with the CJEU).[330]

It is considered here that stronger arguments speak for continued governance of the national law, in particular as contractual and implied duties have not been harmonised under the Directive. The Directive does not contain sufficient guidance for a uniform understanding of implied and contractual post-employment duties. If it was a matter for EU law, interpretation of these duties by the CJEU would force harmonisation by overruling established national practices. This type of harmonisation should be done by way of a legislative measure from the EU. However, the Directive takes the approach of minimum harmonisation and therefore it seems that it was a conscious decision to leave infringing acts beyond Articles 3–4 of the Directive to be determined by national law-makers and courts.

III Summary: Finding the Equilibrium between Protection of Trade Secrets and the Mobility of Employees in the Absence of Contract

A Guidance from Comparative Analysis

In all of the analysed jurisdictions, the courts struggle with determining the information that the departed employee may use after termination of service, applying various methods in this assessment.

In Germany, fragmented legislation, based on punishment of misappropriation of trade secrets by employees during employment as criminal acts, has led to the development of elaborate legal constructions in an attempt to address the issue. Despite differences between the case-law of the general civil and specialised labour courts, in the end the assessment of the use of the information by the ex-employee is made from the point of view of fairness of such use, under consideration of all the circumstances of the case in point. The fairness of a particular behaviour is determined ia by balancing the interests of the parties involved.

The approach presented in the common law jurisdictions concentrates on the assessment of the information, rather than behaviour. In the United Kingdom, the courts have developed a graded categorisation of data, as far as its use after termination of employment is concerned. Accordingly, only highly confidential information is covered by the

[330] Aplin, 'A Critical Evaluation of the Proposed EU Trade Secrets Directive' 257, 270.

implied post-employment duty of confidentiality. This information is determined on a case-by-case basis, in particular – but not only – by assessing whether it can be distinguished from the ex-employee's skill and knowledge.

In the United States, the information which may be used by former employees is determined by the distinction between trade secrets, which are considered the property of the employer, and the employee's general experience necessary for him in further professional activity. In addition, the United States is the only jurisdiction among those analysed, which contains a codified regulation of what trade secrets are. Despite this uniform definition, also in the United States the courts have needed to develop further guidelines to help them draw the distinction.

Both in Germany and in the United Kingdom there exists a differentiation between the duties of the employee during and after employment. In the United States there seems to be no such distinction.[331] Trade secrets are protected as a property right irrespective of the existence of any contractual obligations.

The general freedom of departed employees to compete with their former employers, recognised in all of the jurisdictions analysed, does not cover the use of information which was obtained in a dishonest way, in particular by copying or taking of documents or by deliberately memorising it.[332] Whether such dishonest acquisition took place is a factor in the assessment of the fairness of the behaviour under German law. In the United Kingdom, information thus obtained is considered to have been acquired outside of employment duties and therefore in breach of those duties, which excludes its use after termination of employment. Under the approach taken in the United States, the fact that the ex-employee needed to resort to unfair means of obtaining information points to it being a trade secret.

There seems to be general agreement that employee inventions may not be used by a departed employee. German law provides a statutory regulation in that respect. In the United Kingdom, such information will usually be separable from the departed employee's skill and knowledge,

[331] Charlotte Sander, 'Schutz nicht offenbarter betrieblicher Informationen nach der Beendigung des Arbeitsverhältnisses im deutschen und amerikanischen Recht' (2013) GRUR-Int 217, 226.

[332] Unlawful acquisition, including by unauthorised access, copying or appropriation of documents, objects, materials, substances or electronic files and any other conduct contrary to honest commercial practices has been recognised in Art 4(2)–(3) TSD as a circumstance giving raise to application for the measures, procedures and remedies laid down in the Directive. Art 4(2)(b) contains a general clause which allows to include memorisation in the catalogue of acts of unlawful acquisition.

which is one of the factors in the determination of the highly confidential information which may not be used after termination of service. In the United States, the ownership of employee inventions is regulated under state laws, but the prevailing opinion seems to be that if the employee was hired to develop the particular information or if he used the resources of the employer to develop it, then it should be ascribed to his principal.

The situation is less clear as regards information which may not be the subject of a patent application and in particular information relating to clients. None of the analysed jurisdictions provides for different treatment of the information depending on whether it is of technical or commercial nature. However, the German courts seem to consider that information relating to clients with whom the ex-employee developed a relationship based on trust should remain available to him for competitive purposes after employment. No corresponding assessment has been identified under the law of the United Kingdom. Nevertheless, considering the application of the theory of separability to determine the highly confidential information by the UK courts, the approach to client information might be similar to that in the United States, i.e. that due to its characteristics, it is more likely to be retained in the employee's memory and thus be part of his general skills and knowledge rather that the employer's trade secret. Thus, the fact that the information was developed by the employee, in particular where it was derived from his personal qualities, may be a factor in all three jurisdictions in favour of allowing its use.

Despite the diverging approaches to the legal nature of trade secrets and to treatment of such information after termination of employment, it seems that ultimately the decision must be made under global consideration of the facts of a particular case and that the balancing of the conflicting interests that arise in the context of the employee mobility is a necessary element of this assessment.

The position of the ex-employee in the company of his former principal is one of the factors which the courts consider in the determination of the fairness of use of the information or scope of the post-employment duty of confidentiality. If the position and duties of the employee were such that he was handling confidential information and must have been aware of the importance of this information for his principal, his duty of confidentiality after departure from service is broader. On the other hand, the longer the employment relationship, the more some information becomes imprinted in the employee's memory and thus may be a condition for him to undertake any activity after termination of service.

While not present in German case-law, an important consideration in the United Kingdom and in the United States is whether the information was treated by the employer as a trade secret. Even though the duty of confidentiality may generally be implied, the taking of reasonable measures to maintain secrecy is particularly important in the employment relationship. Due to the fact that the denial of use of particular information by former employees may inhibit competition, imposing of implied duties on former servants should be done carefully. Under the law of the United Kingdom and United States, the absence of measures aiming at keeping the information secret would point to lack of secrecy of that information. In Germany, measures to maintain secrecy are not an element of the definition. However, the taking of measures to keep the information secret may arguably be considered under the global assessment of fairness. Accordingly, absent other considerations, it would not be fair to prohibit the ex-employee from using information which he remembers from previous employment, if it was not treated by the employer as a secret. One of the tools drawing the employee's attention to the confidentiality of the information may be the conclusion of a restrictive covenant, even though it is not a condition for the existence of the post-employment duty of confidentiality.

All of the jurisdictions analysed recognise the ex-employee's freedom to compete with his former principal. Accordingly, the consideration of whether the use of a particular information is essential for the former servant in order to remain professionally active, even in competition with the former employer, has been recognised as a factor in determining the fairness of such use under German law. Although not routinely present in the case-law in the United Kingdom and the United States, it is sometimes put forward as one of the considerations in the determination of separability under UK law and as an aid in the determination of the borderline between trade secrets and general skill and knowledge of the ex-employee in the United States. Thus, a specialist in a narrow field may be allowed to use information which he learned during employment, if denying him this use would effectively restrain him from working in his field of expertise, even if the ex-employer had an interest in preventing such use.

The employee should be allowed to compete with his former principal in a fair way, relying on his general skill and knowledge. Whether particular information has become part of that general stock of knowledge is a factor considered in all three jurisdictions.[333] In Germany it might be deemed unfair to deny the use of information which may not be

[333] Experience and skills honestly acquired by employees in the normal course of their employment are excluded from the scope of the Trade Secrets Directive, see Art 1(3)(b), Recital 14 TSD.

separated from general knowledge, even if it is a trade secret. In the United Kingdom and United States it would be an indication of the information not being highly confidential or a trade secret. Under the approach taken in the United States, the distinction between trade secrets and general skill and knowledge is essential, and once the information is qualified as a trade secret it must remain with the employer as his property. Under the approach developed in the United Kingdom, the fact that the information has become part of the general knowledge is an important, albeit not the only, consideration, since inability to separate it from the employee's general experience indicates that this information is not highly confidential. As an aid, the courts tend to consider that incorporation of the information in a document points to it being separable from the former servant's general stock of knowledge. The fact that the information is particular to the employer's business may be such an aid as well.

On the other hand, the value of the information for the former employer is also taken into consideration, as a reflection of his interest in maintaining his competitive position. This value is one of the elements defining a trade secret under US law, but may be found in the requirement of interest in keeping the information secret under German law and in the belief of the employer that the release of the information would be injurious to him, as considered by the UK courts. The value is to be measured objectively as relating to the role that the information plays in safeguarding the market position of the employer. The courts in the United Kingdom and in the United States have held that the time and effort spent by the employer in developing the information, as well as difficulty in replicating the information by independent development, point to it being a valuable competitive asset. Furthermore, such value may be derived from the fact that the information is unique to the employer's business. In such a case, its use is less likely to be essential for the departed employee to be able to remain professionally active. It is submitted that the value of the information for the former employer should be regarded from the perspective of his competitive position. Thus, the time and effort spent developing such information should be ignored. After all, even information developed by accident may prove valuable. The 'uniqueness' of the data to the employer's business as well as difficulties in independent development by other market participants are considerations better suited to reflect the objective value of a trade secret.

The determination of fairness of the use of information and, of the quality of the information as highly confidential or a trade secret, is made, as explained above, under consideration of the interest of the former employees in choosing their livelihood, including competition with the former employer, and of the ex-employer in maintaining his competitive position.[334] The examination presented above shows that the courts in the United States include a wide range of considerations when applying the UTSA: they routinely place the conflict between the employer and his ex-employee in a broader context of public policy of incentivising innovation and dissemination of knowledge; promotion of entrepreneurship by creation of start-ups; creation of new jobs; interests of consumers in the creation of new products and increased competition;[335] and interests of other employers in being able to hire experienced labour, not restrained by duties towards their former employers.

While the consideration that the role of the protection granted to trade secrets is to safeguard commercial ethics is present in all of the analysed jurisdictions, European courts do not include in-depth examination of public policy in the assessment of the protection of trade secrets in the context of employee mobility. In the United Kingdom it has been recognised that the enforcement of trade secrets should not unreasonably inhibit competition and that there exists a public interest in the use of the employee's skills. In Germany, on the other hand, the courts seem to confine their assessment to private interests, although incidentally recognising the interests of the former colleagues of the departed employee in maintaining their jobs by safeguarding the market position of their employer. The public interest considerations are set out in the German literature. In particular it is stressed that the goal of the UWG, which serves as a basis for the enforcement of trade secrets, is to safeguard the interests not only of competitors but also of consumers and other market participants.

B Assessment

Absence of strict rules and case-by-case assessment are inevitable in the elusive intersection of trade secrecy and employee mobility.

In particular, differentiation between the employee's skill and knowledge and the employer's trade secret, often referred to as the ultima ratio of the conflict of interests, is neither always possible nor systematically

[334] The respect for fundamental rights, including freedom to choose an occupation and right to engage in work, as well as the freedom to conduct business and the right to property, is recognised in Recital 34 TSD. These fundamental rights encompass the private interests taken into consideration when determining the scope of information which may be used by ex-employees.

[335] Despite theoretical possibility, anti-trust considerations are not given particular weight in considerations of public policy.

decisive under German and UK law. It is an important factor in the assessment, but not the only one. Rather, the main guideline in Germany is the fairness of the taking and use of the information, and the resulting acceptance of the use of a trade secret by a departed employee if such use would be fair under the circumstances. In the United Kingdom, the 'level' of confidentiality of the information based on a multi-factor assessment is the decisive consideration. Even in the United States, where the distinction between trade secrets and skill and knowledge appears to be basic, it is drawn in the light of various factors. In this respect the solution adopted in the Trade Secrets Directive appears unsatisfactory. Still, as argued here, it appears possible under Article 1 (3) of the Directive to accept continued use of trade secrets which have become part of the employee's skill and knowledge.

It seems that the current legal frameworks of Germany and the United Kingdom allow for a broader inclusion of the public interest in the assessment of the scope of information which a departed employee may use. Under German law this is possible due to the fact that the concept of fairness of a behaviour is derived from a general clause, which by definition requires flexible application. In the United Kingdom, the concept of highly confidential information is sufficiently flexible to allow for a broader inclusion of economic considerations in determining the post-employment duty of confidentiality. This would not change after implementation of the Trade Secrets Directive, since the determination of the lawfulness of use of the information after termination of employment is left for national law.[336]

It is suggested here that putting the assessment of the scope of information which may be used by former employees in the broader context of information policy would bring positive effects. Accordingly, absent other considerations, a higher level of protection should be granted to information which would not have been disclosed to the employee in the absence of protection granted to trade secrets. This would allow for a fair inclusion of the role that the protection of trade secrets plays in incentivising innovation and reducing the cost of doing business. Furthermore, again, absent strong indications to the contrary, particular weight should be given to allowing the use of the information which is essential for the departed employee to be able to continue his professional activity, even in competition with his former principal, as this reflects both the private interest of the employee and the public interest in dissemination of knowledge, spill-overs and increased competition. Consideration of the

[336] Art 3(2) TSD.

type of industry concerned and the type of information might also be helpful in striking the right balance. Trade secrets, as compared to patents, provide incentives to develop particularly inventions characterised by a relatively short life-cycle, e.g. in the area of IT and software. This may be similar for marketing information.[337] In the case of such information, the fact that it loses value quickly would point to the employer's interest in restricting its use.[338] At the same time, in view of the short life-cycle of that information, the negative impact on the mobility of the employees should not be prohibitive. If, on the other hand, a particular industry is characterised by high employee mobility and is dependent on knowledge spill-overs, it is a factor which would weigh in favour of less restricted use of the experience the employees have gained from previous employment, to the benefit not only of the workforce, but also the entire industry and employers in general.

With regard to the duration of the post-employment duty of confidentiality where no contract was entered into, apart from isolated proposals in the German literature to limit the duration of the implied duty to the duration of the contractual duty not to compete,[339] the prevailing opinion seems to be that this duty lasts as long as the information remains secret. Nevertheless, considering the conflict of interests between the employers and their former servants, it may be contemplated to ensure the necessary balance by adjusting the time during which the former employee should refrain from using information learned during employment.[340] Currently, such considerations seem not to be part of the legislative framework regulating post-employment duties in the

[337] Although in case of commercial and marketing information the argument is also valid that it would be developed in any case, as a by-product of a business activity. For generating such information, no incentive needs to be provided.

[338] The protection of such interest is explained by Abramowicz and Duffy as necessary in order to encourage market experimentation, see Michael Abramowicz and John F Duffy, 'Intellectual Property for Market Experimentation' (2008) 83 *NYU L Rev* 337.

[339] See e.g. Molkenbur, 'Pflicht zur Geheimniswahrung nach Ende des Arbeitsverhältnisses?' 1196, 1199–1200.

[340] The need to balance the interests of employees who developed the information with the interests of their employers entitled to the information seems to have been a consideration underlying Art 4.2 of the Resolution 571 (1974) of the Parliamentary Assembly of the Council of Europe on the protection of manufacturing and commercial secrets. This model law suggested that if a former employee has himself developed a secret or himself played an essential role in the development of a secret during the period of his employment by the person entitled to the secret, no obligation whatsoever to keep the secret shall exist after two years have elapsed since the termination of his contract of employment. See Art 4.2 Resolution 571 (1974) on the protection of manufacturing and commercial secrets, adopted by Parliamentary Assembly of Council of Europe on 3 July 1974, http://assembly.coe.int/Main.asp?link=/Documents/AdoptedText/ta74/ERES571.htm accessed 6 March 2015, on file with the author.

jurisdictions analysed. This seems appropriate, since the assessment of the scope of duty is made on a case-by-case basis. However, considering that the assessment of the actual scope and duration of the duty is made upon enforcement, a flexible determination of the scope (e.g. by differentiating between prohibition of disclosure and prohibition of use) and of the duration could be part of the court's decision to grant or deny a remedy. The plausibility of such a solution is analysed infra.[341]

The consideration of public interest in determining the scope of the post-employment duty of confidentiality and the fairness of the use of the information by former employees advocated here would ensure that the necessary balance struck in the event of employee mobility reflects the impact of this mobility on innovation, entrepreneurship, economic growth and competition, as well as on social policy. After all, as explained in the initial part of this book, the private interests involved in those cases are a reflection of public policy. Overprotection of information may undermine the IP system and the benefits stemming from knowledge spill-overs and entrepreneurship. Even though, admittedly, it is the role of legislators and not the courts to create new rules, their judgements should not be made without regard to the broader economic and social context of the case at hand, especially since, as argued here, the legal frameworks are sufficiently flexible to encompass considerations of public interest.

The analysis presented above shows that the demonstrative illustration, in *Fleming Sales Company Inc v Joseph W Bailey*, of the problem of protection of trade secrets in the context of employee mobility remains topical. In this case the court concluded that the departed employee was free to use general skills and knowledge acquired in the course of employment. According to the decision, '[a]ny other rule would force a departing employee to perform a prefrontal lobotomy on himself or herself. It would disserve the free market goal of maximizing available resources to foster competition. (...) [I]t would not strike a proper balance between the purposes of trade secrets law and the strong policy in favour of fair and vigorous business competition'.[342] It remains the difficult task of the courts to ensure that ex-employees do not have to undergo such painful treatment.

The considerations analysed in this part of the book relate to a situation where the former employee and his principal did not explicitly regulate the use of information learned during service after its termination. The scope of contractual freedom in defining post-employment confidentiality obligations is analysed in Chapter 4.

[341] In Chapter 5.
[342] *Fleming Sales Company Inc v Joseph W Bailey* 611 F Supp 507, 514 (Ill Distr Ct 1985).

4 Contractual Freedom to Regulate Use of Trade Secrets after Termination of Employment

I Introduction

The duty of confidentiality discussed in Chapter 3 applies in situations where the employer and the employee did not agree on any post-termination rules governing the use of information learned by the employee during service. Considering the convoluted statutory regulation of the post-employment duty of confidentiality, combined with the increasing mobility of the workforce, a tendency towards explicit regulation may be observed.[1] Accordingly, the duties of departed employees with regard to trade secrets are often determined by contracts,[2] concluded either upon entering into the employment relationship, during its term, or upon termination.

The possibility to agree on the conditions of use of trade secrets by the employee after his departure is rooted in the generally recognised freedom to contract.[3] Among agreements concluded with the purpose of protecting trade secrets, non-disclosure agreements (NDAs) aim directly

[1] Katherine VW Stone, 'The New Psychological Contract: Implications of the Changing Workplace for Labor and Employment Law' (2001) 48 *UCLA L Rev* 519, 578; Norman D Bishara, 'Covenants Not to Compete in a Knowledge Economy: Balancing Innovation from Employee Mobility against Legal Protection for Human Capital Investment' (2006) 27 *Berk J Emp & Lab L* 287, 296; Bauer/Diller para 5, referring to empirical studies showing the applicability of NCAs for various groups of employees, although the data used predates 1990.

[2] Even though, generally, contractual obligations may accrue both by way of explicit agreement and implicitly, a clear determination of what can be used, and how, makes it possible to achieve the legal certainty which the statutory regulation is often lacking.

[3] In Germany enshrined in Art 2 GG, see Josef Molkenbur, 'Pflicht zur Geheimniswahrung nach Ende des Arbeitsverhältnisses?' (1990) BB 1196, 1198 and Schlötter 194; DiFabio in Theodor Maunz and Günter Dürig, *Grundgesetz-Kommentar* (69 edn, CH Beck 2013) Art 2 para 101. For a general presentation of the freedom of contract in the United Kingdom, see Edwin Peel, *The Law of Contract* (13th edn, Sweet&Maxwell 2011) para 1-004. For the United States, see e.g. Viva R Moffat, 'The Wrong Tool for the Job: The IP Problem with Non-Competition Agreements' (2010) University of Denver Sturm College of Law Legal Research Paper Series Working Paper No 10-10 881 http://papers.ssrn.com/sol3/papers.cfm?abstract_id=1577271 accessed 1 June 2017.

at protection of secrecy. An employee who enters into such a contract obliges himself not to disclose (and possibly use) information defined therein.[4]

The protection of trade secrets may also be achieved by conclusion of a broader agreement not to engage in competition with the employer's business after termination of service (NCA).[5] Due to the effect of limitation of competition, such a restrictive covenant is 'both a contract in its own right and a restriction on future freedom to contract'.[6] In comparison with NDAs, non-compete agreements improve the former employer's position by limiting competition in general, reducing the incentive for the employees to change jobs, and – in case of departure – by facilitating enforcement: it is easier to show that the former employee is engaging in competitive activity than to provide evidence of infringement of a right to a trade secret[7] or of breach of contract prescribing confidentiality.

Trade secrets may also be protected by non-solicitation agreements (NSAs). These contracts may effectively safeguard customer lists and other information relating to business partners of the ex-employer by prohibiting the ex-employees from approaching them.[8] They may also take the form of agreements not to solicit former colleagues to engage in

[4] NDAs are an exception to the otherwise strict approach to post-employment contracts in California, as long as they protect trade secrets, Gary E Weiss, 'Biting the Hand that Stops Feeding: How to protect Trade Secrets from Misappropriation by Laid Off Employees' (2001) 661 *PLI/Lit* 469, 478; Carsten Salger and Anja Breitfeld, 'Regelungen zum Schutz von betrieblichen Know-how – die Sicherung von Geschäfts- und Betriebsgeheimnissen' (2005) BB 154, 158.

[5] NCAs are also referred to as restrictive covenants, see e.g. Robert Unikel, 'Bridging the "Trade Secret" Gap: Protecting "Confidential Information" Not Rising to the Level of Trade Secrets' (1998) 29 *Loy U Chi LJ* 841, note 71; Salger and Breitfeld, 'Regelungen zum Schutz von betrieblichen Know-how – die Sicherung von Geschäfts- und Betriebsgeheimnissen' 154, 156–157.

[6] Catherine L Fisk, '"An Ingenious Man Enabled by Contract": Entrepreneurship and the Rise of Contract' (2007) Duke Law School Legal Studies Research Paper Series, Research Paper 157, 13 http://ssrn.com/abstract=983739 accessed 1 June 2017.

[7] Which includes the need to show both the existence of a trade secret and the misappropriation, see Matt Marx, Jasjit Singh and Lee Fleming, 'Regional Disadvantage? Non-Compete Agreements and Brain Drain' (2010) 4 http://papers.ssrn.com/sol3/papers.cfm?abstract_id=1654719 accessed 1 June 2017.

[8] Also referred to as 'non-dealing clauses', see Gurry on Breach of Confidence para 12.02. Solicitation of customers of the former employer is also referred to as 'customer-poaching', see e.g. Salger and Breitfeld, 'Regelungen zum Schutz von betrieblichen Know-how – die Sicherung von Geschäfts- und Betriebsgeheimnissen' 154, 156–158. The extent to which an NSA may be breached by use of social media such as LinkedIn is debated in the United States, see e.g. Marisa Warren and Arnie Pedowitz, 'Social Media, Trade Secrets, and Yes, the Sky is Falling' (2011) www.americanbar.org/content/dam/aba/administrative/labor_law/meetings/2011/tech/a_03.authcheckdam.pdf accessed 1 June 2017.

a competitive activity.[9] In this case they serve as a measure to protect trade secrets relating to the internal functioning of the company and in particular to the qualities and skills of its employees, remuneration schemes and other working conditions. Non-solicitation agreements may be seen as a sub-category of covenants not to compete.[10]

There may be various reasons for entering into a contractual relationship instead of relying on the protection provided to trade secrets by statute. Principally, post-employment covenants increase certainty.[11] NDAs serve as notification to the employee as to which information is a trade secret, they limit the risk of (at least involuntary) disclosure and provide the former employee with clarity as to what information he may use after departure. In jurisdictions which require measures to maintain secrecy of the information, the conclusion of an agreement will serve as evidence to show the existence of a trade secret.[12] Even in other jurisdictions a description of the subject-matter of a trade secret in a contract may be helpful upon enforcement.[13] Furthermore, an action for breach of contract may be more convenient for the employer than an action for misappropriation of trade secrets, because a contractual claim may be asserted before any misappropriation occurs and does not require a proof of use or disclosure of a secret, only a breach of a provision of the agreement must be shown.[14]

Despite these advantages, in practice it may not be easy to draft a clear confidentiality agreement. This can make it difficult to detect and enforce a breach of such a contract.[15] In this respect, agreements not to compete may be a more attractive, even if indirect, way to protect trade secrets. Since they refer to acts of competition rather than particular information,

9 '"Enticement" covenants', as referred to in Gurry on Breach of Confidence para 12.02; See also Margo E K Reder and Christine Neylon O'Brien, 'Managing the Risk of Trade Secret Loss Due to Job Mobility in an Innovation Economy with the Theory of Inevitable Disclosure' (2012) 12 *Journal of High Technology Law* 7 http://ssrn.com/abstract=2014051 accessed 1 June 2017.

10 Bishara, 'Covenants Not to Compete in a Knowledge Economy: Balancing Innovation from Employee Mobility against Legal Protection for Human Capital Investment' 287, 294.

11 As a result of the case-by-case assessment, the legal framework governing trade secrets is often perceived as convoluted, and the case-law as inconsistent.

12 Weiss, 'Biting the Hand that Stops Feeding: How to protect Trade Secrets from Misappropriation by Laid Off Employees' 469, 479.

13 In fulfilling the duty to substantiate a claim and provide evidence of the alleged misappropriation, Schlötter 193.

14 William A Landes and Richard A Posner, *The Economic Structure of Intellectual Property Law* (The Belknap Press of Harvard University Press 2003) 360, 365.

15 Gurry on Breach of Confidence para 12.03.

their infringement is easier to detect and, if litigation proves successful, the formulation of an injunctive relief is not overly problematic.[16] Yet, because such agreements have the effect of limiting competition, they must be subject to careful scrutiny.[17]

Some authors[18] suggest that taking into consideration the benefits of contractual regulation, agreements are a better tool than statute for safeguarding valuable information and they should replace statute as means of trade secrets protection. This proposal is especially attractive for employers. It would increase legal certainty surrounding the use of information learned from the former employer. However, reliance on contract, and in particular on broad covenants not to compete, raises concerns stemming from the imbalance of powers both during contractual negotiations and upon enforcement, which favours the employers. Reliance solely on contractual regulation might result in employers imposing broad post-employment duties on their employees. Even if they were not compliant with the rules of contract law, the employees might not challenge them in court, which is costly in both time and money. This might have a negative impact on their freedom of self-determination in choosing a profession. On the policy level, unlimited freedom to contract might lead to restriction of competition and mobility.

These risks have been recognised by both legislators and the courts and, as a response, tools have been created, aiming at limitation of the contractual freedom to regulate the use of information learned during service, particularly where the contract would effectively limit the ex-employee's freedom to compete with his former principal.

This chapter presents an analysis of the application of the freedom to conclude post-employment agreements on the use of trade secrets, as well as the limits to that freedom.[19]

16 Gurry on Breach of Confidence para 12.04, but stressing a disadvantage of time-limited NCAs for the protection of trade secrets, which may be interpreted as indication that after expiry of the agreed time limit the employer is no longer interested in the information covered by the agreement (note 8).

17 Gurry on Breach of Confidence para 12.05.

18 Robert G Bone, 'A New Look at Trade Secret Law: Doctrine in Search of Justification' (1998) 86 *Cal L Rev* 241, 303–304, considering introduction of limited exceptions to contractual regulation; Robert G Bone, 'The (Still) Shaky Foundations of Trade Secret Law' (2014) 92 *Tex L R* 1803, 1836–1838.

19 The analysis is made here under the assumption that, unless otherwise indicated, the contract was freely negotiated and entered into and free from legal defects (such as mistake, fraud or duress). That is, the analysis concerns the limitations to post-employment contracts in particular and not to contracts in general.

II Comparative Analysis

A Post-Employment Contracts in Germany

In Germany, post-employment competition by an employee is generally allowed.[20] What is more, the use of trade secrets of the former employer is also generally allowed, unless it would be unfair towards the former principal.[21] As was discussed above,[22] this flexible rule requires assessment on a case-by-case basis and thus may be perceived as causing legal uncertainty. This uncertainty can be limited to some extent[23] by conclusion of an agreement which lays down the rules on the use of information learned during employment after its termination.

German law distinguishes between agreements not to disclose trade secrets, which are regulated by general rules of contract law, and agreements not to compete, which are governed by dedicated statutory provisions.

1 Non-Disclosure Agreements

Covenants not to disclose trade secrets are not subject to specific regulation.[24] They may be entered into at any time during employment, before commencement or after termination of this relationship, by way of an individual agreement or collectively.[25]

Such agreements must be limited to trade secrets and may not cover any other information.[26] The BAG in the *Thrombosol* decision considered that

[20] NZA 1999, 200, 201 (BAG) *Kantenbänder;* Falk Freiherr von Maltzahn, 'Wettbewerbsrechtliche Probleme beim Arbeitsplatzwechsel' (1981) GRUR 788, 794; Dieter Gaul, 'Die nachvertragliche Geheimhaltungspflicht eines ausgeschiedenen Arbeitnehmers' (1988) NZA 225, 225; Molkenbur, 'Pflicht zur Geheimniswahrung nach Ende des Arbeitsverhältnisses?' 1196, 1198.

[21] As an act of unfair competition as considered by the BGH or as a result of a duty of fidelity towards the former employer and the duty to safeguard the former employer's trade secrets (duty of confidentiality) which survives the employment relationship, as considered by the BAG, see Richters and Wodtke, 'Schutz von Betriebsgeheimnissen aus Unternehmenssicht "Verhinderung von Know-how Abfluss durch eigene Mitarbeiter"' 281.

[22] Chapter 3, part II, point A.

[23] That is, within the limits applicable to contractual freedom, in particular statutory prohibitions (S 134 BGB), rules of good conduct and public policy (S 138 BGB), performance in good faith (S 242 BGB) and limitations applicable to standard business terms (S 305 BGB), Eileen Gaugenrieder and Dagmar Unger-Hellmich, 'Know-How Schutz – gehen mit dem Mitarbeiter auch die Unternehmensgeheimnisse?' (2011) WRP 1364, 1376.

[24] As is the case for NCAs, which must satisfy the requirements of Ss 74ff HGB. These are discussed infra in Chapter 4, part II, point A.2.

[25] Schlötter 196.

[26] Charlotte Sander, 'Schutz nicht offenbarter betrieblicher Informationen nach der Beendigung des Arbeitsverhältnisses im deutschen und amerikanischen Recht' (2013) GRUR-Int 217, 225.

as long as the post-employment agreement is restricted to prohibition of disclosure of trade secrets, the employee's freedom to decide on his post-employment activity is not limited; he is merely put in the same competitive position as his colleagues who did not learn the secret information.[27] Since such an agreement does not constitute a limitation of the freedom of the ex-employee to compete with his former employer, it does not require compensation.[28]

The broad statement made in *Thrombosol* that any trade secret may be the subject of a non-disclosure agreement has been questioned. In particular, this decision is compared with the *Kundenlisten*[29] decision of the same court, where it was considered that the duty not to disclose information relating to clients does not encompass a prohibition against disclosing the former principal's clients. These two decisions have been perceived as contradictory.[30] This may seem to be the case, however this apparent contradiction may be explained by the differing facts of those cases. While *Thrombosol* related to technical information which was the core business of the ex-employer and which was not essential for the employee to continue his professional activity in the relevant field, *Kundenlisten* related to client information which was necessary for the continuation of the employee's professional activity. Thus, the balancing of the conflicting interests led to different results in those cases.

It appears that, as a result of the requirement that contracts be performed in good faith (Section 242 BGB), even when assessing agreements restricted to the use of trade secrets the balancing exercise is necessary.[31] Depending on the circumstances, in particular the position and duties of the former employee, his pre-employment experience and the industry in which he is active, even a limitation of the use of trade secrets may effectively deny him the possibility to remain professionally active[32] by making the best use of his skills and experience and thus be contrary to Article 12 GG and Section 242 BGB.

[27] NJW 1983, 134, 135 (BAG) *Thrombosol*; Richters and Wodtke, 'Schutz von Betriebsgeheimnissen aus Unternehmenssicht "Verhinderung von Know-how Abfluss durch eigene Mitarbeiter"' 281, 283.

[28] NJW 1983, 134, 135 (BAG) *Thrombosol*.

[29] NJW 1988, 1686 (BAG) *Kundenlisten*.

[30] Richters and Wodtke, 'Schutz von Betriebsgeheimnissen aus Unternehmenssicht "Verhinderung von Know-how Abfluss durch eigene Mitarbeiter"' 281, 285.

[31] Gaul, 'Die nachvertragliche Geheimhaltungspflicht eines ausgeschiedenen Arbeitnehmers' 225, 226, 229; Richters and Wodtke, 'Schutz von Betriebsgeheimnissen aus Unternehmenssicht "Verhinderung von Know-how Abfluss durch eigene Mitarbeiter"' 281, 285.

[32] Even though, as explained by Gaul, an agreement not to disclose has as its object the exercise rather than choice of occupation, Gaul, 'Die nachvertragliche Geheimhaltungspflicht eines ausgeschiedenen Arbeitnehmers' 225, 229. A prohibitive

In particular, the scope of the NDA is to be taken into consideration in the balancing exercise. The negative effect on the former employee's professional activity may depend on whether the contract is limited only to disclosure or whether it also encompasses use of the information.

1) Subject-Matter of an NDA

Non-disclosure agreements make it possible to explicitly determine which information is a trade secret which the ex-employee is not allowed to disclose or use after termination of employment.[33] This can be done by identifying the information (e.g. information contained in documents marked as confidential), its source (e.g. information concerning a particular project) or circumstances in which it was disclosed to the employee (e.g. information discussed during meetings of an internal body of the company).[34] Often the restricted information is determined by referring to what is not confidential.[35]

In view of *Titanoxid,* non-disclosure agreements limited to trade secrets are generally accepted. It is submitted that nevertheless the assessment of the effect of such a contract should take into consideration the circumstances of the particular case, because under *Titanoxid* only such limitation of disclosure of information is allowed which puts the contracting employee in the same position as his colleagues who did not find out about the information. Therefore, an NDA may be allowed only if the employee is not restrained in his post-employment professional activity.[36] Otherwise, it would need to be seen as an NCA, which must fulfil stricter requirements.

effect of an NDA may be particularly visible in the case of creative employees, who have a strong interest in relying on the information which they have learned or developed in previous service, ibid.

33 NZA 1999, 200, 201 (BAG) *Kantenbänder*; Salger and Breitfeld, 'Regelungen zum Schutz von betrieblichen Know-how – die Sicherung von Geschäfts- und Betriebsgeheimnissen' 154, 158.

34 Peter Kurz, *Vertraulichkeitsvereinbarungen* (3rd edn Carl Heymanns Verlag 2013) paras 97–98; see also Arndt J Hengstler, *Die Geheimhaltungsvereinbarung (Non-Disclosure Agreement)* (Verlag Recht und Wirtschaft Frankfurt am Main 2011) 17. Considering that overly broad NDAs may be considered null and void or invalid and lacking legal effect, clear formulation and determination of the subject-matter is recommendable, see Richters and Wodtke, 'Schutz von Betriebsgeheimnissen aus Unternehmenssicht "Verhinderung von Know-how Abfluss durch eigene Mitarbeiter"' 281, 287; Salger and Breitfeld, 'Regelungen zum Schutz von betrieblichen Know-how – die Sicherung von Geschäfts- und Betriebsgeheimnissen' 154, 158.

35 Nigel Parker, 'The Secret Recipe: Key Ingredients of Agreements to Protect Confidential Information' (2011) 6(4) *JIPLP* 223, 224.

36 Richters and Wodtke, 'Schutz von Betriebsgeheimnissen aus Unternehmenssicht "Verhinderung von Know-how Abfluss durch eigene Mitarbeiter"' (2003) NZA-RR 281, 287.

Generally, broadly formulated non-disclosure clauses are not accepted,[37] since they are likely to encompass information other than trade secrets. However, a relatively broad formulation may be the only way to encompass information which was learned by the employee while in service, but which was not related to his duties as employee.[38] This solution should be accepted since such trade secrets can hardly be deemed necessary for the ex-employee to continue his professional activity. This also corresponds to the rules governing the use of trade secrets where no contract has been entered into.

Under *Titanoxid*, clauses which encompass information which is not a trade secret, e.g. because it is part of the employee's general skill and knowledge,[39] and in particular knowledge from before employment,[40] are likely to go beyond what is necessary to safeguard the interests of the employer. If the ex-employee is not in a position to distinguish the trade secrets from his own experience, the contract may be unclear or overly broad and thus have an effect of a covenant not to compete.[41]

Also a non-disclosure clause covering a wide range of information relating to clients[42] may have the effect of limiting the competitive activity of the ex-employee. If this limitation is not insignificant,[43] it

[37] As explained by Gaugenrieder and Unger-Hellmich, the usual clauses obliging the departed employee to maintain the confidentiality of 'all company and business information, including any trade secrets' do not have a legal effect due to their broad formulation, Gaugenrieder and Unger-Hellmich, 'Know-How Schutz – gehen mit dem Mitarbeiter auch die Unternehmensgeheimnisse?' 1364, 1377. Molkenbur seems to accept such broad clauses, see Molkenbur, 'Pflicht zur Geheimniswahrung nach Ende des Arbeitsverhältnisses?' 1196, 1198.

[38] Frank Wertheimer, 'Bezahlte Karenz oder entschädigungslose Wettbewerbsenthaltung des ausgeschiedenen Arbeitnehmers?' (1999) BB 1600, 1602.

[39] Under the theory of reparability applied by the BAG, an employee's skill and knowledge are not a trade secret. Nevertheless, the BAG fails to provide for reliable guidance on how the distinction should be made, see Richters and Wodtke, 'Schutz von Betriebsgeheimnissen aus Unternehmenssicht "Verhinderung von Know-how Abfluss durch eigene Mitarbeiter"' 281, 287.

[40] Gaul, 'Die nachvertragliche Geheimhaltungspflicht eines ausgeschiedenen Arbeitnehmers' 225, 232.

[41] Schlötter 195, 197.

[42] Which the departed employee is generally allowed to use if he relies on what he remembers, as explained supra Chapter 3 part II, point A.

[43] This was found e.g. for a clause prohibiting a former wine dealer from making any use of the names of the clients which he had learned during employment, both in his own activity and in employment for others. The BAG considered that such a clause effectively amounts to prohibition of competition with the former employer, as it was not limited territorially or in duration and because it excluded the professional activity of the ex-employee precisely in the trade that he specialised in, see NJW 1988, 1686, 1686 (BAG) *Kundenlisten*. See also Richters and Wodtke, 'Schutz von Betriebsgeheimnissen aus Unternehmenssicht "Verhinderung von Know-how Abfluss durch eigene Mitarbeiter"' 281, 287.

may no longer be seen merely as an NDA, but is rather an NCA, which requires compensation in order to be effective.[44]

2) Scope of Prohibited Acts: Disclosure, Use, Sale to Third Parties

If the prohibition encompasses not only the disclosure of the secret information but also its use, a conflict arises between the employer's interests safeguarded by the contract and the employee's right to compete.[45] While the prohibition of use of client information learned during employment was considered a disproportional limitation of the ex-employee's rights, the prohibition of sale of client data to third parties was accepted.[46] Thus, client information should be protected by agreements not to disclose only if they are limited to prohibition of selling client information to third parties.[47] Exclusion of use by the ex-employee himself would amount to limitation of competition.

It is submitted that this could be different in the case of technical secrets which are the core of the employer's business and in the case of data which is not essential for the employee in order to remain professionally active. Prohibition of both disclosure and use of such information is not likely to amount to restriction of competition.

In any case, if use of the particular information would amount to its disclosure, an NDA may encompass both.

3) Duration of the Agreement Not to Disclose

By nature, an agreement not to disclose a secret ceases to be binding upon disclosure of the information, i.e. when the object of the protection and its rationale ceases to exist.[48] Otherwise, due to the potentially indefinite existence of a trade secret, an NDA may be of unlimited duration.[49]

[44] NJW 1988, 1686, 1686 (BAG) *Kundenlisten.*

[45] Gaul seems to consider that a typical NDA would encompass also the prohibition of use of the information. Thus, he suggests that after termination of the NDA the ex-employee should be allowed to use the information for himself or for his new employer, but not to disclose it to others until the information loses the quality of secrecy, see Gaul, 'Die nachvertragliche Geheimhaltungspflicht eines ausgeschiedenen Arbeitnehmers' 225, 232.

[46] NJW 1988, 1686, 1687 (BAG) *Kundenlisten.*

[47] Richters and Wodtke, 'Schutz von Betriebsgeheimnissen aus Unternehmenssicht "Verhinderung von Know-how Abfluss durch eigene Mitarbeiter"' 281, 285; Schlötter 197. Wertheimer proposes that a valid NDA could also encompass the use of the information in employment for others, see Wertheimer, 'Bezahlte Karenz oder entschädigungslose Wettbewerbsenthaltung des ausgeschiedenen Arbeitnehmers?' 1600, 1602. It is submitted that this proposal goes too far since it limits the freedom of post-employment activity only to independent business, which is not always possible.

[48] Schlötter 198. This however needs to be proven by the ex-employee, see Richters and Wodtke, 'Schutz von Betriebsgeheimnissen aus Unternehmenssicht "Verhinderung von Know-how Abfluss durch eigene Mitarbeiter"' 281, 288.

[49] Gaugenrieder and Unger-Hellmich, 'Know-How Schutz – gehen mit dem Mitarbeiter auch die Unternehmensgeheimnisse?' 1364, 1378.

There are however voices suggesting that also such covenants which are confined to trade secrets and which limit post-employment competition only insignificantly should be of limited duration. Gaul explains that also contractual obligations underlie the principle of proportionality laid down in Article 12(1) GG. Consequently, limitations of use of certain information after termination of the employment relationship may be accepted only to the extent that they do not overly restrict the ex-employee's post-employment activity.[50] He proposes to assess the duration of the contractual duty not to disclose trade secrets from the point of view of the consideration which the employee receives from his principal during employment, measured by the knowledge and experience gained during service. Most employees enter employment relationship with some knowledge and skills. They should not be prejudiced just because they were professionally active with a particular employer and thus learned the information during this relationship rather than through independent development. Therefore, an NDA should not last longer than the time a skilled person would need in order to work out the trade secret independently.[51]

The proposal to consider the employee's knowledge gathered before entering service is interesting. However, it seems more appropriate to include it as a factor to determine the scope of the duty not to disclose trade secrets after termination of employment where no contractual relationship was entered into. It is submitted here that the principle allowing NDAs only if they limit the post-employment activity of the employee not more than insignificantly satisfies the proportionality required by Article 12(1) GG. Nevertheless, it is suggested here that evidence concerning the likely time needed for independent development may be used as one of the factors for determining the duration of an injunction, if a breach of contract is found.[52]

The principle of proportionality contained in Article 12(1) GG has also served as a basis for proposing a time-limitation of the duration of an NDA to two[53] or five[54] years.

[50] Gaul, 'Die nachvertragliche Geheimhaltungspflicht eines ausgeschiedenen Arbeitnehmers' 225, 229.

[51] Ibid 225, 230.

[52] See infra Chapter 5 part II, point A.3.

[53] By reference to the duration of NCAs under S 74 HGB, see e.g. Jürgen Kunz, 'Betriebs- und Geschäftsgeheimnisse und Wettbewerbsverbot während der Dauer und nach Beendigung des Anstellungsverhältnisses' (1993) DB 2482, 2486 (criticised by Gaul in 'Die nachvertragliche Geheimhaltungspflicht eines ausgeschiedenen Arbeitnehmers' 225, 232). Similarly Molkenbur, 'Pflicht zur Geheimniswahrung nach Ende des Arbeitsverhältnisses?' 1196, 1199–1200; Richters and Wodtke, 'Schutz von Betriebsgeheimnissen aus Unternehmenssicht "Verhinderung von Know-how Abfluss durch eigene Mitarbeiter"' 281, 288.

[54] Gaul, 'Die nachvertragliche Geheimhaltungspflicht eines ausgeschiedenen Arbeitnehmers' 225, 232, who argues that this time limit is proportional to the average time needed in order to develop a typical trade secret.

Other authors argue that the most balanced approach is to determine the duration of an NDA, like its validity, in the light of various factors, including the competitive value of the information for the employer. Thus, it is proposed that the duration of an NDA is always limited, but that the actual time of the obligation should be determined case-by-case.[55]

It is observed here that the extent to which non-disclosure covenants are accepted is narrow: they may not influence the competitive position of the former employee. If an NDA is limited only to safeguarding the secrecy of the information and does not affect the ex-employee's freedom to work, there seems to be no reason not to recognise its unlimited duration, terminated by the loss of secrecy. Considering that trade secrecy is a relative concept, the use of the information by one more competitor does not destroy the value of the secret, and at the same time brings positive market effects by enhancing competition. If, on the other hand, an NDA also prohibits the use of the information by the employee himself, it seems reasonable to recognise the termination of such a contractual obligation, either from the beginning, as a result of bargaining, or once the employee receives the information from some other source, e.g. his new employer. Otherwise, the recommendation from *Titanoxid* that the prohibition should merely put the employee in a similar position to that of his colleagues would lose its meaning. However, it must be stressed that this does not terminate the obligation to maintain the secrecy of the information, but only the obligation to refrain from its use, unless the information has lost its secret status for reasons which cannot be ascribed to the employee.

4) Legal Consequences of an Overly Broad NDA

An agreement not to disclose trade secrets after termination of employment may broaden the duty of confidentiality applied to departed employees.[56] However, an overly broad contract, e.g. not restricted to clearly defined secret information, may in effect limit the employee's right to compete with his ex-employer and thus have effect of a covenant not to compete.[57] As

[55] Richters and Wodtke, 'Schutz von Betriebsgeheimnissen aus Unternehmenssicht "Verhinderung von Know-how Abfluss durch eigene Mitarbeiter"' 281, 288; similarly Gaugenrieder and Unger-Hellmich, 'Know-How Schutz – gehen mit dem Mitarbeiter auch die Unternehmensgeheimnisse?' 1364, 1378; Kurz, *Vertraulichkeitsvereinbarungen* para 644.

[56] LAG Hamm judgment of 05.10.1988, 15 Sa 1403/88, BeckRS 1988, 06934.

[57] NZA 1999, 200, 201 (BAG) *Kantenbänder*; Wertheimer, 'Bezahlte Karenz oder entschädigungslose Wettbewerbsenthaltung des ausgeschiedenen Arbeitnehmers?' 1600, 1601; Gaugenrieder and Unger-Hellmich, 'Know-How Schutz – gehen mit dem Mitarbeiter auch die Unternehmensgeheimnisse?' 1364, 1374–1375; Schlötter 195. For example, a contractual obligation not to disclose any information learned during employment, concerning any transactions, company or financial affairs, technical

such, lacking compensation, it would be considered invalid and lacking legal effect (*unwirksam*).[58]

Even if it is not qualified as an NCA,[59] an overly broad NDA might be null and void (*nichtig*) as going against the rules of good conduct and public policy (*gute Sitten*) pursuant to Section 138 BGB.[60] When determining whether an NDA is in breach of those rules, a similar assessment is made as when judging fairness of the use of information in the absence of a contract. Thus, all the circumstances of the particular case must be taken into account. The assessment includes in particular a decision on whether the limitation imposed by the contract is disproportionate considering the interests of the parties involved: the interest of the employer in maintaining the secrecy of certain information measured by its competitive value and the interest of the employee in his professional mobility.[61]

The effect of a contract being void is ex tunc and in toto. The majority approach seems to be that a void NDA may not be partially retained to the extent it might have been valid.[62] Bauer and Diller suggest that in case of invalidity, apart from the general duty of confidentiality recognised in the lack of contract, the prohibition against using information outside the ex-employee's professional activity, including by selling it 'as a commodity' to third parties, should remain.[63]

improvements or inventions, was considered too broad and thus contrary to good conduct and public policy (§138 BGB) in LAG Hamm judgment of 05.10.1988, 15 Sa 1403/88, BeckRS 1988, 06934.

[58] NJW 1988, 1686, 1686 (BAG) *Kundenlisten*. Elsewhere described as null and void (*nichtig*), see e.g. Bauer/Diller para 152.

[59] In case the agreement is qualified as a covenant not to compete, the application of S 74–75f HGB takes precedence over S 138 BGB, see Bauer/Diller para 174.

[60] LAG Hamm judgment of 05.10.1988, 15 Sa 1403/88, BeckRS 1988, 06934; Gaugenrieder and Unger-Hellmich, 'Know-How Schutz – gehen mit dem Mitarbeiter auch die Unternehmensgeheimnisse?' 1364, 1377; Schlötter 196.

[61] LAG Hamm judgment of 05.10.1988, 15 Sa 1403/88, BeckRS 1988, 06934, where the court did not provide further guidance as to how the necessary balance should be struck, but considered that an agreement prohibiting the provision of any information also to the members of the employee's family and to his legal counsel was against public policy. Gaugenrieder and Unger-Hellmich argue that the content of the employment agreement itself (in particular the information regarding remuneration) may be the object of an NDA since its disclosure may influence the competitive position of the employer or cause internal tensions, see Gaugenrieder and Unger-Hellmich, 'Know-How Schutz – gehen mit dem Mitarbeiter auch die Unternehmensgeheimnisse?' 1364, 1377.

[62] In other words, a void NDA may not be 'blue pencilled' and limited to concrete trade secrets, see Richters and Wodtke, 'Schutz von Betriebsgeheimnissen aus Unternehmenssicht "Verhinderung von Know-how Abfluss durch eigene Mitarbeiter"' 281, 285; Gaugenrieder and Unger-Hellmich, 'Know-How Schutz – gehen mit dem Mitarbeiter auch die Unternehmensgeheimnisse?' 1364, 1377; Sander, 'Schutz nicht offenbarter betrieblicher Informationen nach der Beendigung des Arbeitsverhältnisses im deutschen und amerikanischen Recht' 217, 225; Bauer/Diller para 126.

[63] Bauer/Diller para 126.

5) *Summary: Agreements Not to Disclose under German Law*

Despite the general freedom to contract, covenants not to disclose certain information after termination of the employment relationship are not always accepted. They must be assessed on a case-by-case basis, with a view to the effect that they might have on the freedom of the departed employee to engage in professional activity, including in competition with his former employer.[64] As a result of this assessment, only such clauses may be accepted as NDAs as do not limit the competitive activity of the ex-employee but which merely put him in the same position as his former colleagues who did not possess the secret data.[65]

The case-law does not provide detailed guidance as to how the right balance between the interests of the employer and the employee is to be achieved in this case. This has led some authors to consider that in the absence of a valid covenant not to compete, the scope of a post-employment NDA may not go beyond the general post-employment duty of confidentiality applicable in the absence of a contract.[66] Others take the view that the limits of an acceptable NDA are crossed when the contract effectively denies the ex-employee the use of the knowledge gained during employment.[67] Bauer and Diller argue that already a noticeable limitation of post-employment competition may be seen as crossing the line of an allowable NDA.[68]

It is considered here that an overall analysis of a particular case may include an assessment of similar factors to those analysed when determining the fairness of the use of particular information after termination of employment. Considering the freedom of contracting, this assessment should however be more focused on establishing the intentions of the contracting parties,[69] and take into account their respective bargaining power. It is proposed here that clear determination of information covered by the agreement and the effect on the competitive position of the departed employee should be given particular weight.

2 Agreements Not to Compete

The limitations applicable to the scope of covenants not to disclose may make their drafting difficult, and an imprecise NDA may be invalid

[64] NJW 1988, 1686, 1686 (BAG) *Kundenlisten*; Gaul, 'Die nachvertragliche Geheimhaltungspflicht eines ausgeschiedenen Arbeitnehmers' 225, 229.

[65] Schlötter 198.

[66] Richters and Wodtke, 'Schutz von Betriebsgeheimnissen aus Unternehmenssicht "Verhinderung von Know-how Abfluss durch eigene Mitarbeiter"' 281, 287.

[67] Gaugenrieder and Unger-Hellmich, 'Know-How Schutz – gehen mit dem Mitarbeiter auch die Unternehmensgeheimnisse?' 1364, 1377, referring to NJW 1988, 1686 (BAG) *Kundenlisten.*

[68] Bauer/Diller para 124.

[69] S 133 BGB.

pursuant to Section 138 BGB. Moreover, if the NDA is qualified as having the effect of limiting the competitive activity of the former employee, without compensation, it is likely to be regarded as an invalid covenant not to compete.

Therefore, in situations in which the parties intend to actually limit the post-employment competitive activity of the employee, it is advisable to conclude an agreement to that effect.[70] Thereby, the protection of trade secrets is achieved without the necessity to define this information.

Unlike covenants not to disclose, agreements aimed at limiting post-employment competition are regulated by statute. Pursuant to Section 110 GewO, Sections 74–75f HGB are applicable to contracts between employers and employees.[71]

1) Requirements of an NCA

Pursuant to Section 74(1) HGB, an agreement between an employer and an employee which limits post-employment competition by the latter must be concluded in writing and requires the delivery to the employee of a document signed by the employer, stipulating the conditions of that agreement.

Such a contract is binding (*verbindlich*) only if the principal commits himself to paying compensation for the duration of the covenant, as prescribed in Section 74(2) HGB. This compensation is a consideration for the limitation of the employee's freedom to compete with his previous principal. On the one hand, its aim is to compensate the employee for possible loss of income due to restriction of competition. On the other hand, considering the statutory determination of its minimum amount, it serves as a deterrent for the employer to insist on the limitation where it is not essential to protect his interests.[72] The amount of compensation is calculated on the basis of the remuneration that the employee was receiving upon termination of employment and may not be lower than half of this remuneration, including basic salary and all other income from the employment.[73] Thus, in case of highly paid employees, the costs of a post-employment limitation of competition may be significant.

[70] Brock in Ann/Loschelder/Grosch 128.

[71] Covenants not to compete with members of the company's organs are not regulated by Ss 74–75f HGB, since they are not employees. The limits of post-employment restrictions imposed on them by way of contract are assessed under S 138 BGB, see Brock in Ann/Loschelder/Grosch 129. See also Johan-Michel Menke, 'Gestaltung nachvertraglicher Wettbewerbsverbote mit GmbH-Geschäftsführern. Verzicht statt Karenzentschädigung' (2009) NJW 636.

[72] Schlötter 203.

[73] S 74(2) HGB; Schlötter 203. For more on calculation of the compensation, see Brock in Ann/Loschelder/Grosch 152–159.

The covenant may be concluded prior to or during employment, by way of an individual agreement or collectively. An agreement not to compete concluded after termination of the employment relationship is not subject to the conditions provided in Sections 74–75f HGB. In such circumstances, the special employment relationship no longer exists and thus the employee as the weaker party no longer needs to be protected.[74]

Even though not explicitly provided for in the HGB, the former employee's obligation to refrain from competitive activity may be safeguarded by agreeing on a contractual penalty in case of breach of the obligation not to compete.[75]

2) Limitations of the Contractual Freedom to Conclude Post-Employment Agreements Not to Compete

Further conditions apply to the conclusion of agreements limiting post-employment competition: an NCA must serve the protection of a legitimate commercial interest of the employer, it must not unfairly limit the employee's post-employment professional activity, and it must not extend beyond the duration of two years, as prescribed in Section 74a(1) HGB.

All of these conditions must be fulfilled cumulatively. In the first place it must be established whether the NCA is supported by the existence of a legitimate commercial interest of the employer. To the extent that is the case, it is then to be scrutinised whether the agreement does not overly limit the post-employment professional activity of the employee. Thus, for the parts of the agreement which are not supported by a legitimate interest of the employer, no assessment of the fairness of the limitation needs to be made.[76]

a) Legitimate Commercial Interest of the Employer The legitimate interest of the employer protected by a covenant not to compete is understood as an interest in preservation of his business activity and competitive position. According to Bauer and Diller, even though this legitimate commercial interest needs not be the only motivation for the employer in

[74] Schlötter 200; see also Brock in Ann/Loschelder/Grosch 129–130.

[75] Richters and Wodtke, 'Schutz von Betriebsgeheimnissen aus Unternehmenssicht "Verhinderung von Know-how Abfluss durch eigene Mitarbeiter"' 281, 288; Salger and Breitfeld, 'Regelungen zum Schutz von betrieblichen Know-how – die Sicherung von Geschäfts- und Betriebsgeheimnissen' 154, 157; Mathias M Siems, 'Die Logik des Schutzes von Betriebsgeheimnissen' (2007) WRP 1146, 1150; Brock in Ann/Loschelder/Grosch 144–146.

[76] NZA 2010, 1175, 1176 (BAG) *Anspruch auf Karenzentschädigung* para 18; Bauer/Diller paras 348, 341.

entering an NCA, it must support the substantive and territorial limitation of the employee's post-employment competitive activity as well as its duration.[77]

The legitimate interest of the employer will usually be found where the agreement aims at protection of trade secrets or relationships with clients or contractors.[78]

Moreover, there must exist a link between the activity prohibited by an NCA and the duties of the employee while in service.[79] A covenant limiting competition may not prohibit service for any competitor of the former employer, with the purpose of forbidding a qualified employee to undertake any activity or to exclude competition as such.[80] Accordingly, an employee active in marketing of food products is likely to be effectively prevented from working in the food marketing department of a competitor, but not necessarily in his department responsible for home cleaning products. The existence of the link should be assessed from the perspective of the duties and responsibilities in the previous and in the new employment.[81] To the extent that such a link cannot be identified, no legitimate interest of the employer exists and thus the NCA is invalid and lacking legal effect. This is a reasonable solution, considering the growing number of corporations which are active in multiple industries.[82]

A link between the employee's service for the employer and the competitive activity envisaged in an NCA does not exist where the covenant prohibits solicitation of the former colleagues of the employee to leave their employment and join their former colleague in his competitive activity.[83] Thus while NSAs having as their purpose the protection of the employer's client base are generally accepted, this is not the case where they are aimed at him keeping his staff.

[77] Bauer/Diller paras 301–302. Understood in this way, the assessment of the employer's interest must correspond to the aspects under which the limitation of the employee's mobility is scrutinised under S 74a(1) second sentence HGB.

[78] Schlötter 200; Bauer/Diller paras 305, 312.

[79] NZA 2010, 1175, 1176 (BAG) *Anspruch auf Karenzentschädigung* para 16.

[80] NZA 2010, 1175, 1176 (BAG) *Anspruch auf Karenzentschädigung* para 15; Schlötter 201; Bauer/Diller paras 305, 307, 311. This was the case when NCAs were entered into only with certain particularly productive employees, see LAG Thüringen decision of 11.06.2001, 8 Sa 418/00, ZIP 2002, 587.

[81] Thus, the areas of activity (e.g. judged by the products sold) of the previous and of the new employer must overlap at least partially, LAG Baden-Württemberg judgment of 30.01.2008, 10 Sa 60/07, NZA-RR 2008, 508.

[82] For example, energy, construction, transport, medical instruments, healthcare, home appliances and finance, to name but a few in the case of Siemens AG, see www.siemens.com/entry/de/de/#-2326790 accessed 1 June 2017.

[83] NZA 2010, 1175, 1177 (BAG) *Anspruch auf Karenzentschädigung* para 21; Bauer/Diller para 305. Brock seems to be of the opinion that such NSAs may generally be accepted, see Brock in Ann/Loschelder/Grosch 147.

Similarly, no such link may be found where an NCA has the purpose of safeguarding the investment made by the employer in the training of the employee,[84] or where its only goal is to punish the departing employee for terminating his service.[85]

Although it is possible to draft an NCA restricting the employee from undertaking activity for particular competitors, this must be accompanied by an interest in protecting trade secrets or client relations. If such a clause aims at weakening a particular competitor, it is not supported by a legitimate interest of the employer.[86]

The interest in limitation of the competitive activity of the employee must be the employer's interest. Thus, generally, an NCA must be restricted to working for the employer's competitors. However Bauer and Diller explain that under certain circumstances, despite a lack of direct competition between the old and the new employer, exclusion of service for competitors of a subsidiary may be supported by a legitimate interest of the parent company. The condition for a binding effect of such a clause is that despite lack of direct competition, the employee's work for the prospective employer would pose a real threat to the interests of his former employer (usually the parent company in a corporate group – *Konzern*)[87] This could be the case e.g. where the former employer produces cars, and the new employer software. They are not direct competitors, since the ex-employer purchases software for his cars from his subsidiary. Prohibition of service for the new employer would be supported by legitimate interest of a direct competitor (subsidiary of the former employer), but the ex-employee's activity could harm the interests of the ex-employer if the new employer with the help of the ex-employee started to produce software, which could be installed in cars produced by the old employer. Similarly, even though usually no competitive relationship exists between the employer and his clients, he may nevertheless have an interest in excluding the possibility of the employee working for those clients, if this could result in the loss of that client, e.g. because the employee would take with him the know-how which the customer had previously been buying from the employer.[88]

To establish whether the employer has a legitimate interest protectable by an NCA, the position of the employee in the company must be taken

84 This investment may be protected by an agreement to reimburse the relevant costs of training in case of termination of the employment relationship, see Bauer/Diller paras 305, 311.

85 Bauer/Diller para 305.

86 Ibid para 313.

87 Ibid paras 316–317; generally, see Brock in Ann/Loschelder/Grosch 140–141.

88 Brock in Ann/Loschelder/Grosch 142; Bauer/Diller para 318.

into consideration. Thus, the higher that position was and the broader the scope of his duties and access to information, the bigger the area of competitive activity that the ex-employee may be prevented from entering into after termination of his employment.[89]

In the case of an NCA aiming at protection of trade secrets, the legitimate interest of the employer ceases to exist with the termination of secrecy, or when the information, despite remaining secret, loses its value, e.g. because the technology to which it related has become obsolete.[90]

b) Unfair Limitation of the Employee's Post-Employment Activity With Regard to Substance, Territory or Duration, Taking into Consideration the Compensation Agreed On The existence of the employee's interest in his professional development and freedom to choose his occupation is recognised in Section 74a(1) HGB. This interest should not be unduly impaired by the agreement not to compete. The existence of any limitation in this respect is to be assessed from the perspective of geographical scope, duration and subject-matter of the contract. The formulation of Section 74a(1) HGB implies an interrelationship between those factors. Thus, a narrow determination of the substance of the prohibition may allow a broader territorial scope to be validly agreed. On the other hand, if the substance and territorial scope are broad, its duration may have to be short.[91] The amount of compensation agreed should be taken into consideration as well. Thus, the negative effect on the ex-employee's freedom to compete may be offset by paying him appropriately high compensation.[92]

Even though the balancing of the interests of the employer and the employee is not explicitly foreseen, it seems inevitable.[93] The fact that the provision refers to the fairness of a limitation gives it to some extent the character of a general clause, which is usually assessed in the light of all the circumstances of a case, including the balancing of any interests involved.

While prohibiting any activity for a competitor without any territorial limitation would arguably be unfair,[94] Schlötter argues for acceptance of

[89] Heinz-Peter Winterstein, 'Nachvertragliches Wettbewerbsverbot und Karenzentschädigung' (1989) NJW 1463, 1464; Schlötter 201.
[90] Bauer/Diller para 323.
[91] Schlötter 201.
[92] NZA 2010, 1175, 1177 (BAG) *Anspruch auf Karenzentschädigung* para 27; Bauer/Diller paras 341–342.
[93] Winterstein, 'Nachvertragliches Wettbewerbsverbot und Karenzentschädigung' 1463, 1464; Schlötter 201; Bauer/Diller para 299, stressing that no considerations of public interest and in particular of safeguarding competition apply in Germany, see also ibid paras 305–306.
[94] Winterstein, 'Nachvertragliches Wettbewerbsverbot und Karenzentschädigung' 1463, 1464; Schlötter 201.

extraterritorial limitations. A cross-border NCA does not seem to be unfair per se, considering that, in the age of globalisation, it is also on the international level that competition and mobility of employees take place.[95] Brock acknowledges the possibility of concluding extraterritorial or even world-wide NCAs, but warns against the risk of unduly broad formulations.[96] In any case, the territorial scope of a non-disclosure obligation should be assessed considering both the legitimate interest of the employer and the interests of the employee. Thus, the appropriate territorial scope will be narrower in the case of services for consumers (such as insurance or general transport services), and may be broader in a narrow field, especially where the protection of technical trade secrets underlies the employer's interest in the restriction of competition (e.g. where an NCA aims to protect processes used in nuclear power plants).[97]

The activity to which the prohibition relates, i.e. the substance of the limitation, should be assessed under consideration of the employee's position and scope of duties during his service for the employer who is to benefit from the NCA. Clauses drafted by reference to these duties are usually accepted.[98] Problems may arise where the covenant contains a prohibition of activity 'for any competitor', i.e. not by reference to the activity of the employee or a particular competing company.[99] Subject to consideration of their territorial scope and duration, such clauses should not be accepted for regular employees, as they overly limit their freedom to undertake a post-employment activity. In case of employees responsible for contact with clients, it would overly limit their freedom to compete if they were prohibited from undertaking any competitive activity. The legitimate interest of the employer may be safeguarded in such a case by limiting the NCA to contacts with the relevant clients.[100] However, if the core of the prohibition is not the protection of contacts with clients but rather information about who the employer's clients are

95 Bauer/Diller para 326; Schlötter 201; left open in the BAG judgment of 30.01.1970, 3 AZR 348/69, AP GewO §133 Nr 24.

96 Brock in Ann/Loschelder/Grosch 139.

97 Bauer/Diller para 326.

98 Although detecting a breach of such a clause may be difficult. Therefore Brock suggests that a better solution is to determine the substantive scope of an NCA by reference to competitors, Brock in Ann/Loschelder/Grosch 138–139.

99 NZA 2011, 413, 415 (BAG) *Vorvertrag bei Wettbewerbsverbot* para 14.

100 Bauer/Diller paras 308, 310, who suggest that the relevant circle of clients as well as the relevant territory for such an agreement should be assessed taking into consideration the activities of the employee in the last two years before termination of the employment relationship, as after that time those relationships weaken and therefore are likely to be no longer relevant for competitive purposes; see also BGH NJW 2000, 2584 *Mandantenschutzklausel*.

(e.g. in the case of a detective agency) or other trade secrets, an unlimited prohibition of competition is likely to be valid.[101]

In the case of employees who held managerial positions, with access to a wide range of information, a broadly framed post-employment NCA may nevertheless be fair.[102] The fairness of the substantive scope of the prohibition is therefore to be assessed under similar considerations as the employer's legitimate interest in restricting competition.

Pursuant to Section 74a(1) HGB, a contractual limitation of the post-employment competitive activity of the employee may not exceed two years. Any NCA concluded for a longer or even unlimited period of time ceases to be binding two years after termination of employment.[103] The actual duration of the obligation not to compete must correspond to the legitimate interest of the employer and not unfairly limit the employee's freedom to compete. Thus, the appropriateness of the duration of the NCA must be assessed in the light of the circumstances of the case, in particular the substance and geographical scope of the limitation. Depending on the type of the information or the industry involved, the appropriate duration may vary. In particular, if the prohibition of competition would amount to not using information which quickly loses its competitive value, e.g. in marketing or IT, an NCA lasting two years and with a broad territorial and substantive scope would be excessive.[104]

However, under certain circumstances, even a short NCA may be unacceptable,[105] for example if the aim were to make it more difficult for the employee to find a new employment, since the new employer may not be willing to wait for e.g. six months for the employee to start his service.[106] Another factor influencing the fairness of an NCA is the duration of the period of notice during which the employer releases the employee from working but continues to pay him the remuneration.[107] Since during that time the employee is effectively prevented from taking up new employment (because he remains employed) and is bound by the

101 Bauer/Diller para 309.

102 BAG judgment of 16.12.1968, 3 AZR 434/67, AP GewO §133 Nr 21; Bauer/Diller paras 315, 346; Schlötter 201.

103 Bauer/Diller para 358; Schlötter 202. After expiry of that time limit the NCA is only partially binding and the employee may choose to continue to observe it in return for further compensation, see Bauer/Diller para 335.

104 Schlötter 202.

105 Bauer/Diller para 327, although generally they accept the statutory time limit of two years as appropriate and suggest that it should be shortened only if the NCA concerns short-lived products.

106 Bauer/Diller para 314. It is submitted that if that was the purpose of the NCA, it would not be supported by the employer's legitimate interest.

107 Referred to in the United Kingdom as 'garden leave'.

duty of good faith applicable during employment, the duration of the prohibition on his competitive activity may de facto be longer than the two years prescribed in Section 74a(1) HGB. Thus, an NCA entering into force after this 'garden leave' might have a negative impact on the interests of the employee in choosing his livelihood and occupation (Article 12 GG) and therefore be unfair, even though not exceeding the statutory limit of two years.[108]

In any case, an NCA remains binding only as long as the legitimate interest of the employer which was the reason for concluding it continues to exist.[109]

c) Competition Law According to some authors, as the goal of NCAs is to limit the competitive activity of a former employee, they may be assessed under competition law, in particular Section 1 GWB which prohibits agreements which have as their object or effect the prevention, restriction or distortion of competition. Even though the employee may not be seen as an undertaking when the NCA is concluded, by the time it takes effect he may be active as a competitor in the market. Thus, if the NCA would prohibit independent competition by the former employee (i.e. not in employment for another), it could be assessed from the perspective of antitrust regulation.[110]

Despite this theoretical possibility, NCAs fulfilling the requirements of Sections 74ff HGB are not seen as anticompetitive, because, even though they limit competition, they play an auxiliary role in safeguarding the main contract of employment (they are inherent to this relationship).[111] If NCAs could not be concluded to protect employer's legitimate interests, employment relationships would be impaired, because employers would be reluctant to disclose information to their employees. The requirements that the provisions of the HGB impose on contracts limiting post-employment competition (legitimate interest of the employer, no unfair limitation of the post-employment freedom to remain professionally

[108] Bauer/Diller para 345.

[109] Ibid para 330.

[110] Holger Poth, *Die Grenzen des Arbeitsrechts aus kartellrechtlicher Sicht* (Peter Lang 1990) 68–72; Bauer/Diller para 364. According to von Maltzahn, agreements between employers and employees are not subject to scrutiny under S 1 GWB, as they are not 'between undertakings', see Freiherr von Maltzahn, 'Wettbewerbsrechtliche Probleme beim Arbeitsplatzwechsel' 788, 794.

[111] Poth, *Die Grenzen des Arbeitsrechts aus kartellrechtlicher Sicht* 175–176; Rainer Bechtold and Wolfgang Bosch, *Kartellgesetz. Gesetz gegen Wettbewerbsbeschränkungen. Kommentar* (8th edn CH Beck 2015) §1 para 75. It is submitted here that the inherent nature of a limitation of competition is more visible during employment. For post-employment covenants this effect should be scrutinised carefully.

active) ensure that they do not unduly affect competition, so generally such agreements are not prohibited under Section 1 GWB.[112]

3) Conditional Covenant Not to Compete

The requirement that the departed employee obtains compensation for the limitation of his competitive activity calculated on the basis of his latest remuneration, combined with the fact that the amounts in question are not known when the NCA is concluded (which happens before or during employment),[113] may make the conclusion of a conditional non-compete agreement[114] an attractive option from the point of view of the employer.

Under such an agreement, the employee undertakes to refrain from engaging in competitive activity after termination of employment. However, the binding effect of the agreement and the payment of the compensation as required by Section 74(2) HGB are conditional on the employer deciding to hold the employee to that undertaking.[115] This would allow the employer to calculate whether the compulsory compensation is an appropriate cost for keeping the departed employee from competing with him. Such agreements are however considered not binding (*unverbindlich*)[116] because they permit circumvention of compulsory rules governing the post-employment agreements not to compete.[117] They restrain the employee in search of a new job by making his performance of a particular competitive activity dependent on his former employer's declaration, which may be made only after the employee's departure. This causes uncertainty for the ex-employee.[118]

Another type of conditional agreements not to compete make their prohibitive effect dependent on the employee behaving in a particular way (e.g. deciding to retire)[119] or on a circumstance connected to his person (e.g. giving notice terminating the employment relationship, leaving the

[112] Bauer/Diller para 364.

[113] NCAs containing fixed amounts of remuneration are problematic, see Schlötter 203.

[114] Even though this term seems to be generally accepted, with regard to most such agreements it is not precise. Rather than including a condition within the meaning of Ss 158 ff BGB (connecting the coming into effect of the contract to some external event), they leave it to the employer to choose whether he will be bound by the agreement, see Bauer/Diller para 485.

[115] For a detailed analysis of the various types of such agreements, see Bauer/Diller paras 487–508.

[116] Bauer/Diller para 485. Von Maltzahn describes them as invalid and lacking legal effect (*unwirksam*), Freiherr von Maltzahn, 'Wettbewerbsrechtliche Probleme beim Arbeitsplatzwechsel' 788, 795.

[117] NZA 2011, 413, 415 (BAG) *Vorvertrag bei Wettbewerbsverbot* para 20.

[118] Freiherr von Maltzahn, 'Wettbewerbsrechtliche Probleme beim Arbeitsplatzwechsel' 788, 795.

[119] Bauer/Diller para 509, although considering the lack of binding effect of such an agreement only to the extent that it does not depend on objective considerations such as reaching the statutory retirement age, ibid.

country or changing his field of activity).[120] They are also considered not binding,[121] since they do not depend on any external factor but rather on the employee's behaviour, which may be influenced by the existence of the non-compete clause itself (e.g. the decision to retire might be the result not of reaching statutory retirement age but rather of the NCA's restriction of the employee's freedom to choose his future occupation).

An NCA which is not binding gives the employee a choice to undertake the competitive activity, ignoring the conditional NCA, or to accept the limitation in return for appropriate compensation.[122]

On the other hand, agreements not to compete whose validity is conditional on an objective event, independent of the will of any of the parties involved and indeed of the existence of the non-compete clause itself, may be considered binding. This is the case e.g. where the parties agree that the non-compete effect will be binding only after the employee is promoted to a certain position in the company, obtains a particular amount of monthly remuneration, participates in certain projects, or after a particular date, such as when he reaches an agreed age.[123]

4) Legal Consequences of an NCA not Fulfilling the Prescribed Conditions

Depending on the type of the requirement which the NCA does not fulfil, the statute prescribes various legal consequences: either its being null and void (*Nichtigkeit*) or invalidity and lack of legal effect (*Unwirksamkeit*), complete or partial.[124]

If an agreement is considered void, none of the parties may derive any rights from it.[125] In the case of post-employment NCAs this is the case in the event of non-compliance with the requirement that the agreement be in written form (Section 74(1) HGB),[126] lack of compensation[127] (i.e. also if an overly broad NDA is considered to have the effect of an

[120] Bauer/Diller para 511–513.
[121] Ibid paras 485, 510, 513.
[122] Freiherr von Maltzahn, 'Wettbewerbsrechtliche Probleme beim Arbeitsplatzwechsel' 788, 795; Bauer/Diller paras 485, 155–176.
[123] Bauer/Diller paras 515, 518. See generally, ibid paras 515–527; Brock in Ann/Loschelder/Grosch 146.
[124] There is no possibility to reduce an overly broad covenant not to compete by limiting its content, NZA 2008, 170, 172 (BAG) *Wirksamkeit einer Vertragsstrafenabrede* paras 34–35. This would interfere with the freedom of the parties to determine their contractual obligations and might furthermore encourage employers to insist on broad NCAs since they could be adapted by a court upon enforcement, Sander, 'Schutz nicht offenbarter betrieblicher Informationen nach der Beendigung des Arbeitsverhältnisses im deutschen und amerikanischen Recht' 217, 225.
[125] NZA 2011, 413, 416 (BAG) *Vorvertrag bei Wettbewerbsverbot* para 28; Bauer/Diller para 151.
[126] NZA 2011, 413, 413 (BAG) *Vorvertrag bei Wettbewerbsverbot* headnote 4.
[127] However, where the compensation exists but is too low the effect is that the limitation does not have a binding effect on the employee, Brock in Ann/Loschelder/Grosch 143,

NCA) or conclusion of such an agreement with a minor or person on the minimum wage.[128]

An NCA which is not at all supported by a legitimate interest of the employer, which unfairly limits the employee's freedom to compete, or which provides for compensation lower than the prescribed in Section 74(2) HGB, is binding only to the extent that the ex-employee himself is ready to accept the limitation.[129] Thus, the binding effect of such an NCA is conditional on the employee's declaration that he wishes to be bound by the contract.[130] Only if the ex-employee decides to accept the NCA does it become effective.[131] The ex-employer may not invoke such a contract or agreement which aims at circumventing the rules regarding compensation.[132]

A partially binding effect of a covenant not to compete may be the result of its non-compliance with the requirements of Section 74a(1) HGB. To the extent that the duration of the agreement fails to be supported by a legitimate interest of the employer or unfairly limits the ex-employee's right to continue his professional activity, it is for the employee to choose whether he wishes to be bound for the agreed term.[133] To the extent that the agreement is too broad in terms of substance, it is partially void.[134]

The relevant provisions of the HGB are considered to contain a complete regulation of the consequences of lack of compliance with their requirements. In particular they are thought to permit a flexible response to changes in circumstances between the conclusion of the agreement and entry into force of its effects. Thus, the general legal principle contained in Section

although refers not to the agreement being null and void (*Nichtigkeit*), but to its invalidity and lack of legal effect (*Unwirksamkeit*).

[128] Bauer/Diller para 152, with further examples.

[129] Bauer/Diller paras 158–166; Schlötter 199.

[130] However, the ex-employee may only accept or reject the conditions agreed on and may not change them, e.g. by unilaterally limiting the duration of the restriction, NZA 2011, 413, 415 (BAG) *Vorvertrag bei Wettbewerbsverbot* para 22. Furthermore, this declaration does not need to take any particular form. Rather, the ex-employee's behaviour is to be interpreted as the sign of acceptance or rejection of the restriction on post-employment competition, NZA 2011, 413, 415 (BAG) *Vorvertrag bei Wettbewerbsverbot* para 22, i.e. as long as the ex-employee does not undertake any competitive activity he has the right to demand the compensation laid down in the NCA, see Bauer/Diller paras 162–163, 166.

[131] NZA 2011, 413, 415 (BAG) *Vorvertrag bei Wettbewerbsverbot* para 19.

[132] S 75d HGB.

[133] Bauer/Diller paras 177–178, 334–335.

[134] Bauer/Diller para 336, referring to NZA 2010, 1175, 1177 (BAG) *Anspruch auf Karenzentschädigung* paras 22–23 (which however remains open as regards partial invalidity). For an analysis of the consequences which partial lack of binding legal effect and partial invalidity can have on post-employment NCAs, see Bauer/Diller para 337.

313 BGB enabling contractual terms to be adjusted if circumstances change is not applicable.[135] Moreover, despite Section 74a(3) HGB, the provisions of HGB take precedence over Section 138 BGB[136] and Sections 305ff BGB.[137] To the extent that those general regulations would lead to the NCA being null and void, while under the HGB it would lack binding legal effect, it is considered that the acceptance of the general provisions of the BGB would fail to serve the employees' interests and would unduly privilege the employers, who could avoid any financial burdens if the NCA did not fulfil the statutory requirements. In view of the deterrent effect of leaving the choice to the employee, in case of lack of binding effect it is considered more appropriate to give precedence to applying the provisions of the HGB as lex specialis over the provisions of the BGB.[138]

5) Summary: NCAs in Germany

Despite the explicit regulation of covenants not to compete in Sections 74–75f HGB, in practice the drafting of such agreements may pose considerable problems. As NCAs may be entered into right at the start of the employment relationship, an agreement which was balanced and clear at that point in time may lose those qualities upon termination of the employment and entry into force of the restrictive covenant.

Possible changes in circumstances after conclusion of the contract but before its entry into force, combined with the requirement that the employer has a legitimate interest which should be protected and that the employee's professional activity after termination of employment must not be unfairly limited, mean that such contracts have to be assessed on a case-by-case basis, weighing up the interests of the parties.[139] A fair result may be achieved by adjusting the flexible framework regarding substance, territorial scope and duration of the agreement as well as by granting the employee appropriate remuneration to compensate for limitating his competitive activity.

[135] Bauer/Diller para 179.

[136] Invalidity of a contract going against rules of good conduct and public policy (*gute Sitten*).

[137] Regulating the applicability and validity of terms and conditions of contracts not subject to negotiations. See LAG Baden-Württemberg judgment of 30.01.2008, 10 Sa 60/07, NZA-RR 2008, 508, 509. Nevertheless, Brock argues that S 307(1) second sentence BGB might still be applicable to standard terms in employment contracts and result in invalidity and lack of legal effect (*Unwirksamkeit*) of their unclear terms (such as 'indirect competition' or 'other activity'), see Brock in Ann/Loschelder/Grosch 136–138.

[138] Brock in Ann/Loschelder/Grosch 133–136; Bauer/Diller paras 174–175, 349, 353–356. Westermann seems to accept the applicability of S 138 BGB also to NCAs, see Ingo Westermann, *Handbuch Know-How Schutz* (CH Beck 2007) 97.

[139] NZA 2010, 1175, 1176 (BAG) *Anspruch auf Karenzentschädigung* para 17; Bauer/Diller paras 305–306.

The system of rules applicable to covenants not to compete seems to attribute central significance to the interests of the employees. This is indicated by the fact that the agreements' validity is made dependent on compensation and that their duration may not exceed two years. Furthermore, the lack of 'blue-pencilling' and general non-acceptance of conditional NCAs, combined with the employee's freedom to choose whether he wishes to be bound by an NCA in most cases where it does not comply with statutory requirements, reflect the concerns about the need to ensure the mobility of labour.

Given the risks connected with imprecise drafting of covenants not to compete, as well as the way the compensation is calculated, it seems that concluding such contracts upon termination of the employment relationship, rather than early on, would be the best way of striking the right balance between the respective interests of employer and employee.

3 Summary: Post-Employment Contractual Protection of Trade Secrets in Germany

The contractual freedom to conclude agreements to protect trade secrets after termination of employment is limited in Germany. Even though generally both covenants not to disclose and covenants not to compete (including non-solicitation agreements) are accepted, whether they can be relied on depends on careful drafting, since their validity and binding effect are determined ia by weighing up the interests of the parties involved.

In the case of NDAs, imprecise determination of the subject-matter might lead to invalidity for breach of rules of good conduct and public policy (Section 138 BGB) or for limiting competition (and being in effect a covenant not to compete offering no compensation).

The NCAs are regulated by the provisions of the HGB. However, the fact that they must be accompanied by remuneration limits their attractiveness as a tool to protect trade secrets.[140]

Even though there is consensus that contracts to protect trade secrets are accepted, there is little guidance available as to how to define the limits of contractual freedom in this context. It is suggested that the rules delineating the limits of use of trade secrets after termination of employment in the absence of a contract constitute a minimum level of protection which can be extended by concluding such a contract.[141] The possibility of entering into non-disclosure agreements without compensation should be limited to

[140] Salger and Breitfeld, 'Regelungen zum Schutz von betrieblichen Know-how – die Sicherung von Geschäfts- und Betriebsgeheimnissen' 154, 156.

[141] Rudolf Kraßer, 'Grundlagen des Zivilrechtlichen Schutzes von Geschäfts- und Betriebsgeheimnissen sowie von Know-How' (1977) GRUR 177, 187.

trade secrets. The conclusion of covenants limiting competition may be more broadly allowable, but it is essential that they are supported by the existence of a legitimate interest of the employer. In the case of trade secrets such an interest is given, however even such a motivation might not lead to a binding NCA, if it would lead to prohibition of any post-employment activity for the ex-employee. It seems that this effect might be neutralised by offering appropriately high compensation and concluding agreements of short duration. It is furthermore suggested that under the legal framework governing post-employment contracts in Germany it is possible to combine the effects of both agreements, since after termination of the NCA the need to ensure the confidentiality of certain information might remain. However, this may be applicable only to vital secrets and should not exclude the use of information by the former employee himself, if otherwise transgression of statutory limits on post-employment competition would be likely. Nevertheless, considering that under German law it is not possible to partially retain the effects of an NCA (no severance or 'blue-pencilling'), it is suggested here that a covenant to keep particular information secret should be concluded separately.

The analysis presented here shows that the effects of any agreements reached are to be assessed by weighing up conflicting interests, which however are limited to those of the parties to the contract. The rules of construction necessitate trying to establish the true intention of the parties (Section 133 BGB) within the limits of contractual freedom.[142] Considering furthermore that blue-pencilling of post-employment agreements by the courts is not accepted, it seems that there is no place for broader inclusion of public interest when assessing their validity and binding effect. This must be accepted because otherwise the freedom to contract recognised in Article 2 GG would be infringed.

B Contracts in the United Kingdom

As in Germany, in the United Kingdom the employers are free to conclude agreements with their employees imposing post-employment obligations, which can be broader than the implicit ones.[143] However, unlike Germany, UK law does not contain an explicit statutory regulation applicable to post-employment agreements. As is the case for all

[142] In particular statutory prohibitions (S 134 BGB), rules of good conduct and public policy (S 138 BGB), performance in good faith (S 242 BGB) and limitations applicable to standard business terms (S 305 BGB).

[143] Paul Stanley, *The Law of Confidentiality: A Restatement* (Hart Publishing 2008) 83; Toulson/Phipps paras 14-028–14-029.

other contracts, the freedom to enter agreements between employers and employees is limited by the common-law doctrine of restraint of trade.[144]

According to this doctrine, 'any contract that is in restraint of trade is invalid and unenforceable unless it is reasonable having regard to the interests of the parties and the public interest'.[145] This doctrine reflects public policy safeguarding competition as such.[146]

The general rule is modified in the employment context, due to its specific balance of powers. A post-employment covenant is invalid unless it aims at protection of a legitimate interest of the employer and the resulting restraint of trade is reasonable and not contrary to the public interest.[147] The aim of the doctrine in this context is to protect the public interest in everyone using their talents and skills to support themselves, and the individual interest of the employee in choosing his professional activity.[148] At the same time, the application of the doctrine should reflect the difference in the bargaining positions of the parties.[149]

The assessment of a contract under the doctrine of restraint of trade in the first place requires determining the meaning of the agreement. The next step is to assess whether its effect is a restriction of trade. The third and final step is to establish whether this effect is reasonable. This is done under consideration of the interests of the parties and the public, and involves an analysis of the substantive and territorial scope of the restriction as well as its duration.[150]

1 Determination of the Meaning of the Agreement

A contract between an employee and his employer, like any other covenant, undergoes interpretation aimed at ascertaining its meaning.

Construction is objective and requires determining how this contract would be understood by a reasonable person having all the background

[144] Gurry on Breach of Confidence para 10.01.

[145] Gurry on Breach of Confidence para 12.09 and the case-law referred to in note 21. See also Peel, *The Law of Contract* paras 11-062–11-063, 11-066.

[146] *Herbert Morris Ltd v Saxelby* [1916] 1 AC 688, (HL) 702 (Lord Atkinson); Alexandra Kamerling and Christopher Goodwill, *Restrictive Covenants under Common and Competition Law* (Sweet&Maxwell 2010) 1–2.

[147] Peel, *The Law of Contract* para 11-066.

[148] *Herbert Morris Ltd v Saxelby* [1916] 1 AC 688 (HL) 699 (Lord Atkinson).

[149] See e.g. *Dawnay Day & Co Ltd v D'Alphen* [1998] ICR 1068 (CA) 1081. Usually, the employee is thought to be the weaker party, but this may not always be the case, in particular for executives or highly paid specialists, Gurry on Breach of Confidence paras 12.10–12.11; Goulding, Clarke, Jones and Taylor in Goulding para 6.239. On the employee not always being the weaker party, see also: Andrew Stewart, 'Confidential Information and Departing Employees: The Employer's Options' (1989) 11(3) *EIPR* 88, 94.

[150] Gurry on Breach of Confidence para 12.12.

knowledge realistically available to the parties when they concluded the contract. This excludes previous negotiations and declarations of subjective intent. Moreover, the meaning of the contract is to be determined giving the words their 'natural and ordinary meaning', unless that would be at odds with the parties' intentions.[151]

In the employment context it has been suggested that any ambiguities in the formulation of terms should be considered to the detriment to the employer, as a party having a stronger bargaining position, and that a contract which 'leaves the employee in a position of honest doubt as to what the limits of his activities may be' should not be enforced.[152]

In practice however the courts adopt various approaches to the interpretation of post-employment agreements for the purpose of assessment under the doctrine of restraint of trade. Some courts already at the first step seem to be willing to apply a narrow interpretation of the obligations imposed on the employee by the contract, which makes it possible to uphold its validity.[153] At the other extreme, the approach is to adhere strictly to the literal meaning of the contract, with the argument that any lack of clarity should be to the detriment of the employer as the stronger party, which often results in the agreement being deemed overly broad and thus invalid.[154]

2 Determination of Whether the Agreement Has an Effect of Restraint of Trade

Once the meaning of the post-employment agreement has been determined, the next step is to assess whether it is a restraint of trade, i.e. whether it imposes any limitations on the former employee in practising his trade. This will usually be the case for non-solicitation agreements

[151] *Investors Compensation Scheme Ltd v West Bromwich Building Society* [1998] 1 WLR 896 (HL) 912–913 (Lord Hoffmann). See also Peel, *The Law of Contract* paras 6-008–6-012; Goulding, Clarke, Jones and Taylor in Goulding paras 6.162–6.192.

[152] *Gilford Motor Company Ltd v Horne* [1933] Ch 935 (CA) 946.

[153] Criticised in *Arbuthnot Funds Managers v Rawlings* [2003] EWCA Civ 518 (EWCA) [23] (Chadwick LJ). For examples, see Gurry on Breach of Confidence para 12.14; Goulding, Clarke, Jones and Taylor in Goulding paras 6.171–6.188. This approach seems however to circumvent the application of the doctrine of restraint of trade by immediately going to the last step which is the severance of the contract to the extent it may be enforced.

[154] *Prophet Plc v Christopher Huggett* [2014] EWCA Civ 1013 (EWCA) [29]–[38]; Gurry on Breach of Confidence para 12.15. This approach seems to leave no room for interpretation. It is argued here that, considering that the drafting of post-employment covenants is difficult, particularly in terms of determination of their subject-matter and under consideration of possible changes in circumstances between their conclusion and entry into force, a flexible construction of contractual obligations should be accepted to a reasonable extent.

and agreements not to compete,[155] but not necessarily for NDAs. The existence of the restraint is judged by looking at the substance and effect of the provision. If the agreement, despite not imposing an explicit prohibition of competitive activity, contains obligations which might stop the employee from undertaking it, e.g. because he would be faced with a contractual penalty (liquidated damages) or would be obliged to repay the costs of training obtained during employment, it is nevertheless a restraint of trade.[156] Similarly, a covenant obliging the former employee to assign to his previous employer any invention conceived after termination of employment would be a restraint of trade.[157]

On the other hand, clauses which merely reiterate regulations already applicable e.g. under criminal law would not be a restraint.[158]

Agreements not to disclose, if drafted narrowly, may be seen as simply reiterating the implied post-employment obligations. Such a contract is not a restraint of trade, because it does not prohibit the ex-employee from using the information in his professional activity. However, if the use of the information would amount to its disclosure, such a clause may nevertheless have an effect of limitation of professional activity[159] and for that reason be subject to the reasonableness test.

3 Determination of Whether the Restraint of Trade is Reasonable

Not all agreements in restraint of trade are automatically invalid. Those which are reasonable, considering the interests of the parties and the public, are accepted, since they may have an overall positive effect.[160] Reasonableness is assessed taking into account all the facts of the case.[161]

The basic considerations are the interests of the employer, the activity which the employee plans to undertake or has undertaken after termination

[155] Gurry on Breach of Confidence para 12.20.

[156] Gurry on Breach of Confidence paras 12.21–12.22. In Germany, covenants obliging the employee to reimburse the costs of training are suggested as an alternative to non-compete clauses, see Bauer/Diller paras 305, 311. In the United Kingdom, even though they are considered to be in restraint of trade, further analysis might lead to finding them reasonable and thus not invalid. For further examples of covenants in restraint of trade, see Goulding, Clarke, Jones and Taylor in Goulding paras 6.66–6.78.

[157] Gurry on Breach of Confidence para 12.22. Such agreements are also considered to be unreasonable restraints of trade, see Gurry on Breach of Confidence paras 12.124–12.126.

[158] Gurry on Breach of Confidence paras 12.23–12.32, giving as an example obligations to safeguard privacy of others.

[159] Gurry on Breach of Confidence paras 12.33–12.35.

[160] *Herbert Morris Ltd v Saxelby* [1916] 1 AC 688 (HL) 707 (Lord Parker of Waddington).

[161] Kamerling and Goodwill, *Restrictive Covenants under Common and Competition Law* 162; Goulding, Clarke, Jones and Taylor in Goulding para 6.05.

of the employment, and the scope, duration and geographical extent of the agreement. Apart from those factors, depending on the facts of the case, the courts also consider further elements such as the circumstances accompanying the conclusion of the contract (e.g. whether the employee received legal advice, whether the agreement was actually negotiated), the duration of the employment and the circumstances in which it was terminated, whether the employee had any prospects of undertaking a professional activity should the agreement be enforceable and whether he actually entered into competition with his former employer.[162]

These considerations are discussed below.

1) *Interests of the Parties to the Agreement*

Despite the general rule requiring reasonableness to be assessed in terms of the interests of both parties involved, most of the case-law concentrates on the interests of the employer. Thus, usually, a restraint which is necessary to protect legitimate interests of the employer will be considered reasonable.[163]

The impact that the restraint has on the interests of the employee is given much less importance. Even though there are cases recognising that the restraint should be fair to the employee as well, generally it is the reasonableness from the point of view of the former employer which is decisive. If at all, the interest of the employee is considered as a reflection of the wider public interest which is taken into consideration upon assessment of reasonableness.[164]

This is a surprising approach. Considering that reasonableness of the restraint is assessed under consideration of both the parties' and the public interest, the concentration on the interest of the employer seems at odds with the general rule. What is more, inclusion of the interest of the employee only as part of the public interest does not seem satisfactory either. Admittedly, the interest of the public is a reflection of the individual interests of the employee, but the same applies to those of the employer. Thus, the voices pleading for including full consideration of the interest of the employee in the determination of reasonableness of post-employment covenants are welcomed. Accordingly, even where the

162 Gurry on Breach of Confidence para 12.95.

163 Gurry on Breach of Confidence paras 12.37–12.38.

164 See e.g. *Herbert Morris Ltd v Saxelby* [1916] 1 AC 688 (HL) 699–700 (Lord Atkinson), where it was considered that a contractual restraint put on the employee's activity in a certain industry 'does not concern him alone. The general public suffer with him' (at 699) and that while the employer may have a reasonable interest in being protected against competition, this restraint may 'be held to be injurious to the public and therefore void' (at 700).

clause protects a legitimate interest of the employer, it might still be considered unreasonable if it has an overly negative impact on the legitimate interests of the employee.[165]

The concentration on the protection of a legitimate interest of the employer is reflected in the rule that the amount of the employee's remuneration in consideration for the restraint may not have influence on the finding of reasonableness. Unlike Germany, where compensation for the post-employment limitation of competition is compulsory and where the amount of this compensation may offset the negative effect on the employee's freedom to compete with his former employer, in the United Kingdom the employer cannot 'buy' a restraint.[166] Since the interest of the former employee is considered only as a reflection of the public interest, there is no place for including his financial position. Rather, the use of his skills and knowledge from which the society as a whole may profit is part of the analysis of the public interest.

Even though some courts and commentators consider that the amount of remuneration of the employee may compensate for the limitation,[167] this seems to be a de lege ferenda proposal, since under the current majority approach the interest of the former employee plays no separate role in the assessment of reasonableness of post-employment covenants.[168] Nevertheless, as in any contract, some consideration must be provided. If the agreement is entered into upon employment, the employment itself may be such consideration. However, if the covenant is entered into at a later stage of the employment relationship, the continuation of the employment as such is generally not seen as consideration and some additional benefit may be necessary, such as promotion, a rise in salary or monetary compensation.[169]

The reasonableness of the restraint of trade is assessed at the time of conclusion of the contract.[170] This approach, again, differs from that under German law, where the effects of an agreement limiting post-employment activities are assessed on their entry into force, i.e. upon

165 See e.g. Gurry on Breach of Confidence para 12.45; Stanley, *The Law of Confidentiality: A Restatement* 83 (considering both the interest of the employer and of the employee as reflections of public interest).

166 Goulding, Clarke, Jones and Taylor in Goulding para 6.234; Gurry on Breach of Confidence para 12.46.

167 Gurry on Breach of Confidence paras 12.47–12.48. Allocation of a sum of money is suggested as consideration for a restrictive covenant in 'Post-Termination Restrictive Covenants' (2008) IDS Emp L Brief 853, 12–18.

168 Gurry on Breach of Confidence para 12.50.

169 *Re-Use Collections Ltd v Sendall* [2014] EWHC 3852 (QB) [81]–[84] (Davies J).

170 *Basic Solutions Ltd v Sands* [2008] EWHC 1388 (QB) [21] (Eady J); Goulding, Clarke, Jones and Taylor in Goulding para 6.238; Gurry on Breach of Confidence para 12.52.

termination of the employment. The approach taken in the United Kingdom appears not to fully acknowledge the fact that the covenant refers to the situation after termination of employment. After all, an agreement entered into upon commencement of employment will not necessarily anticipate and reflect the situation from the moment when the employment terminates, which may happen many years later. This might be explained by the fact that the reasonableness of the restraint is assessed under consideration of the interests of the employer. Those interests must have existed already when the agreement was concluded.[171] Should the interest of the employee be taken into consideration as well, the point in time at which the assessment is made would need to be shifted, since it is only after termination of the employment that the interests of the employee in choosing his professional activity become apparent.

The effects of assessing reasonableness when concluding the contract are corrected upon enforcement. When determining relief for breach of a post-employment agreement, the courts consider the events that occurred after the agreement was entered into. Thus, where the agreement has as its object the protection of trade secrets, but the employee was not exposed to such information, the court is likely to deny enforcement, even if the agreement was reasonable at the time of its conclusion.[172] Even though this correction mitigates the effects of determining reasonableness at the time of concluding the agreement, it leaves the employee in uncertainty as to the scope of post-employment competitive activity which he may undertake.

Thus, under the approach taken by the case-law in the United Kingdom, if, at the time of the conclusion of the covenant limiting the employee's competitive activity after termination of service, there existed a legitimate interest of the employer that needed protection, the restraint of trade may be considered reasonable. This interest, as in Germany, is seen in the need to protect the employer's trade secrets and customer connections[173] and must have a proprietary or quasi-proprietary nature,

[171] And must continue to exist upon entry into force of the effects of the contract, see Gurry on Breach of Confidence para 12.86. The difficulties resulting from the passing of time between conclusion and entry of the effects of a restrictive covenant call for accepting a more general description of the information or activities to be covered by the agreement than the one required upon enforcement, when use or disclosure of confidential information is alleged, see Gurry on Breach of Confidence para 12.86.

[172] *Sunrise Brokers LLP and Michael William Rodgers* [2014] EWHC 2633 (QB) [72]; Gurry on Breach of Confidence para 12.147.

[173] *Herbert Morris Ltd v Saxelby* [1916] 1 AC 688 (HL) 709 (Lord Parker of Waddington); Gurry on Breach of Confidence para 12.59. Some case-law suggests that the legitimate

which includes commercial interest[174] such as protection of goodwill. An agreement which has as its goal to protect the employer from competition as such will not be enforced.[175]

a) Trade Secrets and Other Confidential Information Just as trade secrets and highly confidential information are protected against use by departed employees under the implied duty of confidentiality, their safeguarding determines the existence of a legitimate interest on the part of the employer in restriction of trade by way of a post-employment covenant. On the other hand, no such legitimate interest exists in the case of non-confidential information which the employee learned during employment and simply remembers.[176]

The existence of a legitimate interest of the employer in protecting the second category of information established under *Faccenda Chicken*, namely confidential information which does not rise to the level of high confidentiality (equivalent to trade secrecy), has been subject to discussion, as under *Faccenda Chicken* such a legitimate interest of the employer was found only in the case of highly confidential information.[177] Accepting this would mean that the explicit duty of confidentiality could not go beyond the implied one.[178]

For this reason the interpretation presented in *Faccenda Chicken* has been criticised[179] and in the end is not applied to post-employment

interest of the employer is not limited to those two categories and that e.g. the interest of the employer in 'maintaining a stable, trained workforce' may render a restraint of trade reasonable, see *Dawnay Day & Co Ltd v D'Alphen* [1998] ICR 1068 (CA) 1107, 1111. Thus restrictive covenants may also provide protection against poaching of employees, see also Kamerling and Goodwill, *Restrictive Covenants under Common and Competition Law* 163, 168–169; Gurry on Breach of Confidence para 12.93; Goulding, Clarke, Jones and Taylor in Goulding paras 6.196–6.197, 6.214–6.217, suggesting that the catalogue of interests which may be protected by a restrictive covenant is not closed (at para 6.197). Van Caenegem suggests that the legitimate interests justifying a restraint should be confined to the protection of trade secrets, client connections and stability of workforce, William van Caenegem, *Trade Secrets and Intellectual Property. Breach of Confidence, Misappropriation and Unfair Competition* (1st edn, Kluwer Law International 2014) 218–220.

174 *Dawnay Day & Co Ltd v D'Alphen* [1998] ICR 1068 (CA) 1108; Gurry on Breach of Confidence paras 12.56–12.58.

175 Goulding, Clarke, Jones and Taylor in Goulding para 6.193.

176 Parker, 'The Secret Recipe: Key Ingredients of Agreements to Protect Confidential Information' 223, 227; Gurry on Breach of Confidence para 12.66.

177 *Faccenda Chicken v Fowler* [1987] 1 Ch 117 (CA) 137.

178 Gurry on Breach of Confidence para 12.68.

179 Gurry on Breach of Confidence paras 12.71–12.76. For developments of the argumentation in case-law and critique, see John Hull, *Commercial Secrecy: Law and Practice* (Sweet&Maxwell 1998) paras 7.18–7.30 and Kamerling and Goodwill, *Restrictive Covenants under Common and Competition Law* 154–157.

restrictive covenants.[180] There would be no space for explicit agreements imposing post-employment confidentiality if they could not go beyond the implied duty. This might prejudice the interest not only of the employers in protecting their business, but also of the employees, who benefit from greater certainty where the restricted information is defined in a contract.[181] Moreover, *Faccenda Chicken* was not a decision on the doctrine of restraint of trade, but rather related to the scope of the implied duty. Thus, it did not consider the reasonableness of a restraint. An agreement may not be judged simply by assessing the type of information concerned, but also by considering its effect on post-employment activity, as well as its geographical scope and duration, which may offset the substantive scope of the restraint. From that perspective, a reasonable limitation of post-employment activity may be found also with regard to information which is not highly confidential,[182] since this broader substantive scope of restraint may be balanced by limiting the territorial scope or duration of the agreement.

As a result, to determine whether the employer has a legitimate interest under the doctrine of restraint of trade, the more general distinction between trade secrets and employee's skill and knowledge has been applied.[183] The employer's legitimate interest exists not only where trade secrets and highly confidential information are to be protected, such as technical and scientific formulae, but also in case of information used in trade or business which has been disseminated in a limited manner and which 'if disclosed to a competitor, would be liable to cause real (or significant) harm to the owner of the secret', such as names of customers and their product preferences. [184]

b) Trade Connections The employer's interest in protecting his goodwill stemming from the 'special'[185] relations that he has built up with his customers and suppliers has also been recognised as a legitimate interest

[180] Gurry on Breach of Confidence paras 12.77–12.85. See also *Balston Ltd v Headline Filters Ltd* [1987] FSR 330 (Ch) 348; Stewart, 'Confidential Information and Departing Employees: The Employer's Options' 88, 92–93; Toulson/Phipps para 14-029.

[181] Cf Hull, *Commercial Secrecy: Law and Practice* para 8.79; Toulson/Phipps para 14-027; Gurry on Breach of Confidence para 12.76.

[182] *Balston Ltd v Headline Filters Ltd* [1987] FSR 330 (Ch) 348; Gurry on Breach of Confidence para 12.72.

[183] Gurry on Breach of Confidence paras 12.83, 12.85; Toulson/Phipps para 14-028.

[184] *Lansing Linde v Kerr* [1991] 1 WLR 251 (CA) 260.

[185] Kamerling and Goodwill, *Restrictive Covenants under Common and Competition Law* 163, explaining that the 'special' relationship with suppliers or customers does not need to amount to exclusivity, although 'the more widely dispersed the loyalty of customers or suppliers, the less likely the employer will be able to succeed in claiming the speciality required'.

which may render a restriction of trade legitimate. The existence of such legitimate interest has been found in particular where the employer's business requires close relations with the customers and handling their personal information (as is the case for medical or banking services). Due to the high risk that a departing employee will take the employer's customers with him, the employer's interest in protecting such relations may be a valid reason for limiting the employee's post-employment activity.[186]

The legitimate interest to be protected must be that of the employer. However, in exceptional circumstances, if the restraint is to protect the holding (parent) company and its subsidiaries, and the same interest exists with respect to all of those entities, a restraint may be recognised as reasonable even though it safeguards the interests of other companies as well as the employer.[187]

2) Public Interest

Despite the general statement that assessing the reasonableness of restraint of trade should include consideration of the public interest, it seems not to play an important role in the context of employee mobility, as courts generally find that if an agreement is reasonable from the point of view of the parties, it is also reasonable from the perspective of the public interest.[188] This seems to benefit the employers even more, as they predominate in the analysis of the interests of the parties.

Thus, it is difficult to challenge the reasonableness of a restraint of trade where it serves the interests of the parties to the agreement,[189] which in the case of restrictive covenants boils down to the interest of the employer. An agreement prohibiting the former employee from undertaking a competitive activity in a very narrow field, thus allowing the former employer to keep a monopoly in that field, is given as one example of a situation in which the restraint would be supported by a legitimate interest of the employer but not by public interest. Another example relates to the public interest in certain professional activities not being restrained. This exception however seems to be even narrower, as it relates to e.g. the medical profession, where public health, safety or

[186] Kamerling and Goodwill, *Restrictive Covenants under Common and Competition Law* 163–167; Goulding, Clarke, Jones and Taylor in Goulding para 6.206–6.213; Gurry on Breach of Confidence paras 12.87, 12.91–12.92.

[187] *Beckett Investment Management Group Ltd v Hall* [2007] EWCA Civ 613 (CA) [23]; Kamerling and Goodwill, Restrictive Covenants under Common and Competition Law 166–167; Goulding, Clarke, Jones and Taylor in Goulding paras 6.222–6.228.

[188] Goulding, Clarke, Jones and Taylor in Goulding para 6.236; Gurry on Breach of Confidence para 12.130.

[189] Gurry on Breach of Confidence paras 12.129–12.131.

order might be at stake.[190] Thus, it seems that the situations in which considerations of the public interest would render a restraint of trade unreasonable are rare.

Reducing the assessment of the reasonableness of restrictive covenants to the existence of a legitimate interest of the employer has been criticised, and decisions can be identified which include an assessment of the interest of the employee[191] and of the public in the existence of competition.[192] Even though this approach may not be seen as settled law, it is a welcome development. The inclusion of considerations of the public interest to only a limited degree may be accepted in view of the principle of the freedom of contracting which prohibits an overly broad intervention into the conditions agreed by the parties. However, the fact that the interests of the employees are not given thorough consideration does not seem to be justified and may result in an undue limitation of their post-employment professional activity.

3) *Scope of the Agreement*

UK law accepts the conclusion of various types of post-employment agreements: those having as their main object the protection of confidentiality, including non-disclosure and non-use obligations, agreements limiting post-employment competitive activity and solicitation of clients, as well as contracts combining those obligations. Contracts imposing on the former employee an obligation to transfer to his former employer inventions conceived after termination of employment are considered to be an unreasonable restraint of trade and thus invalid.[193]

a) Covenants Not to Disclose Agreements prohibiting disclosure of information learned during employment, as long as they are limited to confidential information,[194] are generally considered to be a legitimate

190 Gurry on Breach of Confidence paras 12.132–12.134. Stanley refers to the possible abuse of a dominant position where certain information is kept secret, although he admits that the possibility of applying competition law has ‘not been explored in the case law’, Stanley, *The Law of Confidentiality: A Restatement* 84–85.

191 See e.g. *Corporate Express Ltd v Day* [2004] EWHC 2943 (QB) [40], [45], where the employee’s interest was considered, although on the facts of the case not found to prevail over the interest of the employer.

192 See e.g. *Basic Solutions Ltd v Robert Sands* [2008] EWHC 1388 (QB) [37]; *Thermascan Ltd v Norman* [2009] EWHC 3694 (QB) [22].

193 Gurry on Breach of Confidence paras 12.124–12.126.

194 Information which has a competitive value, is treated by the employer as confidential, is separable from non-confidential information, is subject to measures to maintain its secrecy and the disclosure of which is likely to cause harm to the employer, ‘Post-Termination Restrictive Covenants’ 853, 12–18. For a detailed definition, see supra Chapter 2 part I point C.

restraint of trade. Despite the fact that such agreements cover a broader range of information than the implied post-employment obligation of confidentiality, it is considered that the employer's interest in maintaining secrecy exists also for information which is confidential, even though not highly confidential.[195] The impact of such agreements on the post-employment activity of the employee is limited, since he is still allowed to use the information, as long as he safeguards its confidential status.[196] Moreover, the employee is not limited in the use of any other information that he has learned during employment and he may undertake professional activity in competition with the ex-employer.

Therefore, the identification of the information subject to an NDA is of vital importance. This may be done by indicating the categories or types of information which are to be treated as confidential, or, if precise identification is not possible, the criteria which will be used to identify the confidential information covered by the agreement.[197] Claims encompassing information which is vaguely described and may not be clearly identified are seen as attempts to restrain competition and will not be enforced.[198]

NDAs are accepted for an unlimited duration, i.e. until the information ceases to be confidential.[199] After that, the employee is free to use it, unless he was responsible for the loss of secrecy, which may result in a springboard injunction restricting the use of the information for a period of time necessary for its independent development.[200] Furthermore, covenants aiming at safeguarding of confidentiality are accepted even if they are not limited to a defined geographic area.[201]

b) Covenants Not to Use Agreements which limit not only the disclosure but also the use of certain information obtained by the employee during employment undergo a stricter assessment from the point of view of the type of information that they cover, as well as the territorial scope of the prohibition and its duration.

Such agreements may also cover only confidential information and may not extend to employee's skill and knowledge[202] or to non-confidential

[195] See supra Chapter 4 part II, point B.3.1)a).
[196] Prohibition of disclosure does not prevent use of the information in question, unless the use would be such that it would amount to disclosure, *Thomas Marshall v Guinle* [1979] 1 Ch 227 (Ch) 247.
[197] Howe, Gupta, Wilkinson, Pritchard and Taylor in Goulding para 4.29.
[198] Hull, *Commercial Secrecy: Law and Practice* para 7.78.
[199] *Caterpillar Logistics Services v Huesca de Crean* [2012] EWCA Civ 156 (CA) [66] (Burnton LJ); Gurry on Breach of Confidence paras 12.98–12.100.
[200] For an analysis of the springboard doctrine, see infra Chapter 5 part II, point B.3.
[201] Kamerling and Goodwill, *Restrictive Covenants under Common and Competition Law* 193.
[202] For the methods of determining the borderline between the skill and knowledge of the employee and confidential information, see supra Chapter 3 part II, points B.2–3.

information learned during service.[203] Considering that the interest of the employee is not taken into account in the assessment of reasonableness, it seems that if such an agreement is considered unreasonable it would be due to lack of any legitimate interest of the employer. Thus, also where the information is not highly confidential, a restrictive covenant prohibiting its use should clearly define that data and limit the prohibition of its use in time and territory.[204] This is because in the case of such information the existence of a legitimate interest of the employer in limiting its use is not evident (as is the case for highly confidential information, equal to a trade secret, as defined in *Faccenda Chicken*).

The reasonable duration of a covenant restricting use of confidential information depends on the life-time of the information in question and should correspond to the period of time during which it retains a competitive value for the former employer. This will usually be shorter in the case of commercial secrets such as marketing strategies or business plans.[205] In the case of information relating to manufacturing processes, a reasonable prohibition should not last longer than the time needed to develop such information independently. On the other hand, it may be reasonable to protect highly confidential information such as chemical formulae for an unlimited period of time, i.e. as long as it is kept secret.[206]

The geographic scope of a restrictive covenant is to be assessed from the perspective of the market in which the employer is active, i.e. where his legitimate interests protected by the agreement exist. The nature of the information also influences the reasonableness of the restraint from the point of view of its territorial scope. Trade secrets and highly confidential information may require worldwide protection.[207] This is justified given that modern competition often takes place on a global scale and therefore the use of a trade secret anywhere in the world might threaten the legitimate interests of its holder. This may not always be the case for information relating to sales or customers. If the employer is active on a global scale, a worldwide prohibition of use of the information may be justified. On the other hand, a local newspaper might have a legitimate interest in restraining the use of information learned by a former marketing manager in the locality where its magazine is sold, but not in other areas.

203 Gurry on Breach of Confidence para 12.101; Toulson/Phipps para 14-027.
204 Gurry on Breach of Confidence para 12.103.
205 *Brake Brothers Ltd v Ungless* [2004] EWHC 2799 (QB) [42]–[45], [55].
206 Gurry on Breach of Confidence para 12.105.
207 Gurry on Breach of Confidence para 12.106.

c) Covenants Not to Solicit Clients This assessment could be different in case of non-solicitation agreements, the purpose of which is to protect the goodwill of the former employer in relation to his clients, rather than information about those clients. These contracts are generally deemed reasonable, especially if they are limited to the clients of the former employer with whom the employee had direct contact.[208] However, they have also been accepted when they relate to the ex-employer's clients in general, i.e. also those with whom the employee did not interact.[209] On the other hand, the extension of a restrictive covenant to cover persons whom the employee might have known before the employment started[210] and clients attracted by the employer after termination of the employment relationship[211] has been deemed unreasonable.[212]

A reasonable duration of a non-solicitation clause depends ia on the nature of the employer's business. In fast-moving areas, where the fluctuation of clients is high, a shorter duration will be reasonable.[213] Where, on the other hand, the business is characterised by a stable circle of customers, with whom contact is infrequent, a longer restriction might be accepted.[214] Another factor is how much time the employer will need to replace the former employee, in terms of training and teaching him the intricacies of the employer's business. Thus, senior employees might be subject to longer limitations of post-employment activity.[215]

A reasonable geographical scope of a non-solicitation agreement must correspond to the territory on which the employer is active. Thus even a worldwide limitation may be reasonable in the case of a senior consultant in a multinational consulting company.[216]

Solicitation must be distinguished from mere information about changing jobs.[217] This becomes particularly apparent in the context of use of social media[218] for professional purposes. Employees often include clients in their virtual network. If they change employment and

208 As in the case of this category of clients a negative impact on the interests of the employer is more likely, Gurry on Breach of Confidence para 12.109.

209 *International Consulting Services (UK) Ltd v Hart* [2000] IRLR 227 (QB).

210 *M&S Drapers (A Firm) v Reynolds* [1957] 1 WLR 9 (CA) 17–18; Kamerling and Goodwill, *Restrictive Covenants under Common and Competition Law* 166.

211 *Rex Stewart Jeffries Parker Ginsberg Ltd v Parker* [1988] IRLR 483 (CA).

212 Gurry on Breach of Confidence paras 12.109–12.110.

213 As was the case for exchange of foreign currencies, *Associated Foreign Exchange Ltd v International Foreign Exchange (UK) Ltd* [2010] EWHC 1178 (Ch) [65]–[66] (Jeremy Cousins QC).

214 Gurry on Breach of Confidence para 12.112.

215 *Rex Stewart Jeffries Parker Ginsberg Ltd v Parker* [1988] IRLR 483 (CA).

216 *International Consulting Services (UK) Ltd v Hart* [2000] IRLR 227 (QB).

217 'Post-Termination Restrictive Covenants' 853, 12–18.

218 Such as Xing, LinkedIn or Facebook.

update their profile, the relevant information will be forwarded to all their contacts, including clients of their former employer.[219] It is submitted that mere information about a change of job does not amount to breach of a non-solicitation agreement. Thus, a covenant prohibiting this is likely to be considered unreasonable for lack of support by a legitimate interest of the employer. This is different in the case of agreements prohibiting active solicitation.[220]

Non-dealing clauses which prohibit any contact with clients of the former employer may be seen as a sub-category of non-solicitation agreements. They undergo stricter scrutiny than regular NSAs, because they limit post-employment activity more stringently[221] and encompass not only offers to leave the service for the former employer but any contact with his clients or suppliers, including for non-competitive purposes. Moreover, they include situations where the former employee is approached by the client without active solicitation on his own part.[222]

d) Covenants Not to Solicit Employees Protecting investments in recruiting and training employees has been recognised as a legitimate interest justifying restraint of post-employment activities. Thus, covenants prohibiting the poaching and employing former colleagues may be a reasonable restraint.

While non-poaching covenants may be allowed if they are limited to the group of former colleagues who may be influenced by the employee, such as team members or subordinates,[223] covenants prohibiting the employment of any former colleagues (even without active solicitation) are criticised. In the absence of active contact, simply employing a former colleague does not necessarily include influencing him and thus taking advantage of the knowledge he gained during service.[224] Such contracts may also be seen as contrary to the public interest since they indirectly limit other employees, not party to the agreement, in their freedom to

219 Kamerling and Goodwill, *Restrictive Covenants under Common and Competition Law* 177.

220 Cf Goulding, Clarke, Jones and Taylor in Goulding para 6.264, suggesting that a breach of a non-solicitation clause occurs if the conduct of the employee shows 'a specific purpose and intention to obtain orders from customers'.

221 Gurry on Breach of Confidence para 12.107. Kamerling and Goodwill criticise non-dealing clauses as contrary to the public interest and leading to waste of resources if enforced, Kamerling and Goodwill, *Restrictive Covenants under Common and Competition Law* 177.

222 Goulding argues that non-dealing clauses are supported by the employer's legitimate interest in particular where they aim at protecting relationships with clients entertained by the ex-employee on behalf of the employer and at his expense, Goulding, Clarke, Jones and Taylor in Goulding para 6.208.

223 Goulding, Clarke, Jones and Taylor in Goulding para 6.281.

224 Goulding, Clarke, Jones and Taylor in Goulding para 6.284.

change jobs.[225] However, in cases in which the ex-employee had knowledge of his colleagues' scope of duties, remuneration and other perks, and therefore could make a more attractive employment offer than his ex-employer, this may be seen as undue influence on the legitimate interest of the employer in the stability of his workforce and justify both a non-poaching and a non-employment clause.[226] Such a prohibition may also be justified by the interest of the ex-employer in protecting his confidential information, if the data concerning working conditions on offer there had such a status.

e) Covenants Not to Compete Such agreements effectively limit the former employee in undertaking any competitive activity. For this reason they are subject to particularly rigorous assessment under the doctrine of restraint of trade. They may be accepted only if an agreement not to disclose or use confidential information or not to solicit clients of the former employer would not be sufficient to protect his legitimate interests.[227]

Radius clauses,[228] prohibiting any competitive activity in a certain area to protect the employer's goodwill relating to his connections with clients, will usually be unreasonable if the clients can be identified in a contract.[229] On the other hand, if the employer's prospective clients might come from among those who have experienced his services, despite not being direct clients or where the identity of the clients is not known or not recorded,[230] a non-compete clause might be the only way to protect his interests. However, where the employer's business is not conducted in a particular area, because it offers services on the phone or over the internet, an area restriction is likely to be unsuitable.

Covenants not to compete aiming at protection of trade secrets (highly confidential information as defined in *Faccenda Chicken*) are generally accepted, since courts tend to recognise that agreements not to disclose

225 Goulding, Clarke, Jones and Taylor in Goulding para 6.289.

226 *Dawnay Day & Co Ltd v D'Alphen* [1998] ICR 1068 (CA) 1111; Goulding, Clarke, Jones and Taylor in Goulding para 6.288.

227 *Dyson Technology Ltd v Strutt* [2005] EWHC 2814 (Ch) [60]–[63]; Kamerling and Goodwill suggest that this is when the employee, judging by his previous behaviour, may not be trusted to observe a covenant not to disclose confidential information or where customers are difficult to identify or likely to follow the employee after his departure, see Kamerling and Goodwill, *Restrictive Covenants under Common and Competition Law* 171.

228 Also referred to as 'area covenants'.

229 Gurry on Breach of Confidence para 12.115–12.116.

230 As is the case e.g. in relation to hairdressing services, see Goulding, Clarke, Jones and Taylor in Goulding para 6.211.

might be insufficient to effectively protect such information.[231] However, due to the fact that they are a particularly strong restriction of the ex-employee's trade, they undergo careful scrutiny. The scope of prohibition may be defined by determining the sector in which the employee is not to compete or by defining the position or type of activity that he is not to undertake.[232] A reasonable restraint must be justified by the existence of the employer's interest in the protection of highly confidential information, i.e. it must not go beyond the sector in which the employee would use such information. Thus, a prohibition of activity in any field which uses a particular type of information may be unreasonable if the employer is active in only one such sector.[233] Accordingly, a clause which limits post-employment competition also in markets in which the employer is not active will usually not be considered reasonable.[234] This may be different if the employer is able to show that he wanted to extend his activity to other sectors. However, even a restraint relating to a field of industry or technology in which the employer is actually active may nevertheless be considered unreasonable if it prohibits any activity in that sector, irrespective of the role that the former employee is to undertake. Thus, unless the sector is particularly narrow, a narrower determination of the type of activity will be necessary in order to draft a reasonable non-compete agreement. This may be done by relating the non-compete clause to the duties of the employee during employment[235] or to the information that he handled while in service.[236] Of course, a restraint may be justified only by an interest in protecting information to which the employee had access at the time of the conclusion of the agreement, e.g. due to the nature of his duties or position in the company.[237]

The reasonable territorial scope and the duration of such a limitation are determined, as in the case of non-solicitation agreements, by reference to the territorial scope of the former employer's activity[238] and by assessing the time needed to build customer connections.[239] In determination

[231] Goulding, Clarke, Jones and Taylor in Goulding paras 6.249–6.250.

[232] Gurry on Breach of Confidence para 12.120.

[233] For example, when an NCA prohibits competition by a software programmer in any sector, but his ex-employer is active only in the automotive industry.

[234] *Scully UK Ltd v Lee* [1998] IRLR 259 (CA); Gurry on Breach of Confidence para 12.120.

[235] *Dyson Technology Ltd v Strutt* [2005] EWHC 2814 (Ch) [63] (Rattee J).

[236] This information can be defined by technological field, patents to which it relates or by its application, cf Gurry on Breach of Confidence para 12.121.

[237] Beth Richards-Bray, 'Intellectual Property Law: Employment Law – Contract Law' (2007) 12(1) *Cov L J* 76, 79.

[238] Gurry on Breach of Confidence para 12.117.

[239] Cf Gurry on Breach of Confidence para 12.112.

of reasonableness of the duration, the time spent by the employee on garden leave[240] may also be considered. In the case of a lengthy period of such an effective limitation of the employee's competitive activity, a further restriction by way of a covenant not to compete may be deemed unreasonable.[241]

The duration of a covenant not to compete must be limited, even if it protects trade secrets.[242] Despite the fact that the reasonableness of the duration of an NCA is assessed in the light of all the circumstances of the case, it is proposed that it should not be longer than twelve months after termination of employment.[243]

The reasonableness of the geographical scope of the restriction is determined taking into account the industry or trade in which the employer is active. If he is active on a world-wide scale or on the internet, or where the restriction is aimed at protection of technical improvements,[244] a world-wide restriction may be reasonable.[245]

4 Legal Consequences of an Agreement in Restraint of Trade: Invalidity and Severance by Court

It follows that a restraint will be considered unreasonable where it aims at preventing competition as such or stops the ex-employee from using his personal skills and knowledge.[246] A covenant which constitutes an

[240] Garden leave 'typically requires the provision of lengthy notice periods, during which a resigning employee is retained on the company's books, paid, but is required not to attend the workplace'. Thus, during that period the employee remains bound by the expressed and implied terms of his employment contract, see Gurry on Breach of Confidence para 11.103. See also ibid paras 11.104–11.114. In the United Kingdom a restriction of post-employment competitive activity may not be compensated for by awarding the ex-employee additional remuneration. Sending the employee on garden leave is one possibility of circumventing this. It effectively limits competition by the employee who is (still) bound by his employment duties, including prohibition of competition, see Ansgar Ohly, 'Harmonising the Protection of Trade Secrets: Challenges and Perspectives' in Jacques de Werra (ed), *La protection des secrets d'affaires. The Protection of Trade Secrets* (Schulthess 2013) 42.

[241] *Brake Brothers Ltd v Ungless* [2004] EWHC 2799 (QB) [55], where the duration of garden leave was considered but did not influence the duration of the restrictive covenant; Goulding, Clarke, Jones and Taylor in Goulding paras 6.307–6.312; Gurry on Breach of Confidence para 12.118.

[242] Beyond that time, a covenant not to disclose the information may still be considered reasonable.

[243] *Dyson Technology Ltd v Strutt* [2005] EWHC 2814 (Ch) [66] (Rattee J); Gurry on Breach of Confidence para 12.122, proposing that the expected life-time of the information to be protected is included in the assessment of the duration of the restraint.

[244] *Cyrus Energy Ltd v Stewart* [2009] CSOH 53 (CSOH) [33], [36].

[245] *Dyson Technology Ltd v Strutt* [2005] EWHC 2814 (Ch) [65] (Rattee J); Gurry on Breach of Confidence para 12.123.

[246] Kamerling and Goodwill, *Restrictive Covenants under Common and Competition Law* 162.

unreasonable restraint of trade is, as a whole, void and unenforceable.[247] However, unlike Germany, where this effect destroys the agreement altogether, in the United Kingdom it is possible for the court to delete those fragments which are unreasonable and preserve the remainder of the contract, under the 'doctrine of severance'.[248] This can be done when the unreasonable part may be removed without changing of the wording of the agreement, the remaining parts are supported by consideration and the severance does not change the character of the contract.[249]

The first requirement (linguistic severability or the 'blue pencil' test) requires that the part of the agreement to be extracted is a 'linguistically distinct and substantively independent obligation, the removal of which leaves a remainder that itself makes sense without further modification'.[250]

This remainder must be supported by consideration. Thus, where the contract is limited to the obligation which is considered to be an unreasonable restraint of trade, it will be invalid and unenforceable as a whole. Otherwise, it may be subject to severance by court, provided that other requirements are met.[251]

Finally, severance may not result in rewriting the contract and giving it an effect different from the one intended by the parties. Thus, it may be applied only 'in cases where the part so enforceable is clearly severable, and even so only in cases where the excess is of trivial importance, or merely technical, and not part of the main purport and substance of the clause'.[252] Thus, severance may maintain the agreement if the part to be removed does not constitute an essential obligation agreed on. The part to be preserved should be 'in commercial terms the greater part of the obligation'.[253]

[247] Gurry on Breach of Confidence para 12.09 and the case-law referred to in note 21. See also Peel, *The Law of Contract* paras 11-062–11-063, 11-066. Such an invalid clause may not be rescued by granting a limited injunction, *Dawnay Day & Co Ltd v D'Alphen* [1998] ICR 1068 (CA) 1108. The agreement may not be enforced in court. However, the parties may decide to observe it, see Goulding, Clarke, Jones and Taylor in Goulding para 6.80.

[248] On the increasing use of drafting techniques enabling easy severability, see Stewart, 'Confidential Information and Departing Employees: The Employer's Options' 88, 93–94. Such drafting is referred to as a 'risky strategy' in 'Post-Termination Restrictive Covenants' 853, 12–18.

[249] Goulding, Clarke, Jones and Taylor in Goulding paras 6.84–6.86, 6.314; Gurry on Breach of Confidence para 12.135.

[250] Gurry on Breach of Confidence para 12.140.

[251] Gurry on Breach of Confidence para 12.142.

[252] *Mason v Provident* [1913] AC 724 (HL) 745.

[253] Gurry on Breach of Confidence para 12.143.

The doctrine of severance is not uncontroversial. It must be applied carefully in order not to interfere with the intentions of the parties, which might result in 'rewriting' the contract and imposing on the parties conditions that they have not agreed to.[254] Another controversy relates to how it should be applied in the assessment of agreements with employees. In *Mason v Provident*, Lord Moulton considered that the imbalance of powers and resources to litigate between the employer and the employee should be considered, to the effect that it should be the former who should bear the consequences of an overly broad restriction.[255] This proposition has not been followed in subsequent decisions of the courts. As a result, there are no special rules on severability of agreements between employers and employees.[256] In particular, so-called cascading clauses are accepted. The fact that they may be easily severed may encourage employers to impose broad prohibitions, in the assurance that should the agreement be reviewed by a court, it will be adapted to ensure its reasonableness.[257]

Where severance may not be performed, the agreement is void in toto. Despite that, the implied post-employment duties, including the duty not to use or disclose highly confidential information learned during service, remains unaffected.[258]

5 Repudiatory Breach of the Employment Contract by the Employer

Apart from situations in which it is an unreasonable restraint of trade, a post-employment agreement will not be enforced if the employer has committed a repudiatory breach of the employment contract,[259] i.e. a serious breach 'going to the root of the contract of employment, or which shows that the employer no longer intends to be bound by one or more of

[254] Gurry on Breach of Confidence para 12.141. For examples of application of the doctrine of severance to post-employment agreements, see Goulding, Clarke, Jones and Taylor in Goulding paras 6.322–6.329.

[255] *Mason v Provident* [1913] AC 724 (HL) 745.

[256] *Beckett Investment Management Group Ltd v Hall* [2007] EWCA Civ 613 (CA) [35] with further references (Maurice Kay LJ); Gurry on Breach of Confidence para 12.138.

[257] van Caenegem, *Trade Secrets and Intellectual Property. Breach of Confidence, Misappropriation and Unfair Competition* 211–212.

[258] *Triplex Safety Glass Co v Scorah* [1938] Ch 211 (Ch) 217; *Force India Formula One Team Ltd v Aerolab Srl & Another* [2013] EWCA Civ 780 (EWCA) [70] (Lewison J); Kenneth Miller, 'Implied Duties of Confidentiality in the Contract of Employment' (1986) 102 *LQR* 359, 362; Linda Clarke, 'Breach of Confidence and the Employment Relationship' (2002) 31(4) *ILJ* 353, 355; Gurry on Breach of Confidence para 12.149.

[259] *General Billposting Co Ltd v Atkinson* [1909] AC 118 (HL); Goulding, Clarke, Jones and Taylor in Goulding paras 6.91, 6.126–6.127.

the essential terms of the contract'.[260] The effect of such a breach by the employer on the post-employment duties of the employee is discussed in the literature.[261] While under recognised principles, the express duty is no longer binding, it is not clear whether the implied obligation applies or whether the former employee is free to use any information he learned during employment, no matter whether confidential or not.

Some justify limiting the use of information after employment by ascribing to it some proprietary nature – thus, the ex-employee should not be allowed to take with him the employer's trade secrets, just as he is not allowed to take a car, computer or any other material property, even if the employer has committed a repudiatory breach.[262] Others argue that despite termination of the express duty, equitable obligations remain binding on the former employee.[263] Honeyball and Pearce stress that the provisions of the contract of employment, including restrictive covenants, should be interpreted according to the parties' intentions. Since the consideration for a restrictive covenant is the employment itself, it would put the ex-employee in a privileged position if after repudiatory breach by the employer he were entitled to claim the lost remuneration (as damages) and at the same time were discharged from his obligations under a restrictive covenant. They propose seeing restrictive covenants as primary obligations ancillary to the main purpose of the employment agreement, and able to survive termination of the contract.[264]

These approaches have been criticised as unsatisfactory, considering that the nature of confidential information has not been settled and is neither clearly proprietary, nor clearly equitable. Gurry proposes that if an express obligation may not be enforced, the implied obligations should step in.[265] This approach seems convincing, since the implied obligations accrue irrespectively of the existence of a contract or the

[260] *Western Excavating (ECC) Ltd v Sharp* [1978] 1 QB 761 (CA) 769 (Lord Denning MR); e.g. a wrongful dismissal, unilateral reduction of pay, unilateral change of duties and responsibilities. Generally, on repudiation and its consequences, see Goulding, Clarke, Jones and Taylor in Goulding paras 6.91–6.161.

[261] Goulding, Clarke, Jones and Taylor in Goulding paras 6.140–6.160, with further references to case-law. According to Goulding et al., the House of Lords might in the future revoke the current rule, see Goulding, Clarke, Jones and Taylor in Goulding para 6.161.

[262] *Rock Refrigeration Ltd v Jones* [1997] ICR 938 (CA) 952–953 (Morritt LJ).

[263] Clarke, 'Breach of Confidence and the Employment Relationship' 353, 355; Linda Clarke, 'Repudiation of Contract and Breach of Confidence: General Billposting v Atkinson Revisited' (2003) 32 *ILJ* 43, 45; Goulding, Clarke, Jones and Taylor in Goulding para 6.161; Toulson/Phipps para 14-031.

[264] Simon Honeyball and David Pearce, 'Contract, Employment and the Contract of Employment' (2006) 35(1) *ILJ* 30, 45–48, 52.

[265] Gurry on Breach of Confidence para 12.149.

manner in which the employment was terminated. Moreover, releasing a former employee from any obligations, even the implied ones, would put him in a better position than when there was no contract at all.

6 Summary: Post-Employment Contractual Protection of Trade Secrets in the United Kingdom

Post-employment agreements are accepted in the United Kingdom as part of the general freedom of contracting. However, the validity and enforceability of restrictions on the employee's freedom to undertake professional activity after termination of service are scrutinised under the doctrine of restraint of trade and under consideration of the infringement by the employer of his duties which might have led to a repudiatory breach of the employment contract.

The reasonableness of post-employment agreements in restraint of trade is judged in the light of all the circumstances of the case.[266] In particular, the scope and definition of the prohibited acts, the geographical scope and the duration of the restriction are taken into account. Another factor is whether the restriction is limited to activities in which the employer was engaged at the time of termination of his employment, and the type of activities in which the employee was engaged during service. It is also taken into consideration whether a less restrictive type of agreement would afford adequate protection.[267] Even though the restriction may not be balanced by granting the ex-employee additional remuneration, a broader substantive or geographical extent may be compensated by a shorter duration.[268] Reasonableness is judged from the perspective of protecting the legitimate interests of the employer, and therefore the nature and life-time of the information as well as the market and geographic area in which the employer is active are used as points of reference for assessing reasonableness of the restraint in terms of substance, territory and duration.

Reasonableness of a restrictive covenant should be judged weighing up the interests of the parties to the agreement and of the public. However, despite proposals to include the interests of the employees, the balance of bargaining powers and a more thorough analysis of the interest of the public, the prevailing view is to confirm reasonableness of the restraint where it protects legitimate interests of the employer. These interests lie

[266] For a summary of the various factors which may be taken into consideration for various types of agreements, see Goulding, Clarke, Jones and Taylor in Goulding paras 6.356–6.370.

[267] Goulding, Clarke, Jones and Taylor in Goulding para 6.260.

[268] Goulding, Clarke, Jones and Taylor in Goulding para 6.245.

in the protection of confidential information, customer connections and workforce stability. Although they enter into force after termination of employment, the reasonableness of restrictive covenants is assessed at the time of their conclusion. The negative effects that such an assessment might have are however mitigated by the fact that the courts take into consideration changes in the situation upon enforcement of the contract. Moreover, an agreement which is an unreasonable restraint of trade is not automatically void as a whole, but may be severed by the court in order to maintain the validity of the part which is considered reasonable. This is another feature of the United Kingdom's approach with regard to restrictive covenants which strengthens the position of the employers.

While agreements not to disclose and even non-solicitation clauses are generally tolerated, covenants not to compete are critisised. On the one hand, NCAs make it possible to avoid difficulties connected with defining the highly confidential information and drafting an injunction, as they refer to competitive activity rather than particular information or clients. On the other hand, they seriously interfere with the ex-employee's professional freedom. Even a restrictive covenant which is in restraint of trade and thus unenforceable might effectively deter the ex-employee from undertaking a competitive activity without subjecting the agreement to the scrutiny of a court. Furthermore, unless the covenant is clearly unreasonable, the ex-employer will still be able to obtain an interlocutory injunction which might never be reviewed at trial if the employee cannot afford to pursue the case. The possibility to sever the unreasonable parts of the agreements furthermore encourages broad drafting in the knowledge that, should the agreement be assessed by the court, it will not be struck down altogether but limited. Although often the employees who are exposed to confidential information are those in more senior and highly paid positions, who might in fact be able to negotiate a restrictive covenant and later on, if needed, challenge it in court,[269] in many companies restrictive covenants have become 'standard clauses' demanded of all employees, irrespective of their position in the company or whether they actually handled confidential information. Therefore, allowing non-compete agreements with their sweeping effect is considered by some 'a "prevention better than cure" strategy capable of being taken to absurd lengths'. Thus, it is proposed to allow confidentiality clauses, while prohibiting non-compete clauses.[270]

'Garden leave' clauses are put forward as an alternative to restrictive covenants. While they achieve the same purpose as NCAs, their negative

[269] Stewart, 'Confidential Information and Departing Employees: The Employer's Options' 88, 93.
[270] Ibid 88, 94.

impact on the employees' interests is weakened by the fact that they receive remuneration.[271]

On the whole, while providing for limits on the freedom to restrict post-employment competition and use of confidential information by way of contract, the UK approach concentrates on the legitimate interests of employers and considers these of the employee and of the public only rudimentarily and in extreme cases.

C *Contracts in the United States*

In the United States the conclusion as well as enforcement of post-employment agreements is governed by state laws which differ in many respects.[272] The analysis presented here is an attempt to present the general US approach and therefore reference is made to common rules governing such agreements and only some of the more obvious differences among the state laws are pointed out.

As in the other jurisdictions analysed, covenants not to disclose, not to solicit clients or other employees and agreements not to compete may be entered into by the employee and the employer. The US courts however go further and accept agreements assigning inventions conceived or reduced to practice during a certain period of time after termination of the employment relationship.[273] If enforced, such contracts allow the ex-employer to appropriate the results of his former employee's inventive activity made with his resources, by eliminating the difficulties connected to showing when a particular invention was conceived. Since the enforcement of such covenants might severely limit the rights of particularly creative employees, invention assignment agreements are closely scrutinised for reasonableness and not enforced in states which put a high value on the mobility of employees as a matter of public policy.[274]

[271] van Caenegem, *Trade Secrets and Intellectual Property. Breach of Confidence, Misappropriation and Unfair Competition* 208.

[272] For an overview of approaches to post-employment agreements, and in particular covenants not to compete, in state laws, see Jay P Kesan and Carol M Hayes, 'The Law and Policy of Non-Compete Clauses in the United States and Their Implications' in Marilyn Pittard, Ann L Monotti and John Duns (eds), *Business Innovation and the Law. Perspectives from Intellectual Property, Labour, Competition and Corporate Law* (Edward Elgar 2013) 381, 400–404.

[273] So-called trailer or hold-over clauses, see Barton Beebe and others, *Trademarks, Unfair Competition, and Business Torts* (2nd edn Wolters Kluwer 2016) 796; Peterson 8–17. Those agreements are a restraint of trade and therefore are assessed as to reasonableness in the same way as NCAs, Peterson 8–18.

[274] Pooley 8-25, giving California as an example of a state where a post-employment invention assignment agreement may be considered unenforceable per se as being against public policy.

Covenants limiting certain post-employment activity may be entered into both by way of an explicit agreement as well as implicitly.[275] Any such agreement must be accompanied by consideration. For agreements concluded upon commencement of employment, the employment itself is a valid consideration and no particular compensation is required. However, at this stage the parties generally do not anticipate termination of the relationship and it may be difficult for them to determine the information covered by the covenant, which could be created later on. Taking into account the ever faster pace of economic and technical development, such agreements may therefore be inefficient in cases of termination of employment after many years.[276] If however the covenant is entered into at a later stage of the employment relationship, the continuation of the employment as such is generally not seen as consideration and some additional benefit may be necessary, such as promotion, rise in salary or monetary compensation.[277]

Despite the varying approaches presented by state laws, the general framework regulating the limits of the contractual freedom to limit post-employment activity resembles that of the United Kingdom. Accordingly, post-employment agreements are assessed under the doctrine of restraint of trade and accepted only to the extent that they are reasonable.

Other limitations of validity or enforceability of such agreements include the doctrine of estoppel in situations in which the employer did not enforce similar obligations with respect to other employees and thereby waived his right to hold the employee to a similar agreement, and the doctrine of unclean hands or economic duress which forced the employee to enter into a disadvantageous agreement.[278] Unjustified termination of employment by the employer may[279] furthermore be a ground for the employee to challenge a restrictive covenant. However, even if successfully relied on, these defences do not terminate the statutory implied duty of confidentiality of the former employee and therefore

[275] Pooley 8-6–8-7. This may be the case for NDAs which in any case do not extend in scope beyond the implied duty of confidentiality. In case of NCAs however it is difficult to imagine an implied agreement not to compete with a former employer, in view of the general freedom to be professionally active.

[276] Miles J Feldman, 'Towards a Clearer Standard of Protectable Information: Trade Secrets and the Employment Relationship' (1994) 9 *HTLJ* 151, 181.

[277] *Avery Dennison Corp v Kitsonas* 118 F Supp 2d 848, 851–852 (SD Ohio 2000); Pooley 8-34–8-35; Milgrim on Trade Secrets vol 1A 6-45–6-49, 6-54; Kesan and Hayes, 'The Law and Policy of Non-Compete Clauses in the United States and Their Implications' 388–389.

[278] Pooley 8-38.

[279] Stone, 'The New Psychological Contract: Implications of the Changing Workplace for Labor and Employment Law' 519, 581–582.

do not allow him to use the former employer's trade secrets. For this reason a detailed analysis of those ways to avoid a post-employment agreement remains beyond the scope of this book.

1 Doctrine of Restraint of Trade

Generally, any agreement which limits an employee's activity after termination of service constitutes a restraint of trade. Therefore, post-employment covenants and in particular NCAs undergo scrutiny to assess whether they are reasonable, considering the interests of the parties and public policy. Whether a particular agreement has an effect of a restraint of trade is assessed globally. Accordingly, even if it does not contain a clause prohibiting particular competitive behaviour, such as solicitating customers or working in a particular sector of industry, a contract may still constitute a restriction if it ascribes some negative consequence to the ex-employee's commencement of a competitive activity, e.g. payment of a contractual penalty (liquidated damages)[280] or forfeiture of some benefits not dependent on continuation of employment,[281] if such a sanction might effectively deter the former employee from competing.

1) Reasonableness of the Restraint: Interest of the Parties and the Public Interest

A restraint is unreasonable if it is greater than necessary to protect the legitimate interest of the employer or if the employer's interest in protection is outweighed by the likely harm to the employee or the public.[282]

The reasonableness of a restraint of trade imposed by a post-employment agreement is assessed from the point of view of the interests of the parties to the agreement as well as the public interest.[283] Thus, the freedom of contracting, protection of the employer's investments, intellectual property (also in the case of trade secrets),[284] valuable information which is not secret[285] and the interest in avoiding uncertainty

280 Kesan and Hayes, 'The Law and Policy of Non-Compete Clauses in the United States and Their Implications' 391.

281 *Muggill v Reuben H Donnelley Corp* 62 Cal 2d 239, 242–243 (Supr Ct California 1965); *BDO Seidman v Hirshberg* 690 NYS 2d 854, 856 (NY Ct App 1999); Pooley 8-40.2.

282 S 41 comment d Restatement (Third) of Unfair Competition. See also e.g. *Comprehensive Technologies Int v Software Artisans Inc* 3 F 3d 730, 738 (4th Cir 1993).

283 The reasonableness standard is said to be analogous to the antitrust rule of reason stipulated in S 1 Sherman Act, Philip J Closius and Henry M Schaffer, 'Involuntary Nonservitude: the Current Judicial Enforcement of Employee Covenants Not to Compete – a Proposal for Reform' (1984) 57 *S Cal L Rev* 531, 542–543.

284 *Outsource International Inc v Barton* 192 F3d 662, 666, 668 (7th Cir 1999).

285 *Continental Group Inc v Kinsley* 422 F Supp 838, 844 (D Conn 1976).

about litigation in the absence of agreement, are factors arguing in favour of accepting post-employment contractual restrictions.[286] The protection of customer connections[287] and goodwill[288] are also considered to be legitimate interests, which may justify a restraint of trade.[289] On the other hand, no interest deserving protection exists when the restriction prohibits the former employee from contacting clients whom he knew before commencing employment[290] or when the agreement aims at protecting the employer from 'raiding' his employees, where no trade secrets were taken by the departed employee.[291]

Even if supported by a legitimate interest of the employer, an agreement will not be enforced if, given the employee's interest in being able to remain professionally active and seek new employment relying on his knowledge and experience, it constitutes a limitation stronger than necessary in terms of its subject-matter, duration or territory.[292]

The final step in the assessment of reasonableness is the consideration of public interest. This includes an appraisal of whether the effect of the agreement is to limit access to particular services and thus affect consumer choice, or whether it would cause dislocation or create a monopoly in the market.[293] Moreover, as a matter of public policy, some

[286] Pooley 8-33.

[287] *Outsource International Inc v Barton* 192 F3d 662, 666–667 (7th Cir 1999).

[288] Understood as 'advantageous familiarity and personal contact that employees (...) derive from their dealings with the employer's customers', *Standard Register Co v Cleaver* 30 F Supp 2d 1084, 1095 (7th Cir ND Ind 1998).

[289] Protection of confidential information, customer relationships and the employer's investment in the employee's reputation are given as examples of legitimate interests to be taken into account when assessing the reasonableness of a restrictive covenant in S 8.07 of the proposed Restatement (Third) of Employment Law, see Kesan and Hayes, 'The Law and Policy of Non-Compete Clauses in the United States and Their Implications' 392–393.

[290] *Com-Co Insurance Agency Inc v Service Insurance Agency Inc* 748 NE 2d 298, 301–302 (Ill App 2001).

[291] *Mutual Service Casualty Insurance Co v Brass* 625 NW 2d 648, 655 (Wis App 2001).

[292] Pooley 8-34. The interest of the employee prevailed e.g. where the employee was dismissed at the age of 58, without giving a reason for the termination of employment, where he had extensive pre-employment experience and connections in the industry and was deprived of contacts with most valuable clients prior to termination in *Fenner Precision Inc v Mearthane Products Corp* Case No 12-CV-6610 CJS (WDNY 2013) as reported in (*Trading Secrets*, 13 February 2013) www.tradesecretslaw.com/2013/02/articles/noncompete-enforceability/new-york-federal-court-denies-injunction-to-enforce-restrictive-covenants-against-terminated-employee/ accessed 1 June 2017.

[293] *BDO Seidman v Hirshberg* 690 NYS 2d 854, 860 (NY Ct App 1999); Milgrim on Trade Secrets vol 1A 6-10 note 22. Beebe et al. explain that while post-employment agreements may be assessed from an antitrust perspective, very few cases resulted in a finding of actual or attempted monopolisation, see Beebe and others, *Trademarks, Unfair Competition, and Business Torts* 812.

states do not accept agreements not to compete, regardless of the balance of interests between the parties involved.[294]

The assessment of reasonableness is made globally, taking into consideration all the facts of a particular case, such as the duration and geographic scope of the restraint, the information that it covers and the acts that it prohibits, whether the employee had contact with customers, whether he was exposed to trade secrets, whether the agreement prohibits only unfair competition or any competition at all, whether the agreement effectively restrains the employee from using his skill and experience, whether the detriment which the employee suffers is disproportionately high compared with the benefit of the employer, whether the agreement denies the employee any means of support, whether the employee's talents and experience were developed during employment, whether the prohibited activities pose a competitive threat for the employer, whether the prohibited activities are merely incidental to the employee's new duties and whether the employee is paid during the period of restriction.[295] The reason for a dismissal may also be taken into account when assessing the reasonableness of a post-employment agreement: if the employee was dismissed for poor performance, restricting his activities would not be reasonable since such a dismissal implies that the employer did not hold the employee in very high regard.[296]

Bishara and Orozco propose to approach the enforceability of restrictive agreements from the perspective of 'resource-based theory' and present a method for determining whether there exists a legitimate interest of the employer which warrants protection by a post-employment covenant. As a first step the court should determine whether the information in question is public knowledge. If so, no protectable interest exists on the part of the employer. If however the information is private, as a next step the court should assess whether it is 'tacit' (vaguely identified) or whether it is explicit, i.e. incorporated in written materials, charts, lists, reports or presentations. If the information is not sufficiently identified, no legitimate interest is demonstrated.[297] As a final step it should be determined

[294] Pooley 8-33, 8-39. The usual example is California which prohibits any agreement precluding an individual from 'engaging in a lawful profession trade or business of any kind', S 16600 Cal Bus & Prof Code. See also *Edwards v* Arthur *Andersen LLP* 81 Cal Rptr 3d 282, 288–292 (Cal Sup Ct 2008).

[295] *Basicomputer Corp v Scott* 973 F 2d 507, 512 (6th Cir 1992); Pooley 8-35; Milgrim on Trade Secrets vol 1A 6-16 and the case-law referred to in note 23 ibidem.

[296] *Fenner Precision Inc v Mearthane Products Corp* Case No 12-CV-6610 CJS 19–20 (WDNY 2013).

[297] Norman D Bishara and David Orozco, 'Using the Resource-Based Theory to Determine Covenant Not to Compete Legitimacy' (2011) Ross School of Business Working Paper No 1157 56–57 http://papers.ssrn.com/sol3/papers.cfm?abstract_id=1900873## accessed 1 June 2017.

whether the information has 'social (organisational) complexity', i.e. whether it was combined with other resources in the company in such a way as to create an asset giving a competitive advantage (e.g. strategic plans prepared with other employees) or whether it related to 'higher organisational principles' such as managerial techniques.[298] Such information is usually complex, involves knowledge relating to various types of activities of a business (research, production, marketing, human resources) and is possessed by employees in managerial positions. Where the post-employment agreement relates to such information, the employer will have a legitimate interest. However, an agreement protecting such an interest must still be subject to the reasonableness assessment as to the public interest, duration and territory.[299] It is submitted that these considerations may be an aid to determine the existence of the employer's legitimate interest in borderline cases, where it is difficult to describe the valuable information relating to the functioning of a company. They may not be decisive in all cases, in particular that of technical information, which does not possess 'organisational complexity', but which is nonetheless valuable.

In view of the analysis presented here, it appears that in practice US courts take a holistic approach to the assessment of reasonableness. While the support by consideration is determined upon conclusion of the agreement, the existence of interest in support of the restriction and the balance of interests are assessed at the time of enforcement.

2) *Scope of the Agreement*

The freedom of contracting accepted in the United States allows the conclusion of various types of agreements between employers and employees with a view to regulating use of information and activity after termination of the employment relationship. Since they essentially limit the former employee in undertaking a professional activity, their enforceability depends on whether they are reasonable.

a) Agreements Not to Disclose Agreements not to disclose are generally not considered to be a restraint of trade. Such covenants must be limited to information which is a trade secret[300] and therefore they 'merely (...) confirm obligations that the law otherwise would imply'[301] and may

[298] Ibid 57–58.
[299] Ibid 59–60.
[300] *AMP Inc v Fleischhacker* 823 F 2d 1199, 1202–1204 (7th Cir 1987).
[301] Pooley 8-4. For an analysis of the post-employment implied duty of confidentiality, see supra Chapter 3 part II, point C.

not be used to extend the implied duty of confidentiality.[302] These agreements, considered as a basic form of protection of trade secrets,[303] serve to show the secret character of the information and, while not always sufficient alone, constitute a reasonable measure to maintain secrecy, thus giving the data the status of trade secret[304] and make it possible to determine who owns the particular information.[305] Thus, NDAs may be challenged if they cover information which is not a trade secret,[306] and usually are not subject to assessment under the doctrine of restraint of trade.

b) Non-Solicitation Agreements In the United States, non-solicitation agreements may refer to a prohibition of contacting clients of the former employer in order to offer competing goods or services or it may refer to approaching the former employer's employees to encourage them to change jobs.[307]

302 Even though some courts accept protection by way of contract of information which is not a trade secret, see Pooley 8-8; *Structural Dynamics Research Corp v Engineering Mechanics Research Corp* 401 F Supp 1102, 1113–1114 (ED Mich 1975); Feldman, 'Towards a Clearer Standard of Protectable Information: Trade Secrets and the Employment Relationship' 151.

303 Agreements prohibiting use and disclosure of trade secrets are accepted even in states such as California which encourage employee mobility as a matter of public policy, Beebe and others, *Trademarks, Unfair Competition, and Business Torts* 810.

304 Reasonable measures taken by the holder of the information to maintain its secrecy constitute an element of the definition of a trade secret under S 1(4)(ii) UTSA and 18 US Code §1839(3), as amended by the DTSA. A detailed analysis of the definition of a trade secret under the state laws of the United States is presented in Chapter 2 part I point D.

305 Weiss, 'Biting the Hand that Stops Feeding: How to protect Trade Secrets from Misappropriation by Laid Off Employees' 469, 479; Pooley 8-3, 8-5–8-6; Darin W Snyder and David S Almeling, *Keeping Secrets: A Practical Introduction to Trade Secret Law and Strategy* (1st edn, Oxford University Press 2012) 70.

306 S 41 comment d Restatement (Third) of Unfair Competition. Pooley adds that they may also be challenged if they are not limited in terms of duration or territory, Pooley 8-4. While lack of secret subject-matter will usually render the agreement void, a challenge as to duration or territorial scope seems rarely to be successful, as protection of trade secrets presupposes that any disclosure is damaging and that they are protected as long as they remain secret, i.e. for an unlimited period of time (the requirement that an NDA be limited as to duration and territory is described as 'deceptively simple logic' leading to 'a patently wrong result' in Peterson 9-82). There are decisions accepting a confidentiality agreement of unlimited duration, as long as it does not prevent the employee from pursuing his livelihood, see e.g. *Ashland Mgt Inc v Altair Invs NA LLC* 59 A D 3d 97, 104 (NY 1st Dep't 2008), see also Snyder and Almeling, *Keeping Secrets: A Practical Introduction to Trade Secret Law and Strategy* 73.

307 Non-poaching or non-interference covenants, Weiss, 'Biting the Hand that Stops Feeding: How to protect Trade Secrets from Misappropriation by Laid Off Employees' 469, 481.

NSAs are accepted more readily than NCAs since they do not exclude the competitive activity of the former employee altogether.[308] It is recognised that in some cases such a restraint may be the only way for the employer to avoid losing his client base and employees as a result of approaches from a former employee who knows the preferences of those clients and the working conditions of the employees, and who with that 'insider' knowledge is able to outbid his ex-employer. Therefore non-solicitation covenants are usually accepted for a limited period of time following termination of employment.[309]

Non-solicitation of clients will usually be supported by the employer's legitimate interest in the protection of his goodwill and trade secrets. It may be more difficult to show legitimate interest on the part of the employer in the case of non-poaching covenants.[310] It is submitted here that such an agreement is more likely to be reasonable in the case of employees with intimate knowledge of the working conditions of their colleagues, i.e. information which may provide a competitive advantage when making a job offer. This may be the case for those in high positions, managing the work of others or working in an HR department. It is less likely for those in lower positions in the ex-employer's company or not working in a team.

Agreements prohibiting the former employee from soliciting clients of his former employer are accepted as long as they are limited to contacting clients whom the employee attended to while in service.[311] The controversial issue is usually what behaviour amounts to solicitation. The prevailing opinion seems to be that active contacting and making offers to former clients and colleagues constitutes solicitation, while merely informing them of a change of activity, e.g. by posting information on Facebook,[312] or replying to enquiries from former clients or colleagues does not.[313]

308 They are accepted even in California, a state which is traditionally an employee-friendly jurisdiction and where NCAs are as a rule not enforced at all, Pooley 8-40.1 note 32. Nevertheless, an NSA which is so broadly drafted that it entirely prohibits the party from pursuing its trade will not be reasonable, Weiss, 'Biting the Hand that Stops Feeding: How to protect Trade Secrets from Misappropriation by Laid Off Employees' 469, 481. This is likely to be the case for a company having a large share in a market of specialised services or goods. If the employee is restricted from contacting clients of this company, he may be excluded from continuing to work in this field, which would amount to prohibition of competition.

309 Pooley 8-40.1.

310 Ibid.

311 *Garber Bros Inc v Evlek* 122 F Supp 2d 375, 383 (EDNY 2000).

312 *Invidia LLC v Difonzo* MICV 2012-3798-H 10 (Mass County Super Court 2012).

313 Weiss, 'Biting the Hand that Stops Feeding: How to protect Trade Secrets from Misappropriation by Laid Off Employees' 469, 480–481; Pooley 8-40.1 – 8-40.2.

c) Agreements Not to Compete Agreements prohibiting any competitive activity by the former employee constitute the strongest restraint and are therefore assessed most stringently for reasonableness.

While generally any legitimate interest of the employer may justify a restrictive covenant, some courts accept NCAs only to the extent that they serve as a means to protect trade secrets.[314] The interest in protection of goodwill is likely to render an NCA reasonable as long as it relates to clients with whom the former employee had direct contact and who were acquired using the resources of the employer.[315] Including clients attracted solely by the employee, e.g. even before the employment commenced, is likely to render the restriction unreasonable.[316] In any case, the broader the subject-matter covered by the covenant, the more likely it is to be unreasonable.[317] Reasonableness depends also on the type of work the employee performed and his position in the former employer's company.[318]

The duration of such a covenant must be limited and may not extend beyond the life-time of the protected interest, e.g. the expected life-time of the information and – in the case of goodwill – the time necessary for the employer to rebuild his relationship with the clients looked after by the departed employee.[319] To assess a reasonable duration, the courts take into account the type of industry in which the ex-employee is active and will accept a shorter duration as reasonable in fast-moving sectors.[320] Generally, more than one or two years is not considered reasonable.[321]

314 *Reed Roberts Assocs v Strauman* 40 NY 2d 303, 308–309 (NY Ct App 1976).

315 Cf shop right determining ownership of inventions, analysed in Chapter 3, part II, point C.2.

316 *BDO Seidman v Hirshberg* 690 NYS 2d 854, 859–860 (Ct App 1999).

317 A clause prohibiting the employee to act 'directly or indirectly [...] as an advisor, consultant, or salesperson for, or becom[ing] financially interested, directly or indirectly, [in an entity] engaged in [...] the business of selling flavour materials', was considered too broad for a plant manager in *Horner Intl Co v McKoy Case No COA 13-964* 10 (North Carolina App 2014).

318 Generally, the higher the position of the employee, the broader the restrictions accepted. However, some state laws provide for explicit prohibition of NCAs in the case of e.g. physicians or clerical staff, others provide for explicit acceptance of NCAs for executive and management personnel, see Kesan and Hayes, 'The Law and Policy of Non-Compete Clauses in the United States and Their Implications' 389–390.

319 *BDO Seidman v Hirshberg* 690 NYS 2d 854, 860 (Ct App 1999); *IBM v Papermaster* 2008 WL 4974508 11 (SDNY 2008). Another factor which may be taken into consideration to determine a reasonable duration of an NCA is the time necessary to train an employee to take over from the departing one, *Bryceland v Northey* 772 P 2d 36, 40 (Arizona Ct App 1989).

320 As was recognised in the case of online products and services in the IT industry in *EarthWeb Inc v Schlack* 71 F Supp 2d 299, 313 (SDNY 1999).

321 Pooley 8-36 with further references; Orly Lobel, 'Intellectual Property and Restrictive Covenants' (2008) Legal Studies Research Paper Series, Research Paper 08-059, 19 http://ssrn.com/abstract=1226463 accessed 1 June 2017. However, in Florida, the

The territorial scope of the restriction also must correspond to the legitimate interest of the employer. Accordingly, where the protected interest is the employer's goodwill, the territory of the NCA should be limited to that on which the former employee was active during service. Agreements with no territorial limitation may be accepted only exceptionally, in cases in which the employer's business has no territorial limitations either.[322]

Thus, both the duration and the territorial scope depend on the type of industry in which the former employer is active. Generally, the employee may be obliged to refrain from competition in the sector and function in which he worked for his previous employer[323] and a broader limitation may be accepted only exceptionally, in the case of companies with many lines of business. The subject-matter, duration and territory of the restraint are interdependent and a narrower subject-matter may offset a longer duration or broader geographical scope.[324]

Agreements not to compete are the subject of ongoing debate and controversy. They are considered beneficial to employers and to encourage loyalty among employees as well as investment in human capital.[325] On the other hand, they limit employee mobility and knowledge spillovers as well as the innovation resulting from that.[326] Against this background, from the point of view of law and economics, various approaches to the enforceability of NCAs may be identified.

At one extreme is the argument for general acceptance of restrictive covenants put forward by Glick, Bush and Hafen. According to them,

duration of NCAs protecting trade secrets is presumed to be reasonable if it is less than five years, Kesan and Hayes, 'The Law and Policy of Non-Compete Clauses in the United States and Their Implications' 387.

322 Pooley 8-36.

323 *Grant v Carotek* 737 F 2d 410, 412 (4th Cir 1984); *Modern Environments Inc v Stinnett* 561 S E 2d 694, 696 (Va Sup Ct 2002); Pooley 8-37.

324 *Bed Mart Inc v Kelley* 45 P 3d 1219, 1222–1223 (Ariz App 2002); Pooley 8-36 note 14.1; Milgrim on Trade Secrets vol 1A 6-15 note 22.

325 That is, training of the employees. By limiting employee mobility the employer may count on his investment in training being repaid by the services of highly qualified employees. He might furthermore decide to invest the new resources in further training and innovation. If not for the restrictive covenant, it might be his competitor who would benefit from the services of employees trained at his expense. Since the new employer would save the costs of training, he could offer more attractive payment to the employee, Bishara, 'Covenants Not to Compete in a Knowledge Economy: Balancing Innovation from Employee Mobility against Legal Protection for Human Capital Investment' 287, 298, 300–301, 310–311.

326 Ibid 287, 298; Marx, Singh and Fleming, 'Regional Disadvantage? Non-Compete Agreements and Brain Drain'; Sampsa Samila and Olav Sorenson, 'Non-Compete Covenants: Incentives to Innovate or Impediments to Growth' (2010) 10–11, 26 http://papers.ssrn.com/sol3/papers.cfm?abstract_id=1411172 accessed 1 June 2017.

enforcement of NCAs should be denied only in case of 'market failure', i.e. where negotiations are conducted in a situation of imperfect information, where the parties have a limited choice or where there are externalities in the form of negative impact on consumers.[327] It is proposed to address imperfect information and limited choice cases under general contractual defences.[328] In the case of externalities, the authors argue that the reasonableness assessment is not an appropriate response, since it places too much weight on the interests of the parties to the agreement. Instead, they suggest the application of antitrust analysis and the rule of reason test, which would make it possible to incorporate assessment of the effect that the agreement might have on the particular market.[329]

At the other extreme, restrictive covenants are accepted only to the extent that they protect trade secrets. Closius and Schaffer suggest that the courts should place less weight on the reasonableness analysis and concentrate on the nature of the information covered by the contract, because only where this information is a trade secret does a legitimate interest of the employer in limiting its use exist. Therefore, they argue, contracts are superfluous, because protection of confidential information and trade secrets is already safeguarded by the implied post-employment duties.[330] The only situation where a post-employment agreement could be accepted is if the employee has a bargaining power equal to the employer's, e.g. in case of service contracts with highly qualified and acknowledged specialists.[331]

[327] Mark A Glick, Darren Bush and Jonathan Q Hafen, 'The Law and Economics of Post-Employment Covenants: A Unified Framework' (2002) 11 *Geo Mason L Rev* 357, 382–418.

[328] Ibid 357, 418.

[329] Ibid 357, 412–418, admitting that antitrust considerations are not frequently applied to restrictive covenants.

[330] Closius and Schaffer, 'Involuntary Nonservitude: The Current Judicial Enforcement of Employee Covenants Not to Compete – a Proposal for Reform' 531, 547–549.

[331] Ibid 531, 550. The problem of imbalance of bargaining powers pertains to all types of agreements between employers and employees. While freedom of contracting is accepted, it is rarely the case that the employer and the employee negotiate over a post-employment restrictive clause. In the case of large companies, their resources and experience favour them in the negotiations, even with experienced and well-paid candidates. This results in decreased perspectives of mobility for workers, often without adequate compensation. On the other hand, smaller companies and start-ups, who would benefit from employing top specialists, often do not have the experience or the leverage to impose an agreement protecting their interests, Feldman, 'Towards a Clearer Standard of Protectable Information: Trade Secrets and the Employment Relationship' 151, 181. See also Moffat, 'The Wrong Tool for the Job: The IP Problem with Non-Competition Agreements' 884, 885–892.

Stone also argues that post-employment agreements should be accepted only where they protect trade secrets, justifying her proposal by the need to consider the 'new psychological contract' under which employees accept lower job security in return for training provided by the employers. This results in forced mobility of employees and any limitation going beyond the protection of trade secrets should not be accepted, as it would be overly burdensome for the employees. [332]

Moffat proposes a statutory ban on non-compete agreements. He argues that they are an effect of an imbalance in the bargaining powers between employees and employers and therefore are often overbroad and unenforceable. Despite that, they create an 'in terrorem' effect for both the employees, who do not challenge the unenforceable terms because they cannot afford litigation, and for other employers, by discouraging them from employing people who have signed NCAs in the past.[333] He furthermore argues that NCAs do not fit the system of IPRs and undermine it by disrupting the balance created by the incentive theory. Since they control the employees rather than the valuable information, they are a 'blunt instrument for the IP task' and do not provide better solutions than patent, copyright, NDAs and the implied duties.[334] He concludes that even though NCAs are attractive for individual employers, they are counterproductive from the market and competition perspective because they limit the flow of information without providing any benefits in return. For that reason they should be banned by statute as a matter of public policy rather than left to the courts.[335]

There are also attempts to reconcile both approaches. Bishara explains that the justifications for the enforceability of NCAs are different for various categories of employees. Accordingly, he suggests that NCAs should be accepted for service employees[336] but rejected for creative ones.[337] This would allow their flexible application to maximise the benefits they provide in areas where companies invest large sums in

[332] Stone, 'The New Psychological Contract: Implications of the Changing Workplace for Labor and Employment Law' 519, 588, 596.

[333] Moffat, 'The Wrong Tool for the Job: The IP Problem with Non-Competition Agreements' 888–889.

[334] Ibid 912–914.

[335] Ibid 920–922.

[336] Those who are not engaged in manufacturing goods but in providing services requiring specialised knowledge and experience, such as investment bankers, stock analysts, journalists, consultants, or sales representatives in pharmaceutical companies, Bishara, 'Covenants Not to Compete in a Knowledge Economy: Balancing Innovation from Employee Mobility against Legal Protection for Human Capital Investment' 287, 313.

[337] Those who are engaged in research and development and the creation of innovative products, e.g. engineers, computer software designers or chemists, ibid 287, 313.

creating confidential information and relationships with clients,[338] while encouraging mobility of creative employees and the resulting knowledge spill-overs in other areas.[339]

While Bishara presents this as a policy argument,[340] it is considered here that it is possible to include a corresponding assessment under the current legal framework. Since the assessment of reasonableness is made on a case-by-case basis, it is possible to include in the identification of the interests of the employer, of the employee and the public whether the employee is to be regarded as a service or a creative worker, and to strike the balance accordingly.

Garrison and Wendt seem to develop this approach. According to their proposal, NCAs should be accepted only insofar as they protect goodwill and relationships with clients. By doing that, they in fact prevent unfair competition by former employees and, if needed, may be appropriately limited by the courts on the basis of reasonableness.[341] This is not the case where an NCA aims at protection of trade secrets. The authors explain that NCAs create an 'in terrorem' effect, thus stifling mobility and innovation.[342] They argue that NDAs are a better solution and, combined with the application of the doctrine of inevitable disclosure,[343] should allow the courts to strike the necessary balance between the interests of the employers and of the employees. This would eliminate the threatening effect of NCAs protecting trade secrets and replace such broad agreements with carefully drafted injunctions which should be granted only where the disclosure of the information 'is a virtual certainty', where the ex-employee had '[i]ntimate and extensive knowledge of legitimate and highly valuable (and vulnerable) trade secrets' and where there is evidence of intent on the part of the employee.[344]

338 As is the case for financial services companies, which do not profit from knowledge spill-overs, e.g. Wall Street investment banks, see ibid 287, 319, 321.

339 Ibid 287, 320–321. Examples of industries relying on innovation and employee mobility are the high-tech firms located in Silicon Valley, ibid.

340 This includes a call for state legislators to introduce special legislation on NCAs, ibid 287, 314, 317.

341 Michael J Garrison and John T Wendt, 'The Evolving Law of Employee Non-Compete Agreements: Recent Trends and an Alternative Policy Approach' (2008) 45 *Am Bus L J* 107, 174–175.

342 Ibid 107, 177–178.

343 Under which an injunction prohibiting the ex-employee from undertaking a competitive activity is issued where the disclosure of the former employer's trade secrets would be inevitable, were the employee to undertake such an activity. For a more detailed analysis as well as a critical appraisal of this doctrine, see infra Chapter 5, part II, point C.2.

344 Garrison and Wendt, 'The Evolving Law of Employee Non-Compete Agreements: Recent Trends and an Alternative Policy Approach' 107, 179–182.

Yet another approach is taken by Beebe et al., who concentrate on the issue of consideration and suggest that for an NCA to be enforceable, the ex-employee must obtain additional compensation from his former employer for the duration of the NCA, as is the practice in Germany.[345]

3) *Effect of a Contract in Restraint of Trade*

Overly broad covenants are void as against public policy.[346] Therefore, as a rule, agreements which result in an unreasonable restraint of trade are not enforced at all.[347]

Some courts however tend to uphold agreements to the extent that they are reasonable. This can be done by removing the unreasonable parts, if the remaining part of the agreement remains grammatically viable ('blue pencil rule').[348] Other courts apply the rules of equity and interpret the agreement narrowly so as to render it reasonable, even if the offensive parts may not be clearly separated. This is however only possible in cases in which the employer negotiated or imposed the restraint in good faith, e.g. where there actually exists a legitimate interest on his part which needs to be protected and the employer did not attempt to use the agreement to cover information already in the public domain.[349]

The 'blue pencil rule' as well as the 'rewriting' of a contract to render it enforceable are criticised as methods of applying the reasonableness assessment, because they invite employers to draft unreasonably broad covenants, knowing that, should litigation occur, the court will not strike down the entire restraint, but simply limit it to what is reasonable.[350]

345 Beebe and others, *Trademarks, Unfair Competition, and Business Torts* 814.

346 See e.g. *Liautaud v Liautaud* 221 F 3d 981, 986, 989 (7th Cir 2000), although not issued in the context of post-employment restrictive covenant.

347 Closius and Schaffer, 'Involuntary Nonservitude: The Current Judicial Enforcement of Employee Covenants Not to Compete – a Proposal for Reform' 531, 543. This approach is taken ia by the state laws of Georgia and Virginia, see Kesan and Hayes, 'The Law and Policy of Non-Compete Clauses in the United States and Their Implications' 387.

348 Kesan and Hayes, 'The Law and Policy of Non-Compete Clauses in the United States and Their Implications' 387.

349 Closius and Schaffer, 'Involuntary Nonservitude: The Current Judicial Enforcement of Employee Covenants Not to Compete – a Proposal for Reform' 531, 543–544; Garrison and Wendt, 'The Evolving Law of Employee Non-Compete Agreements: Recent Trends and an Alternative Policy Approach' 107, 130–131; Pooley 8-37; Kesan and Hayes, 'The Law and Policy of Non-Compete clauses in the United States and Their Implications' 388.

350 Closius and Schaffer, 'Involuntary Nonservitude: The Current Judicial Enforcement of Employee Covenants Not to Compete – a Proposal for Reform' 531, 547.

2 Summary: Post-Employment Contractual Protection of Trade Secrets in the United States

Despite the fact that they increase legal security by defining the information to be protected and facilitating litigation,[351] agreements regulating activities of former employees are not uniformly accepted by state laws in the United States. Non-disclosure agreements are generally enforced, as their scope may not extend beyond the statutory duties relating to protection of trade secrets. Non-solicitation, non-poaching and invention assignment agreements are also accepted, as long as they are reasonable. The differing attitudes presented in the laws of various states are most clearly visible with regard to the enforceability of covenants not to compete, with some states accepting them as long as they are reasonable, and others prohibiting them for reasons of public policy as restricting competition.

While post-employment agreements are subject to the same limitations as other contracts, they are usually assessed to establish whether the restraint of trade that they impose is reasonable, taking into consideration the interests of the parties to the agreement and of the public. The legitimate interest of the employer is not limited to protection of trade secrets, relations with clients and workforce stability. Other interests, such as protection against unfair competition[352] or protection of investment made in developing information and training employees, are also deemed legitimate. The assessment of reasonableness in the United States furthermore takes full account of the interest of the employee in remaining professionally active, changing employment and earning his living relying on his experience. Finally, a broad assessment of the public interest in unfettered competition, promotion of innovation and economic growth is included in the balancing exercise.

The various goals of public policy result in differing treatment of the agreements found to be unreasonable by the courts. Those stressing the need to encourage employee mobility and the resulting knowledge spillovers are likely not to enforce an unreasonable agreement in toto. Other courts may use a 'blue pencil' or limiting interpretation to enforce the agreement to the extent they consider it reasonable.

On the whole, the approaches presented in US literature and case-law seem to take a comprehensive view of the conflicting interests when enforcing post-employment agreements. The differences between state

[351] Stone, 'The New Psychological Contract: Implications of the Changing Workplace for Labor and Employment Law' 519, 585.

[352] Kesan and Hayes, 'The Law and Policy of Non-Compete Clauses in the United States and Their Implications' 384.

laws, court decisions and the views of the scholars presented here show that the area of contractual determination of the use by departed employees of information learned during service is a reflection of public policy and as such not uniformly settled.

D *Comparative Assessment: Limited Freedom to Regulate Use of Information after Employment*

Despite uniform recognition of the general freedom of contracting, the approaches taken towards post-employment agreements in the jurisdictions analysed show significant differences. The main distinction between the civil law and the common law systems is that German law contains a statutory regulation of agreements limiting competition,[353] while in the United Kingdom and in the United States all post-employment agreements are subject to assessment under doctrine of restraint of trade.

Covenants not to disclose are commonly used as a means to protect trade secrets of the former employer and are least problematic from the perspective of employee mobility. All the jurisdictions analysed accept NDAs to the extent that they protect technical secrets. Non-technical information may also be safeguarded by such agreements, although the conditions they must meet are less clear. In Germany, commercial information and even information which is not a trade secret may be subject to such an agreement, unless it would limit competition and amount to an NCA. Thus, under German law an NDA may broaden the scope of the implied duty of confidentiality. This is also the case in the United Kingdom. There, NDAs may cover confidential information which the employee learned as part of his general work experience (second category of information as defined in *Faccenda Chicken*). However, once such an agreement extends beyond the implied duty it needs to be assessed under the doctrine of restraint of trade. In the United States, on the other hand, non-disclosure agreements may not extend beyond the duty imposed by statute and as such should rather be seen as a measure taken to maintain secrecy, which is a requirement of the statutory definition of a trade secret, and not as an independent means to safeguard the employer's competitive position.

The difference between the European and the US approach is reflected also in the accepted scope of the acts covered by a non-disclosure agreement. In the United States, since the scope of an NDA may not

[353] Statutory regulation of post-employment restraints increases legal certainty, van Caenegem, *Trade Secrets and Intellectual Property. Breach of Confidence, Misappropriation and Unfair Competition* 214–215.

extend beyond the statutory duty, it may cover both the disclosure and use of the information and does not have to be limited in duration. This is not necessarily the case in Europe. In Germany, the use of the information by the former employee is generally allowed, and limitating it in an NDA seems to be possible only if the use would amount to disclosure. In the United Kingdom, NDAs covering use are scrutinised as a restriction of trade.

Finally, all the jurisdictions analysed accept non-disclosure agreements of unlimited duration and territorial scope.

The other types of post-employment contracts may also effectively protect trade secrets, but they do not relate to particular information, but rather limit the former employee in the activities which he may undertake. For that reason they limit competition and therefore undergo a strict assessment. In Germany, covenants not to compete, as well as non-solicitation agreements which are considered a sub-category of NCAs, are accepted only within the statutory boundaries laid down by Sections 74–75f HGB. The law requires ia that the limitation may not extend beyond two years after termination of the employment relationship and that the former employee is paid compensation for the duration of the agreement, with a minimum amount prescribed by law. In the United Kingdom and the United States, no statutory boundaries are prescribed for agreements not to compete. Rather, they are assessed under the doctrine of restraint of trade, whereby any agreement which limits trade is void unless it is reasonable as to subject-matter, duration and territory.

None of the jurisdictions accepts agreements aiming at exclusion of competition as such. Consequently, under German law the restraint must be fair and in the common-law jurisdictions reasonable. This presupposes an assessment of the terms of the agreement and its effects under consideration of all the facts of the case and is subject to the balancing of interests.

All the jurisdictions analysed require that a restrictive covenant is supported by a legitimate interest of the employer. It is uniformly recognised that protection of trade secrets and relationships with clients and contractors are such interests. While the German courts seem not to accept other interests as legitimate, UK case-law does not give an exhaustive list and explicitly recognises also the employer's interest in workforce stability. US law presents a most flexible approach, accepting various interests of the employer as legitimate, including protection of information which is not secret and of investment in the training of employees. The limited list of legitimate interests under German law is a reason for its non-acceptance of non-poaching agreements, which in the United Kingdom and United States are allowed if reasonable.

The interest of the employee in personal development and remaining professionally active is fully considered under German and US law. In the United Kingdom, although full balancing of interests is included in the assessment of reasonableness, it is the interest of the employer which is given most weight, the interests of employees being considered only rudimentarily as part of the public interest in profiting from skills and work.

The public interest is not thoroughly considered under German law, which concentrates on the assessment of whether the employee's interests are not overly limited by the agreement. In particular, unlike the United States, there is no consideration of the public interest in the existence of competition.[354] In the United Kingdom the public interest is considered to be satisfied as long as the employer has a legitimate interest justifying the restraint. Only the US courts seem to assess the reasonableness of the restraint by making a full analysis of the interests of the parties, in view of the public interest in innovation and competition, and weigh them up against one another.

The fairness or reasonableness of the agreement is assessed taking into consideration the subject-matter, the duration and the territorial scope of the restraint. There must exist a link between the employer's interest to be protected by the covenant and the prohibited activity. This is judged from the point of view of the subject-matter and territory of the employer's business as well as the duties and position of the employee during service. The higher his position and awareness of the intricacies of the employer's business, the broader the restraint may be. In terms of territory, if the former employer is active on an international scale, even a worldwide restriction may be legitimate. The fair or reasonable duration of the restraint depends on the type of prohibited activity and the type of protected interest, but usually should not last more than two years (which is the legal maximum in Germany). The substance of the restriction, its duration and territorial scope are interdependent: a broader restriction in one of those areas may be offset by narrower one in another. Moreover, under German law, a broader restriction may be offset by appropriately high compensation during the term of restriction. This seems not to be acceptable in the United Kingdom, where it is considered that in the absence of a legitimate interest of the employer, a restriction may not be 'bought'. In the United States, it appears that appropriately high remuneration may be seen as a suitable consideration for a broader limitation.

[354] Bauer/Diller para 299. Grosch sees consideration of the impact on the market as not workable and overly burdensome for the courts, Grosch in Ann/Loschelder/Grosch 351.

The effects of a contract not fulfilling the requirements of fairness or reasonableness differ between the civil and the common-law jurisdictions. In Germany, agreements lacking compensation are invalid in toto. Otherwise, the employee has a choice as to whether to be bound by a contract not fulfilling the statutory requirements. It is however not possible to delete the offending parts or to rewrite it so that it remains valid. This is different in the United Kingdom and in the United States. While generally an agreement which is an unreasonable restraint of trade is void and unenforceable as a whole, the court may excise the unreasonable parts in order to render the agreement enforceable. Under some circumstances it is even possible to rewrite or interpret the agreement narrowly to ensure its continued validity.

This comparison shows that while all the jurisdictions analysed apply a balancing exercise to the assessment of restrictive covenants, they make the assessment from different perspectives. German law seems to stress the interests of the employees, by putting statutory limitations on agreements limiting competition, providing not only for a requirement of fairness but also for compulsory compensation and a maximum duration. In the United Kingdom, while reasonableness is also assessed, this boils down to identification of the legitimate interest of the employer. This, combined with the possibility to delete the unreasonable part of the contract or apply a narrow interpretation, results in a legal framework which seems to support the interests of the employers. Similarly in the United States, where, despite a comprehensive balancing of the interests not only of the parties to the agreement but also of the public, the possibility that courts can rewrite agreements effectively encourages employers to impose possibly overbroad non-compete obligations on employees.[355] Thus, it seems that among the jurisdictions analysed it is German law which takes the fullest account of the employee's interests in the context of post-employment covenants.[356]

The proposition to fully include public interest in the assessment of post-employment agreements seems to be most likely in the United Kingdom, where the legal framework seems to allow for a broader consideration of this interest than is currently the case. In Germany, the policy considerations are reflected in the statutory framework of post-employment agreements. German law of contracts concentrates on determining the interests of the parties, as a contract binds the parties

[355] The exceptions are states, such as California which, as a matter of public policy do not enforce restrictive covenants.

[356] Sander, 'Schutz nicht offenbarter betrieblicher Informationen nach der Beendigung des Arbeitsverhältnisses im deutschen und amerikanischen Recht' 217, 226–227.

who entered into it. The correction of an inter partes agreement in view of the public interest is possible only in the most egregious cases and results in invalidation of the contract in its entirety.

The Trade Secrets Directive does not seek to regulate the freedom to conclude post-employment agreements aiming at protection of trade secrets.[357] However, its drafters recognised the role which contractual measures play in the protection of confidential information. Accordingly, use or disclosure of a trade secret in breach of a contractual obligation is considered unlawful pursuant to Article 4(3)(b)–(c). Under Article 4(1) of the Directive, the Member States are obliged to ensure that the holders of the information are entitled to apply for measures, procedures, and in particular for the remedies foreseen in the Directive in case of such unlawful use or disclosure. Thus, the remedies and other measures provided in the Directive may be applied both in case of breach of implied post-employment duties and in case of breach of a post-employment agreement aiming at protection of trade secrets. The basic remedies available against former employees are assessed in the following part of this book.

III Post-Employment Agreements and Competition Law

Agreements protecting trade secrets limit the post-employment activities of the employee, possibly in competition with his former employer. Therefore, their assessment from the perspective of antitrust law may be contemplated.

Contracts limiting competition are subject to scrutiny under Article 101 TFEU and corresponding national provisions.[358] Such agreements between undertakings, which may affect trade between the Member States and have as their object or effect the prevention, restriction or distortion of competition, e.g. by limiting or sharing markets, are automatically void (Article 101(2) TFEU).

Restriction of competition is often present in post-employment covenants, especially those which are not limited to prohibition of disclosure of information. Moreover, in the age of globalisation, multinational corporations and cross-border activity, employee mobility frequently likewise has an international dimension. Thus, the effect of a restrictive covenant often must and does extend beyond the territory of one country.

[357] Art 1(3)(c), Recitals 13 and 39 TSD. This has been referred to as a 'gap' in the regulation, although one which needs to be filled by national legislations, MPI Position Paper para 8.

[358] In Germany Art 1 GWB, in the United Kingdom S 2 CA 1998.

Nevertheless, such agreements are not likely to noticeably affect trade between the Member States of the EU or even within one country.[359] It appears highly unlikely that an agreement with a single employee might have an observable influence on trade in Europe or a given country. This might be the case in an extremely narrow field, e.g. in case of an emerging technology or in a market in which competition depends on the personal qualities of those active in it, such as creative industries.[360]

Furthermore, application of Article 101 TFEU would require that employees are considered to be 'undertakings'. Due to the fact that the employment relationship requires subordinance, for agreements concluded during employment, this condition of Article 101 TFEU would not be fulfilled.[361] However, once employment terminates, and the employee becomes engaged in independent activity, this assessment may change.[362] Moreover, an agreement may be assessed under competition rules at any time it is in force, not only when it is signed.[363] Therefore, even if the requirement that the restrictive covenant is 'between undertakings' is not fulfilled when it is concluded, it may be met once the employment relationship terminates. Furthermore, competition law prohibits agreements which may affect competition in the internal market even potentially. This speaks for applying Article 101 TFEU to post-employment agreements whose effects will enter into force after the service relationship has come to an end.[364] Bauer and Diller present the view that only such post-employment agreements are likely to fall under Article 101 TFEU as prevent the ex-employee from undertaking a competitive activity independently, either as a sole entrepreneur or by starting a new company. The assessment would be different if the ex-employee were to start working for an existing competitor, since in such a case he would not become an 'undertaking'.[365]

Furthermore, an agreement falls into the scope of Article 101 TFEU if its object or effect is the prevention, restriction or distortion of competition.

[359] Bauer/Diller para 364. Application of EU competition law requires an actual or potential effect on trade between EU Member States. National competition laws step in when trade on the national level is affected, Beal and Neill in Goulding paras A3.22–A3.24.

[360] Poth, *Die Grenzen des Arbeitsrechts aus kartellrechtlicher Sicht* 142–143.

[361] Case C-22/98 *Jean Claude Becu* [1999] ECR I-5665 [24]–[26]; Beal and Neill in Goulding para A3.08.

[362] Beal and Neill in Goulding para A3.09.

[363] By contrast to the UK doctrine of restraint of trade, Beal and Neill in Goulding paras A3.15–A3.16.

[364] Beal and Neill in Goulding para A3.09.

[365] Bauer/Diller para 364, Poth, *Die Grenzen des Arbeitsrechts aus kartellrechtlicher Sicht* 68–72.

This is independent of the parties' intentions and motivations in concluding it. Thus, Article 101 TFEU would apply irrespective of whether the agreement was negotiated by the employer and employee or imposed by the employer, and irrespective of the employee's willingness to enter into it. Moreover, this effect is assessed in the 'economic and legal context' of the agreement and Article 101 TFEU steps in irrespective of whether the parties were actual or only potential competitors.[366]

Under the case-law developed by the EU courts, a restrictive covenant does not violate Article 101(1) TFEU if the imposed restriction is ancillary to the main purpose of the contract which protects a legitimate commercial interest. No case has been identified which would involve a post-employment restrictive agreement. However, in the context of a non-compete clause included in a transfer of business agreement, the European Commission was of the opinion that a restriction which is justified by the main purpose of an agreement – which was the transfer of goodwill, including customer relations, and secret technical know-how – may be accepted from the perspective of competition law, if it is necessary and proportionate. Accordingly, the scope of the restriction and its duration should correspond to the nature of the transferred know-how as well as to the opportunities for its use, be limited to the market in which the undertaking was active before its sale and allow the purchaser to take over the transferor's business with an undiminished market position.[367] A possible consideration in this context is how competition would function without the restriction. If the main purpose of the agreement would be diminished, the limitation is necessary and compatible with competition rules.[368] These considerations resemble those made to establish the fairness, or reasonableness of the restriction under the German and UK doctrines discussed above.

Nevertheless, even if Article 101(1) TFEU was applicable, a particular restrictive covenant might still be found to be allowable from the antitrust perspective, if it promoted economic progress while at the same time allowing consumers a fair share of the benefits, was proportionate and did not eliminate competition.[369] This could be the case for contracts aiming at the protection of particularly valuable technical secrets which could not be patented. In any case, this assessment would require determining not only whether the information covered by the agreement is a trade secret but also whether it improves the production or distribution

[366] Beal and Neill in Goulding para A3.36–A3.37.
[367] *Reuter/BASF* (Case IV/28.996) Commission Decision 76/743/EEC [1976] OJ L254/40 [46]–[47].
[368] Beal and Neill in Goulding para A3.47.
[369] Art 101(3) TFEU.

of goods or promotes technical or economic progress, while allowing consumers a fair share of the resulting benefit. This assessment differs from the determination of the competitive value referred to upon determination of fairness of a restrictive covenant. It is made from the perspective of the public and the interest of the parties does not play a role.

Application of Article 102 TFEU is doubtful as well.[370] In some cases the CJEU has found abuse of dominant position where the dominant undertaking tried to eliminate a competitor using tools other than competition on the merits, e.g. by contractual limitation of the other party's freedom to conclude service agreements.[371] Arguably, similar considerations could be applied where a former employer imposed or enforced a post-employment covenant going beyond what is supported by his legitimate interest in protecting trade secrets or customer relations.[372] Nevertheless, while enforcement of contractual obligations restraining competition by a dominant undertaking may be a result of an abuse of position, only in the rarest of cases will this be likely to affect trade between the Member States.

In Germany, agreements limiting competition fulfilling the requirements of Sections 74ff HGB are not seen as anticompetitive. Even though they limit competition, they play an accessory role in safeguarding the main contract of employment (they are inherent to this relationship).[373] Thus, at national level Article 1 GWB is not likely to apply either.[374]

Under the framework of UK law, Beal and Neill analyse the applicability of Articles 101–102 TFEU and corresponding national provisions to employee covenants and argue that there is scope for their application under some circumstances, because employees may be considered 'undertakings'. In particular, the UK doctrine of restraint of trade may be seen as emanating from competition law rules, even if assessment under the doctrine of restraint of trade occurs upon conclusion of the contract and that under competition law takes place at any time,[375] and their methods of enforcement[376] and legal consequences[377] differ.

[370] Kamerling and Goodwill, *Restrictive Covenants under Common and Competition Law* 204.

[371] Joined Cases T-191, 212–214/98 *Atlantic Container Line and Others v Commission* [2003] ECR-II-3275 [1106].

[372] Beal and Neill in Goulding para A3.70.

[373] Bechtold and Bosch, *Kartellgesetz. Gesetz gegen Wettbewerbsbeschränkungen. Kommentar §1 para 75;* Poth, *Die Grenzen des Arbeitsrechts aus kartellrechtlicher Sicht* 175–176.

[374] Bauer/Diller para 364; see also Chapter 4, part II, point A.2.2)c) supra.

[375] Beal and Neill in Goulding para A3.15–A3.16.

[376] Private enforcement in case of doctrine of restraint of trade and public enforcement of competition law, see Beal and Neill in Goulding para A3.18–A3.19.

[377] Unenforceability which needs to be invoked by one of the parties in case of doctrine of restraint of trade and automatic invalidity in case of violation of competition law, see Beal and Neill in Goulding para A3.20.

Nevertheless, there is little case-law in that respect.[378] The direct application of antitrust regulation to post-employment agreements is therefore theoretically possible, although 'not explored in the case law'.[379]

In the United States, the federal courts scrutinise restrictive covenants from antitrust perspective. Such agreements have not been recognised as anticompetitive and thus invalid per se, and are assessed under the rule of reason.[380] This analysis necessitates defining of the relevant market and determining the market power of the party to that agreement. After that the reasonableness of the agreement is assessed, i.e. whether the agreement as such is too broad in terms of duration and scope and whether it has a negative impact on the public.[381] Even though the assessment of restrictive covenants under antitrust rules is always possible in the United States, due to the fact that, unlike Articles 101–102 TFEU, Section 1 Sherman Act covers any contract and is not limited to 'undertakings', its application is rare in practice.[382] Rather, the courts follow a long-established line that the public has no right to the secret information as such and that, if not for the restriction, the contracting party would not obtain the information at all.[383] Furthermore, US courts apply the 'ancillary restraints' doctrine which, like the doctrines applied in Europe, accepts a restraint which is ancillary to the main purpose of the contract, is necessary and proportionate.[384] It is submitted here that such an argumentation applies particularly well to non-disclosure agreements with competitors or licensees. It fits less aptly in post-employment contexts, especially as regards agreements not to compete. Nevertheless, an agreement which passes the test of reasonableness under the doctrine of restraint of trade is unlikely to fall into the ambit of antitrust provisions.

This brief examination of post-employment agreements from the antitrust perspective does not suggest that competition rules are an appropriate tool to address the problems posed by restrictive covenants. However, it is proposed here that the public interest in the existence of competition is taken into consideration in the assessment of fairness or reasonableness of the restraint, wherever national law allows for inclusion of public interest in this assessment.

[378] Beal and Neill in Goulding paras A3.01–A3.70.
[379] Stanley, *The Law of Confidentiality: A Restatement* 84–85.
[380] Glick, Bush and Hafen, 'The Law and Economics of Post-Employment Covenants: A Unified Framework' 357, 410.
[381] Ibid 357, 413–414.
[382] Ibid 357, 414.
[383] Melvin F Jager, *Trade Secrets Law* (Thomson Reuters 2015) 11-8–11-9.
[384] Ernst-Joachim Mestmäcker and Heike Schweitzer, *Europäisches Wettbewerbsrecht* (3rd edn, CH Beck 2014) §8 para 48.

IV Post-Employment Agreements and Article 45 TFEU

According to some authors,[385] due to the fact that their effect may extend over the territory of more than one Member State of the European Union, post-employment agreements may be scrutinised under Article 45 TFEU which safeguards freedom of movement for employees within the EU as one aspect of the basic freedom of movement of persons.

Article 45 TFEU prohibits discrimination based on nationality and entails the right to accept offers of employment and move within the Member States for this purpose. On this legal ground, the CJEU recognised in *Bosman* that provisions which preclude or deter a national of a Member State from leaving his country of origin in order to undertake a professional activity constitute an obstacle to the freedom of movement of workers, even if they apply without regard to the nationality of the workers concerned.[386] This decision was issued in the context of litigation between private parties (a football player on the one side and football clubs and associations on the other). Thus, it appears that Article 45 TFEU has both a vertical as well as a horizontal effect and that an ex-employee could rely on it in order to support his claim against a former employer enforcing a post-employment covenant.

Bauer and Diller are sceptical as regards the applicability of Art 45 TFEU to post-employment agreements.[387] They consider that only Article 45(1) TFEU has a horizontal effect, and that Article 45(2) TFEU may be relied on only in a dispute against a Member State. Koenig and Steiner are of the opinion that all regulations safeguarding basic freedoms are to be applied also between private parties, since otherwise the freedom of movement of workers could not be effectively safeguarded.[388]

It is considered here that already Article 45(1) TFEU and its emanation laid down in Article 45(3) TFEU provide sufficient legal ground for action against a former employer. Thus, an agreement which limits the professional activity of a former employee may fall under Article 45 TFEU, unless the limitation on free movement it imposes is supported by a legitimate private interest, is justified by the public interest and is proportionate (i.e. able to ensure the achievement of the aim in question and not going beyond what is necessary for that purpose).[389]

[385] Christian Koenig and Ulrike Steiner, 'Die Vereinbarkeit nachvertraglicher Wettbewerbsverbote mit der Arbeitnehmerfreizügigkeit des EG-Vertrags' (2002) NJW 3583, 3583.

[386] Case C-415/93 *Bosman* [1995] ECR I-04921 [96].

[387] Bauer/Diller para 368.

[388] Koenig and Steiner, 'Die Vereinbarkeit nachvertraglicher Wettbewerbsverbote mit der Arbeitnehmerfreizügigkeit des EG-Vertrags' 3583, 3584.

[389] Case C-415/93 *Bosman* [1995] ECR I-04921 [104].

It is considered that an agreement fulfilling the national requirements under the laws of Germany and the United Kingdom would meet those requirements.

Under German law, a limitation of post-employment competition which fulfils the requirements of Sections 74–75f HGB is likely to be justified by a legitimate aim (protection of the employer's investments, trade secrets and customer relations) and be proportionate. In particular, the binding effect of an agreement only to the extent that it is supported by a legitimate interest of the employer, and the balancing of interests which is inherent in that assessment, are considerations which seem to correspond to those made under Article 45 TFEU,[390] even though public interest is not explicitly included as a factor.

These considerations are less likely to apply to a post-employment agreement which is accepted under the UK doctrine of restraint of trade. Such agreements are balanced in a different way than those in Germany: from the perspective of the interests of the employer and with only a rudimentary consideration of the public interest. Nevertheless, an agreement whose scope is limited to the protection of a legitimate interest of the employer may meet the requirements of Article 45 TFEU as well.

Even though the scope of Article 45 TFEU appears to include post-employment restrictive covenants, this provision is not likely to be applied frequently in the legal orders analysed. They already contain mechanisms which appear to be better suited for resolving post-employment disputes. Former employees may safeguard their right to mobility, both on national and EU markets, relying on statutory provisions and established legal principles. Article 45 TFEU is not likely to add to this level of protection. Thus, it is more likely that Article 45 TFEU will be relied on in countries which do not provide for a specific regulation of post-employment agreements. This situation will not change under the Trade Secrets Directive, which explicitly excludes contractual obligations from its scope of application.[391]

V General Assessment and Recommendation

The accepted reason for limiting employees' mobility by concluding restrictive covenants is to protect the employer's legitimate interests, in particular his trade secrets and relations with clients. Even though these are private interests, they may be seen as a reflection of the public interest in the promotion of innovation and protection of investments.[392]

[390] Bauer/Diller para 368.

[391] Art 1(3)(c), Recitals 13 and 39 TSD.

[392] Koenig and Steiner argue that this private interest may be qualified as 'protection of industrial and commercial property' as recognised in Art 36 TFEU, see Koenig and

Still, the relative ease of imposing contractual post-employment obligations, combined with uncertainty concerning their scope and enforceability, present a substantial threat for the interests of former employees. The usual imbalance of resources between ex-employees and their employers may encourage the latter to impose unclear or overbroad terms, under the assumption that the agreement will not be challenged in court.[393] From this perspective, the interests of the employees are supported by the public interest in 'keeping the economy free from artificial restraints'.[394]

Thus, the core problem which post-employment restrictive covenants present seems to be the assessment of the proportionality (fairness, respectively reasonableness) of a particular contractual understanding in view of the conflicting interests. As a general statement, it can be said that NDAs and NCAs are able to ensure the protection of trade secrets and customer relations.[395] Whether a particular agreement does not go beyond what is necessary to achieve this purpose must be assessed in the light of the circumstances of the case. Agreements not to disclose are more likely to constitute a proportionate measure.[396] In the case of non-competes, their subject-matter, territory and duration must be considered.

At a policy level, post-employment restrictive covenants are controversial. Their proponents point out that contractual regulation allows the parties to achieve the level of protection they need. This enables the employer to protect his trade secrets, customer relations and competitive position, which in turn incentivises innovation and increases investments in developing new products and services and in training employees. Critics point to the fact that post-employment agreements are often unnegotiated blanket agreements, and that the employers often impose overbroad obligations under the assumption that the employee will not challenge the contract. In the United Kingdom and the United States, the possibility of blue-pencilling of over-inclusive contracts makes this

Steiner, 'Die Vereinbarkeit nachvertraglicher Wettbewerbsverbote mit der Arbeitnehmerfreizügigkeit des EG-Vertrags' 3583, 3586. It is submitted that this may be accepted only under a broad understanding of the notions of industrial and commercial property, since under EU law trade secrets are not property (Recital 16 TSD). For a detailed analysis of the public interest supporting the protection of trade secrets, see Chapter 1, part III.

393 van Caenegem, *Trade Secrets and Intellectual Property. Breach of Confidence, Misappropriation and Unfair Competition* 207.

394 Ibid 217.

395 Koenig and Steiner, 'Die Vereinbarkeit nachvertraglicher Wettbewerbsverbote mit der Arbeitnehmerfreizügigkeit des EG-Vertrags' 3583, 3587.

396 Although they may not always achieve the aim in question, especially when it is the protection of relations with clients, see Ibid 3583, 3588.

effect even stronger, as no deterrent is provided. Thus, post-employment agreements and especially NCAs may limit employee mobility and the positive spill-overs resulting therefrom.

Regardless of the discussion at policy level as to the enforceability of post-employment agreements, and NCAs in particular, i.e. as to whether they promote or rather stifle innovation, it is suggested here that on the private level they should be accepted only if they are balanced as to scope, territory and duration and as long as the employee is adequately rewarded for the limitation. Employment alone is rarely to be seen as an appropriate consideration for an NCA. At the time of the commencement of the employment relationship, when such agreements are often concluded, it is usually not possible to determine the effect that a post-employment covenant may have and thus award a proper consideration for the limitation it imposes.

From this perspective, it seems that the German model is particularly well suited for the purpose. A statutory framework for post-employment agreements achieves a certain level of legal certainty. Any agreement limiting post-employment activity of the employee may go beyond the protection of trade secrets, but must be fair: supported by the employer's interest and limited in scope, duration and territory. These considerations are also present in the other legal orders analysed. However, the remuneration which the employee must obtain during the time of restriction compensates him at least to some extent for the negative impact on his mobility that the particular restriction may have. The compulsory remuneration may also have a deterrent effect. It encourages employers to insist on a post-employment restriction only if a less intrusive measure (such as a non-disclosure agreement) may not be fit for purpose and only in situations where the employee has actually acquired some particularly valuable information which may not be protected in a less intrusive way.

In view of the analysis presented in this chapter, it may be concluded that contracts protecting secret information after termination of employment are subject to a balance of interests. While the assessment concentrates on the interests of the parties to the contract, instances of consideration of public interest may be identified as well. In this context it must however be stressed that an agreement is a result of negotiations between the parties themselves and a reflection of freedom of contracting. The rules of interpretation of contracts impose an obligation to interpret the agreement according to the will of the parties. This principle should not be limited unless there are overwhelming reasons do so.

Thus, it is considered here that all the jurisdictions analysed provide tools to mitigate the negative consequences which restrictive covenants might have on the mobility of individual employees. German regulation providing compulsory compensation is a particularly good example. The UK and US legal frameworks are satisfactory as well, although the practice of application of the doctrine of restraint of trade in the United Kingdom does not sufficiently take into account the interests of employees and the public.

The Trade Secrets Directive does not attempt to regulate post-employment restrictive covenants.[397] The possibility of including uniform rules applicable to non-compete and non-disclosure clauses between the trade secret holder and his employee was considered by the European Commission when drafting the initial Proposal for the Trade Secrets Directive, but was discarded. It was considered that such uniform rules would not cover third parties who did not enter into a contract with the holder of the trade secret, would increase transaction costs by imposing contractual obligations and would limit the generally recognised freedom of contracting. Thus, the Commission considered it more efficient to harmonise remedies only, leaving it for the holder of the trade secret to enter into a contractual relationship or to rely on the statutory minimum protection.[398]

Indeed, imposing an obligation to enter into prescribed agreements would encroach on the freedom of contracting and would likely be inefficient. Even though such a 'one size fits all' approach is not endorsed, it is considered here that minimum harmonisation of post-employment contracts would be efficient and would not violate the principle of freedom of contracting. After all, employees are a group which may be easily identified. What is more, they are often named as the biggest threat to the trade secrets of their employers, which would justify harmonisation.

Harmonisation of agreements not to disclose along the lines accepted in the jurisdictions analysed, and agreements not to compete along the lines of the German model, would introduce more legal certainty into employment relationships which nowadays often extend beyond a single jurisdiction.

However, while non-disclosure agreements certainly fit within the framework of harmonisation aiming at protection of trade secrets,

[397] Art 1(3)(c), Recitals 13 and 39 TSD.

[398] Commission, 'Commission Staff Working Document Impact Assessment Accompanying the document proposal for a Directive of the European Parliament and of the Council on the protection of undisclosed know-how and business information (trade secrets) against their unlawful acquisition, use and disclosure' COM (2013) 813 final, SWD(2013) 472 final, SWD(2013) 493 final, SWD(2013) 471 final 240–245 http://eur-lex.europa.eu/legal-content/EN/TXT/PDF/?uri=CELEX:52013SC0471&from=EN accessed 1 June 2017.

agreements not to compete go beyond that, as their effect is not limited to trade secrets only. Thus, harmonisation of non-competition agreements within the framework of harmonisation of protection of trade secrets does not appear appropriate. One possibility is for this harmonisation to be tackled by the EU, under its competence to establish competition rules necessary for the functioning of the internal market.[399] However, this does not appear likely, since, as explained above,[400] the applicability of competition rules to post-employment agreements is doubtful.

[399] Art 3(1)(b) TFEU.
[400] Chapter 4, part III.

5 Remedies

I Introduction

'Courts cannot suppress nor can they deprive individuals of knowledge, experience and expertise acquired in pursuit of their professions or callings. Courts can and will protect, through the media of appropriate injunctive relief and by monetary reimbursement, those entitled to protection against wrongful appropriation, disclosure of trade secrets and the revelation of proprietary data and confidential information for the purpose of personal gain by employees (. . .) in violation of a contractual obligation or duty owing to an employer'.[1]

Even though some guidelines are provided in law, the scope of information which a departed employee may use is determined case-by-case, bearing in mind the interests of both parties and often of the public as well.

The resolution of a trade secrets dispute between a former employer and a former employee requires in the first place determining whether there is interference with the employer's right to the trade secret (be it breach of statutory or implied duty, unfair taking of information or breach of contract). Determination of the scope of information which can be used requires an assessment of whether the information is a trade secret, consideration of the circumstances of its taking and use, and distinguishing between the general skill and knowledge of the employee and information of a more proprietary character which should remain with the employer. This multi-layered assessment poses problems[2] which the courts are called upon to resolve.

There are various paths which the aggrieved employer may follow to prevent infringement or its continuation, compensate him for the losses he has incurred or to punish or deter the ex-employee.

1 *Republic Aviation Corp v Schenk* 152 USPQ 830 (NY Sup Ct 1967).

2 Those problems, as well as the solutions adopted by the analysed jurisdictions are analysed in Chapter 3 and Chapter 4.

TRIPS sets a minimum standard[3] for the protection of trade secrets by placing it in the context of ensuring effective protection against unfair competition pursuant to Art 10*bis* PC.[4] The Member States often go beyond this level of protection, by providing for civil as well as criminal enforcement of trade secrets.[5]

In Germany, their protection is safeguarded primarily by the criminal sanctions contained in Sections 17–19 UWG.[6] The civil law does not contain a specific regulation for protection of trade secrets. Nevertheless, civil enforcement is more frequently relied on.[7] This is possible on the basis of enforcement of contractual obligations,[8] as well as by recourse to general clauses such as Section 3(1) UWG (prohibition of unfair commercial practices),[9] Section 823(2) BGB (breach of statute intended to protect another person),[10] Section 826 BGB (intentional damage contrary to public policy), Section 1004 BGB (interference with ownership)[11] or Section 823(1) BGB (infringement of an absolute right).[12] In some cases it is also possible for an aggrieved party to rely on the protection accorded to IPRs and the sui generis database right.[13]

UK law[14] does not provide for a criminal cause of action for misappropriation of trade secrets.[15] Instead, enforcement is based on the

[3] Art 1(1) TRIPS; Daniel Gervais, *The TRIPS Agreement: Drafting History and Analysis* (4th edn, Sweet&Maxwell 2012) para 2.24.

[4] Art 39(1) TRIPS.

[5] See e.g. Hogan Lovells Report para 78.

[6] For the analysis of the enforcement of trade secrets under criminal law, see e.g. Bukow in Ann/Loschelder/Grosch 412–433; Kurt Kiethe and Olaf Hohmann, 'Der strafrechtliche Schutz von Geschäfts- und Betriebsgeheimnissen' (2006) NStZ 185.

[7] Ohly in Ohly/Sosnitza §17 para 35.

[8] Brock in Ann/Loschelder/Grosch 166–168; Ohly in Ohly/Sosnitza §17 paras 38–43; Bauer/Diller paras 861–970.

[9] Ohly in Ohly/Sosnitza §17 paras 44–46. Grosch pleads for a narrow interpretation and application of S 3(1) UWG, Grosch in Ann/Loschelder/Grosch 349–352.

[10] As such statutory provisions, Ss 17–18 UWG are particularly relevant in the context of employee mobility, Ansgar Ohly, 'Der Geheimnisschutz im deutschen Recht: heutiger Stand und Perspektiven' (2014) GRUR 1, 7.

[11] Ohly in Ohly/Sosnitza §17 para 48.

[12] Since S 823(1) BGB requires infringement of an absolute right, such as property, its application in the context of trade secrets, whose proprietary nature is not uniformly accepted, is controversial, see e.g. Ohly, 'Der Geheimnisschutz im deutschen Recht: heutiger Stand und Perspektiven' 1, 8; Ohly in Ohly/Sosnitza §17 para 49.

[13] Ohly in Ohly/Sosnitza §17 para 47. For an analysis of the grounds for enforcement of trade secrets in German law, see also Ingo Westermann, *Handbuch Know-How Schutz* (CH Beck 2007) 116–118; Grosch in Ann/Loschelder/Grosch 344–352.

[14] For a comparative overview of protection in Germany and in the United Kingdom, see Mathias M Siems, 'Die Logik des Schutzes von Betriebsgeheimnissen' (2007) WRP 1146, 1148–1149, 1152.

[15] Sarah Turner, 'The Protection of Trade Secrets: the Legal Framework in the EU' in Jacques de Werra (ed), *La protection des secrets d'affaires. The Protection of Trade Secrets*

equitable doctrine of breach of confidence, whose principles are laid down in *Coco v Clark*[16] and whose nature in given circumstances may be similar to a fiduciary obligation, intellectual property, contract or tort.[17] Under certain circumstances, the aggrieved employer may rely on the protection granted to databases[18] or to IPRs.

Also in the United States, civil enforcement plays a major role in the protection of trade secrets. The legal framework is provided by the UTSA[19] as adopted by the various states. Apart from that, actions under tort[20] and unfair competition[21] state laws[22] may be available for the aggrieved employers as well as actions for breach of contract.[23] Federal law provides for criminal sanctions under the Computer Fraud and Abuse Act.[24] A civil cause of action has been introduced into the federal law in the United States in May 2016, upon passing of the DTSA.

The Trade Secrets Directive contains ia a definition of trade secrets,[25] lays down the notion of unlawful acquisition, use and disclosure of trade secrets, which entitle the holder of a secret to apply for measures under the Directive,[26] and defines acts which are considered lawful.[27] In the main part, it harmonises[28] the measures, procedures and remedies in cases where unlawful acquisition, use or disclosure of trade

(Schulthess 2013) 95; William van Caenegem, *Trade Secrets and Intellectual Property. Breach of Confidence, Misappropriation and Unfair Competition* (1st edn, Kluwer Law International 2014) 96–98.

16 *Coco v Clark Ltd* [1968] FSR 415 (Ch) 419–421, requiring that 'the information must be of a confidential nature', it must have been imparted in circumstances imparting an obligation of confidence and there must be 'an unauthorised use of that information to the detriment of the person communicating it'. The duty of confidentiality may be implied (as discussed in Chapter 3) or derived from contract (as discussed in Chapter 4) For a detailed analysis of the doctrine of breach of confidence and its application, see e.g. Stanley 3–36.

17 *Vercoe v Rutland Fund* [2010] EWHC 424 (Ch) [344] (Sales J).

18 Howe, Gupta, Wilkinson, Pritchard and Taylor in Goulding paras 4.183 – 4.208.

19 Ss 2–4 in connection with S 1(2) UTSA.

20 S 757 Restatement (First) of Torts.

21 Ss 40, 42 Restatement (Third) of Unfair Competition; Quinto/Singer 96–97.

22 Other possible actions include breach of fiduciary duty or duty of loyalty and conversion, see e.g. Quinto/Singer 82–103.

23 Quinto/Singer 82–88.

24 Victoria A Cundiff, 'Reasonable Measures to Protect Trade Secrets in a Digital Environment' (2009) 49(3) *IDEA* 359, 382–385, indicating other statutes that can protect digitised secrets, ibid 390; Quinto/Singer 105–121. For other, federal and state, criminal causes of action, see Quinto/Singer 374–418.

25 Art 2(1) TSD.

26 Art 4 TSD.

27 Art 3 TSD.

28 Pursuant to Art 1(1) TSD, its provisions, with some exceptions, have a character of minimum harmonisation.

secrets is found to have occurred.[29] The harmonisation relates to civil enforcement[30] and the provisions of the Directive are meant to be lex specialis towards the Enforcement Directive.[31]

Despite the undoubtedly deterrent effect that criminal enforcement of trade secrets brings with it, together with the broad investigative powers of the police and public prosecutors, in most cases the aggrieved holders of trade secrets turn to civil enforcement. There seem to be various reasons for this. First of all, criminal enforcement serves the public interest rather than the interest of the individual employer and may not always provide for measures safeguarding his rights. At the same time, it often attracts publicity, which is particularly undesirable where trade secrets are concerned. Apart from that, a decisive reason for the holders of trade secrets to turn to civil rather than criminal enforcement is the broad range of remedies available in civil courts, including preliminary injunctions, which allow for an immediate reaction to prevent disclosure of the secret information.[32]

This chapter discusses the basic remedies available under civil law for the former employers in cases of breach of the statutory, implied or contractual duty aiming at protection of trade secrets. Criminal and administrative measures, even if foreseen in the jurisdictions analysed, remain beyond the scope of the discussion. This is also the case for

[29] Chapter III TSD.

[30] See Common position of the Council of the European Union of 19 May 2014, document 9870/14 3 http://register.consilium.europa.eu/doc/srv?l=EN&f=ST%209870%202014%20INIT accessed 1 June 2017.

[31] Recital 39 TSD. This corresponds to the approach presented in Statement 2005/295/EC by the Commission concerning Article 2 of Directive 2004/48/EC of the European Parliament and of the Council on the enforcement of intellectual property rights [2005] OJ L 94/37, which does not include trade secrets in the catalogue of IPRs covered by the scope of the Enforcement Directive. See also Ohly, 'Der Geheimnisschutz im deutschen Recht: heutiger Stand und Perspektiven' 1, 4. Despite this approach taken by the European legislator, the UK courts have applied the Enforcement Directive in cases concerning trade secrets, see e.g. *Vestergaard Frandsen A/S & Ors v Bestnet Europe Ltd & Ors* [2011] EWCA Civ 424 (CA) [56]. The authors of the MPI Position Paper suggested with respect to the proposed text of the Directive that the lex specialis character is insufficient in view of the considerations of unfair competition underlying the proposal. They argued that the final draft should clearly state that the Enforcement Directive is not applicable to the protection of trade secrets, MPI Position Paper para 16. This was also advocated in Tanya Aplin, 'A Critical Evaluation of the Proposed EU Trade Secrets Directive' (2014) 4 *IPQ* 257, 273. Other authors argue that the solutions contained in the Directive put trade secrets in the same position as IPRs, Anette Gärtner, 'Zum Richtlinienentwurf über den Schutz von Geschäftsgeheimnissen' (2014) NZG 650, 651.

[32] For a discussion of the advantages and disadvantages of criminal and civil enforcement of trade secrets, see Quinto/Singer 365–370.

possible contractual remedies,[33] which, being part of the agreement, are devised by the parties and are subject to the limitations of the freedom of contracting, provided primarily by statute[34] in Germany and by the doctrine of restraint of trade[35] and other doctrines[36] in the United Kingdom and the United States. Orders facilitating the preparation of legal proceedings, such as inspection and information[37] and corrective measures available in case of infringement, such as recall of infringing products from the market, destruction of infringing goods, documents and materials[38] or publication of the decision,[39] are also beyond the scope of the book, since they are ancillary to the decision of the court to grant an injunction or damages.

The remedies presented here include permanent and preliminary injunctions, as well as damages. Considering the focus of this book, which is the role of the balancing of interests in determining the type of information which can be used by a departed employee as well as the extent to which it can be used, the following discussion is focused on those aspects of granting remedies which are particularly relevant in the context of employee mobility. No attempt is made to provide a complete analysis of remedies for misappropriation of trade secrets.

The conflict of interests remains and needs to be resolved also when a decision to grant a remedy is made. The aggrieved employers are interested in obtaining a quick and broad injunction in order to stop the use or prevent the disclosure of the information by the former employee. Otherwise loss of the trade secret or damage to the employer's competitive position may ensue. Even though damages are also foreseen as a remedy, they are likely to play a secondary role from the employer's perspective: on the one hand they come into play only when the damage

[33] For a detailed discussion of those remedies in Germany, see Bauer/Diller paras 861–970; for a discussion of liquidated damages in the United Kingdom, see Nathan, Adamson and Taylor in Goulding paras 11.83–11.95.

[34] As discussed in Chapter 4 part II, point A.

[35] As discussed in Chapter 4 part II, points B–C.

[36] Such as laches, estoppel, unclean hands or economic duress.

[37] In Germany, claims for information (S 242 BGB) and inspection (S 809) BGB, are measures separate from injunctions, see Harte-Bavendamm in Harte/Henning §17 paras 64–65; Bauer/Diller paras 862–866. The legal grounds for obtaining information about other infringers are unclear, see Björn Kalbfus, 'Die neuere Rechtsprechung des BGH zum Schutz von Betriebs- und Geschäftsgeheimnissen' (2013) WRP 584, 589–590; Ohly, 'Der Geheimnisschutz im deutschen Recht: heutiger Stand und Perspektiven' 1, 9. In the United Kingdom information may be obtained with the help of Anton Piller (search) orders, Gurry on Breach of Confidence para 18.80. In the United States, see Peterson 13–6.

[38] Art 12 TSD.

[39] Art 15 TSD.

has already occurred, i.e. often when the information has been disclosed, thus losing its competitive value. On the other hand, the calculation of damages for trade secrets misappropriation poses particular difficulties: not only is it difficult to prove the value of information which has been kept secret, but attempting to show this value may mean revealing further confidential information, thus risking the loss of even more secrets. From the perspective of the ex-employee, an injunction may restrain him from undertaking a professional activity, possibly in the only field in which he is an expert, and might have severe overreaching consequences if it effectively covers not only trade secrets but also information forming part of his general skill and knowledge.

It is also interesting to see to what extent the public interest plays a role in considerations made upon granting and framing of a remedy, for example where the former employer pursues a broad injunction or high damages in an attempt to eliminate a competitor from the market. A similar risk pertains to granting a preliminary injunction: due to its provisional character, its issuance creates a situation of legal uncertainty and before the case is finally decided, the loss of market position resulting from the prohibition of sales or the negative image created by the injunction may terminate the existence of a business.

Thus, the balancing of interests appears inevitable not only in order to determine the scope of the post-employment duties, but also upon grant of remedy against the former employee. The extent to which such balancing is possible is analysed in this part of the book. Moreover, it is explored whether the difficulties in determining the scope of the post-employment duties may be mitigated by the grant or particular framing of a remedy.

II Injunction

Trade secrets have an inherently perishable nature: any disclosure terminates their existence. A secret process might fall into the public domain after publication of a scientific article describing it; a secret design of a product will lose this quality when the product is put on the market, a customer list might cease to be secret if it becomes easily accessible on the Internet.

The more people know the information, the higher the risk of losing control over it.[40] Therefore, the primary goal of a person asserting rights to a trade secret is to prevent its disclosure. Where the use of the

[40] Peterson 13–4.

information results in its disclosure, or where such contractual obligations exist, it is also in the interest of the plaintiff to prevent the use of the information.[41] Moreover, the prevention of use of the information safeguards the competitive position of the former employer. In economic terms, an injunction makes it possible to keep the information secret and to reduce the costs that would otherwise need to be spent to obtain damages.[42]

A Injunction in Cases of Infringement of a Right to a Trade Secret by a Former Employee in Germany

1 Requirements for Grant

The employer may apply for an injunction obliging the former employee to stop the infringing activity or to refrain from undertaking a threatened infringement, by relying on Section 8 in conjunction with Section 3 UWG or under analogical application of Section 1004 BGB in conjunction with Section 823(2) or 826 BGB.[43] In case of contracts limiting certain post-employment activity of the employee this is possible by reference to Section 241(1) BGB.[44]

Grant of an injunction requires showing an actual or impending infringement of a right to a trade secret.[45] Thus, it is necessary for the plaintiff to show not only the fact of infringing behaviour or of breach of contract, but also to provide evidence of the existence of the trade secret. No injunction may be granted after the obligation of confidentiality has terminated[46] or the information has lost the quality of secrecy, irrespective of whether it was the plaintiff or another person[47] who disclosed the information.[48]

[41] Peterson 13–6.
[42] Michael Risch, 'Why Do We Have Trade Secrets?' (2007) 11 *Marq IP L Rev* 1, 60–61.
[43] Kalbfus paras 298, 423. For a broader discussion of grounds for enforcement, see e.g. Westermann, *Handbuch Know-How Schutz* 116–118.
[44] Kalbfus para 299.
[45] Ohly in Ohly/Sosnitza §8 para 3.
[46] For example, as a result of expiry of the post-employment NDA.
[47] If it was the defendant who disclosed the information, it may nevertheless be possible to issue a time-limited ('springboard') injunction which, despite the information having fallen into the public domain, prohibits the defendant from using that information for a period of time which he would have needed to develop the information without recourse to unfair means, see e.g. Eberhard Körner, 'Befristete und unbefristete Unterlassungstitel bei Wettbewerbsverstößen' (1985) GRUR 909, 915. Westermann seems to support an unlimited duration of the injunction in case of disclosure by the defendant, see Westermann, *Handbuch Know-How Schutz* 119–120.
[48] BGH GRUR 1960, 554, 555 *Handstrickverfahren*; Rudolf Kraßer, 'Grundlagen des Zivilrechtlichen Schutzes von Geschäfts- und Betriebsgeheimnissen sowie von Know-How' (1977) GRUR 177, 181–182. If the information is no longer secret the only

An injunction may be granted upon an objective finding of infringement of a right, regardless of whether the employee acted with fault (*Verschulden*), i.e. intentionally (*Vorsatz*) or recklessly (*Fahrlässigkeit*) or even whether he was aware that his actions amounted to breach of a duty.[49] Thus, any activity which goes against the statutory, contractual, explicit or implied post-employment duty may be terminated by way of an injunction. In practice however, it seems that some intention will need to be shown, at least in order to obtain an injunction against threatening infringement.[50]

Furthermore, there must exist a likelihood of continuation or a real threat of commencement of the infringement. According to Kabfus, such a threat is always given where the information was obtained in a dishonest way, which might give rise to criminal consequences (e.g. Sections 17–18 UWG). He argues that if a person decides to take the risk of criminal liability, it is with a view to profiting from the use of the information so obtained. Therefore, he suggests an introduction of a rebuttable presumption that there exists a threat of infringement where the information was obtained in circumstances giving rise to criminal liability.[51]

Finally, there must exist no other, less burdensome, way to ensure that the defendant meets the obligation. This is usually so in case of orders not to disclose trade secrets, since only an injunction may effectively prevent their publication.[52]

Moreover, pursuant to Section 8(4) UWG, an abusive claim for an injunction is not accepted. Thus, where abusive behaviour is found on the part of the ex-employer, such as initiating proceedings with a view to profiting from their costs, the court will deny an injunction.[53]

available remedy is damages, Körner, 'Befristete und unbefristete Unterlassungstitel bei Wettbewerbsverstößen' 909, 915.

[49] BGH GRUR 1961, 40, 42 *Wurftaubenpresse*; Westermann, *Handbuch Know-How Schutz* 118; Harte-Bavendamm in Harte/Henning §17 para 59a; Ohly in Ohly/Sosnitza §8 para 1, §17 para 43.

[50] Kalbfus para 423. According to Westermann, where information was obtained dishonestly, a threat of infringement is assumed. See Westermann, *Handbuch Know-How Schutz* 119. Thus, in such a case it would not be necessary to demonstrate intent to use or disclose the information.

[51] Kalbfus para 429. Such presumption exists according to Westermann, see Westermann, *Handbuch Know-How Schutz* 119.

[52] Kalbfus paras 301–302. Ohly stresses that proportionality is a generally recognised principle of civil law in Germany, Ansgar Ohly, '"Patenttrolle" oder: Der patentrechtliche Unterlassungsanspruch unter Verhältnismäßigkeitsvorbehalt? – Aktuelle Entwicklungen im US-Patentrecht und ihre Bedeutung für das deutsche und europäische Patentsystem' (2008) GRUR Int 787, 796.

[53] Ohly in Ohly/Sosnitza §8 para 155, 159.

2 Scope of Prohibited Acts

The scope of prohibited acts as well as the territorial scope of the injunctive order corresponds to the scope of the duty not to use or disclose trade secrets, stemming from statute or contract.[54]

An injunction may, depending on the circumstances, cover the disclosure of the information, its use, as well as the use or manufacture of products or processes or the rendering of services which have been developed relying on this information.[55] This includes products in the development of which the information in question played a not insignificant technical or commercial role.[56]

In the case of trade secrets relating to the use of a generally known process,[57] secrecy does not so much cover the fact of the use of the process by the plaintiff but rather the applicability of the process for a particular purpose.[58] In such a case an injunction covers both the prohibition of disclosure of information as to the applicability of this method for the particular purpose, and also the use of the method in the defendant's own activities.[59]

Considering that the competitive advantage that a trade secret provides for the employer stems from the fact that the information is not known to his competitors, maintaining the secrecy of the data in question plays a primary role. Therefore, in situations where no dishonest activity of the employee may be found and the employee simply remembers the information, it has been proposed to accept the use of the information by the ex-employee, while at the same time denying him the right to disclose it at will.[60] It is considered here that such a solution would necessarily limit the competitive advantage of the ex-employer by introducing one more competitor into the market. However, it would not altogether destroy the value of the

[54] Analysed in Chapters 3–4.

[55] BGH GRUR 2002, 91, 94–95 *Spritzgießwerkzeuge*; Stier/Hasselblatt in Horst-Peter Götting and Axel Nordemann, *UWG Handkommentar* (3rd edn Nomos 2016) §17 para 98; Ohly in Ohly/Sosnitza §17 para 52.

[56] As was recognised in the case of an apparatus for measuring temperature, which comprised ia a filling station developed using secret information of the former employer, in BGH GRUR 1985, 294, 296 *Füllanlage*. See also Kalbfus para 431; Harte-Bavendamm in Harte/Henning §17 para 59.

[57] Cf BGH GRUR 1955, 424, 425 *Möbelpaste;* WRP 1993, 36 (OLG Hamm) *Tierohrmarken*.

[58] WRP 1993, 36, 38 (OLG Hamm) *Tierohrmarken*; Christoph Ann, 'Know-how – Stiefkind des Geistigen Eigentums?' (2007) GRUR 39, 41.

[59] Westermann, *Handbuch Know-How Schutz* 119; Kalbfus para 434.

[60] With regard to information concerning clients, see NJW 1988, 1686, 1687 (BAG) *Kundenlisten* and NZA 1994, 502, 506 (BAG) *Titanoxid*. See also Karl Nastelski, 'Der Schutz des Betriebsgeheimnisses' (1957) GRUR 1, 7; Harte-Bavendamm in Harte/Henning §17 para 54.

information stemming from secrecy. It would take into consideration the interest of the employee in being able to maintain professionally active, drawing on his previous work experience. At the same time, the ex-employee would be personally interested in maintaining the confidentiality of the information, as it would support his own competitive position as well.

In this context it is to be stressed that the prohibited acts should be sufficiently substantiated (*Konkretisierungsgebot*) and determined (*Bestimmtheitserfordernis*) in the order.[61] Injunction is a remedy which strongly interferes with the employee's right to continue his professional activity; therefore, its precise drafting is essential in order to limit the employee's rights only to the extent necessary to safeguard the employer's right to a trade secret. This calls for a clear and precise formulation of the order, with a view to enabling its enforcement.[62] On the other hand, the primary role of an injunction is to protect the secret status of the information. A detailed description of the object of the injunction in the court's order might lead to its disclosure. Therefore, a balance needs to be struck between the requirements of substantiation and determination on the one hand and the need to preserve secrecy on the other.[63] This can be achieved by describing the infringing product, rather than the secret information,[64] or even by reference to documents[65] with their simultaneous exclusion from file inspection.[66] In the case of a customer list, a full disclosure of names and contact data of the clients is not required, but the identification of the clients must be unambiguous.[67]

[61] Ohly in Ohly/Sosnitza §17 para 53. For general information on those requirements, see also BGH GRUR 1998, 489, 491 *Unbestimmter Unterlassungsantrag III*; Ulf Doepner, 'Anmerkungen zum wettbewerbsrechtlichen Geheimnisschutz im Zivilprozess' in Erhard Keller, Clemens Plassmann and Andreas von Falck (eds), *Festschrift für Winfried Tilmann* (Carl Heymanns Verlag 2003) 112–118.

[62] Harte-Bavendamm in Harte/Henning §17 para 60.

[63] Harte-Bavendamm in Harte/Henning §17 para 60; Ohly in Ohly/Sosnitza §17 para 53.

[64] BGH GRUR 1961, 40, 42 *Wurftaubenpresse*, where the defendant prepared identical copies of the machine of the plaintiff; BGH GRUR 2002, 91, 95 *Spritzgießwerkzeuge*. A reference to the infringing product is on the other hand not sufficient when the product may also be produced by generally known methods, Harte-Bavendamm in Harte/Henning §17 para 61.

[65] BGH GRUR 2008, 727 para 9 *Schweißmodulgenerator*; accepted by Harte-Bavendamm in Harte/Henning §17 para 60; Stier/Hasselblatt in Horst-Götting and Nordemann, *UWG Handkommentar* §17 para 100 and Ohly in Ohly/Sosnitza §17 para 53, although he admits that such a formulation may pose problems upon enforcement of the injunction.

[66] Pursuant to S 299(2) ZPO, Harte-Bavendamm in Harte/Henning §17 para 60; see also Kai Schmidt-Hern, 'Kundenliste muss im Geheimnisschutz-Prozess eindeutig beschrieben werden' (2011) GRUR-Prax 154.

[67] Schmidt-Hern, 'Kundenliste muss im Geheimnisschutz-Prozess eindeutig beschrieben werden' 154.

While a reference to an infringing product in the court's order is considered sufficient, it is submitted that reference to other documents may be problematic and therefore such a drafting technique should be applied with caution and only in exceptional cases where it is not possible to describe the infringing technological embodiments without recourse to e.g. models or source code.

In *Schweißmodulgenerator* the BGH was of the opinion that an injunction is sufficiently substantiated if it refers to a product containing infringing elements, without the need to describe those elements in the order.[68] It was considered that even if the description in the court's order refers to a product which encompasses both infringing and non-infringing elements, the injunction in any case does not extend beyond information which is a trade secret.[69] Therefore, the Court considered it to be sufficient that the order refers to the infringing product, if it is possible to establish which elements of that product are infringing by reference to additional documents. A reference to the infringing product alone would have as a consequence that any modification of the defendant's product would remove it from the scope of the injunction. If it is possible to determine by reference to additional documents which elements of the product are infringing, the injunction will remain effective even if the product is modified.[70]

This decision weakens the requirement of clarity of the injunctive order. A capricious application of the possibility to refer to other documents for the purpose of determining the scope of an injunction might lead to legal uncertainty on the part of the former employee. Therefore, it is submitted that the application of the guidelines provided in *Schweißmodulgenerator* might lead to imposition of overly broad injunctions in which the exact scope of the trade secret in question cannot be determined by recourse to the documents discussed at trial and thus available to the defendant. Even though elements which are not secret may always be used, determining which information was in fact a trade secret is often the central problem. This should be clearly determinable for the former employee, as an overbroad or unclear injunction may limit his possibilities to pursue his livelihood. Considering that he is often the weaker party, he might de facto be forced to observe an overbroad injunction as a whole (i.e. not distinguishing between information which is and is not a trade secret), not being able to afford further litigation challenging the injunctive order. Since the issuance of

[68] BGH GRUR 2008, 727 para 13 *Schweißmodulgenerator*.
[69] Ibid para 17 Schweißmodulgenerator.
[70] Ibid para 18 Schweißmodulgenerator.

an injunction does not require the finding of fault or intention to cause damage on the part of the employee, the scope of the order must be strictly limited to the information which he is not allowed to use. Otherwise this remedy would be punitive.

3 Duration of the Injunction

Since the injunction should last as long as the underlying obligation, in the case of post-employment agreements the duration of the injunction is limited to the duration of the contractual obligation.[71]

Where no contract was entered into, the post-employment duty is not limited in time.[72] Even though there are voices advocating a limited duration of the post-employment duty of confidentiality in the absence of a contract,[73] absent evidence to the contrary the duty not to disclose lasts as long as the information retains the quality of secrecy. Only the restriction of use may be limited in time. Thus, injunctions are generally imposed for an unlimited period of time.

If the information was obtained in breach of Section 17 UWG, i.e by dishonest means such as theft, purposive memorisation or copying of documents, its use is 'permanently unlawful'. Thus, an injunction prohibiting its use is of unlimited duration.[74] The former employee may request the court to terminate the injunction if it is no longer necessary to protect the information, e.g. after it has entered the public domain, or if he has obtained it in a fair way, e.g. from a competitor who developed it independently.[75] If that is the case, the employee may initiate an action based on circumstances or defences subsequent to termination of the oral proceedings preceding the issuance of the injunction (*Vollstreckungsabwehrklage*) pursuant to Section 767 ZPO.[76]

[71] Bauer/Diller para 871.

[72] Frank Wertheimer, 'Bezahlte Karenz oder entschädigungslose Wettbewerbsenthaltung des ausgeschiedenen Arbeitnehmers?' (1999) BB 1600, 1600. See also supra in Chapter 3, part II, point A.5.

[73] Josef Molkenbur, 'Pflicht zur Geheimniswahrung nach Ende des Arbeitsverhältnisses?' (1990) BB 1196, 1200.

[74] WRP 2008, 938, 939 (BGH) *Entwendete Datensätze mit Konstruktionszeichnungen.*

[75] Kalbfus paras 436–437. According to Kraßer, even if the information was initially obtained dishonestly, as of the moment of honest acquisition, its use must be accepted, as it is not possible to distinguish between the use of the information obtained honestly and dishonestly, see Kraßer, 'Grundlagen des Zivilrechtlichen Schutzes von Geschäfts- und Betriebsgeheimnissen sowie von Know-How' 177, 182. It is submitted that this problem may be mitigated by issuing a time-limited ('springboard') injunction corresponding to the duration of the unfairly obtained competitive advantage.

[76] BGH GRUR 1983, 179, 181 *Stapel-Automat*; Westermann, *Handbuch Know-How Schutz* 120; Kalbfus para 438. Generally, on this type of action, see Fromut Volp, 'Änderung

The situation is different if the information was not learned through dishonest means, but its use is considered unfair pursuant to Section 3 UWG.[77] In those cases it is possible for the court to impose a time-limited final injunction,[78] subject to balancing the rights of the employer and of the employee.[79] Some authors recognise this only where the point in time when the obligation of confidentiality will cease to exist may be determined upon issuance of the injunction.[80] Others plead for a broader acceptance of time-limited injunctions,[81] for example in a situation where the former employee relied on information he had learned during service, but where it was possible for him to develop this information independently, albeit over a longer time or at higher cost. Accordingly, it is proposed to issue an injunction proscribing the use of this information for the time which would have been necessary for its independent development, i.e. in order to mitigate the effects of the competitive head start ('springboard')[82] obtained by the use of this secret information.

Issuance of a 'springboard' injunction appears less controversial in the case of trade secrets relating to clients and suppliers. According to Körner, issuing time-limited injunctions is possible in the case of such information, as it is relatively easy to show the time needed for acquiring and developing relations with new clients, which, according to him, corresponds to the appropriate duration of the restriction.[83] Evidence as to the time needed to develop relations with those persons is usually available, e.g. by showing the time needed to acquire the clients in

der Rechts- oder Sachlage bei Unterlassungstitel' (1984) GRUR 486 and Benjamin E Leyendecker, 'Grundfälle zur Vollstreckungsabwehrklage' (2010) JA 631.

[77] WRP 2008, 938, 939 (BGH) *Entwendete Datensätze mit Konstruktionszeichnungen.*

[78] BGH GRUR 2002, 91, 94 *Spritzgießwerkzeuge;* Harte-Bavendamm in Harte/Henning §17 para 59.

[79] WRP 2008, 938, 939 (BGH) *Entwendete Datensätze mit Konstruktionszeichnungen.*

[80] For example, when in a contractual relationship a notice was given, but the period of notice had not expired yet, see Kalbfus para 438; Westermann, *Handbuch Know-How Schutz* 120; Harte-Bavendamm in Harte/Henning §17 para 59. This seems also possible in the case of post-employment restrictive covenants, which are entered into for a limited period of time. The date of termination of the obligation of confidentiality is determinable also e.g. in case of a product or marketing strategy whose date of launch is already known.

[81] Kraßer, 'Grundlagen des Zivilrechtlichen Schutzes von Geschäfts- und Betriebsgeheimnissen sowie von Know-How' 177, 182–183; Körner, 'Befristete und unbefristete Unterlassungstitel bei Wettbewerbsverstößen' 909; Ohly, 'Der Geheimnisschutz im deutschen Recht: heutiger Stand und Perspektiven' 1, 9; Ohly in Ohly/Sosnitza §17 para 52. Kalbfus describes such injunctions as arbitrary and suggests a narrow formulation of the subject-matter of the injunction as a better solution to address possible unjust consequences of a prohibition not limited in time, Kalbfus para 438.

[82] As referred to in the United Kingdom, *Seager v Copydex* [1967] 1 WLR 923 (CA) 931–932.

[83] WRP 1995, 114, 115 (OLG Celle) judgment of 26.05.1994, 13U 29/94; Körner, 'Befristete und unbefristete Unterlassungstitel bei Wettbewerbsverstößen' 909, 914.

question or by making a comparison with the time needed to attract other clients. In that respect, the considerations made with regard to determining the post-employment duty of confidentiality where no contract has been entered into by the parties may be helpful: the type of business in which the client base changes quickly or remains stable, or whether the services in question require development of a personal relationship based on trust.[84]

With regard to technical information, Körner argues that a time-limited injunction may be issued only if the defendant actually undertook independent research and development and is able to provide evidence as to the time he would have needed to develop the information independently. Otherwise, an injunction of an unlimited duration should be issued. This applies also where the information has become public as a result of the ex-employee's actions.[85] The author considers that a mere theoretical possibility of independent development of the information is not sufficient for limitation of the injunction in time.[86]

It is argued here that in the case of a former employee he will rarely be able to provide evidence of his own independent research and development. At the same time, the necessity to commence court proceedings in order to terminate the injunction due to changed circumstances is particularly burdensome for a private individual. Such proceedings are both time-consuming[87] and cost-intensive (court costs, costs of representation, preparation of proceedings and gathering of evidence). Therefore, it is suggested here that in cases where the former employee is able to provide evidence as to the likely time needed for independent development of the information in question, the possibility of limiting the duration of injunctive order even in the case of technical secrets should be explored by the court hearing the case, before issuing the injunction. The evidence of the time needed for independent development may be available where the employee is able to obtain it from other market participants who conduct research and development, or by comparing the time needed to develop similar solutions, or even by showing the time spent by the plaintiff-employer to develop the information in question, which is

[84] For an analysis of the post-employment duty of confidentiality where no contract was concluded, see Chapter 3, part II, point A.

[85] In this case the injunction would serve to put the infringer into the position in which he would have been in the absence of the infringement, by taking away his head start advantage, Körner, 'Befristete und unbefristete Unterlassungstitel bei Wettbewerbsverstößen' 909, 915. The disclosure by the holder of the information or by a third party always leads to termination of the duty imposed by the injunctive order, ibid 914.

[86] Ibid 909, 914, 915.

[87] Ibid 909, 915–916.

often possible if the employee himself was involved in the research and development activities of the employer.

A similar result to the issuance of a springboard injunction may be achieved by the application of rules on compensation for damage. Kraßer suggests that the competitive advantage which the holder of the information has lost as a result of the infringement may be compensated by specific performance in the form of an order prohibiting the use of information for a certain time (e.g. by prohibiting the ex-employee from contacting certain clients). The duration of such an order should be determined by the court and correspond to the envisaged duration of the unfairly obtained competitive advantage. It would not terminate with the disclosure of the information.[88]

The above argumentation concerning limitation of the injunctions in time is applicable to orders prohibiting the use of the information but not to those restricting disclosure. Safeguarding secrecy and thereby the competitive value of the information is the primary goal of an injunction. At the same time it generally does not overly limit the employee's rights. Thus, an injunction prohibiting disclosure should be limited in time only if it is clear that the information will become public at a specific and determinable point in time, e.g. on entry into force of a secret marketing strategy, publication of a patent application or presentation of a design at a forthcoming trade fair. The situation is different as regards use of the information. Prohibition of use may influence the former employee's possibilities to undertake a professional activity, thus negatively impacting his interests. At the same time, the unfairness of the employee's head start may often be mitigated by issuance of a time-limited injunction. Thus, it is submitted that 'springboard' injunctions prohibiting use of information should be accepted, as they satisfy the interest of the ex-employer while also taking into consideration the interest of the former employee.

4 Summary

The conflict between the interests of employers and employees still applies upon grant of injunctions. In particular, also in this situation the interest of the employer in maintaining secrecy and in maintaining his competitive position based on the use of the secret information collides with the employee's interest in continuing his professional activity relying on his experience.

Despite that, the balancing of rights is not clearly included as part of assessing whether or not the injunction should be granted: upon finding of breach of duty or unfairness of behaviour, the order is issued, unless a less burdensome measure is available. One such measure could be to

[88] Kraßer, 'Grundlagen des Zivilrechtlichen Schutzes von Geschäfts- und Betriebsgeheimnissen sowie von Know-How' 177, 183.

award damages in lieu of injunction. The possibility to apply such a remedy is explored infra.[89]

The balancing of the interests of the parties to the dispute is considered when framing the injunction: if the employee acquired the information without recourse to dishonest means, he may be free to continue using it, while being obliged to maintain its secrecy. Also the duration of the injunction granted may be influenced by the consideration of the parties' interests: while generally injunctions are issued for an unlimited period of time, it is possible to issue a time-limited order prohibiting the use of the information for such time as is necessary to compensate for the unfair advantage provided by its use ('springboard'). This solution is available only in cases in which the employee did not act dishonestly when obtaining the information.

The public interest does not seem to be included in the balancing exercise.

B Injunction in Cases of Infringement of a Right to a Trade Secret by a Former Employee in the United Kingdom

1 Requirements for Grant

Also in the United Kingdom it is possible for the ex-employer to obtain an injunction both in case of breach of the ex-employee's implied duty of confidence and in case of breach of contract.[90] The remedy may be granted where the threatened or actual infringement of a right is established and where, absent injunction, there is a reason to believe that the infringement will occur[91] or be repeated,[92] unless special circumstances speak against granting an injunction.[93] Determination of those exceptional circumstances lies in the discretion of the court,[94] which should also take into account that the remedy should be proportionate to the wrong.[95]

89 In Chapter 5, part V, point A.

90 I C F Spry, *The Principles of Equitable Remedies* (4th edn, Sweet&Maxwell 1990) 435; Stanley 117; Gurry on Breach of Confidence paras 18.07, 18.48.

91 'quia timet' injunction, issued before the act of infringement has occurred, see Spry, *The Principles of Equitable Remedies* 369–373.

92 'actual or prospective harm', 'Post-Termination Restrictive Covenants' (2008) IDS Emp L Brief 853, 12–18; *Caterpillar Logistics Services v Huesca de Crean* [2012] EWCA Civ 156 (CA) [67] (Burnton LJ).

93 *Pride of Derby v British Celanese* [1953] Ch 149 (CA) 181 (Evershed MR), *Vestergaard Frandsen A/S & Ors v Bestnet Europe Ltd & Ors* [2009] EWHC 1456 (Ch) [41] (Arnold J); John Hull, *Commercial Secrecy: Law and Practice* (Sweet&Maxwell 1998) para 11.50; Gurry on Breach of Confidence para 18.48. For a less stringent position, see Stanley 117.

94 Gurry on Breach of Confidence para 18.51. The general equitable defences such as laches, acquiescence or unclean hands also apply in this context, Hull, *Commercial Secrecy: Law and Practice* para 11.51.

95 *Vestergaard Frandsen A/S & Ors v Bestnet Europe Ltd & Ors* [2011] EWCA Civ 424 (CA) [56] (Jacob LJ), suggesting that the principle of proportionality as required by Art 3(2) Enforcement Directive is in fact applied also in English law with respect to trade secrets.

A court will not grant an injunction where it considers that it is more just to grant damages or another remedy.[96] From this perspective it seems that an injunction against disclosure of the information will usually be appropriate.[97] As regards the use of the information, damages are often considered more fit for purpose.[98]

An injunction may also be refused by the court exercising its discretion, if it finds that under the circumstances of the case this remedy would be 'highly unreasonable',[99] for example where granting an injunction would result in substantial hardship for the defendant,[100] disproportionate to the interest of the plaintiff. This may also be the case where the proceedings have an abusive character (putting forward reckless claims to confidentiality and conducting the litigation in such a way as to maximise the defendant's costs, with a view to eliminating a competitor from the market).[101]

When considering the reasonableness of granting an injunction, the interest of third parties and of the public may be taken into account as well.[102] However, it must be remembered that where a final injunction is ordered, it must have been established that the employee is in breach of his duties (i.e. he is an actual or a potential wrongdoer). Therefore, refusal of an injunction against a former employee who is found to have breached his duties seems to be exceptional and is more likely to be applied in the case of preliminary injunctions, where the final decision on infringement has not yet been made.[103] Nevertheless, the possibility to include the balancing of interests upon grant of an injunction is considered particularly interesting in the context of employee mobility. Even where breach of duty is found, a distinction with regard to the balance of interests may be drawn between situations where the ex-employee took documents containing confidential information, and situations where he simply remembers the data as a result of working for the former

See also David Cran and Paul Joseph, 'Breach of Confidence Claim against Ex-employees and Consultants' (2011) 6(10) *JIPLP* 688, 690.

96 Spry, *The Principles of Equitable Remedies* 375, 380.

97 Ibid 376.

98 See e.g. *Universal Thermosensors v Hibben* [1992] 1 WLR 840 (Ch) 854 – 855; *Crowson Fabrics Ltd v Rider* [2008] FSR 17 (Ch) 448 [127]; *Vestergaard Frandsen A/S & Ors v Bestnet Europe Ltd & Ors* [2009] EWHC 1456 (Ch) [93] (Arnold J).

99 Spry, *The Principles of Equitable Remedies* 384.

100 Stanley 118.

101 *Ocular Sciences Ltd v Aspect Vision Care Ltd* [1997] RPC 289 (Ch) 406–407 (Laddie J); Gurry on Breach of Confidence para 17.22. For other equitable defences, see Gurry on Breach of Confidence paras 17.16–17.31. UK law also accepts damages and injunctions against a party who makes unjustified threats of commencing proceedings, Gill Grassie, 'Trade Secrets: The New EU Enforcement Regime' (2014) 9(8) *JIPLP* 677, 681.

102 Spry, *The Principles of Equitable Remedies* 391–393.

103 Ibid 396.

employer. The possibility to deny an injunction against use and to grant an injunction against disclosure may, in appropriate circumstances, be a way to reconcile the primary interest of the employer in maintaining confidentiality of the information with the interest of the employee in remaining professionally active in the field of his expertise.

Also in case of breach of contract the court has discretion to issue an injunction. Damage to the former employer is not a condition for grant of the order. If the agreement is enforceable (if the restriction it imposes is reasonable), the injunction will be issued, unless it would cause disproportionate hardship to the defendant.[104] This flexibility mitigates the negative consequences of the determination of reasonableness of the restrictive covenant at the time of its conclusion.[105] Accordingly, an injunction may be denied in case of an agreement which was reasonable upon conclusion, if at the time of enforcement it no longer serves its purpose; if the remaining duration of the covenant is short; if the employer delayed seeking a remedy despite being aware of the infringement; or if the damage caused by the employee may be mitigated by awarding monetary compensation.[106] In one case, applying its discretionary powers, the court denied injunction for breach of a non-solicitation and non-compete agreement because its enforcement would have caused the defendant to lose his new job, in a situation where the restrictive covenant was to expire shortly.[107]

No injunction may be granted once the information has become public, irrespective of who disclosed it.[108] In such a case damages are the remedy available for the aggrieved employer.[109]

2 Scope of Prohibited Acts

The scope of the prohibition corresponds to the scope of the duty which is to be observed, whether it stems from an implied obligation or is prescribed by an enforceable contract.[110] Thus, a final injunction may prohibit the disclosure of the information, its use, or both.[111]

[104] *Dyson Technology Ltd v Strutt* [2005] EWHC 2814 (Ch) [70]–[76]; Goulding, Clarke, Jones and Taylor in Goulding para 6.330.

[105] As discussed in Chapter 4, part II, point B.3.1).

[106] Goulding, Clarke, Jones and Taylor in Goulding para 6.332.

[107] *Corporate Express Ltd v Day* [2004] EWHC 2943 (QB) [46]–[48].

[108] *Ocular Sciences Ltd v Aspect Vision Care Ltd* [1997] RPC 289 (Pat) 396–400 (Laddie J); *Vestergaard Frandsen A/S & Ors v Bestnet Europe Ltd & Ors* [2009] EWHC 1456 (Ch) [72], [76] (Arnold J); Gurry on Breach of Confidence para 18.08.

[109] *Vestergaard Frandsen A/S & Ors v Bestnet Europe Ltd & Ors* [2009] EWHC 1456 (Ch) [72] (Arnold J).

[110] Alex Batteson, 'Gaining Confidence in the Law of Confidence' (2006) 1(11) *JIPLP* 714, 718.

[111] *Ocular Sciences Ltd v Aspect Vision Care Ltd* [1997] RPC 289 (Pat) 395 (Ch) (Laddie J).

It is generally accepted that an injunction may prohibit the use of documents, drawings and the like, obtained, copied or retained as a result of breach of duty of good faith during employment.[112]

The prohibition of use of technical information is also accepted as an appropriate remedy, e.g. in the form of an injunction against manufacturing and sale of products incorporating the trade secret. The extent to which the use of the information may be prohibited in the case of derivative products must be determined on the facts of the case. In *Ocular Sciences*, Laddie J referred to the rules applicable in patent cases and considered that for the injunction to be awarded there must be a 'substantial nexus' between the secret information and the derivative product.[113]

On the other hand, an injunction against contacting clients, if their contact data has been obtained from documents taken from the employer in breach of implied duty is problematic. While it is applied sometimes, in cases of a clear and serious breach of duty, when the unfair advantage gained by the employee continues and for the duration of such an advantage,[114] it is suggested to treat such injunctions as 'an exception rather than the norm'.[115] This is because their practical effect is the same as that of a non-solicitation or a non-compete agreement. Where the parties did not agree on such a covenant, it should not be imposed by the court. Moreover, such injunctions generally go against the recognised principle that the employee should be free to compete with his employer after termination of service. If an injunction against contacting clients is imposed, particularly during preliminary proceedings where the facts of the case have not yet been thoroughly examined, it might have severe consequences for the mobility of the individual employee.[116]

An injunction must clearly indicate to the defendant what he is and what he is not allowed to do.[117] It is the duty of the plaintiff to describe the confidential information sufficiently clearly, specifically and unambiguously so that the order, if issued, may be enforced. This applies also where the information in question partially overlaps with information in the public domain. In such a case a 'disclaimer' may be included in the

112 Gurry on Breach of Confidence para 11.52.

113 *Ocular Sciences Ltd v Aspect Vision Care Ltd* [1997] RPC 289 (Pat) 404 (Ch) (Laddie J).

114 *Roger Bullivant Ltd v Ellis* [1987] ICR 464 (CA) 476 (Nourse LJ); Gurry on Breach of Confidence para 11.55.

115 Gurry on Breach of Confidence para 11.57.

116 Ibid.

117 *Potters-Ballotini v Weston Baker* [1977] RPC 202 (CA) 206 (Lord Denning MR); *Caterpillar Logistics Services v Huesca de Crean* [2012] EWCA Civ 156 (CA) [68] (Bournton LJ); Howe, Gupta, Wilkinson, Pritchard and Taylor in Goulding para 4.52; Goulding, Croxford, De Marco, Mountford, Nathan, Powell, Windle and Taylor in Goulding para10.208.

injunction in order to make sure that the order is not too broad.[118] The clarity of the injunction plays a central role.[119] It seems that UK courts are less likely than German ones to consider the interest of the employer in maintaining the secrecy of information, at the expense of clear determination of the prohibited acts.

3 Duration of the Injunction

Final[120] injunctions are generally awarded for an unlimited duration and may at any time be dissolved upon application to the court that granted the remedy.[121]

A time-limited injunction may be granted for the remaining duration of a restrictive covenant or if it is clear that the information will fall into the public domain at a certain point in time,[122] e.g. in case of pending publication of a patent application or the forthcoming entry into force of a secret marketing strategy.

The courts may also award time-limited (springboard) injunctions.[123] Such an order may be granted with regard to information which has not yet entered the public domain, but whose 'degree' of secrecy has been diminished by the fact that the defendant possesses and uses it[124] as a result of breach of a duty, in a situation where he could have obtained that information from public sources by reverse-engineering a product or otherwise.[125] The idea is that the ex-employee obtained an unfair head start over his competitors by relying on information learned during employment instead of working it out from the publicly accessible sources, as any competitor could.

Once a springboard injunction has been issued, the defendant is precluded from using the information for a defined period of time, although others who discover this information independently may not be stopped from using it. The defendant will be allowed to use that

[118] Stanley 118–119.

[119] Grassie, 'Trade Secrets: The New EU Enforcement Regime' 677, 678.

[120] Also referred to as permanent injunctions, see e.g. Hull, *Commercial Secrecy: Law and Practice* para 11.48.

[121] Spry, *The Principles of Equitable Remedies* 374.

[122] Hull, *Commercial Secrecy: Law and Practice* para 11.48.

[123] For an analysis of the historical development of the springboard doctrine, see Gurry on Breach of Confidence paras 14.17–14.50.

[124] This is possible under the concept of relative secrecy.

[125] *Vestergaard Frandsen A/S & Ors v Bestnet Europe Ltd & Ors* [2009] EWHC 1456 (Ch) [78] (Arnold J); Gurry on Breach of Confidence para 18.71, explaining at para 18.72 that the possibility of developing the information with recourse to publicly available sources should be judged from the perspective of the defendant and that, accordingly, the fact that it would have been possible for a third party to develop the information should not play any role in granting a springboard injunction.

information after termination of the injunction or after the information becomes 'completely accessible to the public and thus ceases to be confidential'.[126] Therefore, a springboard injunction is an attempt to put the defendant into the position he would have been in if he had obtained the information from the publicly accessible sources.[127]

Taking this into consideration, the court may grant a springboard injunction if the plaintiff shows that the defendant is making unlawful use of the information, has gained an unfair competitive advantage as a result of this use and that on the day the injunction is granted this unfair advantage still exists and will continue to exist unless the injunction is granted.[128]

A time-limited springboard injunction may be awarded where the defendant is still using the information. However, in view of the possibility of obtaining the information from public sources, the court considers that its duration should be limited to the time a third person would need to obtain the information from those sources.[129] The appropriate duration of such an injunction depends on the circumstances of a particular case, but not on the seriousness of the breach or the conduct of the defendant.[130] It should commence at the point in time when the possibility to obtain the information in a legitimate way arose (e.g. in the case of reverse engineering, when the product was put on the market) and finish with the termination of the unfair advantage created by the use of the information.[131] A distinction has also been drawn between information which may be qualified as trade secrets under *Faccenda Chicken* and information which is 'merely' confidential, with the suggestion that springboard injunctions protecting trade secrets should be more readily accepted, while when considering such injunctions with regard to information of a lower degree of secrecy the courts should make sure that legitimate competition is not inhibited.[132]

126 Gurry on Breach of Confidence para 14.38; Batteson, 'Gaining Confidence in the Law of Confidence' 714, 715.

127 Stanley 41.

128 *Sun Valley Foods v Vincent* [2000] FSR 825 (Ch) 834. In any case the unfair advantage 'does not last for ever' and thus a springboard injunction must terminate, *Potters-Ballotini v Weston Baker* [1977] RPC 202 (CA) 206 (Lord Denning MR).

129 *Vestergaard Frandsen A/S & Ors v Bestnet Europe Ltd & Ors* [2009] EWHC 1456 (Ch) [80] (Arnold J), suggesting that this should apply also in the case of technical information which has a limited 'shelf-life', so that it may become part of the public domain within a predictable period of time.

130 Gurry on Breach of Confidence para 18.74.

131 *Roger Bullivant Ltd v Ellis* [1987] ICR 464 (CA) 476 (Nourse LJ); Gurry on Breach of Confidence para 18.74.

132 *Roger* Bullivant *Ltd v Ellis* [1987] ICR 464 (CA) 481 (May LJ).

It has also been considered that a springboard injunction may sometimes be awarded when the defendant has already stopped using the information.[133] The role of such an injunction would be to mitigate the advantage that the ex-employee has obtained from such use.[134] This is more likely to be the case as regards information relating to clients.[135] Technical information is being used as long as the products incorporating it are being manufactured. In the case of data of clients or contractors, once contact with such a person has commenced, the information taken from the ex-employer is no longer being used (i.e. it can only be used once – upon contacting the client).

There seems to be no conclusive approach with regard to granting an injunction for such past misuse. The courts have held that an injunction should not 'merely (. . .) punish a defendant for his previous unlawful action, where the injunction does not protect the claimant against any further harm, unlawfully caused' and that in such a situation only financial compensation is an appropriate remedy.[136] Granting an injunction for past misuse would 'unjustly benefit the plaintiff by putting it into a better position as against the [ex-employee] than if there had been no breach of confidence'.[137] A court order against contacting clients is less controversial during preliminary proceedings,[138] since its purpose is to preserve the status quo pending trial and its effect may be corrected at trial. Awarding a time-limited injunction for past misuse at trial is approached with caution. In particular where the ex-employee has developed contacts with the clients of his former employer, it is advised to award damages rather than issue an injunction.[139] This is because granting an injunction in such circumstances does not guarantee that

[133] Although granting an injunction in such circumstances remains controversial, *Vestergaard Frandsen A/S & Ors v Bestnet Europe Ltd & Ors* [2009] EWHC 1456 (Ch) [93] (Arnold J); Gurry on Breach of Confidence paras 18.76–18.77.

[134] *Vestergaard Frandsen A/S & Ors v Bestnet Europe Ltd & Ors* [2009] EWHC 1456 (Ch) [81] (Arnold J).

[135] Gurry on Breach of Confidence para 18.75.

[136] *BBC v Collins* [2010] EWHC 2424 (Ch) [65]. In *Crowson Fabrics Ltd v Rider* [2008] FSR 17 (Ch) [113] the Court found breach of duty by the former employees despite the information not being confidential. At the same time it expressed doubts as to the worth of a springboard injunction in such a case and endorsed damages instead (ibid [125]–[127]). For a different interpretation of this case, see Gurry on Breach of Confidence para 18.76.

[137] *Universal Thermosensors v Hibben* [1992] 1 WLR 840 (Ch) 854–855.

[138] As analysed infra in Chapter 5, part III, point B.2.

[139] *Universal Thermosensors v Hibben* [1992] 1 WLR 840 (Ch) 855; *Vestergaard Frandsen A/S & Ors v Bestnet Europe Ltd & Ors* [2009] EWHC 1456 (Ch) [93] (Arnold J); Gurry on Breach of Confidence para 18.79.

those clients will start using the ex-employer's services again. Therefore such an injunction might merely have a punitive effect on the employee.

Thus, it appears that the UK courts are ready to award a springboard injunction at trial if the defendant uses information obtained in breach of duty, even though it was possible for him to develop the information by honest means and where that information has not yet entered the public domain. The injunction should be granted for a time deemed necessary for such development.

4 Summary

In the United Kingdom, permanent injunctions are equitable remedies, awarded if the court deems it reasonable and just. One factor in deciding whether to award a final injunction is that it is not the purpose of such an order to punish the infringer. Thus, an injunction should not limit fair competition from the employee, thereby putting the employer in a better position than he would have been in if no infringement had taken place.

Injunctions are not issued automatically if breach of duty or threat thereof is found. It is possible to 'correct' the finding of a breach by framing an injunction. This is the case, for example, if a restrictive covenant is found to have been reasonable at the time of its conclusion, but due to changed circumstances its enforcement by way of injunctive relief would be oppressive for the ex-employee.

Another instance of the flexibility of UK equity doctrine is the possibility to award time-limited springboard injunctions in order to mitigate the unfair head start which the employee obtained over competitors. This is more readily accepted in the case of technical secrets, where the duration of the springboard may be determined by assessing the time needed for research and development. If contact with clients has been made, monetary compensation is generally considered a more appropriate remedy, since a prohibition against contacting clients would overly limit competition. The aim of such a springboard injunction is, unlike in Germany, not to compensate the former employer for the head start obtained by the ex-employee. That is the role of damages. Rather, it is to correct the duration of the injunction in a situation where the information was available from public sources (albeit with difficulties), to include the hypothetical time the defendant would have needed to develop the information without reliance on the data obtained from his employer. Thus, it appears that UK springboard doctrine aims at determining the time when the information would have entered the public domain and become free for everyone to use, even the infringer. Under the German approach, it seems that, in view of the compensatory nature of the time-limited injunction, it may remain in force even though the information subsequently loses secrecy.

The approach of UK doctrine is more flexible than in Germany and encompasses in particular a broad balancing of interests, including the public interest in competition. The balancing of interests affects not only the scope of the injunction, but also the decision whether it is to be granted at all.

C *Injunction in Cases of Infringement of a Right to a Trade Secret by a Former Employee in the United States*

1 Requirements for Grant

Pursuant to Section 2(a) UTSA and as prescribed under the DTSA,[140] both actual and threatened[141] misappropriation[142] may be enjoined.[143] The decision whether to grant a permanent[144] injunction lies in the discretion of the court. This remedy may be awarded if the court finds that the ex-employee is in breach of a statutory or a contractual[145] duty, the ex-employer has suffered an irreparable injury and other remedies, in particular damages, are inadequate to compensate for this injury.[146] Moreover, the court will balance the interests of the parties and the interests of the public in order to determine whether such a far-reaching remedy is appropriate.[147]

140 18 US Code §1836(b)(3)(A), as amended by the DTSA.

141 Showing threatened misappropriation usually means demonstrating that a former employee who has the knowledge of trade secrets has accepted a position with his ex-employer's competitor in such a capacity that it would be logical for him to use his former employer's trade secrets. However, in states which do not accept the doctrine of inevitable disclosure, it might be necessary to additionally show that the defendant acted dishonestly before leaving service, Quinto/Singer 146–147.

142 Which includes unauthorised disclosure or use of the trade secret as prescribed in S 1 (2)(ii) UTSA.

143 Peterson 13–71.

144 Injunctions issued after final consideration of the merits of the case are referred to as 'permanent' in the United States and as 'final' in the United Kingdom.

145 In the case of enforcement of a contract, the injunction will in fact order specific performance of the agreement, Jack W Berryhill, 'Trade Secret Litigation: Injunctions and other Equitable Remedies' (1977) 48 *Univ Colo L R* 189, 194.

146 The fact that damages may be awarded does not exclude issuing an injunction, since the purpose of an injunction is to prevent future breaches and the purpose of damages is to compensate for breaches which have already taken place. Thus, where the former employees acted in breach of duty and there is a high likelihood that the infringement will continue, the Court may award both damages and an injunction, see e.g. *Litigation Management Inc v Bourgeois* 2011 WL 2270553 paras 17–18, 25, 27, 31 (Ohio Ct App 2011).

147 *eBay Inc v MercExchange LLC* 547 US 388, 391, 394 (US Supr Ct 2006), even though this decision was issued in the context of a patent infringement dispute, the Court refers to the general principles governing the granting of a permanent injunction; Pooley 7–9 – 7-10, 7-32; Barton Beebe and others, *Trademarks, Unfair Competition, and Business Torts* (2nd edn Wolters Kluwer 2016) 848–849. See also Berryhill, 'Trade Secret Litigation: Injunctions and other Equitable Remedies' 189, 195–196.

Thus, even where misappropriation is found, an injunction will not be issued automatically and no irreparable injury is presumed. In one case, even though the employee took documents from his former employer, the plaintiff was not able to show that he would use or was likely to use them. Consequently, the Court refused an injunction.[148]

Like in the other jurisdictions analysed, an injunction will not be issued if the information has already ceased to be secret,[149] since one of the conditions for granting injunctive relief is showing the existence of a trade secret.[150] In such a case damages are the appropriate remedy to compensate the former employer.

Moreover, under the DTSA an injunction will be refused if it would prevent a person from entering into an employment relationship or if it would conflict with the state law on restraint of trade.[151]

The influence that an issued injunction might have on the interests of third parties and of the public is taken into account as well. Apart from balancing the interests of the employer in the protection of his property and investment against the interests of the employee in his freedom to choose a professional activity, the US courts fully consider the possible impact of the injunction in the context of the public interest.[152] In particular, abusive enforcement of trade secrets in bad faith, e.g. if the information is not in fact a trade secret,[153] for the purpose of restraining competition or to create or strengthen a monopolistic position, may be a reason for the court to deny an injunction. An injunction covering information which is not a trade secret or prohibiting any competition altogether may be considered invalid as a restraint of trade under Sections 1–2 Sherman Act.[154]

[148] In this case it was a preliminary injunction, but the same considerations apply when granting a permanent injunction, *American Airlines Inc v Imhof* 620 F Supp 2d 574, 585–586 (SDNY 2009).

[149] Comment to S 2(a) UTSA, Peterson 13–19, 13–72. Pooley seems to support the issuance of a time-limited head start injunction even if the information entered the public domain before the injunction was issued, Pooley 7-34 – 7-35.

[150] Loss of secrecy occurs e.g. if the information is published on the Internet. An injunction may prevent such publication. If the information is already on the Internet, Rowe proposes an introduction of a new remedy, takedown from the Internet, which in expedited process would disable access to the information, pending a ruling by the court, and thus maintaining the secrecy, Elizabeth A Rowe, 'Introducing a Takedown for Trade Secrets on the Internet' (2007) 5 *WLR* 1041.

[151] 18 US Code §1836(b)(3)(A)(i), as amended by the DTSA.

[152] *eBay Inc v MercExchange LLC* 547 US 388, 391 (US Supr Ct 2006).

[153] Peterson 14–21.

[154] *By-Buk Co v Printed Cellophane Tape Co* 163 Cal App 2d 157, 169 (Cal 1958), where the injunction covered the manufacture of products which the machine containing the secrets was designed to produce, even if the products were manufactured by another method.; *CVD Inc v Raytheon Co* 769 F2d 842 paras 25–26, 32–36, 70 (1st Cir 1985);

2 Scope of Prohibited Acts

The US courts have wide discretion in framing an injunction. The principles governing this freedom are, on the one hand, the necessity to formulate the order in a manner sufficiently clear for the defendant to know what he is and is not allowed to do. On the other hand, the courts must make sure that the injunction does not entirely take away the defendant's ability to engage in fair competition with his former employer.[155] The balancing of the interests of the holder of the secret information, the former employee and the public serves as an aid in framing an appropriate injunction.[156]

The scope of the injunction depends on the facts of the case. Factors to be borne in mind when framing an injunctive order include the extent to which the defendant is in possession of the information, the nature of the information, which influences how it may be defined in the order,[157] the harm to the defendant which might be caused by an overly broad injunction, the risk of circumventing the order if it is drafted too narrowly and the type of infringement (in particular the likelihood that the former employee will try to evade the order, if he has already shown intent to harm the former employer).[158]

The prohibition may cover disclosure or use of the information. In states which apply the doctrine of inevitable disclosure, an injunction may restrict the former employee from undertaking new employment, even though no agreement to that effect has been concluded.[159] Moreover, orders prohibiting solicitation of customers or accepting business from the former employer's clients may be issued.[160]

Generally, the prohibition of use relates to the secret information in question ('use injunction'). However, where the information is inextricably connected to the defendant's process or product, the court may issue an injunction prohibiting the manufacturing of the product ('production injunction').[161] In such a case, in order to determine the

Mark A Glick, Lara A Reymann and Richard Hoffman, *Intellectual Property Damages: Guidelines and Analysis* (John Wiley & Sons, Inc 2003) 308–309.

155 Peterson 13–53; Pooley 7-25 – 7-27.

156 Ruth E Leistensnider, 'Trade Secret Misappropriation: What is the Proper Length of an Injunction after Public Disclosure?' (1987) 51 *Alb L Rev* 271, 288–289; Pooley 7-26.

157 For example, whether reference must be made to drawings, products or a list.

158 Pooley 7-26 – 7-27.

159 It appears that this would not be possible under the DTSA which prescribes that any conditions put on an employment by way of injunction must be based on evidence of threatened misappropriation and not merely on the information the person knows, 18 US Code §1836(b)(3)(A)(i)(I), as amended by the DTSA.

160 Pooley 7-22.

161 Peterson 13–54 – 13.55; Berryhill, 'Trade Secret Litigation: Injunctions and other Equitable Remedies' 189, 197.

substantive scope of the order, where, looking at the defendant's product it is not clear to what extent it relies on the secret information, the US courts apply by analogy the doctrine of equivalents from patent law. Thus, if the defendant's product performs substantially the same function in substantially the same way and achieves the same result as the one produced by the secret information, it may be covered by the injunction.[162] On the other hand, if the secret information relates only to a small part of the infringer's product, a 'production' injunction might not serve the public interest and therefore is likely to be denied.[163]

Where the court is enforcing a non-compete covenant, it may issue an injunction prohibiting the ex-employee from undertaking competitive activity. The same effect may be achieved if implied duties are being enforced, under the highly controversial[164] doctrine of inevitable disclosure.

The doctrine is applied by some courts[165] in circumstances where the ex-employee has learned a trade secret of the former employer in the course of service and where the parties did not explicitly agree by way of a restrictive covenant on the scope of the information which the employee is allowed to use after departure. If the secret information is 'inextricably tied up'[166] with the ex-employee's skills and knowledge, and the position of the ex-employee with his new employer is such that there is a high

[162] *Motorola Inc v Computer Displays International Inc* 739 F 2d 1149, 1157 (7th Cir 1984); Peterson 13–55; Pooley 6-27. Thus, the injunction extends to the production of an entire product and is not limited to component parts, Pooley 7-23.

[163] *eBay Inc v MercExchange LLC* 547 US 388, 396 (US Supr Ct 2006). The court was of the opinion that if the injunction was to be issued also in such instances, it might be used by plaintiffs initiating proceedings in bad faith to intimidate defendants.

[164] As argued by Beebe et al., taking into consideration that S 2(a) UTSA allows for enjoining both actual and threatened misappropriation and the fact that the doctrine imposes a non-compete agreement if the parties did not bargain to conclude one, the inevitable disclosure doctrine might not be efficient, see Beebe and others, *Trademarks, Unfair Competition, and Business Torts* 820–821. Many courts, particularly in California, reject the doctrine of inevitable disclosure, see ibid 819. For critical appraisal of this doctrine, see also Katherine V W Stone, 'The New Psychological Contract: Implications of the Changing Workplace for Labor and Employment Law' (2001) 48 *UCLA L Rev* 519; Margo E K Reder and Christine Neylon O'Brien, 'Managing the Risk of Trade Secret Loss Due to Job Mobility in an Innovation Economy with the Theory of Inevitable Disclosure' (2012) 12 *Journal of High Technology Law* 33–36 http://ssrn.com/abstract=2014051 accessed 1 June 2017. For a more lenient approach, endorsing the pragmatic application of the doctrine by the courts, see Ivan P L Png and Sampsa Samila, 'Trade Secrets Law and Mobility: Evidence from "Inevitable Disclosure"' (2015) 24 http://papers.ssrn.com/sol3/papers.cfm?abstract_id=1986775 accessed 1 June 2017 and Pooley 7-15–7-16.

[165] For an overview of the application of this doctrine in various states, see Quinto/Singer 148–161.

[166] Milgrim on Trade Secrets vol 1A 5-43.

probability that it will be used, such use may be denied. This is achieved by way of an injunction prohibiting the employee from undertaking certain activities with the new employer.[167] Due to the intertwining of the secrets with the employee's experience, the injunction necessarily affects the former employee's general skill and knowledge.

Some courts suggest that such an injunction may be issued only where the existence of a trade secret is proven, where it relates to an advanced technological process developed through extensive investment in R&D, and where there is a high degree of probability that the employee's service for the new employer will lead to wrongful use or disclosure of this information.[168] This standard was lowered in *PepsiCo Inc v Redmond*,[169] where the Court accepted the application of this doctrine to marketing information. This decision was criticised as effectively imposing on the ex-employee a restrictive covenant where there had been none.[170] Considering this severe effect, it is proposed that the doctrine of inevitable disclosure should be applied only in extreme cases, where the information to be used is 'a unique trade secret', where the second employer has tried to develop a solution equivalent to that covered by secrecy but has failed to do so, and when the former employee 'could not be rationally expected not to use the trade secret' when working for the new employer.[171] In *EarthWeb Inc v Schlack*[172] it was suggested that the factors to be considered when applying the doctrine should include whether the old and the new employer are direct competitors providing the same or similar products or services, whether the ex-employee's position with the new employer is so similar to his position with the old employer that he cannot be expected to fulfil his new duties without relying on the secret information, and whether the information is highly valuable to both employers. The court concluded that the inevitable disclosure doctrine should not be applied with the effect of a restrictive covenant.[173]

[167] Milgrim on Trade Secrets vol 1A 5–50. Considering its concept, Pooley suggests that the doctrine would more accurately be described as doctrine of inevitable misappropriation, Pooley 7-14.

[168] See e.g. *EI DuPont de Nemours and Co v American Potash & Chemical Corp* 220 A 2d 428 (Del Ch 1964).

[169] *PepsiCo Inc v Redmond* 54 F 3d 1262 (7th Cir 1995).

[170] And in particular where there was no consideration (financial or otherwise) for restricting the post-employment activities of the employee, see Milgrim on Trade Secrets vol 1A 5–70, 5–72.2.

[171] Milgrim on Trade Secrets vol 1A 5–70 – 5–72.1.

[172] *EarthWeb Inc v Schlack* 71 F Supp 2d 299 (SDNY 1999).

[173] *EarthWeb Inc v Schlack* 71 F Supp 2d 299, 310–311 (SDNY 1999).

Thus, the doctrine of inevitable disclosure, despite its name, relates to prohibition of use of the information, rather than prohibition of disclosure. Seen from this perspective, although it is capable of protecting the employer's proprietary interests in the information, it aims not so much at protecting secrecy as at protecting the competitive position of the former employer. By restraining the ex-employee from taking a particular job, it prohibits the use not only of a trade secret but also of the employee's general skills and experience. Thus, the application of this doctrine blurs the basic distinction between trade secrets and general skill and knowledge. In this way, the effect of an injunction issued as a result of applying the doctrine is akin to a restrictive covenant.[174] However, it must be kept in mind that any injunction which prohibits use of the information affects the competitive position of the former employee. In cases where no agreement was concluded and particularly where the infringement is only threatening, the assessment of the likelihood that misappropriation will occur (e.g. through use of the information) is central to the court's decision on whether to grant the injunction and how to frame it. In such cases, consideration of whether the use or disclosure of the information is inevitable, by including it in the assessment of the likelihood of the threatened misappropriation, may be helpful.[175] Once threatened infringement is found, the core consideration should be the proper framing of the injunction, so that it does not restrain competition altogether, but only to the extent necessary to protect the employer's interests. Thus, a prohibition against working for a competitor should be accepted only to the extent that it is not a blanket restriction, but covers a narrowly defined position at the new employer's, involving the use of a particular trade secret.

One suggestion for a balanced application of the doctrine has been put forward by Rowe.[176] According to her, an injunction prohibiting the former employee from taking a particular position with the new employer may be issued only where the employee signed a non-disclosure agreement defining the protected information[177] and acted in bad faith in taking

[174] William G Porter II and Michael Griffaton, 'Identifying and Protecting Employers' Interests in Trade Secrets and Proprietary Information' (2001) 68 *Def Couns J* 439, 445.

[175] Indeed, the doctrine of inevitable disclosure is usually used to support an application for a preliminary injunction. Nevertheless, it may be the basis for issuing a permanent order as well, Quinto/Singer 149.

[176] Elizabeth A Rowe, 'When Trade Secrets Become Shackles: Fairness and the Inevitable Disclosure Doctrine' (2005) 7 *Tul J Tech & Intell Prop* 167.

[177] Considering the severe effects of the application of the doctrine on the position of the employee, fairness requires that the employee is made aware of the information to be kept secret and explicitly agrees to keep it secret, Rowe, 'When Trade Secrets Become Shackles: Fairness and the Inevitable Disclosure Doctrine' 167, 208.

or using the information.[178] In such a case, the injunction can be issued if the former and the new employer are direct competitors, the position in which the employee is to work would involve use of the information,[179] and the employee was exposed to specific trade secrets and will inevitably use them in his new employment.[180] Furthermore, the scope of the injunction should be determined in a flexible way. The duration should correspond to the duration of secrecy. The scope of the prohibited acts should be specified, e.g. prohibition of working for a competitor in any position, or on a particular post.[181] Thus, as the author admits, the proposed model for applying the doctrine of inevitable disclosure would resemble the assessment of the reasonableness of restrictive covenants.[182]

It is considered that Rowe's proposal takes due account of the criticism of the doctrine of inevitable disclosure. Moreover, the factors which she proposes may be relevant when granting any injunction against use of the information. However, where an injunction would result in imposing a de facto restrictive covenant on the former employee, the doctrine, even as proposed by Rowe, should be applied only in the most egregious cases, e.g. where an employee who knows the core trade secrets of his former employer is hired by a direct competitor to act in the same capacity as in his former job. Otherwise, in the absence of an agreement and consideration (remuneration), restrictive covenants might be imposed. Such a result should not be accepted in view of the interests of the former employee.

The criticism of the doctrine of inevitable disclosure appears to have been taken into account upon drafting the DTSA. It prescribes that any conditions put on an employment by way of injunction must be based on

[178] According to Rowe, where no restrictive covenant was entered into, an injunction prohibiting work for a competitor may be issued only where the former employee used dishonest means to obtain the information, or has otherwise behaved in such a way that it may be presumed that he will use the information to harm the former employer. However, keeping silent regarding plans to join a competitor is not to be seen as evidence of dishonesty, Rowe, 'When Trade Secrets Become Shackles: Fairness and the Inevitable Disclosure Doctrine' 167, 214–218. An example of dishonest behaviour could be repeated accessing of secret information of the employer shortly before leaving service, which may indicate not only bad faith but also to the intention of using the information for the new employer, *Bimbo Bakeries USA Inc v Botticella* 613 F3d 102 (3d Cir 2010).

[179] Accordingly, the fact that the companies are not in the same industry, or compete for a different market segment or where the employee would hold a position unrelated to the previous one, weigh against granting an injunction, Rowe, 'When Trade Secrets Become Shackles: Fairness and the Inevitable Disclosure Doctrine' 167, 210–212.

[180] Ibid 167, 212–214.

[181] Ibid 167, 219.

[182] Ibid 167, 226.

evidence of threatened misappropriation and not merely on the information the person knows.[183]

When issuing an injunction, clarity of the order is also taken into account in the United States. The need to safeguard the secrecy of the information is addressed by the possibility of issuing a general injunctive order, with reference to a confidential attachment containing a more detailed description of the information covered by the prohibition.[184]

3 Duration of the Injunction

Under the UTSA an injunction 'should last for as long as is necessary, but no longer than is necessary, to eliminate the commercial advantage or 'lead time' with respect to good faith competitors that a person has obtained through misappropriation'.[185] Thus, the injunction may be terminated by the court which issued it, upon application, once the information loses the quality of secrecy. However, as long as the infringer still holds a competitive advantage the injunction against him may continue despite disclosure of the information.[186]

Even though, in the past, in cases of trade-secret misappropriation, the courts did issue perpetual injunctions,[187] which extended in time also beyond the date on which the information became publicly available,[188] currently most states apply the UTSA approach, thus tending to issue time-limited injunctions, both preliminary and permanent, aiming at putting the defendant in position he would have been in if he had not used unfair means to obtain the information, but rather had relied on

183 18 US Code §1836(b)(3)(A)(i)(I), as amended by the DTSA.

184 *Henry Hope X-Ray Products Inc v Marrion Carrel Inc* 674 F 2d 1336, 1343 (9th Cir 1982), in which reference to a confidential attachment was accepted despite the requirement of Rule 65(d) of the Federal Rules of Civil Procedure that the injunction must describe the restrained acts in reasonable detail and not by referring to the complaint or some other document; Pooley 7-27.

185 Comment to S 2 UTSA; Similarly S 44(3) Restatement (Third) of Unfair Competition; Edmund W Kitch, 'The Expansion of Trade Secrecy Protection and the Mobility of Management Employees: a New Problem for the Law' (1996) 47 *S C L Rev* 659, 671; Peterson 13–76.

186 S 2(a) UTSA.

187 A 'perpetual' injunction is an order granted for an unlimited period of time. A 'permanent' injunction is a notion used to describe injunctions issued at trial (in the United Kingdom referred to as 'final' injunctions), as opposed to preliminary orders granted before trial, Pooley 7-34. It is considered that a perpetual injunction may be appropriate only in cases of trade secrets which are not likely to be reverse-engineered in any foreseeable future. Otherwise they would be inconsistent with the public interest in promoting competition, S 44 comments c and f Restatement (Third) of Unfair Competition, Pooley 7-33.

188 Kitch, 'The Law and Economics of Rights in Valuable Information' 683, 693, with further references; Peterson 13–20 – 13–46.

publicly available sources to develop it. To that end, the injunction may extend beyond the point in time when the information loses its secret status.[189] The appropriate duration of the 'head start' is determined at the discretion of the court.[190]

In the case of technical information, the appropriate duration of the injunction is thought to correspond to the time necessary for an independent third party to reverse-engineer the trade secret or to develop the information independently.[191] If a preliminary injunction was issued and served the same purpose as the final injunction, its duration will be included by the court in the calculation of the appropriate duration of the permanent order.[192] Other factors include the time the plaintiff needed to develop the information, the sophistication of the parties (e.g. whether the ex-employee had the knowledge and the technical capacities to develop the information independently), the type of product concerned (e.g. source-code as opposed to a machine which can easily be disassembled) and the relative ease or difficulty of reverse engineering.[193] Where the injunction is based on a breach of a contractual duty, it will not extend beyond the reasonable duration of the covenant agreed on.[194]

Also when deciding the appropriate duration of a head start injunction, the US courts fully acknowledge and consider the conflict of interests inherent in the employee-mobility scenario. An overly long prohibition would deny the employees the possibility to use their skills and knowledge and the public the possibility to profit from the utilisation of those skills. On the other hand, refusing an injunction, or framing it too narrowly, might give a dishonest ex-employee a head start over his legitimate competitors.[195]

189 *Winston Research Corp v Minnesota Mining and Manufacturing Company* 350 F 2d 134, 142 (9th Cir 1965); Peterson 13–46. On the development of that rule, see Berryhill, 'Trade Secret Litigation: Injunctions and other Equitable Remedies' 189, 204–207

190 Peterson 13–49.

191 *Winston Research Corp v Minnesota Mining and Manufacturing Company* 350 F 2d 134, 142 (9th Cir 1965); *K-2 Ski Company v Head Ski Co Inc* 506 f 2d 471, 474 (9th Cir 1974).

192 *K-2 Ski Company v Head Ski Co Inc* 506 f 2d 471, 475 (9th Cir 1974); Berryhill, 'Trade Secret Litigation: Injunctions and other Equitable Remedies' 189, 201; Pooley 7-35 – 7-36.

193 Peterson 13–49.

194 Leistensnider, 'Trade Secret Misappropriation: What is the Proper Length of an Injunction after Public Disclosure?' 271, 279. Nevertheless, in exceptional circumstances, where the misappropriation extends beyond the contractual duty, an injunction lasting longer than the contractual obligation may be issued, see *Cherne Indus Inc v Grounds & Assocs Inc* 278 NW 2d 81, 93 (Supr Ct Minn 1979). Other exceptional circumstances may relate to the existence and extent of a preliminary injunction, see Berryhill, 'Trade Secret Litigation: Injunctions and other Equitable Remedies' 189, 209–210.

195 *Winston Research Corp v Minnesota Mining and Manufacturing Company* 350 F 2d 134, 142–143 (9th Cir 1965).

Some authors suggest that any attempt to determine the proper duration of the head start is in fact speculation and suggest instead issuing perpetual injunctions, which could be modified or terminated later on, once it can be shown that the information has lost its secret status.[196] Leistensnider argues that the approach taken in the UTSA does not fully consider the interests of employers, as it does not appropriately[197] take into consideration misappropriation amounting to theft or other 'egregious conduct'. Thus, she proposes that the head start injunction as prescribed in the UTSA be taken as a starting point for determining the length of an injunction in cases where the information was disclosed. If malicious and wilful conduct on the part of the employee is found, she proposes that an injunction of a punitive character be awarded: a perpetual injunction with no possibility of dissolution. At the same time she suggests that this injunction be drafted narrowly so that it does not completely preclude the former employee from undertaking professional activity.[198] Despite the proposal that the perpetual injunction be framed in a narrow way, it is observed that the purpose of an injunction is prevention rather than punishment.[199] Even though US law accepts punitive remedies, they relate to monetary measures and not to prohibition of competition. For this reason it is considered here that the UTSA with its system of time-limited injunctions, combined – where necessary – with exemplary damages or attorney's fees, is better suited for application in the context of employee mobility. At the same time, in particularly blatant cases of misappropriation, US law provides also for criminal causes of action.

4 Summary

Injunction is a flexible equitable remedy in cases of actual or threatened misappropriation of trade secrets in the United States. The decision on whether to grant and how to design it is strongly dependent on the facts of the case and the courts have broad discretion in that respect. Thus, there are no strict rules in this matter.[200]

Balancing of interests is included at every stage of granting and framing of the injunction and, as when determining the scope of the right to a trade secret vis-à-vis a departed employee, includes full consideration of the

196 Pooley 7-35.

197 Under S 3(b) UTSA the court may award punitive damages in such a case.

198 Leistensnider, 'Trade Secret Misappropriation: What is the proper Length of an Injunction after Public Disclosure?' 271, 289–291.

199 Berryhill, 'Trade Secret Litigation: Injunctions and other Equitable Remedies' 189, 204.

200 Berryhill, 'Trade Secret Litigation: Injunctions and other Equitable Remedies' 189, 214.

interests of the parties and the public. In particular, litigating in bad faith or in an attempt to restrict competition might be a reason for the court to deny injunctive relief.

Generally, US law seems to prefer time-limited injunctions, to deprive a disloyal employee from the head start he might otherwise enjoy as a result of having access to the information ahead of his competitors. The orders may cover disclosure of the information, its use, or the manufacture of products incorporating the information.

This flexibility of the US approach to granting injunctions in cases of trade-secret misappropriation against former employees largely corresponds to the approach in UK law. Nevertheless, the US courts appear to take a more employer-friendly stance. It seems possible to sustain an injunction even once the information is no longer secret, and the courts seem more willing to issue an injunction even where the information relates to clients and not technical secrets. Moreover, in states applying the doctrine of inevitable disclosure, an injunction may expressly prohibit the employee from working for a competitor, even where the parties did not conclude a restrictive covenant.

D Injunction in Cases of Infringement of a Right to a Trade Secret by a Former Employee under the Trade Secrets Directive

The Trade Secrets Directive is directed ia at harmonisation of remedies in cases of unlawful acquisition, use or disclosure of a trade secret. In Article 12, it provides for minimum harmonisation[201] relating to injunctions and corrective measures resulting from a decision on the merits of the case. The application of injunctive relief is subject to the conditions and safeguards contained in Article 13 of the Directive, which need to be respected in any case, even if the Member States decide to apply stronger protection than that provided for in the Directive.[202] In this sense Article 13 has the character of full (maximum) harmonisation.

1 Requirements for Grant

According to Article 12(1) of the Directive, when a judicial decision is taken, finding that unlawful acquisition, use or disclosure of a trade secret has occurred, an injunction may be issued. Furthermore, corrective measures may be adopted with regard to the infringing goods or materials incorporating the trade secret.[203]

201 Art 1, Recital 10 TSD.
202 Art 1(1), Recital 10 TSD.
203 Art 12(1)(c)–(d), (2)–(4) TSD. Since application of corrective measures, such as destruction of infringing goods or destruction or delivery up of the materials containing

No further requirements for grant are prescribed, thus allowing the Member States to apply their developed rules. However, according to the Directive, application for any measure or remedy prescribed in it must be dismissed if the acquisition, use or disclosure of the secret is carried out ia to protect a legitimate interest.[204] Although this solution has been criticised as insufficiently clear,[205] it seems that it may apply where the employee uses information which he acquired honestly and which he must be able to rely on in order to remain professionally active.[206]

Furthermore, the Directive expressly provides for a duty to balance various factors when granting the remedy. Since the court 'may'[207] grant an injunction, but in considering the request for an injunction and in assessing the proportionality of the remedy it 'shall' apply the safeguards prescribed by the Directive,[208] it seems that the balancing of rights and interests is obligatory not only when determining the contents of the injunctive order, but also when deciding whether this remedy is to be granted in the first place.

As prescribed by Article 6(2) of the Directive, the remedies for infringement of a right to a trade secret must be fair and equitable, not unnecessarily complicated or costly, and effective and dissuasive. Pursuant to Article 7(1),[209] all remedies provided in the Directive must be applied in a manner which is proportionate; avoids creating barriers to legitimate trade in the internal market; and provides safeguards against their abuse.[210] According to Article 13(1) of the Directive, in assessing the proportionality of an injunction, the courts shall be required to take into consideration: the circumstances of the case and in particular the value of the trade secret; the measures taken to protect the trade secret; other specific features of the trade secret; the conduct of the infringer in acquiring, using or disclosing the trade secret; the impact of the unlawful use or disclosure of the information; the legitimate interests of the parties and the impact which the grant or refusal of the injunction might have on

the trade secret, is not specific to the context of employee mobility, the analysis of those measures is beyond the scope of this book.

204 Art 5(d) TSD.

205 ICC Comments on Proposal for EU Trade Secrets Directive, Paper 450/1083 DYE/cle – 20 March 2014 www.icc-deutschland.de/fileadmin/icc/ICC_2012/ICC_Comments_on_Proposal_for_EU_Trade_Secrets_Directive.pdf accessed 3 March 2016, on file with the author.

206 MPI Position Paper para 38.

207 Art 12(1) TSD.

208 Art 13(1) TSD.

209 Both Art 7(1) and Art 13 have a character of full harmonisation according to Art 1 (1) TSD.

210 This requirement of proportionality corresponds to that contained in Art 3 Enforcement Directive.

their positions; the legitimate interests of third parties;[211] and the public interest and the safeguarding of fundamental rights. Furthermore, the application of remedies should be without prejudice to the mobility of workers.[212]

The codification of proportionality and the balancing exercise is novel compared with the rules applied in the European jurisdictions analysed. Even though both UK and German law foresees that the injunction must be granted[213] and framed under consideration of all the circumstances of the case, it is left for the competent court to decide which elements are to be considered.

The list of factors provided in the Directive is not exhaustive, but it contains a compulsory framework of safeguards for granting remedies, thus increasing legal certainty and serving the goal of harmonisation. In particular, it clarifies that the legitimate interests of the parties and the impact of the grant of remedy on their positions, as well as the interest of third parties and the public, shall be included in the assessment, 'where appropriate'.[214] Even though this is not expressly stated in the Directive, it is submitted that the broad inclusion of the interest of the parties and the public is particularly relevant upon grant of an injunction against former employees and thus will be appropriate in such cases. Moreover, the balancing includes a duty to consider fundamental rights, in particular the freedom to choose one's occupation and the right to engage in work, the preservation of secrecy of business and the right to an effective remedy,[215] which are of material importance in the employee-mobility context. The inclusion of the proportionality test is also to be welcomed as serving the goal of harmonisation, in particular since it corresponds to the proportionality requirement contained in the Enforcement Directive. Accordingly, an injunction should be granted only where it is suitable for achieving the goal[216] and there is no less severe method of achieving it.[217]

211 This should include, where appropriate, the interests of consumers, Recital 21 TSD.

212 Recital 21 TSD.

213 In that respect German law seems to be less flexible, since it includes the consideration of various interests upon framing, but prescribes grant of a remedy whenever infringement is found, unless a less burdensome measure is applicable. UK law leaves both the decision to grant and the design of a remedy to the discretion of the court, and the courts seem to apply the principle of proportionality prescribed by Art 3(2) Enforcement Directive, cf *Vestergaard Frandsen A/S & Ors v Bestnet Europe Ltd & Ors* [2011] EWCA Civ 424 (CA) [56](Jacob J).

214 Art 13(1) TSD.

215 Recital 34 TSD.

216 Which would not be the case for an injunction against disclosure after the information has fallen into the public domain.

217 In particular where damages would not serve the purpose of protecting the former employer's rights.

Apart from the compulsory consideration of proportionality, according to Article 7(1)(c), application of all the remedies provided in the Directive must include considerations of abuse of litigation.[218] This statement is however weakened by the wording of Article 7(2) which prescribes that in cases where the claim is manifestly unfounded and the plaintiff is found to have initiated the legal proceedings abusively or in bad faith, the Member States shall ensure that the courts may, upon application by the defendant, apply appropriate measures as provided for under national law. These measures may include awarding damages to the defendant, imposing sanctions on the plaintiff or ordering the dissemination of information in accordance with Article 15 of the Directive.[219]

While the recognition of the negative impact that abusive litigation may have is to be welcomed, it is not clear how it is to be enforced.[220] Article 7(2) of the Directive provides that the Member States may provide that these measures are dealt with in separate proceedings. Such a solution seems not to be completely satisfactory, particularly in ex-employer–ex-employee cases. Where the enforced information is in fact not a trade secret, any remedy should be denied. However, where the secret status of the information is unclear, where the information is intertwined with the employee's skill and knowledge, or where litigation is conducted by the plaintiff in such a way as to maximise the defendant's costs, pursuit of a claim might in fact have the goal of limiting competition and thus be abusive, especially if the information is not of decisive importance for the competitive position of the employer. Thus, even if the injunction is denied, the winning defendant might be financially damaged, as in the case of enforcement of broadly drafted post-employment agreements, which might result in the elimination of a competitor from the market by the time a decision on the merits of the case is issued. Considering the abusive character of litigation in separate proceedings forces the former employee to instigate new court action (in the form of separate proceedings or a counterclaim), thus putting on him

[218] This requirement has the character of full harmonisation according to Art 1(1) TSD. See also Recital 22 TSD.

[219] The possibility to order publication of information concerning the decision of the court has been criticised by Gärtner, with the argument that it might deter the holder of the information form enforcing his rights, Gärtner, 'Zum Richtlinienentwurf über den Schutz von Geschäftsgeheimnissen' 650, 652. It is submitted that Art 15 provides sufficient safeguards in (2) and (3).

[220] The MPI Position Paper correctly points out that where the claims are raised without legal cause, the courts are likely to dismiss the action, possibly imposing the duty to reimburse the costs of the other party, and will not issue a positive decision stating the abusive character of litigation. Thus, according to the Position Paper, it should be clarified that the measures against a litigant abusing his rights should result from a separate claim or counterclaim and that the sanctions should include damages covering full costs of legal help, MPI Position Paper paras 42–44.

additional burden and costs. Implementation of measures laid down in Article 7(2) of the Directive in the main proceedings would be a better deterrent against abusive litigation.

Furthermore, abusive-litigation aspects should be considered when granting a remedy in the main proceedings, in particular a final injunction, which is granted after a full assessment of the merits of the case. Such consideration is possible because the catalogue of factors taken into account when granting an injunction pursuant to Article 13(1) of the Directive is not exhaustive. Furthermore, Article 7(2) of the Directive has the character of minimum harmonisation, so the Member States may prescribe, and the courts may include, abusive litigation as a factor in denying or limiting a final injunction, as seems to already be the case in Germany (Section 8(4) UWG) and in the United Kingdom. Nevertheless, from the perspective of conflict of interest in the employee-mobility scenario, it seems that the goal of harmonisation would be better served by explicitly including the abusive character of the claimant's behaviour in the catalogue of factors to be taken into account when granting an injunction pursuant to Article 13(1) of the Directive.

Another way to safeguard the rights of defendants is suggested in the MPI Position Paper. Its authors propose to include in Recital 12 (Recital 22 in the final text of the Directive) an obligation that the sanctions for abusive litigation be subject to the same general obligations of effectiveness and dissuasiveness as those prescribed in Article 6 of the Directive for the remedies contained therein.[221]

As part of the discretionary power to grant a remedy under the rules of fairness and equity, and at the request of the defendant, Member States should provide that the court may order damages instead (in lieu) of injunction (Article 13(3) of the Directive).[222] Under the Directive, this possibility is available only where the defendant is a person who obtained information from another who was using or disclosing the secret unlawfully and where that person neither knew nor had reason to know that the use or disclosure was unlawful, where issuance of an injunction would cause disproportionate harm to the alleged infringer and where pecuniary compensation appears reasonably satisfactory. The damages awarded shall not exceed the amount of royalties or fees which would have been due if the defendant had requested authorisation and are payable for the time for which the use of the information could have been prohibited. The possibility to apply such a remedy in the context of employee mobility is analysed infra.[223]

[221] MPI Position Paper para 41.
[222] See also Recital 29 TSD.
[223] Chapter 5, part V.

The question of whether an injunction may be issued after the information has lost its secrecy does not seem to be addressed by the Directive, although it may be included in the proportionality test, since an injunction, at least against disclosure, does not serve any purpose once the information is no longer confidential. Both under German and UK law, an injunction may not be issued once the information has lost its secret status. In this respect the Directive foresees termination of the injunction by revocation 'or otherwise', upon request by the defendant, when the information ceases to be secret for reasons which cannot be attributed to him.[224] This seems to correspond to the action based on circumstances or defences which occurred after termination of oral proceedings preceding the issuance of the injunction (*Vollstreckungsabwehrklage*) pursuant to Section 767 ZPO under German law. Since the Directive includes a condition that the disclosure occurred for reasons which may not be attributed to the defendant, it seems that the prohibition of use of the information may continue despite its disclosure if that was attributable to the defendant. This seems to correspond to the position presented in Germany,[225] but not in the United Kingdom, which seems to accept the termination of a springboard with disclosure of the information.[226]

2 Scope of Prohibited Acts

The injunctive relief, under the Directive, may relate to prohibition of use or disclosure of the information, as well as to the production of goods incorporating the secret information.[227] In this sense the rules applicable both in Germany and the United Kingdom seem to comply with the Directive.

3 Duration of the Injunction

According to Article 13(1) and Recital 27 of the Directive, an injunction may be granted for an unlimited period of time or for a limited duration. The possibility to limit the duration of the injunction in time seems to be derived from the principle of proportionality.[228] Thus, a decision to limit the effect of the order in time may be a result ia of balancing the interests of the parties to the dispute and of the public.

[224] Art 13(2), Recital 27 TSD.
[225] Körner, 'Befristete und unbefristete Unterlassungstitel bei Wettbewerbsverstößen' 909, 915.
[226] Batteson, 'Gaining Confidence in the Law of Confidence' 714, 715; Gurry on Breach of Confidence para 14.38.
[227] Art 12(1)(a)–(b) TSD.
[228] Grassie, 'Trade Secrets: The New EU Enforcement Regime' 677, 680.

In cases where limitation of the duration is foreseen, it should correspond to the time sufficient to eliminate any commercial advantage which could have been derived from the unlawful acquisition, use or disclosure of the trade secret. This corresponds to the concept of 'springboard' injunctions as applied by the German and the UK courts.

4 Summary

The Trade Secrets Directive provides for minimum harmonisation relating to the granting of injunctions where the court finds unlawful acquisition, use or disclosure of a trade secret. It appears that the laws in the analysed jurisdictions will not need to be substantially amended in that respect. Moreover, in Article 13 the Directive introduces compulsory safeguards which need to be considered when granting and framing injunctions, imposing the duty to balance various factors, including the interests of the parties and the public. In this respect it appears that the automatic grant of a remedy is not supported by the Directive[229] and a full consideration of various factors, some of which are exemplified in Article 13(1), will be necessary.

The application of all the remedies is subject to the rules of proportionality (Article 7(1) of the Directive) known in EU law. Another interesting development is the introduction of considerations relating to abusive litigation. Under Article 7(2) of the Directive, the Member States must ensure the possibility to apply for measures against abusive litigation. The fact that this may be done in separate proceedings seems not completely satisfactory in the context of employee mobility. Nevertheless it is suggested that abusive litigation may be included as a factor to be borne in mind in the balancing exercise pursuant to Article 13(1) of the Directive.

E Summary: Balancing Injunctions in Cases of Infringement of a Right to a Trade Secret by a Former Employee

All of the analysed legal orders recognise the primary role which an injunction plays in safeguarding the rights to a trade secret. Whether based on statute or on rules of equity, injunctions may be granted where actual or threatened breach of statutory, implied or contractual duty is found.

The scope of an injunction corresponds to the scope of the infringement. Thus, prohibition may cover the disclosure and use of the

[229] See also Art 7(1) TSD prescribing proportionality and having character of full harmonisation.

information, including production of goods which incorporate the trade secret. Under the doctrine of inevitable disclosure applicable in some jurisdictions in the United States, the prohibition may also include working for a competitor, where such work would necessarily include the use of the secret information.

While the grant of an injunction is not possible once the information has lost its secret status, the jurisdictions analysed take various approaches to a situation where the loss of secrecy occurs after the final injunction has been issued. Generally, in such a case it is for the ex-employee to apply to the court for an order terminating the injunction. However, in the United Kingdom an injunction terminates automatically with the loss of secrecy. In the United States it may continue despite loss of secrecy, for the time necessary to offset the head start which the former employee has obtained over competitors who did not have access to the information. This seems also to be the approach presented in the Trade Secrets Directive.

The legal orders analysed present differing approaches as to how long an injunction should last.

In Germany, if the information was obtained dishonestly, the order is generally granted for an unlimited period of time. An order not to disclose information is also usually of unlimited duration. Limitation of the duration of an injunction is possible only if the information was obtained in an honest way, but its use would be unfair. The appropriate duration of an injunction in such a case should correspond to the time necessary to develop this information independently, thus mitigating the competitive advantage obtained through early access to the secret. The requirements determining this period of time are relatively strict and thus it seems that it is more likely that a time-limited injunction will be issued in case of secrets relating to clients, since the time needed to establish client relations is thought to be easier to determine than the time necessary to develop a technical secret.

In the United Kingdom, the injunction is usually granted for an unlimited period of time, unless the future date of disclosure of the information is clearly determinable. It is also possible for the court to grant a time-limited springboard injunction for the time which would have been needed in order to develop the information independently. The UK courts are more willing to grant injunctions against use of technical secrets; prohibition of use of client information is approached with caution as it amounts to limitation of competition.

US state laws present a similar approach to the courts in the United Kingdom, but under the UTSA an injunction may as a rule be granted only for a limited time.

The full balancing of interests, including the consideration of the rights of the parties to the dispute, the public interest in competition and the interests of third parties, is included in the decision on granting and framing the remedy under the laws of United Kingdom and the United States. It seems that in Germany, balancing the interests of the parties is a factor in determining the scope and duration of the remedy, but that the decision to grant is predetermined by the finding of infringement, unless a less burdensome measure may be applied. The approach taken in the Trade Secrets Directive goes even further than the common-law jurisdictions, by expressly subjecting both the grant and the framing of the injunction to the principle of proportionality and by including a non-exhaustive list of factors for consideration.

Due to the fact that in all the jurisdictions analysed the grant and framing of an injunction is a result of the consideration of all the circumstances of the case, it is difficult to derive any comprehensive guidelines from their comparison. However, the distinction between an injunction prohibiting use and an injunction prohibiting disclosure needs to be stressed. It is considered that the primary goal of an injunction protecting a trade secret is to maintain the secret character of the information and thus its value. The prohibition of use of the information, especially where such use does not disclose the secret, should be approached with caution. Unlike preservation of secrecy alone, injunction against use may limit the possibilities of the former employee to undertake a competitive activity. Thus, it is considered that where the information is not disclosed upon use, no dishonesty on the part of the employee is found and where the possibility to use the information influences the employee's post-employment professional perspectives, the injunction should be limited to the prohibition of disclosure, leaving it for the employee to use the information and maintain its secrecy. Such an approach encourages competition and at the same time preserves the trade secret, which in some cases may ensure the necessary equilibrium between the interests of the employers, the employees and the public.

III Preliminary Injunction[230]

Preliminary injunctions have a similar goal to final ones: ensuring the observance of a duty. However, being provisional measures, they are

[230] Injunctions issued before the final decision on the merits of the case are referred to as interlocutory, temporary, preliminary, provisional, pendente lite or interim, see Bryan A Garner (ed), *Black's Law Dictionary* (9th edn Thomson Reuters 2009) 855, 889. Those terms are used interchangeably in this book.

issued in speedy proceedings before the conclusive decision on the merits of the case, at a stage when a detailed evaluation of the parties' submissions and evidence is not possible. Furthermore, they are sometimes issued ex parte, without the opportunity for the defendant to present his case. In those circumstances the conflict of interests becomes even more visible than in the case of final injunctions. Immediate prohibition of disclosure or use of information without detailed evaluation of the circumstances of the case might limit competition from the former employees and reduce their chances in the job market. On the other hand, a quick reaction to threatened disclosure of the information might be the former employer's only chance to prevent loss of secrecy and with it the loss of the information's competitive value.

Thus, the balancing of interests of the parties is an essential element of the decision on whether to grant a preliminary injunction and how to frame it. This assessment is at the centre of the analysis presented below.

Preliminary injunctions may be used to prevent disclosure or use of trade secrets, but also to preserve evidence to be used in the proceedings on the merits of the case.[231] As this function of preliminary injunctions has no direct bearing on the mobility of employees, it goes beyond the scope of this book and will not be analysed in detail.

A Preliminary Injunctions in Cases of Threatened Infringement of a Right to a Trade Secret by a Former Employee in Germany

1 Requirements for Grant

Preliminary injunctions may be granted in accordance with Sections 935 ff ZPO. They are issued prior to the final decision on the facts of the case, subject to limited evaluation of evidence and within a short period of time. Therefore, the discretion and flexibility of the courts in issuing preliminary injunctive orders is broader than in case of final injunctions.

The plaintiff must show that he has a valid claim against infringement of a right to a trade secret (prima facie case; *Verfügungsanspruch*) and that there exists an imminent threat of injury of this right or impediment to enforcement of this right unless a preliminary injunction is issued urgently (a reason for interim relief; *Verfügungsgrund*) (Section 935 ZPO).[232] The

[231] Cf in the United Kingdom Anton Piller (search) orders, Gurry on Breach of Confidence para 18.80; in the United States Peterson 13–6. In Germany claims for information (S 242 BGB) and inspection (S 809) BGB, are measures separate from injunctions, see Bauer/Diller paras 862–866; Harte-Bavendamm in Harte/Henning §17 paras 64–65.

[232] Sosnitza in Ohly/Sosnitza §12 paras 110–114.

court will determine both the existence of the right as well as the threat of infringement on the balance of convenience (Sections 936, 920(2) and 294 ZPO),[233] assessing prima facie the facts and argumentation presented by the plaintiff as well as any evidence available, such as documents or affidavits.[234]

A preliminary injunction prohibiting the former employee from disclosing or using a secret information or from undertaking a competitive activity has the same effect as a permanent injunction.[235] However, before the merits of the case are fully considered, the former employer applying for such a provisional measure must show an objectively justified threat that, lacking the measure, his right will be lost or its enforcement will be hampered. This must be assessed under consideration of all the facts of the case and the interests of the parties.[236] This is despite the fact that under Section 12(2) UWG the urgency of issuing a remedy is presumed.[237] The decision whether there exists a need for urgent issuance of a remedy is made inter partes[238] and includes the assessment of the positions and the behaviour of the parties involved, their interests and the effect that granting a preliminary injunction would have on their interests and positions.[239] The interests of third parties and of the public are not part of this analysis.[240]

Taking into consideration the serious effect of injunctive relief, Bauer and Diller argue that showing that infringement is threatened is not enough to obtain a preliminary injunction. Rather, the ex-employer

233 Bauer/Diller para 895.

234 Sosnitza in Ohly/Sosnitza §12 para 133.

235 Although generally undesirable, this effect is accepted, since time is of the essence in the trade secrets cases and other remedies may not provide adequate redress for the damage in the form of loss of secrecy or loss of market position, Barbara Reinhard and Tina Kliemt, 'Die Durchsetzung arbeitsrechtlicher Ansprüche im Eilverfahren' (2005) NZA 545, 550–551.

236 Henrik Holzapfel, 'Zum einstweiligen Rechtsschutz im Wettbewerbs- und Patentrecht' (2003) GRUR 287, 289–290, 292; Sosnitza in Ohly/Sosnitza §12 para 115; Bauer/Diller para 892. See also Konrad Retzer, 'Wiederlegung der „Dringlichkeitsvermutung"durch Interessenabwägung?' (2009) GRUR 329, 331–332 with further references. Retzer seems to accept the application of the presumption of urgency, but proposes a very low threshold for rebutting it, based on argumentation of the respondent, ibid 332–333.

237 Holzapfel, 'Zum einstweiligen Rechtsschutz im Wettbewerbs- und Patentrecht' 287, 291; Grosch in Ann/Loschelder/Grosch 409; Sosnitza in Ohly/Sosnitza §12 para 115.

238 Sosnitza in Ohly/Sosnitza §12 para 116. Thus, an argument that the applicant for a preliminary injunction did not pursue similar behaviour by others may not be used as an argument for denying an injunctive order, ibid para 120.

239 Thus, the balancing of interests is referred to by some as a third requirement for granting a preliminary injunction, see Holzapfel, 'Zum einstweiligen Rechtsschutz im Wettbewerbs- und Patentrecht' 287, 289 with further references.

240 Retzer, 'Wiederlegung der „Dringlichkeitsvermutung"durch Interessenabwägung?' 329, 329.

applying for this provisional measure should show which concrete negative effects such infringement would have.[241] It should be sufficient to show which clients could be targeted by the departed employee or which technical secrets are at stake, and how this would negatively impact the former employer. Evidence that the former employee has already approached certain clients or has made preparations to use the secret information may be sufficient,[242] although production of such evidence is not necessary to obtain a preliminary injunctive order.[243] In the case of technical trade secrets, Grosch also calls for caution. He argues that establishing the existence of threat of infringement of a technical secret in preliminary proceedings may be even more difficult than in the case of patents. From this perspective, and considering the effect of a preliminary injunction, courts should not presume urgency and refrain from detailed assessment of the case. If the aggrieved employer fails to sufficiently substantiate infringement and urgency, provisional protection should be denied.[244] Thus, full consideration of the interests of the parties seems applicable.[245] Cases where a preliminary injunction has been denied include abusive litigation.[246]

Issuing a preliminary injunction based on (threatened) breach of contract also requires showing the threatened breach and the need for urgent action.[247] The inapplicability of the presumption of urgency from Section 12(2) UWG implies full balancing of interests of the parties involved. In particular, in case of application for a preliminary injunction based on infringement of an NCA, the court may deny relief where the former employer has failed to pay the employee the compulsory compensation for the limitation of his competitive activity.[248]

According to Holzapfel, the balancing of interests is an independent element of the decision made by the court issuing a preliminary injunction. Thus, he argues that there are no particular differences in those proceedings between cases of unfair competition, patent law and

[241] Bauer/Diller para 892 with reference to LAG Hamm judgment of 12.09.2006, 7 Sa 1356/06 para 28.
[242] LAG Niedersachsen judgment of 08.12.2005, 7 Sa 1871/05 paras 62–63.
[243] Bauer/Diller paras 892–893.
[244] Grosch in Ann/Loschelder/Grosch 409.
[245] Retzer, 'Wiederlegung der „Dringlichkeitsvermutung"durch Interessenabwägung?' 329, 333.
[246] OLG Düsseldorf judgment of 24.05.2005, I-20 U 25/05 MMR 2005, 776, where a lawyer of an applicant for a preliminary injunction managed a webpage in order to create a competitive relationship with the respondents, with a view to obtaining costs of representation.
[247] Retzer, 'Wiederlegung der „Dringlichkeitsvermutung"durch Interessenabwägung?' 329, 331; Sosnitza in Ohly/Sosnitza §12 para 115.
[248] Bauer/Diller para 893.

generally applicable rules of civil procedure. The central consideration is that a decision in a preliminary injunction case is issued without assessing the merits of the case. Thus, the essential factors to be taken into consideration should be the likelihood of success on the merits of the case and the need to protect the interests of the parties.[249] Drawing a comparison with patent law, he argues that it will often be the respondent who is facing more serious consequences if an injunction is issued, including stopping production and insolvency resulting therefrom.[250] It is argued here that even though patents and trade secrets show many similarities, the considerations applicable when issuing a preliminary injunction in patent cases are not directly transferable to proceedings against former employees in trade-secrets cases. While determining the likelihood of infringement may be difficult in both the case of patents and trade secrets, the loss incurred by the patent owner in case of denial of a preliminary injunction may usually be compensated in damages.[251] The risk on the part of the holder of a trade secret is more significant: lack of an immediate reaction might lead to disclosure of the information. For this reason, it is considered here that the interests of both parties to the dispute should be given particular weight when granting an injunction against use or disclosure of a trade secret by a former employee.

The condition that a preliminary injunction may only be issued where it is urgently necessary to repel a threatened or continued infringement, which cannot be done in proceedings on the merits, requires that this remedy be applied for without undue delay. If this is not the case, the request will be denied due to lack of legal interest in obtaining provisional protection.[252] The time after which the delay is too long to warrant protection depends on the facts of the case and varies between one and two months from detection of the infringement or threat thereof.[253] Such a strict approach has been criticised with the argument that detection of infringement and collection of evidence is particularly difficult in trade-secrets cases, where the infringing activity or preparations for it might be taking place secretly. Gathering evidence appears particularly difficult in

[249] Holzapfel, 'Zum einstweiligen Rechtsschutz im Wettbewerbs- und Patentrecht' 287, 294. Holzapfel correctly points out that the presence or absence of fault should not be included as part of the balancing of interests, since it is part of assessing the existence of a claim, which in any case is only subject to a prima facie consideration in preliminary injunction proceedings, ibid 290–291.

[250] Ibid 287, 293–294.

[251] Ibid 287, 293.

[252] LAG Hamm judgment of 12.09.2006, 7 Sa 1356/06 para 27; Sosnitza in Ohly/Sosnitza §12 para 117; Bauer/Diller para 894.

[253] Désirée Demuth, 'Neue Maßstäbe für einstweilige Verfügungsverfahren in Wettbewerbssachen' (2011) GRUR 404; Sosnitza in Ohly/Sosnitza §12 para 117–118.

the case of departed employees who are no longer under the control of their former employer. With this in mind Grosch calls for consideration of the measures taken by the holder of the information upon detection of the (threat of) infringement, with a view to verifying the information and enforcing his rights.[254] This should allow for a more flexible assessment of whether the application for the injunctive order has been filed without undue delay.

Apart from those conditions, the interests of the respondent are furthermore safeguarded by the possibility to apply for compensation of the damage he incurs as a result of complying with a preliminary injunction which turns out to be unjustified or is terminated due to inaction by the plaintiff in pursuing the merits of the case (Section 945 ZPO).[255] This future claim may be safeguarded by a decision of the court to issue the preliminary injunction upon filing by the applicant of a security.[256]

A preliminary injunction may, in particularly urgent cases, be issued ex parte, without hearing the defendant (Section 937(2) ZPO).[257] According to Bauer and Diller, this may be only exceptionally the case in post-employment cases, as the courts have the power to schedule the hearing within a shortened period of time.[258] It is submitted here that issuing an injunctive order without hearing the ex-employee may have particularly negative consequences in the context of employee mobility, since it reduces the possibility of the court to consider the interests of the particular employee. Taking into account that an injunctive order prohibiting a particular activity by an ex-employee may affect his livelihood and freedom to work (Article 12 GG), it is essential to enable him to present his case before the decision is made.

2 Scope of a Preliminary Injunction

After considering the available facts of the case as well as the evidence provided, it is in the discretion of the court to determine the scope of the provisional injunctive measure.

In particular, even if the ex-employer has a right to prevent any competitive activity by the former employee, stemming e.g. from a contract, the court may decide to issue a preliminary injunction

254 Grosch in Ann/Loschelder/Grosch 409–410.

255 Sosnitza in Ohly/Sosnitza §12 paras 193–211.

256 Ss 921 ZPO, 936 ZPO; Christian Berger and others, *Einstweiliger Rechtsschutz im Zivilrecht* (Erich Schmidt Verlag 2006) 342. Retzer argues for a more frequent application of such a solution in Retzer, 'Wiederlegung der „Dringlichkeitsvermutung“durch Interessenabwägung?' 329, 333.

257 Sosnitza in Ohly/Sosnitza §12 paras 139–140.

258 Bauer/Diller para 890.

prohibiting only particular activities of the employee, e.g. – if the employee has started independent competitive activity – only those activities which are particularly harmful for the ex-employer and not this activity altogether.[259] The discretion in determining the scope of the order must be exercised carefully, since a preliminary injunction prohibiting the use or disclosure of information in fact has the same effect as the performance of the main obligation,[260] rather than preservation of the status quo pending a final decision, as is the usual case for preliminary measures. Despite its gravity, this effect is necessary, since where preservation of the confidentiality of the information is at stake no other measures fit the purpose.[261]

The necessity to make it clear for the ex-employee what he may and what he may not do requires also in the case of preliminary injunctions that the prohibited acts are expressed clearly and unambiguously, in the same way as in a final injunction.[262]

3 Duration

As a rule, preliminary injunctions are issued without setting a final date. However, on application by the respondent (ex-employee), the court may oblige the former employer to start proceedings on the merits within a prescribed period of time (Sections 936, 926(1) ZPO). If that is not done, the court will terminate the preliminary injunction upon application by the respondent (Sections 936, 926(2) ZPO).[263] Similarly, the court will terminate the preliminary injunctive order upon application by the former employee in case of change of circumstances after the order has been issued (Sections 936, 927 ZPO).[264] This may be the case if the information becomes public or when the decision on the merits is issued.[265]

4 Summary

Preliminary injunctions in Germany are issued if the applicant for such measure shows that he has a valid claim against infringement of his right to a trade secret, where there is a threat of injury or continuation of injury of that right and for that reason a court's action is urgently needed. Since

259 Bauer/Diller para 896.
260 Ohly in Ohly/Sosnitza §17 para 43.
261 Bauer/Diller para 888.
262 Reinhard and Kliemt, 'Die Durchsetzung arbeitsrechtlicher Ansprüche im Eilverfahren' 545, 551; Sosnitza in Ohly/Sosnitza §12 para 130. See also supra Chapter 5, part II, point A.2.
263 Sosnitza in Ohly/Sosnitza §12 paras 153–158.
264 Sosnitza in Ohly/Sosnitza §12 paras 159–165; Kalbfus para 438.
265 Sosnitza in Ohly/Sosnitza §12 para 162.

the order is issued based on a prima facie assessment of evidence, but has the same effect and scope as the final decision on the merits of the case (prohibition of use or of disclosure of the information), the balancing of interests of the parties to the dispute becomes essential in the decision-making process.

The interests of the parties must be considered with a view to the summary nature of the proceedings and the resulting court decision. That is why it is necessary for the court to consider whether the applicant for the measure sufficiently has substantiated his claim and the need to issue the injunction on a preliminary basis, taking into consideration the short period of time which he had to prepare his case. Based on this, the likelihood of success on the merits of the case is assessed, as well as the effect that issuing or denying the order would have on the parties. As part of this assessment, it needs to be decided whether the urgency in issuing the order is justified.

The courts have considerable discretion in assessing the facts of the case and deciding on the order.

It is also possible for the court, when granting an injunction, to impose an obligation on the applicant (ex-employer) to commence the proceedings on the merits of the case within a prescribed period of time. This is done upon application by the respondent (ex-employee). Considering the often weaker position of the employee as party to the proceedings, it would be desirable to enable the courts to impose such an obligation ex officio. Furthermore, it would be desirable to impose relatively short time limits for filing the action in the main proceedings, so that the duration of the preliminary injunction and the resulting legal uncertainly are reduced to a minimum.[266]

Another way to reduce the negative impact of a preliminary injunction on the interests of the ex-employee is to make issuing the injunctive order conditional on the filing of a security. More frequent application of this measure is advocated in the literature.[267]

Despite the fact that interim injunctions effectively preserve the rights of former employers, due to their effect which equals that of a final injunctive order, their issuance should be reduced to the necessary minimum. German law seems to provide tools allowing for issuance of balanced preliminary injunctions.

[266] As point of reference, the Trade Secrets Directive prescribes in Art 11(3)(a) a default time limit of 20 working days or 31 calendar days.

[267] Retzer, 'Wiederlegung der „Dringlichkeitsvermutung“durch Interessenabwägung?' 329, 333.

B *Preliminary Injunctions in Cases of Threatened Infringement of a Right to a Trade Secret by a Former Employee in the United Kingdom*

1 Requirements for Grant

The conditions under which the court may issue an interim injunction have been established by the House of Lords in *American Cyanamid v Ethicon.*[268] Such injunctions may take various forms, depending on the circumstances of the case, and may be issued both to stop an ongoing infringing activity and to prevent it.[269]

In accordance with the rules laid down in *American Cyanamid*, in determining whether an interim injunction is to be issued the court should consider whether there is a serious question to be tried, whether damages would be an adequate remedy for the losing party in case of grant or denial of the injunction and whether the balance of convenience supports the position of the plaintiff or of the defendant.[270] As with final injunctions, the courts have broad discretion when deciding on the preliminary orders. Thus, the balancing of interests plays a significant role here as well.

The requirement that the plaintiff shows that with his application there is a serious question to be tried is a low threshold.[271] It is recognised that no assessment of the merits of the case may be made at the interim stage. Rather, the court must be convinced that the claim is not frivolous or vexatious. To that end, it should base its assessment on the undisputed evidence and facts.[272] This threshold was not immediately accepted by the UK courts, and even though today *American Cyanamid* is an established authority, cases may be identified in which determination of merits is to some extent present.[273] In *Series 5 Software Ltd v Clarke,* Laddie J urged acceptance of an assessment of the merits of the case, including contentious issues, as long as it does not require the resolution of complex issues of

[268] *American Cyanamid Co v Ethicon Ltd* [1975] AC 396 (HL). The facts underlying the case related to an infringement of a patent. However, the rules developed by the House of Lords are applied to interim injunctions in general.

[269] In the cases where the infringement has not yet occurred, but threatens, a court may issue a so called quia timet injunction, Gurry on Breach of Confidence para 18.12. See also Spry, *The Principles of Equitable Remedies* 459–461.

[270] *American Cyanamid Co v Ethicon Ltd* [1975] AC 396 (HL) 407–408 (Lord Diplock); Gurry on Breach of Confidence para 18.11.

[271] Stanley 124. Nevertheless, '[a]n employer is not entitled to injunctive relief simply because he seeks it'. Rather, he must establish an arguable case that infringement has occurred or threatens to, *Caterpillar Logistics Services v Huesca de Crean* [2012] EWCA Civ 156 (CA) [66]–[68] (Burnton J).

[272] *American Cyanamid Co v Ethicon Ltd* [1975] AC 396 (HL) 407 (Lord Diplock).

[273] Gurry on Breach of Confidence para 18.13.

disputed facts or law,[274] which seems to correspond to a prima facie standard of evidence. In 2013, in a trade-secrets case concerning an academic publication disclosing an algorithm included in car immobilisers, Birss J considered that even though the standard for granting preliminary injunctions is a flexible one, the court 'should be exceedingly slow to make interim orders if [it] is not satisfied that the claimant will probably succeed at trial'.[275] Consequently, in his decision, he assessed the merits of the case, including the existence of the public interest in the freedom of expression and academic freedom, and the public interest in the security of cars.[276] *Volkswagen* is in fact a case based on freedom of expression, which is not the usual scenario in the employee mobility cases.[277] Nevertheless, it is submitted here that the low threshold of 'serious question to be tried', overly privileges the plaintiffs, i.e. employers, especially since the courts rarely find that this requirement is not fulfilled.[278] Considering the gravity of the interests at stake in cases against former employees, it seems advisable to include a more than rudimentary assessment of likelihood of success at trial, keeping, however, in mind the necessity to issue a quick decision in the interim proceedings.

In case of quia timet injunctions issued before infringement occurs, in addition to the 'serious question to be tried' it is necessary for the plaintiff to substantiate the existence of the threat of infringement and to provide evidence in support thereof.[279]

The two other elements of the test require balancing of various factors. The court should start by determining whether damages issued at trial would compensate the plaintiff for any loss he would have incurred if the interim injunction had not been issued and the defendant had been allowed to continue his activity. According to Lord Diplock, if damages were an adequate remedy, an interlocutory injunction should be denied,

274 *Series 5 Software Ltd v Clarke* [1996] FSR 273 (Ch) 286 (Laddie J). This approach has been endorsed in the literature, see Laura Reynolds and Justin Watts, 'A New Approach to Interlocutory Injunctions?' (1996) 2(2) *CTLR* 66, 68.

275 *Volkswagen AG v Garcia and others* [2013] EWHC 1832 (Ch) [26] (Birss J).

276 *Volkswagen AG v Garcia and others* [2013] EWHC 1832 (Ch) [28] – [29], [43] (Birss J). See also Stanley 124–125.

277 According to Aplin, where freedom of expression is concerned, S 12(3) HRA establishing the higher threshold ('more likely than not') for granting an interlocutory injunction applies to all types of information, including commercial information, Aplin, 'Commercial confidences after the Human Rights Act' 411, 418–419.

278 Particularly in the case of restrictive covenants the courts in interim proceedings usually consider that there is a serious issue to be tried, unless the agreement is obviously unreasonable or not supported by the employer's interest, see Goulding, Croxford, De Marco, Mountford, Nathan, Powell, Windle and Taylor in Goulding para10.32.

279 Spry, *The Principles of Equitable Remedies* 459–461; Gurry on Breach of Confidence para 18.12, with further references.

no matter how convincing the plaintiff's argumentation.[280] In case of trade secrets, damages may only rarely compensate the loss to the holder of the information, especially the loss of secrecy resulting from disclosure may not be compensated that way.[281] Therefore, the court should consider whether, should the defendant succeed at trial, he would be adequately compensated, by way of the plaintiff's undertaking in damages, for any loss which he might have incurred as a result of the interim injunction. If such damages would adequately compensate the defendant, an interim injunction may be issued.[282]

The adequacy of damages for the plaintiff, or defendant must be assessed on a case-by-case basis.[283] Considerations here include the likely amount of damages, the envisaged difficulty of determining their amount and whether the relevant party may be expected to cover them.[284] The effect on the parties is also a factor for consideration. Should the information at hand, due to its breadth or value, be essential for the employer's business and its use or dissemination result in him being put out of business, it is an indication that damages are not an appropriate remedy for the plaintiff.[285] Where the plaintiff's product is already on the market, his loss resulting from denial of an injunction against selling a competing product is likely to be difficult to compensate by way of damages. Where the information relates only to an idea for a product which is neither on the market nor planned to be launched, damages may be a sufficient remedy for the plaintiff.[286] Damages may also be appropriate if the information is being licensed, or could be licensed.[287] A corresponding argumentation may be applied for the

280 *American Cyanamid Co v Ethicon Ltd* [1975] AC 396 (HL) 408 (Lord Diplock).

281 Usually it is difficult to quantify the loss to the holder of the trade secret resulting from its use or disclosure. It might also be difficult to collect evidence in that respect. However, an undertaking by the defendant to keep a record of business transactions and pay some of the revenue into a court account pending trial might be relied on as an argument for denying a preliminary injunction because the plaintiff would be getting adequate damages as compensation, see Stanley 126; Goulding, Croxford, De Marco, Mountford, Nathan, Powell, Windle and Taylor in Goulding para10.35. For an example of such undertakings, see e.g. *Allfiled UK Ltd v Eltis & 16 Others* [2015] EWHC 1300 (Ch) [160] (Hildyard J).

282 *American Cyanamid Co v Ethicon Ltd* [1975] AC 396 (HL) 408 (Lord Diplock).

283 Generally, see Spry, *The Principles of Equitable Remedies* 465–472.

284 For example, due to the financial situation of that party or its conduct so far. Gurry on Breach of Confidence paras 18.20, 18.24, 18.29; *Secktrack NV v Satamatics Ltd* [2007] EWHC3003 (Comm) [74] (Flaux J).

285 *Secktrack NV v Satamatics Ltd* [2007] EWHC 3003 (Comm) [74] (Flaux J).

286 *Coco v Clark Ltd* [1968] FSR 415 (Ch) 428 (Meggary J).

287 Gurry on Breach of Confidence para 18.22. In *AB and CD* [2014] EWHC 1 (QB) [24] Stuart-Smith J, strictly adhering to the *American Cyanamid* structure, distinguished between whether damages are an adequate remedy and whether the damage caused is

defendant. If issuing an injunction would force him to stop production or distribution, this might speak against granting one. Further factors indicating that damages are likely to be inadequate for either party include disruption of business, loss of customers and potential employees and loss of goodwill.[288]

In view of these guidelines, it seems that if the departed employee has not yet commenced a new professional activity, damages might be considered appropriate as compensation for any loss on his part resulting from the interim injunction. This is less likely to be the case if the ex-employee has already started a new business or established goodwill.[289]

The plaintiff's financial position is taken into consideration in the same way as the ability of the defendant to pay damages granted at trial. Thus, the plaintiff is required to give an undertaking to make good any damage incurred by the defendant should the preliminary injunction be later considered unjustified.[290] If there are doubts as to the sufficiency or enforceability of the undertaking in damages, the court may require that the undertaking is supported by security, such as a bank guarantee or payment into the court's account.[291] If the claimant fails to give this undertaking, the court may refuse the application for an interim injunction.[292]

If it is not possible to decide whether damages would be an adequate remedy for either of the parties,[293] the court must decide which party, the plaintiff or the defendant, is favoured under the balance of convenience. This is strongly fact-dependent.[294] Nevertheless, some guidance is available. Lord Diplock suggested that where other factors are evenly balanced, the court should preserve the status quo.[295] This is because it is a

irremediable. He expressed the view that the latter consideration is part of the assessment under balance of convenience. Despite this dogmatic separation, it is submitted here that the two issues can often not be clearly distinguished.

288 *Allfiled UK Ltd v Eltis & 16 Others* [2015] EWHC 1300 (Ch) [118]–[119] (Hildyard J); Gurry on Breach of Confidence para 18.24.

289 Stanley 126–127; Goulding, Croxford, De Marco, Mountford, Nathan, Powell, Windle and Taylor in Goulding para10.37.

290 Civil Procedure Rules, Practice Direction 25A, point 5.1(1); Goulding, Croxford, De Marco, Mountford, Nathan, Powell, Windle and Taylor in Goulding para10.90. Generally, see *Allfiled UK Ltd v Eltis & 16 Others* [2015] EWHC 1300 (Ch) [162]–[166] (Hildyard J); Spry, *The Principles of Equitable Remedies* 472–478.

291 Goulding, Croxford, De Marco, Mountford, Nathan, Powell, Windle and Taylor in Goulding para10.114.

292 Goulding, Croxford, De Marco, Mountford, Nathan, Powell, Windle and Taylor in Goulding para10.90; Gurry on Breach of Confidence para 18.29.

293 Which is frequently the case in the employee competition cases, see Goulding, Croxford, De Marco, Mountford, Nathan, Powell, Windle and Taylor in Goulding para10.38.

294 *American Cyanamid Co v Ethicon Ltd* [1975] AC 396 (HL) 408 (Lord Diplock).

295 *American Cyanamid Co v Ethicon Ltd* [1975] AC 396 (HL) 408 (Lord Diplock); Gurry on Breach of Confidence paras 18.31–18.32. At which point in time the status quo is

lesser inconvenience for the defendant to be temporarily enjoined from doing something which he has not undertaken before. Should issuing a preliminary injunction force the defendant to stop an established professional activity, e.g. in the form of an enterprise, and to start all over again after the trial on the merits, the balance of convenience weighs in favour of refusing the provisional measure.[296]

The strength of the party's case was put forward as another consideration in borderline cases. Due to the fact that the evaluation of evidence is not part of the interlocutory proceedings, the decision regarding the strength of the party's case may be based only on facts and evidence which are not disputed by the parties.[297] Despite this statement in *American Cyanamid*, the merits of the case are considered in an application for interim relief where the likely effect of the interim decision would be to 'decide the dispute against the defendant for good and all'.[298] According to Stanley, in cases involving employers and their former employees, this will usually be the case.[299] Therefore, he argues, it is

measured, is to be decided on the facts of the case. It may be defined as the 'state of affairs before the most significant recent change', see Goulding, Croxford, De Marco, Mountford, Nathan, Powell, Windle and Taylor in Goulding para10.48. In *Allfiled UK Ltd* the Court was of the opinion that this should be the status quo ante the commencement of the breach, but if the aggrieved party delays applying for an interim injunction, a new status quo might be created, *Allfiled UK Ltd v Eltis & 16 Others* [2015] EWHC 1300 (Ch) [153]–[154] (Hildyard J).

296 *American Cyanamid Co v Ethicon Ltd* [1975] AC 396 (HL) 408 (Lord Diplock). In *Potters-Ballotini v Weston Baker* [1977] RPC 202 (CA) 207 (Lord Denning MR) a preliminary injunction was refused with the argument that it would have a disastrous effect on the defendant, requiring him to close a plant which had been built with money raised on loan and which would mean dismissing employees working there. On the other hand, in *Roger Bullivant Ltd v Ellis* [1987] ICR 464 (CA) 482 (May LJ) the court considered that the fact that an injunction would drive the defendant into liquidation was 'of itself nihil ad rem'.

297 *American Cyanamid Co v Ethicon Ltd* [1975] AC 396 (HL) 409 (Lord Diplock). To express an opinion as to the prospect of success of either party was considered 'embarrassing to the judge who will have eventually to try the case' and therefore rejected, ibid 410.

298 See e.g. *Lansing Linde v Kerr* [1991] 1 WLR 251 (CA) 258 (Straughton LJ), where the restrictive covenant being enforced would expire before trial on the merits could be held; Gurry on Breach of Confidence para 18.36. Generally however, the principles established in *American Cyanamid* apply also to cases involving restrictive covenants, *Lawrence David Ltd v Ashton* [1989] ICR 123 (CA) 132, 135 (Balcombe LJ); Hull, *Commercial Secrecy: Law and Practice* para 10.83; Goulding, Croxford, De Marco, Mountford, Nathan, Powell, Windle and Taylor in Goulding para10.25.

299 Similarly 'Post-Termination Restrictive Covenants' 853, 12–18, stressing the particular usefulness of preliminary injunctions where restrictive covenants are concerned. Since their duration normally does not exceed one year, their enforcement is usually transferred to the preliminary phase, making the consideration of the merits of the case necessary.

generally necessary for the plaintiff-employer to make a stronger case than simply presenting a serious question to be tried.[300]

The behaviour of the defendant may also be used as a factor in determining the balance of convenience. If he has already started the infringing activity (e.g. by contacting clients) and refuses to refrain from it, it points to the necessity of issuing an interim injunction.[301] Of course, if the information has already been disclosed and therefore is no longer secret, no injunction will be issued.

2 Scope of Prohibited Acts

Like a final injunction, a provisional injunctive order may restrain the defendant from using and disclosing the information. It may furthermore include an order to perform certain acts, such as delivery up of documents.[302]

Also, as in the case of a final injunction, the clarity of an injunctive order is of prime importance. Thus, the request for a preliminary injunction should contain details of the information to be protected and the acts to be prohibited. Unless those matters are identified clearly enough, the request for a preliminary injunction will be denied.[303]

3 Duration

Considering their function, preliminary injunctions are granted for the time until the decision on the merits of the case is reached at trial. Nevertheless, the courts have agreed to issue springboard injunctions[304] in interlocutory proceedings, in accordance with the rules laid down in *American Cyanamid*.[305]

Of course, such an order should neither give the plaintiff more protection than he needs nor limit legitimate competition.[306] Thus, the courts should more readily issue springboard injunctions in the case of confidential information below the level of trade secrets,[307] while applying the

[300] Stanley 125.

[301] *Secktrack NV v Satamatics Ltd* [2007] EWHC 3003 (Comm) [74] (Flaux J).

[302] *Allfiled UK Ltd v Eltis & 16 Others* [2015] EWHC 1300 (Ch) [160] (Hildyard J); Gurry on Breach of Confidence para 18.41.

[303] *Ocular Sciences Ltd v Aspect Vision Care Ltd* [1997] RPC 289 (Pat) 361 (Laddie J); Gurry on Breach of Confidence para 18.41.

[304] For a discussion of the rules governing the issuance of springboard injunctions, see supra Chapter 5, part II, point B.3.

[305] *Roger Bullivant Ltd v Ellis* [1987] ICR 464 (CA) 481–482 (May LJ); Goulding, Croxford, De Marco, Mountford, Nathan, Powell, Windle and Taylor in Goulding paras 10.60–10.85.

[306] *Roger Bullivant Ltd v Ellis* [1987] ICR 464 (CA) 481–482 (May LJ).

[307] Within the meaning of *Faccenda Chicken v Fowler* [1987] 1 Ch 117 (CA). Those concepts are analysed supra in Chapter 3 part II, points B.2–3.

'usual "until trial or further order"' standard in respect of 'true trade secrets'.[308]

Considering that determining the appropriate duration of the competitive advantage requires a detailed assessment of the facts of the case, acceptance of springboard injunctions during interlocutory proceedings seems to be at odds with the ruling in *American Cyanamid* that no assessment of the merits of the case should be made at the interim stage. In particular, determining the period of time necessary to put the defendant into the position he would have been in, had the infringement not occurred, appears to be an element of the final resolution of the case, which as a rule is made only after trial on the merits. Despite this, the UK courts often issue time-limited injunctions as interlocutory measures.[309]

4 Summary

Interim injunctions are equitable remedies, granted subject to the discretion of the court, within the framework laid down by the House of Lords in *American Cyanamid*. In accordance with this decision, as a general rule, a preliminary injunction will be issued only if there is a serious question to be tried, damages would not be an appropriate remedy and the balance of convenience speaks for issuing this interim measure.

Cases involving employers and their former employees have proved not to completely fit into the framework laid down by the House of Lords. Under *American Cyanamid*, the courts were advised not to make an assessment of the merits of the case during the interim phase. This is often not possible in the post-employment scenario, where the case is de facto resolved at the preliminary stage, due to the fact that by the time the case proceeds to trial, the subject-matter of the proceedings might have ceased to exist, e.g. due to expiry of a restrictive covenant. Thus, the employer-plaintiff requesting an interim injunction must show at least a prima facie case of infringement of his right to a trade secret or threat thereof. The need to assess the merits of the case has furthermore been explicitly recognised in disputes involving freedom of expression, which however seems rarely to be applicable in the employee-mobility scenario.

The assessment of the other two elements of the test is strongly fact-dependent. Even though balance of convenience should only be analysed where damages would not be an appropriate remedy for the plaintiff if his application for the preliminary injunction is rejected, or for the defendant if it is granted, they are often considered together, due to the fact that

[308] *Roger Bullivant Ltd v Ellis* [1987] ICR 464 (CA) 481–482 (May LJ).
[309] Gurry on Breach of Confidence para 18.79.

they frequently depend on similar facts and require consideration of similar interests of the parties concerned.

The balancing of rights of the parties to the dispute is present in the assessment made prior to the decision on application for the interim injunction, as well as in its framing. This may result in granting a springboard injunction against the former employee already at the interim stage. The interests of the employees are also taken into account by way of a compulsory undertaking in damages which is in most cases a condition for granting a preliminary injunction, if other requirements are met. The public interest does not seem to feature in the assessment made by the UK courts at this stage.

C *Preliminary Injunctions in Cases of Threatened Infringement of a Right to a Trade Secret by a Former Employee in the United States*

1 Requirements for Grant

Section 2(a) UTSA and the DTSA[310] allow for enjoining both actual and threatened misappropriation, without differentiating between preliminary and final injunctions. Accordingly, as in the case of final injunctions, the actual and threatened misappropriation may be temporarily enjoined before the final decision on the merits of the case is made.[311]

Due to the fact that a quick reaction to threatened or actual misappropriation is of vital importance in cases involving trade secrets, the issue of a preliminary injunction may make an application for a permanent order obsolete.[312]

State and federal courts apply various tests to determine whether an interlocutory injunction is to be issued.[313] Essentially, the plaintiff applying for preliminary injunctive relief must show irreparable injury if no injunction is granted, that other remedies are inadequate, the likelihood of success at trial and that the injunction will benefit him more than it will harm the defendant, which includes the balancing of private as well as public interests.[314]

[310] 18 US Code §1836(b)(3)(A)(i), as amended by the DTSA.

[311] Quinto/Singer 144.

[312] Berryhill, 'Trade Secret Litigation: Injunctions and other Equitable Remedies' 189, 201. Since they generally serve the same purpose, albeit at a different stage of proceedings, the presence or absence of a preliminary injunction as well as its duration are taken into account upon assessing the application for a permanent injunctive order, ibid.

[313] Quinto/Singer 164–165. The tests applied when deciding on a preliminary injunction include also the test applied for issuing permanent injunctions, as laid down in *eBay Inc v MercExchange LLC* 547 US 388, 391 (US Supr Ct 2006).

[314] Peterson 13-12.

In order to obtain a preliminary injunction, the plaintiff must show that he will suffer irreparable harm (injury) if no injunction is issued immediately. Even if the fact of misappropriation is undisputed, this does not lead to a presumption of irreparable injury; it must be substantiated by the plaintiff.[315] Thus, considering that a preliminary injunction is issued before the full assessment of the merits of the case, the urgent need for this remedy is at the centre of the court's decision.[316]

An interim injunction may be issued only if no other remedy would be appropriate. In particular, if damages would be adequate and the defendant is able to compensate the plaintiff in this way,[317] the grant of an interlocutory injunction is precluded.[318] If damages are 'seriously deficient' as a remedy[319] or where it would be difficult to quantify them, the chances of obtaining a preliminary injunction increase. Other types of irreparable harm relate to loss of business reputation and goodwill and loss of a competitive advantage derived from the use of the secret information.[320] Detriment to a competitive position and thereby irreparable harm is indicated by the presence of an agreement not to compete[321] and is not removed by the ex-employee's promise that he will not use the secrets, in a situation where his new position might inevitably require the use of such information.[322]

Due to the time-pressure during interim proceedings, rather than showing actual breach of duty the plaintiff is required to show likelihood of success on the merits at trial. The plaintiff must present a prima facie case that he has a protectable right and that the defendant has acquired or used the secret information.[323] This is determined as part of the equitable assessment made by the court. If the plaintiff is able to show the threatened irreparable injury (i.e. that the former employee possessed secret information and that he is likely to use or disclose it)[324] and that the balance of hardship is in his favour, showing 'serious questions going

[315] *IBM v Papermaster* 2008 WL 4974508 7 (SDNY 2008); *American Airlines Inc v Imhof* 620 F Supp 2d 574, 579 (SDNY 2009).

[316] Irreparable harm has been described as 'the single most important prerequisite for the issuance of a preliminary injunction' in *IBM v Papermaster* 2008 WL 4974508 7 (SDNY 2008).

[317] For example, if the defendant is a large and solvent company and payment of licensing fees would be appropriate in the circumstances of the case.

[318] Berryhill, 'Trade Secret Litigation: Injunctions and other Equitable Remedies' 189, 202–203;

[319] *Foodcomm Int v Barry* 328 F3d 300, 304 (7th Cir 2003).

[320] Peterson 13-12 – 13-13; Pooley 7-12; Quinto/Singer 166–167.

[321] *IBM v Papermaster* 2008 WL 4974508 9 (SDNY 2008).

[322] *IBM v Papermaster* 2008 WL 4974508 10 note 10 (SDNY 2008).

[323] Pooley 7-8 – 7-9; Quinto/Singer 164–165.

[324] *American Airlines Inc v Imhof* 620 F Supp 2d 574, 580 (SDNY 2009).

to the merits which make them a fair ground for litigation and thus for more deliberate investigation'[325] should be sufficient. Nevertheless, mere allegations do not meet this standard[326] and the plaintiff needs to provide some evidence, although expert testimony is not required.[327]

Finally, the harm which the plaintiff will suffer if the preliminary injunction is improperly denied must be balanced against the harm which the defendant will suffer if the order is so issued.[328] The assessment is based on consideration of all the facts of the case and includes balancing of interests of the parties to the dispute[329] as well as the interests of third parties and the public.[330] In particular it must be borne in mind that the decision is made without full presentation and assessment of arguments and evidence and that the court's opinion on the merits of the case is merely tentative. Thus, even though the considerations underlying the grant of a preliminary injunction are similar to those applicable when balancing interests with a view to granting the final injunction, those factors are assessed from a different perspective.[331]

When balancing the hardships of the respective parties, the court may consider whether the injury to the defendant could be compensated by a bond, i.e. a security filed by the plaintiff in order to compensate the defendant for any costs and damage which may be incurred by him should the preliminary injunction later be considered to have been wrongfully issued. Issuing a bond is a condition for granting an interlocutory injunction by federal and most of state courts.[332] The purpose of this security is to discourage unfounded applications for interim relief and to ensure that the defendant is able to recoup any damage which he might incur as a result of a wrongfully issued injunction, even if the plaintiff is insolvent.[333]

The type of preliminary injunction issued in the most urgent cases is a temporary restraining order. It may be granted ex parte, based merely on

[325] Berryhill, 'Trade Secret Litigation: Injunctions and other Equitable Remedies' 189, 203–204.
[326] Ibid.
[327] Quinto/Singer 168.
[328] Berryhill, 'Trade Secret Litigation: Injunctions and other Equitable Remedies' 189, 202; Quinto/Singer 168.
[329] The interests of the employer may lie in safeguarding his competitive position. With regard to the interests of the employee, the perspective of losing the job with his new employer who would not be willing to await the court's decision at trial and difficulties in finding a new job speak against granting a preliminary injunction, *American Airlines Inc v Imhof* 620 F Supp 2d 574, 586–587 (SDNY 2009).
[330] *United States v First National City Bank* 379 US 378, 383 (Supr Ct 1965) expressing the general rule, although not a case relating to trade secrets and employee mobility; Quinto/Singer 169.
[331] Berryhill, 'Trade Secret Litigation: Injunctions and other Equitable Remedies' 189, 202.
[332] Federal Rules of Civil Procedure Rule 65(c); Quinto/Singer 169–170.
[333] Quinto/Singer 169.

written submissions and without oral argumentation by the parties.[334] It may only be issued for a short period of time, usually between 10 and 20 days,[335] after which an application for a preliminary injunction must be filed.[336]

The issuance of a temporary restraining order, as an equitable remedy, is at the discretion of the court. Due to the fact that the order may be issued without giving the defendant an opportunity to present his case, the plaintiff should provide argumentation and, if available, evidence that he is likely to prevail on the merits; that he would suffer irreparable harm if the order was denied; that possibly other interested parties will be harmed if the order is not issued; and that the balance of interests, including the public interest, speaks in favour of issuing the order. To secure the interests of the defendant, the issuance of the order may be made conditional on the filing of a bond by the plaintiff.[337]

2 Scope of Prohibited Acts

As in the case of final injunctions, depending on the circumstances, the order may prohibit the use or disclosure of the information, or a particular activity referred to in the restrictive covenant serving as a basis for the injunction, in particular solicitation of clients or undertaking a competitive activity. In states which accept the doctrine of inevitable disclosure it is also possible for the plaintiff to obtain an injunction in preliminary proceedings which prohibits the former employee from working for a competitor, even if no agreement to that effect was entered into by the parties to the employment contract.[338]

As in the case of permanent injunctions, the order must define the prohibited conduct clearly and specifically.[339] As the considerations applicable when framing a preliminary injunction correspond to those applicable in the case of a final order, reference is made to the analysis presented supra.[340]

3 Duration

Preliminary injunctions remain in force until the final decision at trial is issued or until the injunction is made permanent by the court.[341]

[334] Rule 65(b) Federal Rules of Civil procedure; Pooley 7-7; Quinto/Singer 161–163.

[335] Pooley 7–8. In federal courts the temporary restraining order expires after 14 days, unless it is extended for a like period, Rule 65(b) Federal Rules of Civil Procedure; Quinto/Singer 161.

[336] Quinto/Singer 161.

[337] Quinto/Singer 163.

[338] Quinto/Singer 146.

[339] Peterson 13-11.

[340] Chapter 5, part II, point C.2.

[341] Berryhill, 'Trade Secret Litigation: Injunctions and other Equitable Remedies' 189, 204.

Nevertheless, it is also possible for the court in preliminary proceedings, exercising its discretion, to issue a time-limited springboard injunction. The principles governing the issuance of springboard injunctions in preliminary proceedings correspond to those applicable when issuing permanent injunctions (see the analysis presented supra).[342]

4 Summary

Preliminary injunctions play a major role in the enforcement of trade secrets, also in the post-employment setting. In fact, once issued, they frequently take the place of the final resolution of the case, since after the time for which the interlocutory injunction is issued the parties are often no longer interested in pursuing the case. The US courts recognise this effect of a preliminary injunction in that they approach them in a very similar way to final injunctive orders. Consequently, the assessment of the merits of the case is an essential part of the proceedings on the interim injunction, even though the standard of evidence differs: the prima facie assessment is necessary in view of the urgency of the remedy.

The interests of the parties and of the public are considered here as well, although the perspective is different from when the issuing of a final injunction is being decided. The irreparability of harm and the balance of hardships are assessed taking into account that an injunction must be issued quickly, without the possibility to fully consider all the facts of the case.

D Preliminary Injunctions in Cases of Threatened Infringement of a Right to a Trade Secret by a Former Employee under the Trade Secrets Directive

The Trade Secrets Directive recognises the danger of disclosure of the information before a court's decision can be obtained.[343] With this in mind, Article 10 contains a catalogue of minimum measures which may be ordered by the Court as a preliminary remedy, and Article 11 contains the safeguards which must be observed when applying those measures. Interim injunctions are subject to the general provisions of Articles 6–9 of the Directive,[344] as are all the remedies foreseen there.

1 Requirements for Grant

The Directive makes the granting of a preliminary injunction subject to provision by the applicant of evidence which may reasonably be

[342] Chapter 5, part II, point C.3.
[343] Recital 26 TSD.
[344] Discussed supra in Chapter 5, part II, point D.1.

considered to be available and which should allow the court to make a decision on the application for the preliminary measure. Thus, the holder of the information must show the existence of the trade secret, his right to this information, that the information has been acquired unlawfully by the respondent and is so used or disclosed, or that such acquisition, use or disclosure is threatened.[345] Substantiation and evidence are required so that the court can make a decision with a sufficient degree of certainty. This provision has a character of full harmonisation.[346] Thus, to the extent that the laws of the Member States allow a decision to grant an injunction to be based only on argumentation provided by the parties, which seems to be, at least theoretically, the case in the United Kingdom,[347] the implementation of Article 11(1) of the Directive would require amendments of their law.

The grant of a preliminary injunction must be the result, as is already the case in the jurisdictions analysed, of a consideration of all the circumstances of the case. In Article 11(2), the Directive prescribes a catalogue of factors which the courts are to take into consideration when granting a preliminary injunction. This corresponds to the one foreseen in the case of final injunctions under Article 13(1), including the legitimate interests of third parties and the public interest. Such considerations are not included by the German courts, which generally concentrate on assessing the need for urgency rather than on the balancing of interests.[348]

Interestingly, the time the applicant took to apply for the preliminary measure is not included in this list.[349] In Germany and in the United Kingdom, a preliminary measure may be denied if the applicant waits too long before filing such an application. Even though this factor has been left out, it is considered that it may still be applied by the national courts, as one of the 'specific circumstances of the case' (Article 11(2) of the Directive).

[345] Art 11(1) TSD. According to Gärtner, this threshold is too high. She suggests that introduction of a reversed burden of proof would better safeguard the interests of the holders of the information, see Gärtner, 'Zum Richtlinienentwurf über den Schutz von Geschäftsgeheimnissen' 650, 652.

[346] Art 1(1) TSD.

[347] Under the *American Cyanamid* test, as analysed supra in Chapter 5, part III, point B.1.

[348] See comments of Hufnagel and Ahrens in Björn Kalbfus and Henning Harte-Bavendamm, 'Protokoll der Sitzung des Fachausschusses für Wettbewerbs- und Markenrecht zum Richtlinienvorschlag über den Schutz von Geschäftsgeheimnissen' (2014) GRUR 453, 456.

[349] The need to include urgency as one of the factors in Art 10(2) (Art 11(2) in the final text of the Directive) has been recognised by the authors of the MPI Position Paper in point 52.

Like all the other remedies laid down in the Directive, grant of a preliminary injunction must be fair and equitable, not unnecessarily complicated or costly as well as effective and dissuasive.[350] Furthermore, the granted remedy must be proportionate in the circumstances of the case.[351]

The interests of the respondent are furthermore taken into account by permitting the court to make issuing of the preliminary remedy conditional on the filing by the applicant of guarantees in the form of a security or equivalent intended to cover the costs and damage to the respondent, if the request for a preliminary injunction later turns out to have been unjustified.[352] This is a solution similar to the one applied in Germany and 'broadly equivalent' to the undertaking in damages applied by the UK courts, although not a compulsory element of a decision to grant an interim injunction.[353] Apart from that, the Directive prescribes compensation for the respondent if the interim order is revoked for reasons pertaining to the applicant, in particular if he does not file the action on the merits within the prescribed time limit,[354] or if it is subsequently found that the application for the preliminary injunction was unjustified due to lack of infringement or threat thereof.[355]

Finally, the Directive foresees in Article 10(2) a compulsory alternative[356] to the preliminary measures, in the form of allowing the continuation of the allegedly unlawful use or disclosure of the information, subject to the filing of a guarantee by the respondent, intended to ensure the compensation of the holder of the information. According to the Directive, such a measure may be applied by the court only if there is little risk that the information will enter the public domain as a result of such use or disclosure,[357] and may never be applied if disclosure would ensue.[358]

The authors of the MPI Position Paper assess this provision critically, explaining that accepting any use of the information might threaten its secret character.[359] This criticism is recognised, but it is considered here that the proposed solution may be an interesting option in the employee

350 Art 6 TSD.
351 Art 7(1)(a), Recital 26 TSD.
352 Art 11(4), Recital 26 TSD.
353 Grassie, 'Trade Secrets: The New EU Enforcement Regime' 677, 681.
354 Art 11(3)(a) TSD.
355 Art 11(5) TSD.
356 Full harmonisation, according to Art 1(1) TSD; MPI Position Paper para 49.
357 Recital 26 TSD.
358 Art 10(2) TSD.
359 MPI Position Paper para 50, stating that the safeguards contained in Art 11(1)–(2) and (4) TSD sufficiently safeguard the interests of the respondent.

mobility context. Where use of the information does not automatically disclose it, it is also in the interest of the former employee or his new employer to safeguard the secrecy of the information. In such circumstances, accepting the use of the information against a guarantee would allow greater flexibility in the application of preliminary measures. However, due to difficulties in determining the appropriate amount of the security, particularly in the interim phase when time is of the essence, it seems that allowing the use of the information subject to a guarantee placed by the defendant will be possible only where that amount can be determined without much effort. This might be possible in the case of some former employees, in particular where the employer licenses information. If it is possible to determine the appropriate amount of the licence fee, because the information relates to similar or identical subject-matter to that licensed, determining the amount of the guarantee will not pose major problems. Where the ex-employee is aware of the licensing rates used by his former employer e.g. because he was involved in the licensing negotiations, setting the amount may even not be contentious between the parties.

2 Scope of Prohibited Acts

The catalogue of minimum provisional and precautionary measures that must be available to the holder of a trade secret is laid down in Article 10 (1) of the Directive. They include prohibition of use and disclosure as well as of their continuation.[360] The courts must also be able to prohibit production, offering, placing on the market as well as export and import of infringing goods and to order seizure or delivery up of such goods to prevent them entering or circulating in the market.[361]

3 Duration

The Directive does not provide for a possibility to issue time-limited preliminary injunctions as it does in the case of final orders in Article 12 (1) and as is the practice in the United Kingdom for both final and interim injunctive orders.

Rather, in Article 11(3) it foresees revocation of the interim injunction upon request[362] by the respondent if the applicant does not institute

360 Art 10(1)(a) TSD.

361 Art 10(1)(b)–(c) TSD. These measures are of secondary importance in the context of employee mobility and therefore remain beyond the scope of this book.

362 Referred to as ‚a positive aspect‘ of Art 11 by Ahrens, in Kalbfus and Harte-Bavendamm, ‘Protokoll der Sitzung des Fachausschusses für Wettbewerbs- und Markenrecht zum Richtlinienvorschlag über den Schutz von Geschäftsgeheimnissen’ 453, 456.

proceedings on the merits within a reasonable time limit prescribed by the court issuing the intermediate measure or, if no such time limit is set by the court, within 20 working days or 31 calendar days, whichever is the longer.[363] This is a solution similar to the possibility for the court to set a time limit for the applicant to file the action on the merits if the respondent so requests, as prescribed in Sections 926(1), 936 ZPO.[364] However, German law does not prescribe how long such a time limit should last. Despite the duration contained in Article 11(3)(a) of the Directive, which national legislators may not depart from, with the aim of providing more far-reaching protection,[365] it seems that upon implementation of the Directive, the national courts will be able to lay down time limits longer than 20 working days or 31 calendar days, if that is reasonable under the circumstances. Only if such a time limit is not set by the court will the prescribed period of time apply. However, whatever its duration, it appears that it will be necessary to start the proceedings on the merits within a determined time. This is to be welcomed, as it reduces the legal uncertainty pertaining to the issuance of preliminary remedies and limits the possibility for the former employers to instigate interim proceedings as a means to harass their ex-employees and limit competition. At the same time, it must be kept in mind that the process of gathering evidence is difficult and time-consuming in cases involving trade secrets. Thus, it will be essential for the court to make a thorough assessment of the circumstances in order to determine the appropriate period of time for filing the action on the merits.

If the interim injunction is revoked for such reasons, the Member States shall ensure that the respondent is entitled to apply for compensation, as prescribed in Article 11(5) of the Directive. Such an application may be dealt with in separate proceedings. This safeguard is supported by the possibility to apply for the measures prescribed in Article 7(2) of the Directive. According to this provision, if the application for the interim injunction is manifestly unfounded or if it has been filed in bad faith or abusively, the Member States shall ensure that the respondent may apply for damages or the imposition of other sanctions on the plaintiff, including dissemination of information in accordance with Article 15. These measures may also be dealt with in separate proceedings.

[363] Art 11(3)(a) TSD.
[364] According to Rauer, despite a differing approach, German law will not need to be aligned with Art 11(3)(a) of the Directive, Nils Rauer, 'Richtlinienentwurf: Europaweit einheitlicher Schutz von Geschäftsgeheimnissen' (2014) GRUR-Prax 2, 3.
[365] Art 1(1) TSD.

As argued supra,[366] the need to initiate separate proceedings to pursue his claim for compensation is burdensome for the respondent, particularly if he is a former employee, who usually has fewer financial and organisational resources and legal experience than his former employer. However, the need to start separate proceedings is less questionable in the case of interim measures than in that of final injunctions. Whether litigation was abusive or unfounded may be decided only upon assessment of the merits of the case, which is not the subject of interim proceedings.

As in the case of final orders,[367] a preliminary injunction is to be revoked if the information ceases to be a trade secret for reasons which cannot be attributed to the respondent.[368]

4 Summary

The Trade Secrets Directive contains several solutions which satisfy its harmonisation goal and appear relevant in the context of employee mobility.

It prescribes substantiation of the application for a preliminary injunction and provision of supporting evidence, so that the court can take the decision on the interim measure with a sufficient level of certainty. This limits the possibility for former employers to initiate interim proceedings abusively.

Recognising the need to issue the decision on a preliminary injunction after assessing all the circumstances of the case, the Directive contains a catalogue of factors which are to be taken into account, including the interests of the parties, the public and third parties. What is not included in the list is the time between discovering the infringement or threat thereof and filing the application for the preliminary measure. This is a surprising omission, considering that interim proceedings are based on the consideration that the decision must be issued urgently.

With respect to the catalogue of factors prescribed for the balancing of interests in Article 11(2) of the Directive, von Mühlendahl has expressed the opinion that considering the lack of clarity of the terminology used in that provision and the differing legal traditions within Europe, harmonisation in that respect should not be expected.[369]

Apart from the explicit recognition of the need to balance the parties' interests, the Directive contains further safeguards for the respondent,

[366] In Chapter 5, part II, point D.1.
[367] Art 13(2) TSD.
[368] Art 11(3)(b) TSD.
[369] Kalbfus and Harte-Bavendamm, 'Protokoll der Sitzung des Fachausschusses für Wettbewerbs- und Markenrecht zum Richtlinienvorschlag über den Schutz von Geschäftsgeheimnissen' 453, 456.

including making grant of the injunction conditional on a security filed by the applicant, compensation for the alleged infringer if the measure is revoked for reasons pertaining to the applicant, and the possibility to allow the continuation of the use by the alleged infringer, against a guarantee.

These are to be welcomed. They may be applied within the court's discretion, and are likely to be useful tools for evening out the imbalance inherent in interim proceedings.

The Directive does not cover the possibility to issue time-limited preliminary injunctions. Instead, the order may be terminated upon request by the respondent, if the proceedings on the merits are not started within the prescribed time limit or if the information is no longer a trade secret for reasons which may not be attributed to the respondent. While the latter is only reasonable, it seems that there is no need to make termination of a preliminary injunction conditional on application by the respondent, if the plaintiff fails to start the proceedings on the merits within the prescribed time limit. After all, both the date and the lack of the necessary action on the part of the plaintiff are clearly determinable, and termination of such an injunction could easily be achieved without obliging the respondent to initiate new court proceedings. Moreover, considering that the preliminary injunction often has the effect of a final resolution of the dispute, the plaintiff may well have no incentive to initiate the proceedings on the merits and have the substance of the case thoroughly assessed. Automatic termination of a preliminary injunction would in such circumstances serve legal certainty.

E Summary: Balancing Preliminary Injunctions in Cases of Alleged or Threatening Infringement of a Right to a Trade Secret by a Former Employee

Preliminary injunctions are a powerful measure in protecting trade secrets. The fragility of the right which is lost with disclosure requires an immediate reaction where the infringing activity has already started or is imminent. However, for the same reason, a preliminary injunction often has the same effect as the final order, even though it was issued without a full assessment of the merits of the case. Since the competitive advantage provided by the information is often short-lived (e.g. in the case of marketing information) the proceedings on the merits may never take place because, by the time the trial on the merits could be held, the holder of the information is no longer interested in its enforcement.

This calls for a cautious application of this remedy. In Germany, United Kingdom and the United States, as well as under the Trade Secrets Directive, consideration of the interests of the parties has been recognised as helpful in that respect.

In the analysed jurisdictions, various tests have been developed in order to determine whether an interim measure should be granted or not. Nevertheless, they all recognise the summary nature of the proceedings and the need to make a prima facie assessment of the available facts and resulting evidence. Therefore, it is a principle common to those countries that the court has broad discretion to grant the preliminary measure and to frame its scope.

The plaintiff or the applicant for the interim injunction must always show that he has a valid claim and that his rights will be or continue to be adversely affected unless the court reacts immediately. This is assessed having regard to all the circumstances of the case. The common law courts put particular weight on the inadequacy of damages as remedy and on the balance of hardship between the parties.

The balance of interest is a consideration recognised in all the jurisdictions analysed. However, while in Germany and the United Kingdom it seems that the balancing exercise concentrates on the interests of the parties, which also includes abusive litigation, in the United States the public interest is also taken on board. This is also the approach presented in the Trade Secrets Directive, which includes the public interest and the interest of third parties in the catalogue of factors to be considered when granting an interim measure. The recognition of the interests of the parties to the dispute is reflected also by the fact that in cases involving former employees, preliminary injunctions may generally not be issued ex parte.[370]

The need to safeguard the interests of the defendant (respondent) is addressed by the possibility of making a preliminary injunction conditional on the filing of a security by the applicant. However, this is a compulsory requirement for issuing an interim measure only in the United States. The Trade Secrets Directive also leaves it to the court's discretion to decide what conditions to attach to the grant of a preliminary injunction.

A reverse solution is introduced in the Trade Secrets Directive, by way of allowing continuation of the allegedly infringing activity subject to the filing of a guarantee by the defendant (respondent). This does not

[370] With the exception of temporary restraining orders in the United States.

seem to occur in any of the legal orders analysed here and has been the object of criticism. As argued supra, while such a solution may make it possible to address some of the problems pertaining to the balancing of interests, it is envisaged that it will be applied only rarely, due to the difficulties in establishing the appropriate amount of guarantee at the interim stage.

Both German law and the Trade Secrets Directive provide for compensation for the respondent if the action on the merits is not filed within the set time limit or proves unjustified. It seems that in the United Kingdom and the United States any such claim would need to be subject to general rules of restitution.

Preliminary injunctions are granted as a rule until the decision on the merits is made at trial. The courts in the United Kingdom and the United States also issue time-limited springboard injunctions, recognising that the interim measure is often the only decision in a particular case. German law takes a different approach: upon request by the respondent, the court may set a time limit during which the applicant should file the action on the merits. If that is not done, the injunction is terminated by the court upon application by the respondent. The respondent may also apply for termination of the injunction if the underlying circumstances change. The Trade Secrets Directive takes a similar approach. As explained supra, automatic termination of the preliminary injunction in such circumstances could be contemplated. It would reduce the burden on the respondent of having to initiate separate proceedings in order to obtain an order terminating the injunction.

IV Damages

In many trade-secrets cases, the injunctions, both final and preliminary, are of primary significance. This is because of the necessity to preserve the confidentiality of the information and due to the difficulties in determining appropriate compensation for loss of secrecy or competitive position. Nevertheless, with respect to infringing acts which have already taken place, the former employer may only apply for damages. Where the information has been disclosed, this might be his only option.

As a result of the perishable nature of secret information, damages are likely to play a secondary role in trade-secrets cases. Consequently, the analysis presented below is made only insofar as pertinent to the main focus of this book: the balancing of interests.

A *Damages in Cases of Infringement of a Right to a Trade Secret by a Former Employee in Germany*

Under German law, damages are available for losses resulting from breach of statutory and contractual duties[371] and have the role of compensating the aggrieved party for the infringement which took place.[372] Thus, they may be awarded only after the infringement is found to have occurred, at trial on the merits and only if the defendant acted with fault.[373]

The law does not foresee special rules for granting and calculating damages for infringement of trade secrets.[374] The general consideration is that the granted damages should put the aggrieved party into the position it would have been in had there been no infringement.[375] Of course, the loss of secrecy cannot be reversed. Thus, in such cases the prevailing methods of compensation are monetary damages for the plaintiff's loss, which includes the loss of competitive advantage due to the use or disclosure of the information by the defendant.[376]

The aggrieved ex-employer may rely on one of three methods of calculation:[377] by applying a licence analogy; by reference to the actual loss he has suffered, including lost income; or by transferring to him the profits which the infringer has made. For claims stemming from contract, only the first two methods of calculation are available.[378]

[371] In case of claims based on unfair competition S 9 UWG, see Ohly in Ohly/Sosnitza §17 para 51; in case of claims based on contract S 280 (1) BGB, see Bauer/Diller para 907; in case of claims based on civil law Ss 823, 826 BGB, see Westermann, *Handbuch Know-How Schutz* 121.

[372] Ss 249ff BGB; Bauer/Diller para 908.

[373] S 9 UWG; Westermann, *Handbuch Know-How Schutz* 121; Bauer/Diller para 907. For an analysis regarding the burden of proof see Bauer/Diller paras 909–911.

[374] It is accepted that the same methods of calculation apply as in the case of intellectual property rights, see BGH GRUR 1977, 539, 542 *Prozessrechner;* BAG judgment of 24.06.1986, 3 AZR 486/84, AP BGB § 611 *Betriebsgeheimnis Nr.4;* Grosch in Ann/Loschelder/Grosch 369; Köhler in Helmut Köhler and Joachim Bornkamm, *Gesetz gegen den unlauteren Wettbewerb* (35th edn CH Beck 2017) §9 paras 1.36–1.36b, and that the case-law concerning IPRs may be applied also in case of trade secrets, Ohly, 'Der Geheimnisschutz im deutschen Recht: heutiger Stand und Perspektiven' 1, 9. Kalbfus pleads for an express statutory provision accepting those methods of calculation, along the lines of the provisions contained in the IPR statutes, Kalbfus para 458.

[375] BGH GRUR 1995, 349, 352 *Objektive Schadensberechnung* with further references.

[376] Kraßer, 'Grundlagen des Zivilrechtlichen Schutzes von Geschäfts- und Betriebsgeheimnissen sowie von Know-How' 177, 182–183; Westermann, *Handbuch Know-How Schutz* 121.

[377] The choice of the method lies with the plaintiff, BGH GRUR 1993, 55, 59 *Tchibo/Rolex II;* Grosch in Ann/Loschelder/Grosch 369–370.

[378] Bauer/Diller para 908; Kalbfus para 449 note 1207. Kalbfus argues for acceptance of the three methods of damages calculation also in cases of infringement of contract, Kalbfus para 456.

The German courts seem not to accept damages for the springboard advantage obtained by the defendant, after the information has been disclosed. Disclosure is considered to be the moment in time when the defendant's activity stops being illicit. The consequences of the infringement from the plaintiff's perspective may however stretch beyond that point.[379] With this in mind it has been suggested by Falck that damages should be granted also for the time after the information has lost the quality of secrecy. This would be the case where, due to infringement, the defendant was able to prepare production, but otherwise would not have been able to start production immediately after the information became publicly accessible.[380] Considering the strict differentiation between the three methods of calculation of damages applied in Germany, it seems that the springboard advantage may be included in the calculation of damages based on the infringer's profits. It is less likely to be taken into consideration when damages are computed by reference to the losses of the holder of the information.

The three methods of calculation of damages are discussed in turn.

1 Licence Analogy

The calculation of damages by licence analogy is based on the assumption that the parties have entered into a licensing agreement. Accordingly, the plaintiff is awarded an amount corresponding to the licence fees which would have been due under such an agreement.[381] Due to the fact that the calculation is a legal fiction, it assumes that the parties were actually willing to enter into such an agreement. Nevertheless, awarding such damages does not create any contractual relationship between them.[382] Thus, even if damages are determined on the basis of licence analogy, this does not exclude granting the plaintiff an injunction against future uses.

The amount of the licence fee is determined by considering the reasonable positions of the parties at the time the licence would have been entered into, considering the duration of the licence relationship (which corresponds to the duration of the infringing activity, until the information enters the public domain[383]); the envisaged use (corresponding

[379] BGH GRUR 1960, 554, 557 *Handstrickverfahren.*

[380] BGH GRUR 1960, 554, 557 *Handstrickverfahren* with comment by Falck.

[381] BGH GRUR 1995, 349, 351 *Objektive Schadensberechnung*; Westermann, *Handbuch Know-How Schutz* 122. For a discussion relating to ex-post and ex-ante analysis of damages, see Grosch in Ann/Loschelder/Grosch 373.

[382] BGH WRP 2002, 214, 218 *Spiegel-CD-Rom.*

[383] Where the information became publicly accessible as a result of the defendant's actions, it is suggested that damages should be computed taking into consideration the point in

to the extent to which the information was used by the defendant); any fixed costs related to the use of the information (which is more relevant where the information is used for manufacturing of products, and less so when the information relates to services); and all the other facts of the particular case.[384] If the information is already being licensed, the rates used in those agreements may be adopted.[385] These considerations have the goal of establishing the amount of licence fees which the holder of the information could have obtained if he had granted a licence on the use of the information.[386]

In most cases the licence fee varies between 1 and 5 per cent of the net price of the product sold by the defendant.[387] In case of complex products, where the trade secret relates only to a part of the final product, the licence fee is still calculated on the basis of the final price, but its rate is lowered to reflect the extent to which the information influenced the final product.[388]

The fact that the defendant was able to use the information for some time without having to pay the licensing fees (and thus could use the corresponding capital for other purposes) puts him in a better position than a licensee who voluntarily entered an agreement with the holder of the information. To address this, the case-law has developed methods of correcting fictitious licence fees, by complementing them by adding a lump sum corresponding to the savings the defendant made as a result of the infringing use, plus prejudgment interest corresponding to the market interest on the capital used instead of paying the licensing fees.[389] This correction is applied in case of IPRs. Nevertheless, it is submitted that damages calculated by way of licence analogy may be supplemented by prejudgment interest in trade-secrets cases as well. The addition of the lump sum appears more problematic, since its calculation is based on the likelihood that the right will be invalidated, or not enforced due to the short time remaining until it expires. This may not be directly transferrable to the trade-secrets cases since the duration of this right as well as

time when the information would have fallen into the public domain 'in due course' i.e. not as a result of the infringement, Kraßer, 'Grundlagen des Zivilrechtlichen Schutzes von Geschäfts- und Betriebsgeheimnissen sowie von Know-How' 177, 184.

384 Westermann, *Handbuch Know-How Schutz* 122.

385 Grosch in Ann/Loschelder/Grosch 374.

386 Bauer/Diller para 908.

387 BAG judgment of 24.06.1986, 3 AZR 486/84, AP BGB § 611 *Betriebsgeheimnis Nr. 4*; Westermann, *Handbuch Know-How Schutz* 122–123. Although in BGH GRUR 1993, 55, 56 *Tchibo/Rolex II*, the court accepted the licence fee in the amount of 12.5 per cent and in BGH GRUR 1991, 914, 917 *Kastanienmuster* that of 10 per cent.

388 Grosch in Ann/Loschelder/Grosch 374.

389 Eberhard Körner, 'Die Aufwertung der Schadensberechnung nach der Lizenzanalogie bei Verletzung gewerblicher Schutzrechte durch die Rechtsprechung zum „Verletzervorteil"und zu den „aufgelaufenen Zinsen"' (1983) GRUR 611, 612–614.

the likelihood that an injunction will be issued is much more uncertain in case of trade secrets than in the case of IPRs.

It is considered here that a ficticious licence calculated by reference to the above factors is an attractive way to determine damages for the use of a secret in the manufacture of products. Licence analogy appears less apt for determination of damages where the information in question relates to clients or marketing. Such information is not likely to be subject to a licence, since it is not used repeatedly: once a particular client is contacted, or a particular marketing plan executed, its competitive value is 'used up' and thus cannot give rise to recurring payments. It may be different in case of marketing know-how relating to methods of doing business. They may be comparable to a technical process and thus be used repeatedly, which would justify regular payments.

2 Plaintiff's Loss

This method of calculation requires that the plaintiff substantiates and provides evidence of his loss resulting from the infringement. This may be done e.g. by showing the loss of income or the reduction of prices necessary to remain on the market. The plaintiff's loss may not be determined by reference to the situation of the defendant.[390]

This method of calculation, despite the fact that it is likely to be most accurate, puts a considerable burden on the plaintiff, often requiring production of confidential documents, such as price lists, contracts, or accounting records, in order to support his claim for damages. This increases the risk of disclosure of further secrets. As a result of these difficulties pertaining to the collection and presentation of evidence, the calculation of damages based on the plaintiff's loss is rare.[391]

3 Infringer's Profit

Given that it would be unfair for an infringer to keep the fruits of his misconduct, damages may be calculated on the basis of the profit he has made as a result of obtaining, using or disclosing secret information in breach of a duty.[392]

In order to use this method of calculation, the plaintiff must show that as a result of the infringement he incurred damage and that the defendant derived profit.[393]

[390] Westermann, *Handbuch Know-How Schutz* 123.
[391] BAG judgment of 24.06.1986, 3 AZR 486/84, AP BGB § 611 *Betriebsgeheimnis Nr.4;* Grosch in Ann/Loschelder/Grosch 383.
[392] Westermann, *Handbuch Know-How Schutz* 123.
[393] BGH GRUR 1962, 509, 512 *Dia-Rämchen II*; Westermann, *Handbuch Know-How Schutz* 123.

The amount of profit made by the defendant may be determined by way of a discretionary assessment by the court under consideration of all the circumstances of the case (Section 287(1) ZPO).[394] For determining damage, only those profits are taken into account which were incurred as a result of the infringement (i.e. direct causality is required).[395] The court has broad discretion in assessing the available evidence in order to determine the profit.[396] Within this framework, the entire income of the defendant is taken into consideration. In particular, the argument that the defendant could have at some point worked out the secret information independently carries no weight.[397]

It is recognised that calculating damages on the basis of the profits made by the infringer may lead to overcompensation of the plaintiff. This result is however accepted with the argument that it would be unfair to allow the infringer to keep any profits from his infringing activity.[398]

4 Summary

German law requires that the plaintiff is fully compensated for the damage resulting from the infringement of his right to a trade secret. In order to determine the appropriate amount the plaintiff may choose one of the three methods available also in case of infringement of IP rights: licence analogy, plaintiff's loss or infringer's profits.

[394] According to Bauer and Diller, even where there are difficulties in determining the amount of the infringer's profit, and thus the damages, the court must make an assessment and may not dismiss the claim for lack of substantiation, Bauer/Diller para 908. See also Wolf J Reuter, 'Wettbewerbsrechtliche Ansprüche bei Konflikten zwischen Arbeitgebern und Arbeitnehmern – Terra Incognita?' (2008) NJW 3538, 3544; Grosch in Ann/Loschelder/Grosch 372. The discretionary assessment of damages in accordance with S 287 ZPO is available for all of the methods of calculation of damages, Kraßer, 'Grundlagen des Zivilrechtlichen Schutzes von Geschäfts- und Betriebsgeheimnissen sowie von Know-How' 177, 182.

[395] BGH GRUR 1962, 509, 512 *Dia-Rämchen II*; BGH GRUR 1995, 349, 351 *Objektive Schadensberechnung*; BGH GRUR 2001, 329 *Berechnung des Verletzergewinns nach Schutzrechtsverstoß*; Grosch in Ann/Loschelder/Grosch 377–378.

[396] BGH GRUR 1993, 55, 59 *Tchibo/Rolex II*; Westermann, *Handbuch Know-How Schutz* 123. For a discussion of which costs on the part of the defendant should be deducted from his profit when calculating damages using this method, see Grosch in Ann/Loschelder/Grosch 379–383.

[397] WRP 2008, 938, 939–940 (BGH) *Entwendete Datensätze mit Konstruktionszeichnungen*; Grosch in Ann/Loschelder/Grosch 375–376, supporting such an interpretation, but suggesting that an exception could be made if the defendant were able to show that the trade secret had only a limited influence on his profits. Critically, especially in cases where the trade secret was used in a complex product or process, see Ohly, 'Der Geheimnisschutz im deutschen Recht: heutiger Stand und Perspektiven' 1, 9.

[398] Joachim von Ungern-Sternberg, 'Einwirkung der Durchsetzungsrichtlinie auf das deutsche Schadensersatzrecht' (2009) GRUR 460, 463, with further references.

Determination of damages is difficult where the right to a trade secret is found to have been infringed, and, depending on the facts of the case and the information in question, not all the methods may be applicable.

Calculations based on either the plaintiff's loss or the infringer's profit pose considerable evidentiary problems. Moreover, showing his loss may require the plaintiff to refer to other confidential information, thus risking its disclosure. Calculation based on the infringer's profits may not be helpful in situations where the infringement results from disclosure of the information. While this may cause considerable damage to the plaintiff, it is not likely to bring a corresponding profit to the defendant. As a result, damages based on licence analogy seems to be the most frequently applied method of calculation.[399]

Still, licence analogy may not always be helpful either. Where the information may only be 'used' once or where the infringement results from disclosure,[400] there might be no basis for calculating a licence fee. That is because a licence implies use of the information. If disclosure occurred but was not accompanied by use, plaintiff's loss seems to be the only reasonable alternative available for calculation of damages.[401]

B *Damages in Cases of Infringement of a Right to a Trade Secret by a Former Employee in the United Kingdom*

In the United Kingdom, monetary compensation may be awarded at trial[402] on various grounds, as common law damages or as equitable compensation.[403] Irrespective of which ground is applied[404] to grant damages, their role is to put the claimant into the position he would have

[399] Mary-Rose McGuire, Björn Joachim, Jens Künzel and Nils Weber, 'Der Schutz von Geschäftsgeheimnissen durch Rechte des Geistigen Eigentums und durch das Recht des unlauteren Wettbewerbs (Q215)' (2010) GRUR Int 829, 834.

[400] Cf Grosch in Ann/Loschelder/Grosch 372 (for calculation of damages on the basis of licence analogy, it must be possible to license the information in the first place).

[401] Grosch in Ann/Loschelder/Grosch 384.

[402] Nathan, Adamson and Taylor in Goulding para 11.02.

[403] In common law, monetary compensation for the claimant's loss is referred to as damages, Stanley 132; Gurry on Breach of Confidence para19.01. In equity, it may be granted in the form of equitable compensation or account of profits, Gurry on Breach of Confidence paras 19.23, 20.02. Due to the fact that those remedies have the same function and are measured in the same way (see Spry, *The Principles of Equitable Remedies* 631), the terms 'damages' and 'compensation' are used interchangeably here.

[404] For a discussion of the issues of jurisdiction to award damages, see Stanley 129; Gurry on Breach of Confidence paras 19.01–19.15, 19.24.

been in had the defendant not infringed his right to a trade secret (breached the obligation of confidence).[405]

As part of the court's discretion in granting remedies,[406] damages are looked at in the broader framework of measures available to sanction particular misconduct.[407] As a result, they may be granted together with an injunction, but also in lieu of an injunction, e.g where the information was disclosed before the decision on the merits was issued by the court, where the enforced restrictive covenant is about to expire, or where under balance of interests the court refuses to grant injunctive relief.[408] Consequently, the court may award damages for future losses resulting from use of the information, if it denies an injunction, or if in spite of the injunction issued, further damage is likely.[409]

As a condition for granting damages, there must exist a causal link between the plaintiff's loss and the defendant's behaviour, e.g. disclosure of the information or breach of a restrictive covenant. To that extent all the plaintiff's losses, both past and future, may be compensated.[410]

1 Compensatory Damages

Damages should correspond to the plaintiff's loss resulting from the infringement (loss of profits).[411] If the lost profit cannot be clearly shown, it is assessed on the basis of the market value of the information,[412] and the methods applied in that respect vary depending on the characteristics of that information.[413] If it could have been purchased in

405 Stanley 131; Gurry on Breach of Confidence para 19.25.
406 Spry, *The Principles of Equitable Remedies* 622, 628, 529.
407 Gurry on Breach of Confidence para 19.25.
408 Nathan, Adamson and Taylor in Goulding para 11.06; Gurry on Breach of Confidence para 19.16. Spry explains that damages will be awarded instead of injunction, as a general rule, where the hardship caused to the defendant by the grant of an injunction 'would so far outweigh the inconvenience caused to the plaintiff if the injunction is denied, that 'it would be highly unreasonable in all the circumstances to do more than to award damages', Spry, *The Principles of Equitable Remedies* 625–626. Thus, it appears that a similar balancing exercise is applicable as in the case of granting injunctions.
409 *Cranleigh Precision Engineering Ltd v Bryant and Another* [1963] 1 WLR 1293 (QB) 1312, 1320 (Roskill J); Gurry on Breach of Confidence paras 19.17–19.19, 19.22. An example of future damage despite the issued injunction may be loss of (further) clients due to reputational damage caused by disclosure of a trade secret.
410 For a discussion relating to the standard of proof in that respect, see Nathan, Adamson and Taylor in Goulding paras 11.09–11.29.
411 *Universal Thermosensors v Hibben* [1992] 1 WLR 840 (Ch) 851 (Nicholls VC); Stanley 131. This measure might be appropriate in the case of information relating to customers and similar, where the plaintiff can show the difference in his profits before and after the infringement, Gurry on Breach of Confidence para 19.28.
412 *Seager v Copydex (No 2)* [1969] 1 WLR 809 (CA) 813 (Denning MR); Stanley 132.
413 *Seager v Copydex (No 2)* [1969] 1 WLR 809 (CA) 814 (Salmon LJ).

the market, e.g. from a consultant, the damages will correspond to the fee which would be charged by such a consultant.[414] If the information is of the sort which may not be freely bought, but requires special skills which only some have (as would be the case for a patentable invention), the damages should correspond to the price which a willing buyer would pay a willing seller.[415] In the case of even more specific subject-matter, e.g. invention unsuccessfully pursued by many, capitalised royalty might be used as a measure.[416] If the information was licensed, the amount of damages might be set at the amount, which a willing licensee would pay a willing licensor.[417]

In the case of damages resulting from breach of contract, the calculation may furthermore be based on the net loss to the plaintiff, so that the employer is placed in the same position as if the contract had been performed.[418] To that extent only reasonable costs will be included in the calculation, and any expenses which the plaintiff would necessarily incur irrespective of the breach are deducted from the sum awarded.[419]

Despite decisions to the contrary,[420] the prevailing view seems to be that the award and payment of damages do not transfer the information to the defendant.[421] This corresponds to the approach presented in German law and is endorsed. Of course, certain infringing acts, such as disclosure of the information, cannot be undone by court decision. However, if the resulting damage is compensated for, this does not result in the transfer of such information which has entered the public domain. Even if damages are computed by reference to a licence which might have been awarded in given circumstances, this is to be treated only as a method of calculating damages and not as an agreement imposed on the parties. Otherwise the infringer would be favoured, by acceptance of his taking information without the holder's consent. It would also be contrary to the recognised purpose of damages, which is to compensate the aggrieved party and not to create a new legal situation.

[414] *Seager v Copydex (No 2)* [1969] 1 WLR 809 (CA) 813 (Denning MR); Gurry on Breach of Confidence para 19.27.
[415] Ibid.
[416] Ibid.
[417] *Seager v Copydex (No 2)* [1969] 1 WLR 809 (CA) 813 (Denning MR); Gurry on Breach of Confidence para 19.28.
[418] Nathan, Adamson and Taylor in Goulding para 11.08.
[419] Nathan, Adamson and Taylor in Goulding paras 11.30–11.31.
[420] *Seager v Copydex (No 2)* [1969] 1 WLR 809 (CA) 813 (Denning MR).
[421] Nathan, Adamson and Taylor in Goulding para 11.117; Gurry on Breach of Confidence para 19.32.

2 Restitutionary ('Gain-Based') Damages[422]

In cases of breach of a contractual duty, the plaintiff may apply for damages calculated by reference to the defendant's gain obtained from the infringement, and the court will make such a calculation if it considers it just. On this basis, the infringer's profit may be transferred to the plaintiff where the claimant has not suffered any actual loss, if this loss is disproportionately lower than the profit made by the infringer, or if the plaintiff is unable to establish his loss.[423] Despite this, damages calculated in this way must not in effect punish the defendant, but be nothing more than 'just compensation' for the plaintiff.[424] This calls for a careful consideration of the case within the court's discretionary powers.

In determining the amount of such damages the court may consider a hypothetical situation in which the parties were negotiating over an appropriate sum at the time the infringement took place. The knowledge of the parties at that point in time plays a decisive role, but it is irrelevant whether the innocent party would have agreed to negotiate. The defendant's infringing behaviour is not to be considered either. The court may include also further factors, depending on the facts of the case, in particular any delay on the part of the plaintiff in pursuing his right.[425]

3 Account of Profits

A remedy similar to damages, which is applied under the rules of equity in the United Kingdom, is account of profits. Its purpose is to take from the infringer the profits which he has gained from his misconduct, with the consideration that it would be unfair for him to retain those profits.[426] It has been described as a 'standard remedy' ia in cases of breach of duty of confidence by an ex-employee.[427]

422 Linda Clarke, 'Remedial Responses to Breach of Confidence: The Question of Damages' (2005) 24 *CJQ* 316, 318; Nathan, Adamson and Taylor in Goulding para 11.39. The term 'restitutionary damages' is somewhat contradictory, since the role of damages is to compensate the claimant's loss, while the goal of restitution is to reverse the defendant's gains. Despite this difference, they usually 'amount to the same thing', Stanley 132.

423 Nathan, Adamson and Taylor in Goulding para 11.39.

424 *WWF World Wide Fund for Nature v World Wrestling Federation Entertainment Inc* [2006] EWHC 184 (Ch) [177] (Smith J); Nathan, Adamson and Taylor in Goulding para 11.64.

425 *WWF World Wide Fund for Nature v World Wrestling Federation Entertainment Inc* [2006] EWHC 184 (Ch) [178]–[179] (Smith J).

426 Gurry on Breach of Confidence para 20.01. Despite the fact that it resembles the method of calculating damages based on infringer's profits applied in Germany and under the Enforcement Directive, in the United Kingdom it is a separate remedy, ibid.

427 Nathan, Adamson and Taylor in Goulding para 11.98 with further references. Similarly Stanley 130.

It is an alternative to a claim for damages, but the claimant's choice[428] as to which remedy to apply for, must be accepted by the court.[429] The court will decide to order account of profits when it is just and equitable that the defendant should not keep any revenue from his misconduct,[430] irrespective of whether the plaintiff suffered any loss.[431] This is decided on a case-by-case basis, and having regard to the interests of the parties to the dispute.[432] Where the right is more of a proprietary nature, so that it is unlikely that it could be bought, it should be afforded stronger protection and the court should consider a remedy in the form of account of profits.[433] This seems to be a high threshold, available probably only upon infringement of the most essential and valuable trade secrets, given that account of profits was denied even in *Seager v Copydex*[434] where the subject-matter was 'closely akin to a patent'.[435]

As with damages based on infringer's gains and the calculation of damages based on infringer's profits in Germany, the calculation of profit upon application of account of profits requires a causal link between the information which was taken from the plaintiff and the profit made by the defendant.[436] As a result, if the information contributed only partly to the defendant's profit, only that portion will be awarded to the plaintiff.[437] As correctly pointed out, this guideline seems more readily applicable to information of an inventive nature relating to products. It is more difficult to assess the part of the profit which should be ascribed to particular information in the case of commercial information relating to clients or to marketing.[438] Determining the appropriate share of profits to be

428 Stanley 130.

429 Nathan, Adamson and Taylor in Goulding para 11.97; Gurry on Breach of Confidence para 20.03.

430 *Vercoe v Rutland Fund* [2010] EWHC 424 (Ch) [339] (Sales J); Gurry on Breach of Confidence para 20.04.

431 This indicates a deterrent function of account of profits as a remedy, which is based on a consideration that there is a public interest in the protection of a relationship of confidence, Clarke, 'Remedial Responses to Breach of Confidence: The Question of Damages' 316, 318, 332–334.

432 *Vercoe v Rutland Fund* [2010] EWHC 424 (Ch) [341] (Sales J).

433 *Vercoe v Rutland Fund* [2010] EWHC 424 (Ch) [340]–[341] (Sales J). Similarly, the extent to which the information was used seems to be considered as a factor: if the trade secret made only a small contribution to the defendant's product, account of profits is not likely to be awarded, Gurry on Breach of Confidence para 20.08.

434 *Seager v Copydex* [1967] 1 WLR 923 (CA).

435 *Vercoe v Rutland Fund* [2010] EWHC 424 (Ch) [341] (Sales J).

436 Stanley 136; Gurry on Breach of Confidence para 20.10.

437 Stanley 136–137; Nathan, Adamson and Taylor in Goulding para 11.114.

438 Gurry on Breach of Confidence paras 20.11–20.12. E.g. the contribution which a particular marketing strategy has made towards profits from the sales of a product may be difficult to separate from the contribution of the technical features of that

awarded to the plaintiff is further complicated by various deductions which the defendant may make.[439] In that respect it has been recognised in particular that the positive contribution in time and skill made by the defendant acting honestly may be deducted from the amount to be awarded to the plaintiff 'on a liberal scale'.[440]

Application of account of profits has been described as 'most unsatisfactory and cumbersome in practice'[441] due to the evidentiary difficulties connected with the need to show the profits made by the defendant as a result of his misconduct. As a consequence, this remedy is applied in cases where the profits on the part of the defendant are substantial and evident.[442] It will furthermore be refused if the claimant's behaviour would make it unjust, if it would cause disproportionate hardship to the defendant, or if other circumstances compel a refusal.[443]

4 Exemplary Damages

The basic function of damages, which is to put the plaintiff into the same position as if the infringement had not occurred, is adjusted in cases of particularly egregious infringements,[444] in particular where the defendant has calculated that his profits from infringement would exceed any damages payable. In such cases the court may additionally award the claimant exemplary damages with the purpose to adequately deter wrongdoing.[445]

Account of profits already has a deterrent element in that it denies the defendant the profits from his wrongdoing even if the claimant did not incur damage. Exemplary damages go further and may be awarded if it is clear that the defendant acted upon cynical calculation, but it is difficult to obtain proof of his profits.[446]

product, its design, compatibility with other products, networking effects, client fidelity etc.

439 Stanley 137–138; Gurry on Breach of Confidence para 20.14.

440 *Boardman v Phipps* [1967] 2 AC 46 (HL) 99, 104, 112, where the defendant acted honestly in making an investment based on confidential information; Stanley 138, arguing that if the defendant is innocent, account of profits should be refused altogether.

441 Gurry on Breach of Confidence para 20.06. To that effect, see also Nathan, Adamson and Taylor in Goulding para 11.114.

442 Gurry on Breach of Confidence para 20.06.

443 Stanley 130.

444 But not in case of breach of contract, Nathan, Adamson and Taylor in Goulding para 11.71.

445 Stanley 133.

446 Stanley 133–134.

From that perspective, grant of exemplary damages is likely only in the rarest cases,[447] akin to industrial espionage.

5 Summary

The grant of damages if a breach of confidence is found to have occurred is subject to discretionary assessment by the court. In this exercise, the court may combine damages with an injunction, award damages instead of injunctive relief, or deny any remedy whatsoever. Thus, under the rules applicable in the United Kingdom, consideration of the interests of the parties has a strong influence on the decision as to which measures are to be applied in case of infringement.

Nevertheless, it must be kept in mind that damages are granted after a final consideration of the merits of the case in which the defendant is found to have breached a duty of confidence. Thus, denial of a remedy, or replacing injunctive relief with damages for which the plaintiff has not applied, may be decided only in exceptional cases, where the negative consequences of grant of a remedy for the defendant would be disproportionately more severe than the detriment to the plaintiff in case of refusal of that remedy.[448] In that respect any dishonesty on the part of either the plaintiff or the defendant is taken into account[449] and the balance of hardship as well as considerations such as existence of fraud, misrepresentation on either side, or laches or acquiescence on the part of the plaintiff[450] may influence the grant of a remedy.

The successful plaintiff has a choice between applying for compensatory damages which are measured by his loss or by the market value of the information, including its licensing value, or for restitutionary damages or account of profits, which are calculated on the basis of the gain which the defendant obtained as a result of breach of confidence and which do not require the plaintiff to have incurred any loss.[451] The acceptance of such monetary compensation is justified by the interest which the public has in

[447] Stanley 134; Gurry on Breach of Confidence paras 19.35–19.36. According to Toulson and Phipps, exemplary damages are conceivable only in certain cases relating to personal information, Toulson/Phipps paras 9-051–9-052.

[448] Spry, *The Principles of Equitable Remedies* 626.

[449] Ibid.

[450] Ibid 629–631.

[451] Fitzgerald and Firth propose combination of those methods of calculation, as long as this does not result in double counting. Accordingly, lost profit should be the primary method of calculation, supplemented by royalty measure of damages. If these methods do not provide for an effective and dissuasive remedy, damages may be calculated by reference to defendant's profits, John Fitzgerald and Alison Firth, 'Is Art. 13 of the Enforcement Directive a Redundancy Notice for the Account of Profits Remedy in the UK?' (2014) GRUR Int 881, 884.

the protection of confidential relationships as such. On a similar note, exceptionally, the court may grant exemplary damages, which are rooted in a desire to deter particularly egregious misconduct.

In view of the analysis presented above, it appears that UK law contains flexible instruments which allow consideration of the interests of the parties and of the public also upon grant of a remedy at trial. Thus, it appears possible to grant and frame an appropriate remedy that will correct any imbalance of interests after a breach of confidence has been found to have occurred.

C *Damages in Cases of Infringement of a Right to a Trade Secret by a Former Employee in the United States*

Under Section 3 UTSA and under the DTSA,[452] the holder of a trade secret is entitled to damages for misappropriation of this information. Section 3(a) prescribes two alternative methods of calculating damages. They may cover either both the actual loss to the plaintiff and the unjust enrichment of the defendant, or, alternatively, be computed on the basis of a reasonable royalty for the defendant's unauthorised use or disclosure of a trade secret.[453] Where wilful or malicious misappropriation is found to have occurred, the court may furthermore double the award by granting exemplary damages under Section 3(b) UTSA.[454] Since, in the United States, trade secrets are considered to be a right of intellectual property, together with patents and copyright, damages for misappropriation of trade secrets are determined in a similar way to those granted for infringement of IPRs.[455]

The purpose of granting damages is to put the holder of the information into the position which he would have been in had no infringement occurred.[456] Damages have the role of compensating the plaintiff for past as well as future infringements and, as in the United Kingdom, may be combined with injunctive relief, although an injunction and damages may not cover the same period of time.[457] Where there has been some substantial use of the information by the defendant, the

[452] 18 US Code §1836(b)(3)(B), as amended by the DTSA.
[453] See also 18 US Code §1836(b)(3)(B)(i)–(ii), as amended by the DTSA.
[454] See also 18 US Code §1836(b)(3)(C), as amended by the DTSA.
[455] Glick, Reymann and Hoffman, *Intellectual Property Damages: Guidelines and Analysis* 335, with the exception that no statutory damages exist in trade secrets cases and that in some cases damages may be limited to the time the defendant obtained a head start over his competitors as a result of the infringement, ibid 342; Peterson 15–4.
[456] Pooley 7-40.
[457] Comment to S 3 UTSA.

plaintiff will usually have a valid claim for damages. He must show that he suffered a loss and that there exists a causal link between this loss and the infringement.[458]

It is considered under the UTSA that the grant of damages, like injunctive relief, is appropriate for the period of time during which the information remains secret and for the period for which the defendant has obtained a competitive advantage (head start) resulting from the misappropriation. Accordingly, damages may be calculated on the basis of the plaintiff's actual loss and combined with the unjust benefit which the defendant obtained through misappropriation.[459] Depending on the situation, e.g. if the information has lost secret status and was not used by the defendant, assessing the plaintiff's loss may be the only available measure of damages. Where the secrecy of the information was maintained and the information was used in production of goods or services, the defendant's profits may be included in the calculation as well.[460]

In any case, as in the case of injunctions, damages are precluded as of the moment when the information is no longer secret or the period of the head start gained by the defendant from using it is over.[461]

1 Plaintiff's Loss

To obtain damages for his loss, the plaintiff must show a demand for his product, the lack of acceptable non-infringing substitutes, his manufacturing and marketing capability to exploit the demand, and how much profit he would have made by using the information.[462] The plaintiff's loss will usually be shown by a decline in sales or reduction in prices forced on him by the unfair competition resulting from the misappropriation.[463] It may also correspond to the value of lost business opportunities,[464] or, if the secret was disclosed, to the market value of the

[458] Pooley 7-38–7-39, explaining also that the plaintiff must show the damage and the causal link, while the defendant must show any deductions which could reduce the amount of damages.

[459] Comment to S 3 UTSA; Glick, Reymann and Hoffman, *Intellectual Property Damages: Guidelines and Analysis* 335.

[460] Ibid 336.

[461] Craig N Johnson, 'Assessing Damages for Misappropriation of Trade Secrets' (1998) 27 *Colo Law* 71, 72–73.

[462] By reference to rules governing calculation of damages in case of infringement of a patent, *Panduit Corp v Stahlin Bros* 575 F2d 1152, 1156 (6th Cir 1978).

[463] Pooley 7-40–7-41; Glick, Reymann and Hoffman, *Intellectual Property Damages: Guidelines and Analysis* 337; Quinto/Singer 188.

[464] *Eagle Group v Pullen* 58 P 3d 292, 299 (Wash App 2002).

information.[465] It is also possible for the plaintiff to obtain damages for harm to his reputation.[466]

If there are only two competitors in the market, the sales made by the defendant may be used as a point of reference to determine the lost profit of the plaintiff. Otherwise, reference must be made to the reduction in sales of the plaintiff.[467]

The value of the information may be assessed from the perspective of the plaintiff or of the defendant. It is argued that if the information was disclosed, the assessment should be made from the perspective of the plaintiff, taking into account his costs of developing the information.[468] If the information remains secret and the injury to the plaintiff is not evident, determination of damages by reference to the value of the information to the defendant appears more appropriate.[469]

2 Defendant's Gain

The defendant's profit is calculated by his net income from the wrongful use of the information[470] and may correspond to the costs of the research and development which the defendant 'saved' due to misappropriation,[471] or to the increase in value of the defendant's business resulting from the misappropriation.[472]

This is often determined using the 'standard of comparison' method, i.e. by comparing the costs which the defendant incurred in developing the product or business using the secret information, with the costs he would have incurred if he had not misappropriated it. To that end, the plaintiff's costs in developing the information and the possibility of reverse engineering may be taken into consideration.[473]

465 *Precision Plating & Metal Finishing Inc v Martin-Marietta Corp* 435 F 2d 1262, 1263 (5th Cir 1970); Pooley 7-41.

466 For example, if his product may be confused with the defendant's poorer-quality product, see *World Wide Prosthetic Supply Inc v Mikulsky* 631 NW 2d 253, 258–259 (Wis App 2001); Pooley 7-41.

467 Glick, Reymann and Hoffman, *Intellectual Property Damages: Guidelines and Analysis* 336, referring to the methods of damages calculation applied in patent infringement cases.

468 If the information contains both secrets and information in the public domain, the damages should be assessed proportionally, Johnson, 'Assessing Damages for Misappropriation of Trade Secrets' 71, 72.

469 *University Computing Co v Lykes-Youngstown Corp* 504 F 2d 518, 535–536 (5th Cir 1974); Glick, Reymann and Hoffman, *Intellectual Property Damages: Guidelines and Analysis* 337.

470 Johnson, 'Assessing Damages for Misappropriation of Trade Secrets' 71, 73; Pooley 7-41.

471 Quinto/Singer 189.

472 Quinto/Singer 188–189.

473 *University Computing Co v Lykes-Youngstown Corp* 504 F 2d 518, 538 (5th Cir 1974); Pooley 7-42.

However, if the defendant is able to show that his profit is only partially attributable to the use of the secret information, the damages will be reduced accordingly.[474] Further setoffs include R&D expenses not related to the use of the secret information, costs of labour, maintenance and repair, advertising and marketing.[475]

The UTSA however prohibits 'double counting', i.e. inclusion in the calculation of the same item as both the plaintiff's loss and the defendant's gain.[476] Moreover, if a springboard injunction is issued, damages corresponding to the time and risk saved in developing the product or service incorporating the secret will be denied.[477]

3 Reasonable Royalty

Alternatively, if neither the plaintiff's loss nor the defendant's profit can be proven,[478] damages may be calculated as a sum corresponding to a reasonable royalty which the defendant would have paid to the plaintiff for disclosure or use of the trade secret,[479] had the parties negotiated a licence agreement.

The reasonable royalty is determined by the court under the assumption that the holder of the information was willing to grant a licence to the defendant.[480] The factors taken into account include: the bargaining positions of the parties at the time of misappropriation;[481] conditions of other similar licence agreements;[482] the value of the information, including the costs of its development and the extent to which it is or will be used by the defendant; as well as availability of non-infringing alternatives.[483] If the misappropriated information is integrated into a complex product, the royalty should be calculated on the basis of the value of the

474 Pooley 7-42; Glick, Reymann and Hoffman, *Intellectual Property Damages: Guidelines and Analysis* 339.

475 Johnson, 'Assessing Damages for Misappropriation of Trade Secrets' 71, 73. See also Peterson 15–20.

476 Comment to S 3 UTSA; Glick, Reymann and Hoffman, *Intellectual Property Damages: Guidelines and Analysis* 339.

477 Pooley 7-42–7-43.

478 Glick, Reymann and Hoffman, *Intellectual Property Damages: Guidelines and Analysis* 340; Quinto/Singer 189. This is particularly the case if the defendant has not yet started to use the information or has not yet made any profit from it, Pooley 7-43.

479 Comment to S 3 UTSA; Quinto/Singer 189.

480 *University Computing Co v Lykes-Youngstown Corp* 504 F 2d 518, 537 (5th Cir 1974) with further references.

481 *Sabatino Bianco v Globus Medical* WL 2980740 6 (E D Tex 2014).

482 Ibid.

483 *University Computing Co v Lykes-Youngstown Corp* 504 F 2d 518, 539 (5th Cir 1974); Johnson, 'Assessing Damages for Misappropriation of Trade Secrets' 71, 73; Peterson 15–23; Pooley 7-44. Glick, Reymann and Hoffman criticise the assumption that the holder of the information would be willing to enter into a licence agreement, since,

part incorporating it. If this is not possible, e.g. because there is no established market value for the component, the royalty rate may be determined on the basis of the price of the entire product. In such a case, the circumstance that the trade secret contributed only partially to the value of the final product is to be reflected by setting the royalty at an appropriate rate.[484]

Calculation of damages based on a reasonable royalty may not be combined with other methods of calculation and may not cover future sales by the defendant if an injunction prohibiting such sales was awarded by the court.[485] However, it has been accepted by some courts that the reasonable royalty rate in trade secrets cases may be increased in order to punish the defendant. The reason is that awarding a reasonable royalty in fact favours the defendant, who despite reprehensible conduct is put in the same situation as if he had acquired the information legally from the plaintiff, often in a situation where the plaintiff would not have been ready to license it.[486]

4 Exemplary Damages and Attorney's Fees

In situations where the trade secret was misappropriated wilfully and maliciously, i.e. intentionally or with deliberate disregard for the rights of others,[487] the court may award the plaintiff exemplary damages. In such circumstances the court may also award him reasonable attorney's fees.[488] These punitive measures are not available in cases of breach of post-employment agreements.[489]

The amount of exemplary damages is at the discretion of the court,[490] up to the upper limit of double the amount of ordinary damages.[491]

unlike patent cases, this is almost never the case in practice, see Glick, Reymann and Hoffman, *Intellectual Property Damages: Guidelines and Analysis* 340.

484 *Lucent Technologies Inc v Gateway Inc* 580 F3d 1301, 1336–1339 (Fed Cir 2009), which relates to calculation of damages in a patent infringement case.

485 Quinto/Singer 190.

486 Glick, Reymann and Hoffman, *Intellectual Property Damages: Guidelines and Analysis* 340, citing *University Computing Co v Lykes-Youngstown Corp* 504 F 2d 518, 536 (5th Cir 1974).

487 *Mangren Research & Dev Corp v National Chem Co* 87 F 3d 937, 946 (7th Cir 1996), where the defendants were found to have acted knowingly and unethically; *Sabatino Bianco v Globus Medical* WL 2980740 6 (E D Tex 2014).

488 S 4 UTSA; 18 US Code §1836(b)(3)(D), as amended by the DTSA. The determination of the appropriate amount of the attorney's fees lies within the discretion of the court, Quinto/Singer 191. See also Peterson 15–26.

489 Jay P Kesan and Carol M Hayes, 'The law and policy of non-compete clauses in the United States and their implications' in Marilyn Pittard, Ann L Monotti and John Duns (eds), *Business Innovation and the Law. Perspectives from Intellectual Property, Labour, Competition and Corporate Law* (Edward Elgar 2013) 395.

490 Peterson 15–29.

491 Pooley 7-44 – 7-45; Quinto/Singer 191.

In determining whether the defendant's behaviour was wilful and malicious and thus the award of exemplary damages or attorney's fees is appropriate, what counts is whether he knew that the information was secret and he had a duty to keep it that way.[492]

5 Summary

The aggrieved holder of a trade secret may apply for damages compensating him for losses already incurred and those which he will incur, if the court denies a permanent injunction. Damages may be combined with an injunction, but may not cover the same period of time.

The UTSA and the DTSA foresee two methods of calculating damages: they may be determined by combining the plaintiff's loss and the infringer's profits resulting from misappropriation, or by determining an appropriate royalty which would have been agreed on by the parties.

The choice of the method of calculation depends on the circumstances of the case. For example, in rapidly changing industries where the 'first-move' advantage is decisive, or in situations where a trade secret, once taken, may not be returned (e.g. when it relates to a more efficient method of production), the value of the information may be the only way to compute the damages.[493] The same applies in cases of disclosure where the defendant did not profit from making the information public.

The balancing of interests does not feature prominently in determining damages, since it concentrates on putting the plaintiff into the position he would have been in, if the misappropriation had not taken place. It seems that it may be taken into account to some extent when deciding whether to award exemplary damages or attorney's fees to the plaintiff, since that requires the defendant's behaviour to have been wilful and malicious.

D Damages in Cases of Infringement of a Right to a Trade Secret by a Former Employee under the Trade Secrets Directive

The rules on damages for infringing the right to a trade secret are contained in Article 14 of the Trade Secrets Directive. They mirror the regulation provided in Article 13(1) of the Enforcement Directive,[494] but allow the Member States to limit liability for damages if the infringement was committed by an employee. Article 14 is not included in the

[492] Johnson, 'Assessing Damages for Misappropriation of Trade Secrets' 71, 73.
[493] Glick, Reymann and Hoffman, *Intellectual Property Damages: Guidelines and Analysis* 393.
[494] Grassie, 'Trade Secrets: The New EU Enforcement Regime' 677, 681; Kalbfus and Harte-Bavendamm, 'Protokoll der Sitzung des Fachausschusses für Wettbewerbs- und Markenrecht zum Richtlinienvorschlag über den Schutz von Geschäftsgeheimnissen' 453, 457.

catalogue of provisions which according to Article 1(1) of the Trade Secrets Directive must be fully complied with, and thus has a character of minimum harmonisation, allowing the Member States to maintain or introduce more far-reaching protection. Nevertheless, the rules on damages applied by the Member States must comply with Articles 6 and 7 of the Directive, i.e. their application must be fair and equitable, not unnecessarily complicated or costly, effective and dissuasive as well as proportionate. Article 5(d) of the Directive seems to apply to damages as well, with the effect that if the alleged infringement took place for the purpose of protecting a legitimate interest, this remedy should be denied. It has been suggested that this might be the case in a situation where the employee uses information which he acquired honestly and which he must be able to rely on in order to remain professionally active.[495] In view of Article 1(3) of the Directive, it seems that this might be the case even if such information is a trade secret. This provision declares that the Directive does not give grounds to limit employee mobility and in particular to limit use of information which is not a trade secret[496] or to limit use of honestly acquired experience and skills.[497] Since these are defined as separate categories, it appears that trade secrets which have become part of the employee's skill and knowledge might be used if necessary for the employee to remain professionally active.

According to the minimum level of harmonisation prescribed by the Directive, damages are to be granted for infringement of a right to a trade secret where the defendant is found to have acted with fault (i.e. where he knew or ought to have known that he was engaging in an infringing activity). The amount of damages must be appropriate to the actual prejudice suffered by the holder of the information as a result of the infringement,[498] which seems to correspond to the requirement of causality applied in the jurisdictions studied. The goal of the damages award, as in the legal orders analysed, is to place the aggrieved party in the position it would have been in, had the infringement not taken place.[499]

Pursuant to Article 14(1) second paragraph of the Directive, the Member States may limit employees' liability for damages towards their employers for unlawful acquisition, use or disclosure of a trade secret if they acted without intent.[500] This seems to be novel as compared to the

495 MPI Position Paper para 38.
496 Art 1(3)(a) TSD.
497 Art 1(3)(b) TSD.
498 Art 14(1) TSD.
499 Recital 30 TSD.
500 See also Recital 30 TSD.

rules applicable in the jurisdictions analysed.[501] It is unclear whether this should apply also to the relationship between former parties to an employment agreement, but it seems that this has been left to the Member States and should be decided in accordance with their national law and practice. It is an interesting solution, which is already foreseen in the laws of some of the Member States.[502] Considering that Article 14 has the character of minimum harmonisation and that the restriction of the employee's liability for damages contained therein seems to confirm the present practices of the Member States rather than to have a harmonising function, the analysed laws will not need to be amended in order to accommodate such a solution. Nevertheless, should such a restriction of liability be contemplated, it is suggested that it should not be drafted as a blanket limitation, but rather should include consideration of certain determinable factors. Apart from lack of intent on the part of the employee, they may include the ex-employee's need to rely on the information to remain professionally active in the particular field. Moreover, tying the upper amount of damages to the employee's last remuneration might give rise to awards, which on the one hand would be easily determinable and thus not unnecessarily complicated and dissuasive, and on the other hand not disproportionately burdensome for the employee and thus fair. Nevertheless, even if restriction of liability for damages is contemplated, it should not be detached from the actual damage to the plaintiff. The restriction should merely determine a ceiling and not take the place of the calculation of the actual damage.

The Directive recognises three methods of setting[503] damages, as discussed supra, although no strict distinction is drawn between damages set by reference to the plaintiff's loss and those set by reference to the infringer's profits. Rather, the decision on the amount of damages is to be made taking into account all the appropriate factors, such as the negative

[501] Although e.g. in Germany, von Ungern-Sternberg advocates including the level of the infringer's fault in the determination of damages, which could result in limiting them, von Ungern-Sternberg, 'Einwirkung der Durchsetzungsrichtlinie auf das deutsche Schadensersatzrecht' 460, 465, with reference to the Enforcement Directive. For a contrary opinion, see e.g. Volkmar Tetzner, 'Der Verletzerzuschlag bei der Lizenzanalogie' (2009) GRUR 6, 13.

[502] For example, Art 119 of the Polish Labour Code (ustawa z dnia 26 czerwca 1974r Kodeks Pracy, Dz U 1974 nr 24 poz 141, with amendments), limiting the damages to triple the amount of the employee's remuneration on the day the damage occurred. This however does not apply to former employees.

[503] According to von Ungern-Sternberg, the use of the term 'setting' rather than 'calculating' damages is appropriate, where, as in the case of Art 14(2) TSD, the decision on the amount of damages to be awarded is not bound to the actual loss of the plaintiff, von Ungern-Sternberg, 'Einwirkung der Durchsetzungsrichtlinie auf das deutsche Schadensersatzrecht' 460, 461, with reference to the Enforcement Directive.

consequences for the aggrieved party, including lost profits, any unfair profits made by the defendant, but also non-economic factors such as the moral prejudice caused by the misappropriation.[504] This list is not exhaustive; further factors may also be taken into account. Damages calculated by reference to royalties are an alternative measure under the Directive.

Some authors have suggested that this multifaceted approach does not require the plaintiff to have suffered any injury in order to obtain damages.[505] This might lead to situations where the plaintiff is put in a better position than if no infringement had taken place. This interpretation seems to correspond to the dissuasive function attributed to damages under Article 6(2)(c) of the Directive, but does not promote the goal of damages laid down in Recital 30, which is to put the injured party into the position it would have been in, if no infringement had taken place.[506] Furthermore, it does not correspond to Article 14(1) of the Directive, which prescribes that the damages must be appropriate to the prejudice actually suffered by the holder of the information.

The Directive seems to take a flexible approach like that under UK law, where various methods of calculating damages may be applied simultaneously. In this respect, German scholars have expressed concern that applying the calculation rules laid down in the Directive might lead to cumulated damages.[507]

Non-economic factors introduced in the Directive, such as moral prejudice caused to the holder of a trade secret, have been criticised as not fitting well into the system of compensation for damage caused to a former employer. They seem to be better suited for application to damages for injury to a person.[508] Even where the infringement of a right to a trade secret causes loss of reputation on the part of the former employer,

504 Art 14(2) TSD.

505 With reference to Art 13 Enforcement Directive, which however contains the same wording as Art 14(2) TSD, von Ungern-Sternberg, 'Einwirkung der Durchsetzungsrichtlinie auf das deutsche Schadensersatzrecht' 460, 461.

506 Tetzner, 'Der Verletzerzuschlag bei der Lizenzanalogie' 6, 8 and von Ungern-Sternberg, 'Einwirkung der Durchsetzungsrichtlinie auf das deutsche Schadensersatzrecht' 460, 462, with reference to the Enforcement Directive.

507 This could happen according to von Mühlendahl, since under German law the three methods of calculation are strictly separated and may not be applied cumulatively, which is not the case under the Trade Secrets Directive, Kalbfus and Harte-Bavendamm, 'Protokoll der Sitzung des Fachausschusses für Wettbewerbs- und Markenrecht zum Richtlinienvorschlag über den Schutz von Geschäftsgeheimnissen' 453, 457.

508 As Timm-Wagner has pointed out, the inclusion of non-economic factors when fixing damages may be accepted under the Enforcement Directive, since it applies also to infringement of the author's moral rights. According to her, this is not justified in the case of trade secrets. Refer ibid.

this type of damage can still be quantified by reference e.g. to loss of clients and revenue.[509] It does not appear necessary to include non-economic factors in the assessment of damages, which, after all, must be expressed as a particular sum of money. Inclusion of non-economic factors might complicate the process of damages calculation and result in legal uncertainty surrounding the court's decision. This in turn might lead to the court's decisions on damages being perceived as having a punitive character, which is not the aim of the Directive.[510]

The award of damages based on reasonable royalty is seen as an alternative method of setting damages and considered appropriate e.g. where it would be difficult to determine the actual prejudice.[511] It is to be set at least at the amount of fees or royalties which would have been due if the parties had negotiated over the use of the information. Importantly, Article 14(2) of the Trade Secrets Directive prescribes that damages set by reference to a reasonable royalty are awarded as a lump sum. Thus, it appears that the courts will be able to impose recurring payments only in the form of instalments of the lump sum, and not to impose recurring payments indefinitely. This does not exclude setting damages for the future, but implies that the duration of the future payments must be specified in the ruling on damages.

Furthermore, according to some authors, given that the remedy should have a dissuasive effect, the amount of damages set by reference to a reasonable royalty may exceed the level of actual loss suffered by the plaintiff.[512] This seems to be a response to the fact that reasonable royalty, even though it partially limits evidentiary difficulties, is based on a fiction: it is not freely negotiated by the parties. If its amount is limited to a 'fictitious licence' the defendant may be put in a better position than if he had negotiated a licence, by not being subject to usual licence clauses such as cross-licensing or inspection. Furthermore, this measure of calculation may be used even if the holder of the information would not have been willing to license it in the first place. Thus, damages set by reference to a reasonable royalty should be more than just a fictitious licence and be determined in the light of other factors. These may include: whether the rightholder would have been willing to grant the licence in the first place, whether the infringement influenced the licensing capacity of the rightholder, the existence of a competitive

[509] This seems to be also the opinion of Ohly and Sack, see ibid.
[510] Recital 30 TSD.
[511] Recital 30 TSD.
[512] von Ungern-Sternberg, 'Einwirkung der Durchsetzungsrichtlinie auf das deutsche Schadensersatzrecht' 460, 464, with reference to the Enforcement Directive.

relationship between the parties, the costs of detection and enforcement of the infringement, the negative impact on the image of the rightholder or his products resulting from the infringement, and the fact that the infringer was not subject to additional obligations usually imposed in licensing agreements.[513] Similar considerations may apply when setting damages by reference to a reasonable royalty in trade secrets cases.

The CJEU went further and considered that the fact that the Enforcement Directive does not provide for punitive damages, cannot be interpreted as a prohibition for the Member States on introducing such a measure.[514] This decision was issued in the context of infringement of economic rights of copyright and contrary to the opinion of the Advocate General.[515] The Court considered that national law may provide for double the amount of reasonable royalty measure of damages, with the argument that reasonable royalty alone does not cover costs of detecting the infringement, moral prejudice and interest on the sums due.[516] The Court further considered that such an award would be reconcilable with the causality requirement because the plaintiff must show the link between the infringing event and loss suffered, but not its exact amount.[517]

Article 14 Trade Secrets Directive, as Article 13 Enforcement Directive, has a character of minimum harmonisation. Thus, it could be contemplated to accept punitive damages also in cases of infringement of trade secrets, following the CJEU argumentation. Nevertheless, due to the fact that the Trade Secrets Directive takes precedence over the Enforcement Directive[518] this decision of the CJEU may not be transferred directly to enforcement of trade secrets. It is considered here that the decision of the Court is questionable from the perspective of the principle of proportionality laid down in Article 7(1) of the Trade Secrets Directive.[519] Furthermore, accepting punitive damages would

513 In the context of patent enforcement under the Enforcement Directive see Tetzner, 'Der Verletzerzuschlag bei der Lizenzanalogie' 6, 10–12.

514 Case C-367/15 *Stowarzyszenie 'Oławska Telewizja Kablowa' v Stowarzyszenie Filmowców Polskich* [2017] ECLI:EU:C:2017:36 [28]. The Enforcement Directive contains the same relevant wording as the Trade Secrets Directive.

515 Case C-367/15 *Stowarzyszenie 'Oławska Telewizja Kablowa' v Stowarzyszenie Filmowców Polskich* [2017] ECLI:EU:C:2016:900, Opinion of AG Sharpston.

516 Case C-367/15 *Stowarzyszenie 'Oławska Telewizja Kablowa' v Stowarzyszenie Filmowców Polskich* [2017] ECLI:EU:C:2017:36 [30].

517 Case C-367/15 *Stowarzyszenie 'Oławska Telewizja Kablowa' v Stowarzyszenie Filmowców Polskich* [2017] ECLI:EU:C:2017:36 [32].

518 Recital 39 TSD.

519 And which has a character of full harmonisation, Art 1(1) TSD. Proportionality was stressed by AG Sharpston in her opinion in Case C-367/15 *Stowarzyszenie 'Oławska*

undermine the harmonisation goal of the Directive by encouraging discrepancies between the legal orders of the Member States.

It is submitted here that the effect of Article 14(2) of the Trade Secrets Directive, allowing for multifactored setting of damages, is to some extent mitigated by the statement in Article 14(1) of the Directive that the damages must be 'appropriate to the actual prejudice suffered' as a result of the infringement, and the prohibition of punitive damages laid down in Recital 30.

Article 14(2) Trade Secrets Directive applies 'when setting the damages pursuant to paragraph 1'. Thus, it appears that the actual prejudice suffered by the plaintiff is the upper limit of the defendant's liability, even if it may go beyond purely financial loss. In this context, it is submitted that additional economic factors, such as the competitive position of the parties, their willingness to negotiate, the costs of detection of the infringement, the negative impact on the image of the employer and his products or the degree of the infringer's fault may be taken into consideration. Moral prejudice is not considered to fit the framework of compensation for infringement of a right to a trade secret in the context of employee mobility. It fits better in the context of personality or moral rights, such as personal confidential information of economic value under the UK law.

E Summary: Damages in Cases of Infringement of a Right to a Trade Secret by a Former Employee

Damages are available for infringement of a right to a trade secret by a former employee in all of the jurisdictions analysed, as well as under the Trade Secrets Directive, with the purpose of putting the aggrieved employer in the position he would have been in had the infringement not taken place. Thus, a causal link between the infringement and the award must be established.

Nevertheless, under the law of the United Kingdom and the United States, as well as under the Trade Secrets Directive, it seems that damages may be awarded in an amount which goes beyond the mere financial loss of the plaintiff, and in the United Kingdom as well as under the Directive, no loss incurred by the plaintiff needs to be shown.

German law seems to present a less flexible approach than the other jurisdictions studied in that it does not allow the various methods of calculation of damages to be combined. Thus, the plaintiff must choose between basing his claim on his loss, the defendant's gain or by reference

Telewizja Kablowa' v Stowarzyszenie Filmowców Polskich [2017] ECLI:EU:C:2016:900, Opinion of AG Sharpston [55].

to a fictitious licence between the parties. The other systems analysed also recognise those three methods of calculation of damages. However, while in the United Kingdom they may be combined in a relatively flexible manner, under US law and under the Trade Secrets Directive, only the first two methods may be combined, and calculation by reference to a reasonable royalty is an alternative, to be applied particularly where determining the plaintiff's loss or the infringer's profits proves difficult.

Generally, the plaintiff needs to substantiate and provide evidence as to the amount of damages claimed. However, if calculating the infringer's profits poses difficulties, the courts in Germany may assess the appropriate amount of damages. The UK courts have even broader discretionary power and may apply it when deciding both whether to grant an injunction and what its amount should be.

The Trade Secrets Directive contains two solutions which seem absent from the jurisdictions analysed: the possibility to include non-economic factors when setting the amount of damages and the possibility to limit the liability for damages of employees who acted without intent. While the first solution is viewed critically, restricting the liability of employees seems to respond to the conflict of interests pertaining to disputes between employers and their employees over trade secrets. Nevertheless, it is not clear whether this applies to former employees as well. Furthermore, according to the Trade Secrets Directive, introducing a limitation of the employee's liability will be optional and thus will not result in the need to approximate the national laws.

German law does not provide for exemplary damages. They may however be awarded under the rules applicable in the United Kingdom and in the United States. While the Trade Secrets Directive expressly states that it is not its purpose to introduce punitive damages,[520] the requirement that the remedies must have a dissuasive effect may result in the acceptance of damages going beyond a strict calculation.

Balancing of interests is not prominent in the determination of damages for infringement of a right to a trade secret. This must be accepted, since they are awarded only after full consideration of the facts of the case and their main role is to put the injured party into the position it would have been in if no infringement had occurred. Nevertheless, under the Directive, awarding of damages, like other remedies, is subject to Articles 6 and 7, which require ia that they are fair, equitable and proportionate. This leaves some space for including the balancing of interests where under the facts of the case the interests of the employer and the employee are of equal weight but remain in conflict.

[520] Recital 30 TSD.

V Damages in lieu of Injunction

Injunctions and damages complement each other as remedies in cases of interference with a right to a trade secret. While the purpose of an injunction is to prevent future or continued infringement, damages aim at compensating the holder of the information for the loss he has already suffered.

However, in certain situations, especially where the information was obtained honestly and has not yet been disclosed, issuing an injunction might be particularly harmful to the ex-employee.

If he knows information which could qualify as a trade secret, but which may not be easily defined and may not be separated from his skill and knowledge, such as pricing policy or information relating to the preferences of clients, an injunction effectively prohibiting the use of this data would necessarily inhibit competition by the employee. Similarly, an order restraining him from contacting clients he has already approached may not serve the purpose, since it does not guarantee that those clients will return to the former employer and thus would only have the effect of punishing the ex-employee.

If the information has already been incorporated into products (complex products, which include other elements apart from the one incorporating the secret) or services (e.g. the employee is about to implement a business model which includes the use of the information) or if he has made preparations for using the information, which has included making investments, the harm to the employee resulting from having to remove the information from his products or services if an injunction is issued might exceed the likely harm to his former employer.

And if, for example, the post-employment agreement not to compete is about to expire, the balance of interests may again point to accepting the use of the information by the departed employee.

In such circumstances, rather than limiting a particular activity, it may be more plausible to compensate the former employer for the damage likely to result from the ex-employee's future use of the information. The possibility to issue damages in lieu of injunction in the jurisdictions analysed is discussed below.

A Damages in lieu of Injunction in Germany – A Proposal de lege ferenda?

Instances where the court could refuse an injunction for infringement of the right to a trade secret and instead order payment of damages for future use of the information have not been identified under German law.

Such a possibility is foreseen under Section 100 UrhG in case of infringement of copyright.[521] An infringer who has acted neither intentionally nor negligently may rely on this provision to avert a claim for an injunction or the destruction of infringing goods,[522] if application of the measure would cause him disproportionate harm[523] and if it can be expected that payment of financial compensation instead would be reasonably satisfactory for the injured party.[524] As a result of application of Section 100 UrhG, the infringing party obtains a right to use the work.[525] Nevertheless, due to the requirement that the infringer acted without fault, combined with broad interpretation of the concept of fault, Section 100 UrhG has not often been applied in practice.[526]

Such a possibility has also been recognised in the case of patents, where it was considered that refusal of a licence to the use a standard-essential patent would constitute an abuse of the patentee's dominant position.[527] In such a situation, the prohibition of discrimination prescribed in competition law warrants granting of a compulsory licence, based on the balancing of both the public and private interests of the defendant, who, faced by a standard generally accepted in the industry, cannot be expected to turn to other solutions than the patented one.[528] In effect, an injunction will not be issued.[529] However, the condition for refusing the injunctive order is that the defendant accepts a licensing offer made by the patentee, or presents an unconditional and concrete counter-offer for a licence, on fair, reasonable and non-discriminatory

[521] A corresponding provision is not foreseen in any other statute protecting IPRs, see Alexander Reetz, Camille Pecnard, Riccardo Fruscalzo, Ruud van der Velden and Mark Marfé, 'Die Befugnisse der nationalen Gerichte unter dem EPÜ und des Einheitlichen Patentgerichts (EPG) nach Art. 63 (1) EPGÜ zum Erlass von Unterlassungsverfügungen – eine rechtsvergleichende Untersuchung' (2015) GRUR Int 210, 211; Thomas Dreier and Gernot Schulze, *Urheberrechtsgesetz* (5th edn CH Beck 2015) §100 para 2.

[522] Dreier and Schulze, *Urheberrechtsgesetz* §100 para 3.

[523] For example, if the infringement relates only to a small element of a complex product and it would be costly to remove this element, ibid §100 para 5.

[524] For example, if the copyright owner grants licences to use the infringed work, ibid §100 para 6.

[525] Ibid §100 para 9.

[526] Ibid §100 para 4.

[527] BGH GRUR 2009, 694 *Orange Book Standard*; Reetz, Pecnard, Fruscalzo, van der Velden and Marfé, 'Die Befugnisse der nationalen Gerichte unter dem EPÜ und des Einheitlichen Patentgerichts (EPG) nach Art. 63 (1) EPGÜ zum Erlass von Unterlassungsverfügungen – eine rechtsvergleichende Untersuchung' 210, 212.

[528] Jochen Kilchert, 'Allgemeine Grundsätze im Patentrecht' in Carl Schramm, *Der Patentverletzungsprozess* (7th edn Carl Heymanns Verlag 2013) 1–2.

[529] Ohly, '"Patenttrolle"oder: Der patentrechtliche Unterlassungsanspruch unter Verhältnismäßigkeitsvorbehalt? – Aktuelle Entwicklungen im US-Patentrecht und ihre Bedeutung für das deutsche und europäische Patentsystem' 787, 794.

(FRAND) terms and complies with the conditions of this offer.[530] These requirements of a FRAND offer in the context of abuse of dominant position under Article 102 TFEU have been reviewed by the CJEU. It decided that an injunction must be denied in the case of a patentee owning a standard-essential patent, unless he has given notice to the alleged infringer, specifying the details of the alleged infringement and, if the alleged infringer has indicated a willingness to obtain a licence, has made him a FRAND offer in writing, specifying in particular the royalty and how it is to be calculated. Furthermore, the infringer must have responded to that offer in good faith, or made a counter-offer. If the counter-offer is rejected by the patentee, the alleged infringer should provide for a security and be able to render an account in respect of the acts of use of the patent.[531]

Even though effectively the *Orange Book Standard* case concerns a denial of an injunction and grant of a licence instead, it cannot be seen as an instance of awarding damages in lieu of injunction. The considerations presented by the BGH refer to abuse of a right, which pursuant to Section 242 BGB[532] can in any case result in denial of an injunction. Where the right to a trade secret is abused, the court is more likely to deny injunctive relief altogether, since considerations relating to the proprietary nature of patents, which warrant the grant of a licence even if the right is abused, are not present in the case of trade secrets.

A remedy in the form of damages in lieu of injunction is based not so much on abuse of a right by one party as on a balancing of rights in a situation where there are good reasons for recognising the interests of both parties. Nevertheless, abusive behaviour may be one instance where the balance of interests points to denial of an injunction.

In the context of enforcement of patents, Ohly puts forward the general applicability of the proportionality principle in German civil law in support of an argument that a claim for an injunction based on Section 1004 BGB may be replaced by a claim for monetary compensation, if under the circumstances of the case the enforcement of the injunction would place an undue burden on the defendant and thus be abusive.[533]

[530] BGH GRUR 2009, 694, 696 *Orange Book Standard;* Thomas Kaess, 'Allgemeine Grunsätze der Eingriffsprüfung' in Carl Schramm, *Der Patentverletzungsprozess* (7th edn Carl Heymanns Verlag 2013) 130.

[531] Case C-170/13 *Huawei Technologies Co. Ltd v ZTE* [2015] not published in ECR.

[532] BGH GRUR 2009, 694, 696 *Orange Book Standard.*

[533] Ohly, '"Patenttrolle"oder: Der patentrechtliche Unterlassungsanspruch unter Verhältnismäßigkeitsvorbehalt? – Aktuelle Entwicklungen im US-Patentrecht und ihre Bedeutung für das deutsche und europäische Patentsystem' 787, 796, with further references. With regard to real property, see Tobias Lettl, 'Die Beeinträchtigung des Eigentums nach §1004(I)(1) BGB' (2005) JuS 871, 877.

A counter-argument is the absolute character of the right to property, to which Section 1004 BGB refers. Thus, it is argued, the right to demand termination of interference with a property right should be unconditional.[534]

Such a flexible application of the principle of proportionality is endorsed here in the context of enforcement of trade secrets. It would allow the courts to address the problem of conflicting interests, particularly where a former employee is the defendant. The criticism concerning the unconditional right to injunction where property is interfered with is less convincing in the case of trade secrets than it is for patents. First, the remedy exists in case of infringement of copyright which has proprietary character. Furthermore, under German law, trade secrets are not considered to have a proprietary character, and in enforcing them Section 1004 BGB is applied only by analogy.

It is proposed that the factors to be considered when applying the proportionality principle should include the extent to which the infringing embodiment is part of the product of the infringer, as well as the level of fault on his part.[535] Where former employees are concerned, the interest in remaining professionally active with reliance on previous experience; the freedom to choose a professional activity and compete with the former employer; the level of harm likely to be suffered by each of the parties to the dispute; and the time remaining until the duty expires, should be considered as well.

B Damages in lieu of Injunction in the United Kingdom – Within the Discretionary Power of the Court

The rules applicable in the United Kingdom for awarding financial compensation do not require that the damage has already occurred.[536] Thus, the court may award pecuniary compensation for use of information in the future, instead of issuing an injunction.

534 Ohly, '"Patenttrolle"oder: Der patentrechtliche Unterlassungsanspruch unter Verhältnismäßigkeitsvorbehalt? – Aktuelle Entwicklungen im US-Patentrecht und ihre Bedeutung für das deutsche und europäische Patentsystem' 787, 796 with further references.

535 Ohly, '"Patenttrolle"oder: Der patentrechtliche Unterlassungsanspruch unter Verhältnismäßigkeitsvorbehalt? – Aktuelle Entwicklungen im US-Patentrecht und ihre Bedeutung für das deutsche und europäische Patentsystem' 787, 797.

536 This seems to be the majority, even if not straightforward, opinion, see Spry, *The Principles of Equitable Remedies* 624; Gurry on Breach of Confidence paras 19.16–19.18, 19.20; uncontroversial in the case of post-employment agreements, see Nathan, Adamson and Taylor in Goulding para 11.06.

The flexibility of equity rules governing grant of remedies under UK law allows the courts in exercising their discretion to award damages in lieu of injunction, on conditions corresponding to the second and third requirement foreseen in Article 12 Enforcement Directive and Article 13 (3) of the Trade Secrets Directive. Thus, generally such damages may be awarded where the hardship caused to the defendant by the grant of an injunction would be so disproportionate to the harm caused to the plaintiff if the injunction was denied that it would be reasonable on the facts of the case to award the plaintiff only damages.[537]

No strict rules exist in this respect. The UK Supreme Court, in *Coventry v Lawrence*[538] stressed that damages in lieu of injunction are a remedy within the court's discretion and that any strict guidance as to when they should be awarded 'is likely to do more harm than good'.[539] Nevertheless, the Court considered that in a situation where prima facie the plaintiff is entitled to an injunction, the burden is on the defendant to show why it should not be granted but replaced with damages. In this respect, evidence as to the defendant's behaviour is of particular relevance, e.g. whether he has tried to avoid the jurisdiction of the Court, or whether he has acted fairly and in good faith under the circumstances.[540] Further factors which the court may consider when exercising its discretion include the 'extent of the injury' to the plaintiff, whether this injury may be easily quantified in financial terms[541] and whether it would be oppressive to the defendant to grant the injunction. The Supreme Court stated as well that when exercising discretion to grant damages in lieu of injunction, the court may take into account the public interest, for example, if the injunction would oblige the defendant to close his business and dismiss his employees, or would stop him from pursuing an otherwise legitimate activity.[542]

Accordingly, a similar balancing exercise must be performed as in the case of grant of an injunction, i.e. the impact on the positions of the

[537] Reetz, Pecnard, Fruscalzo, van der Velden and Marfé, 'Die Befugnisse der nationalen Gerichte unter dem EPÜ und des Einheitlichen Patentgerichts (EPG) nach Art. 63 (1) EPGÜ zum Erlass von Unterlassungsverfügungen – eine rechtsvergleichende Untersuchung' 210, 214; Spry, *The Principles of Equitable Remedies* 624, 625–626.

[538] *Coventry v Lawrence* [2014] UKSC 13 (UKSC). Even though this case considered general tort law and in particular action against nuisance by noise, it is submitted here that the guidance provided by the UKSC is of sufficiently general nature to be applicable also to disputes between employers and their former employees in the context of infringements of trade secrets.

[539] Ibid [119]–[120], [123].

[540] Ibid [121].

[541] Spry, *The Principles of Equitable Remedies* 625.

[542] *Coventry v Lawrence* [2014] UKSC 13 (UKSC) [124], [126].

parties to the dispute must be considered by the decision-maker. The discretion to award damages in lieu of injunction 'is not exercised lightly'[543] and thus such a remedy is likely to be awarded only in exceptional cases, where issuing an injunction would have a particularly negative impact on the position of the ex-employee, e.g. where the enforced restrictive covenant is about to expire[544] or where the balance of interests speaks against granting injunctive relief.[545]

As regards the amount of damages granted instead of an injunction, the UKSC considered that, while double counting must be avoided, damages may include the plaintiff's loss, combined with the loss of his 'ability to enforce his rights', which may be determined by reference to the defendant's benefit.[546]

C Damages in lieu of Injunction in the United States – An 'Exceptional Circumstance'

In the United States, the possibility to award damages (royalty) in lieu of injunction is provided in Section 2(b) UTSA and in the DTSA,[547] in exceptional circumstances, for the period of time during which use of the information could have been prohibited by an injunction. This is justified by the consideration that even though use of the information may harm the holder of the trade secret, issuing an injunction would be inequitable under the circumstances of the case.[548]

The law does not contain a catalogue of 'exceptional circumstances', but the UTSA refers, by way of example, to overriding public interest and to a material change of position before knowledge of the misappropriation was acquired. The latter example is likely to refer to 'innocent misappropriators', i.e. third parties who incorporated the information into their products or services before finding out that the information was a trade secret.[549]

Royalty in lieu of injunction was granted on justification by overriding public interest in a case where the information related to weapons used in an ongoing military conflict.[550] Nevertheless, the courts show some

[543] Spry, *The Principles of Equitable Remedies* 623, 626; Gurry on Breach of Confidence paras 19.18, 19.22;

[544] Nathan, Adamson and Taylor in Goulding para 11.06.

[545] Gurry on Breach of Confidence para 19.18, 19.22.

[546] *Coventry v Lawrence* [2014] UKSC 13 (UKSC) [128].

[547] 18 US Code §1836(b)(3)(A)(iii), as amended by the DTSA.

[548] Comment to S 2(b) UTSA.

[549] Comment to S 2(b) UTSA; Pooley 7-37; Quinto/Singer 187.

[550] Judgment ordering damages to be determined in the future in *Republic Aviation Corp v Schenk* 152 USPQ 830 (NY Sup Ct 1967).

flexibility in applying the requirement of 'exceptional circumstances' justifying issuing an order for damages rather than an injunction, and have granted this remedy where, due to changed circumstances, an injunction would not reverse the damage.[551] The public interest in the existence of competition, combined with the adequacy of royalties in the circumstances of the specific case, have also given rise to awarding damages in lieu of injunction.[552]

Thus, even though use of the information by a former employee has not been explicitly recognised as an 'exceptional circumstance' justifying the award of royalties in lieu of injunction, the US courts have interpreted this requirement in a flexible way. It seems therefore that in the United States it is possible to grant this remedy in disputes between employers and their former employees, if the public interest in competition and workforce mobility prevails over the interest of the holder of the trade secret and if it is possible to compensate his loss by way of damages.

D Damages in lieu of Injunction under the Trade Secrets Directive

In Article 13(3), the Trade Secrets Directive prescribes as full harmonisation[553] that the Member States shall provide for a possibility for the courts to award pecuniary compensation as an alternative to a final injunction. According to the Directive, this alternative solution may be applied with respect to third parties who at the time of the alleged misappropriation, neither knew, nor under the circumstances had reason to know that the person from whom the trade secret had been obtained was using or disclosing it unlawfully. Moreover, this alternative remedy may be granted only in circumstances in which an injunction would cause disproportionate harm to the defendant and pecuniary compensation appears reasonably satisfactory to the plaintiff. Where the use of the information constitutes a breach going beyond infringement of a right to a trade secret or would be likely to harm consumers, it should not be

551 *Kilbarr Corp v Bus Sys Inc* 679 F Supp 422, 426 (DNJ 1988). In this case a preliminary injunction was denied based on false testimony. At trial, the court considered that too much time had passed and too much had happened to grant a permanent injunction. In particular, this would require shutting down an operative company.

552 *Electronic Data Systems Corp v Heinemann* 268 Ga 755, 756–757 (Ga 1997); *Sabatino Bianco v Globus Medical* No 2:2012cv00147 – Document 45 (E D Tex 2012), where the plaintiff and defendant were not competitors, the plaintiff did not manufacture the products incorporating the trade secret, and monetary compensation was found an appropriate response to the plaintiff's injury (this case however was not between former parties to an employment agreement).

553 Art 1(1) TSD.

accepted and an injunction is to be issued.[554] The amount of the award should not exceed the sum calculated as a reasonable royalty for the period of time for which use of the information could have been prevented by its holder.[555]

This provision appears to have been inspired by Article 12 Enforcement Directive,[556] which however is not limited to third parties who acquired the information in good faith, but applies to all persons who acted unintentionally and without negligence. The other conditions laid down in the Enforcement Directive (disproportionate harm to the plaintiff and pecuniary compensation reasonably satisfactory for the defendant) correspond to those laid down in Article 13(3)(b)–(c) of the Trade Secrets Directive. Thus, the scope of application of the alternative remedy of pecuniary compensation in lieu of injunction under the Enforcement Directive is broader than the one laid down in the Trade Secrets Directive.

Still, the remedy of damages in lieu of injunction as drafted in the Enforcement Directive has a very narrow scope of application. This is due in particular to the requirement that the infringer acted unintentionally and without negligence. Some have argued that this condition contradicts the basic principle of civil law according to which damages may be granted only against infringers who acted intentionally, or at least negligently. Blok explains that this criticism is based on a misunderstanding. According to him, damages in lieu of injunction are 'compensation for continuing infringements'. Thus, they are to be paid after the court has established that the defendant has committed an infringement. Accordingly, while at the time of infringement the defendant acted without fault, at least as from the decision of the court, he is aware of his infringement. Since damages in lieu of injunction take effect after the court issues a decision, the civil law principles are respected.[557]

It is submitted here that damages in lieu of injunction are in line with the principles of civil law. Even though referred to as 'damages', this remedy is more akin to a compulsory licence. It is granted upon balancing of interests. A party acting with fault is not likely to have a legitimate interest in continuing the use of the information. Accordingly, it is considered proportionate for the plaintiff to accept the use of his information by a party who started using it without fault and who has a

[554] Recital 29 TSD.

[555] Grassie, 'Trade Secrets: The New EU Enforcement Regime' 677, 680.

[556] MPI Position Paper para 55.

[557] Peter Blok, 'A Harmonized Approach to Prohibitory Injunctions: Reconsidering Article 12 of the Enforcement Directive' (2016) 11(1) *JIPLP* 56, 58.

legitimate interest in continuing to use it because otherwise it would suffer disproportionate harm.

When granting damages in lieu of injunction, the court replaces the plaintiff's valid claim for injunction. Thus, this remedy must be seen as an exception and, to be interpreted narrowly. This is reflected in the requirement that all of the conditions laid down in Article 12 of the Enforcement Directive must be complied with cumulatively.[558]

It is submitted that, unlike Article 13(3) of the Trade Secrets Directive, the conditions laid down in Article 12 of the Enforcement Directive could encompass use by a former employee who learned the secret information in the normal course of employment, without recourse to undue means and then uses it in his new occupation (i.e. he is acting unintentionally and without negligence). Lack of fault on the part of the employee using trade secrets is more likely than in the case of many IPRs, especially patents. This is because trade secrets are neither registered nor published, the employee may learn the information involuntarily, while performing his normal duties, and the obligation of confidence may be implied. If the employer does not draw the employee's attention to the confidential status of particular information, an employee who remembers it might indeed regard it as part of his skill and knowledge.

Application of the remaining conditions (harm to the plaintiff if an injunction is refused and appropriateness of pecuniary compensation) in fact requires a balancing of interests, which the courts routinely undertake in employee-mobility cases. Nevertheless, the Enforcement Directive is not applicable to enforcement of rights to trade secrets,[559] and the fact that the Trade Secrets Directive limits this remedy to third parties excludes former employees.

It is considered here that the conditions set out in the Enforcement Directive are better suited to addressing the conflict of interests inherent in disputes between employers and their ex-employees. There seem to be no compelling reasons to deny such a solution where trade secrets are concerned, if it is has been accepted with regard to IPRs, which are of a proprietary nature and thus awarded stronger protection. Admittedly, any use by a person other than the holder of the information increases the risk of disclosure of the secret. However, accepting the use of the information as a result of balancing of interests does not exclude issuing an injunction against disclosure. Furthermore, the risk of disclosure by an

[558] Ibid 56, 59.

[559] Recital 25 Enforcement Directive, Statement 2005/295/EC by the Commission concerning Article 2 of Directive 2004/48/EC of the European Parliament and of the Council on the enforcement of intellectual property rights [2005] OJ L 94/37.

ex-employee using and profiting from use of the information is relatively low, since he too will be interested in maintaining the secrecy of information which has a competitive value.

It is considered that adopting the wording of Article 12 Enforcement Directive, and thus broadening the scope of this remedy beyond third parties, would be beneficial, as it would increase the flexibility of the courts granting remedies for infringement of trade secrets. At the same time, it would not threaten the interests of the holders of the information. The requirement that the information was obtained and used unintentionally and without negligence excludes damages in lieu of injunction where it was obtained dishonestly. The cases where a trade secret could be obtained and used unintentionally and without negligence, but nevertheless adversely impact the interests of the former employer, are admittedly rare. It seems that this would be the case of 'innocent' third parties under Article 13(3) of the Trade Secrets Directive, but also in the post-employment scenario, where balancing of interests speaks against issuing an injunction, even though use of the information by the ex-employee is found to have occurred or may be expected (e.g. where the information was learned as part of the person's professional experience and is necessary for him to remain professionally active in a given field).

E Summary

Awarding by the court of damages instead of injunction is an exceptional measure. It may be applied against the will of the plaintiff and in its effects resemble a compulsory licence granted in cases of prevailing public interest. In the case of former employees, an award of damages instead of an injunction may in some situations serve the public interest in competition, employee mobility, spill-overs and the resulting social and economic benefits. On a private level, it allows the ex-employee to continue professional activity, and at the same time secures compensation for his former employer.

As the analysis presented here shows, the application of such a remedy is not settled practice in the jurisdictions analysed. It seems to most readily fit the UK system, where the courts have broad discretion in granting equitable remedies and where damages may be awarded for the future. In the United States, the application of damages in lieu of injunction is possible where the court finds 'exceptional circumstances'. In Germany, the prevailing view seems to be that an injunction is to be issued if infringement threatens and should not be replaced with monetary compensation against the will of the applicant for injunctive relief. The Trade Secrets Directive foresees damages in lieu of injunction only in the case of 'innocent third parties' who obtained the information from an infringer without knowledge of its secret status. Drafted in this way, the remedy does not apply to former employees.

It is considered here that awarding damages instead of an injunction should be possible in disputes between employers and their former employees, subject to consideration of all the facts of the case, balancing of interests and the principle of proportionality. Considering that such a possibility has been recognised in the Enforcement Directive in the case of IPRs and may be applied in the United States, where trade secrets are considered to have a proprietary nature, the adoption of this remedy should be possible in the case of trade secrets, especially in jurisdictions which do not recognise them as property.

Since damages in lieu of an injunction are an exceptional measure, the balancing of interests of the parties to the dispute as well as the public interest should be given particular weight when awarding them.

Thus, it should be applied only in cases where the ex-employee acted unintentionally and without negligence in obtaining the information. There seem to be no compelling arguments to accept use of the information by a former employee who stole it or deliberately memorised it.

The information which may be subject to damages in lieu of injunction is that which is not automatically disclosed upon use, such as process information, business methods, know-how concerning production or conducting business, i.e. information with regard to which it is possible to prohibit disclosure while accepting use. Allowing the use of information which necessarily leads to disclosure would have an unduly negative impact on the interests of the ex-employer, so an injunction appears more suitable in the case of such information. At the same time, such information is more likely to be separable from the employee's skill and knowledge and thus he is more likely not to depend on its use in order to remain professionally active. In case of information which is not self-disclosing, the former employee himself will be interested in maintaining its secrecy, since it would support his own competitive position.

Further considerations which may be relevant in order to determine whether damages in lieu of injunction should be granted include: whether the information is essential for the employee to remain professionally active in a given field; whether the harm to the ex-employer by denying the injunction would be greater than the harm to the ex-employee if his use of the information is denied; whether the damage has already occurred; whether pecuniary compensation is reasonably fair to the former employer and whether its amount may be readily quantified. Furthermore, if the employee's obligations e.g. under an agreement not to compete are about to expire, this might speak in favour of denying an injunction.

If the court decides to grant damages in lieu of an injunction, it can award the employer a lump sum, or impose regular payments (royalties). Since at the time of the court's decision neither the loss on the part of the ex-employer nor the profit on the part of the former employee is determinable, it seems that calculating the damages by reference to a fictitious licence would be the appropriate way to determine the amount of compensation for the employer. If the remedy is granted in the form of a royalty payment, its duration should correspond to the time for which an injunction would be issued, i.e. until the information is disclosed, as long as its use provides a competitive advantage over other market participants, or until expiry of the enforced contractual duty. If the information is of a type which is likely to be developed independently, the appropriate duration of the royalty payments can correspond to the time the ex-employee would need in order to work out the problem himself, judging by his skills and experience and his access to technology, financial means and human resources.

The possibility to grant damages in lieu of injunction, as advocated here, would give the courts greater flexibility in handling disputes between employers and their former employees, while not threatening the interests of the former. This is despite the fact that this remedy is granted in a situation where the employer has a valid claim for an injunction. Nevertheless, the right to an injunction is not absolute and the scope of application of the proposed remedy is very narrow. Furthermore, granting damages in lieu of injunction does not negate the main goal of an injunction which is to prevent disclosure of the information. This remedy may be accompanied by an injunction against disclosure of the information, and the ex-employee himself will be interested in keeping the information secret. Thus, while providing more flexibility, the possibility to grant damages in lieu of injunction would not dilute the protection of trade secrets enforced against departed employees.

In this way, in some circumstances, damages in lieu of injunction can be a balanced response to conflict of interests between former parties to an employment relationship.

VI Summary: Balancing of Interests When Granting a Remedy for Infringement of a Right to a Trade Secret

A decision whether to grant a final remedy is made by the court after the facts of the case have been established and after the scope of the infringement has been determined. As discussed in the previous chapters of this book, determining the scope of both the implied and the contractual duty involves balancing of rights and assessing the possible effects that the finding of infringement will have on the parties to the dispute. Nevertheless, even if infringement is found to have occurred, the conflict of interests remains.

This conflict is particularly clear in the case of preliminary measures. They are issued quickly, without a full assessment of the merits of the case or presentation and discussion of evidence. At the same time, in trade secrets cases they often have the effect of a final resolution of the dispute. Therefore, balancing of interests when granting interlocutory injunctions is crucial, even if made only prima facie. As part of the balancing exercise, assessing the effects on the parties of granting or refusing the order is of particular importance.

Injunctions, both preliminary and final, appear most effective from the perspective of the holder of the information, since they may prevent disclosure, and with it the destruction of the secret's value. Injunctions against use make it possible to safeguard the competitive position of the former employer supported by the use of the information. At the same time, these measures most strongly interfere with the ex-employee's right to remain professionally active, where he needs to be able to use the information in his new job. Damages on the other hand, apart from considerable difficulties in determining their amount, do not satisfy the interest of the employer if the use or disclosure has not yet occurred.

Issuing injunctions automatically may have a negative impact on employee mobility, employment and innovation, by limiting knowledge spill-overs. It may also increase opportunity costs, especially for creative employees, by narrowing their choice of post-employment activities. In the case of abusive litigation, basing unjustified claims on trade secrets may be an attempt by an undertaking to create, maintain or abuse a dominant position. Even if this is not the case, it has a negative impact on competition by inviting litigation and thus creating costs.

Laying down guidelines for granting remedies would increase legal certainty, thus reducing the investments made by information holders in de facto protection. This might encourage business innovation and market experimentation and boost economic growth.

In view of these considerations, it appears that case-by-case assessment remains essential when deciding to grant a remedy. The conflict of interests calls for a flexible application of remedies in trade secrets infringement cases.

The conflict of interests is to some extent addressed in all the jurisdictions analysed. The private interests of the employer and of the employee are prominent in civil enforcement in inter partes proceedings. The public interest in supporting innovation, entrepreneurship or competition is considered only rudimentarily in this context. While abusive litigation is recognised in all the jurisdictions analysed as a reason for not granting a remedy to the plaintiff, the public interest in a narrower sense and the interests of third parties seem to be factors considered only in the United States and under the Trade Secrets Directive.

It is nevertheless considered that it is possible to include more flexibility in the decision-making process when granting remedies within the existing legal frameworks discussed here.

It is submitted that, apart from the cases where trade secrets were obtained in a clearly unauthorised manner, such as theft, balancing of interest should be a compulsory element in determining and granting injunctions, both preliminary and final.

In the case of preliminary injunctions, it is considered that the assessment of the merits of the case, even if made on a prima facie basis, is an essential safeguard against abuses and for that reason should be present in the decision-making process. It is furthermore stressed that due to the lack of finality of the decision, the courts should as a rule make granting a preliminary injunction conditional on the filing of a security by the plaintiff, as is possible in all of the analysed jurisdictions. In the case of information which is not self-disclosing and where an injunction would amount to prohibition of competition by the ex-employee, the possibility to deny the order against filing of a security by the defendant might adequately address its anti-competitive effect. Another measure which would serve as a deterrent against abusive litigation would be the introduction of a requirement that an action on the merits is to be filed within a time limit set by the court, accompanied by automatic termination of the injunction, or a right for the defendant to compensation, if the action on the merits is not filed in that time. In cases where it is not likely that proceedings on the merits will take place, especially if the date of disclosure of the information (e.g. publication of the patent application including the secret information, or launch of a product) is known, it is suggested that time-limited injunctions are issued, in order to limit the cost to the former employee of filing a separate action for termination of the injunction.

Application of the principle of proportionality and full assessment of the conflicting interests of the parties to the proceedings are considered essential also when the court is deciding whether to grant and how to frame a final injunction. This is recognised in all of the analysed jurisdictions, although it appears that the balancing of rights is not the main consideration in the decisions of the courts in Germany.

The analysis presented here suggests that there are good reasons for distinguishing between injunctions prohibiting disclosure and those prohibiting use of the information. If the information is not self-disclosing, was obtained in an honest way and is necessary for the former employee to remain professionally active in a given field, the balancing of rights speaks for issuing an injunction against its disclosure, but not against use. Even though this would introduce one more competitor into the market, post-employment competition as such is accepted in all the jurisdictions analysed. Moreover, the possibility to rely on the information in question will improve the competitive position of the ex-employee. Thus, he will be personally interested in keeping it confidential.

In the case of data which is self-disclosing, its use may be prohibited as well, although in such cases the courts should tend to limit the duration of the injunction in time, for as long as a third party with similar skills and resources to the former employee would need to develop the information independently. In the case of information which was obtained by the employee in a dishonest way, the proportionality principle does not seem to speak against issuing a perpetual injunction (i.e. an order of unlimited duration). However, it is suggested that if the information has been disclosed by a third party or its holder, the ex-employee has obtained it from a third party and where his competitive advantage has been neutralised, such an injunction should nevertheless be terminated upon application by the former employee. Otherwise the order would have a punitive character, which is not the purpose of remedies granted under civil law.

Balancing of rights is not included in determining the amount of damages for infringement of a right to a trade secret. This is accepted, since the purpose of awarding damages is to put the plaintiff into position he would have been in if no infringement had taken place. Nevertheless, under the Trade Secrets Directive, non-economic factors are included in the assessment of the amount of damages and a possibility is foreseen for the Member States to restrict the amount of damages where employee acted without intent. This solution seems to introduce a way to include balancing of interests in determining the amount of damages. Although the inclusion of non-economic factors seems not to correspond to the goal of damages, it is considered here that relating the upper limit of damages to the amount of remuneration, which the ex-employee received at the time of termination of the employment relationship, may be an adequate response to the conflict of interests present in the post-employment use of confidential information. Even though the laws of the United Kingdom and United States, as well as the Trade Secrets Directive, seem to accept the granting of damages going beyond the loss of the plaintiff and even though in the United Kingdom and the United

States exemplary (punitive) damages may sometimes be granted, it must be stressed that it is not the goal of damages to punish the former employee. Therefore, it is submitted that the showing of a loss by the plaintiff should always be a necessary requirement for issuing a decision to award damages, even if their amount will be determined by a different method.

Finally, it is argued here that in some cases the conflict of interests between the employers and their former employees could be addressed by accepting the use of the information by the ex-employee, against payment. Currently the possibility to grant damages in lieu of injunction seems to fit only the UK system, the DTSA and, at least theoretically, the laws harmonised under the UTSA. Under the express terms of the UTSA and under the Trade Secrets Directive, it is foreseen in the case of third parties who obtained the information from the infringer without knowledge of its misappropriation. In Germany, damages in lieu of injunction could arguably be granted under application of the proportionality principle, but this does not seem to be the case in practice. The acceptance of a remedy in the form of awarding damages in lieu of injunction in cases involving employers and their former employees is advocated here. It is submitted that the award of such a remedy should be at the discretion of the court and should be considered only in a narrow category of cases, where the balance of interests points to issuing neither an injunction nor damages.

Final Conclusions

Balancing of interests is an indispensable element in determining the scope of post-employment obligations with respect to confidential information learned during service – irrespective of whether trade secrets are protected by law of unfair competition, contract, equity or special rules, and whether or not they are treated as property. Balancing of interests is part of how those obligations are determined, and falls within the framework regulating contracts with employees. It also influences court decisions granting a remedy if post-employment obligations are found to have been breached.

Freedom to work and compete with a former employer, and rights of personal development and self-determination, are recognised in all the jurisdictions analysed. Thus, the law protects the employee's interest in being able to continue in his chosen line of work whilst making optimum use of what he has learned through professional experience.

At the same time, the law also gives weight to the employer's interest in protecting his investment in developing valuable information, and safeguarding his business assets in general.

The public interest, on the other hand, does not feature prominently in the enforcement of rights to trade secrets after termination of employment. Society's general interest in ethical behaviour and the existence of competition is however taken into account. Accordingly, ex-employees may not use information which has been obtained dishonestly. But nor may their post-employment obligations go so far as to effectively prohibit them from competing with former employers. Contractual restrictions may go further, but they will not be valid unless the ex-employer has legitimate interests which justify their scope, unless they are fair and compensation is provided (in Germany) or unless their impact on competition is reasonable (in the United Kingdom and United States). The courts uniformly treat abusive litigation as an obstacle to obtaining the remedy sought.

Although widely discussed in US literature, and to some extent cited in US case-law, economic considerations such as encouraging innovation, knowledge-sharing and entrepreneurship do not play a major role in practice in the enforcement of trade secrets against ex-employees in the other jurisdictions analysed.

The need for a case-by-case assessment of the scope of post-employment obligations with respect to trade secrets is recognised and endorsed here. The wide variety of circumstances in which information can be used, and the conflicting interests at stake, require that every case be assessed on its own particular facts.

The scope of the right to use information learned during employment that has ended should be determined flexibly, applying certain guidelines as 'rules of thumb'. To achieve fair solutions, balancing the interests of the parties to any dispute must play a significant role, and the public interest must be duly considered.

I Striking the Balance Where No Post-Employment Agreement Was Concluded

If the parties have not contractually agreed the scope of the post-employment obligations, the first step is to determine how the employee obtained the information; any dishonesty precludes his using it. The next step is to consider whether the information is relevant for the employer's competitive position, and necessary to the employee if he is to be able to continue working in his area of professional expertise. The value of the information to the employer should be assessed from the perspective of his competitive position, not by reference to the time and effort spent on developing the data. The interests of third parties may also be taken into account, by assessing the impact which allocating the information to the employer or the ex-employee would have on their own position, particularly if they are former colleagues who still have jobs with the employer. At the same time, the longer the ex-employee's employment relationship lasted and the higher the position he reached, the broader his post-employment confidentiality obligations. The industry sector concerned must also be taken into consideration. In fast-moving industries, length of service with a particular employer might be less relevant than the position held. The same goes for highly technical positions. On the other hand, when it comes to information about conducting business, long-lasting employment enabling the employee to understand the intricacies of the employer's operations might be a factor in determining the scope of his obligations post-employment.

Also relevant is whether the information can be separated from the ex-employee's general skill and knowledge. That is the case if he can dissect it in his mind from all the other knowledge he has accumulated during his professional experience. Generally, the fruits of the employee's activities during employment belong to the employer,[1] but the greater the information's connection to the employee's personal qualities, the more its use post-employment should be accepted. This applies in particular to information the employee remembers naturally, rather than having to memorise it deliberately or even take documents with him. Tacit knowledge is an extreme example, being so connected to the individual concerned that it can be transferred only together with that person. That is why tacit knowledge can never be a trade secret of the employer.

However, despite the increasing relevance of 'separability', both in Germany (where fairness of use is decisive) and in the United Kingdom (where only highly confidential information must remain with the employer), it is however not the only consideration.[2] Other factors include the type of information (technical information tends to be regarded as belonging to the ex-employer, and commercial information as necessary for the ex-employee to use – unless he has removed large quantities of it); how it was taken and is now being used; who developed it, its value to the employer and his competitors; the existence of a post-employment contract; and the nature of employment. The nature of the information is also relevant: is it specific to the employer's business or more general; is it known to outsiders; and can it be easily reverse-engineered or obtained from publicly available sources?

Outside the United States, there is a reluctance to set the determination of post-employment confidentiality obligations in the context of broader public policy. Nevertheless, under the current legal framework in Germany and United Kingdom such considerations can be included as part of a 'more economic approach' to the enforcement of trade secrets.

Assessing the scope of the information which may be used by former employees in a broader policy context would have positive effects. Accordingly, in the absence of other considerations, information should enjoy greater protection if it would not have been disclosed to the employee if it had not been protected as a trade secret. This would allow fair consideration of the role played by trade secrets in incentivising innovation and reducing the costs of doing business. At the same time, particular weight should be given to allowing a departed employee to continue to use information which is essential for him to be able to

[1] This is always the case for employee inventions.

[2] This can possibly be said of the US system, where the borderline between information which can and cannot be used post-employment is determined by categorising the information as either a trade secret – which belongs to the employer – or general skill and knowledge – which can be used by the employee. Even so, rights are balanced – also in the United States – in performing that categorisation process.

continue his professional activity – even in competition with his former employer – as this is not only in his own private interest but also in the public interest as regards knowledge dissemination, spill-overs and increased competition.

Considering the industry sector and type of information might also be helpful in striking this balance. Trade secrets, as compared to patents, provide incentives to develop improvements which tend to have a relatively short life-cycle, e.g. in IT hardware and software. The same may hold true for marketing information. In these instances, the fact that the information quickly loses value would suggest that the employer has an interest in restricting its use. At the same time, the short life-cycle means that the negative impact on employee mobility should not be excessive. At a general level, such an approach would invite market experimentation. However, if a particular industry is characterised by high employee mobility and dependent on knowledge spill-overs, that would be a factor in favour of fewer restrictions on the use of knowledge and experience gained in previous employment, as this would benefit the industry as a whole as well as those working in it. In R&D-intensive industries, on the other hand, the decisive consideration might be to allow employers to accumulate resources in order to encourage the development of new products and services.

It is considered here that determining the scope of post-employment confidentiality obligations by balancing private interests in the context of policy considerations will do justice to the breadth of the concept of trade secrecy, which may cover all sorts of information, from patentable subject-matter to pure facts and business know-how. Such an approach to solving disputes between employers and ex-employees will be fairly flexible, and thus responsive to ongoing changes in society and employment markets, as well as to the ever faster pace of technical development.

II Striking the Balance in Post-Employment Agreements

Contractual regulation of post-employment obligations is accepted because of its benefits, which lie primarily in the legal certainty created by a clearly drafted agreement.

Non-disclosure agreements are accepted in all the jurisdictions analysed. This is endorsed here since they are particularly apt to increase legal certainty. Such agreements which also cover use of information should however be approached with caution, since they might limit competition by the ex-employee. Only if using the information would amount to disclosing it, should a covenant prohibiting both disclosure and use be accepted.

Agreements which limit competition from the former employee are scrutinised to establish that they are fair and reasonable. The employer must have legitimate interests to protect – such as trade secrets or client relationships – and these must be balanced against those of the ex-employee.[3] In making this assessment, only in the United States is the public interest in innovation and competition taken into account.

Contracts can be considered only to a limited extent in the broader context of public policy; they reflect the parties' will and should be construed accordingly. Therefore, public-policy considerations should not play any role, unless there are overwhelming reasons justifying this – for example if the contract was signed under duress. In particular, assessing post-employment agreements under competition law is unlikely to lead to finding them invalid. Nevertheless, antitrust and other public-policy considerations may feature in determining whether the interests the contract seeks to protect are legitimate, and upon determination of the contract's reasonableness, whenever assessment of the public interest is included.[4] In particular, it is suggested that the fact that an agreement, despite restrictive effects, contributes to technical or economic progress[5] can be one argument in favour of its validity.

Although the public interest is unlikely to greatly affect the assessment of individual contracts, general frameworks laid down in law are expressions of the lawmaker's attitude towards particular behaviour. Thus, providing a statutory framework for the conclusion of post-employment restrictive covenants is a better way to limit their negative effects than trying to shoe-horn public-interest considerations into assessments of individual agreements. The German legislator has taken that approach, and state law in California has gone even further, the effect being a total prohibition of post-employment agreements limiting competition.

It is considered here that post-employment agreements that restrict competition should always be clearly defined, and limited in duration and geographical scope. It is also suggested that employment as such, or its continuation, are not sufficient as consideration in a contract limiting post-employment competition. Accordingly, separate compensation for limiting competitive activity should be agreed. Such compulsory remuneration also has a deterrent effect, discouraging ex-employers from insisting on agreements unless they protect information or competitive

3 Currently, not part of determining the reasonableness of a restrictive covenant in the United Kingdom.
4 As foreseen under the doctrine of restraint of trade in the United Kingdom and United States.
5 See Art 101(3) TFEU.

positions of real value. Of course, not every post-employment contract is challenged in court. Ex-employees might not be aware that the obligations laid down are unenforceable, and they might comply with unduly broad agreements. Given that post-employment restrictive covenants are becoming 'standard practice', it would be a positive development to introduce a statutory framework delineating the limits to contractual freedom in this area. Not doing so could have a stifling effect on knowledge spill-overs, entrepreneurship and innovation in the long term.

A similar effect to granting separate remuneration for the restriction may be achieved by agreeing 'garden leave' during which the employee no longer works but continues to be paid, because he is still in employment and subject to the obligations arising from that relationship. However, if an employee is placed on such leave, further contractual limitations of his post-employment activity should not be accepted.

Lastly, it is considered that 'blue pencilling' or severance of post-employment agreements should generally not be accepted. It encourages the imposition of unduly broad restrictions on ex-employees, safe in the knowledge that if the ex-employee challenges them the courts may well modify them but will not strike down the agreement as a whole.

Minimum harmonisation of post-employment non-disclosure agreements, along the lines accepted in the jurisdictions analysed – i.e. they must be clearly drafted, protect a legitimate interest of the employer, and be limited in scope, duration and territory so that they take account of the employees' and the public's interests – would increase legal certainty in employment relationships which nowadays often extend beyond a single jurisdiction. Such harmonisation of minimum standards would be efficient without infringing the principle of freedom of contracting. It does not appear appropriate to regulate non-competition agreements within the framework of harmonisation of trade-secret protection, as it would go beyond the safeguarding of undisclosed information.

III Striking the Balance When Granting Remedies

The remedy awarded for breaching a post-employment obligation must be an adequate response to the breach in question or, if damages are awarded, to the actual damage suffered by the ex-employer. Therefore, when granting such a remedy, balancing of interests can be applied only to a limited extent.

The courts award remedies inter partes, and therefore consider the private interests of the parties to the proceedings. The public interest in ethical behaviour seems to be reflected in the principle that remedies will be denied in case of abusive litigation, which may furthermore give rise to compensation for the defendant. But remedies should be applied in a flexible way, taking due account of the principle of proportionality.

The risk of abusive litigation is particularly high with preliminary injunctions, where unfounded applications may be used to harass former employees and exclude competition. That is why it is essential that such interim orders are not issued automatically. Even though their urgency is acknowledged, they should not be issued without any substantiation and an assessment of the merits of the case. Making a preliminary injunction conditional on the plaintiff filing a security is one way to limit the negative impact it might have on employee mobility. Another way – if the information is not self-disclosing and the injunction would severely affect the employee's right to work – is to accept use of the information in return for a security filed by the defendant. This may be appropriate if, for example, he is a specialist in a very narrow field and would have to resign from his new position if the injunction were issued.

Applying such measures introduces more balance into the granting of interim injunctions, and is also likely to have a deterrent effect on the initiation of unjustified preliminary proceedings. This could reduce litigation and costs for the former employer, who will be more likely to apply for relief only if he really believes that valuable information has to be protected, whilst also saving the ex-employee from having to defend himself against unjustified claims.

Lastly, given that proceedings on the merits can never take place in cases involving trade secrets, it is proposed that preliminary injunctions be time-limited if it is clear when the information in question is going to be disclosed. Otherwise, the order should set the plaintiff a time limit for filing an action on the merits, and should terminate automatically if he does not comply with it.

With respect to final injunctions, it is proposed that the court's discretion should encompass both whether to grant and how to frame them. Considering the negative impact on competition that an injunction prohibiting use of information might have, it is suggested that preference be given to injunctions against disclosure. They could help to strike a balance between employers' and employees' interests if the information is not self-disclosing, was obtained honestly and is necessary for the ex-employee to remain professionally active. In other cases, injunctions prohibiting both use and disclosure are accepted. If the information was obtained dishonestly, injunctions of unlimited duration are considered appropriate. Otherwise, they should be limited in time until the information becomes public (if this date is known), or for as long as necessary to neutralise the competitive advantage gained by the ex-employee.

It is proposed here that the courts, applying the principle of proportionality and balancing the competing interests, should be able to refuse the plaintiff an injunction and award him damages instead. They could issue such decisions, accepting use of the information and compensating the ex-employer for the future by way of damages (whether a lump sum or recurring payments akin to royalties), in cases where an ex-employee is in breach of a post-employment obligation but there are strong reasons to accept his continued use of the information. If the information was obtained honestly, is not automatically disclosed when used, is essential for the employee to remain professionally active, and the prejudice to the employer from allowing use is less than that to the ex-employee from denying it, and the amount of the damages payable can be readily quantified, ordering damages in lieu of injunction may have positive effects.

Damages are awarded if infringement has already taken place. Therefore, they are not suitable for achieving a balance of interests, their purpose being to put the aggrieved party into the position it would have been in if no infringement had taken place. It would therefore be preferable to introduce interest-balancing considerations at a legislative level. If the employee has acted honestly, one possibility could be to link the amount of damages awardable by the court to his final remuneration from his aggrieved employer. It is considered that this would increase legal certainty in the post-employment phase.

Lastly, determining the amount of damages is an objective exercise. So no account should be taken of non-economic factors such as moral prejudice to the ex-employer. Departing from a strictly economic and objective assessment might result in over-compensation, giving this remedy a punitive character.

As a general consideration it is advocated here that the courts should be reluctant to deny the use of information to former employees, unless they are found to have acted dishonestly, the information is an essential secret of the ex-employer and not necessary for the employee to remain professionally active, or if the information is self-disclosing. This is because competition as such is not reprehensible behaviour. Admittedly, accepting that the former employee can use the information adds another competitor to the market. However, he too will be interested in safeguarding the information's confidential nature, because it will support his own competitive position. At a general level, this might increase spillover innovation and encourage entrepreneurship. At the same time, accepting such use does not destroy the secret character of the information and thus does not take away the lead time possibly gained by the ex-employer through using it. The fact that there is one more competitor in the market is not considered likely to prejudice unduly the ex-employer's competitive position.[6]

The proposed application of remedies for infringement of post-employment obligations relating to information learned during employment is aimed at increasing legal certainty by providing guidelines, while respecting the need for flexibility and a case-by-case assessment when awarding remedies. In particular, under the guidelines proposed here, any dishonesty in obtaining the information precludes this flexible approach. Nor is it likely to be applicable to information which is essential for the former employer, such as technical secrets, chemical formulae or source code. For such information, the higher level of protection is likely to act as an incentive to innovate. At the same time, those active in fast-moving industries where innovation is based on knowledge-sharing, spill-over effects and mobility are likely to profit from the flexibility proposed.

IV Developments at EU Level

The Trade Secrets Directive does not contain tailor-made solutions for addressing employee-mobility issues. Nevertheless, by harmonising trade-secret enforcement to some extent, it is likely to increase legal certainty and thus have a positive effect on employee mobility[7] within the EU. The Directive acknowledges the importance of such mobility and of fundamental freedoms to choose an occupation, engage in work, conduct business and own property,[8] as well as possible tensions between employer and employee interests in these areas.

Thus Article 1(3)[9] states that the Directive is not to be understood as giving rise to any limitation of employee mobility, in particular to employees' use of information which is not a trade secret, and of their knowledge and experience honestly acquired during employment. While the statement that employees are allowed to use such knowledge and experience is welcome, placing it in the context of exclusion from the scope of the Directive rather than making it part of lawful use under Articles 3 and 4 is rather confusing. It does not fit well with the definition of trade secrets laid down in Article 2(1) of the Directive. It gives the impression that particular information learned by an employee may be either a trade secret or part of his skill and experience. Such a dichotomy

[6] With the exception of extremely narrow markets.
[7] MPI Position Paper para 4.
[8] Recital 34 TSD.
[9] See also Recital 14 TSD.

does not sit easily in the framework of the European jurisdictions analysed and the unfair competition approach taken in the Directive. It is submitted that whether specific information is part of an employee's skill and experience should be considered, together with other factors, when assessing the lawfulness of its acquisition, use and disclosure and in particular whether this complies with honest commercial practices (fairness). After all, information which is a trade secret might at the same time be part of the ex-employee's skill and experience, and it might therefore be fair to accept its use by him.

The implementation of the Directive is not likely to have a major impact on how the European jurisdictions analysed here approach the scope of post-employment implied obligations, since any act of acquisition, use or disclosure which is required or allowed by Union or national law is lawful under the Directive.[10] The acts of lawful and unlawful acquisition, use and disclosure laid down in Articles 3 to 5 of the Directive generally correspond to those in the analysed jurisdictions; in particular, acquiring information by unauthorised access or copying of documents and the like is unlawful. It is considered that including an open catalogue of factors to be taken into account when determining lawfulness under Article 3 would help to harmonise post-employment obligations. These could include the factors discussed above,[11] and in particular whether the information has become part of the employee's skill and experience, whether he needs it in order to continue working in a given field, and the competitive value of the information for the employer.

The Directive does not give rise to the imposition of any additional restrictions to employment contracts beyond those laid down in Union or national law,[12] and the possibility of concluding non-competition agreements remains exclusively in the jurisdiction of the Member States.[13] It is submitted that completely omitting post-employment agreements from the scope of the Directive does not serve the goal of harmonisation. After all, contractual regulation of post-employment use of information is an increasingly popular way of protecting trade secrets. Limiting freedom of contract or making agreements obligatory is not recommended. Nevertheless, in the case of non-disclosure agreements with employees, introducing a minimum level of regulation along the lines accepted in the jurisdictions analysed would significantly increase legal certainty and have a positive

[10] Art 3(2) TSD. See also Björn Kalbfus, 'Die EU-Geschäftsgeheimnis-Richtlinie. Welcher Umsetzungsbedarf besteht in Deutschland?' (2016) GRUR 1009, 1012.
[11] Chapter 3; Final conclusions, part I.
[12] Art 1(3)(c) TSD.
[13] Recitals 13, 39 TSD.

effect on mobility, knowledge spill-overs and innovation within the EU. It is not considered that it would increase transaction costs, since employers would remain free to opt for an agreement or rely on implicit post-employment obligations. The harmonisation of non-compete agreements goes beyond the framework of protection of trade secrets, as their effects are not confined to trade secrets only. Nor does such regulation appear possible under the EU's powers to establish competition rules necessary for the functioning of the internal market,[14] because the applicability of competition rules to post-employment agreements is doubtful.

Apart from harmonising the definition of trade secrets and defining infringing and non-infringing acts at a minimum level, the main part of the Directive lays down a framework for granting remedies for unlawful acquisition, use and disclosure of trade secrets. It provides for safeguards intended to ensure balance when such remedies are issued, by prescribing proportionality[15] and balancing of interests – including the public's – when preliminary[16] and final injunctions are issued.[17] These provisions, combined with Article 5(d) which prescribes denial of a remedy if the acquisition, use or disclosure occurred for the purpose of protecting a legitimate interest, have a character of full harmonisation. This is a welcome solution allowing the incorporation of national approaches to trade-secret enforcement while at the same time providing a uniform legal framework. This is likely to increase legal certainty, and strengthens the minimum harmonisation approach taken otherwise in the Directive.

Codifying proportionality and the balancing exercise is novel compared to the rules currently applied in the European jurisdictions analysed. The list of factors provided in the Directive is not exhaustive, but makes it clear that the parties' legitimate interests and the impact on their positions of granting a remedy, together with the interests of third parties and the public, are to be included in the assessment 'where appropriate'.[18] Including the parties' and the public's interests is particularly relevant when granting injunctions against former employees, and will thus be appropriate in such cases. Moreover, the balancing exercise includes a requirement to consider fundamental rights, in particular the freedom to choose an occupation, the right to work, the preservation of business secrets, and the right to effective remedies;[19] these are all of material importance in the employee-mobility context. The inclusion of the proportionality test is also

[14] Art 3(1)(b) TFEU.
[15] Arts 6 and 7(1) TSD.
[16] Art 11(2) TSD.
[17] Art 13(1) TSD.
[18] Arts 11(2) and 13(1) TSD.
[19] Recital 34 TSD.

to be welcomed as serving the goal of harmonisation, in particular since it corresponds to the proportionality requirement contained in the Enforcement Directive. Accordingly, a remedy should be granted only if it is suitable for achieving the goal in question and no less severe way of doing so is available. This is particularly important in the context of injunctions.

Furthermore, the Directive provides for sanctions for abusive litigation.[20] The fact that these are applied in separate proceedings seems less than entirely satisfactory in the context of employee mobility. Nevertheless, it is suggested that any abusive character of the litigation be taken into account in the balancing exercise pursuant to Articles 11(2) and 13(1) of the Directive. Still, from the perspective of conflict of interest in an employee-mobility scenario, it seems that the goal of harmonisation would be better served by explicitly including abusive conduct by a claimant, together with unjustified delay in applying for a preliminary injunction, in the catalogue of factors to be taken into account when granting remedies.

From the perspective of safeguarding the rights of respondents (defendants) in preliminary proceedings, under the Directive the granting of an interim injunction can be made conditional on the applicant filing a security,[21] the alleged infringer can be compensated if the measure is revoked for reasons relating to the applicant or if, at trial, no infringement is found to have occurred,[22] and the alleged infringer can be allowed to continue using the information, against a guarantee.[23] Furthermore, the order may be terminated, at the respondent's request, if proceedings on the merits are not started within the prescribed time limit or if the information is no longer a trade secret for reasons not attributable to the respondent.[24] The introduction of these measures at EU level is welcome, as they are likely to increase legal certainty and ensure greater flexibility and balance when provisional measures are issued. Nevertheless, it is submitted that preliminary injunctions should terminate automatically if proceedings on the merits are not started within the prescribed time limit. The solution adopted in the Directive forces ex-employees to bear costs of a new court action.

The Directive provides for minimum harmonisation of damages as a remedy for infringing the right to a trade secret. An interesting solution in the employee-mobility context – and another instance in which tension between employees' and employers' interests is recognised – is that the Member States will be able to restrict the liability of employees who acted

[20] Art 7(2) TSD.
[21] Art 11(4) TSD.
[22] Art 11(5) TSD.
[23] Art 10(2) TSD.
[24] Art 11(3) TSD.

without intent.[25] However, it is not clear whether this measure will apply to former employees as well as to existing ones. It is being introduced as minimum harmonisation and is to be applied in accordance with the Member States' 'national law and practice'. It is therefore unclear whether it will have a harmonising effect at all. It would be better if it also covered former employees and constituted full harmonisation. It should not be drafted as a blanket limitation, but rather should provide for certain determinable factors to be considered, including lack of intent on the employee's part, and an ex-employee's need to rely on the information in order to remain professionally active in the particular field. Moreover, tying the maximum damages to the last remuneration received by the employee might make it possible to set damages which would be both dissuasive and fair at the same time. However, that restriction should merely determine the upper limit, not take the place of calculating the damages actually sustained. The Directive also includes non-economic factors, such as moral prejudice, for consideration when setting the amount of damages.[26] But it is argued here that injury to trade secrets as assets should be measured in purely economic terms; non-economic factors should not be part of the mix.

Lastly, the Directive enables courts to award injured parties damages in lieu of injunction.[27] This is limited to 'innocent third parties' and thus will not apply to former employees. It is considered here that harmonisation would be better served by extending this solution to also cover the post-employment setting, e.g. by aligning the wording of the Directive with Article 12 of the Enforcement Directive. This remedy is already available in some Member States, and even though it is to be applied exceptionally – and therefore narrowly – it would give the courts a useful tool for addressing some trade-secret disputes in which there is a particularly serious conflict of interests between the employer and his former employee.

On the whole, it is considered here that while the Directive is a welcome development in the protection of trade secrets, and recognises some of the difficulties which can arise in the post-employment scenario, introducing the solutions discussed here would increase legal certainty and better serve the goal of harmonisation.[28]

[25] Art 14(1) TSD.

[26] Art 12(2) TSD.

[27] Art 13(3) TSD.

[28] For a discussion on how to implement the Directive into German law, see e.g. Mary-Rose McGuire, 'Der Schutz von Know-how im System des Immaterialgüterrechts. Perspektiven für die Umsetzung der Richtlinie über Geschäftsgeheimnisse' (2016) GRUR 1000 and Kalbfus, 'Die EU-Geschäftsgeheimnis-Richtlinie. Welcher Umsetzungsbedarf besteht in Deutschland?' 1009.

V General Assessment

The importance of the balancing of interests for determining post-employment obligations and awarding remedies should be recognised and seen in the broader context of public policy with respect to innovation, entrepreneurship and employment. Trade secrets, being assets, are likely to benefit from being treated as such and from a 'more economic approach' to their enforcement within the framework of information policy. Such an approach, based on case-by-case assessment, is expected to increase dynamic efficiency on a general level.[29] A legislative framework offering flexible tools aiming at enhancing the role of balance of interests is considered a good way of increasing legal certainty.

The benefits of a balanced system for enforcing trade secrets should not be underestimated. After all, in a knowledge-based economy any restriction of employee mobility is a double-edged sword: an employer who successfully limits competition from his ex-employees may soon find himself unable to hire qualified and experienced staff.

29 Carl J Belliston, *Patent Rights and Patent Infringement Remedies: Working toward a Unified Theory* (Department of Economics, The University of Utah, UMI Dissertation Services 2004) 11. In his argumentation, Belliston refers to 'inventions'. However, it seems that his definition of inventions may also encompass trade secrets, ibid. 3.

Bibliography

I Legislation

International

Agreement on Trade-related Aspects of Intellectual Property Rights (**TRIPS**)

Paris Convention for the Protection of Industrial Property of 20 March 1883, as revised and amended (**Paris Convention, PC**)

Germany

Grundgesetz für die Bundesrepublik Deutschland [GG] [Basic Law for the Federal Republic of Germany], 23 May 1949, BGBl III 100–1 as amended, English translation available at www.gesetze-im-internet.de/englisch_gg/index.html accessed 1 June 2017 (**GG**)

Bürgerliches Gesetzbuch [BGB] [Civil Code], 18 August 1896, RGBl at 195, as amended, English translation available on www.gesetze-im-internet.de/englisch_bgb/index.html accessed 1 June 2017 (**BGB**)

Gesetz gegen den unlauteren Wettbewerb [UWG] [Act against Unfair Competition], 3 March 2010, BGBl I at 254 with amendments, English translation available at www.gesetze-im-internet.de/englisch_uwg/index.html accessed 1 June 2017 (**UWG**)

Handelsgesetzbuch [HGB] [Commercial Code], 5 May 1897, BGBl III at 4100–1, as amended (**HGB**)

Gesetz gegen Wettbewerbsbeschränkungen [GWB] [Act against Restraints of Competition], 26 August 1998, BGBl I 1750, 3245 as amended, English translation available at www.gesetze-im-internet.de/englisch_gwb/index.html accessed 1 June 2017 (**GWB**)

Gewerbeordnung [GewO] [Act on Trade], 21 June 1896, BGBl I 202 as amended (**GewO**)

Gesetz über Urheberrecht und verwandte Schutzrechte [UrhG] [Copyright Act], 9 September 1965, BGBl I 1273 as amended, English translation available at www.gesetze-im-internet.de/englisch_urhg/index.html accessed 1 June 2017 (**UrhG**)

Patentgesetz [PatG] [Patent Act], 5 May 1936, BGBl 1981 I 1 as amended, English translation available at www.gesetze-im-internet.de/englisch_patg/index.html accessed 1 June 2017 (**PatG**)

Gesetz über Arbeitnehmererfindungen [ArbnErfG] [Act on Employee Inventions], 25 July 1957, BGBl I 2521 as amended (**ArbnErfG**)

Gesetz über den rechtlichen Schutz von Design [DesignG] [Design Act] 12 March 2004, BGBl I 122 as amended (**DesignG**)

Strafgesetzbuch [StGB] [Criminal Act] 15 May 1871, BGBl I 3322 as amended, English translation available at www.gesetze-im-internet.de/englisch_stgb/index.html accessed 1 June 2017 (**StGB**)

Zivilprozessordnung [ZPO] [Civil Procedure Statute], 12 September 1950, BGBl at 455, as amended, English translation available on www.gesetze-im-internet.de/englisch_zpo/index.html accessed 1 June 2017 (**ZPO**)

United Kingdom

Human Rights Act 1998 (**HRA**)

Copyright, Designs and Patents Act 1988 (**CDPA**)

Patents Act 1977

Competition Act 1998

United States

US Patent Act, US Code Title 35 (**US Patent Act**)

US Copyright Act, US Code Title 17 (**USCA**)

Sherman Act, US Code Title 15 (**Sherman Act**)

Federal Rules of Civil Procedure

California Business and Professions Code

California Labor Code

Uniform Trade Secrets Act (**UTSA**)

Defend Trade Secters Act (**DTSA**)

Restatement (First) of Torts

Restatement (Third) of Unfair Competition

Restatement (Third) of Agency

Antitrust Guidelines for the Licensing of Intellectual Property, US Department of Justice and the Federal Trade Commission, 6 April 1995 www.justice.gov/atr/public/guidelines/0558.htm#t22 accessed 1 June 2017

European Union

Treaty on the Functioning of the European Union, consolidated version [2012] OJ C 326 (**TFEU**)

Commission Regulation (EU) No 316/2014 of 21 March 2014 on the application of Article 101(3) of the Treaty on the Functioning of the European Union to categories of technology transfer agreements [2014] OJ L 93/17 (**TTBER**)

Commission Regulation (EC) No 1217/2010 of 14 December 2010 on the application of Article 101(3) TFEU to certain categories of research and development agreements [2010] OJ L355/36 (**RDBER**)

Directive 96/9/EC of the European Parliament and of the Council of 11 March 1996 on the legal protection of databases [1996] OJ L77/20 (**Database Directive**)

Directive 2004/48/EC of the European Parliament and of the Council of 29 April 2004 on the enforcement of intellectual property rights [2004] OJ L 157 (**Enforcement Directive**)

Statement 2005/295/EC by the Commission concerning Article 2 of Directive 2004/48/EC of the European Parliament and of the Council on the enforcement of intellectual property rights [2005] OJ L 94/37

Directive (EU) 2016/943 of the European Parliament and of the Council of 8 June 2016 on the protection of undisclosed know-how and business information (trade secrets) against their unlawful acquisition, use and disclosure [2016] OJ L 157 (**Trade Secrets Directive, TSD**)

Commission, 'Commission Staff Working Document Impact Assessment Accompanying the document proposal for a Directive of the European Parliament and of the Council on the protection of undisclosed know-how and business information (trade secrets) against their unlawful acquisition, use and disclosure' COM (2013) 813 final, SWD(2013) 472 final, SWD(2013) 493 final, SWD(2013) 471 final http://eur-lex.europa.eu/legal-content/EN/TXT/PDF/?uri=CELEX:52013SC0471&from=EN accessed 1 June 2017

Final compromise text of the Proposal for a Directive of the European Parliament and of the Council on the protection of undisclosed know-how and business information (trade secrets) against their unlawful acquisition, use and disclosure, Document 15382/1/15 REV 1 http://data.consilium.europa.eu/doc/document/ST-15382-2015-REV-1/en/pdf accessed 1 June 2017

European Convention on Human Rights of 4 November 1950

Other

Resolution 571 (1974) on the protection of manufacturing and commercial secrets, adopted by the Parliamentary Assembly of Council of Europe on 3 July 1974, http://assembly.coe.int/Main.asp?link=/Documents/AdoptedText/ta74/ERES571.htm accessed 6 March 2015, on file with the author

Ustawa z dnia 26 czerwca 1974r. Kodeks Pracy, Dz U 1974 nr 24 poz 141, with amendments (**Polish Labour Code**)

II Case Law

Germany

BGH GRUR 2006, 1044 *Kundendatenprogramm*

BGH GRUR 2003, 356, *Präzisionsmessgeräte*

BGH GRUR 1995, 349 *Objektive Schadensberechnung*

BGH WRP 2002, 214 *Spiegel-CD-Rom*
BGH GRUR 1991, 914 *Kastanienmuster*
BGH GRUR 1993, 55 *Tchibo/Rolex II*
BGH GRUR 1962, 509 *Dia-Rämchen II*
BGH GRUR 2001, 329 *Berechnung des Verletzergewinns nach Schutzrechtsverstoß*
BGH GRUR 1977, 539 *Prozessrechner*
BGH GRUR 1999, 934 *Weinberater*
BGH GRUR 1963, 367 *Industrieböden*
BGH GRUR 1964, 215 *Milchfahrer*
BGH NJW 2009, 1420 *Versicherungsvertreter*
BGH GRUR 1955, 424 *Möbelpaste* with reference to RGZ 149, 334 = GRUR 1936, 255, *Kaffee-Kanne*,
BGH GRUR 1961, 40 *Wurftaubenpresse*
MMR 2001, 310 (BGH) *Wetterführungspläne I*
MMR 2002, 99 (BGH) *Wetterführungspläne II*
BGH GRUR 2012, 1048 *MOVICOL-Zulassungsantrag*
OLG Köln GRUR-RR 2010, 480 *Werbeadressen als Geschäftsgeheimnis*
NJW 1967, 125 (BAG)
BGH GRUR 2009, 694 *Orange Book Standard*
RGZ 149, 329 *Stiefeleisenpresse*
BGH GRUR 2008, 727 *Schweißmodulgenerator*
BGH GRUR 1985, 294 *Füllanlage*
BGH GRUR 1983, 179 *Stapel-Automat*
BGH GRUR 2002, 91 *Spritzgießwerkzeuge*
BGH GRUR 1998, 489 *Unbestimmter Unterlassungsantrag III*
BGH GRUR 1955, 388 *Dücko*
BGH GRUR 1955, 468 *Schwermetall-Kokillenguß*
BGH GRUR 1960, 554 *Handstrickverfahren*
BGH GRUR 1955, 402 *Anreißgerät*
BGH NJW 2000, 2584 *Mandantenschutzklausel*
NJW 1983, 134 (BAG) *Thrombosol*
NJW 1988, 1686 (BAG) *Kundenlisten* = NZA 1988, 502 (BAG) *Kundenschutzabrede*
NJW 2006, 3803 (BAG) *Herausgabeanspruch*
NZA 1999, 200 (BAG) *Kantenbänder*
NZA 1994, 502 (BAG) *Titanoxid*
NZA 2011, 413 (BAG) *Vorvertrag bei Wettbewerbsverbot*
NZA 2010, 1175 (BAG) *Anspruch auf Karenzentschädigung*
NZA 2008, 170 (BAG) *Wirksamkeit einer Vertragsstrafenabrede*
OLG München judgment of 28.06.2012, 6U 1560/12
WRP 1995, 114 (OLG Celle) judgment of 26.05.1994, 13U 29/94
WRP 2008, 938 (BGH) *Entwendete Datensätze mit Konstruktionszeichnungen*
WRP 1993, 36 (OLG Hamm) *Tierohrmarken*
LAG Hamm judgment of 05.10.1988, 15 Sa 1403/88, BeckRS 1988, 06934
LAG Thüringen decision of 11.06.2001, 8 Sa 418/00, ZIP 2002, 587
LAG Baden-Württemberg judgment of 30.01.2008, 10 Sa 60/07, NZA-RR 2008, 508
OLG Düsseldorf judgment of 24.05.2005, I-20 U 25/05 MMR 2005, 776

LAG Niedersachsen judgment of 08.12.2005, 7 Sa 1871/05
LAG Hamm judgment of 12.09.2006, 7 Sa 1356/06
BAG judgment of 16.12.1968, 3 AZR 434/67, AP GewO §133 Nr 21
BAG judgment of 30.01.1970, 3 AZR 348/69, AP GewO §133 Nr 24
BAG judgment of 24.06.1986, 3 AZR 486/84, AP BGB § 611 *Betriebsgeheimnis Nr.4*
BVerfG NVwZ 2006, 1041.

United Kingdom

AB and CD [2014] EWHC 1 (QB)
Allfiled UK Ltd v Eltis & 16 Others [2015] EWHC 1300 (Ch)
American Cyanamid Co v Ethicon Ltd [1975] AC 396 (HL)
Arbuthnot Funds Managers v Rawlings [2003] EWCA Civ 518 (EWCA)
Associated Foreign Exchange Ltd v International Foreign Exchange (UK) Ltd [2010] EWHC 1178 (Ch)
AT Poeton (Gloucester Plating) Ltd and Another v Horton and Another [2000] ICR 1208 (CA)
Attorney General v Newspaper Publishing Plc [1989] 2 FSR 27 (Ch)
Balston Ltd v Headline Filters Ltd [1987] FSR 330 (Ch)
Basic Solutions Ltd v Robert Sands [2008] EWHC 1388 (QB)
BBC v Collins [2010] EWHC 2424 (Ch)
Beckett Investment Management Group Ltd v Hall [2007] EWCA Civ 613 (CA)
Boardman v Phipps [1967] 2 AC 46 (HL)
Brake Brothers Ltd v Ungless [2004] EWHC 2799 (QB)
Caterpillar Logistics Services v Huesca de Crean [2012] EWCA Civ 156 (CA)
Coco v Clark Ltd [1968] FSR 415 (Ch)
Coogan and Phillips v News Group Newspapers Ltd and Mulcaire [2012] EWCA Civ 48 (EWCA).
Corporate Express Ltd v Day [2004] EWHC 2943 (QB)
Coventry v Lawrence [2014] UKSC 13 (UKSC)
Cranleigh Precision Engineering Ltd v Bryant and Another [1965] 1 WLR 1293 (QB)
Crowson Fabrics Ltd v Rider [2008] FSR 17 (Ch)
Cyrus Energy Ltd v Stewart [2009] CSOH 53 (CSOH)
Dawnay Day & Co Ltd v D'Alphen [1998] ICR 1068 (CA)
Donoghue v Allied Newspapers Ltd [1938] Ch 106 (Ch)
Douglas v Hello! Ltd (No3) [2006] 1 QB 125 (CA)
Dyson Technology Ltd v Strutt [2005] EWHC 2814 (Ch)
Faccenda Chicken v Fowler [1984] ICR 589 (Ch)
Faccenda Chicken v Fowler [1987] 1 Ch 117 (CA)
Fairstar v Adkins [2012] EWHC 2952 (TCC)
Fairstar v Adkins [2013] EWCA Civ 886 (CA)
Force India Formula One Team Ltd v Aerolab Srl & Another [2013] EWCA Civ 780 (EWCA)
GD Searle & Co Ltd v Celltech Ltd and Others [1982] FSR 92 (CA)

General Billposting Co Ltd v Atkinson [1909] AC 118 (HL)
Generics (UK) Ltd v Yeda Research and Development Co Ltd [2012] EWCA Civ 726 (EWCA)
Gilford Motor Company Ltd v Horne [1933] Ch 935 (CA)
Helmet Integrated Systems Ltd v Tunnard [2007] FSR (16) 437 (CA)
Herbert Morris Ltd v Saxelby [1916] 1 AC 688 (HL)
International Consulting Services (UK) Ltd v Hart [2000] IRLR 227 (QB)
Investors Compensation Scheme Ltd v West Bromwich Building Society [1998] 1 WLR 896 (HL)
Lancashire Fires Ltd v SA Lyons & Comp Ltd and Others [1996] FSR 629 (CA)
Lansing Linde v Kerr [1991] 1 WLR 251 (CA)
Lawrence David Ltd v Ashton [1989] ICR 123 (CA)
M&S Drapers (A Firm) v Reynolds [1957] 1 WLR 9 (CA)
Mars v Teknowledge [1999] EWHC 226 (Pat)
Mason v Provident [1913] AC 724 (HL)
Mustad v Allock and Dosen (1928) [1964] 1 WLR 109 (HL)
Ocular Sciences Ltd v Aspect Vision Care Ltd [1997] RPC 289 (Pat).
Phillips v Mulcaire [2012] UKSC 28 (UKSC)
Potters-Ballotini v Weston Baker [1977] RPC 202 (CA)
Pride of Derby v British Celanese [1953] Ch 149 (CA)
Prince Albert v Strange [1849] EWHC Ch J20 (EWHC)
Prince Jefri Bolkiah v KPMG [1999] 2 AC 222 (HL)
Printers & Finishers v Holloway [1965] 1 WLR 1 (CA)
Prophet Plc v Christopher Huggett [2014] EWCA Civ 1013 (EWCA)
Re-Use Collections Ltd v Sendall [2014] EWHC 3852 (QB)
Rex Stewart Jeffries Parker Ginsberg Ltd v Parker [1988] IRLR 483 (CA)
Rock Refrigeration Ltd v Jones [1997] ICR 938 (CA)
Roger Bullivant Ltd v Ellis [1987] ICR 464 (CA)
Schering Chemicals Ltd v Falkman Ltd and Others [1982] QB 1 (CA)
Scully UK Ltd v Lee [1998] IRLR 259 (CA)
Seager v Copydex (No 2) [1969] 1 WLR 809 (CA)
Seager v Copydex [1967] 1 WLR 923 (CA)
Secktrack NV v Satamatics Ltd [2007] EWHC3003 (Comm)
Series 5 Software Ltd v Clarke [1996] FSR 273 (Ch)
Sun Valley Foods v Vincent [2000] FSR 825 (Ch)
Sunrise Brokers LLP and Michael William Rodgers [2014] EWHC 2633 (QB)
Thermascan Ltd v Norman [2009] EWHC 3694 (QB)
Thomas Marshall v Guinle [1979] 1 Ch 227 (Ch)
Threeway Pressings Ltd [2012] BL O/124/12 (UKIPO)
Triplex Safety Glass Co v Scorah [1938] Ch 211 (Ch)
Universal Thermosensors v Hibben [1992] 1 WLR 840 (Ch)
Vercoe v Rutland Fund [2010] EWHC 424 (Ch)
Vestergaard Frandsen A/S & Ors v Bestnet Europe Ltd & Ors [2009] EWHC 1456 (Ch)
Vestergaard Frandsen A/S & Ors v Bestnet Europe Ltd & Ors [2011] EWCA Civ 424 (CA)

Vestergaard Frandsen A/S & Ors v Bestnet Europe Ltd & Ors [2013] UKSC 31 (UKSC)
Volkswagen AG v Garcia and others [2013] EWHC 1832 (Ch)
Wallace Bogan & Co v Cove [1997] IRLR 453 (CA)
Western Excavating (ECC) Ltd v Sharp [1978] 1 QB 761 (CA)
WWF World Wide Fund for Nature v World Wrestling Federation Entertainment Inc [2006] EWHC 184 (Ch)

United States

Al Minor & Assocs v Martin 881 NE 2d 850 (Supr Ct Ohio 2008)
American Airlines Inc v Imhof 620 F Supp 2d 574 (SDNY 2009)
AMP Inc v Fleischhacker 823 F 2d 1199 (7th Cir 1987)
Ashland Mgt Inc v Altair Invs NA LLC 59 A D 3d 97 (1st Dep't 2008)
Aspect Software Inc v Barnett, 787 F Supp 2d 118 (D Mass 2011)
Avery Dennison Corp v Kitsonas 118 F Supp 2d 848 (SD Ohio 2000)
Basicomputer Corp v Scott 973 F 2d 507 (6th Cir 1992)
BDO Seidman v Hirshberg 690 NYS 2d 854 (NY Ct App 1999)
Bed Mart Inc v Kelley 45 P 3d 1219 (Ariz App 2002)
Bimbo Bakeries USA Inc v Botticella 613 F3d 102 (3d Cir 2010)
Bonito Boats v Thunder Craft Boats 489 US 141 (US Supr Ct 1989)
Bryceland v Northey 772 P 2d 36 (Arizona Ct App 1989)
By-Buk Co v Printed Cellophane Tape Co 163 Cal App 2d 157(Cal 1958)
Cherne Indus Inc v Grounds & Assocs Inc 278 NW 2d 81 (Supr Ct Minn 1979)
Com-Co Insurance Agency Inc v Service Insurance Agency Inc 748 NE 2d 298, 301 – 302 (Ill App 2001)
Comprehensive Technologies Int v Software Artisans Inc 3 F 3d 730 (4th Cir 1993)
Continental Group Inc v Kinsley 422 F Supp 838 (D Conn 1976)
CVD Inc v Raytheon Co 769 F2d 842 (1st Cir 1985)
Dynamics Research Corp v Analytic Sciences Corp 400 NE 2d 1274 (Mass CA 1980)
Eagle Group v Pullen 58 P 3d 292 (Wash App 2002)
EarthWeb Inc v Schlack 71 F Supp 2d 299 (SDNY 1999)
eBay Inc v MercExchange LLC 547 US 388 (US Supr Ct 2006)
Ed Nowogroski Insurance Inc v Michael Rucker et al 137 Wash 2d 427 (Washington Supr Ct 1999)
Edwards v Arthur Andersen LLP 81 Cal Rptr 3d 282 (Cal Sup Ct 2008)
EI DuPont de Nemours & Co v Christopher 431 F 2d 1012 (5th Cir 1970)
EI DuPont de Nemours and Co v American Potash & Chemical Corp 220 A 2d 428 (Del Ch 1964)
EI DuPont de Nemours Powder Co v Masland 244 US 100 (US Supr Ct 1917)
Electronic Data Systems Corp v Heinemann 268 Ga 755 (Ga 1997)
Faiveley Transport Malmo Ab v WABTEC Corporation 559 F 3d 110 (2nd Cir 2009)
Feist Publications Inc v Rural Telephone Service Co, 499 US 340 (US Supr Ct 1991)
Fenner Precision Inc v Mearthane Products Corp Case No 12-CV-6610 CJS (WDNY 2013)
Fleming Sales Company Inc v Joseph W Bailey 611 F Supp 507 (Ill Distr Ct 1985)

Foodcomm Int v Barry 328 F3d 300 (7th Cir 2003)
Franke v Wiltschek 209 F 2d 439 (CA2 NY 1953)
Garber Bros Inc v Evlek 122 F Supp 2d 375 (EDNY 2000)
Grant v Carotek 737 F 2d 410 (4th Cir 1984)
Henry Hope X-Ray Products Inc v Marrion Carrel Inc 674 F 2d 1336 (9th Cir 1982)
Heyden Chemical Corp v Burrell & Neidig 2 64 A 2d 465 (NJ Super 1949)
Horner Intl Co v McKoy Case No COA 13–964 (North Carolina Ct App 2014)
IBM v Papermaster 2008 WL 4974508 (SDNY 2008)
Imperial Chemical Industries Ltd v National Distillers and Chemical Corp 342 F 2d 737 (CA 2nd Circuit 1965)
In re Innovative Construction Systems Inc 793 F2d 875 (7th Cir 1986)
Jostens Inc v National Computer Systems Inc 318 NW 2d 691 (Supr Ct Minn 1982)
K-2 Ski Company v Head Ski Co Inc 506 f 2d 471 (9th Cir 1974)
Kewanee Oil Co v Bicron Corp 416 US 470 (US Supr Ct 1974)
Kilbarr Corp v Bus Sys Inc 679 F Supp 422 (DNJ 1988)
Kodekey Electronics Inc v The Mechanex Corp 486 F2d 449 (10th Cir 1973)
Liautaud v Liautaud 221 F 3d 981 (7th Cir 2000)
Litigation Management Inc v Bourgeois 2011 WL 2270553 (Ohio Ct App 2011)
Lucent Technologies Inc v Gateway Inc 580 F3d 1301 (Fed Cir 2009)
Mangren Research & Dev Corp v National Chem Co 87 F 3d 937 (7th Cir 1996)
Modern Environments Inc v Stinnett 561 S E 2d 694 (Va Sup Ct 2002)
Motorola Inc v Computer Displays International Inc 739 F 2d 1149 (7th Cir 1984)
Muggill v Reuben H Donnelley Corp 62 Cal 2d 239 (Supr Ct California 1965)
Mutual Service Casualty Insurance Co v Brass 625 NW 2d 648 (Wis App 2001)
Outsource International Inc v Barton 192 F3d 662 (7th Cir 1999)
Panduit Corp v Stahlin Bros 575 F2d 1152 (6th Cir 1978)
Pappan Enters v Hardee's Food Sys 143 F3d 800, 803 (3rd Cir 1998)
Paramanandam v Herrmann 827 NE 2d 1173 (Ind CA 2005)
PepsiCo Inc v Redmond 54 F 3d 1262 (7th Cir 1995)
Precision Plating & Metal Finishing Inc v Martin-Marietta Corp 435 F 2d 1262 (5th Cir 1970)
Professional Real Estate Investors Inc v Columbia Pictures Industries Inc 508 US 49 (US Supr Ct 1993)
Reed Roberts Assocs v Strauman 40 NY 2d 303 (Ct App 1976)
Republic Aviation Corp v Schenk 152 USPQ 830 (NY Sup Ct 1967)
Roboserve Ltd v Tom's Foods Inc 940 F 2d 1441 (11th Cir 1991)
Ruckelshaus v Monsanto 467 US 986 (US Supr Ct 1984)
Sabatino Bianco v Globus Medical No 2:2012cv00147 – Document 45 (E D Tex 2012)
Sabatino Bianco v Globus Medical WL 2980740 (E D Tex 2014)
SI Handling Systems v Heisley 753 F 2d 1244 (3rd Cir 1985)
Silicon Image Inc v Analogix Semiconductor Inc No C-07-00635 JCS (not reported in F Sup 2d) 2008 WL 166950 (ND Cal 2008)
Silvaco Data Systems v Intel Corp 109 Cal Rptr 3d 27 (Cal App 2010)
Standard Register Co v Cleaver 30 F Supp 2d 1084, 1095 (7th Cir ND Ind 1998)
Structural Dynamics Research Corp v Engineering Mechanics Research Corp 401 F Supp 1102 (ED Mich 1975)

United States v First National City Bank 379 US 378 (Supr Ct 1965)
University Computing Co v Lykes-Youngstown Corp 504 F 2d 518 (5th Cir 1974)
Winston Research Corp v Minnesota Mining and Manufacturing Company 350 F 2d 134 (9th Cir 1965)
World Wide Prosthetic Supply Inc v Mikulsky 631 NW 2d 253 (Wis App 2001)

GC

Case T-201/04 *Microsoft v Commission* [2007] ECR II-03601

ECJ/CJEU

Case C-126/97 *Eco Swiss China Time Ltd and Benetton International NV* [1999] ECR I-3079
Case C-22/98 *Jean Claude Becu* [1999] ECRI-5665
Case C-415/93 *Bosman* [1995] ECR I-04921
Joined Cases C-267/91 and C-268/91 *Keck and Mithouard* [1993] ECR I-06097
Case 27/76 *United Brands Company and United Brands Continentaal BV v Commission of the European Communities* [1978] ECR 1978 00207
Case T-111/96 *ITT Promedia v Commission* [1998] ECR II-02937
Joined Cases T-191, T 212 – 214/98 *Atlantic Container Line and Others v Commission* [2003] ECR-II-3275
Case C-5/08 *Infopaq* [2009] ECR I-06569
Case C-393/09 *BSA* [2010] ECR I-13971
Combined cases C-403/08 and C-429/08 *Murphy* [2011] I-09083
Case C-170/13 *Huawei Technologies Co. Ltd v ZTE* [2015] ECLI:EU:C:2015:477
Case C-367/15 *Stowarzyszenie 'Oławska Telewizja Kablowa' v Stowarzyszenie Filmowców Polskich* [2017] ECLI:EU:C:2016:900, Opinion of AG Sharpston
Case C-367/15 *Stowarzyszenie 'Oławska Telewizja Kablowa' v Stowarzyszenie Filmowców Polskich* [2017] ECLI:EU:C:2017:36

European Commission

Reuter/BASF (Case IV/28.996) Commission Decision 76/743/EEC [1976] OJ L254/40

III Books

–, *Münchner Kommentar zum Bürgerlichen Gesetzbuch* (6th edn, CH Beck 2012)
Altman L and Pollack M, *Callmann on Unfair Competition, Trademarks and Monopolies* (4th edn, Clark Boardman Callaghan 2012)
Ann C, Loschelder M and Grosch M, *Praxishandbuch Know-how-Schutz* (1st edn, Carl Heymanns Verlag 2010)
Aplin T and others, *Gurry on Breach of Confidence: The Protection of Confidential Information* (2nd edn, Oxford University Press 2012)

Basedow J (ed), *Private Enforcement of EC Competition Law* (Kluwer Law International 2007)

Bauer J-H and Diller M, *Wettbewerbsverbote* (7th edn, CH Beck 2015)

Bechtold R and Bosch W, *Kartellgesetz. Gesetz gegen Wettbewerbsbeschränkungen. Kommentar* (8th edn, CH Beck 2015)

Beebe B and others, *Trademarks, Unfair Competition, and Business Torts* (2nd edn, Wolters Kluwer 2016)

Belliston CJ, *Patent Rights and Patent Infringement Remedies: Working toward a Unified Theory* (Department of Economics, The University of Utah, UMI Dissertation Services 2004)

Bently L and Sherman B, *Intellectual Property Law* (4th edn, Oxford University Press 2014)

Berger C and others, *Einstweiliger Rechtsschutz im Zivilrecht* (Erich Schmidt Verlag 2006)

Busche J, Stoll P-T and Wiebe A, *TRIPs. Internationales und europäisches Recht des geistigen Eigentums. Kommentar* (2nd edn, Carl Heymanns Verlag 2013)

Coleman A, *The Legal Protection of Trade Secrets* (Sweet&Maxwell 1992)

Cornish W and others, *Intellectual Property: Patents, Copyright, Trade Marks and Allied Rights* (8th edn, Sweet&Maxwell 2013)

Correa CM, *Trade Related Aspects of Intellectual Property Rights. A Commentary on the TRIPS Agreement* (Oxford University Press 2007)

Correa CM and Yusuf AA (eds), *Intellectual Property and International Trade: The TRIPS Agreement* (3rd edn, Wolters Kluwer 2016)

Darbyshire P, *Darbyshire on the English Legal System* (10th edn, Sweet&Maxwell 2011)

de Werra J (ed), *La protection des secrets d'affaires. The Protection of Trade Secrets* (Schulthess 2013)

Dreier T and Schulze G, *Urheberrechtsgesetz* (5th edn, CH Beck 2015)

Dreyer G, Kotthoff J, Meckel A and Zeisberg H-J, *Urheberrecht* (3rd edn, C F Müller 2013)

Dreyfuss RC and Strandburg KJ (eds), *The Law and Theory of Trade Secrecy: A Handbook of Contemporary Research* (Edward Elgar 2011)

Estlund CL and Wachter ML (eds), *Research Handbook on the Economics of Labor and Employment Law* (Cheltenham: Edward Elgar 2012)

Fabry B and Trimborn M, *Arbeitnehmererfindungsrecht im internationalen Vergleich* (1st edn, Carl Heymanns Verlag 2007)

Garner BA (ed), *Black's Law Dictionary* (9th edn, Thomson Reuters 2009)

Gassmann O and Bader MA, *Patentmanagement. Innovationen erfolgreich nützen und schützen* (3rd edn, Springer 2011)

Geiger Ch (ed), *Research Handbook on Human Rights and Intellectual Property* (Edward Elgar 2015)

Gervais D, *The TRIPS Agreement: Drafting History and Analysis* (4th edn, Sweet&Maxwell 2012)

Glick MA, Reymann LA and Hoffman R, *Intellectual Property Damages: Guidelines and Analysis* (John Wiley & Sons, Inc 2003)

Götting H-P and Nordemann A, *UWG Handkommentar* (3rd edn, Nomos 2016)

Goulding P, *Employee competition. Covenants, Confidentiality and Garden Leave* (3rd edn, Oxford University Press 2016)

Harte-Bavendamm H and Henning-Bodewig F, *Gesetz gegen den unlauteren Wettbewerb (UWG)* (4th edn, CH Beck 2016)

Hengstler AJ, *Die Geheimhaltungsvereinbarung (Non-Disclosure Agreement)* (Verlag Recht und Wirtschaft Frankfurt am Main 2011)

Hodkinson K and Wasik M, *Industrial Espionage Protection and Remedies* (Longman Intelligence Reports, Longman Group UK Ltd 1986)

Hull J, *Commercial Secrecy: Law and Practice* (Sweet&Maxwell 1998)

Huston JP, *The Law of Trade Secret Litigation Under the Uniform Trade Secrets Act* (Juris Publishing 2016)

Jager M, *Trade Secrets Law* (Thomson Reuters 2015)

Kalbfus BH, *Know-how-Schutz in Deutschland zwischen Strafrecht und Zivilrecht – welcher Reformbedarf besteht?* (Carl Heymanns Verlag 2011)

Kamerling A and Goodwill C, *Restrictive Covenants under Common and Competition Law* (Sweet&Maxwell 2010)

Keller E, Plassmann C and von Falck A (eds), *Festschrift für Winfried Tilmann* (Carl Heymanns Verlag 2003)

Köhler H and Bornkamm J, *Gesetz gegen den unlauteren Wettbewerb* (35th edn, CH Beck 2017)

Kurz P, *Vertraulichkeitsvereinbarungen* (3rd edn, Carl Heymanns Verlag 2013)

Landes WA and Posner RA, *The Economic Structure of Intellectual Property Law* (The Belknap Press of Harvard University Press 2003)

Lawson FH and Teff H, *Remedies of English Law* (2nd edn, London Butterworths 1980)

Loewenheim U and Raiser T (eds), *Festschrift für Fritz Traub zum 65. Geburtstag* (Deutscher Fachverlag 1994)

Malbon J, Lawson C and Davison M, *The WTO Agreement on Trade–Related Aspects of Intellectual Property Rights* (Edward Elgar 2014)

Maunz T and Dürig G, *Grundgesetz-Kommentar* (69th edn, CH Beck 2013)

Mehigan S and Griffiths D, *Restraint of Trade and Business Secrets* (3rd edn, Sweet&Maxwell 1996)

Mestmäcker E-J and Schweitzer H, *Europäisches Wettbewerbsrecht* (3rd edn, CH Beck 2014)

Milgrim RM and Bensen EE, *Milgrim on Trade Secrets* (102nd edn, Lexis Nexis 2013)

Ohly A and Sosnitza O, *UWG. Gesetz gegen den unlauteren Wettbewerb* (7th edn, CH Beck 2016)

Peel E, *The Law of Contract* (13th edn, Sweet&Maxwell 2011)

Pendergrast M, *For God, Country & Coca-Cola: The Definitive History of the Great American Soft Drink and the Company That Makes It* (3rd edn, Basis Books 2013)

Peterson GR, *Trade Secret Protection in an Information Age* (Glasser Legal Works 1997)

Pires de Carvalho N, *The TRIPS Regime of Antitrust and Undisclosed Information* (Kluwer Law International 2008)

Pittard M, Monotti AL and Duns J (eds), *Business Innovation and the Law. Perspectives from Intellectual Property, Labour, Competition and Corporate Law* (Edward Elgar 2013)

Pooley J, *Trade Secrets* (6th edn, Law Journal Press 2002)

Poth H, *Die Grenzen des Arbeitsrechts aus kartellrechtlicher Sicht* (Peter Lang 1990)
Prinz zu Waldeck und Pyrmont W, Adelman MJ, Brauneis R, Drexl J and Nack R (eds), *Patents and Technological Progress in a Globalized World. Liber Amicorum Joseph Straus* (Springer 2009)
Quinto D W, Singer S H and McCauley C A *Trade Secrets: Law and Practice* (Lexis Nexis 2016)
Ribeiro R, *Damages and Other Remedies for Breach of Commercial Contracts* (Thorogood 2005)
Schlötter R, *Der Schutz von Betriebs- und Geschäftsgeheimnissen und die Abwerbung von Arbeitnehmern* (Carl Heymanns Verlag 1997)
Schramm C, *Der Patentverletzungsprozess* (7th edn, Carl Heymanns Verlag 2013)
Schumpeter JA, *Capitalism, Socialism and Democracy* (5th edn, Routledge reprinted 1996)
Schweyer F, *Die rechtliche Bewertung des Reverse Engineering in Deutschland und den USA* (Mohr Siebeck 2012)
Sigmund PE (ed), *The Selected Political Writings of John Locke* (W W Norton & Company 2005)
Snyder DW and Almeling DS, *Keeping Secrets: A Practical Introduction to Trade Secret Law and Strategy* (1st edn, Oxford University Press 2012)
Spry ICF, *The Principles of Equitable Remedies* (4th edn, Sweet&Maxwell 1990)
Stanley P, *The Law of Confidentiality: A Restatement* (Hart Publishing 2008)
Surblytė G, *The Refusal to Disclose Trade Secrets and Abuse of Market Dominance - Microsoft and Beyond* (Stämpfli Publishers Ltd Berne 2011)
Taeger J, *Softwareschutz durch Geheimnisschutz* (Lüneburg, 1991)
Toulson RG and Phipps CM, *Confidentiality* (3rd edn, Sweet&Maxwell, 2012)
UNCTAD, *Resource Book on TRIPS and Development* (Cambridge University Press 2005)
van Caenegem W, *Trade Secrets and Intellectual Property. Breach of Confidence, Misappropriation and Unfair Competition* (1st edn, Kluwer Law International 2014)
Westermann I, *Handbuch Know-How Schutz* (CH Beck 2007)
Wheeler J, *Essentials of the English Legal System* (2nd edn, Pearson Longman 2006)

IV Book Chapters

Aplin T, 'Right to Property and Trade Secrets' in Christophe Geiger (ed), *Research Handbook on Human Rights and Intellectual Property* (Edward Elgar 2015) 421
Bone RG, 'Trade Secrecy, Innovation and the Requirement of Reasonable Secrecy Precautions' in Rochelle C Dreyfuss and Katherine J Strandburg (eds), *The Law and Theory of Trade Secrecy: A Handbook of Contemporary Research* (Edward Elgar 2011) 48
Dessemontet F, 'Protection of Trade Secrets and Confidential Information' in Carlos M Correa and Abdulqawi A Yusuf (eds), *Intellectual Property and International Trade: The TRIPS Agreement* (3rd edn, Wolters Kluwer 2016) 339
Doepner U, 'Anmerkungen zum wettbewerbsrechtlichen Geheimnisschutz im Zivilprozess' in Erhard Keller, Clemens Plassmann and Andreas von Falck (eds), *Festschrift für Winfried Tilmann* (Carl Heymanns Verlag 2003) 112

Fezer K-H, 'Der Zivilrechtliche Geheimnisschutz im Wettbewerbsrecht' in Ulrich Loewenheim and Thomas Raiser (eds), *Festschrift für Fritz Traub zum 65. Geburtstag* (Deutscher Fachverlag 1994) 81

First H, 'Trade Secrets and Antitrust Law' in Rochelle C Dreyfuss and Katherine J Strandburg (eds), *The Law and Theory of Trade Secrecy: A Handbook of Contemporary Research* (Edward Elgar 2011) 333

Ghidini G and Falce V, 'Trade Secrets as Intellectual Property Rights: a Disgraceful Upgrading – Notes on an Italian "Reform"' in Rochelle C Dreyfuss and Katherine J Strandburg (eds), *The Law and Theory of Trade Secrecy: A Handbook of Contemporary Research* (Edward Elgar 2011) 140

Hyde A, 'Intellectual Property Justifications for Restricting Employee Mobility: A Critical Appraisal in Light of Economic Evidence' in Cynthia L Estlund and Michael L Wachter (eds), *Research Handbook on the Economics of Labor and Employment Law* (Edward Elgar 2012) 369

Kesan JP and Hayes CM, 'The Law and Policy of Non-Compete Clauses in the United States and Their Implications' in Marilyn Pittard, Ann L Monotti and John Duns (eds), *Business Innovation and the Law. Perspectives from Intellectual Property, Labour, Competition and Corporate Law* (Edward Elgar 2013) 381

Locke J, 'The Second Treatise of Government. An Essay Concerning the True Original, Extent, and End of Civil Government' in Paul E Sigmund (ed), *The Selected Political Writings of John Locke* (W W Norton & Company 2005) 28

Madison MJ, 'Open Secrets' in Rochelle C Dreyfuss and Katherine J Strandburg (eds), *The Law and Theory of Trade Secrecy: A Handbook of Contemporary Research* (Edward Elgar 2011) 241

Ohly A, 'Harmonising the Protection of Trade Secrets: Challenges and Perspectives' in Jacques de Werra (ed), *La protection des secrets d'affaires. The Protection of Trade Secrets* (Schulthess 2013) 39

Ohly A, 'Reverse Engineering: Unfair Competition or Catalyst for Innovation?' in Wolrad Prinz zu Waldeck und Pyrmont, Martin J Adelman, Robert Brauneis, Josef Drexl and Ralph Nack (eds), *Patents and Technological Progress in a Globalized World. Liber Amicorum Joseph Straus* (Springer 2009) 535

Reichman JH, 'How Trade Secrecy Law Generates a Natural Semicommons of Innovative Know-How' in Rochelle C Dreyfuss and Katherine J Strandburg (eds), *The Law and Theory of Trade Secrecy: A Handbook of Contemporary Research* (Edward Elgar 2011) 193

Risch M, 'Trade Secret Law and Information Development Incentives' in Rochelle C Dreyfuss and Katherine J Strandburg (eds), *The Law and Theory of Trade Secrecy: A Handbook of Contemporary Research* (Edward Elgar 2011) 160

Turner S, 'The Protection of Trade Secrets: the Legal Framework in the EU' in Jacques de Werra (ed), *La protection des secrets d'affaires. The Protection of Trade Secrets* (Schulthess 2013) 95

V Journal Articles

–, 'Post-Termination Restrictive Covenants' (2008) IDS Emp L Brief 853, 12–18

Abramowicz M and Duffy JF, 'Intellectual Property for Market Experimentation' (2008) 83 *NYU L Rev* 337

Almeling DS, Snyder DW, Sapoznikow M, McCollum WE and Weader J, 'A Statistical Analysis of Trade Secret Litigation in Federal Courts' (2010) 45(2) *Gonz L Rev* 291

Ann C, 'Know-how – Stiefkind des Geistigen Eigentums?' (2007) GRUR 39

Aplin T, 'Commercial confidences after the Human Rights Act' (2007) 29(10) *EIPR* 411

Aplin T, 'A Critical Evaluation of the Proposed EU Trade Secrets Directive' (2014) 4 *IPQ* 257

Arundel A, 'The Relative Effectiveness of Patents and Secrecy for Appropriation' (2001) 30 *Research Policy* 611

Asendorf CD, 'Wettbewerbs- und Patentstreitsachen vor Arbeitsgerichten? Die sachliche Zuständigkeit bei der Verletzung von Betriebsgeheimnissen durch Arbeitnehmer' (1990) GRUR 229

Batteson A, 'Gaining Confidence in the Law of Confidence' (2006) 1(11) *JIPLP* 714

Berryhill JW, 'Trade Secret Litigation: Injunctions and other Equitable Remedies' (1977) 48 *Univ Colo L R* 189

Bishara ND, 'Covenants Not to Compete in a Knowledge Economy: Balancing Innovation from Employee Mobility against Legal Protection for Human Capital Investment' (2006) 27 *Berk J Emp & Lab L* 287

Blok P, 'A Harmonized Approach to Prohibitory Injunctions: Reconsidering Article 12 of the Enforcement Directive' (2016) 11(1) *JIPLP* 56

Bone RG, 'A New Look at Trade Secret Law: Doctrine in Search of Justification' (1998) 86 *Cal L Rev* 241

Bone RG, 'The (Still) Shaky Foundations of Trade Secret Law' (2014) 92 *Tex L R* 1803

Brammsen J, 'Der Arbeitnehmerbegriff. Versuch einer einheitlichen Neubestimmung' (2010) RdA 267

Bronckers M and McNelis N, 'Is the EU Obliged to Improve the Protection of Trade Secrets? An Inquiry into TRIPS, the European Convention on Human Rights and the EU Charter of Fundamental Rights' (2012) 34(10) *EIPR* 673

Chally JR, 'The Law of Trade Secrets: Toward a More Efficient Approach' (2004) 57 *V and L Rev* 1269

Clarke L, 'Breach of Confidence and the Employment Relationship' (2002) 31 (4) *ILJ* 353

Clarke L, 'Repudiation of Contract and Breach of Confidence: General Billposting v Atkinson Revisited' (2003) 32 *ILJ* 43

Clarke L, 'Remedial Responses to Breach of Confidence: The Question of Damages' (2005) 24 *CJQ* 316

Closius PJ and Schaffer HM, 'Involuntary Nonservitude: The Current Judicial Enforcement of Employee Covenants Not to Compete – a Proposal for Reform' (1984) 57 *S Cal L Rev* 531

Coulthard A, 'Garden Leave, The Right to Work and Restraints of Trade' (2009) 22 *Aust J Lab L* 87

Cran D and Joseph P, 'Breach of Confidence Claim against Ex-employees and Consultants' (2011) 6(10) *JIPLP* 688

Cundiff VA, 'Reasonable Measures to Protect Trade Secrets in a Digital Environment' (2009) 49(3) *IDEA* 359 de Werra J, 'How to Protect Trade Secrets in High Tech Sports? An Intellectual Property Analysis Based on the Experiences in the America's Cup and in the Formula One Championship' (2010) 32(4) *EIPR* 155

Demuth D, 'Neue Maβstäbe für einstweilige Verfügungsverfahren in Wettbewerbssachen' (2011) GRUR 404

Denninger E, 'Die Zweitanmelderproblematik im Arzneimittelrecht' (1984) GRUR 627

Dobash TJ, 'Trade Secret Theft & Employer Vicarious Liability in Hagen v. Burmeister & Associates, Inc.' (2002–2003) 29 *Wm Mitchell L Rev* 375

Drexl J, 'Intellectual Property and Antitrust Law. IMS Health and Trinko – Antitrust Placebo for Consumers Instead of Sound Economics in Refusal-to-Deal Cases' (2004) IIC 788

Eady D, 'Injunctions and the Protection of Privacy' (2010) 29 *CJQ* 411

Ellington P, 'Obligations of Confidentiality – English law' (1991) 1 *IBLJ* 141

Enders T, 'Know How Schutz als Teil des geistigen Eigentums' (2012) GRUR 25

Feldman MJ, 'Towards a Clearer Standard of Protectable Information: Trade Secrets and the Employment Relationship' (1994) 9 *HTLJ* 151

Fitzgerald J and Firth A, 'Is Art. 13 of the Enforcement Directive a Redundancy Notice for the Account of Profits Remedy in the UK?' (2014) GRUR Int 881

Freiherr von Maltzahn F, 'Wettbewerbsrechtliche Probleme beim Arbeitsplatzwechsel' (1981) GRUR 788

Friedman DD, Landes WM and Posner RA, 'Some Economics of Trade Secret Law' (1991) 5(1) *J Econ Pers* 61

Friesen LS, 'Distinguishing between an Employee's General Knowledge and Trade Secrets' (1994) 23 *Colo Law* 2123

Garrison MJ and Wendt JT, 'The Evolving Law of Employee Non-Compete Agreements: Recent Trends and an Alternative Policy Approach' (2008) 45 *Am Bus L J* 107

Gärtner A, 'Zum Richtlinienentwurf über den Schutz von Geschäftsgeheimnissen' (2014) NZG 650

Gaugenrieder E and Unger-Hellmich D, 'Know-How Schutz – gehen mit dem Mitarbeiter auch die Unternehmensgeheimnisse?' (2011) WRP 1364

Gaul D, 'Die nachvertragliche Geheimhaltungspflicht eines ausgeschiedenen Arbeitnehmers' (1988) NZA 225

Gaul D, 'Erfindungen eines gekündigten Arbeitnehmers' (1979) GRUR 750

Glick MA, Bush D and Hafen JQ, 'The Law and Economics of Post-Employment Covenants: A Unified Framework' (2002) 11 *Geo Mason L Rev* 357

Grassie G, 'Trade Secrets: The New EU Enforcement Regime' (2014) 9(8) *JIPLP* 677

Grunewald R, 'Fern der Quelle – Geheimnisschutz und Outsourcing' (2007) WRP 1307

Guthrie P, 'Employee's Duty, in Absence of Express Contract, Not to Disclose or Use in the New Employment Special Skills or Techniques Acquired in Earlier Employment' 30 ALR 3d 631

Holzapfel H, 'Zum einstweiligen Rechtsschutz im Wettbewerbs- und Patentrecht' (2003) GRUR 287

Honeyball S and Pearce D, 'Contract, Employment and the Contract of Employment' (2006) 35(1) *ILJ* 30

Hull J, 'Speed Seal Products v Paddington: Retraining Use of Information in the Public Domain' (1986) 8(8) *EIPR* 249

Hull J, 'Trade Secret Licensing: The Art of the Possible' (2009) 4(3) *JIPLP* 203

Hull J, 'Making Preparations to Compete – A Note on Helmet Systems v Tunnard' (2009) 31(12) *EIPR* 623

Hull J and Abbott S, 'Property Rights in Secrets – Douglas v Hello! In the Court of Appeal' (2005) 27(10) *EIPR* 379

Hussinger K, 'Is Silence Golden? Patents Versus Secrecy at the Firm Level' (2006) 15(8) *Econ Innov New Techn* 735

Hyde A, 'Should Non-Competes be Enforced?' (2010) 33 *Regulation* 6

Johnson CN, 'Assessing Damages for Misappropriation of Trade Secrets' (1998) 27 *Colo Law* 71

Kalbfus B, 'Die neuere Rechtsprechung des BGH zum Schutz von Betriebs- und Geschäftsgeheimnissen' (2013) WRP 584

Kalbfus B and Harte-Bavendamm H, 'Protokoll der Sitzung des Fachausschusses für Wettbewerbs- und Markenrecht zum Richtlinienvorschlag über den Schutz von Geschäftsgeheimnissen' (2014) GRUR 453

Kalbfus B, 'Die EU-Geschäftsgeheimnis-Richtlinie. Welcher Umsetzungsbedarf besteht in Deutschland?' (2016) GRUR 1009

Khan AN, 'Former Employee's Duty of Secrecy' (1988) 9(6) *Company Lawyer* 130

Kiethe K and Hohmann O, 'Der strafrechtliche Schutz von Geschäfts- und Betriebsgeheimnissen' (2006) NStZ 185

Kitch EW, 'The Law and Economics of Rights in Valuable Information' (1980) 9 (4) *JLS, The Law and Economics of Privacy* 683

Kitch EW, 'The Expansion of Trade Secrecy Protection and the Mobility of Management Employees: a New Problem for the Law' (1996) 47 *S C L Rev* 659

Koenig C and Steiner U, 'Die Vereinbarkeit nachvertraglicher Wettbewerbsverbote mit der Arbeitnehmerfreizügigkeit des EG-Vertrags' (2002) NJW 3583

Körner E, 'Die Aufwertung der Schadensberechnung nach der Lizenzanalogie bei Verletzung gewerblicher Schutzrechte durch die Rechtsprechung zum „Verletzervorteil"und zu den „aufgelaufenen Zinsen"' (1983) GRUR 611

Körner E, 'Befristete und unbefristete Unterlassungstitel bei Wettbewerbsverstößen' (1985) GRUR 909

Kraßer R, 'Grundlagen des Zivilrechtlichen Schutzes von Geschäfts- und Betriebsgeheimnissen sowie von Know-How' (1977) GRUR 177

Kunz J, 'Betriebs- und Geschäftsgeheimnisse und Wettbewerbsverbot während der Dauer und nach Beendigung des Anstellungsverhältnisses' (1993) DB 2482

Leistensnider RE, 'Trade Secret Misappropriation: What is the Proper Length of an Injunction after Public Disclosure?' (1987) 51 *Alb L Rev* 271

Lemley MA, 'The Surprising Virtues of Treating Trade Secrets as IP Rights' (2008) 61 *Stanf L R* 311

Lemley MA, 'The Myth of the Sole Inventor' (2012) 110 *MILR* 709

Lettl T, 'Die Beeinträchtigung des Eigentums nach §1004(I)(1) BGB' (2005) JuS 871

Leyendecker BE, 'Grundfälle zur Vollstreckungsabwehrklage' (2010) JA 631

Mansfield E, 'How Rapidly Does New Industrial Technology Leak Out?' (1985) 34 *J Ind Econ* 217

Maume P, 'Know-how-Schutz – Abschied vom Geheimhaltungswillen?' (2008) WRP 1275

Mayer MA, 'Geschäfts- und Betriebsgeheimnis oder Geheimniskrämerei?' (2011) GRUR 884
McGuire M-R, Joachim B, Künzel J and Weber N, 'Der Schutz von Geschäftsgeheimnissen durch Rechte des Geistigen Eigentums und durch das Recht des unlauteren Wettbewerbs (Q215)' (2010) GRUR Int 829
McGuire M-R, 'Know-how: Stiefkind, Störenfried oder Sorgenkind? Lücken und Regelungsalternativen vor dem Hintergrund des RL-Vorschlags' (2015) GRUR 424
McGuire M-R, 'Der Schutz von Know-how im System des Immaterialgüterrechts. Perspektiven für die Umsetzung der Richtlinie über Geschäftsgeheimnisse' (2016) GRUR 1000
Menke J-M, 'Gestaltung nachvertraglicher Wettbewerbsverbote mit GmbH-Geschäftsführern. Verzicht statt Karenzentschädigung' (2009) NJW 636
Merges RP, 'The Law and Economics of Employee Inventions' (1999) 13(1) *Harv J L Techn* 1
Mes P, 'Arbeitsplatzwechsel und Geheimnisschutz' (1979) GRUR 584
Middlemiss S, 'The Psychological Contract and Implied Contractual Terms: Synchronous or Asynchronous Models?' (2011) 53(1) *Int JLM* 32
Miller K, 'Implied Duties of Confidentiality in the Contract of Employment' (1986) 102 *LQR* 359
Milligan RB and Sieve CE, 'Adequately Identifying Trade Secrets in California Trade Secret Misappropriation Litigation' (2009) 4(10) *JIPLP* 703
Molkenbur J, 'Pflicht zur Geheimniswahrung nach Ende des Arbeitsverhältnisses?' (1990) BB 1196
Motolenich-Salas K, 'Trade Secret Misappropriation, Possession of Confidential Information, and Preliminary Injunctions' (2008) 3(7) *JIPLP* 440
Nastelski K, 'Der Schutz des Betriebsgeheimnisses' (1957) GRUR 1
Nisar S, 'Pre-filing Disclosure of an Invention is Found to be in Breach of Equitable Doctrine of Confidence' (2012) 7(7) *JIPLP* 485
Oehlrich M, 'Know-how und Tacit Knowledge als vernachlässigte Vertragsbestandteile bei Lizenzverträgen' (2010) GRUR 33
Ohly A, 'Der Geheimnisschutz im deutschen Recht: heutiger Stand und Perspektiven' (2014) GRUR 1
Ohly A, '"Patenttrolle"oder: Der patentrechtliche Unterlassungsanspruch unter Verhältnismäßigkeitsvorbehalt? – Aktuelle Entwicklungen im US-Patentrecht und ihre Bedeutung für das deutsche und europäische Patentsystem' (2008) GRUR Int 787
Parker N, 'The Secret Recipe: Key Ingredients of Agreements to Protect Confidential Information' (2011) 6(4) *JIPLP* 223
Porter II WG and Griffaton M, 'Identifying and Protecting Employers' Interests in Trade Secrets and Proprietary Information' (2001) 68 *Def Couns J* 439
Rauer N, 'Richtlinienentwurf: Europaweit einheitlicher Schutz von Geschäftsgeheimnissen' (2014) GRUR-Prax 2
Redeker SS, Pres S and Gittinger C, 'Die Entwürfe zur Know-how-Richtlinie, deren Konsequenzen für das innerbetriebliche Vertragsmanagement (Teil 1)' (2015) WRP 681
Reetz A, Pecnard C, Fruscalzo R, van der Velden R and Marfé M, 'Die Befugnisse der nationalen Gerichte unter dem EPÜ und des Einheitlichen Patentgerichts

(EPG) nach Art. 63 (1) EPGÜ zum Erlass von Unterlassungsverfügungen – eine rechtsvergleichende Untersuchung' (2015) GRUR Int 210

Reimann T, 'Einige Überlegungen zur Offenkundigkeit im Rahmen von §§17 ff. UWG und von §3 PatG' (1998) GRUR 298

Reinhard B and Kliemt T, 'Die Durchsetzung arbeitsrechtlicher Ansprüche im Eilverfahren' (2005) NZA 545

Retzer K, 'Wiederlegung der "Dringlichkeitsvermutung"durch Interessenabwägung?' (2009) GRUR 329

Reuter WJ, 'Wettbewerbsrechtliche Ansprüche bei Konflikten zwischen Arbeitgebern und Arbeitnehmern – Terra Incognita?' (2008) NJW 3538

Reynolds L and Watts J, 'A New Approach to Interlocutory Injunctions?' (1996) 2(2) *CTLR* 66

Richards-Bray B, 'Intellectual Property Law: Employment Law – Contract Law' (2007) 12(1) *Cov L J* 76

Richters S and Wodtke C, 'Schutz von Betriebsgeheimnissen aus Unternehmenssicht "Verhinderung von Know-how Abfluss durch eigene Mitarbeiter"' (2003) NZA-RR 281

Risch M, 'Why Do We Have Trade Secrets?' (2007) 11 *Marq IP L Rev* 1

Rowe EA, 'When Trade Secrets Become Shackles: Fairness and the Inevitable Disclosure Doctrine' (2005) 7 *Tul J Tech & Intell Prop* 167

Rowe EA, 'Introducing a Takedown for Trade Secrets on the Internet' (2007) 5 *WLR* 1041

Rützel S, 'Illegale Unternehmensgeheimnisse?' (1995) GRUR 557

Salger C and Breitfeld A, 'Regelungen zum Schutz von betrieblichen Know-how – die Sicherung von Geschäfts- und Betriebsgeheimnissen' (2005) BB 154

Sander C, 'Schutz nicht offenbarter betrieblicher Informationen nach der Beendigung des Arbeitsverhältnisses im deutschen und amerikanischen Recht' (2013) GRUR-Int 217

Schmidt-Hern K, 'Kundenliste muss im Geheimnisschutz-Prozess eindeutig beschrieben werden' (2011) GRUR-Prax 154

Siems MM, 'Die Logik des Schutzes von Betriebsgeheimnissen' (2007) WRP 1146

Sołtysiński SJ, 'Are Trade Secrets Property?' (1986) IIC 331

Sousa e Silva N, 'What Exactly is a Trade Secret under the Proposed Directive?' (2014) 9(11) *JIPLP* 923

Stewart A, 'Confidential Information and Departing Employees: The Employer's Options' (1989) 11(3) *EIPR* 88

Stone KVW, 'The New Psychological Contract: Implications of the Changing Workplace for Labor and Employment Law' (2001) 48 *UCLA L Rev* 519

Stone KVW, 'Knowledge at Work: Disputes over Ownership of Human Capital in the Changing Workplace' (2001–2002) 34 *Conn L Rev* 721

Stone KVW, 'Human Capital and Employee Mobility: A Rejoinder' (2002) 34 *CTLR* 1233

Tetzner V, 'Der Verletzerzuschlag bei der Lizenzanalogie' (2009) GRUR 6

Tönnies JG, 'Erfindungen – ein Kollektivgut oder die Gedanken sind frei' (2013) GRUR 796

Turner B and Purvis I, 'More Chicken Pieces' (1989) 11(1) *EIPR* 3

Unikel R, 'Bridging the "Trade Secret" Gap: Protecting "Confidential Information" Not Rising to the Level of Trade Secrets' (1998) 29 *Loy U Chi LJ* 841

Volp F, 'Änderung der Rechts- oder Sachlage bei Unterlassungstitel' (1984) GRUR 486

von Ungern-Sternberg J, 'Einwirkung der Durchsetzungsrichtlinie auf das deutsche Schadensersatzrecht' (2009) GRUR 460

Waas B, 'Überlegungen zur Fortentwicklung des deutschen Arbeitsrechts. Diskussion im Inland, Anstöße aus dem Ausland' (2007) RdA 76

Weiss GE, 'Biting the Hand that Stops Feeding: How to Protect Trade Secrets from Misappropriation by Laid Off Employees' (2001) 661 *PLI/Lit* 469

Wennakoski AA, 'Trade Secrets under Review: A Comparative Analysis of the Protection of Trade Secrets in the EU and in the US' (2016) 38(3) *EIPR* 154

Wertheimer F, 'Bezahlte Karenz oder entschädigungslose Wettbewerbsenthaltung des ausgeschiedenen Arbeitnehmers?' (1999) BB 1600

Wilf S, 'Trade Secret, Property and Social Relations' (2002) 34 *Conn L Rev* 787

Winterstein H-P, 'Nachvertragliches Wettbewerbsverbot und Karenzentschädigung' (1989) NJW 1463

Wolff HA, 'Der verfassungsrechtliche Schutz der Betriebs- und Geschäftsgeheimnisse' (1997) NJW 98

VI Online Journals

Beckerman-Rodau A, 'The Choice between Patent Protection and Trade Secret Protection: A Legal and Business Decision' (2002) http://papers.ssrn.com/sol3/papers.cfm?abstract_id=704644&download=yes accessed 3 March 2016, on file with the author

Bessen J and Nuvolari A, 'Knowledge-Sharing Among Inventors: Some Historical Perspectives' (2011) Boston University School of Law Working Paper No 11–51 http://ssrn.com/abstract=1944201 accessed 1 June 2017

Bishara ND and Orozco D, 'Using the Resource-Based Theory to Determine Covenant not to Compete Legitimacy' (2011) Ross School of Business Working Paper No 1157 http://papers.ssrn.com/sol3/papers.cfm?abstract_id=1900873## accessed 1 June 2017

Bishara ND, 'Fifty Ways to Leave Your Employer: Relative Enforcement of Covenants Not to Compete, Trends and Implications for Employee Mobility Policy' (2011) 13(3) University of Pennsylvania Journal of Business Law 751 http://scholarship.law.upenn.edu/jbl/vol13/iss3/5 accessed 1 June 2017

Cohen WM, Nelson RR and Walsh JP 'Protecting their Intellectual Assets: Appropriability Conditions and Why US Manufacturing Firms Patent (or Not)' (2000) NBER Working Paper Series Working Paper No 7552 www.nber.org/papers/w7552.pdf accessed 1 June 2017

Epstein RA, 'Trade Secrets as Private Property: Their Constitutional Protection' (2003) John M Olin Law & Economics Working Paper No 190 (2d Series) http://papers.ssrn.com/sol3/papers.cfm?abstract_id=421340 accessed 1 June 2017

Fisk CL, '"An Ingenious Man Enabled by Contract": Entrepreneurship and the Rise of Contract' (2007) Duke Law School Legal Studies Research Paper Series, Research Paper 157 http://ssrn.com/abstract=983739 accessed 1 June 2017

Lerner J, 'Using Litigation to Understand Trade Secrets: A Preliminary Exploration' (2006) Harvard Business School Working Papers http://papers.ssrn.com/sol3/papers.cfm?abstract_id=922520 accessed 1 June 2017

Lichtman D, 'How the Law Responds to Self-Help' (2004) John M Olin Law & Economics Working Paper No 232 http://papers.ssrn.com/sol3/papers.cfm?abstract_id=629287 accessed 1 June 2017

Lobel O, 'Intellectual Property and Restrictive Covenants' (2008) Legal Studies Research Paper Series, Research Paper 08-059 http://ssrn.com/abstract=1226463 accessed 1 June 2017

Marx M, Singh J and Fleming L, 'Regional Disadvantage? Non-Compete Agreements and Brain Drain' (2010) http://papers.ssrn.com/sol3/papers.cfm?abstract_id=1654719 accessed 1 June 2017

Moffat VR, 'The Wrong Tool for the Job: The IP Problem with Non-Competition Agreements' (2010) University of Denver Sturm College of Law Legal Research Paper Series Working Paper No 10–10 http://papers.ssrn.com/sol3/papers.cfm?abstract_id=1577271 accessed 1 June 2017

Png IPL and Samila S, 'Trade Secrets Law and Mobility: Evidence from "Inevitable Disclosure"' (2015) http://papers.ssrn.com/sol3/papers.cfm?abstract_id=1986775 accessed 1 June 2017

Reder MEK and O'Brien CN, 'Managing the Risk of Trade Secret Loss Due to Job Mobility in an Innovation Economy with the Theory of Inevitable Disclosure' (2012) 12 Journal of High Technology Law http://ssrn.com/abstract=2014051 accessed 1 June 2017

Risch MV, 'Comments on Trade Secrets Sharing in High Velocity Labor Markets' (2008) http://ssrn.com/abstract=1269039 accessed 1 June 2017

Samila S and Sorenson O, 'Non-Compete Covenants: Incentives to Innovate or Impediments to Growth' (2010) http://papers.ssrn.com/sol3/papers.cfm?abstract_id=1411172 accessed 1 June 2017

Searle N and Reid GC, 'Firm Size and Trade Secret Intensity: Evidence from the Economic Espionage Act' (2012) Scottish Institute for Research in Economics Discussion Paper http://repo.sire.ac.uk/bitstream/10943/372/1/SIRE-DP-2012_60.pdf accessed 1 June 2017

Warren M and Pedowitz A, 'Social Media, Trade Secrets, and Yes, the Sky is Falling' (2011) www.americanbar.org/content/dam/aba/administrative/labor_law/meetings/2011/tech/a_03.authcheckdam.pdf accessed 1 June 2017

VII Reports

Report on Trade Secrets for the European Commission, Hogan Lovells International LLP, Study on Trade Secrets and Parasitic Copying (Look-alikes) MARKT/2010/20/D http://ec.europa.eu/internal_market/iprenforcement/docs/parasitic/Study_Parasitic_copying_en.pdf accessed 1 June 2017 (**Hogan Lovells Report**)

Study on Trade Secrets and Confidential Business Information in the Internal Market, Baker & McKenzie – Milan MARKT/2011/128/D http://ec.europa.eu/internal_market/iprenforcement/docs/trade-secrets/130711_final-study_en.pdf accessed 1 June 2017 (**Baker&McKenzie Study**)

Stellungnahme des Max-Planck-Instituts für Innovation und Wettbewerb vom 3 Juni 2014 zum Vorschlag der Europäischen Kommission für eine Richtlinie über den Schutz vertraulichen Know-hows und vertraulicher Geschäftsinformationen (Geschäftsgeheimnisse) vor rechtswidrigem Erwerb sowie rechtswidriger Nutzung und Offenlegung vom 28.11.2013, COM (2013) 813 final www.ip.mpg.de/fileadmin/ipmpg/content/stellungnahmen/stellungnahme-geschaeftsgeheimnisse_2014-05–12_final_7.pdf accessed 1 June 2017 (**MPI Position Paper**)

ICC Comments on Proposal for EU Trade Secrets Directive, Paper 450/1083 DYE/cle – 20 March 2014 www.icc-deutschland.de/fileadmin/icc/ICC_2012/ICC_Comments_on_Proposal_for_EU_Trade_Secrets_Directive.pdf accessed 3 March 2016, on file with the author

Russel Beck, Year in Review (2015) Trade Secrets 5–8 http://wk-kliblogs-test.elasticbeanstalk.com/patent/wp-content/uploads/sites/52/2016/02/Year-in-Review-2015_Trade-Secrets.pdf accessed 1 June 2017

VIII Websites and Blogs

United States Department of Labor, Bureau of Labor Statistics www.bls.gov/opub/regional_reports/200908_silicon_valley_high_tech.htm accessed 1 June 2017

'Texas Adopts the Uniform Trade Secrets Act' (*Trading Secrets*, 3 May 2013) www.tradesecretslaw.com/2013/05/articles/trade-secrets/texas-adopts-the-uniform-trade-secrets-act/ accessed 1 June 2017

'The Cinderella of IP (or not)' (*The IP Kat*, 18 December 2012) http://ipkitten.blogspot.de/2012/12/the-cinderella-of-ip-or-not.html accessed 1 June 2017

'Why Europe Must Reform its Trade Secrets Rules' (*Managing Intellectual Property*, 10 February 2015) www.managingip.com/Blog/3426227/Guest-blog-Why-Europe-must-reform-its-trade-secrets-rules.html accessed 1 June 2017

'New York Federal Court Denies Injunction to Enforce Restrictive Covenants Against Terminated Employee' (*Trading Secrets*, 13 February 2013) www.tradesecretslaw.com/2013/02/articles/noncompete-enforceability/new-york-federal-court-denies-injunction-to-enforce-restrictive-covenants-against-terminated-employee/ accessed 1 June 2017

'Jorda on: Trade Secrets are not Trade Secrets' (*Jorda on Trade Secrets* 18 October 2007) http://blogs.law.unh.edu/tradesecrets/2007/10/jorda-on-trade-secrets-are-not.html accessed 1 June 2017.

Index

Cambridge Intellectual Property and Information Law

Titles in the Series (Formerly Known as *Cambridge Studies in Intellectual Property Rights*)

Brad Sherman and Lionel Bently *The Making of Modern Intellectual Property Law*
Irini A. Stamatoudi *Copyright and Multimedia Products: A Comparative Analysis*
Pascal Kamina *Film Copyright in the European Union*
Huw Beverly-Smith *The Commercial Appropriation of Personality*
Mark J. Davison *The Legal Protection of Databases*
Robert Burrell and Allison Coleman *Copyright Exceptions: The Digital Impact*
Huw Beverly-Smith, Ansgar Ohly and Agnès Lucas-Schloetter *Privacy, Property and Personality: Civil Law Perspectives on Commercial Appropriation*
Catherine Seville *The Internationalisation of Copyright Law: Books, Buccaneers and the Black Flag in the Nineteenth Century*
Philip Leith *Software and Patents in Europe*
Geertrui Van Overwalle *Gene Patents and Clearing Models*
Lionel Bently, Jennifer Davis and Jane C. Ginsburg *Trade Marks and Brands: An Interdisciplinary Critique*
Jonathan Curci *The Protection of Biodiversity and Traditional Knowledge in International Law of Intellectual Property*
Lionel Bently, Jennifer Davis and Jane C. Ginsburg *Copyright and Piracy: An Interdisciplinary Critique*
Megan Richardson and Julian Thomas *Framing Intellectual Property: Legal Constructions of Creativity and Appropriation 1840–1940*
Dev Gangjee *Relocating the Law of Geographical Indications*
Andrew Kenyon, Megan Richardson and Ng-Loy Wee-Loon *The Law of Reputation and Brands in the Asia Pacific Region*
Annabelle Lever *New Frontiers in the Philosophy of Intellectual Property*
Sigrid Sterckx and Julian Cockbain *Exclusions from Patentability: How the European Patent Office is Eroding Boundaries*
Sebastian Haunss *Conflicts in the Knowledge Society: The Contentious Politics of Intellectual Property*
Helena R. Howe and Jonathan Griffiths *Concepts of Property in Intellectual Property Law*
Rochelle Cooper Dreyfuss and Jane C. Ginsburg *Intellectual Property at the Edge: The Contested Contours of IP*
Normann Witzleb, David Lindsay, Moira Paterson and Sharon Rodrick *Emerging Challenges in Privacy Law: Comparative Perspectives*
Paul Bernal *Internet Privacy Rights: Rights to Protect Autonomy*
Peter Drahos *Intellectual Property, Indigenous People and their Knowledge*
Susy Frankel and Daniel Gervais *The Evolution and Equilibrium of Copyright in the Digital Age*

Edited by Kathy Bowrey and Michael Handler *Law and Creativity in the Age of the Entertainment Franchise*

Sean Bottomley *The British Patent System and the Industrial Revolution 1700–1852: From Privileges to Property*

Susy Frankel *Test Tubes for Global Intellectual Property Issues: Small Market Economies*

Jan Oster *Media Freedom as a Fundamental Right*

Sara Bannerman *International Copyright and Access to Knowledge*

Andrew T. Kenyon *Comparative Defamation and Privacy Law*

Pascal Kamina *Film Copyright in the European Union, Second Edition*

Tim W. Dornis *Trademark and Unfair Competition Conflicts*

Ge Chen *Copyright and International Negotiations: An Engine of Free Expression in China?*

David Tan *The Commercial Appropriation of Fame: A Cultural Critique of the Right of Publicity and Passing Off*

Jay Sanderson *Plants, People and Practices: The Nature and History of the UPOV Convention*

Daniel Benoliel *Patent Intensity and Economic Growth*

Jeffrey A. Maine and Xuan-Thao Nguyen *The Intellectual Property Holding Company: Tax Use and Abuse from Victoria's Secret to Apple*

Megan Richardson *The Right to Privacy: Origins and Influence of a Nineteenth Century Idea*

Martin Husovec *Injunctions Against Intermediaries in the European Union: Accountable But Not Liable?*